Ontology

Or the

Theory of Being

By

Peter Coffey, Ph.D. (Louvain)

Professor of Logic and Metaphysics, Waynooth College, Ireland

Contents

Preface.

General Introduction.

Chapter I. Being And Its Primary Determinations.

Chapter II. Becoming And Its Implications.

Chapter III. Existence And Essence.

Chapter IV. Reality As One And Manifold.

Chapter V. Reality And The True.

Chapter VI. Reality And The Good.

Chapter VII. Reality And The Beautiful.

Chapter VIII. The Categories Of Being. Substance And Accident.

Chapter IX. Nature And Person.

Chapter X. Some Accident-Modes Of Being: Quality.

Chapter XI. Quantity, Space And Time.

Chapter XII. Relation; The Relative And The Absolute.

Chapter XIII. Causality; Classification Of Causes.

Chapter XIV. Efficient Causality; Phenomenism And Occasionalism.

Chapter XV. Final Causes; Universal Order.

To
The Students
Past And Present
Of
Maynooth College

Preface.

It is hoped that the present volume will supply a want that is really felt by students of philosophy in our universities—the want of an English text-book on General Metaphysics from the Scholastic standpoint. It is the author's intention to supplement his *Science of Logic* and the present treatise on Ontology, by a volume on the Theory of Knowledge. Hence no disquisitions on the latter subject will be found in these pages: the Moderate Realism of Aristotle and the Schoolmen is assumed throughout.

In the domain of Ontology there are many scholastic theories and discussions which are commonly regarded by non-scholastic writers as possessing nowadays for the student of philosophy an interest that is merely historical. This mistaken notion is probably due to the fact that few if any serious attempts have yet been made to transpose these questions from their medieval setting into the language and context of contemporary philosophy. Perhaps not a single one of these problems is really and in substance alien to present-day speculations. The author has endeavoured, by his treatment of such characteristically "medieval" discussions as those on *Potentia* and *Actus*, Essence and Existence, Individuation, the Theory of Distinctions, Substance and Accident, Nature and Person, Logical and Real Relations, Efficient and Final Causes, to show that the issues involved are in every instance as fully and keenly debated—in an altered setting and a new terminology—by recent and living philosophers of every school of thought as they were by St. Thomas and his contemporaries in the golden age of medieval scholasticism. And, as the purposes of a text-book demanded, attention has been devoted to stating the problems clearly, to showing the significance and bearings of discussions and solutions, rather than to detailed analyses of arguments. At the same time it is hoped that the treatment is sufficiently full to be helpful even to advanced students and to all who are interested in the "Metaphysics of the Schools". For the convenience of the reader the more advanced portions are printed in smaller type.

The teaching of St. Thomas and the other great Schoolmen of the Middle Ages forms the groundwork of the book. This *corpus* of doctrine is scarcely yet accessible outside its Latin sources. As typical of the fuller scholastic text-books the excellent treatise of the Spanish author, Urraburu,[2] has been most frequently consulted. Much assistance has also been derived from Kleutgen's *Philosophie der*

Vorzeit,³ a monumental work which ought to have been long since translated into English. And finally, the excellent treatise in the Louvain *Cours de Philosophie*, by the present Cardinal Archbishop of Mechlin,⁴ has been consulted with profit and largely followed in many places. The writer freely and gratefully acknowledges his indebtedness to these and other authors quoted and referred to in the course of the present volume.

General Introduction.

I. REASON OF INTRODUCTORY CHAPTER.—It is desirable that at some stage in the course of his investigations the student of philosophy should be invited to take a brief general survey of the work in which he is engaged. This purpose will be served by a chapter on *the general aim and scope of philosophy*, its distinctive characteristics as compared with other lines of human thought, and its relations to these latter. Such considerations will at the same time help to define *Ontology*, thus introducing the reader to the subject-matter of the present volume.

II. PHILOSOPHY: THE NAME AND THE THING.—In the fifth book of Cicero's *Tusculan Disputations* we read that the terms *philosophus* and *philosophia* were first employed by Pythagoras who flourished in the sixth century before Christ, that this ancient sage was modest enough to call himself not a "wise man" but a "lover of wisdom" (φίλος, σοφία), and his calling not a profession of wisdom but a search for wisdom. However, despite the disclaimer, the term *philosophy* soon came to signify *wisdom* simply, meaning by this the highest and most precious kind of knowledge.

Now human knowledge has for its object everything that falls in any way within human experience. It has *extensively* a great variety in its subject-matter, and *intensively* a great variety in its degrees of depth and clearness and perfection. *Individual facts* of the past, communicated by human testimony, form the raw materials of *historical* knowledge. Then there are all the individual things and events that fall within one's own personal experience. Moreover, by the study of human language (or languages), of works of the human mind and products of human genius and skill, we gain a knowledge of *literature*, and of the *arts*—the fine arts and the mechanical arts. But not merely do we use our senses and memory thus to accumulate an unassorted stock of informations about isolated facts: a miscellaneous mass of mental furniture which constitutes the bulk of human knowledge in its *least developed* form—*cognitio vulgaris*, the knowledge of the comparatively uneducated and unreflecting classes of mankind. We also use our reasoning faculty to reflect, compare, classify these informations, to interpret them, to reason about them, to infer from them *general truths* that embrace individual things and events *beyond our personal experience*; we try to explain them by seeking out their *reasons* and *causes*. This mental activity gradually converts our knowledge into *scientific* knowledge, and thus gives rise to those great groups of systematized truths called the *sciences*: as, for example, the physical and mathematical sciences, the elements of which usually form part of our early education. These sciences teach us a great deal about ourselves and the universe in which we live. There is no need to dwell on the precious services conferred upon mankind by discoveries due to the progress of the various *special* sciences: mathematics as applied to engineering of all sorts; astronomy; the physical sciences of light, heat, sound, electricity, magnetism, etc.; chemistry in all its branches; physiology and anatomy as applied in medicine and surgery. All these undoubtedly contribute much to man's *bodily* well-being. But man has a *mind* as well as a body, and he is moreover a *social* being: there are, therefore, other special sciences—"human" as distinct from "physical" sciences—in which man himself is studied in his mental activities and social relations with his fellow-men: the sciences of social and political economy, constitutional and civil law, government, statesmanship, etc. Furthermore, man is a *moral* being, recognizing distinctions of good and bad, right and wrong, pleasure and happiness, duty and responsibility, in his own conduct; and finally he is a *religious* being, face to face with the fact that men universally entertain views, beliefs, convictions of some sort or other, regarding man's subjection to, and dependence on, some higher power or powers dwelling somehow or somewhere within or above the whole universe of his direct and immediate experience: there are therefore also sciences which deal with these domains, morality and religion. Here, however, the domains are so extensive, and the problems raised by their phenomena are of such far-reaching importance, that the sciences which deal with them can hardly be called special sciences, but rather constituent portions of the one wider and deeper *general* science which is what men commonly understand nowadays by philosophy.

The distinction between the special sciences on the one hand and philosophy, the general science, on the other, will help us to realize more clearly the nature and scope of the latter. The special sciences are concerned with discovering the *proximate* reasons and causes of this, that, and the other definite department in the whole universe of our experience. The subject-matter of some of them is totally different from that of others: physiology studies the functions of living organisms; geology studies the formation of the earth's crust. Or if two or more of them investigate the same subject-matter they do so from different standpoints, as when the zoologist and the physiologist study the same type or specimen in the animal kingdom. But the common feature of all is this, that each seeks only the reasons, causes, and laws which give a *proximate* and *partial* explanation of the facts which it investigates, leaving untouched and unsolved a number of deeper and wider questions which may be raised about the *whence* and *whither* and *why*, not only of the facts themselves, but of the reasons, causes and laws assigned by the particular science in explanation of these facts.

Now it is those deeper and wider questions, which can be answered only by the discovery of the *more remote* and *ultimate* reasons and causes of things, that philosophy undertakes to investigate, and—as far as lies within man's power—to answer. No one has ever disputed the supreme importance of such inquiries into the ultimate reasons and causes of things—into such questions as these, for instance: What is the nature of man himself? Has he in him a principle of life which is spiritual and immortal? What was his first origin on the earth? Whence did he come? Has his existence any purpose, and if so, what? Whither does he tend? What is his destiny? Why does he distinguish between a right and a wrong in human conduct? What is the ultimate reason or ground of this distinction? Why have men generally some form or other of religion? Why do men generally believe in God? Is there really a God? What is the origin of the whole universe of man's experience? Of life in all its manifestations? Has the universe any intelligible or intelligent purpose, and if so, what? Can the human mind give a certain answer to any of these or similar questions? What about the nature and value of human *knowledge* itself? What is its scope and what are its limitations? And since vast multitudes of men *believe* that the human race has been specially enlightened by God Himself, by Divine Revelation, to know for certain what man's destiny is, and is specially aided by God Himself, by Divine Grace, to work out this destiny—the question immediately arises: What are the real relations between reason alone on the one hand and reason enlightened by such Revelation on the other, in other words between natural knowledge and supernatural faith?

Now it will be admitted that the special sciences take us some distance along the road towards an answer to such questions, inasmuch as the truths established by these sciences, and even the wider hypotheses conceived though not strictly verified in them, furnish us with most valuable data in our investigation of those questions. Similarly the alleged fact of a Divine Revelation cannot be ignored by any man desirous of using all the data available as helps towards their solution. The Revelation embodied in Christianity claims not merely to enlighten us in regard to many ultimate questions which mankind would be able to answer without its assistance, but also to tell us about our destiny some truths of supreme import, which of ourselves we should never have been able to discover. It is obvious, then, that whether a man has been brought up from his infancy to believe in the Christian Revelation or not, his whole outlook on life will be determined very largely by his belief or disbelief in its authenticity and its contents. Similarly, if he be a Confucian, or a Buddhist, or a Mohammedan, his outlook will be in part determined by what he believes of their teachings. Man's conduct in life has undoubtedly many determining influences, but it will hardly be denied that among them the predominant influence is exerted by the views that he holds, the things he believes to be true, concerning his own origin, nature and destiny, as well as the origin, nature and destiny of the universe in which he finds himself. The Germans have an expressive term for that which, in the absence of a more appropriate term, we may translate as a man's *world-outlook*; they call it his *Weltanschauung*. Now this world-outlook is formed by each individual for himself from his interpretation of *his experience as a whole*. It is not unusual to call this world-outlook a man's *philosophy of life*. If we use the term *philosophy* in this wide sense it obviously includes whatever light a man may gather from the *special sciences*, and whatever light he may gather from a divinely revealed *religion* if he believes in such, as well as the light his own reason may shed upon a special and direct study of those ultimate questions themselves, to which we have just referred. But we mention this wide sense of the term *philosophy* merely to put it aside; and to state that we use the term in the sense more commonly accepted nowadays, the sense in which it is understood to be distinct from the *special sciences* on the one side and from *supernatural theology* or the systematic study of divinely revealed religion on the other. Philosophy is distinct from the special sciences because while the latter seek the proximate, the former seeks the ultimate grounds, reasons and causes of all the facts of human experience. Philosophy is distinct from supernatural theology because while the former uses *the unaided power of human reason* to study the ultimate questions raised by human experience, the latter uses *reason enlightened by Divine Revelation* to study the contents of this Revelation in all their bearings on man's life and destiny.

Hence we arrive at this simple and widely accepted definition of philosophy: *the science of all things through their ultimate reasons and causes as discovered by the unaided light of human reason.*[5] The first part of this definition marks off philosophy from the special sciences, the second part marks it off from supernatural theology.

We must remember, however, that these three departments of knowledge—scientific, philosophical, and revealed—are not isolated from one another in any man's mind; they overlap in their subject-matter, and though differing in their respective standpoints they permeate one another through and through. The separation of the special sciences from philosophy, though adumbrated in the speculations of ancient times and made more definite in the middle ages, was completed only in modern times through the growth and progress of the special sciences themselves. The line of demarcation between philosophy and supernatural theology must be determined by the proper relations between Reason and Faith: and naturally these relations are a subject of debate between philosophers who believe in the existence of an authentic Divine Revelation and philosophers who do not. It is the duty of the philosopher as such to determine by the light of reason whether a Supreme Being exists and whether a Divine Revelation to man is possible. If he convinces himself of the existence of God he will have little difficulty in inferring the *possibility* of a Divine Revelation. The *fact* of a Divine Revelation is a matter not for philosophical but for historical research. Now when a man has convinced himself of the existence of God and the fact of a Divine Revelation—the *preambula fidei* or prerequisite conditions of

Faith, as they are called—he must see that it is eminently reasonable for him to believe in the contents of such Divine Revelation; he must see that the truths revealed by God cannot possibly trammel the freedom of his own reason in its philosophical inquiries into ultimate problems concerning man and the universe; he must see that these truths may possibly act as beacons which will keep him from going astray in his own investigations: knowing that truth cannot contradict truth he knows that if he reaches a conclusion really incompatible with any certainly revealed truth, such conclusion must be erroneous; and so he is obliged to reconsider the reasoning processes that led him to such a conclusion.[6] Thus, the position of the Christian philosopher, aided in this negative way by the truths of an authentic Divine Revelation, has a distinct advantage over that of the philosopher who does not believe in such revelation and who tries to solve all ultimate questions independently of any light such revelation may shed upon them. Yet the latter philosopher as a rule not only regards the "independent" position, which he himself takes up in the name of "freedom of thought" and "freedom of research," as the superior position, but as the only one consistent with the dignity of human reason; and he commonly accuses the Christian philosopher of allowing reason to be "enslaved" in "the shackles of dogma". We can see at once the unfairness of such a charge when we remember that the Christian philosopher has convinced himself *on grounds of reason alone* that God exists and has made a revelation to man. His belief in a Divine Revelation is a *reasoned* belief, a *rationabile obsequium* (Rom. XII. I); and only if it were a blind belief, unjustifiable on grounds of reason, would the accusation referred to be a fair one. The Christian philosopher might retort that it is the unbelieving philosopher himself who really destroys "freedom of thought and research," by claiming for the latter what is really an abuse of freedom, namely *license* to believe what reason shows to be erroneous. But this counter-charge would be equally unfair, for the unbelieving philosopher does not claim any such undue license to believe what he knows to be false or to disbelieve what he knows to be true. If he denies the fact or the possibility of a Divine Revelation, and therefore pursues his philosophical investigations without any regard to the contents of such revelation, it is because he has convinced himself on grounds of reason that such revelation is neither a fact nor a possibility. He and the Christian philosopher cannot both be right; one of them must be wrong; but as reasonable men they should agree to differ rather than hurl unjustifiable charges and counter-charges at each other.

All philosophers who believe in the Christian Revelation and allow its authentic teachings to guide and supplement their own rational investigation into ultimate questions, are keenly conscious of the consequent superior depth and fulness and certitude of Christian philosophy as compared with all the other conflicting and fragmentary philosophies that mark the progress of human speculation on the ultimate problems of man and the universe down through the centuries. They feel secure in the possession of a *philosophia perennis*,[7] and none more secure than those of them who complete and confirm that philosophy by the only full and authentic deposit of Divinely Revealed Truth, which is to be found in the teaching of the Catholic Church.

The history of philosophical investigation yields no one universally received conception of what philosophy is, nor would the definition given above be unreservedly accepted. Windelband, in his *History of Philosophy*⁸ instances the following predominant conceptions of philosophy according to the chronological order in which they prevailed: (*a*) the systematic investigation of the problems raised by man and the universe (early Grecian philosophy: absence of differentiation of philosophy from the special sciences); (*b*) the practical art of human conduct, based on rational speculation (later Grecian philosophy: distrust in the value of knowledge, and emphasis on practical guidance of conduct); (*c*) the helper and handmaid of the Science of Revealed Truth, *i.e.* supernatural theology, in the solution of ultimate problems (the Christian philosophy of the Fathers of the Church and of the Medieval Schools down to the sixteenth century: universal recognition of the value of the Christian Revelation as an aid to rational investigation); (*d*) a purely rational investigation of those problems, going beyond the investigations of the special sciences, and either abstracting from, or denying the value of, any light or aid from Revelation (differentiation of the domains of science, philosophy and theology; modern philosophies from the sixteenth to the nineteenth century; excessive individualism and rationalism of these as unnaturally divorced from recognition of, and belief in, Divine Revelation, and unduly isolated from the progressing positive sciences); (*e*) a critical analysis of the significance and scope and limitations of human knowledge itself (recent philosophies, mainly concerned with theories of knowledge and speculations on the nature of the cognitive process and the reliability of its products).

These various conceptions are interesting and suggestive; much might be said about them, but not to any useful purpose in a brief introductory chapter. Let us rather, adopting the definition already set forth, try next to map out into its leading departments the whole philosophical domain.

III. DIVISIONS OF PHILOSOPHY: SPECULATIVE AND PRACTICAL PHILOSOPHY.— The general problem of classifying all the sciences built up by human thought is a logical problem of no little complexity when one tries to work it out in detail. We refer to this general problem only to mention a widely accepted principle on which it is usually approached, and because the division of philosophy itself is a section of the general problem. The principle in question is that sciences may be distinguished indeed by partial or total *diversity of subject-matter*, but that such diversity is not essential, that *diversity of standpoint* is necessary and sufficient to constitute distinct sciences even when these deal with one and the same subject-matter. Now applying this principle to philosophy we see firstly that it has the same subject-matter as all the special sciences taken collectively, but that it is distinct from all of them inasmuch as it studies their data not from the standpoint of the proximate causes, but from the higher standpoint of the ultimate causes of these data. And we see secondly that philosophy, having this one higher standpoint throughout all its departments, is *one* science; that its divisions are only material divisions; that there is not a plurality of philosophies as there is a plurality of sciences, though there is a plurality of departments in philosophy.[9] Let us now see what these departments are.

If we ask why people seek knowledge at all, in any department, we shall detect two main impelling motives. The first of these is simply the desire to know: *trahimur omnes cupiditate sciendi.* The natural feeling of wonder, astonishment, "*admiratio*," which accompanies our perception of things and events, prompts us to seek their causes, to discover the reasons which will make them *intelligible* to us and enable us to *understand* them. But while the possession of knowledge for its own sake is thus a motive of research it is not the only motive. We seek knowledge *in order to use it* for the guidance of our conduct in life, for the orientation of our activities, for the improvement of our condition; knowing that knowledge is power, we seek it in order to make it minister to our needs. Now in the degree in which it fulfils such ulterior purposes, or is sought for these purposes, knowledge may be described as *practical*; in the degree in which it serves no ulterior end, or is sought for no ulterior end, other than that of perfecting our minds, it may be described as *speculative.* Of course this latter purpose is in itself a highly practical purpose; nor indeed is there any knowledge, however speculative, but has, or at least is capable of having, some influence or bearing on the actual tenor and conduct of our lives; and in this sense all knowledge is practical. Still we can distinguish broadly between knowledge which has no direct, immediate bearing on our acts, and knowledge that has.[10] Hence the possibility of distinguishing between two great domains of philosophical knowledge— *Theoretical* or *Speculative Philosophy*, and *Practical Philosophy*. There are, in fact, two great domains into which the data of all human experience may be divided; and for each distinct domain submitted to philosophical investigation there will be a distinct department of philosophy. A first domain is the order *realized* in the universe independently of man; a second is the order which man himself *realizes*: *things*, therefore, and *acts*. The order of the external universe, the order of nature as it is called, exists independently of us: we merely study it (*speculari*, θεωρέω), we do not create it. The other or *practical* order is established by our acts of *intelligence* and *will*, and by our *bodily action* on external things under the direction of those faculties in the arts. Hence we have a *speculative* or *theoretical* philosophy and a *practical* philosophy.[11]

IV. Departments of Practical Philosophy: Logic, Ethics and Esthetics.—In the domain of human activities, to the right regulation of which practical philosophy is directed, we may distinguish two departments of mental activity, namely *intellectual* and *volitional*, and besides these the whole department of *external*, executive or bodily activity. In general the right regulation of acts may be said to consist in directing them to the realization of some ideal; for all cognitive acts this ideal is the *true*, for all appetitive or volitional acts it is the *good*, while for all external operations it may be either the *beautiful* or the *useful*—the respective objects of the fine arts and the mechanical arts or crafts.

Logic, as a practical science, studies the mental acts and processes involved in discovering and proving truths and systematizing these into sciences, with a view to directing these acts and processes aright in the accomplishment of this complex task. Hence it has for its subject-matter, in a certain sense, *all* the data of human experience, or whatever can be an object of human thought. But it studies these data not directly or in themselves or for their own sake, but only in so far as our acts of reason, which form its direct object, are brought to bear upon them. In all the other sciences we employ thought to study the various objects of thought as things, events, realities; and hence these may be called "real" sciences, *scientiae reales*; while in Logic we study thought itself, and even here not speculatively for its own sake or as a reality (as we study it for instance in Psychology), but practically, as a process capable of being directed towards the discovery and proof of truth; and hence in contradistinction to the other sciences as "real," we call Logic *the* "rational" science, *scientia rationalis*. Scholastic philosophers express this distinction by saying that while Speculative Philosophy studies *real* being (*Ens Reale*), or the objects of direct thought (*objecta primae intentionis mentis*), Logic studies the being which is the *product of thought* (*Ens Rationis*), or objects of reflex thought (*objecta secundae intentionis mentis*).[12] The mental processes involved in the attainment of scientific truth are conception, judgment and inference; moreover these processes have to be exercised methodically by the combined application of analysis and synthesis, or induction and deduction, to the various domains of human experience. All these processes, therefore, and the methods of their application, constitute the proper subject-matter of Logic. It has been more or less a matter of debate since the days of Aristotle whether Logic should be regarded as a department of philosophical science proper, or rather as a preparatory discipline, an instrument or *organon* of reasoning—as the collection of Aristotle's own logical treatises was called,—and so as a vestibule or introduction to philosophy. And there is a similar difference of opinion as to whether or not it is advisable to set down Logic as the first department to be studied in the philosophical curriculum. Such doubts arise from differences of view as to the questions to be investigated in Logic, and the point to which such investigations should be carried therein. It is possible to distinguish between a more elementary treatment of thought-processes with the avowedly practical aim of setting forth canons of inference and method which would help and train the mind to reason and investigate correctly; and a more philosophical treatment of those processes with the speculative aim of determining their ultimate significance and validity as factors of knowledge, as attaining to truth, as productive of science and certitude. It is only the former field of investigation that is usually accorded to

Logic nowadays; and thus understood Logic ought to come first in the curriculum as a preparatory training for philosophical studies, accompanied, however, by certain elementary truths from Psychology regarding the nature and functions of the human mind. The other domain of deeper and more speculative investigation was formerly explored in what was regarded as a second portion of logical science, under the title of "Critical" Logic—*Logica Critica*. In modern times this is regarded as a distinct department of Speculative Philosophy, under the various titles of *Epistemology, Criteriology*, or the *Theory of Knowledge*.

Ethics or Moral Philosophy (ἦθος, *mos, mores,* morals, conduct) is that department of practical philosophy which has for its subject-matter all human acts, *i.e.* all acts elicited or commanded by the will of man considered as a free, rational and responsible agent. And it studies human conduct with the practical purpose of discovering the ultimate end or object of this conduct, and the principles whereby it must be regulated in order to attain to this end. Ethics must therefore analyse and account for the distinction of *right* and *wrong* or *good* and *bad* in human conduct, for its feature of *morality*. It must examine the motives that influence conduct: pleasure, well-being, happiness, duty, obligation, moral law, etc. The supreme determining factor in all such considerations will obviously be *the ultimate end of man*, whatever this may be: his destiny as revealed by a study of his nature and place in the universe. Now the nature of man is studied in Psychology, as are also the nature, conditions and effects of his free acts, and the facilities, dispositions and forms of character consequent on these. Furthermore, not only from the study of man in Psychology, but from the study of the external universe in Cosmology, we amass data from which in Natural Theology we establish the existence of a Supreme Being. We then prove in Ethics that the last end of man, his highest perfection, consists in knowing, loving, serving, and thus glorifying God, both in this life and in the next. Hence we can see how these branches of speculative philosophy subserve the practical science of morals. And since a man's interpretation of the moral distinctions—as of right or wrong, meritorious or blameworthy, autonomous or of obligation—which he recognizes as pertaining to his own actions—since his interpretation of these distinctions is so intimately bound up with his religious outlook and beliefs, it is at once apparent that the science of Ethics will be largely influenced and determined by the system of speculative philosophy which inspires it, whether this be Theism, Monism, Agnosticism, etc. No doubt the science of Ethics must take as its data all sorts of moral beliefs, customs and practices prevalent at any time among men; but it is not a speculative science which would merely aim at *a posteriori* inferences or inductive generalizations from these data; it is a practical, *normative* science which aims at discovering the truth as to what is the right and the wrong in human conduct, and at pointing out the right application of the principles arising out of this truth. Hence it is of supreme importance for the philosopher of morals to determine whether the human race has really been vouchsafed a Divine Revelation, and, convincing himself that Christianity contains such a revelation, to recognize the possibility of supplementing and perfecting what his own natural reason can discover by what the Christian religion teaches about the end of man as the supreme determining principle of human conduct. Not that he is to take the revealed truths of Christianity as principles of moral *philosophy*; for these are the principles of the *supernatural Christian Theology* of human morals; but that as a Christian philosopher, *i.e.* a philosopher who recognizes the truth of the Christian Revelation, he should reason out philosophically a science of Ethics which, so far as it goes, will be in harmony with the moral teachings of the Christian Religion, and will admit of being perfected by these. This recognition, as already remarked, will not be a hindrance but a help to him in exploring the wide domains of the individual, domestic, social and religious conduct of man; in determining, on the basis of theism established by natural reason, the right moral conditions and relations of man's conduct as an individual, as a member of the family, as a member of the state, and as a creature of God. The nature, source and sanction of authority, domestic, social and religious; of the dictate of conscience; of the natural moral law and of all positive law; of the moral virtues and vices—these are all questions which the philosopher of Ethics has to explore by the use of natural reason, and for the investigation of which the Christian philosopher of Ethics is incomparably better equipped than the philosopher who, though possessing the compass of natural reason, ignores the beacon lights of Divinely Revealed Truths.

Esthetics, or the *Philosophy of the Fine Arts*, is that department of philosophy which studies the conception of the *beautiful* and its external expression in the works of nature and of man. The arts themselves, of course, whether concerned with the realization of the useful or of the beautiful, are distinct from sciences, even from practical sciences.[13] The *technique* itself consists in a skill acquired by practice—by practice guided, however, by a set of practical canons or rules which are the ripe fruit of experience.[14] But behind every art there is always some background of more or less speculative truth. The conception of the *useful*, however which underlies the mechanical arts and crafts, is not an ultimate conception calling for any further analysis than it receives in the various special sciences and in metaphysics. But the conception of the *beautiful* does seem to demand a special philosophical consideration. On the subjective or mental side the esthetic sense, artistic taste, the sentiment of the beautiful, the complex emotions accompanying such experience; on the objective side the elements or factors requisite to produce this experience; the relation of the esthetic to the moral, of the beautiful to the good and the true—these are all distinctly philosophical questions. Up to the present time, however, their treatment has been divided between the other departments of philosophy—psychology, cosmology, natural theology, general metaphysics, ethics—rather than grouped together to form an additional distinct department.

V. Departments of Speculative Philosophy: Metaphysics.—The philosophy which studies the order realized in things apart from our activity, speculative philosophy, has been variously divided up into separate departments from the first origins of philosophical speculation.

When we remember that all intellectual knowledge of things involves the apprehension of *general* truths or laws about these things, and that this apprehension of intelligible aspects common to a more or less extensive group of things involves the exercise of *abstraction*, we can understand how the whole domain of speculative knowledge, whether scientific or philosophical, can be differentiated into certain layers or levels, so to speak, according to various degrees of abstractness and universality in the intelligible aspects under which the data of our experience may be considered. On this principle Aristotle and the scholastics divided all speculative knowledge into three great domains, *Physics*, *Mathematics* and *Metaphysics*, with their respective proper objects, *Change*, *Quantity* and *Being*, objects which are successively apprehended in three great stages of abstraction traversed by the human mind in its effort to understand and explain the Universal Order of things.

And as a matter of fact perhaps the first great common and most obvious feature which strikes the mind reflecting on the visible universe is the feature of all-pervading change (κίνησις), movement, evolution, progress and regress, growth and decay; we see it everywhere in a variety of forms, mechanical or local change, quantitative change, qualitative change, vital change. Now the knowledge acquired by the study of things under this common aspect is called *Physics*. Here the mind abstracts merely from the individualizing differences of this change in individual things, and fixes its attention on the great, common, sensible aspect itself of visible change.

But the mind can abstract even from the sensible changes that take place in the physical universe and fix its attention on a *static* feature in the changing things. This static element (τὸ ἀκίνητον), which the intellect apprehends in *material* things as naturally inseparable from them (ἀκίνητον ἀλλ' οὐ χωριστόν), is their *quantity*, their extension in space. When the mind strips a material object of all its visible, sensible properties—on which its mechanical, physical and chemical changes depend—there still remains as an object of thought a something formed of parts outside parts in three dimensions of space. This *abstract* quantity, *quantitas intelligibilis*—whether as continuous or discontinuous, as *magnitude* or *multitude*—is the proper object of *Mathematics*.

But the mind can penetrate farther still into the reality of the material data which it finds endowed with the attributes of change and quantity: it can eliminate from the object of its thought even this latter or mathematical attribute, and seize on something still more fundamental. The very essence, substance, nature, being itself, of the thing, the underlying subject and root principle of all the thing's operations and attributes, is something deeper than any of these attributes, something at least mentally distinct from these latter (τὸ ἀκίνητον καὶ χωριστόν): and this something is the proper object of man's highest speculative knowledge, which Aristotle called ἡ πρώτη φιλοσοφία, *philosophia prima*, the *first* or *fundamental* or *deepest* philosophy.[15]

But he gave this latter order of knowledge another very significant title: he called it *theology* or *theological science*, ἐπιστήμη θεολογίκή, by a denomination derived *a potiori parte*, from its nobler part, its culmination in the knowledge of God. Let us see how. For Aristotle *first philosophy* is the science of *being and its essential attributes*.[16] Here the mind apprehends its object as *static* or abstracted from change, and as *immaterial* or abstracted from quantity, the fundamental attribute of material reality—as ἀκίνητον καὶ χωριστόν. Now it is the substance, nature, or essence of *the things of our direct and immediate experience*, that forms the proper object of this highest science. But in these things the substance, nature, or essence, is not found in *real and actual* separation from the material attributes of change and quantity; it is *considered* separately from these only by an effort of mental abstraction. Even the nature of man himself is not wholly immaterial; nor is the spiritual principle in man, his soul, entirely exempt from material conditions. Hence in so far as first philosophy studies the being of the things of our direct experience, its object is immaterial only *negatively* or *by mental abstraction*. But does this study bring within the scope of our experience any being or reality that is *positively and actually* exempt from all change and all material conditions? If so the study of this being, the Divine Being, will be the highest effort, the crowning perfection, of *first philosophy*; which we may therefore call the *theological* science. "If," writes Aristotle,[17] "there really exists a substance absolutely immutable and immaterial, in a word, a Divine Being—as we hope to prove—then such Being must be the absolutely first and supreme principle, and the science that attains to such Being will be theological."

In this triple division of speculative philosophy into Physics, Mathematics, and Metaphysics, it will naturally occur to one to ask: Did Aristotle distinguish between what he called Physics and what we nowadays call the special physical sciences? He did. These special *analytic* studies of the various departments of the physical universe, animate and inanimate, Aristotle described indiscriminately as "partial" sciences: αἱ ἐν μέρει ἐπιστημάι—ἐπιστημαὶ ἐν μέρει λεγόμεναι. These descriptive, inductive, comparative studies, proceeding *a posteriori* from effects to causes, he conceived rather as a preparation for scientific knowledge proper; this latter he conceived to be a *synthetic*, deductive explanation of things, in the light of some common aspect detected in them as principle or cause of all their concrete characteristics.[18] Such synthetic knowledge of things, in the light of some such common aspect as change, is what he regarded as scientific knowledge, meaning thereby what we mean by philosophical knowledge.[19] What he called *Physics*, therefore, is what we nowadays understand as *Cosmology* and *Psychology*.[20]

Mathematical science Aristotle likewise regarded as science in the full and perfect sense, *i.e.* as philosophical. But just as we distinguish nowadays between the special physical and human sciences on the one hand, and the philosophy of external nature and man on the other, so we may distinguish between the special mathematical sciences and a Philosophy of Mathematics: with this difference, that while the former groups of special sciences are mainly inductive the mathematical group is mainly deductive. Furthermore, the Philosophy of Mathematics—which investigates questions regarding the ultimate significance of mathematical concepts, axioms and assumptions: unity, multitude, magnitude, quantity, space, time, etc.—does not usually form a separate department in the philosophical curriculum: its problems are dealt with as they arise in the other departments of Metaphysics.

Before outlining the modern divisions of Metaphysics we may note that this latter term was not used by Aristotle. We owe it probably to Andronicus of Rhodes (✝ 40 B.C.), who, when arranging a complete edition of Aristotle's works, placed next in order after the *Physics*, or physical treatises, all the parts and fragments of the master's works bearing upon the immutable and immaterial object of the *philosophia prima*; these he labelled τὰ μετὰ τὰ (βιβλία) φυσικα, *post physica*, the books *after the physics*: hence the name *metaphysics*,[21] applied to this highest section of speculative philosophy. It was soon noticed that the term, thus fortuitously applied to such investigations, conveyed a very appropriate description of their scope and character if interpreted in the sense of "*supra*-physica," or "*trans*-physica": inasmuch as the object of these investigations is a *hyperphysical* object, an object that is either positively and really, or negatively and by abstraction, beyond the material conditions of quantity and change. St. Thomas combines both meanings of the term when he says that the study of its subject-matter comes naturally *after* the study of physics, and that we naturally pass from the study of the sensible to that of the suprasensible.[22]

The term *philosophia prima* has now only an historical interest; and the term *theology*, used without qualification, is now generally understood to signify *supernatural* theology.

VI. DEPARTMENTS OF METAPHYSICS: COSMOLOGY, PSYCHOLOGY, AND NATURAL THEOLOGY.—Nowadays the term *Metaphysics* is understood as synonymous with speculative philosophy: the investigation of the being, nature, or essence, and essential attributes of the realities which are also studied in the various special sciences: the search for the *ultimate* grounds, reasons and causes of these realities, of which the proximate explanations are sought in the special sciences. We have seen that it has for its special object that most abstract aspect of reality whereby the latter is conceived as changeless and immaterial; and we have seen that a being may have these attributes either by mental abstraction merely, or in actual reality. In other words the philosophical study of things that are really material not only suggests the possibility, but establishes the actual existence, of a Being that is really changeless and immaterial: so that metaphysics in all its amplitude would be *the philosophical science of things that are negatively* (by abstraction) *or positively* (in reality) *immaterial*. This distinction suggests a division of metaphysics into *general* and *special* metaphysics. The former would be the philosophical study of *all* being, considered by mental abstraction as immaterial; the latter would be the philosophical study of the really and positively changeless and immaterial Being,—God. The former would naturally fall into two great branches: the study of *inanimate* nature and the study of *living* things, *Cosmology* and *Psychology*; while special metaphysics, the philosophical study of the *Divine* Being, would constitute *Natural Theology*. These three departments, one of special metaphysics and two of general metaphysics, would not be three distinct philosophical sciences, but three departments of the one speculative philosophical science. The standpoint would be the same in all three sections, *viz. being* considered as *static and immaterial* by *mental abstraction*: for whatever *positive* knowledge we can reach about being that is really immaterial can be reached only through concepts derived from material being and applied analogically to immaterial being.

Cosmology and *Psychology* divide between them the whole domain of man's immediate experience. Cosmology, utilizing not only the data of direct experience, but also the conclusions established by the analytic study of these data in the physical sciences, explores the origin, nature, and destiny of the material universe. Some philosophers include among the data of Cosmology all the phenomena of vegetative life, reserving sentient and rational life for Psychology; others include even sentient life in Cosmology, reserving the study of human life for Psychology, or, as they would call it, Anthropology.[23] The mere matter of location is of secondary importance. Seeing, however, that man embodies in himself all three forms of life, vegetative, sentient, and rational, all three would perhaps more naturally belong to Psychology, which would be the philosophical study of life in all its manifestations (ψυχή, the vital principle, the soul). Just as the conclusions of the physical sciences are the data of Cosmology, so the conclusions of the natural or biological sciences—Zoology, Botany, Physiology, Morphology, Cellular Biology, etc.—are the data of Psychology. Indeed in Psychology itself—especially in more recent years—it is possible to distinguish a positive, analytic, empirical study of the phenomena of consciousness, a study which would rank rather as a special than as an ultimate or philosophical science; and a synthetic, rational study of the results of this analysis, a study which would be strictly philosophical in character. This would have for its object to determine the origin, nature and destiny of living things in general and of man himself in particular. It would inquire into the nature and essential properties of living matter, into the nature of the subject of conscious states, into the operations and faculties of the human mind, into the nature of the human soul and its mode of union with the body, into the rationality of the human intellect and the freedom of the human will, the spirituality and immortality of the human soul, etc.

But since the human mind itself is the natural instrument whereby man acquires *all* his knowledge, it will be at once apparent that the study of the phenomenon of *knowledge* itself, of the *cognitive* activity of the mind, can be studied, and must be studied, not merely as a natural phenomenon of the mind, but from the point of view of *its special significance as representative* of objects other than itself, from the point of view of *its validity or invalidity, its truth or falsity*, and with the special aim of determining the scope and limitations and conditions of its objective validity. We have already referred to the study of human knowledge from this standpoint, in connexion with what was said above concerning Logic. It has a close kinship with Logic on the one hand, and with Psychology on the other; and nowadays it forms a distinct branch of speculative Philosophy under the title of *Criteriology, Epistemology*, or the *Theory of Knowledge*.

Arising out of the data of our direct experience, external and internal, as studied in the philosophical departments just outlined, we find a variety of evidences all pointing beyond the domain of this direct experience to the supreme conclusion that there exists of necessity, distinct from this directly experienced universe, as its Creator, Conserver, and Ruler, its First Beginning and its Last End, its *Alpha* and *Omega*, One Divine and Infinite Being, the Deity. The existence and attributes of the Deity, and the relations of man and the universe to the Deity, form the subject-matter of *Natural Theology*.

VII. DEPARTMENTS OF METAPHYSICS: ONTOLOGY AND EPISTEMOLOGY.— According to the Aristotelian and scholastic conception speculative philosophy would utilize as data the conclusions of the special sciences—physical, biological, and human. It would try to reach a deeper explanation of their data by synthesizing these under the wider aspects of change, quantity, and being, thus bringing to light the ultimate causes, reasons, and explanatory principles of things. This whole study would naturally fall into two great branches: General Metaphysics (*Cosmology* and *Psychology*), which would study things exempt from quantity and change not really but only by mental abstraction; and Special Metaphysics (*Natural Theology*), which would study the positively immaterial and immutable Being of the Deity.

This division of Metaphysics, thoroughly sound in principle, and based on a sane and rational view of the relation between the special sciences and philosophy, has been almost entirely[24] supplanted in modern times by a division which, abstracting from the erroneous attitude that prompted it in the first instance, has much to recommend it from the standpoint of practical convenience of treatment. The modern division was introduced by Wolff (1679-1755), a German philosopher,—a disciple of Leibniz (1646-1716) and forerunner of Kant (1724-1804).[25] Influenced by the excessively deductive method of Leibniz' philosophy, which he sought to systematize and to popularize, he wrongly conceived the metaphysical study of reality as something wholly apart and separate from the inductive investigation of this same reality in the positive sciences. It comprised the study of the most fundamental and essential principles of being, considered in themselves; and the deductive application of these principles to the three great domains of actual reality, the corporeal universe, the human soul, and God. The study of the first principles of being in themselves would constitute *General Metaphysics*, or *Ontology* (ὄντος-λόγος). Their applications would constitute three great departments of *Special Metaphysics*: *Cosmology*, which he described as "transcendental" in opposition to the experimental physical sciences; *Psychology*, which he termed "rational" in opposition to the empirical biological sciences; and finally Natural Theology, which he entitled *Theodicy* (Θεός-δίκη-δικαιόω), using a term invented by Leibniz for his essays in vindication of the wisdom and justice of Divine Providence notwithstanding the evils of the universe.

"The spirit that animated this arrangement of the departments of metaphysics," writes Mercier, "was unsound in theory and unfortunate in tendency. It stereotyped for centuries a disastrous divorce between philosophy and the sciences, a divorce that had its origin in circumstances peculiar to the intellectual atmosphere of the early eighteenth century. As a result of it there was soon no common language or understanding between scientists and philosophers. The terms which expressed the most fundamental ideas—matter, substance, movement, cause, force, energy, and such like—were taken in different senses in science and in philosophy. Hence misunderstandings, aggravated by a growing mutual distrust and hostility, until finally people came to believe that scientific and metaphysical preoccupations were incompatible if not positively opposed to each other."[26]

How very different from the disintegrating conception here criticized is the traditional Aristotelian and scholastic conception of the complementary functions of philosophy and the sciences in unifying human knowledge: a conception thus eloquently expressed by NEWMAN in his *Idea of a University*:—[27]

"All that exists, as contemplated by the human mind, forms one large system or complex fact.... Now, it is not wonderful that, with all its capabilities, the human mind cannot take in this whole vast fact at a single glance, or gain possession of it at once. Like a short-sighted reader, its eye pores closely, and travels slowly, over the awful volume which lies open for its inspection. Or again, as we deal with some huge structure of many parts and sides, the mind goes round about it, noting down, first one thing, then another, as best it may, and viewing it under different aspects, by way of making progress towards mastering the whole.... These various partial views or abstractions ... are called sciences ... they proceed on the principle of a division of labour.... As they all belong to one and the same circle of objects, they are one and all connected together; as they are but aspects of things, they are severally incomplete in their relation to the things themselves, though complete in their own idea and for their own respective purposes; on both accounts they at once need and subserve each other. And further, the comprehension of the bearings of one science on another, and the use of each to each, and the location and limitation and adjustment and due appreciation of them all, one with another, this belongs, I conceive, to a sort of science distinct from all of them, and in some sense, a science of sciences, which is my own conception of what is meant by Philosophy...."

Without in any way countenancing such an isolation of metaphysics from the positive sciences, we may, nevertheless, adopt the modern division in substance and in practice. While recognizing the intimate connexion between the special sciences and metaphysics in all its branches, we may regard as *General Metaphysics* all inquiries into the fundamental principles of *being* and of *knowing*, of *reality* and of *knowledge*; and as *Special Metaphysics* the philosophical study of physical nature, of human nature, and of God, the Author and Supreme Cause of all finite reality. Thus, while special metaphysics would embrace Cosmology, Psychology, and Natural Theology, general metaphysics would embrace Ontology and Epistemology. These two latter disciplines must no doubt investigate what is in a certain sense one and the same subject-matter, inasmuch as *knowledge* is knowledge of reality, nor can the *knowing mind* (the *subjectum cognoscens*) and the known reality (the *objectum cognitum*) be wholly separated or studied in complete isolation from each other. Yet the whole content of human experience, which forms their common subject-matter, can be regarded by mental abstraction from the two distinct standpoints of the knowing mind and the known reality, and can thus give rise to two distinct sets of problems. Epistemology is thus concerned with the truth and certitude of human knowledge; with the subjective conditions and the scope and limits of its validity; with the subjective or mental factors involved in knowing.[28] Ontology is concerned with the objects of knowledge, with reality considered in the widest, deepest, and most fundamental aspects under which it is conceived by the human mind: with the being and becoming of reality, its possibility and its actuality, its essence and its existence, its unity and plurality; with the aspects of truth, goodness, perfection, beauty, which it assumes in relation with our minds; with the contingency of finite reality and the grounds and implications both of its actual existence and of its intelligibility; with the modes of its concrete existence and behaviour, the supreme categories of reality as they are called: substance, individual nature, and personality; quantity, space and time, quality and relation, causality and purpose. These are the principal topics investigated in the present volume. The investigation is confined to fundamental concepts and principles, leaving their applications to be followed out in special metaphysics. Furthermore, the theory of knowledge known as *Moderate Realism*,[29] the Realism of Aristotle and the Scholastics, in regard to the validity of knowledge both sensual and intellectual, is assumed throughout: because not alone is this the true theory, but—as a natural consequence—it is the only theory which renders the individual things and events of human experience really intelligible, and at the same time keeps the highest and most abstract intellectual speculations of metaphysics in constant and wholesome contact with the concrete, actual world in which we live, move, and have our being.

VIII. Remarks on Some Misgivings and Prejudices.—The student, especially the beginner, will find the investigations in this volume rather abstract; but if he remembers that the content of our intellectual concepts, be they ever so abstract and universal, is really embodied in the individual things and events of his daily experience, he will not be disposed to denounce all ultimate analysis of these concepts as "unprofitable" or "unreal". He will recognize that the reproach of "talking in the air," which was levelled by an eminent medieval scholastic[30] at certain philosophers of his time, tells against the metaphysical speculations of Conceptualism, but not against those of Moderate Realism. The reproach is commonly cast at *all* systematic metaphysics nowadays—from prejudices too numerous and varied to admit of investigation here.[31] The modern prejudice which denies the very possibility of metaphysics, a prejudice arising from Phenomenism, Positivism, and Agnosticism—systems which are themselves no less metaphysical than erroneous—will be examined in due course.[32]

But really in order to dispel all such misgivings one has only to remember that metaphysics, systematic or otherwise, is nothing more than a man's reasoned outlook on the world and life. Whatever his conscious opinions and convictions may be regarding the nature and purpose of himself, and other men, and the world at large—and if he use his reason at all he must have some sort of opinions and convictions, whether positive or negative, on these matters—those opinions and convictions are precisely that man's metaphysics. "Breaking free for the moment from all historical and technical definition, let us affirm: *To get at reality*—this is the aim of metaphysics." So writes Professor Ladd in the opening chapter of his *Theory of Reality*.[33] But if this is so, surely a systematic attempt to "get at reality," no matter how deep and wide, no matter how abstract and universal be the conceptions and speculations to which it leads us, cannot nevertheless always and of necessity have the effect of involving us in a mirage of illusion and unreality.

Systematic metaphysics—to quote again the author just referred to—[34] is ... the necessary result of a patient, orderly, well-informed, and prolonged study of those ultimate problems which are proposed to every reflective mind by the real existences and actual transactions of selves and of things. Thus considered it appears as the least abstract and foreign to concrete realities of all the higher pursuits of reason. Mathematics is abstract; logic is abstract; mathematical and so-called "pure" physics are abstract. But metaphysics is bound by its very nature and calling always to keep near to the actual and to the concrete. Dive into the depths of speculation indeed it may; and its ocean is boundless in expanse and deep beyond all reach of human plummets. But it finds its place of standing, for every new turn of daring explanation, on some bit of solid ground. For it is actuality which it wishes to understand—although in reflective and interpretative way. To quote from Professor Royce: "The basis of our whole theory is the bare, brute fact of experience which you have always with you, namely, the fact: *Something is real.* Our question is: What is this reality? or, again, What is the ultimately real?"[35]

The wonderful progress of the positive sciences during the last few centuries has been the occasion of prejudice against metaphysics in a variety of ways. It is objected, for instance, that metaphysics has no corresponding progress to boast of; and from this there is but a small step to the conclusion that all metaphysical speculation is sterile. The comparison is unfair for many reasons. Research into the ultimate grounds and causes of things is manifestly more difficult than research into their proximate grounds and causes. Again, while the positive sciences have increased our knowledge mainly in extent rather than in depth, it is metaphysics and only metaphysics that can increase this knowledge in its unity, comprehensiveness, and significance.

A positive increase in our knowledge of the manifold data of human experience is not the aim of metaphysics; its aim is to give an ultimate meaning and interpretation to this knowledge. It is not utilitarian in the narrower sense in which the positive and special sciences are utilitarian by ministering to our material needs; but in the higher and nobler sense of pointing out to us the bearing of all human knowledge and achievement on our real nature and destiny. True, indeed, individual leaders and schools of metaphysics have strayed from the truth and spoken with conflicting and uncertain voices, especially when they have failed to avail themselves of Truth Divinely Revealed. This, however, is not a failure of metaphysics but of individual metaphysicians. And furthermore, it is undeniable withal, that the metaphysical labours of the great philosophers in all ages have contributed richly to the enlightenment and civilization of mankind—particularly when these labours have been in concord and co-operation with the elevating and purifying influences of the Christian religion. Of no metaphysical system is this so entirely true as of that embodied in Scholastic Philosophy. The greatest intellect of the Middle Ages, St. Thomas Aquinas, gave to this philosophy an expression which is rightly regarded by the modern scholastic as his intellectual charter and the most worthy starting-point of his philosophical investigations. The following passage from an eminent representative of modern scholastic thought[36] is sufficiently suggestive to admit of quotation:—

Amid the almost uninterrupted disintegration of systems during the last three centuries, the philosophy of St. Thomas has alone been able to stand the shock of criticism; it alone has proved sufficiently solid and comprehensive to serve as an intellectual basis and unifying principle for all the new facts and phenomena brought to light by the modern sciences. And unless we are much mistaken, those who take up and follow this philosophy will come to think, as we do, that on the analysis of mental acts and processes, on the inner nature of corporeal things, of living things, and of man, on the existence and nature of God, on the foundations of speculative and moral science, none have thought or written more wisely than St. Thomas Aquinas. But though we place our programme and teaching under the patronage of the illustrious name of this prince of scholastics, we do not regard the Thomistic philosophy as an ideal beyond possibility of amelioration, or as a boundary to the activity of the human mind. We do think, however, on mature reflection, that we are acting no less wisely than modestly in taking it as our starting-point and constant standard of reference. This we say in answer to those of our friends and enemies who are occasionally pleased to ask us if we really do mean to lead back the modern mind into the Middle Ages, and to identify philosophy *simply* with the thought of any *one* philosopher. Manifestly, we mean nothing of the kind. Has not Leo XIII., the great initiator of the new scholastic movement, expressly warned us[37] to be mindful of the present: "Edicimus libenti gratoque animo recipiendum esse quidquid sapienter dictum, quidquid utiliter fuerit a quopiam inventum atque excogitatum"?

St. Thomas himself would be the first to rebuke those who would follow his own philosophical opinions in all things against their own better judgment, and to remind them of what he wrote at the head of his *Summa*: that in philosophy, of all arguments that based on human authority is the weakest, "locus ab auctoritate quæ fundatur super ratione humana, est infirmissimus."[38]

Again, therefore, let us assert that respect for tradition is not servility but mere elementary prudence. Respect for a doctrine of whose soundness and worth we are personally convinced is not fetishism; it is but a rational and rightful tribute to the dominion of Truth over Mind.

Modern scholastics will know how to take to heart and profit by the lessons of the seventeenth and eighteenth century controversies; they will avoid the mistakes of their predecessors; they will keep in close contact with the special sciences subsidiary to philosophy and with the views and teachings of modern and contemporary thinkers.[39]

An overweening confidence in the power of the special sciences to solve ultimate questions, or at least to tell us all that can be known for certain about these problems, a confidence based on the astonishing progress of those sciences in modern times, is the source of yet another prejudice against metaphysics. It is a prejudice of the half-educated mind, of the camp-followers of science, not of its leaders. These latter are keenly conscious that the solution of ultimate questions lies entirely beyond the methods of the special sciences. Not that even the most eminent scientists do not indulge in speculations about ultimate problems—as they have a perfect right to do. But though they may be themselves quite aware that such speculations are distinctly metaphysical, there are multitudes who seem to think that a theory ceases to be metaphysical and becomes scientific provided only it is broached by a scientific expert as distinct from a metaphysician.[40] But all sincere thinkers will recognize that no ultimate question about the totality of human experience can be solved by any science which explores merely a portion of this experience. Nay, the more rapid and extensive is the progress of the various special sciences, the more imperative and insistent becomes the need to collect and collate their separate findings, to interrogate them one and all as to whether and how far these findings fit in with the facts and conditions of human life and existence, to determine what light and aid they contribute to the solution of the great and ever recurring questions of the *whence?* and *whither?* and *why?* of man and the universe. One who is a sincere scientist as well as an earnest philosopher has written *à propos* of this necessity in the following terms:—

The farther science has pushed back the limits of the discernible universe, the more insistently do we feel the demand within us for some satisfactory explanation of the whole. The old, eternal problems rise up before us and clamour loudly and ever more loudly for some newer and better solution. The solution offered by a bygone age was soothing at least, if it was not final. In the present age, however, the problems reappear with an acuteness that is almost painful: the deep secret of our own human nature, the questions of our origin and destiny, the intermeddling of blind necessity and chance and pain in the strange, tangled drama of our existence, the foibles and oddities of the human soul, and all the mystifying problems of social relations: are not these all so many enigmas which torment and trouble us whithersoever we turn? And all seem to circle around the one essential question: Has human nature a real meaning and value, or is it so utterly amiss that truth and peace will never be its portion?[41]

A final difficulty against philosophical research is suggested by the thought that if the philosopher has to take cognizance of all the conclusions of all the special sciences his task is an impossible one, inasmuch as nowadays at all events it would take a lifetime to become proficient in a few of these sciences not to speak of all of them.

There is no question, however, of becoming proficient in them; the philosopher need not be a specialist in any positive science; his acquaintance with the contents of these sciences need extend no farther than such established conclusions and such current though unverified hypotheses as have an immediate bearing on ultimate or philosophical problems.

Moreover, while it would be injurious both to philosophy and to science, as is proved by the history of both alike, to separate synthetic from analytic speculation by a divorce between philosophy and science; while it would be unwise to ignore the conclusions of the special sciences and to base philosophical research *exclusively* on the data of the plain man's common and unanalysed experience, it must be remembered on the other hand that the most fundamental truths of speculative and practical philosophy, the truths that are most important for the right and proper orientation of human life, can be established and defended independently of the special researches of the positive sciences. The human mind had not to await the discovery of radium in order to prove the existence of God. Such supreme truths as the existence of God, the immortality of the human soul, the freedom of the human will, the existence of a moral law, the distinction between right and wrong, etc., have been *always* in possession of the human race. It has been, moreover, confirmed in its possession of them by Divine Revelation. And it has not needed either the rise or the progress of modern science to defend them. These fundamental rational truths constitute a *philosophia perennis*: a fund of truth which is, like all truth, *immutable*, though our human insight into it may develop in depth and clearness.

But while this is so it is none the less true that philosophy, to be progressive in its own order, must take account of every new fact and conclusion brought to light in every department of scientific—and historical, and artistic, and literary, and every other sort of—research. And this for the simple reason that every such accession, whether of fact or of theory, is an enlargement of human experience; as such it clamours on the one hand for philosophical interpretation, for explanation in the light of what we know already about the ultimate grounds and causes of things, for admission into our world-outlook, for adjustment and co-ordination with the previous contents of the latter; while, on the other hand, by its very appearance on the horizon of human experience it may enrich or illumine, rectify or otherwise influence, this outlook or some aspect of it.[42]

If, then, philosophy has to take account of advances in every other department of human research, it is clear that its mastery at the present day is a more laborious task than ever it was in the past. In order to get an intelligent grasp of its principles in their applications to the problems raised by the progress of the sciences, to newly discovered facts and newly propounded hypotheses, the student must be familiar with these facts and hypotheses; and all the more so because through the medium of a sensational newspaper press that has more regard for novelty than truth, these facts and hypotheses are no sooner brought to light by scientists than what are often garbled and distorted versions of them are circulated among the masses.[43]

Similarly, in order that a sound system of speculative and practical philosophy be expounded, developed, and defended at the present time, a system that will embrace and co-ordinate the achieved results of modern scientific research, a system that will offer the most satisfactory solutions of old difficulties in new forms and give the most reasonable and reliable answers to the ever recurring questionings of man concerning his own nature and destiny—it is clear that the insufficiency of individual effort must be supplemented by the co-operation of numbers. It is the absence of fulness, completeness, adequacy, in most modern systems of philosophy, their fragmentary character, the unequal development of their parts, that accounts very largely for the despairing attitude of the many who nowadays despise and turn away from philosophical speculation. Add to this the uncertain voice with which these philosophies speak in consequence of their advocates ignoring the implications of the most stupendous fact in human experience,—the Christian Revelation. But there is one philosophy which is free from these defects, a philosophy which is in complete harmony with Revealed Truth, and which forms with the latter the only true *Philosophy of Life*; and that one philosophy is the system which, assimilating the wisdom of Plato, Aristotle and all the other greatest thinkers of the world, has been traditionally expounded in the Christian schools—the *Scholastic* system of philosophy. It has been elaborated by no one man, and is the original fruit of no one mind. Unlike the philosophies of Kant or Hegel or Spencer or James or Comte or Bergson, it is not a "one-man" philosophy. It cannot boast of the novelty or originality of the many eccentric and ephemeral "systems" which have succeeded one another so rapidly in recent times in the world of intellectual fashion; but it has ever possessed the enduring novelty of the *truth*, which is ever ancient and ever new. Now although this philosophy may have been mastered in its broad outlines and applications by specially gifted individuals in past ages, its progressive exposition and development, and its application to the vastly extended and ever-growing domains of experience that are being constantly explored by the special sciences, can never be the work of any individual: it can be accomplished only by the earnest co-operation of Christian philosophers in every part of the civilized world.[44]

In carrying on this work we have not to build from the beginning. "It has sometimes been remarked," as Newman observes,[45] "when men have boasted of the knowledge of modern times, that no wonder we see more than the ancients because we are mounted upon their shoulders." Yes; the intellectual toilers of to-day are heirs to the intellectual wealth of their ancestors. We have tradition: not to despise but to use, critically, judiciously, reverently, if we are to use it profitably. Thomas Davis has somewhere said that they who demolish the past do not build up for the future. And we have the Christian Revelation, as a *lamp* to our *feet* and a *light* to our *paths*[46] in all those rational investigations which form the appointed task of the philosopher. Hence,

Let knowledge grow from more to more,
But more of reverence in us dwell;
That mind and soul, according well,
May make one music as before,
But vaster.[47]

Chapter I.

Being And Its Primary Determinations.

1. OUR CONCEPT OF BEING: ITS EXPRESSION AND FEATURES.—The term "*Being*" (Lat. *ens*; Gr. ὤν; Ger. *Seiend*; Fr. *étant*) as present participle of the verb *to be* (Lat. *esse*; Gr. ἕιναι; Ger. *Sein*; Fr. *être*) means *existing* (*existens, existere*). But the participle has come to be used as a noun; and as such it does not necessarily imply actual existence *hic et nunc*. It does indeed imply some relation to actual existence; for we designate as "being" (in the substantive sense) only whatever we conceive as actually existing or at least as capable of existing; and it is from the participial sense, which implies actual existence, that the substantive sense has been derived. Moreover, the intelligible use of the word "being" as a term implies a reference to some actually existing sphere of reality.[48] It is in the substantive meaning the term will be most frequently used in these pages, as the context will show. When we speak of "a being" in the concrete, the word has the same meaning as "thing" (*res*) used in the wide sense in which this latter includes persons, places, events, facts and phenomena of whatsoever kind. In the same sense we speak of "a reality," this term having taken on a concrete, in addition to its original abstract, meaning. "Being" has also this abstract sense when we speak of "the being or reality of things". Finally it may be used in a collective sense to indicate the sum-total of all that is or can be—all reality.

(*a*) The notion of being, spontaneously reached by the human mind, is found on reflection to be the *simplest* of all notions, defying every attempt at analysis into simpler notions. It is involved in every other concept which we form of any object of thought whatsoever. Without it we could have no concept of anything.

(*b*) It is thus the first of all notions *in the logical order*, *i.e.* in the process of rational thought.

(*c*) It is also the *first* of all notions *in the chronological order*, the first which the human mind forms in the order of time. Not, of course, that we remember having formed it before any other more determinate notions. But the child's awakening intellectual activity must have proceeded from the simplest, easiest, most superficial of all concepts, to fuller, clearer, and more determinate concepts, *i.e.* from the vague and confused notion of "being" or "thing" to notions of definite modes of being, or kinds of thing.

(*d*) This direct notion of being is likewise the *most indeterminate* of all notions; though not of course entirely indeterminate. An object of thought, to be conceivable or intelligible at all by our finite minds, must be rendered definite in some manner and degree; and even this widest notion of "being" is rendered intelligible only by being conceived as positive and as contrasting with absolute non-being or nothingness.[49]

According to the Hegelian philosophy "pure thought" can apparently think "pure being," *i.e.* being in absolute indeterminateness, being as not even differentiated from "pure not-being" or absolute nothingness. And this absolutely indeterminate confusion (we may not call it a "synthesis" or "unity") of something and nothing, of being and not-being, of positive and negative, of affirmation and denial, would be conceived by our finite minds as the objective correlative of, and at the same time as absolutely identical with, its subjective correlative which is "pure thought". Well, it is with the human mind and its objects, and how it thinks those objects, that we are concerned at present; not with speculations involving the gratuitous assumption of a Being that would transcend all duality of subject and object, all determinateness of knowing and being, all distinction of thought and thing. We believe that the human mind can establish the existence of a Supreme Being whose mode of Thought and Existence transcends all human comprehension, but it can do so only as the culminating achievement of all its speculation; and the transcendent Being it thus reaches has nothing in common with the monistic ideal-real being of Hegel's philosophy. In endeavouring to set out from the high *a priori* ground of such an intangible conception, the Hegelian philosophy starts at the wrong end.

(*e*) Further, the notion of being is the *most abstract* of all notions, poorest in intension as it is widest in extension. We derive it from the data of our experience, and the process by which we reach it is a process of abstraction. We lay aside all the differences whereby things are distinguished from one another; we do not consider these differences; we prescind or abstract from them mentally, and retain for consideration only what is common to all of them. This common element forms the explicit content of our notion of being.

It must be noted, however, that we do not *positively exclude* the differences from the *object* of our concept; we cannot do this, for the simple reason that the differences too are "being," inasmuch as they too are modes of being. Our attitude towards them is *negative*; we merely abstain from considering them explicitly, though they remain in our concept implicitly. The separation effected is only mental, subjective, notional, formal, negative; not objective, not real, not positive. Hence the process by which we narrow down the concept of being to the more comprehensive concept of this or that generic or specific mode of being, does not add to the former concept anything really new, or distinct from, or extraneous to it; but rather brings out explicitly something that was implicit in the latter. The composition of being with its modes is, therefore, only *logical* composition, not real.

On the other hand, it would seem that when we abstract a generic mode of being from the specific modes subordinate to the former, we *positively exclude* the differentiating characteristics of these species; and that, conversely, when we narrow down the genus to a subordinate species we do so by *adding on* a differentiating mode which was not contained even implicitly in the generic concept. Thus, for example, the differentiating concept "rational" is not contained even implicitly in the generic concept "animal": it is added on *ab extra* to the latter[50] in order to reach the specific concept of "rational animal" or "man"; so that in abstracting the generic from the subordinate specific concept we prescind *objectively* and *really* from the differentiating concept, by positively excluding this latter. This kind of abstraction is called objective, real, positive; and the composition of such generic and differentiating modes of being is technically known as *metaphysical* composition. The different modes of being, which the mind can distinguish at different levels of abstraction in any specific concept—such as "rational," "sentient," "living," "corporeal," in the concept of "man"—are likewise known as "metaphysical grades" of being.

It has been questioned whether this latter kind of abstraction is always used in relating generic, specific, and differential modes of being. At first sight it would not appear to be a quite satisfactory account of the process in cases where the generic notion exhibits a mode of being which can be embodied only in one or other of a number of alternative specific modes by means of *differentiae* not found in any things lying outside the genus itself. The generic notion of "plane rectilinear figure" does not, of course, include explicitly its species "triangle," "quadrilateral," "pentagon," etc.; nor does it include even implicitly any definite one of them. But the concept of each of the differentiating characters, *e.g.* the *differentia* "three-sidedness," is unintelligible except as a mode of a "plane rectilinear figure".[51] This, however, is only accidental, *i.e.* due to the special objects considered;[52] and even here there persists this difference that whereas what differentiates the species of plane rectilinear figures is not explicitly and formally plane-rectilinearity, that which differentiates finite from infinite being, or substantial from accidental being, is itself also formally and explicitly *being*. But there are other cases in which the abstraction is manifestly objective. Thus, for example, the differentiating concept "rational" does not even implicitly include the generic concept "animal," for the former concept may be found realized in beings other than animals; and the differentiating concept "living" does not even implicitly include the concept "corporeal," for it may be found realized in incorporeal beings.

(*f*) Since the notion of being is so simple that it cannot be analysed into simpler notions which might serve as its *genus* and *differentia*, it *cannot* strictly speaking *be defined*. We can only describe it by considering it from various points of view and comparing it with the various modes in which we find it realized. This is what we have been attempting so far. Considering its fundamental relation to existence we might say that "Being is that which exists or is at least capable of existing": *Ens est id quod existit vel saltem existere potest.* Or, considering its relation to its opposite we might say that "Being is that which is not absolute nothingness": *Ens est id quod non est nihil absolutum.* Or, considering its relation to our minds, we might say that "Being is whatever is thinkable, whatever can be an object of thought".

(*g*) The notion of being is so universal that it transcends all actual and conceivable determinate modes of being: it embraces infinite being and all modes of finite being. In other words it is *not itself a generic, but a transcendental notion*. Wider than all, even the widest and highest genera, it is not itself a genus. A genus is determinable into its species by the addition of differences which lie outside the concept of the genus itself; being, as we have seen, is not in this way determinable into its modes.

2. IN WHAT SENSE ARE ALL THINGS THAT EXIST OR CAN EXIST SAID TO BE "REAL" OR TO HAVE "BEING"?—A generic concept can be predicated *univocally*, *i.e.* in the same sense, of its subordinate species. These latter differ from one another by characteristics which lie outside the concept of the genus, while they all agree in realizing the generic concept itself: they do not of course realize it in the same way,[53] but as such it is really and truly in each of them and is predicated in the same sense of each. But the characteristics which differentiate all genera and species from one another, and from the common notion of being, in which they all agree, are likewise *being*. That in which they differ is being, as well as that in which they agree. *Hence we do not predicate "being" univocally of its various modes.* When we say of the various classes of things which make up our experience that they are "real" (or "realities," or "beings"), we do not apply this predicate in altogether the same sense to the several classes; for as applied to each class it connotes the whole content of each, not merely the part in which this agrees with, but also the part in which it differs from, the others. Nor yet do we

apply the concept of "being" in a totally different sense to each separate determinate mode of being. When we predicate "being" of its modes *the predication is not merely equivocal.* The concept expressed by the predicate-term "being" is not totally different as applied to each subject-mode; for in all cases alike it implies either actual existence or some relation thereto. It only remains, therefore, that we must regard the notion of being, when predicated of its several modes, *as partly the same and partly different*; and this is what we mean when we say that *the concept of being is analogical, that being is predicated analogically of its various modes.*

Analogical predication is of two kinds: a term or concept may be affirmed of a variety of subjects either by analogy *of attribution* or by analogy *of proportion*. We may, for instance, speak not only of a man as "healthy," but also of his food, his countenance, his occupation, his companionship, etc., as "healthy". Now health is found really only in the man, but it is *attributed* to the other things owing to some extrinsic but real connexion which they have with his health, whether as cause, or effect, or indication, of the latter. This is analogy of attribution; the subject of which the predicate is properly and primarily affirmed being known as the primary analogue or *analogum princeps*, those to which it is transferred being called the *analogata*. It underlies the figures of speech known as metynomy and synechdoche. Now on account of the various relations that exist between the different modes of being, relations of cause and effect, whole and part, means and end, ground and consequence, etc.—relations which constitute the *orders* of existing and possible things, the *physical* and the *metaphysical* orders—being is of course predicated of its modes by *analogy of attribution*; and in such predication infinite being is the primary analogue for finite beings, and the substance-mode of being for all accident-modes of being.

Inasmuch, however, as being is not merely attributed to these modes extrinsically, but belongs to all of them intrinsically, it is also predicated of them by *analogy of proportion*. This latter sort of analogy is based on similarity of relations. For example, the act of understanding bears a relation to the mind similar to that which the act of seeing bears to the eye, and hence we say of the mind that it "sees" things when it understands them. Or, again, we speak of a verdant valley in the sunshine as "smiling," because its appearance bears a relation to the valley similar to that which a smile bears to the human countenance. Or again, we speak of the parched earth as "thirsting" for the rains, or of the devout soul as "thirsting" for God, because these relations are recognized as similar to that of a thirsty person towards the drink for which he thirsts. In all such cases the analogical concept implies not indeed the same attribute (differently realized) in all the analogues (as in univocal predication) but rather a similarity in the relation or proportion in which each analogue embodies or realizes some attribute or attributes peculiar to itself. Seeing is to the eye as understanding is to the mind; smiling is to the countenance as the pleasing appearance of its natural features is to the valley. Rain is to the parched earth, and God is to the devout soul, as drink is to the thirsty person. It will be noted that in all such cases the analogical concept is affirmed primarily and properly of some one thing (the *analogum princeps*), and of the other only secondarily, and relatively to the former.

Now, if we reflect on the manner in which being is affirmed of its various modes (*e.g.* of the infinite and the finite; or of substance and accident; or of spiritual and corporeal substances; or of quantities, or qualities, or causes, etc.) we can see *firstly* that although these differ from one another *by all that each of them is, by the whole being of each*, yet there is an all-pervading similarity between the relations which these modes bear each to its own existence. All have, or can have, actual existence: each according to the grade of perfection of its own reality. If we conceive infinite being as the cause of all finite beings, then the former exists in a manner appropriate to its all-perfect reality, and finite beings in a manner proportionate to their limited realities; and so of the various modes of finite being among themselves. Moreover, we can see *secondly*, as will be explained more fully below,[54] that being is affirmed of the finite by virtue of its dependence on the infinite, and of accident by virtue of its dependence on substance.[55] Being or reality is therefore predicated of its modes by *analogy of proportion*.[56]

Is a concept, when applied in this way, one, or is it really manifold? It is not simply one, for this would yield univocal predication; nor is it simply manifold, for this would give equivocal predication. Being, considered in its vague, imperfect, inadequate sense, as involving some common or similar proportion or relation to existence in all its analogues, is one; considered as representing clearly and adequately what is thus similarly related to each of the analogues, it is manifold.

Analogy of proportion is the basis of the figure of speech known as metaphor. It would be a mistake, however, to infer from this that what is thus analogically predicated of a number of things belongs intrinsically and properly only to one of them, being transferred by a mere extrinsic denomination to the others; and that therefore it does not express any genuine knowledge on our part about the nature of these other things. It does give us real knowledge about them. Metaphor is not equivocation; but perhaps more usually it is understood not to give us real knowledge because it is understood to be based on resemblances that are merely *fanciful*, not real. Still, no matter how slender and remote be the proportional resemblance on which the analogical use of language is based, in so far forth as it has such a *real* basis it gives us real insight into the nature of the analogues. And if we hesitate to describe such a use of language as "metaphorical," this is only because "metaphor" perhaps too commonly connotes a certain transferred and improper extension of the meaning of terms, based upon a *purely fanciful* resemblance.

All our language is primarily and *properly* expressive of concepts derived from the sensible appearances of material realities. As applied to the suprasensible, intelligible aspects of these realities, such as substance and cause, or to spiritual realities, such as the human soul and God, it is analogical in another sense; not as opposed to univocal, but as opposed to *proper*. That is, it expresses concepts which are not formed directly from the presence of the things which they signify, but are gathered from other things to which the latter are necessarily related in a variety of ways.[57] Considering the origin of our knowledge, the material, the sensible, the phenomenal, comes first in order, and moulds our concepts and language primarily to its own proper representation and expression; while the spiritual, the intelligible, the substantial, comes later, and must make use of the concepts and language thus already moulded.

If we consider, however, not the order in which we get our knowledge, but the order of *reality* in the objects of our knowledge, being or reality is primarily and more properly predicated of the infinite than of the finite, of the Creator than of the creature, of the spiritual than of the material, of substances than of their accidents and sensible manifestations or phenomena. Yet we do not predicate being or reality of the finite, or of creatures, in a mere transferred, extrinsic, improper sense, as if these were mere manifestations of the infinite, or mere effects of the First Cause, to which alone reality would properly belong. For creatures, finite things, are in a true and proper sense also real.

Duns Scotus and those who think with him contend that the concept of being, derived as it is from our experience of finite being, if applied only analogically to infinite being would give us no genuine knowledge about the latter. They maintain that whenever a universal concept is applied to the objects in which it is *realized intrinsically*, it is affirmed of these objects *univocally*. The notion of being, in its most imperfect, inadequate, indeterminate sense, is, they say, *one and the same* in so far forth as it is applicable to the infinite and the finite, and to all the modes of the finite; and it is therefore predicated of all univocally.[58] But although they apply the concept of being univocally to the infinite and the finite, *i.e.* to God and creatures, they admit that the *reality* corresponding to this univocal concept is *totally different* in God and in creatures: that God differs by *all that He is* from creatures, and they by *all that they are* from Him. While, however, Scotists emphasize the formal oneness or identity of the indeterminate common concept, followers of St. Thomas emphasize the fact that the various modes of being differ totally, by all that each of them is, from one another; and, from this radical diversity in the modes of being, they infer that the common concept should not be regarded as *simply* the same, but only as *proportionally* the same, as expressive of a *similar relation* of each intrinsically different mode of reality to actual existence.

Thomists lay still greater stress, perhaps, upon the second consideration referred to above, as a reason for regarding being as an analogical concept when affirmed of Creator and creature, or of substance and accident: the consideration that the finite is *dependent* on the infinite, and accident on substance. If being is realized in a true and proper sense, and intrinsically, as it undoubtedly is, in whatever is distinguishable from nothingness, why not say that we should affirm being or reality of all things "either as a genus in the strict sense, or else in some sense not analogical but proper, after the manner in which we predicate a genus of its species and individuals?... Since the object of our universal idea of being is admitted to be really in all things, we can evidently abstract from what is proper to substance and to accident, just as we abstract from what is proper to plants and to animals when we affirm of these that they are living things."[59]

"In reply to this difficulty," Father Kleutgen continues,[60] "we say in the first place that the idea of being is in truth less analogical and more proper than any belonging to the first sort of analogy [*i.e.* of attribution], and that therefore it approaches more closely to generic concepts properly so called. At the same time the difference which separates both from the latter concepts remains. For a name applied to many things is analogical if what it signifies is realized *par excellence* in one, and in the others only subordinately and dependently on that. Hence it is that Aristotle regards predication as analogical when something is affirmed of many things (1) either because these have a certain relation to some one thing, (2) or because they depend on some one thing. In the former case the thing signified by the name is really and properly found only in one single thing, and is affirmed of all the others only in virtue of some real relation of these to the former, whether this be (*a*) that these things merely resemble that single thing [metaphor], or (*b*) bear some other relation to it, such as that of effect to cause, etc. [metonymy]. In the latter case the thing signified by the name is really in each of the things of which it is affirmed; but it is in one alone *par excellence*, and in the others only by depending, for its very existence in them, on that one. Now the object of the term *being* is found indeed in accidents, *e.g.* in quantity, colour, shape; but certainly it must be applied primarily to substance, and to accidents only dependently on the latter: for quantity, colour, shape can have being only because the corporeal substance possesses these determinations. But this is not at all the case with a genus and its species. These differ from the genus, not by any such dependence, but by the addition of some special perfection to the constituents of the genus; for example, in the brute beast sensibility is added to vegetative life, and in man intelligence is added to sensibility. Here there is no relation of dependence for existence. Even if we considered human life as that of which life is principally asserted, we could not say that plants and brute beasts so depended for their life on the life of man that we could not affirm life of them except as dependent on the life of man: as we cannot attribute being to accidents except by reason of their dependence on substance. Hence it is that we can consider apart, and in itself, life in general, and attribute this to all living things without relating it to any other being."[61]

"It might still be objected that the one single being of which we may affirm life primarily and principally, ought to be not human life, but absolute life. And between this divine life and the life of all other beings there is a relation of dependence, which reaches even to the very existence of life in these other beings. In fact all life depends on the absolute life, not indeed in the way accident depends on substance, but in a manner no less real and far more excellent. This is entirely true; but what are we to conclude from it if not precisely this, which scholasticism teaches: that the perfections found in the various species of creatures can be affirmed of these in the same sense (*univocé*), but that they can be affirmed of God and creatures only analogically?"

"From all of which we can understand why it is that in regard to genera and species the analogy is in the things but not in our thoughts, while in regard to substance and accidents it is both in the things and in our thoughts: a difference which rests not solely on our manner of conceiving things, nor *a fortiori* on mere caprice or fancy, but which has its basis in the very nature of the things themselves. For though in the former case there is a certain analogy in the things themselves, inasmuch as the same nature, that of the genus, is realized in the species in different ways, still, as we have seen, that is not sufficient, without the relation of dependence, to yield a basis for analogy in our thoughts. For it is precisely because accident, as a determination of substance, presupposes this latter, that being cannot be affirmed of accident except as dependent on substance."

These paragraphs will have shown with sufficient clearness why we should regard being not as an univocal but as an analogical concept, when referred to God and creatures, or to substance and accident. For the rest, the divergence between the Scotist and the Thomist views is not very important, because Scotists also will deny that being is a genus of which the infinite and the finite would be species; finite and infinite are not *differentiae* superadded to being, inasmuch as each of these differs *by its whole reality*, and not merely by a determining portion, from the other; it is owing to the limitations of our abstractive way of understanding reality that we have to conceive the infinite by first conceiving being in the abstract, and then mentally determining this concept by another, namely, by the concept of "infinite mode of being"[62]; the infinite, and whatever perfections we predicate formally of the infinite, transcend all *genera*, *species* and *differentiae*, because the distinction of being into infinite and finite is prior to the distinction into genera, species and differentiae; this latter distinction applying only to finite, not to infinite being.[63]

The observations we have just been making in regard to the analogy of being are of greater importance than the beginner can be expected to realize. A proper appreciation of the way in which being or reality is conceived by the mind to appertain to the data of our experience, is indispensable to the defence of Theism as against Agnosticism and Pantheism.

3. REAL BEING AND LOGICAL BEING.—We may next illustrate the notion of being by approaching it from another standpoint—by examining a fundamental distinction which may be drawn between *real being* (*ens reale*) and *logical being* (*ens rationis*).

We derive all our knowledge, through external and internal sense perception, from the domain of actually existing things, these things including our own selves and our own minds. We form, from the data of sense-consciousness, by an intellectual process proper, mental representations of an abstract and universal character, which reveal to us partial aspects and phases of the natures of things. We have no intuitive intellectual insight into these natures. It is only by abstracting their various aspects, by comparing these in judgments, and reaching still further aspects by inferences, that we progress in our knowledge of things—gradually, step by step, *discursivé, discurrendo*. All this implies reflection on, and comparison of, our own ideas, our mental views of things. It involves the processes of defining and classifying, affirming and denying, abstracting and generalizing, analysing and synthesizing, comparing and relating in a variety of ways the objects grasped by our thought. Now in all these complex functions, by which alone the mind can *interpret rationally* what is given to it, by which alone, in other words, it can know reality, the mind necessarily and inevitably forms for itself (and expresses in intelligible language) a series of concepts which have for their objects only the *modes* in which, and the *relations* by means of which, it makes such gradual progress in its interpretation of what is given to it, in its knowledge of the real. These concepts are called *secundae intentiones mentis*—concepts of the second order, so to speak. And their objects, the modes and mutual relations of our *primae intentiones* or direct concepts, are called *entia rationis*—logical entities. For example, *abstractness* is a mode which affects not the reality which we apprehend intellectually, but the concept by which we apprehend it. So, too, is the *universality* of a concept, its communicability or applicability to an indefinite multitude of similar realities—the "*intentio universalitatis,*" as it is called—a mode of concept, not of the realities represented by the latter. So, likewise, is the *absence* of other reality than that represented by the concept, the *relative nothingness or non-being* by contrast with which the concept is realized as positive; and the *absolute nothingness or non-being* which is the logical correlative of the concept of being; and the static, unchanging self-identity of the object as conceived in the abstract.[64] These are not modes of reality *as it is* but *as it is conceived*. Again, the manifold logical relations which we establish between our concepts—relations of (extensive or intensive) identity or distinction, inclusion or inherence, etc.—are logical entities, *entia rationis*: relations of genus, species, differentia, proprium, accidens; the affirmative or negative relation between predicate and subject in judgment;[65] the mutual relations of antecedent and consequent in inference. Now all these logical entities, or *objecta secundae intentionis mentis*, are relations established by the mind itself between its own thoughts; they have, no doubt, a foundation in the real objects of those thoughts as well as in the constitution and limitations of the mind itself; but they have themselves, and can have, no other being than that which they have as products of thought. Their sole being consists in *being thought of*. They are necessary creations or products of the thought-process as this goes on in the human mind. We see that it is only by means of these relations we can progress in understanding things. In the thought-process we cannot help bringing them to light—and thinking them after the manner of realities, *per modum entis*. Whatever we think we must think through the concept of "being"; whatever we conceive we must conceive as "being"; but on reflection we easily see that such entities as "nothingness," "negation or absence or privation of being," "universality," "predicate"—and, in general, all relations established by our own thought between our own ideas representative of reality—can have themselves no reality proper, no actual or possible existence, other than that which they get from the mind in virtue of its making them objects of its own thought. Hence the scholastic definition of a logical entity or *ens rationis* as "that which has objective being merely in the intellect": "*illud quod habet esse objective tantum in intellectu, seu ... id quod a ratione excogitatur ut ens, cum tamen in se entitatem non habeat*".[66] Of course the mental process by which we think such entities, the mental state in which they are held in consciousness, is just as real as any other mental process or state. But the entity which is thus held in consciousness has and can have no other reality than what it has by being an object of thought. And this precisely is what distinguishes it from *real being*, from *reality*; for the latter, besides the ideal existence it has in the mind which thinks of it, has, or at least can have, a real existence of its own, independently altogether of our thinking about it. We assume here, of course—what is established elsewhere, as against the subjective idealism of phenomenists and the objective idealism of Berkeley—that the *reality* of *actual* things does not consist in their being perceived or thought of, that their "*esse*" is not "*percipi*," that they have a reality other than and independent of their actual presence to the thought of any human mind. And even purely possible things, even the creatures of our own fancy, the fictions of fable and romance, *could*, absolutely speaking and without any contradiction, have an existence in the actual order, in addition to the mental existence they receive from those who fancy them. Such entities, therefore, differ from *entia rationis*; they, too, are *real* beings.

What the reality of purely possible things is we shall discuss later on. Actually existing things at all events we assume to be *given* to the knowing mind, not to be *created* by the latter. Even in regard to these, however, we must remember that the mind in knowing them, in interpreting them, in seeking to penetrate the nature of them, is not purely passive; that reality as known to us—or, in other words, our knowledge of reality—is the product of a twofold factor: the subjective which is the mind, and the objective which is the extramental reality acting on, and thus revealing itself to, the mind. Hence it is that when we come to analyse in detail our knowledge of the nature of things—or, in other words, the natures of things as revealed to our minds—it will not be always easy to distinguish in each particular case the properties, aspects, relations, distinctions, etc., which are *real* (in the sense of being there in the reality independently of the consideration of the mind) from those that are merely *logical* (in the sense of being produced and superadded to the reality by the mental process itself).[67] Yet it is obviously a matter of the very first importance to determine, as far as may be possible, to what extent our knowledge of reality is not merely a mental *interpretation*, but a mental *construction*, of the latter; and whether, if there be a constructive or constitutive factor in thought, this should be regarded as interfering with the validity of thought as representative of reality. This problem—of the relation of the *ens rationis* to the *ens reale* in the process of cognition—has given rise to discussions which, in modern times, have largely contributed to the formation of that special branch of philosophical enquiry which is called Epistemology. But it must not be imagined that this very problem was not discussed, and very widely discussed, by philosophers long before the problem of the validity of knowledge assumed the prominent place it has won for itself in modern philosophy. Even a moderate familiarity with scholastic philosophy will enable the student to recognize this problem, in a variety of phases, in the discussions of the medieval schoolmen concerning the concepts of matter and form, the simplicity and composition of beings, and the nature of the various distinctions—whether logical, virtual, formal, or real—which the mind either invents or detects in the realities it endeavours to understand and explain.

4. REAL BEING AND IDEAL BEING.—The latter of these expressions has a multiplicity of kindred meanings. We use it here in the sense of "being *known*," *i.e.* to signify the "esse *intentionale*," the mental presence, which, in the scholastic theory of knowledge, an entity of whatsoever kind, whether real or logical, must have in the mind of the knower in order that he be aware of that entity. A mere logical entity, as we have seen, has and can have no other mode of being than this which consists in being an object of the mind's awareness. All real being, too, when it becomes an object of any kind of human cognition whatsoever—of intellectual thought, whether direct or reflex; of sense perception, whether external or internal—must obtain this sort of mental presence or mental existence: thereby alone can it become an "objectum *cognitum*". Only by such mental mirroring, or reproduction, or reconstruction, can reality become so related and connected with mind as to reveal itself to mind. Under this peculiar relation which we call cognition, the mind, as we know from psychology and epistemology, is not passive: if reality revealed itself immediately, as it is, to a purely passive mind (were such conceivable), the existence of error would be unaccountable; but the mind is not passive: under the influence of the reality it forms the intellectual concept (the *verbum mentale*), or the sense percept (the *species sensibilis expressa*), in and through which, and by means of which, it attains to its knowledge of the real.

But prior (ontologically) to this *mental* existence, and as partial cause of the latter, there is the *real* existence or being, which reality has independently of its being known by any individual human mind. Real being, then, as distinguished here from ideal being, is that which exists or can exist extramentally, whether it is known by the human mind or not, *i.e.* whether it exists also mentally or not.

That there is such real being, apart from the "thought"-being whereby the mind is constituted formally knowing, is proved elsewhere; as also that this *esse intentionale* has modes which cannot be attributed to the *esse reale*. We merely note these points here in order to indicate the errors involved in the opposite contentions. Our concepts are characterized by abstractness, by a consequent static immutability, by a plurality often resulting from purely mental distinctions, by a universality which transcends those distinctions and unifies the variety of all subordinate concepts in the widest concept of *being*. Now if, for example, we attribute the unifying mental mode of universality to real being, we must draw the pantheistic conclusion that all real being is one: the logical outcome of extreme realism. If, again, we transfer purely mental distinctions to the unity of the Absolute or Supreme Being, thus making them real, we thereby deny infinite perfection to the most perfect being conceivable: an error of which some catholic philosophers of the later middle ages have been accused with some foundation. If, finally, we identify the *esse reale* with the *esse intentionale*, and this with the thought-process itself, we find ourselves at the starting-point of Hegelian monism.[68]

5. FUNDAMENTAL DISTINCTIONS IN REAL BEING.—Leaving logical and ideal being aside, and fixing our attention exclusively on real being, we may indicate here a few of the most fundamental distinctions which experience enables us to recognize in our study of the universal order of things.

(*a*) *Possible or Potential Being and Actual Being.*—The first of these distinctions is that between possibility and actuality, between that which can be and that which actually is. For a proper understanding of this distinction, which will be dealt with presently, it is necessary to note here the following divisions of *actual* being, which will be studied in detail later on.

(*b*) *Infinite Being and Finite Beings.*—All people have a sufficiently clear notion of Infinite Being, or Infinitely Perfect Being: though not all philosophers are agreed as to how precisely we get this notion, or whether there actually exists such a being, or whether if such being does exist we can attain to a certain knowledge of such existence. By infinite being we mean a being possessing all conceivable perfections in the most perfect conceivable manner; and by finite beings all such beings as have actually any conceivable limitation to their perfection. About these nominal definitions there is no dispute; and scholasticism identifies their respective objects with *God* and *creatures*.

(*c*) *Necessary Being and Contingent Beings.*—Necessary being we conceive as that being which exists of necessity: being which if conceived at all cannot be conceived as non-existent: being in the very concept of which is essentially involved the concept of actual existence: so that the attempt to conceive such being as non-existent would be an attempt to conceive what would be self-contradictory. Contingent being, on the other hand, is being which is conceived not to exist of necessity: being which may be conceived as not actually existent: being in the concept of which is not involved the concept of actual existence. The same observations apply to this distinction as to the preceding one. It is obvious that any being which we regard as actual we must regard either as necessary or as contingent; and, secondly, that necessary being must be considered as absolutely independent, as having its actual existence *from itself*, by its own nature; while contingent being must be considered as dependent for its actual existence on some being *other* than itself. Hence necessary being is termed *Ens a se*, contingent being *Ens ab alio*.

(*d*) *Absolute Being and Relative Beings.*—In modern philosophy the terms "absolute" and "relative," as applied to being, correspond roughly with the terms "God" and "creatures" in the usage of theistic philosophers. But the former pair of terms is really of wider application than the latter. The term *absolute* means, etymologically, that which is loosed, unfettered, disengaged or free from bonds (*absolutum, ab-solvere, solvo = se-luo*, from λύω): that, therefore, which is not bound up with anything else, which is in some sense self-sufficing, independent; while the *relative* is that which is in some way bound up with something else, and which is so far not self-sufficing or independent. That, therefore, is *ontologically* absolute which is in some sense self-sufficing, independent of other things, *in its existence*; while the ontologically relative is that which depends in some real way for its existence on something else. Again, that is *logically* absolute which *can be conceived and known by us without reference to anything else*; while the logically relative is that which we can conceive and know only through our knowledge of something else. And since we usually name things according to the way in which we conceive them, we regard as absolute any being which is *by itself* and *of itself* that which we conceive it to be, or that which its name implies; and as relative any being which is what its name implies only *in virtue of some relation* to something else.[69] Thus, a man is a *man* absolutely, while he is a *friend* only relatively to others.

It is obvious that the primary and general meaning of the terms "absolute" and "relative" can be applied and extended in a variety of ways. For instance, *all* being may be said to be "relative" *to the knowing mind*, in the sense that all knowledge involves a transcendental relation of the known object to the knowing subject. In this widest and most improper sense even God Himself is relative, not however as being, but as known. Again, when we apply the same attribute to a variety of things we may see that it is found in one of them in the most perfect manner conceivable, or at least in a fuller and higher degree than it is found in the others;

and that it is found in these others only with some sort of subordination to, and dependence on, the former: we then say that it belongs to this *primarily* or *absolutely*, and to the others only *secondarily* or *relatively*. This is a less improper application of the terms than in the preceding case. What we have especially to remember here is that there are many different kinds of dependence or subordination, all alike giving rise to the same usage.

Hence, applying the terms absolute and relative to the predicate "being" or "real" or "reality," it is obvious in the first place that the *potential* as such can be called "being," or "reality" only in relation to the *actual*. It is the actual that is being *simpliciter, par excellence*; the potential is so only in relation to this.[70] Again, *substances* may be termed beings absolutely, while *accidents* are beings only relatively, because of their dependence on substances; though this relation is quite different from the relation of potential to actual being. Finally all finite, contingent realities, actual and possible, are what they are only because of their dependence on the Infinite and Necessary Being: and hence the former are relative and the latter absolute; though here again the relation is different from that of accident to substance, or of potential to actual.

Since the order of being includes all orders, and since a being is *absolutely* such-or-such in any order only when that being realizes in all its fulness and purity such-or-such reality, it follows that the being which realizes in all its fulness the reality of *being* is the Absolute Being in the highest possible sense of this term. This concept of Absolute Being is the richest and most comprehensive of all possible concepts: it is the very antithesis of that other concept of "being in general" which is common to everything and distinguished only from nothingness. It includes in itself all actual and possible modes and grades and perfections of finite things, apart from their limitations, embodying all of them in the one highest and richest concept of that which makes all of them real and actual, *viz.* the concept of Actuality or Actual Reality itself.

Hegel and his followers have involved themselves in a pantheistic philosophy by neglecting to distinguish between those two totally different concepts.[71] A similar error has also resulted from failure to distinguish between the various modes in which being that is relative may be dependent on being that is absolute. God is the Absolute Being; creatures are relative. So too is substance absolute being, compared with accidents as inhering and existing in substance. But God is not therefore to be conceived as the one all-pervading substance, of which all finite things, all phenomena, would be only accidental manifestations.

Chapter II.

Becoming And Its Implications.

6. THE STATIC AND THE CHANGING.—The things we see around us, the things which make up the immediate data of our experience, not only *are* or *exist*; they also *become*, or *come* into actual existence; they *change*; they pass out of actual existence. The abstract notion of being represents its object to the mind in a static, permanent, changeless, self-identical condition; but if this condition were an adequate representation of reality change would be unreal, would be only an illusion. This is what the Eleatic philosophers of ancient Greece believed, distinguishing merely between being and nothingness. But they were mistaken; for change in things is too obviously real to be eliminated by calling it an illusion: even if it were an illusion, this illusion at least would have to be accounted for. In order, therefore, to understand reality we must employ not merely the notion of being (something *static*), but also the notion of becoming, change, process, appearing and disappearing (something *kinetic*, and something *dynamic*). In doing so, however, we must not fall into the error of the opposite extreme from the Eleatics—by regarding change as the adequate representation of reality. This is what Heraclitus and the later Ionians did: holding that nothing *is*, that all *becomes* (πάντα ῥεῖ), that change is all reality, that the stable, the permanent, is non-existent, unreal, an illusion. This too is false; for change would be unintelligible without at least an abiding *law* of change, a permanent *principle* of some sort; which, in turn, involves the reality of some sort of abiding, stable, permanent being.

We must then—with Aristotle, as against both of those one-sided conceptions—hold to the reality both of being and of becoming; and proceed to see how the stable and the changing can both be real.

To convince ourselves that they are both real, very little reflection is needed. We have actual experience of both those elements of reality in our consciousness and memory of our own selves. Every human individual in the enjoyment of his mental faculties knows himself as an abiding, self-identical being, yet as constantly undergoing real changes; so that throughout his life he is really the same being, though just as certainly he really changes. In external nature, too, we observe on the one hand innumerable processes of growth and decay, of motion and interaction; and on the other hand a similarly all-pervading element of sameness or identity amid all this never-ending change.

7. THE POTENTIAL AND THE ACTUAL. (*a*) POSSIBILITY, ABSOLUTE, RELATIVE, AND ADEQUATE.—It is from our experience of actuality and change that we derive not only our notion of temporal duration, but also our notion of *potential being* or *possibility*, as distinct from that of *actual being* or *actuality*. It is from our experience of what actually exists that we are able to determine what can, and what cannot exist. We know from experience what gold is, and what a tower is; and that it is intrinsically possible for a golden tower to exist, that such an object of thought involves no contradiction, that therefore its existence is not impossible, even though it may never actually exist as a fact. Similarly, we know from experience what a square is, and what a circle is; and that it is intrinsically impossible for a square circle to exist, that such an object of thought involves a contradiction, that therefore not only is such an object never actually existent in fact, but that it is in no sense real, in no way possible.

Thus, *intrinsic* (or *objective, absolute, logical, metaphysical*) possibility is the mere non-repugnance of an object of thought to actual existence. Any being or object of thought that is conceivable in this way, that can be conceived as capable of actually existing, is called intrinsically (or objectively, absolutely, logically, metaphysically) possible being. The absence of such intrinsic capability of actual existence gives us the notion of the intrinsically (objectively, absolutely, logically, metaphysically) impossible. We shall return to these notions again. They are necessary here for the understanding of real change in the actual universe.

Fixing our attention now upon the real changes which characterize the data of our experience, let us inquire what conditions are necessary in order that an intrinsically possible object of thought become here and now an actual being. It matters not whether we select an example from the domain of organic nature, of inorganic nature, or of art—whether it be an oak, or an iceberg, or a statue. In order that there be here and now an actual oak-tree, it is necessary not only (1) that such an object be intrinsically possible, but (2) that there have been planted here an actual acorn, *i.e.* an actual being having in it subjectively and really the passive potentiality of developing into an actual oak-tree, and (3) that there be in the actual things around the acorn active powers or forces capable of so influencing the latent, passive potentiality of the acorn as gradually to evolve the oak-tree therefrom. So, too, for the (1) intrinsically possible iceberg, there are needed (2) water capable of becoming ice, and (3) natural powers or forces capable of forming it into ice and setting this adrift in the ocean. And for the (1) intrinsically possible statue there are needed (2) the block of marble or other material capable of becoming a statue, and (3) the sculptor having the power to mould this material into an actual statue.

In order, therefore, that a thing which is not now actual, but only intrinsically or absolutely possible, become actual, there must actually exist some being or beings endowed with the *active power or potency* of making this possible thing actual. The latter is then said to be *relatively, extrinsically* possible—in relation to such being or beings. And obviously a thing may be possible relatively to the power of one being, and not possible relatively to lesser power of another being: the statue that is intrinsically possible in the block of marble, may be extrinsically possible relatively to the skilled sculptor, but not relatively to the unskilled person who is not a sculptor.

Furthermore, relatively to the same agent or agents, the production of a given effect, the doing of a given thing, is said to be *physically* possible if it can be brought about by such agents acting according to the ordinary course of nature; if, in other words they have the physical power to do it. Otherwise it is said to be physically impossible, even though metaphysically or intrinsically possible, *e.g.* it is physically impossible for a dead person to come to life again. A thing is said to be *morally* possible, in reference to free and responsible agents, if they can do it without unreasonable inconvenience; otherwise it is considered as morally impossible, even though it be both physically and metaphysically possible: as often happens in regard to the fulfilment of one's obligations.

That which is *both intrinsically and extrinsically possible* is said to be *adequately possible*. Whatever is intrinsically possible is also extrinsically possible in relation to God, who is *Almighty, Omnipotent*.

8. (*b*) SUBJECTIVE "POTENTIA," ACTIVE AND PASSIVE.—Furthermore, we conceive the Infinite Being, Almighty God, as capable of *creating*, or producing actual being *from nothingness*, *i.e.* without any actually pre-existing material out of whose passive potentiality the actual being would be developed. Creative power or activity does not need any pre-existing subject on which to exercise its influence, any subject in whose *passive potentiality* the thing to be created is antecedently implicit.

But all other power, all activity of created causes, does require some such actually existing subject. If we examine the activities of the agencies that fall within our direct experience, whether in external nature or in our own selves, we shall find that in no case does their operative influence or causality extend beyond the production of changes in existing being, or attain to the production of new actual being out of nothingness. The forces of nature cannot produce an oak without an acorn, or an iceberg without water; nor can the sculptor produce a statue except from some pre-existing material.

The *natural* passive potentiality of things is, moreover, limited in reference to the active powers of the created universe. These, for example, can educe life from the passive potentiality of inorganic matter, but only by assimilating this matter into a living organism: they cannot restore life to a human corpse; yet the latter has in it the capacity to be restored to life by the direct influence of the Author of Nature. This special and supernatural potentiality in created things, under the influence of Omnipotence, is known as *potentia obedientalis*.[72]

This consideration will help us to realize that all reality which is produced by change, and subject to change, is essentially a mixture of *becoming* and *being*, of *potential* and *actual*. The reality of such being is not *tota simul*. Only immutable being, whose duration is *eternal*, has its reality *tota simul*: it alone is *purely actual*, the "*Actus Purus*"; and its duration is one eternal "*now*," without beginning, end, or succession. But mutable being, whose duration in actual existence is measured by *time*, is actualized only successively: its actuality at any particular instant does not embody the whole of its reality: this latter includes also a "*was*" and "*will be*"; the thing was *potentially* what it now is *actually*, and it will become actually something which it now is only potentially; nor shall we have understood even moderately the nature or essence of any mutable being—an oak-tree, for example—until we have grasped the fact that the whole reality of its nature embraces more than what we find of it actually existing at any given instant of its existence. In other words, we have to bear in mind that the reality of such a being is not pure actuality but a mixture of potential and actual: that it is an *actus non-purus*, or an *actus mixtus*.

We have to note well that the *potential being* of a thing is something *real*—that it is not merely a *modus loquendi*, or a *modus intelligendi*. The oak is in the acorn in some true and real sense: the potentiality of the oak is something real in the acorn: if it were not so, if it were nothing real in the acorn, we could say with equal truth that a man or a horse or a house is potentially in the acorn; or, again with equal truth, that the oak is potentially in a mustard-seed, or a grain of corn, or a pebble, or a drop of water. Therefore the oak is *really* in the acorn—not actually but potentially, *potentia passiva*.

The oak-tree is also really in those *active* forces of nature whose influence on the acorn develop the latter into an actual oak-tree: it is in those causes not actually, of course, but *virtually*, for they possess in themselves the *operative power—potentia activa sive operativa*—to educe the oak-tree out of the acorn. These two potential conditions of a being—in the active causes which produce it, and in the pre-existing actual thing or things from which it is produced—are called each a real or subjective potency, *potentia realis*, or *potentia subjectiva*, in distinction from the mere logical or objective possibility of such a being.

And just as the passive potentiality of the statue is something real in the block of marble, though distinct from the actuality of the statue and from the process by which this is actualized, so is the active power of making the statue something real in the sculptor, though distinct from the operation by which he makes the statue. If an agent's *power* to act, to produce change, were not a reality in the agent, a reality distinct from the *action* of the latter; or if a being's capacity to undergo change, and thereby to become something other, were not a reality distinct from the process of change, and from the actual result of this process—it would follow not only that the actual alone is real, and the merely possible or potential unreal, but also that no change can be real, that nothing can really become, and nothing really disappear.[73]

9. (*c*) ACTUALITY: ITS RELATION TO POTENTIALITY.—It is from our experience of change in the world that we derive our notions of the potential and the actual, of active power and passive potentiality. The term "act" has primarily the same meaning as "action," "operation," that process by which a change is wrought. But the Latin word *actus* (Gr. ἐνέργεια, ἐντελέχεια) means rather that which is achieved by the *actio*, that which is the correlative and complement of the passive potentiality, the actuality of this latter: that by which potential being is rendered formally actual, and, by way of consequence, this actual being itself. "*Potentia activa*" and its correlative "*actus*" might, perhaps, be appropriately rendered by "*power*" (*potestas agendi*) and "*action*" or "*operation*"; "*potentia passiva*" and its correlative "*actus*," by "*potentiality*" and "*actuality*" respectively.

In these correlatives, the notion underlying the term "actual" is manifestly the notion of something completed, achieved, perfected—as compared with that of something incomplete, imperfect, determinable, which is the notion of the potential. Hence the notions of *potentia* and *actus* have been extended widely beyond their primary signification of power to act and the exercise of this power. Such pairs of correlatives as the determinable and the determined, the perfectible and the perfected, the undeveloped or less developed and the more developed, the generic and the specific, are all conceived under the aspect of this widest relation of the potential to the actual. And since we can distinguish successive stages in any process of development, or an order of logical sequence among the contents of our concept of any concrete reality, it follows that what will be conceived as an *actus* in one relation will be conceived as a *potentia* in another. Thus, the disposition of any faculty—as, for example, the scientific habit in the intellect—is an *actus* or perfection of the faculty regarded as a *potentia*; but it is itself a *potentia* which is actualized in the *operation* of actually studying. This illustrates the distinction commonly drawn between an "*actus primus*" and an "*actus secundus*" in any particular order or line of reality: the *actus primus* is that which presupposes no prior actuality in the same order; the *actus secundus* is that which does presuppose another. The act of knowing is an *actus secundus* which presupposes the cognitive faculty as an *actus primus*: the faculty being the *first* or fundamental equipment of the soul in relation to knowledge. Hence the child is said to have knowledge "*in actu primo*" as having the faculty of reason; and the student to have knowledge "*in actu secundo*" as exercising this faculty.

The *actus* or perfecting principles of which we have spoken so far are all conceived as presupposing an existing subject on which they supervene. They are therefore *accidents* as distinct from *substantial constitutive* principles of this subject; and they are therefore called *accidental* actualities, *actus "accidentales"*. But the actual existence of a being is also conceived as the complement and correlative of its essence: as that which makes the latter actual, thus transferring it from the state of mere possibility. Hence existence also is called an *actus* or actuality: the *actus "existentialis,"* to distinguish it from the existing thing's activities and other subsequently acquired characters. In reference to these existence is a "first actuality"—"*Esse est actus primus*"; "*Prius est esse quam agere*": "Existence is the first actuality"; "Action presupposes existence"—while each of these in reference to existence, is a "second actuality," an *actus secundus*.

When, furthermore, we proceed to examine the constitutive principles essential to any being in the concrete, we may be able to distinguish between principles which are determinable, passive and persistent throughout all essential change of that being, and others which are determining, specifying, differentiating principles. In water, for example, we may distinguish the passive underlying principle which persists throughout the decomposition of water into oxygen and hydrogen, from the active specifying principle which gives that substratum its specific nature as water. The former or material principle (ὕλη, *materia*) is *potential*, compared with the latter or formal principle (μορφή, εἶδος, ἐντελέχεια, *forma, species, actus*) as *actual*. The concept of *actus* is thus applied to the essence itself: the *actus "essentialis"* or "*formalis*" of a thing is that which we conceive to be the ultimate, completing and determining principle of the essence or nature of that thing. In reference to this as well as the other constitutive principles of the thing, the actual existence of the thing is a "second actuality," an *actus secundus*.

In fact all the constitutive principles of the essence of any existing thing, and all the properties and attributes involved in the essence or necessarily connected with the essence, must all alike be conceived as logically antecedent to the existential *actus* whereby they are constituted something in the actual order, and not mere possible objects of our thought. And from this point of view the existence of a thing is called the ultimate actualization of its essence. Hence the scholastic aphorism: "*Esse est ultimus actus rei*".

The term *actus* may designate that complement of reality by which potential being is made actual (*actus "actuans"*), or this actual being itself (*actus "simpliciter dictus"*). In the latter sense we have already distinguished the Being that is immutable, the Being of God, as the *Actus Purus*, from the being of all mutable things, which latter being is necessarily a mixture of potential and actual, an *actus mixtus*.

Now if the essences of corporeal things are composite, if they are constituted by the union of some determining, formative principle with a determinable, passive principle—of "form" with "matter," in scholastic terminology—we may call these formative principles *actus "informantes"*; and if these cannot actually exist except in union with a material principle they may be called actus "*non-subsistentes*": *e.g.*, the formative principle or "*forma substantialis*" of water, or the vital principle of a plant. If, on the other hand, there exist essences which, being simple, do not actualize any material, determinable principle, but subsist independently of any such, they are called *actus "non-informantes,"* or *actus "subsistentes"*. Such, for example, are God, and pure spirits whose existence is known from revelation. Finally, there may be a kind of actual essence which, though it naturally actualizes a material principle *de facto*, can nevertheless continue to subsist without this latter: such an actual being would be at once an *actus informans* and an *actus subsistens*; and such, in fact, is the human soul.

Throughout all distinctions between the potential and the actual there runs the conception of *the actual as something more perfect than the potential*. There is in the actual something positive and real over and above what is in the potential. This is an ultimate fact in our analysis; and its importance will be realized when we come to apply the notions we have been explaining to the study of change.

The notion of grades of perfection in things is one with which everyone is familiar. We naturally conceive some beings as higher upon the scale of reality than others; as having "more" reality, so to speak—not necessarily, of course, in the literal sense of size or quantity—than others; as being more perfect, nobler, of greater worth, value, dignity, excellence, than others. Thus we regard the infinite as more perfect than the finite, spiritual beings as nobler than material beings, man as a higher order of being than the brute beast, this again as surpassing the whole vegetable kingdom, the lowest form of life as higher on the scale of being than inorganic matter, the substance-mode of being as superior to all accident-modes, the actualized state of a being as more perfect than its potential state, *i.e.* as existing in its material, efficient and ideal or exemplar causes. The grounds and significance of this mental appreciation of relative values in things must be discussed elsewhere. We refer to it here in order to point out another scholastic aphorism, according to which the higher a thing is in the scale of actual being, and the more perfect it is accordingly, the more efficient it will also be as a principle of action, the more powerful as a cause in the production of changes in other things, the more operative in actualizing their passive potentialities; and conversely, the less actual a thing is, and therefore the more imperfect, the greater its passive capacity will be to undergo the influence of agencies that are actual and operative around it. "As passive potentiality," says St. Thomas,[74] "is the mark of potential being, so active power is the mark of actual being. For a thing acts, in so far as it is actual; but is acted on, so far as it is potential." Our knowledge of the nature of things is in fact exclusively based on our knowledge of their activities: we have no other key to the knowledge of what a thing is than our knowledge of what it does: "*Operari sequitur esse*": "*Qualis est operatio talis est natura*"—"Acting follows being": "Conduct is the key to nature".

A being that is active or operative in the production of a change is said to be the efficient cause of the change, the latter being termed the effect. Now the greater the change, *i.e.* the higher and more perfect be the grade of reality that is actualized in the change, the higher too in the scale of being must be the efficient cause of that change. There must be a proportion in degree of perfection or reality between effect and cause. The former cannot exceed in actual perfection the active power, and therefore the actual being, of the latter. This is so because we conceive the effect as being produced or actualized *through the operative influence* of the cause, and *with real dependence* on this latter; and it is inconceivable that a cause should have power to actualize other being, distinct from itself, which would be of a higher grade of excellence than itself. The nature of efficient causality, of the influence by which the cause is related to its effect, is not easy to determine; it will be discussed at a subsequent stage of our investigations; but whatever it be, a little reflection should convince us of the truth of the principle just stated: that an effect cannot be more perfect than its cause. The mediæval scholastics embodied this truth in the formula: *Nemo dat quod non habet*—a formula which we must not interpret in the more restricted and literal sense of the words *giving* and *having*, lest we be met with the obvious objection that it is by no means necessary for a boy to have a black eye himself in order to give one to his neighbour! What the formula means is that an agent cannot give to, or produce in, any potential subject, receptive of its causal influence, an actuality which it does not itself possess virtually, or in its active power: that no actuality surpassing in excellence the actual perfection of the cause itself can be found thus virtually in the active power of the latter. There is no question of the cause or agent transferring bodily as it were a part of its own actuality to the subject which is undergoing change[75]; nor will such crude imagination images help us to understand what real change, under the influence of efficient causality, involves.[76] An analysis of change will enable us to appreciate more fully the real difficulty of explaining it, and the futility of any attempt to account for it without admitting the real, objective validity of the notions of actual and potential being, of active powers or forces and passive potentialities in the things that are subject to change.

10. ANALYSIS OF CHANGE.—*Change* (*Mutatio, Motus*, μεταβολή, κίνησις) is one of those simplest concepts which cannot be defined. We may describe it, however, as *the transition of a being from one state to another*. If one thing entirely disappeared and another were substituted for it, we should not regard the former as having been changed into the latter. When one thing is put in the place of another, each, no doubt, undergoes a change of place, but neither is changed into the other. So, also, if we were to conceive a thing as absolutely ceasing to exist, as lapsing into nothingness at a given instant, and another as coming into existence out of nothingness at the same instant (and in the same place), we should not consider this double event as constituting a real change of the former thing into the latter. And although our *senses* cannot testify to anything beyond *sequence* in sense phenomena, our *reason* detects in real change something other than a total substitution of things for one another, or continuous total cessations and inceptions of existence in things. No doubt, if we conceive the whole phenomenal or perceptible universe and all the beings which constitute this universe as essentially contingent, and therefore dependent for their reality and their actual existence on a Supreme, Necessary Being who created and conserves them, who at any time may cease to conserve any of them, and produce other and new beings *out of nothingness*, then such absolute cessations and inceptions of existence in the world would not be impossible. God might *annihilate*, *i.e.* cease to conserve in existence, this or that contingent being at any instant, and at any instant *create* a new contingent being, *i.e.* produce it in its totality from no pre-existing material. But there is no reason to suppose that this is what is constantly taking place in Nature: that all change is simply a series of annihilations and creations. On the contrary, the modes of being which appear and disappear in real change, in the transition of anything from one state to a really different state of being, do not appear *de novo, ex nihilo*, as absolute beginnings out of nothingness;

or disappear *totaliter*, *in nihilum*, as absolute endings or lapses of reality into nothingness. The real changes which take place in Nature are due to the operation of natural causes. These causes, being finite in their operative powers, cannot create, *i.e.* produce new being from nothingness. They can, however, with the concurrence of the Omnipotent Being, modify existing modes of being, *i.e.* make actual what was only potential in these latter. The notion of change is not verified in the conception of successive annihilations and creations; for there is involved in the former concept not merely the notion of a real difference between the two *actual* states, that before and that after the change, but also the notion of some *potential* reality persisting throughout the change, something capable of being actually so and so before the change and actually otherwise after the change. For real change, therefore, we require (1) two positive and really different states of the same being, a "*terminus a quo*" and a "*terminus ad quem*"; and (2) a real process of transition whereby something potential becomes actual. In creation there is no real and positive *terminus a quo*; in annihilation there is no real and positive *terminus ad quem*; these therefore are not changes in the proper sense of the term. Sometimes, too, change is affirmed, by purely extrinsic denomination, of a thing in which there is no real change, but only a relation to some other really changing thing. In this sense when an object unknown or unthought of becomes the actual object of somebody's thought or cognition, it is said to "change," though the transition from "unknown" to "known" involves no real change of state in the object, but only in the knowing subject. If thought were in any true sense "constitutive" of reality, as many modern philosophers contend, the change in the object would of course be real.

Since, therefore, change consists in this, that a thing which is actually in a given state ceases to be actually such and begins to be actually in another state, it is obvious that there persists throughout the process some reality which is in itself potential and indifferent to either actual state; and that, moreover, something which was actual disappears, while some new actuality appears, in this persisting potentiality. The abiding potential principle is called the *matter* or *subject* of the change; the transient actualizing principles are called *forms*. Not all these "forms" which precede or result from change are necessarily positive entities in themselves: they may be mere *privations* of other forms ("*privatio*," στέρησις): not all changes result in the acquisition of a new degree of positive actual being; some result in loss of perfection or actuality. Still, even in these cases, the state characterized by the less perfect degree of actuality has a determinate actual grade of being which is proper to itself, and which, as such, is not found actually, but only potentially, in the state characterized by the more perfect degree of actuality. When, then, a being changes from a more perfect to a less perfect state, the actuality of this less perfect state cannot be adequately accounted for by seeking it in the antecedent and more perfect state: it is not in this latter state *actually*, but only *potentially*; nor do we account for it by saying that it is "equivalently" in the greater actuality of the latter state: the two actualizing principles are really distinct, and neither is wholly or even partially the other. The significance of this consideration will appear presently in connection with the scholastic axiom: *Quidquid movetur ab alio movetur.*

Meanwhile we must guard against conceiving the potential or material factor in change as a sort of actual but hidden core of reality which itself persists unchanged throughout; and the formative or actualizing factors as superficially adorning this substratum by constantly replacing one another. Such a substitution of imagination images for intellectual thought will not help, but rather hinder, all accurate analysis. It is not the potential or material factor in things that changes, nor yet the actualizing or formal factors, but the things themselves; and if "things" are subject to "real change" it is manifest that this fact can be made intelligible, if at all, only by intellectually analysing the things and their changes into constitutive principles or factors which are nor themselves "things" or "changes". Were we to arrive only at principles of the latter sort, so far from explaining anything we would really only have pushed back the problem a step farther. It may be that none of the attempts yet made by philosophers or scientists to offer an ultimate explanation of change is entirely satisfactory,—the scholastic explanation will be gradually outlined in these pages,—but it will be of advantage at least to recognize the shortcomings of theories that are certainly inadequate.

We are now in a position to state and explain the important scholastic aphorism embodying what has been called the Principle of Change ("*Principium Motus*"): *Quidquid movetur, ab alio movetur.* "Whatever undergoes change is changed by something else". The term *motus* is here taken in the wide sense of any real transition from potentiality to actuality, as is evident from the alternative statements of the same principle: *Nihil potest seipsum reducere e potentia in actum*: "Nothing can reduce itself from potentiality to actuality," or, again, *Potentia, qua talis, nequit per semetipsam ad actum reduci, sed reducitur ab alio principio in actu.* "The potential as such cannot be reduced by itself to the actual, but only by some other already actual principle".[7] This assertion, rightly understood, is self-evidently true; for the state of passive potentiality, as such, involves the absence of the correlative actuality in the potential subject; and since the actual, as such, involves a perfection which is not in the potential, the latter cannot confer upon itself this perfection: nothing can be the adequate principle or source of a perfection which is not in this principle or source: *nemo dat quod non habet.*

We have already anticipated the objection arising from the consideration that the state resulting from a change is sometimes in its totality less perfect than the state which existed prior to the change. Even in such cases there results from the change a new actuality which was not in the prior state, and which cannot be conceived as a mere part or residue of the latter, or regarded as equivalently contained in the latter. Even granting, as we must, that the net result of such a change is a loss of actuality or perfection in the subject of change, still there is always a gain which is not accounted for by the loss; there is always a new actual state which, as such, was not in the original state.

A more obvious objection to the principle arises from the consideration of vital action; but it is based on a misunderstanding of the principle under discussion. Living things, it is objected, move themselves: their *vital* action is spontaneous and immanent: originating within themselves, it has its term too within themselves, resulting in their gradual development, growth, increase of actuality and perfection. Therefore it would appear that they move and perfect themselves; and hence the so-called "principle of change" is not true universally.

In reply to all this we admit that vital action is immanent, remaining within the agent to perfect the latter; also that it is spontaneous, inasmuch as when the agent is actually exercising vital functions it need not be actually undergoing the causal influence of any other created agent, or actually dependent on any such agent. But it must, nevertheless, in such action, be dependent on, and influenced by, *some actual being other than itself.* And the reason is obvious: If by such action it increases its own actual perfection, and becomes actually other than it was before such action, then it cannot have given itself the actuality of this perfection, which it possessed before only potentially. No doubt, it is not merely passively potential in regard to such actual perfections, as is the case in non-vital change which results in the subject from the transitive action of some outside cause upon the latter. The living thing has the active power of causing or producing in itself these actual perfections: there is interaction between its vital parts: through one organ or faculty it acts upon another, thus educing an actuality, a new perfection, in this other, and thus developing and perfecting its own being. But even considered as active it cannot be the adequate cause of the actuality acquired through the change. If this actuality is something *really* over and above the reality of its active and passive potential principles, then it remains true that change implies the influence of an actual being other than the subject changed: *Quid quid movetur, ab alio movetur.*

The question here arises, not only in reference to vital agents, but to *all finite, created causes:* Does the active cause of change (together with the passive potentiality of the subject of change, whether this subject be the agent itself as in immanent activity, or something other than the agent as in transitive activity),—does this active power account *adequately* for the new actuality educed in the change? It obviously does not; for the actuality acquired in the change is, as such, a new entity, a new perfection, in some degree positively surpassing the total reality of the combined active powers and passive potentialities which it replaces. In other words, if the actuality resulting from the change is not to be found in the immediate active and passive antecedents of the change, then we are inevitably referred, for an adequate explanation of this actuality, to some actual being above and beyond these antecedents. And to what sort of actual being are we referred? To a being in which the actuality of the effect resides only in the same way as it resides in the immediate active and passive antecedents of the change, that is *potentially*? No; for this would be useless, merely pushing the difficulty one step farther back. We are obliged rather to infer the existence of an Actual Being in whom the actuality of the said effect resides *actually*: not formally, of course, as it exists in itself when it is produced through the change; but eminently, *eminenter*, in such a way that its actualization outside Himself and under His influence does not involve in Him any loss of perfection, any increase of perfection, or any manner of change whatsoever. We are compelled in this way to infer, from the existence of change in the universe of our direct experience, the existence of a transcendent Immovable Prime Mover, a *Primum Movens Immobile*. All the active causes or principles of change which fall under our notice in the universe of direct experience are themselves subject to change. None of them causes change in any other thing without itself undergoing change. The active power of finite causes is itself finite. By educing the potentiality of other things into actuality they gradually use up their own energy; they diminish and lose their active power of producing effects: this belongs to the very nature of finite causes as such. Moreover, they are themselves passive as well as active; interaction is universal among the finite causes which constitute the universe of our direct experience: they all alike have passive potentiality and undergo change. Now, if any one finite cause in this system cannot adequately account for the new actuality evolved from the potential in any single process of change, neither can the whole system adequately account for it. What is true of them distributively is true of them taken all together when there is question of what belongs to their nature; and the fact that their active powers and passive potentialities *fall short* of the actuality of the effects we attribute to them is a fact that appertains to their very nature as finite things. The phenomenon of continuous change in the universe involves the continuous appearance of *new actual being*. To account for this constant stream of actuality we are of necessity carried beyond the system of finite, changing being itself; we are forced to infer the existence of a source and principle which must itself be purely actual and exempt from all change—a Being who can cause all the actuality that results from change without losing or gaining or changing in any way Himself, because He possesses all finite actuality in Himself in a supereminent manner which transcends all the efforts of finite human intelligence to comprehend or characterize in any adequate or positive manner. The scholastics expressed this in the simple aphorism: *Omne novum ens est a Deo*. And it is the realization of this profound truth that underlies their teaching on the necessity of the Divine *Concursus*, *i.e.* the influence of the Infinite First Cause or Prime Mover permeating the efficiency of all finite or created causes. Here, for example, is a brief recent statement of that doctrine:—

"If we must admit a causal influence of these things on one another, then a closer examination will convince us that a finite thing can never be the adequate cause of any effect, but is always, metaphysically regarded, only a part-cause, ever needing to be completed by another cause. Every effect is—at least under one aspect, at least as an effect—something new, something that was not there before. Even were the effect contained, whether formally or virtually, in the cause, it is certainly not identical with this latter, for if it were there would be no causality, nothing would 'happen'. In all causing and happening, something which was heretofore only possible, becomes real and actual. But things cannot determine themselves to influence others, or to receive the influence of others, since they are not dependent in their being on one another. Hence the necessary inference that all being, all happening, all change, requires the concurrence of an Absolute Principle of being. When two things act on each other the Absolute Being must work in and with them, the same Absolute Being in both—to relate them to each other, and supplement their natural insufficiency."

"Such is the profound teaching about the Divine Concursus with every creature.... God works in all and with all. He permeates all reality, everywhere; there is no being beyond Him or independent of His conserving and concurring power. Just as creatures are brought into being only through God's omnipotence, and of themselves have no independent reality, so do they need the self-same ever-present, all-sustaining power to continue in this being and develop it by their activity. Every event in Nature is a transitory, passing phenomenon, so bound up with conditions and circumstances that it must disappear to give place to some other. How could a mode of being so incomplete discharge its function in existence without the concurrence of the First Cause?"[78]

We have seen now that *in the real order* the potential presupposes the actual; for the potential cannot actualize itself, but can be actualized only by the action of some already actual being. Nor can we avoid this consequence by supposing the potential being to have had no actual beginning in time, but to be eternally in process of actualization; for even so, it must be eternally actualized *by some other actual being*—a position which Aristotle and some scholastics admit to be possible. Whether, then, we conceive the actualization as beginning in time or as proceeding from all eternity, it is self-contradictory to suppose the potential as capable of actualizing itself.

It is likewise true that the actual precedes the possible *in the order of our knowledge*. The concept of a thing as possible presupposes the concept of that thing as actual; for the possible is understood to be possible only by its intelligible relation to actual existence. This is evidently true of extrinsic possibility; but our knowledge even of the intrinsic possibility of a thing cannot be the first knowledge we possess in the order of time. Our first knowledge is of the actual; for the mind's first cognitive act must have for object either itself or something not itself. But it knows itself as a consciously acting and therefore actual being. And it comes to know things other than itself only by the fact that such other things act upon it either immediately or mediately through sense-consciousness; so that in every hypothesis its first known object is something actual.[79]

The priority of the actual as compared with the potential in the real order, suggests a proof of the existence of God in the manner indicated above. It also affords a refutation of Hegelian monism. The conception of the world, including all the phenomena of mind and matter, as the gradual self-manifestation or evolution of a potential being eternally actualizing itself, is a self-contradictory conception. Scholastics rightly maintain that the realities from which we derive our first most abstract and transcendental notion of being in general, are actual realities. Hegelians seize on the object of this notion, identify it with pure thought, proclaim it the sole reality, and endow it with the power of becoming actually everything. It is manifest, therefore, that they endow purely potential being with the power of actualizing itself.

Nor can they fairly avoid this charge by pointing out that although their starting-point is not actual being (with which the scholastic philosophy of being commences), yet neither is it possible or potential being, but being which has neither of these determinations, being which abstracts from both, like the real being of the scholastics (7, 13). For though real being can be *an object of abstract human thought* without either of the predicates "existent" or "non-existent," yet it cannot be anything *in the real order* without either of them. There it must be either actually existent or else merely potential. But Hegelians claim absolutely indeterminate being to be *as such* something in the real order; and though they try to distinguish it from potential being they nevertheless think of it as potential being, for they distinctly and repeatedly declare that it can become all things, and does become all things, and is constantly, eternally transforming itself by an internal dialectic process into the phenomena which constitute the worlds of mind and matter. Contrasting it with the abstract "inert" being which they conceive to be the object of the traditional metaphysics, they endow "indeterminate being" with the active power of producing, and the passive potentiality of becoming, actually everything. Thus, in order to show *a priori* how this indeterminate being must evolve itself by internal logical necessity into the world of our direct and immediate experience, they suppose it to be subject to change and to be at the same time self-actualizing, in direct opposition to the axiom that potential reality, reality which is subject to change, cannot actualize itself: *Quidquid movetur ab alio moveatur oportet.*

11. KINDS OF CHANGE.—Following Aristotle,[80] we may recognize a broad and clear distinction between four great classes of change (μεταβολή, *mutatio*) in the phenomena of our sense experience: local change (κίνησις κατὰ τόπον, φορά, *latio*); quantitative change (κατὰ τὸ πόσον, αὔζησις ἤ φθίσις, *augmentatio vel diminutio*); qualitative change (κατὰ τὸ ποίον, ἀλλοίωσις, *alteratio*); and substantial change (κατ' οὐσίαν, γένεσις ἤ φθορά). The three former are accidental, *i.e.* do not reach or affect the essence or substance of the thing that is changed; the fourth is substantial, a change of essence. Substantial change is regarded as taking place instantaneously, as soon as the condition brought about

by the accidental changes leading up to it becomes naturally incompatible with the essence or nature of the subject. The accidental changes, on the other hand, are regarded as taking place gradually, as realizing and involving a succession of states or conditions in the subject. These changes, especially when they take place in corporeal things, are properly described as movement or motion (*motus, motio*). By movement or motion in the strict sense we therefore mean any change which takes place gradually or successively in a corporeal thing. It is only in a wider and improper sense that these terms are sometimes applied to activity of whatsoever kind, even of spiritual beings. In this sense we speak of thoughts, volitions, etc., as movements of the soul, *motus animae*; or of God as the Prime Mover ever in motion, the *Primum Movens semper in motu.*

With local change in material things, as also with quantitative change, growth and diminution of quantity (mass and volume), everyone is perfectly familiar. From the earliest times, moreover, we find both in science and philosophy the conception of matter as composed of, and divisible into, ultimate particles, themselves supposed to admit of no further real division, and hence called *atoms* (ἄ-τομος, τέμνω). From the days of Grecian atomism men have attempted to show that all change in the Universe is ultimately reducible to changes of place, order, spatial arrangement and collocation, of those hypothetical atomic factors. It has likewise been commonly assumed that change in mass is solely due to change in the number of those atoms, and change in volume (of the same mass) to the relative density or closeness with which the atoms aggregate together; though some have held—and it is certainly not inconceivable—that exactly the same material entity, an atom let us say, may be capable of *real* contraction and expansion, and so of *real* change of volume: as distinct from the *apparent* contraction and expansion of bodies, a change which is supposed to be due to change of density, *i.e.* to decrease or increase in the dimensions of the pores or interstices between the smaller constituent parts or molecules. However this may be, the attempts to reduce all change in physical nature to mere *mechanical* change *i.e.* to spatial motions of the masses (*molar* motions), the molecules (*molecular* motions), and the atoms or other ultimate components of matter (whether vibratory, undulatory, rotatory or translational motions), have never been satisfactory.

Qualitative change is wider than material change, for it includes changes in spiritual beings, *i.e.* in beings which are outside the category of quantity and have a mode of existence altogether different from the extensional, spatial existence which characterizes matter. When, for instance, the human mind acquires knowledge, it undergoes qualitative change. But matter, too, has qualities, and is subject to qualitative change. It is endowed with *active* qualities, *i.e.* with powers, forces, energies, whereby it can not merely perform mechanical work by producing local changes in the distribution of its mass throughout space, but also produce physical and chemical changes which seem at least to be different in their nature from mere mechanical changes. It is likewise endowed with *passive* qualities which appear to the senses to be of various kinds, differing from one another and from the mechanical or quantitative characteristics of size, shape, motion, rest, etc. While these latter are called "primary qualities" of bodies—because conceived to be more fundamental and more closely inherent in the real and objective nature of matter—or "common sensibles" (*sensibilia communia*), because perceptible by more than one of our external senses—the former are called "secondary qualities," because conceived to be less characteristic of the real and objective nature of matter, and more largely subjective products of our own sentient cognitive activity—or "proper sensibles" (*sensibilia propria*), because each of them is apprehended by only one of our external senses: colour, sound, taste, odour, temperature, material state or texture (*e.g.* roughness, liquidity, softness, etc.). Now about all these perceived qualities and their changes the question has been raised: Are they, as such, *i.e.* as perceived by us, really in the material things or bodies which make up the physical universe, and really different in these bodies from the quantitative factors and motions of the latter? Or, as such, are they not rather partially or wholly subjective phenomena—products, at least in part, of our own sense perception, states of our own consciousness, having nothing really corresponding to them in the external matter of the universe beyond the quantitative, mechanical factors and motions whereby matter acts upon our faculties of sense cognition and produces these states of consciousness in us? This is a question of the first importance, the solution of which belongs to Epistemology. Aristotle would not allow that the objective material universe can be denuded, in the way just suggested, of qualities and qualitative change; and scholastic philosophers have always held the same general view. What we have to note here, however, in regard to the question is simply this, that even if the world of matter were thus simplified by transferring all qualitative change to the subjective domain of consciousness, the reality of qualitative change and all the problems arising from it would still persist. To transfer qualitative change from object to subject, from matter to mind, is certainly something very different from explaining it as reducible to quantitative or mechanical change. The simplification thus effected would be more apparent than real: it would be simplifying the world of matter by transferring its complexity to the world of mind. This consideration is one which is sometimes lost sight of by scientists who advance mechanical hypotheses as ultimate explanations of the nature and activities of the physical universe.

If all material things and processes could be ultimately analysed into configurations and local motions of space-occupying atoms, homogeneous in nature and differing only in size and shape, then each of these ultimate atomic factors would be itself exempt from intrinsic change as to its own essence and individuality. In this hypothesis there would be really no such thing as *substantial* change. The collection of atoms would form an immutable core of material reality, wholly simple and ever actual. Such an hypothesis, however, is utterly inadequate as an explanation of the facts of life and consciousness. And even as an account of the processes of the inorganic universe it encounters insuperable difficulties. The common belief of men has always been that even in this domain of reality there are fundamentally different *kinds* of matter, kinds which differ from one another not merely in the shape and size and configuration and arrangement of their ultimate *actual* constituents, but even in the very substance or nature of these constituents; and that there are some material changes which affect the actual substance itself of the matter which undergoes them. This belief scholastics, again following Aristotle, hold to be a correct belief, and one which is well grounded in reason. And this belief in turn involves the view that every type of actual material entity—whether merely inorganic, or endowed with life, or even allied with a higher, spiritual mode of being as in the case of man himself—is *essentially composite*, essentially a synthesis of *potential* and *actual* principles of being, and therefore capable of *substantial* change. The actually existing material being scholastics describe as *materia secunda*, the ὕλη ἐσχάτη of Aristotle; the purely potential factor, which is actualized in this or that particular kind of matter, they describe as *materia prima*, the ὕλη πρώτη of Aristotle; the actualizing, specifying, formative principle, they designate as *forma substantialis* (εἶδος). And since the purely potential principle cannot actually exist except as actualized by some formative principle, all substantial change or transition from one substantial type to another is necessarily both a *corruptio* and a *generatio*. That is, it involves the actual disappearance of one substantial form and the actual appearance of another. Hence the scholastic aphorism regarding substantial change: *Corruptio unius est generatio alterius*: the corruption or destruction of one kind of material thing involves the generation of another kind.

The concepts of *materia prima* and *forma substantialis* are concepts not of phenomenal entities directly accessible to the senses or the imagination, but of principles which can be reached only mediately and by intellect proper. They cannot be pictured in the imagination, which can only attain to the sensible. We may help ourselves to grasp them intellectually by the analogy of the shapeless block of marble and the figure educed therefrom by the sculptor, but this is only an analogy: just as the statue results from the union of an *accidental* form with an existing matter, so this matter itself, the substance *marble*, is composed of a *substantial* form and a primordial, *potential* matter. But there the analogy ceases.

Furthermore, when we consider that the proper and primary objects of the human intellect itself are corporeal things or bodies, and that these bodies actually exist in nature only as composite substances, subject to essential or substantial change, we shall realize why it is that the concept of *materia prima* especially, being a mediate and negative concept, is so difficult to grasp; for, as the scholastics describe it, translating Aristotle's formula, it is in itself *neque quid, neque quantum, neque quale, neque aliquid eorum quibus ens determinatur*.[81] But it is through intellectual concepts alone, and not through imagination images, that we may hope to analyse the nature and processes even of the world of corporeal reality; and, as St. Thomas well observes, it was because the ancient Greek atomists did not rise above the level of thinking in imagination images that they failed to recognize the existence, or explain the nature, of substantial change in the material universe[82]: an observation which applies with equal force to those scientists and philosophers of our own time who would fain reduce all physical processes to mere mechanical change.

Those, then, are the principal kinds of change, as analysed by Aristotle and the scholastics. We may note, finally, that the distinction between *immanent* and *transitive* activity is also applied to change—that is, to change considered as a process, not to the result of the change, to change *in fieri*, not *in facto esse*. Immanent movement or activity (*motio, actio immanens*) is that of which the term, the educed actuality, remains within the agent—which latter is therefore at once both *agens* and *patiens*. Vital action is of this kind. Transitive movement or activity, on the other hand (*motio, actio transiens*), is that of which the term is some actuality educed in a being other than the agent. The *patiens* is here really distinct from the *agens*; and it is in the former, not in the latter, that the change takes place: *actio fit in passo*. All change in the inorganic universe is of this sort.

Chapter III.

Existence And Essence.

12. EXISTENCE.—In the preceding chapters we examined reality in itself and in its relation to change or becoming. We have now to examine it in relation to its actual existence and to its intrinsic possibility (7, *a*).

Existing or *being* (in the participial sense: esse, *existere*, τὸ εἶναι) is a simple, indefinable notion. A being is said to exist when it is not merely possible but actual, when it is not merely potential in its active and passive causes but has become actual through those causes (*existere: ex-sisto: ex-stare*: to stand forth, distinct from its causes); or, if it have no causes, when it simply is (*esse*),—in which sense God, the Necessary, purely Actual Being, simply *is*. Thus, existence implies the notion of actuality, and is conceived as that by which any thing or essence *is, distinct from nothingness, in the actual order.*[83] Or, again, it is *the actuality of any thing or essence*. About any conceivable being we may ask two distinct questions: (*a*) What is it? and (*b*) Does such a being actually exist? The answer to the former gives us the *essence*, what is presented to the mind through the concept; the answer to the latter informs us about the actual *existence* of the being or essence in question.

To the mind of any individual man the real existence (as also the real essence) of any being whatsoever, not excepting his own, can be known only through its ideal presence in his mind, through the concept or percept whereby it becomes for him a "known object," an *objectum cognitum*. But this actual presence of known being to the knowing mind must not be confounded with the real existence of such being (4). Real being does not get its real existence in our minds or from our minds. Our cognition does not produce, but only discovers, actually existing reality. The latter, by acting on the mind, engenders therein the cognition of itself. Now all our knowledge comes through the senses; and sense cognition is excited in us by the direct action of material or phenomenal being on our sense faculties. But through sense cognition the mind is able to attain to a knowledge both of the possibility and of the actual existence of suprasensible or spiritual realities. Hence we cannot describe existence as the power which material realities have to excite in us a knowledge of themselves. Their existence is prior to this activity: *prius est esse quam agere*. Nor can we limit existence to material realities; for if there are spiritual realities these too have existence, though this existence can be discerned only by intellect, and not by sense.

13. ESSENCE.—In any existing thing we can distinguish *what the thing is*, its *essence*, from its actual *existence*. If we abstract from the actual existence of a thing, not considering whether it actually exists or not, and fix our attention merely on *what the thing is*, we are thinking of its *real essence*. If we positively exclude the notion of actual existence from our concept of the essence, and think of the latter as not actually existing, we are considering it formally as a *possible essence*. There is no being, even the Necessary Being, whose essence we cannot think of in the former way, *i.e. without including* in our concept the notion of actual existence; but we cannot without error *positively exclude* the notion of actual existence from our concept of the Necessary Being, or think of the latter as a *merely possible* essence.

Taken in its widest sense, the essence of a thing (οὐσία, *essentia*, τὸ τί ἐστι, *quod quid est, quidditas*) means *that by which a thing is what it is: id quo res est id quod est*: that which gives us the answer to the question, What is this thing? *Quid est haec res?* τί ἐστι τόδε τι.[84] Now of course any individual thing is what it is just precisely by all the reality that is in it; but we have no direct or intuitive intellectual insight into this reality; we understand it only by degrees; we explore it from various points of view, abstracting and generalizing partial aspects of it as we compare it with other things and seek to classify and define it: *ratio humana essentias rerum quasi venatur*, as the scholastics say: the human mind hunts, as it were, after the essences or natures of things. Understanding the individual datum of sense experience (what Aristotle called τόδε τι, or οὐσία πρώτη, and the scholastics *hoc aliquid*, or *substantia prima*), *e.g.* this individual, Socrates, first under the vaguest concept of being, then gradually under the more and more determinate concepts of substance, corporeal, living, sentient, rational, it finally forms the complex concept of his *species infima*, expressed by his lowest class-name, "man," and explicitly set forth in the definition of his specific nature as a "rational animal". Nor does our reason fail to realize that by reaching this concept of the *specific* essence or nature of the individual, Socrates, it has not yet grasped all the reality whereby the individual is what he is. It has reached what he has in common with all other individuals of his class, what is essential to him *as a man*; it has distinguished this from the unanalysed something which makes him *this particular individual* of his class, and which makes his specific essence this *individual essence* (*essentia* "*atoma*," or "*individua*"); and it has also distinguished his essence from those accidental and ever varying attributes which are not essential to him as a man, and from those which are not essential to him as Socrates. It is only the unfathomed individual essence, as existing *hic et nunc*, that is *concrete*. All the mind's generic and specific representations of it—*e.g.* of Socrates as a corporeal substance, a living being, a sentient being, a rational animal—are *abstract*, and all more or less inadequate, none of them exhausting its knowable reality. But it is only in so far as the mind is able to represent concrete individual things by such abstract concepts, that it can attain to *intellectual* knowledge of their nature or reality. Hence it is that by the term "essence," simply and *sine addito*, we always mean the essence as grasped by abstract generic or specific concepts (εἶδος, *species*), and as thus capable of definition (λόγος, *ratio rei*). "The essence," says St. Thomas, "is that by which the thing is constituted in its proper genus or species, and which we signify by the definition which states what the thing is".[85] Thus understood, the essence is abstract, and gives the specific or generic type to which the individual thing belongs; but we may also mean by essence, the concrete essence, the individual person or thing (*persona, suppositum, res individua*). The relations between the objects of those two concepts of essence will be examined later.

Since the specific essence is conceived as the most fundamental reality in the thing, and as the seat and source of all the properties and activities of the thing, it is sometimes defined or described, in accordance with this notion of it, as the primary constitutive of the thing and the source of all the properties of the thing. Conceived as the foundation of all the properties of the thing it is sometimes called *substance* (οὐσία, *substantia*). Regarded as the source of the thing's activities, and the principle of its growth or development, it is called the *nature* of the thing (φύσις, *natura*, from φύω, *nascor*).[86]

Since what makes a thing that which it is, by the same fact differentiates this thing from every other thing, the essence is rightly conceived as that which gives the thing its characteristic being, thereby marking it off from all other being. In reality, of course, each individual being is distinct by all that it is from every other. But since we get our intellectual knowledge of things by abstracting, comparing, generalizing, and classifying partial aspects of them, we apprehend part of the imperfectly grasped abstract essence of each individual as common to other classes (generic), and part as peculiar to that class itself (differential); and thus we differentiate classes of things by what is only part of their essence, by what we call the *differentia* of each class, *distinguishing mentally* between it and the generic element: which two are really *one*, really identical, in every individual of the species thus defined and classified.

But in the Aristotelian and scholastic view of the constitution of any *corporeal* thing, there is a danger of taking what is really only part of the essence of such a thing for the whole essence. According to this view all corporeal substance is essentially composite, constituted by two really distinct, substantial principles, primal matter (πρώτη ὕλη, *materia prima*) and substantial form (εἶδος, μορφή) united substantially, as potential and actual principles, to form one composite nature or essence. Now the kind, or species, or specific type, to which a body belongs—*e.g.*, a horse, an oak, gold, water, etc.—depends upon the substantial form which actualizes the matter or potential principle. In so far as the corporeal essence is known to us at all it is known through the form, which is the principle of all the characteristic properties and activities of that particular kind of body. Hence it is quite natural that the εἶδος, μόρφη, or *forma substantialis* of a body should often be referred to as the specific essence of the body, though of course the essence of the body really includes the material as well as the formal factor.

We may look at the essence of any being from two points of view. If we consider it as it is conceived actually to exist in the being, we call it the *physical essence*. If we consider it after the manner in which it is apprehended and defined by our intellects through generic and differentiating concepts, we call it the *metaphysical essence*. Thus, the essence of man conceived by the two defining concepts, "rational animal," is the metaphysical essence; the essence of man as known to be composed of the two really distinct substantial principles, soul and body, is the physical essence. Understood in this way both are one and the same essence considered from different points of view—as existing in the actual order, and as conceived by the mind.[87]

The physical essence of any being, understood as the constitutive principle or principles from which all properties spring, is either *simple* or *composite* according as it is understood to consist of one such constitutive principle, or to result from the substantial union of two constitutive principles, a material and a formal. Thus, the essence of God, the essence of a purely spiritual being, the essence of the human soul, are physically simple; the essence of man, the essences of all corporeal beings, are physically composite.

According to our mode of conceiving, defining and classifying essences by means of the abstract generic and differential grades of being which we apprehend in them, all essences, even physically simple essences, are conceived as logically and metaphysically composite. Moreover we speak and think of their generic and differential factors as "material" and "formal" respectively, after the analogy of the composition of corporeal or physically composite essences from the union of two really distinct principles, matter and form; the analogy consisting in this, that as matter is the indeterminate principle which is determined and actuated by form, so the *generic* concept is the indeterminate concept which is made definite and specific by that of the *differentia*.[88] But when we think of the *genus* of any corporeal essence as "material," and the *differentia* as "formal," we must not consider these "metaphysical parts" as really distinct; whereas the "physical parts" of a corporeal substance (such as man) are really distinct. The genus (animal), although a metaphysical part, expresses the *whole essence* (man) in an indeterminate way; whereas the "matter" which is a physical part, does not express the whole essence of man, nor does the soul which is also a physical part, but only both together. Not a little error has resulted from the confusion of thought whereby *genus* and *differentia* have been regarded as material and formal constitutives in the literal sense of those expressions.

14. CHARACTERISTICS OF ABSTRACT ESSENCES.—When we consider the essences of things not as actually existing, but as intrinsically possible—the abstract, metaphysical essences, therefore—we find that when as objects of our thought they are analysed into their simplest constituents and compared or related with themselves and with one another they present themselves to our minds in these relations as endowed with certain more or less remarkable characteristics.

(*a*) In the first place, being abstract, they present themselves to the mind as being what they are independently of actual existence at any particular time or place. Their intelligibility is something apart from any relation to any actual time or place. Being intrinsically possible, they might exist at any time or place; but as possible, they are out of time and out of place—*detemporalized* and *delocalized*, if we may be permitted to use such expressions.[89]

(*b*) Furthermore, since the intellect forms its notions of them, through the aid of the senses and the imagination, from actual realizations of themselves or their constituent factors, and since it understands them to be intrinsically possible, or free from intrinsic incompatibility of their constituent factors, it conceives them to be capable of indefinitely repeated actualizations throughout time and space—unless it sees some special reason to the contrary, as it does in the case of the Necessary Being, and (according to some philosophers) in the case of purely immaterial beings or pure spirits. That is to say it *universalizes* them, and sees them to be capable of existing at any and every conceivable time and place. This relation of theirs to space is not likely to be confounded with the *immensity* or *ubiquity* of God. But their corresponding relation to time is sometimes described as *eternity*; and if it is so described it must be carefully distinguished from the *positive* eternity of God, the Immutable Being. To distinguish it from the latter it is usually described as *negative* eternity,—this indifference of the possible essence to actual existence at any particular point of time.

But apart from this relation which we conceive it as having to existence in the order of actual reality, can we, or do we, or must we conceive it as in itself an intrinsic possibility *from all eternity*, in the sense that it *never began* to be intrinsically possible, and will never cease to be so? Must we attribute to it a *positive* eternity, not of course of actuality or existence, but of *ideal* being, as an object of thought to an Eternally Existing Mind? What is this supposed eternal possibility of the possible essence? Is it nothing actual: the possible as such is nothing actual. But is it anything real? Has it only ideal being—*esse ideale* or *intentionale*? And has it this only in and from the human mind, or independently of the human mind? And also independently of the *actual* essences from which the human mind gets the data for its thought,—so that we must ascribe to it an *eternal* ideal being? To these questions we shall return presently.

(*c*) Thirdly, essences considered apart from their actual existence, and compared with their own constitutive factors or with one another, reveal to the mind relations which the mind sees to be *necessary*, and which it formulates for itself in *necessary* judgments,—judgments *in materia necessaria*. By virtue of the principle of identity an abstract essence is *necessarily* what it is, what the mind conceives it to be, what the mind conceives as its definition. Man, as an object of thought, is *necessarily* a rational animal, whether he actually exists or not. And if he is thought of as existing, he cannot at the same time be thought of as non-existing,—by the principle of contradiction. An existing man is necessarily an existing man,—by the principle of identity. These logical principles are rooted in the nature of reality, whether actual or possible, considered as an *object of thought*. There is thus a necessary relation between any complex object of thought and each of the constituent factors into which the mind can analyse it. And, similarly, there is a necessary negative relation—a relation of exclusion—between any object of thought and anything which the mind sees to be incompatible with that object as a whole, or with any of its constituent factors.

Again, the mind sees necessary relations between abstract essences compared with one another. Five and seven are *necessarily* twelve. Whatever begins to exist actually *must* have a cause. Contingent being, if such exists, is *necessarily* dependent for its existence on some other actually existing being. If potential being is actualized it *must* be actualized by actual being. The three interior angles of a triangle are *necessarily* equal to two right angles. And so on.

But is the abstract essence itself—apart from all mental analysis of it, apart from all comparison of it with its constituent factors or with other essences—in any sense *necessary*? There is no question of its actual existence, but only of itself as an object of thought. Now our thought does not seem to demand *necessarily*, or have a *necessary* connexion with, any particular object of which we do *de facto* think. What we do think of is determined by our experience of *actual* things. And the things which we conceive to be possible, by the exercise of our reason upon the data of our senses, memory and imagination, are determined as to their nature and number by our experience of actual things, even although they themselves can and do pass beyond the domain of actually experienced things. The only necessary object of thought is reality in general: for the exercise of the function of thought necessarily demands an object, and this object must be reality of some sort. Thought, as we saw, begins with actual reality. Working upon this, thought apprehends in it the foundations of those necessary relations and judgments already referred to. Considering, moreover, the actual data of experience, our thought can infer from these the actual existence of one Being Who must exist by a necessity of His Essence.

But, furthermore, must all the possible essences which the mind does or can actually think of, be conceived as *necessarily possible* in the same sense in which it is suggested that they must be conceived as eternally possible? To this question, too, we shall return presently.

(*d*) Finally, possible essences appear to the mind as *immutable*, and consequently *indivisible*. This means simply that the relations which we establish between them and their constitutive factors are not only necessary but immutable: that if any constitutive factor of an essence is conceived as removed from it, or any new factor as added, we have no longer the original essence but some other essence. If "animal" is a being essentially embodying the two objective concepts of "organism" and "sentient," then on removing either we have no longer the essence "animal". So, too, by adding to these some other element compatible with them, *e.g.* "rational," we have no longer the essence "animal," but the essence "man". Hence possible essences have been likened to numbers, inasmuch as if we add anything to, or subtract anything from, any given number, we have now no longer the original number but another.[90] This, too, is only an expression of the laws of identity and contradiction.

We might ask, however, whether, apart from analysis and comparison of an abstract object of thought with its constitutive notes or factors, such a possible essence is in itself *immutably* possible. This is similar to the question whether we can or must conceive such a possible essence as eternally and necessarily possible.

15. GROUNDS OF THOSE CHARACTERISTICS.—In considering the grounds or reasons of the various characteristics just enumerated it may be well to reflect that when we speak of the *intrinsic possibility* of a possible essence we conceive the latter as something complex, which we mentally resolve into its constitutive notes or factors or principles, to see if these are compatible. If they are we pronounce the essence intrinsically possible, if not we pronounce it intrinsically impossible. For our minds, absence of internal incompatibility in the content of our concept

of any object is the test of its intrinsic possibility. Whatever fulfils this test we consider capable of existing. But what about the possibility of the notes, or factors, or principles themselves, whereby we define those essences, and by the union of which we conceive those essences to be constituted? How do we know that those abstract principles or factors—no one of which can actually exist alone, since all are abstract—can in certain combinations form *possible* objects of thought? We can know this only because we have either experienced such objects as actual, or because we infer their possibility from objects actually experienced. And similarly our knowledge of what is impossible is based upon our experience of the actual. Since, moreover, our experience of the actual is finite and fallible, we may err in our judgments as to what essences are, and what are not, intrinsically possible.[91]

If now we ask ourselves what intelligible reason can we assign for the characteristics just indicated as belonging to possible essences, we must fix our attention first of all on the fundamental fact that the human intellect always apprehends its object *in an abstract condition*. It contemplates the essence apart from the existence in which the essence is subject to circumstances of time and place and change; it grasps the essence in a static condition as simply identical with itself and distinct from all else; it sees the essence as indifferent to existence at any place or time; reflecting then on the actualization of this essence in the existing order of things, it apprehends the essence as capable of indefinite actualizations (except in cases where it sees some reason to the contrary), *i.e.* it *universalizes* the essence; comparing it with its constituent notes or elements, and with those of other essences, it sees and affirms certain relations (of identity or diversity, compatibility or incompatibility, between those notes or elements) as holding good *necessarily* and *immutably*, and independently of the actual embodiment of those notes or elements in any object existing at any particular place or time. All these features of the relations between the constituents of abstract, possible essences, seem so far to be adequately accounted for by the fact that the intellect apprehends those essences *in the abstract*: the data in which it apprehends them being given to it through sense experience. What may be inferred from the fact that the human intellect has this power of abstract thought, is another question[92]. But granting that it does apprehend essences in this manner, we seem to have in this fact a sufficient explanation of the features just referred to.

We have, however, already suggested other questions about the reality of those possible essences. Is their possibility, so far as known to us, explained by our experience of actual things? Or must we think them as eternally, necessarily and immutably possible? From the manner in which we must apprehend them, can we infer anything about the reality of an Eternal, Immutable, Necessary Intelligence, in whose Thought and Essence alone those essences, as apprehended by our minds, can find their ultimate ground and explanation? These are the questions we must now endeavour to examine.

16. Possible Essences as such are Something Distinct from mere Logical Being, and from Nothingness.—There have been philosophers who have held that the actual alone is real, and only while it is actual; that a purely (intrinsically) possible essence as such is nothing real; that the actual alone is possible; that the purely possible as such is impossible. This view is based on the erroneous assumption that whatever is or becomes actual is so, or becomes so, by some sort of unintelligible fatalistic necessity. Apart from the fact that it is incompatible with certain truths of theism, such as the Divine Omnipotence and Freedom in creating, it also involves the denial of all real becoming or change, and the assertion that all actuality is eternal; for if anything becomes actual, it was previously either possible or impossible; if impossible, it could never become actual; if possible, then as possible it was something different from the impossible, or from absolute nothingness. Moreover, the intrinsically possible is capable of becoming actual, and may be actualized if there exists some actual being with power to actualize it; but absolute nothingness—or, in other words, the intrinsically impossible—cannot be actualized, even by Omnipotence; therefore the possible essence as such is something positive or real, as distinct from nothingness. Finally, intrinsically possible essences can be clearly distinguished from one another by the mind; but their negation which is pure non-entity or nothingness cannot be so distinguished. It is therefore clear that possible essences are in some true sense something positive or real. From which it follows that nothingness, in the strict sense, is not the mere absence or negation of actuality, but also the absence or negation of that positive or real something which is intrinsic possibility; in other words that nothingness in the strict sense means intrinsic impossibility.

Even those who hold the opinion just rejected—that the purely possible essence as such has no reality in any conceivable sense—would presumably admit that it is an object of human thought at all events; they would accord to it the being it has from the human mind which thinks it. It would therefore be an *ens rationis* according to this view, having only the ideal being which consists in its being constituted and contemplated by the human mind. That it has the ideal being, the *esse ideale* or *esse intentionale*, which consists in its being contemplated by the human mind as an object of thought, no one will deny. But a little reflection will show, firstly, that this ideal being is something more than the ideal being of an *ens rationis*, of a mere logical entity; and, secondly, that a possible essence must have some other ideal being than that which it has in the individual human mind.

The possible essence is not a mere logical entity; for the latter cannot be conceived as capable of existing apart from the human mind, in the world of actual existences (3), whereas the former can be, and is in fact, conceived as capable of such existence. Its ideal being in the human mind is, therefore, something other than that of a mere logical entity.

The ideal being which it has in the human mind as an object of thought is undoubtedly derived from the mind's knowledge of actual things. We think of the essences of actually experienced realities apart from their actual existence. Thus abstracted, we analyse them, compare them, reason from them. By these processes we can not merely attain to a knowledge of the actual existence of other realities above and beyond and outside of our own direct and immediate intuitional experience, but we can also form concepts of multitudes of realities or essences as intrinsically possible, thus giving these latter an ideal existence in our own minds. Here, then, the question arises: Is this the only ideal being that can be ascribed to such essences? In other words, are essences intrinsically possible because *we think* them as intrinsically possible? Or is it not rather the case that we think them to be intrinsically possible because they are intrinsically possible? Does our thought constitute, or does it not rather merely discover, their intrinsic possibility? Does the latter result from, or is it not rather presupposed by, our thought-activity? The second alternative suggested in each of these questions is the true one. As our thought is not the source of their actuality, neither is it the source of their intrinsic possibility. Solipsism is the *reductio ad absurdum* of the philosophy which would reduce all *actuality* experienced by the individual mind to phases, or phenomena, or self-manifestations, of the individual mind itself as the one and only actuality. And no less absurd is the philosophy which would accord to all *intrinsically possible* realities no being other than the ideal being which they have as the thought-objects of the individual human mind. The study of the *actual* world of direct experience leads the impartial and sincere inquirer to the conclusion that it is in some true sense a manifestation of mind or intelligence: not, however, of his own mind, which is itself only a very tiny item in the totality of the actual world, but of one Supreme Intelligence. And in this same Intelligence the world of possible essences too will be found to have its original and fundamental ideal being.

17. Possible Essences have, besides Ideal Being, no other sort of Being or Reality Proper and Intrinsic to Themselves.—Before inquiring further into the manner in which we attain to a knowledge of this Intelligence, and of the ideal being of possible essences in this Intelligence, we may ask whether, above and beyond such ideal being, possible essences have not perhaps from all eternity some being or reality proper and intrinsic to themselves; not indeed the actual being which they possess when actualized in time, but yet some kind of

intrinsic reality as distinct from the *extrinsic* ideal being, or *esse intentionale*, which consists merely in this that they are objects of thought present as such to a Supreme Intelligence or Mind.

Some few medieval scholastics[93] contended that possible essences have from all eternity not indeed the existence they may receive by creation or production in time, but an intrinsic essential being which, by creation or production, may be transferred to the order of actual existences, and which, when actual existence ceases (if they ever receive it), still continues immutable and incorruptible: what these writers called the *esse essentiae*, as distinct from the *esse existentiae*, conceiving it to be intermediate between the latter on the one hand and mere ideal or logical being on the other, and hence calling it *esse diminutum* or *secundum quid*. Examining the question from the standpoint of theism, these authors seem to have thought that since God understands these essences as possible from all eternity, and since this knowledge must have as its term or object something real and positive, these essences must have some real and proper intrinsic being from all eternity: otherwise they would be simply nothingness, and nothingness cannot be the term of the Divine Intelligence. But the obvious reply is that though possible essences as such are *nothing actual* they must be distinguished as realities, capable of actually existing, from *absolute nothingness*; and that as thus distinguished from absolute nothingness they are really and positively intelligible to the Divine Mind, as indeed they are even to the human mind. To be intelligible they need not have actual being. They must, no doubt, be capable of having actual being, in order to be understood as realities: it is precisely in this understood capability that their reality consists, for the real includes not only what actually exists but whatever is capable of actual existence. Whatever is opposed to absolute nothingness is real; and this manifestly includes not only the actual but whatever is intrinsically possible.

Realities or essences which have not actual being have only ideal being; and ideal being means simply presence in some mind as an object of thought. Scholastic philosophers generally[94] hold that possible essences as such have no other being than this; that before and until such essences actually exist they have of themselves and in themselves no being except the ideal being which they have as objects of the Divine Intelligence and the virtual being they have in the Divine Omnipotence which may at any time give them actual existence. One convincing reason for this view is the consideration that if possible essences as such had from all eternity any proper and intrinsic being in themselves, God could neither create nor annihilate. For in that hypothesis essences, on becoming actual, would not be produced *ex nihilo*, inasmuch as before becoming actual they would in themselves and from all eternity have had their own proper real being; and after ceasing to be actual they would still retain this. But creation is the production of *the whole reality* of actual being from nothingness; and is therefore impossible if the actual being is merely produced from an essence already real, *i.e.* having an eternal positive reality of its own. The same is true of annihilation. The theory of eternally existing uncreated *matter* is no less incompatible with the doctrine of creation than this theory of eternally real and uncreated forms or essences.

Again, what could this supposed positive and proper reality of the possible essence be? If it is anything distinct from the mere ideal being of such an essence, as it is assumed to be, it must after all be *actual* being of some sort, which would apparently have to be actualized again in order to have actual existence! Finally, this supposed eternal reality, proper to possible essences, cannot be anything uncreated. For whatever is uncreated is God; and since it is these supposed proper realities of possible essences that are made actual, and constitute the existing created universe, the latter would be in this view an actualization of the Divine Essence itself,—which is pantheism pure and simple. And neither can this supposed eternal reality, proper to possible essences, be anything created. For such creation would be eternal and necessary; whereas God's creative activity is admitted by all scholastics to be essentially free; and although they are not agreed as to whether "creation from all eternity" ("*creatio ab aeterno*") is possible, they are agreed that it is not a fact.

Possible essences as such are therefore nothing actual. Furthermore, as such they have in themselves no positive being. But they are not therefore unreal. They are positively intelligible as capable of actual existence, and therefore as distinct from logical entities or *entia rationis* which are not capable of such existence. They are present as objects of thought to mind; and to some mind other than the individual human mind. About this ideal being which they have in this Mind we have now in the next place to inquire.

18. INFERENCES FROM OUR KNOWLEDGE OF POSSIBLE ESSENCES.—We have stated that an impartial study of the *actual* world will lead to the conclusion that it is dependent on a Supreme Intelligence; and we have suggested that in this Supreme Intelligence also possible essences as such have their primary ideal being. When the existence of God has been established—as it may be established by various lines of argument—from *actual* things, we can clearly see, as will be pointed out presently, that in the Divine Essence all possible essences have the ultimate source of their possibility. But many scholastic philosophers contend that the nature and properties of possible essences, as apprehended by the human mind, furnish a distinct and conclusive argument for the existence of a Supreme Uncreated Intelligence.[35] Others deny the validity of such a line of reasoning, contending that it is based on misapprehension and misinterpretation of those characteristics.

All admit that it is not human thought that makes essences possible: they are intelligible to the human mind because they are possible, not *vice versa*.[96] For the human mind the immediate source and ground of their intrinsic possibility and characteristics is the fact that they are given to it in *actual* experience while it has the power of considering them *apart from their actual existence*.

But (1) are they not independent of experienced actuality, no less than of the human mind, so that we are forced to infer from them the reality of a Supreme Eternal Mind in which they have eternal ideal being?

(2) Is not any possible essence (*e.g.* "water," or "a triangle") so necessarily what it is that even if it never did and never will exist, nay even were there no human or other finite mind to conceive it, it would still be what it is (*e.g.* "a chemical compound of oxygen and hydrogen," or "a plane rectilinear three-sided figure")—so that there must be some Necessarily Existing Intelligence in and from which it has this necessary truth as a possible essence?[97] These essences, as known to us, are so far from being grounded in, or explained by, the things of our actual experience, that we rather regard the latter as grounded in the former. Do we not consider possible essences as the prototypes and exemplars to which actual things must conform in order to be actual, in order to exist at all?[98]

(3) Finally, the relations which we apprehend as obtaining between them, we see to be necessary and immutable relations. They embody necessary truths which are for our minds the standards of all truth. Such necessary truths cannot be grounded either in the contingent human mind, or in the contingent and mutable actuality of the things of our immediate experience. Therefore we can and must infer from them the reality of a Necessary, Immutable Being, of whose essence they must be imitations.

If, then, this ideal order of intrinsically possible essences is logically and ontologically prior to the contingent actualizations of any of them (even though it be posterior to them *in the order of our knowledge*, which is based on *actual experience*), there must be likewise ontologically prior to all contingent actualities (including our own minds) some *Necessary Intelligence* in which this order of possible essences has its ideal being.

19. CRITICAL ANALYSIS OF THOSE INFERENCES.—The validity of the general line of argument indicated in the preceding paragraphs has been seriously questioned. Among other criticisms the following points have been urged[99]:—

(1) *Actual* things furnish the basis of irrefragable proofs of the existence of God—the Supreme, Necessary, Eternal, Omniscient, and Omnipotent Being. But we are here inquiring whether a mind which has not yet so analysed actual being as to see how it involves this conclusion, or a mind which abstracts altogether from the evidence furnished by actual things for this conclusion, can prove the existence of such a being from the separate consideration of possible essences, their attributes and relations. Now it is not evident that to such a mind possible essences reveal themselves as having *eternal* ideal

being. Such a mind is, no doubt, conscious that it is not itself the cause of their possibility. But it sees that actual things *plus* the abstract character of its own thought account sufficiently for all their features as it knows them. To the question: Is not their ideal being *eternal?* it can only answer: That will depend on whether the world of actual things can be shown to involve the existence of an Eternal Intelligence. Until this is proved we cannot say whether possible essences have any ideal being other than that which they have in human minds.

(2) The actual things from which we get our concepts of possible essences do not exist *necessarily*. But, granted their existence, we know from them that certain essences are *de facto* possible. They are not *necessarily* given to us as possible, any more than actual things are necessarily given to us as actual. Of course, when they are thought of at all, they are, as objects of thought, necessarily and immutably identical with themselves, and related to one another as mutually compatible or incompatible, etc. But this necessity of relations, hypothetical as it is and contingent on the mental processes of analysis and comparison, involved as it is in the very nature of being and thought, and expressed as it is in the principles of identity and contradiction, is just as true of actual contingent essences as of possible essences;[100] and it is something very different from the sort of necessity claimed for possible essences by the contention that they must be conceived as having ideal being *necessarily*. The ideal being they have in the human mind is certainly not necessary: the human mind might never have conceived these possible essences.

But must the human mind conceive a possible essence as having *some* ideal being *necessarily?* No; unless that mind has already convinced itself, from a study of *actual* things, that an Eternal, Necessary, Omniscient Intelligence exists: to which, of course, such essences would be eternally and necessarily present as objects of thought. If the human mind had already reached this conviction it could then see that "even if there were no human intellect, things would still be true in relation to the Divine Intellect. But if both intellects were, *per impossibile*, conceived as non-existent truth would persist no longer."[101] Suppose, therefore, that it has not yet reached this conviction, or abstracts altogether from the existence of God as known from *actual* things; and then, further, imagines the actual things of its experience and all human intellects and finite intellects of whatsoever kind as non-existent: must it still conceive possible things as possible? No; possibility and impossibility, truth and falsity will now have ceased to have any meaning. After such attempted abstraction the mind would have before it only what Balmes describes as "the abyss of nothing". And Balmes is right in saying that the mind is unable "to abstract all existence". But the reason of the inability is not, as Balmes contends, because when it has removed actual things and finite minds there still remains in spite of it a system or order of possible essences which forces it to infer and posit the existence of an Eternal, Necessary Mind as the source and ground of that order. The reason rather is because the mind sees that the known *actual* things, from which it got all its notions of possible essences, necessarily imply, as the only intelligible ground of their actuality, the existence of a Necessary Being, in whose Intelligence they must have been contained ideally, and in whose Omnipotence they must have been contained virtually, from all eternity. From contingent *actuality*, as known to it, the mind can argue to the eternal actuality of Necessary Being, and to the impossibility either of a state of absolute nothingness, or of an order of purely possible things apart from all actuality.

(3) Of course, whether the mind has thus thought out the ultimate implications of the actuality of experienced things or not, once it has thought and experienced those things it cannot by any effort banish the memory of them from its presence: they are there still as objects of its thought even when it abstracts from their actual existence. But if, while it has not yet seen that their actuality implies the existence of a Necessary, Omniscient and Omnipotent Being, it abstracts not only from their actual existence but from the existence of all finite minds (itself included), then in that state, so far as its knowledge goes, there would be neither actual nor ideal nor possible being. Nor can the fact that an ideal order of possible things still persists in its own thought mislead it into concluding that such an ideal order really persists in the hypothesis it has made. For it knows that this ideal order still persists for itself simply because it cannot "think itself away". It sees all the time that if it could effectively think itself away, this ideal order would have to disappear with it, leaving nothing—so far as it knows—either actual or possible. Mercier has some apposite remarks on this very point. "From the fact," he writes, "that those abstract essences, grasped by our abstractive thought from the dawn of our reason, have grown so familiar to us, we easily come to look upon them as pre-existing archetypes or models of our thoughts and of things; they form a fund of predicates by which we are in the habit of interpreting the data of our experience. So, too, the hypothetically necessary relations established by abstract thought between them we come to regard as a sort of eternal system of principles, endowed with a sort of legislative power, to which created things and intelligences must conform. But they have really no such pre-existence. The eternal pre-existence of those essence-types, which Plato called the 'intelligible world,' the τόπος νοητός, and the supposed eternal legislative power of their relations, are a sort of mental optical illusion. Those abstract essences, and the principles based upon them, are the products of our mental activity working on the data of our actual experience. When we enter on the domain of *speculative reflection* ... they are there before us; ... but we must not forget that reflection is *consequent* on the spontaneous thought-activity which—by working abstractively on the actual data of sensible, contingent, changeable, temporal realities—set them up there.... We know from psychology how those ideal, abstract essence-types are formed.... But because we have no actual memory of their formation, which is so rapid as practically to escape consciousness in spontaneous thought, we are naturally prone to imagine that they are not the product of our own mental action on the data of actual experience, but that they exist in us, or rather above us, and independently of us. We can therefore understand the psychological illusion under which Plato wrote such passages as the following: 'But if anyone should tell me why anything is beautiful, either because it has a blooming, florid colour, or figure, or anything else of the kind, I dismiss all other reasons, for I am confounded by them all; but I simply, wholly, and perhaps naïvely, confine myself to this, that nothing else causes it to be beautiful, except either the presence or communication of that abstract beauty, by whatever means and in whatever way communicated; for I cannot yet affirm with certainty, but only that by means of beauty all beautiful things become beautiful (τῷ καλῷ τὰ καλὰ γίγνεται καλά). For this appears to me the safest answer to give both to myself and others, and

adhering to this I think that I shall never fall .... And that by magnitude great things become great, and greater things greater; and by littleness less things become less.'[102] St. Augustine's doctrine on the invariable laws of numbers, on the immutable principles of wisdom, and on truth generally, draws its inspiration from this Platonic idealism."[103]

But this Platonic doctrine, attributing to the abstract essences conceived by our thought a reality independent both of our thought and of the actual sense data from which directly or indirectly we derive our concepts of them, is rejected as unsound by scholastics generally. When we have proved from actual things that God exists, and is the Intelligent and Free Creator of the actual world of our direct experience, we can of course consider the Divine Intellect as contemplating from all eternity the Divine Essence, and as seeing therein the eternal archetypes or ideas of all actual and possible essences. We may thus regard the Divine Mind as the eternal τόπος νοητός, or *mundus intelligibilis*. This, of course, is not Plato's thought; it is what St. Augustine substituted for Platonism, and very properly. But we must not infer, from this truth, that when we contemplate possible essences, with all the characteristics we may detect in them, we are contemplating this *mundus intelligibilis* which is the Divine Mind. This was the error of the ontologists. They inferred that since possible essences, as known by the human mind, have ideal being independently of the latter and of all actual contingent reality, the human mind in contemplating them has really an intuition of them as they are seen by the Divine Intellect Itself in the Divine Essence; so that, in the words of Gioberti, the *Primum Ontologicum*, the Divine Being Himself, is also the *primum logicum*, or first reality apprehended by human thought.[104]

Now those authors who hold that the ideal order of possible essences contemplated by the human mind is seen by the latter, as so contemplated, to have some being, some ideal being, really independent of the human mind itself, and of the actual contingent things from which they admit that the human mind derives its knowledge of such essences,— these authors *do not hold*, but *deny*, that this independent ideal being, which they claim for these essences, is *anything Divine*, that it is the Divine Essence as seen by the Divine Intellect to be imitable *ad extra*.[105] Hence they cannot fairly be charged with the error of ontologism.

Renouncing Plato's exaggerated realism, and holding that our knowledge of the ideal order of possible essences is derived by our mind from its consideration of *actual* things, they yet hold that this ideal order is seen to have some sort of being or reality independent both of the mind and of actual things.[106] This is not easy to understand. When we ask, Is this supposed independent being (or reality, or possibility) of possible essences the ideal being they have in the Divine mind?—we are told that it is not;[107] but that it is something from which we can *infer, by reasoning*, this eternal, necessary, and immutable ideal being of these same essences in the Divine Mind.

The considerations urged in the foregoing paragraphs will, however, have shown that the validity of this line of reasoning from possible essences to the reality of an Eternal, Divine, Immutable Intelligence is by no means evident or free from difficulties. Of course, when the existence of God has been proved from actual things, the conception of the Divine Intelligence and Essence as the ultimate source of all possible reality, no less than of all actual reality, will be found to shed a great deal of new light upon the intrinsic possibility of possible essences. Since, however, our knowledge of the Divine is merely analogical, and since God's intuition of possible essences, as imitations of His own Divine Essence, completely transcends our comprehension, and is totally different from our abstractive knowledge of such essences, our conception of the manner in which these essences are related to the Divine Nature and the Divine Attributes, must be determined after the analogy of the manner in which our own minds are related to these essences.

20. ESSENCES ARE INTRINSICALLY POSSIBLE, NOT BECAUSE GOD CAN MAKE THEM EXIST ACTUALLY; NOR YET BECAUSE HE FREELY WILLS THEM TO BE POSSIBLE; NOR BECAUSE HE UNDERSTANDS THEM AS POSSIBLE; BUT BECAUSE THEY ARE MODES IN WHICH THE DIVINE ESSENCE IS IMITABLE *ad extra*.—(*a*) The ultimate source of the *extrinsic* possibility of all contingent realities is the Divine Omnipotence: just as the proximate source of the extrinsic possibility of a statue is the power of the sculptor to educe it from the block of wood or marble. But just as the power of the sculptor presupposes the *intrinsic* possibility of the statue, so does the Divine Omnipotence presuppose the intrinsic possibility of all possible things. It is not, as William of Ockam († 1347), a scholastic of the decadent period, erroneously thought, because God can create things that such things are intrinsically possible, but rather because they are intrinsically possible He can create them.

(*b*) Not less erroneous is the *voluntarist* theory of Descartes, according to which possible essences are intrinsically possible because God freely willed them to be possible.[108] The *actuality* of all created things depends, of course, on the free will of God to create them; but that possible essences are what they are, and are related to each other necessarily as they are, because God has willed them to be such, is absolutely incredible. Descartes seems to have been betrayed into this strange error by a false notion of what is requisite for the absolute freedom and independence of the Divine Will: as if this demanded that God should be free to will, *e.g.* that two *plus* two be five, or that the radii of a circle be unequal, or that creatures be independent of Himself, or that blasphemy be a virtuous act! The intrinsic possibility of essences is *not* dependent on the Free Will of God; the actualization of possible essences is; but God can will to actualize only such essences as He sees, from comprehending His own Divine Essence, to be intrinsically possible. But it derogates in no way from the supremacy of the Divine Will to conceive its free volition as thus consequent on, and illumined by, the Divine Knowledge; whereas it is incompatible with the wisdom and sanctity of God, as well as inconceivable to the human mind, that the necessary laws of thought and being—such as the principles of contradiction and identity, the principle of causality, the first principles of the moral order—should be what they are simply because God has freely willed them to be so, and might therefore have been otherwise.

From the fact that we have no direct intuition of the Divine Being, some philosophers have concluded that all speculation on the relation of God to the world of our direct experience is necessarily barren and fruitless. This is a phase of agnosticism; and, like all error, it is the exaggeration of a truth: the truth being that while we may reach real knowledge about the Divine Nature and attributes by such speculation, we can do so only on condition that we are guided by analogies drawn from God's creation, and remember that our concepts, as applied to God, are analogical (2).

"We can know God only by analogy with contingent and finite beings, and consequently the realities and laws of the contingent and finite world must necessarily serve as our term of comparison. But, among finite realities, we see an essential subordination of the extrinsically possible to the intelligible, of this to the intrinsically possible, and of this again to the essential type which is presupposed by our thought. Therefore, *a pari*, we must consider the omnipotent will of God, which is the first and universal cause of all [contingent] existences, as under the direction of the Divine Omniscience, and this in turn as having for its object the Divine Essence and in it the essential types whose intrinsic possibility is grounded on the necessary imitability of the Divine Being.

"When, therefore, in defence of his position, Descartes argues that 'In God willing and knowing are one and the same; the reason why He knows anything is because He wills it, and for this reason only can it be true: *Ex hoc ipso quod Deus aliquid velit, ideo cognoscit, et ideo tantum talis res est vera*'—he is only confusing the issue. We might, indeed, retort the argument: 'In God willing and knowing are one and the same; the reason why He wills anything is because He knows it, and for this reason only can it be good: *Ex hoc ipso quod aliquid cognoscit, ideo vult, et ideo tantum talis res est bona*,' but both inferences are equally unwarranted. For, though willing and knowing are certainly one and the same *in God*, this one and the same thing is formally and for our minds neither will nor intellect, but a reality transcending will and intellect, a substance infinitely above any substances known to us: ὑπερούσια, *supersubstantia*, as the Fathers of the Church and the Doctors of the Schools call it. But of this transcendent substance we have no intuitive knowledge. We must therefore either abandon all attempts to find out anything about it, or else apprehend it and designate it after the analogy of what we know from direct experience about created life and mind. And as in creatures will is not identical with intellect, nor either of these with the nature of the being that possesses them; so what we conceive in God under the concept of will, we must not identify in thought with what we conceive in Him under the concept of intellect, nor may we with impunity confound either in our thought with the Nature or Essence of the Divine Being."[109]

(*c*) Philosophers who deny the validity of all the arguments advanced by theists in proof of the existence of a transcendent Supreme Being, distinct from the world of direct human experience, endeavour to account in various ways for the intrinsic possibility of abstract essences. Agnostics either deny to these latter any reality whatsoever, or else declare the problem of their reality insoluble. Monists of the materialist type—who try to reduce all mind to matter and its mere mechanical energies—treat the question in a still more inadequate and unsatisfactory manner; while the advocates of idealistic monism, like Hegel and his followers, refer us to the supposed Immanent Mind of the universe for an ultimate explanation of all intrinsic possibility. Certainly this must have its ultimate source in some mind; and it is not in referring us to an Eternal Mind that these philosophers err, but in their conception of the relation of this mind to the world of direct actual experience. It is not, however, with such theories we are concerned just now, but only with theories put forward by theists. And among these latter it is surprising to find some few[110] who maintain that the intrinsic possibility of abstract essences depends ultimately and exclusively on these essences themselves, irrespective of things actually experienced by the human mind, irrespective of the human mind itself, and irrespective of the Divine Mind and the Divine Nature.

As to this view, we have already seen that if we abstract from all human minds, and from all actual things that can be directly experienced by such minds, we are face to face either with the alternative of absolute nothingness wherein the true and the false, the possible and the impossible, cease to have any intelligible meaning, or else with the alternative of a Supreme, Eternal, Necessary, Omniscient and Omnipotent Being, whose actual existence has been, or can be, inferred from the actual data of human experience. Now the theist, who admits the existence of such a Being, cannot fail to see that possible essences must have their primary ideal being in the Divine Intellect, and the ultimate source of their intrinsic possibility in the Divine Essence Itself. For, knowing that God can actualize intrinsically possible essences by the creative act, which is intelligent and free, he will understand that these essences have their ideal being in the Divine Intellect; that the Divine Intellect sees their intrinsic possibility by contemplating the Divine Essence as the Uncreated Prototype and Exemplar of all intrinsically possible things; and that these latter are intrinsically possible precisely because they are possible adumbrations or imitations of the Divine Nature.

(*d*) But are we to conceive that essences are intrinsically possible precisely because the Divine Intellect, by understanding them, makes them intrinsically possible? Or should we rather conceive their intrinsic possibility as antecedent to this act by which the Divine Intellect understands them, and as dependent only on the Divine Essence Itself, so that essences would be intrinsically possible simply because the Divine Essence is what it is, and because they are possible imitations or expressions of it? Here scholastics are not agreed.

Some[111] hold that the intrinsic possibility of essences is *formally* constituted by the act whereby the Divine Intellect, contemplating the Divine Essence, understands the latter to be indefinitely imitable *ad extra*; so that as the actuality of things results from the *Fiat* of the Divine Will, and as their extrinsic possibility is grounded in the Divine Omnipotence, so their intrinsic possibility is grounded in the Divine Intellect. The latter, by understanding the Divine Essence, would not merely give an ideal being to the intrinsic possibility of essences, but would make those essences *formally* possible, they being only *virtually* possible in the Divine Essence considered antecedently to this act of the Divine Intellect. Or, rather, as some Scotists explain the matter,[112] this ideal being which possible essences have from the Divine Intellect is not as extrinsic to them as the ideal being they have from the human intellect, but is rather the very first being they can be said *formally* to have, and is somehow intrinsic to them after the analogy of the being which mere logical entities, *entia rationis*, derive from the human mind: which being is intrinsic to these entities and is in fact the only being they have or can have.

Others[113] hold that while, no doubt, possible essences have ideal being in the Divine Intellect from the fact that they are objects of the Divine Knowledge, yet we must not conceive these essences as deriving their intrinsic possibility from the Divine Intellect. For intellect as such presupposes its object. Just, therefore, as possible essences are not intrinsically possible because they are understood by, and have ideal being in, the human mind, so neither are they intrinsically possible because they are understood by, and have ideal being in, the Divine Mind. In order to be understood actually, in order to have ideal being, in order to be objects of thought, they must be intelligible; and in order to be intelligible they must be intrinsically possible. Therefore they are formally constituted as intrinsically possible essences, not by the fact that they are understood by the Divine Intellect, but by the fact that antecedently to this act (in our way of conceiving the matter: for there is *really* no priority of acts or attributes in God) they are already possible imitations of the Divine Essence Itself.

This view seems preferable as being more in accordance with the analogy of what takes place in the human mind. The speculative intellect in man does not constitute, but presupposes its object. Now, while *actual* things are the objects of God's *practical science*—the "*scientia visionis*," which reaches what is freely decreed by the Divine Will,—*possible* things are the objects of God's *speculative* science—the "*scientia simplicis intelligentiae*," which is not, like the former, productive of its object, but rather contemplative of objects presented to it by and in the Divine Essence.

Why, then, ultimately will the notions "square" and "circle" not coalesce so as to form one object of thought for the human mind, while the notions "equilateral" and "triangle" will so coalesce? Because the Essence of God, the Necessary Being, the First Reality, and the Source of all contingent reality, affords no basis for the former as a possible expression or imitation of Itself; in other words, because Being is not expressible by nothingness, and a "square circle" is nothingness: while the Divine Essence does afford a basis for the latter; because Necessary Being is in some intelligible way imitated, expressed, manifested, by whatever has any being to distinguish it from nothingness, and an "equilateral triangle" has such being and is not nothingness.

It is hardly necessary to add that when we conceive the Divine Essence, contemplated by the Divine Intellect, as containing in itself the exemplars or prototypes of all possible things, we are not to understand the Divine Essence as the *formal* exemplar of each, or, *a fortiori*, as a vast collection of such formally distinct exemplars; but only as *virtually* and *equivalently* the exemplar of each and all. We are not to conceive that possible essences are seen by the Divine Intellect imaged in the Divine Essence *as in a mirror*, but rather *as in their supreme source and principle*: so that they are faint and far off reflections of It, and, when actualized, become for us the only means we have, in this present state, for reaching any knowledge of the Deity: *videmus nunc per speculum*.[114]

21. DISTINCTION BETWEEN ESSENCE AND EXISTENCE IN ACTUALLY EXISTING CONTINGENT OR CREATED BEINGS.—Passing now from the consideration of possible essences as such, to the consideration of actually existing essences, we have to examine a question which has given rise to a great deal of controversy, partly on account of its inherent difficulty, and partly because of a multitude of ambiguities arising from confusion of thought: What is the nature of the distinction between essence and existence in the actually existing things of our experience?

We have seen already that the *concepts* of essence and existence are distinct from each other ; in other words, that in all cases there is at least a *logical* distinction between the essence and the existence of any being. We must, however, distinguish between created or contingent beings and the Uncreated, Necessary, Self-Existent Being. The latter exists *essentially*, eternally, by His own Essence, so that in Him essence and existence are *really identical*. His essence is *formally* His Existence; and, therefore, in thinking of His Essence we cannot positively exclude the notion of existence or think of Him as non-existent. The distinction between essence and existence, which we find in our thoughts, is, therefore, when applied to God, a *purely logical* distinction, due solely to our finite human mode of thinking, and having no ground or basis or reason in the reality which is the object of our thought. On this there is complete unanimity among scholastic philosophers.

But while we conceive that God actually exists by that whereby He is God, by His Essence Itself, we do not conceive that any created or contingent being exists by that whereby it is what it is, by its essence. We do not, for example, regard the essence of Socrates, whether specific or individual (that whereby he is a *man*, or that whereby he is *this* man, Socrates), as that whereby he actually exists. In other words, the essence of the existing Socrates, being a contingent essence, does not necessarily demand or imply that it actually exist. Our concept of such an essence does not include the note of actual existence. Therefore if we find such an essence actually existing we consider this actually existing essence as caused or produced, and conserved in existence, by some other being, *viz.* by the Necessary Being: so that if it were not so created and conserved it would be a pure possibility and nothing actual.[115] The same difference between the Necessary Being and contingent beings will be seen from considering their existence. The abstract concept of existence is rendered definite and determinate by the essence which it actualizes. Now every finite essence is of some particular kind; and its existence is rendered determinate by the fact that it is the existence of a definite kind of essence. The existence of a contingent being we conceive as the actuality of its essence; and its essence as a definite potentiality of existence. Thus if we conceive existence as a perfection it is restricted by the finite nature of the potentiality which it actualizes. But the existence of the Necessary Being is the plenitude of actuality, an existence not restricted by being the existence of any essence that is determinate because finite, but of an essence that is determinate by being above all genera and species, by being infinite, by being Itself pure actuality, in no sense potential but perfectly and formally identical with actual existence. While, therefore, the essence of the Necessary Being is a necessarily existing essence, that of a contingent being is not necessarily existent, but is conceived as a potentiality which has been *de facto* actualized or made existent by the Necessary Being, and which may again cease to be actually existent.[116] On this too there is unanimity among scholastic philosophers.

We distinguish mentally or logically between the essence of an actually existing contingent being and its existence; considering the former as the potential principle, in relation to the latter as the actualizing principle, of the contingent existing reality. But is the distinction between such an essence and its existence something more than a logical distinction? Is it a real distinction? This is the question in dispute. And in order to avoid misunderstanding, we must be clear on these two points: firstly, of what essence and existence is there question? and secondly, what exactly are we to understand by a real distinction in this matter?

22. STATE OF THE QUESTION.—In the first place, there is no question here of the relation of a *possible* essence as such to existence. The possible essence of a contingent being, as such, has no reality outside the Divine Essence, Intellect, Will, and Omnipotence. Before the world was created the possible essences of all the beings that constitute it were certainly really distinct from the actual existence of these beings which do constitute the created universe. On this point there can be no difference of opinion. To contend that it is on the eternal reality of the possible essence that actual existence supervenes, when a contingent being begins to exist, would be equivalent to contending that it is the Divine Essence that becomes actual in the phenomena of our experience: which is the error of Pantheism.

Again, before a contingent thing comes into actual existence it may be virtually and potentially in the active powers and passive potentialities of other actually existing contingent things: as the oak, for instance, is in the passive potentiality of the acorn and in the active powers of the natural agencies whereby it is evolved from the acorn; or the statue in the block of marble and in the mind and artistic power of the sculptor. But neither is there any question here of the relation of such potential being or essence as a thing has in its causes to the actual existence of this thing when actually produced. Whatever being or essence it has in its active and passive causes is certainly really distinct from the existence which the thing has when it has been actually produced. Nor is there any doubt or dispute about this point. At the same time much controversy is due to misunderstandings arising from a confusion of thought which fails to distinguish between the essence as purely possible, the essence as virtually or potentially in its causes, and the essence as actually existing. It is about the distinction between the latter and its existence that the whole question is raised. And it must be borne in mind that this essence, whether it is really distinct from its existence or not, is itself a positive reality from the moment it is created or produced. The question is whether the creative or productive act—whereby this essence is placed "outside its causes," and is now no longer merely possible, or merely virtual or potential in its causes, but something real *in itself*—has for its term *one reality*, or *two realities*, *viz*. the essence as real subjective potentiality of existence, and the existential act or perfection whereby it is constituted actually existent.[117]

The question is exclusively concerned with the essence which began to exist when the contingent being came into actual existence, and which ceases to exist when, or if, this being again passes out of actual existence; and the question is whether this essence which actually exists is really distinct from the existence whereby it actually exists. Finally, the question concerns the essence and existence of any and every actual contingent reality, whether such reality be a substance or an accident. Of course it is primarily concerned with the essence and existence of substances;

but it also applies to the essence and existence of accidents in so far as these latter will be found to be really distinct from the substances in which they inhere, and to have reality proper to themselves.

23. THE THEORY OF DISTINCTIONS IN ITS APPLICATION TO THE QUESTION.—In the next place, what are we to understand by a *real* distinction in this matter? Ambiguity and obscurity of thought in regard to the theory of *distinctions*, and in regard to the application of the theory to the present question, has been probably the most fertile source of much tedious and fruitless controversy in this connexion.

Anticipating what will be considered more fully at a later stage, we must note here the two main classes of distinction which, by reflecting on our thought-processes, we discover between the objects of our thought. The *real* distinction is that which exists in things independently of the consideration of our minds; that which is discovered, but not made, by the mind; that which is given to us in and with the data of our experience. For example, the act of thinking is a reality other than, and therefore *really* distinct from, the mind that thinks; for the mind persists after the act of thinking has passed away.

Opposed to this is the mental or logical distinction, which is the distinction made by the mind itself between two different concepts of one and the same reality; which is not in the reality independently of our thought, but is introduced into it by our thought, regarding the same reality under different aspects or from different points of view. The mind never makes such a distinction without some ground or reason for doing so.

Sometimes, however, this reason will be found exclusively in the mind itself—in the limitations of its modes of thought—and not in the reality which is the matter or object of the thought. The distinction is then said to be *purely* logical or mental. Such distinctions are *entia rationis*, logical entities. An example would be the distinction between the concept "man" and the concept "rational animal," or, in general, between any definable object of thought and its definition; the distinction, therefore, between the essence and the existence of the Necessary Being is a purely logical distinction, for in a definition it is the essence of the thing we define, and existence is of the essence or definition of the Necessary Being.

Sometimes, again, the reason for making a mental distinction will be found in the reality itself. What is one and the same reality presents different aspects to the mind and evokes different concepts of itself in the mind: though really one, it is virtually manifold; and the distinction between the concepts of these various aspects is commonly known as a *virtual* distinction. For example, when we think of any individual man as a "rational animal," though our concept of "animal nature" is distinct from that of "rational nature," we do not regard these in him as two realities co-existing or combining to form his human nature, but only as two distinct aspects under which we view the one reality which is his human nature. And we view it under these two aspects because we have actual experience of instances in which animal nature is really distinct and separated from rationality, *e.g.*, in the brute beast. Or, again, since we can recognize three grades of life in man—vegetative, sentient, and rational—we conceive the one principle of life, his soul, as virtually three principles; and so we distinguish mentally or virtually between three souls in man, although in reality there is only one. Or, once more, when we think of the Wisdom, the Will, and the Omnipotence of God, we know that although these concepts represent different aspects of the Deity, these aspects are not distinct realities in Him; but that because of His infinite perfection and infinite simplicity they are all objectively one and the same self-identical reality.

A virtual distinction is said to be *imperfect* (thus approaching nearer to the nature of a purely logical distinction) when each of the concepts whereby we apprehend the same reality only prescinds *explicitly* from what is expressed by the other, although one of them is found on analysis to include *implicitly* what is expressed by the other. Such is the distinction between the *being* and the *life* of any living thing; or the distinction between the spirituality and the immortality of the human soul; or the distinction between *Infinite* Wisdom and *Infinite* Power: the distinction between the divine attributes in general. A virtual distinction is said to be *perfect* (thus approaching nearer to the nature of a real distinction) when neither of the concepts includes either explicitly or implicitly what is expressed by the other. Such, for instance, is the distinction between the principle of intellectual life and the principle of animal or sentient life in man; for not only can these exist separately (the former without the latter, *e.g.* in pure spirits, the latter without the former, *e.g.* in brute beasts), but also it will be found that by no analysis does either concept in any way involve the other.[118]

Our only object in setting down the various examples just given is to illustrate the general scholastic teaching on the doctrine of distinction. In themselves they are not beyond dispute, for the general doctrine of distinction is not easy of application in detail; but they will be sufficient for our present purpose. Probably the greatest difficulty in applying the general doctrine will be found to lie in discriminating between virtual distinctions—especially perfect virtual distinctions—and real distinctions.[119] And this difficulty will be appreciated still more when we learn that a real distinction does not necessarily involve *separability* of the objects so distinguished. In other words there may be, in a composite existing individual being, constitutive factors or principles, or integral parts, each of which is a positive real entity, really distinct from the others, and yet incapable of existing separately or in isolation from the others. "Separability," says Mercier,[120] "is one of the signs of a real distinction; but it is neither essential to, nor a necessary property of the latter. Two separable things are of course really distinct from each other; but two entities may be really distinct from each other without being separable or capable of existing apart from each other. Thus we believe that the intellect and the will in man are really distinct from each other, and both alike from the substance of the human soul; yet they cannot exist isolated from the soul." Therefore, even though the objects which we apprehend as distinct, by means of distinct concepts, be understood to be such that they cannot actually exist in isolation from each other, but only as united in a composite individual being, still if it can be shown that each of them has its own proper reality independently of our thought, so that the distinction between them is not the result of our thought, or introduced by our thought into the individual thing or being which we are considering, then the distinction must be regarded as real. If, on the other hand, it can be shown that the different aspects which we apprehend in any *datum* by means of distinct concepts have not, apart from the consideration of the mind, apart from the analytic activity of our own thought, each its own proper reality, but are only distinct mental views of what is objectively one and the same reality, then the distinction must be regarded as logical, not real,—and this even although there may be in the richness and fulness of that one reality comparatively to the limited capacity of our minds, as well as in the very constitution and modes of thought of our minds themselves, a reason or basis for, and an explanation of, the *multiplicity of concepts* whereby we attain to an understanding of some *one reality*.

24. SOLUTIONS OF THE QUESTION.—Postponing further consideration of the serious problems on the validity of knowledge and its relation to reality, to which those reflections inevitably give rise, let us now return to the main question: the nature of the distinction between the essence and the existence of any actually existing contingent being. We need not be surprised to find that the greatest minds have been unable to reach the same solution of this question. For it is but a phase of the more general metaphysical problem—at once both ontological and epistemological—of the nature of reality and the relation of the human mind thereto. Nor will any serious modern philosopher who is at all mindful of the wealth of current controversial literature on this very problem, or of the endless variety of conflicting opinions among contemporary thinkers in regard to it, be disposed to ridicule the medieval controversies on the doctrine of distinction as applied to essence and existence. No doubt there has been a good deal of mere verbal, and perhaps trifling, argumentation on the matter: it lends itself to the dialectical skill of the controversialist who "takes sides," as well as to the serious thought of the open-minded investigator. It is not, however, through drawing

different conclusions from the same premises that conflicting solutions of the question have been reached, but rather through fundamentally different attitudes in regard to the premises themselves which different philosophers profess to find in the common data of their experience. When we have once grasped what philosophers mean by a logical or a real distinction as applied to the relation between essence and existence we shall not get any very material assistance towards the choice of a solution by considering at length the arguments adduced on either side.[121]

Those who believe there is a real distinction[122] between the essence and the existence of all actually existing contingent beings mean by this that the real essence which comes into actual existence by creation, or by the action of created causes, is a reality distinct from the existence whereby it actually exists. The actually existing essence is the total term of the creative or productive act; but what we apprehend in it under the concept of *essence* is really distinct from what we apprehend in it under the concept of *existence*: the existence being a real principle which *actualizes* the essence, and this latter being itself another real principle which is in itself a positive, subjective *potentiality* of existence.[123] Neither, of course, can actually exist without the other: no actual existence except that of a real essence; no existing essence except by reason of the existence which makes it actual. But these two real principles of existing contingent being, inseparable as they are and correlative, are nevertheless distinct realities—distinct in the objective order and independently of our thought,—and form by their union a really *composite* product: the existing thing.

We might attempt to illustrate this by the analogy of a body and its shape or colour. The body itself is really distinct from its actual shape and colour: it may lose them, and yet remain the same body; and it may acquire other shapes and colours. At any time the body has actually some particular shape and colour; but that by which it is formally so shaped and coloured is something really different from the body itself. Furthermore, before the body *actually* possessed this particular shape and colour, these were in it *potentially*: that is to say, there were then in the body the real, passive, subjective potentialities of this particular shape and colour. So too *that by which* a real (contingent) essence actually exists (*i.e.* the existential *act*, existence) is really distinct from *that which* actually exists (*i.e.* the essence, the *potentiality* of that existential act). The analogy is, however, at best only a halting one. For while it is comparatively easy to understand how the passive, subjective *potentiality* of a shape or colour can be *something real* in the *already actually existing* body, it is not so easy to understand how the *potentiality of existence*, *i.e.* the real essence, can be anything that is itself real and really distinct from the existence.[124] The oak is *really* in the acorn, for the passive, subjective potentiality of the oak is in the actual acorn; but is this potentiality anything really distinct from the acorn? or should we not rather say that the *actual* acorn *is potentially* the oak, or *is* the potentiality of the oak? At all events even if it is really distinct from the actual acorn, it is in the actual acorn. But is it possible to conceive a *real, subjective potentiality* which *does not reside in anything actual*.[125] Now if the real essence is really distinct from its existence it must be conceived as a *real, subjective potentiality* of existence. Yet it cannot be conceived as a potentiality *in* anything actual: except indeed in the actually existing essence which is the composite result of its union with the existential act. It is not a real, subjective potentiality antecedently to the existential act, and on which the latter is, as it were, superimposed:[126] in itself, it is, in fact, nothing real except as actualized by the latter; but, as we have already observed, the process of actualization, whether by direct creation or by the action of created causes, must be conceived as having for its total term or effect a composite reality resulting from what we can at best imperfectly describe as the union of two correlative, con-created, or co-produced principles of being, a potential and an actual, really distinct from each other: that whereby the thing *can* exist, the potentiality of existence, the essence; and that whereby the thing *does* exist, the actuality of essence, the existence. The description is imperfect because these principles are not con-created or co-produced separately; but, rather, the creation or production of an existing essence, the efficiency by which it is "placed outside its causes," has one single, though composite, term: the actually existing thing.

This view, thus advocating a real distinction between essence and existence, may obviously be regarded as an emphatic expression of the objective validity of intellectual knowledge. It might be regarded as an application of the more general view that the objective concepts between which the intellect distinguishes in its interpretation of reality should be regarded as representing *distinct realities*, except when the distinction is seen to arise not from the nature of the object but from the nature of the subject, from the limitations and imperfections of our own modes of thought. But in the case of any particular (disputed) distinction, the *onus probandi* should lie rather on the side of those who contend that such distinction is logical, and not real. On the other hand, many philosophers who are no less firmly convinced of the objective validity of intellectual knowledge observe that it is possible to push this principle too far, or rather to err by excess in its application. Instead of placing the burden of proof solely on the side of the logical distinction, they would place it rather more on the side of the real distinction—in conformity with the maxim of method, *Entia non sunt multiplicanda praeter necessitatem*. And they think that it is an error by excess to hold the distinction between essence and existence to be real. This brings us to the second alternative opinion: that the distinction in question is not real, but only virtual.[127]

According to this view, the essence and the existence of any existing contingent being are one and the same reality. There is, however, in this reality a basis for the two distinct objective concepts—of essence and of existence—whereby we apprehend it. For the contingent being does not exist necessarily: we see such beings coming into existence and ceasing to exist: we can therefore think of *what they are* without thinking of them as *actually existent*: in other words, we can think of them as possible, and of their existence as that by which they become actual. This is a sufficient reason for distinguishing mentally, in the existing being, the essence which exists and the existence by which it exists.[128] But when we think of the essence of an actually existing being as objectively possible, or as potential in its causes, we are no longer thinking of it as anything real in itself, but only of its ideal being as an object of thought in our minds, or of the ideal being it has in the Divine Mind, or of the potential being it has in created causes, or of the virtual being it has in the Divine Omnipotence, or of the ultimate basis of its possibility in the Divine Essence. But all these modes of "being" we know to be really distinct from the real, contingent essence itself which begins to exist actually in time, and may cease once more to exist in time when and if its own nature demands, and God wills, such cessation. But that the real, contingent essence itself which so exists, is something really distinct from the existence whereby it exists; that it forms with the latter a really composite being; that it is in itself a real, subjective potentiality, receptive of existence as another and actualizing reality, really distinct from it, so that the creation or production of any single actually existing contingent being would have for its term two really distinct principles of being, a potential and an actual, essence and existence, created or produced *per modum unius*, so to speak: for asserting all this it is contended by supporters of the virtual distinction that we have no sufficient justifying reason.[129] Hence they conclude that a real distinction must be denied: *Entia non sunt multiplicanda praeter necessitatem*.

Though each of these opinions has been defended with a great deal of ability, and an exhaustive array of arguments, a mere rehearsal of these latter would not give much material assistance towards a solution of the question. We therefore abstain from repeating them here. There are only a few points in connexion with them to which attention may be directed.

In the first place, some defenders of the real distinction urge that were the distinction not real, things would exist essentially, *i.e.* necessarily; and thus the most fundamental ground of distinction between God and creatures, between the Necessary Being and contingent beings, would be destroyed: creatures would be no longer in their very constitution composite, mixtures of potentiality and actuality, but would be purely actual, absolutely simple and, in a word, identical with the Infinite Being Himself. Supporters of the virtual distinction deny that those very serious consequences follow from their view. They point out that though the existence of the creature is really identical with its essence, the essence does not exist necessarily or *a se*; the whole existing essence is *ab alio*, is caused, contingent; and the fundamental distinction between such a being and the Self-Existing Being is in this view perfectly clear. Nor is the creature, they contend, purely actual and absolutely simple; it need not have existed, and it may cease to exist; it has, therefore, a potentiality of non-existence, which is inconceivable in the case of the Necessary and purely Actual Being; it is, therefore, mutable as regards existence; besides which the essences even of the most simple created beings, namely pure spirits are composite in the sense that they have faculties and operations really distinct from their substance.

Secondly, it is alleged by some defenders of the real distinction that this latter view of the nature of existing contingent reality is a cardinal doctrine in the whole philosophical system of St. Thomas, and of scholastics generally: so fundamental, in fact, that many important doctrines, unanimously held to be true by all scholastics, cannot be successfully vindicated apart from it.[130] To which it is replied that there are no important truths of scholastic philosophy which cannot be defended quite adequately apart altogether from the view one may hold on the present question; and that, this being the case, it is unwise to endeavour to base admittedly true doctrines, which can be better defended otherwise, upon an opinion which can at best claim only the amount of probability it can derive from the intrinsic merits of the arguments by which it is itself supported.[131]

Before passing from this whole question we must note the existence of a third school of thought, identified mainly with the followers of Duns Scotus.[132] These authors contend that the distinction between essence and existence is not a real distinction, nor yet, on the other hand, is it merely a virtual distinction, but one which they call *formalis, actualis ex natura rei*, that between a reality and its intrinsic modes. It is better known as the "Scotistic" distinction. We shall see the nature of it when dealing *ex professo* with the general doctrine of distinctions.

The multiplicity of these views, and the unavoidable difficulty experienced in grasping and setting forth their meaning with any tolerable degree of clearness, would suggest the reflection that in those controversies the medieval scholastics were perhaps endeavouring to think and to express what reality is, apart from thought and "independently of the consideration of the mind"—a task which, conceived in these terms, must appear fruitless; and one which, anyhow, involves in its very nature the closest scrutiny of the epistemological problem of the power of the human mind to get at least a true and valid, if not adequate and comprehensive, insight into the nature of reality.

Chapter IV.

Reality As One And Manifold.

25. THE TRANSCENDENTAL ATTRIBUTES OR PROPERTIES OF BEING: UNITY, TRUTH, AND GOODNESS.—So far, we have analysed the notions of Real Being, of Becoming or Change, of Being as Possible and as Actual, of Essence and Existence. Before approaching a study of the Categories or *Suprema Genera Entis*, the highest and widest modes in which reality manifests itself, we have next to consider certain attributes or properties of being which reveal themselves as co-extensive with reality itself. Taking human experience in its widest sense, as embracing all modes that are cognitive or allied with consciousness, as including intellect, memory, imagination, sense perception, will and appetite, as speculative, ethical or moral, and esthetic or artistic,—we find that the reality which makes up this complex human experience of ours is universally and necessarily characterized by certain features which we call the *transcendental attributes or properties of being*, inasmuch as they transcend all specific and generic modes of being, pervade all its categories equally, and are inseparable from any datum of experience. We shall see that they are not really distinct from the reality which they characterize, but only logically distinct from it, being aspects under which we apprehend it, negations or other logical relations which we necessarily annex to it by the mental processes whereby we seek to render it actually intelligible to our minds.

The first in order of these ontological attributes is *unity*: the concept of that whereby reality considered in itself becomes a definite object of thought. The second in order is *truth*: which is the conception of reality considered in its relation to cognitive experience, to intellect. The third is *goodness*: the aspect under which reality is related as an object to appetitive experience, to will.

Now when we predicate of any reality under our consideration that it is "one," or "good," or "true"—in the ontological sense to be explained,—that which we predicate is not a mere *ens rationis*, but something real, something which is really identical with the subject, and which is distinguished from the latter in our judgment only by a logical distinction. The attribution of any of these properties to the subject does not, however, add anything real to the latter: it adds merely some logical aspect involved in, or supposed by, the attribution. At the same time, this logical aspect gives us real information by making explicit some real feature of being not explicitly revealed in the concept of being itself, although involved in, and following as a property from, the latter.

There do not seem to be any other transcendental properties of being besides the three enumerated. The terms "reality," "thing," "something," are synonymous expressions of the concept of being itself, rather than of properties of being. "Existence" is not a transcendental attribute of being, for it is not co-extensive with reality or real being. And although reality *must* be "*either* possible *or* actual," "*either* necessary *or* contingent," "*either* infinite *or* finite," etc., this necessity of verifying in itself one or other member of any such alternatives is not a property of being, but rather something essentially rooted in the very concept of reality itself. Some would regard as a distinct transcendental attribute of being the conception of the latter as an object of esthetic contemplation, as manifesting order and harmony, as *beautiful*. This conception of being will be found, however, to flow from the more fundamental aspects of reality considered as *true* and as *good*, rather than directly from the concept of being itself.

26. TRANSCENDENTAL UNITY.—When we think of anything as one we think of it as undivided in itself. The unity or oneness of being is the undividedness of being: *Unum est id quod est indivisum in se: Universaliter quaecunque non habent divisionem, inquantum non habent, sic unum dicuntur.*[133] When, therefore, we conceive being as undivided into constitutive parts, and unmultiplied into repetitions of itself, we conceive it as *a* being, as *one*. For the concept of being, formally as one, it does not seem necessary that we conceive being as *divided or distinct from all other being*. This second negation, of identity with other being, rather follows the conception of being as one: being is distinct from other being because it is already itself one: it is a prior negation that formally constitutes its unity, namely, *the negation of internal division or multiplication of itself*. God was truly *one* from all eternity, before there was any *other* being, any created being, distinct from Him. The division or distinction of an object of thought from whatever is not itself is what constitutes the notion of *otherness*.[134]

It is manifest that being and unity are really identical, that when we think of being we think of what is really undivided in itself, that once we introduce dividedness into the object of our concept we are no longer thinking of being but of *beings*, *i.e.* of a multitude or plurality each member of which is a *being* and *one*. For being, as an object of thought, is either simple or composite. If simple, it is not only undivided but indivisible. If composite, we cannot think of it as *a* being, capable of existing, so long as we think its parts as separate or divided: only when we think of them as actually united and undivided have we the concept of *a* being: and *eo ipso* we have the concept of being as one, as a unity.[135]

Hence the scholastic formulæ: *Ens et unum convertuntur*, and *Omne ens est unum*. The truth embodied in these is so self-evident that the expression of it may seem superfluous; but they are not mere tautologies, and in the interests of clear and consistent thinking our attention may be profitably directed to them. The same remark applies to much in the present and subsequent chapters on the transcendental attributes of being.

27. KINDS OF UNITY.—(*a*) The unity we have been describing has been called *transcendental*, to distinguish it from *predicamental* unity—the unity which is proper to a special category of being, namely, *quantity*, and which, accordingly, is also called *quantitative* or *mathematical* unity. While the former is common to all being, with which it is really identical, and to which it adds nothing real, the latter belongs and is applicable, properly speaking, only to the mode of being which is corporeal, which exists only as affected by quantity, as occupying space, as capable of measurement; and therefore, also, this latter unity adds something real to the being which it affects, namely, the attribute of quantity, of which unity is the measure and the generating principle.[136] For quantity, as we shall see, is a mode of being really distinct from the corporeal substance which it affects. The quantity has its own transcendental unity; so has the substance which it quantifies; so has the composite whole, the quantified body, but this latter transcendental unity, like the composite being with which it is identical, is not a *unum per se* but only a *unum per accidens* (*cf. b, infra*).

We derive our notion of quantitative or mathematical unity, which is the principle of counting and the standard of measuring, from dividing mentally the continuous quantity or magnitude which is one of the immediate data of sense experience. Now the distinction between this unit and transcendental unity supposes not merely that quantity is really distinct from the corporeal substance, but also that the human mind is capable of conceiving as real certain modes of being other than the corporeal, modes to which quantitative concepts and processes, such as counting and measuring, are not *properly* applicable, as they are to corporeal reality, but only in an *analogical* or *transferred* sense . The notion of transcendental unity, therefore, bears the same relation to that of quantitative unity, as the notion of being in general bears to that of quantified or corporeal being.

(*b*) Transcendental unity may be either *essential* (or *substantial*, "unum *per se*," "unum *simpliciter*"), or *accidental* ("unum *per accidens*," "unum *secundum quid*"). The former characterizes a being which has nothing in it beyond what is essential to it as such, *e.g.* the unity of any substance: and this unity is twofold—(1) *unity of simplicity* and (2) *unity of composition*—according as the substance is essentially simple (such as the human soul or a pure spirit) or essentially composite (such as man, or any corporeal substance: since every such substance is composed essentially of a formative and an indeterminate principle).[137]

Accidental unity is the unity of a being whose constituent factors or contents are not really united in such a way as to form one essence, whether simple or composite. It is threefold: (1) *collective* unity, or unity *of aggregation*, as of a *heap* of stones or a *crowd* of men; (2) *artificial* unity, as of a house or a picture; and (3) *natural* or *physical* unity, as of any existing substance with its connatural accidents, *e.g.* a living organism with its size, shape, qualities, etc., or the human soul with its faculties.[138]

(*c*) Transcendental unity may be either individual (singular, numerical, concrete, real) or universal (specific, generic, abstract, logical). The former is that which characterizes being or reality considered as actually existing or as proximately capable of existing: the unity of an *individual* nature or essence: the unity whereby a being is not merely undivided in itself but incapable of repetition or multiplication of itself. It is only the individual as such that can actually exist: the abstract and universal is incapable of actually existing as such. We shall examine presently what it is that *individuates* reality, and what it is that renders it capable of existing actually in the form of "things" or of "persons"—the forms in which it actually presents itself in our experience.

Abstract or universal unity is the unity which characterizes a reality conceived as an abstract, universal object by the human intellect. The object of a specific or generic concept, "man" or "animal," for example, is one in this sense, undivided in itself, but capable of indefinite multiplication or repetition in the only mode in which it can actually exist—the individual mode. The universal is *unum aptum inesse pluribus*.

Finally, we can conceive any nature or essence without considering it in either of its alternative states—either as individual or as universal. Thus conceived it is characterized by a unity which has been commonly designated as *abstract*, or (by Scotists) as *formal* unity.

28. MULTITUDE AND NUMBER.—The *one* has for its correlative the *manifold*. Units, one of which is not the other, constitute multitude or plurality. If unity is the negation of actual division in being, multitude results from a second negation, that, namely, by which the undivided being or unit is marked off or divided from other units.[139] We have defined unity by the negation of actual *intrinsic* dividedness; and we have seen it to be compatible with *extrinsic* dividedness, or otherness. Thus the vague notion of dividedness is anterior to that of unity. Now multitude involves dividedness; but it also involves and presupposes the intrinsic undividedness or *unity* of each constituent of the manifold. In the real order of things the *one* is prior to all *dividedness*; but on account of the sensuous origin of our concepts we can define the former only by exclusion of the latter. The order in which we obtain these ideas seems, therefore, to be as follows: "first *being*, then *dividedness*, next *unity* which excludes dividedness, and finally *multitude* which consists of units".[140]

The relation of the *one* to the *manifold* is that of undivided being to divided being. The same reality cannot be one and manifold under the same aspect; though obviously a being may be actually one and potentially manifold or *vice versa*, or one under a certain aspect and manifold under another aspect.

From the transcendental plurality or multitude which we have just described we can distinguish *predicamental* or *quantitative* plurality: a distinction which is to be understood in the same way as when applied to unity. Quantitative multitude is the actually separated or divided condition of quantified being. *Number* is a multitude measured or counted by unity: it is a *counted*, and, therefore, necessarily a *definite* and *finite* multitude. Now it is *mathematical* unity that is, properly, the principle of number and the standard or measure of all counting; and therefore it is only to realities which fall within the category of quantity—in other words, to material being—that the concept of number is properly applicable. No doubt we can and do conceive transcendental unity after the analogy of the quantitative unity which is the principle of counting and measuring; and no doubt we can use the transcendental concept of "actually undivided being" as a principle of enumeration, and so "count" or "enumerate" spiritual beings; but this counting is only analogical; and many philosophers, following Aristotle and St. Thomas, hold that the concepts of *numerical* multiplicity and *numerical* distinction are not properly applicable to immaterial beings, that these latter differ individually from one another *not numerically*, but each by its whole nature or essence, that is, *formally*.[141]

29. THE INDIVIDUAL AND THE UNIVERSAL.—We have distinguished transcendental unity into individual and universal. Reality as endowed with universal unity is reality as apprehended by abstract thought to be capable of indefinite repetition or multiplication of itself in actual existence. Reality as endowed with individual unity is reality apprehended as actually existing, or as proximately capable of actually existing, and as therefore incapable of any repetition or multiplication of itself, of any division of itself into other "selves" or communication of itself to other "selves". While, therefore, the universal has its reality only in the individuals to which it communicates itself, and which thus embody it, the individual has its reality in itself and of its own right, so to speak: when it actually exists it is *"sui juris,"* and as such incommunicable, *"incommunicabilis"*. The actually existing individual is called in Latin a *"suppositum"*—a term which we shall render by the English "thing" or "individual thing". It was called by Aristotle the οὐσία πρωτή, *substantia prima*, "first substance," or "first essence," to distinguish it from the substance or essence conceived by abstract thought as universal; the latter being designated as οὐσία δέυτερα, *substantia secunda*, "second substance" or "second essence".

Now it is a fundamental assumption in Aristotelian and scholastic philosophy that whatever actually exists, or whatever is real in the sense that as such it is proximately capable of actual existence, is and must be individual: that the universal as such is not real, *i.e.* as such cannot actually exist. And the manifest reason for this assumption is that whatever actually exists must be, with entire definiteness and determinateness, its own self and nothing else: it cannot be capable of division or repetition of itself, of that which it really is, into "other" realities which would still be "that individual thing". But reality considered as universal *is* capable of such repetition of itself indefinitely. Therefore reality cannot actually exist as universal, but only as individual.

This is merely plain common sense; nor does the idealistic monism which appears to attribute reality to the universal as such, and which interprets reality exclusively according to the forms in which it presents itself to abstract thought, really run counter to this consideration; for what it really holds is not that universals as such are real, but that they are phases of the all-one reality which is itself *one individual being*.

But many modern philosophers hold that individuality, no less than universality, is a form of thought. No doubt "individuality" *in the abstract* is, no less than universality, an object abstracted from the data of experience by the mind's analysis of the latter. But this is not what those philosophers mean. They mean that the individual as such is not a real datum of experience. From the Kantian view that individuality is a purely mental form with which the mind invests the datum, they draw the subjectivist conclusion that the world, thus interpreted as consisting of "individuals," is a phenomenal or mental product for the objective validity of which there can be to man's speculative reason no sufficient guarantee.

To this theory we oppose that of Aristotle and the scholastics, not merely that the individual alone is actually existent, but that as actually existent and as individual it is actually given to us and apprehended by us in internal and external sense experience; and that although in the inorganic world, and to some extent in the lower forms of life, we may not be able to determine for certain what portions of this experience are distinct individuals, still in the world of living things generally, and especially of the animal kingdom, there can be no difficulty in determining this, for the simple reason that here reality is given to us in sense experience as consisting of distinct individuals.

At the same time it is true that we can understand these individual realities, interpret them, read the meaning of them, only by the intellectual function of judgment, *i.e.* by the analytic and synthetic activity whereby we abstract and universalize certain aspects of them, and use these aspects as predicates of the individuals. Now, seeing that intellectual thought, as distinct from sense experience, apprehends its objects only as abstract and potentially universal, only as static, self-identical, possible essences, and nevertheless predicates these of the concrete, individual, contingent, actually existing "things" of sense experience, identifying them with the latter in affirmative judgments; seeing moreover, that—since the intellectual knowledge we thus acquire about the data of sense experience is genuine and not chimerical—those "objects" of abstract thought must be likewise real, and must be really in those individual sense data (according to the theory of knowledge which finds its expression in Moderate Realism),—there arises immediately the problem, or rather the group of problems, regarding the relations between reality as revealed to intellect, *i.e.* as abstract and universal, and reality as revealed to sense, *i.e.* as concrete and individual. In other words, we have to inquire how we are to interpret intellectually the fact that reality, which as a possible essence is *universal* for abstract thought, is nevertheless, as actually existing, *individualized* for sense—and consequently for intellect reflecting on the data of sense.[142]

30. THE "METAPHYSICAL GRADES OF BEING" IN THE INDIVIDUAL.—What, then is the relation between all that intellect can apprehend in the individual, *viz.* its lowest class essence or specific nature, and its whole nature as an individual, its *essentia atoma* or individual nature? We can best approach this problem by considering first these various abstract thought-objects which intellect can apprehend in the individual.

What are called the metaphysical grades of being, those positive moments of perfection or reality which the mind detects in the individual, as, for instance, substantiality, materiality, organic life, animality, rationality, individuality, in the individual man—whether we describe them as "phases" or "aspects" or "formalities" of being—are undoubtedly distinct objects for abstract thought. Why does it thus distinguish between them, and express them by distinct concepts, even when it finds them embodied in a single individual? Because, reflecting on the manner in which reality presents itself, through sense experience, as actually existing, it finds resemblances and differences between individually distinct data. It finds in some of them grades of reality which it does not find in others, individual, specific, and generic grades; and some—transcendental—grades common to all. Now between these various grades of being as found in one and the same individual it cannot be denied that there exists a logical distinction with a foundation or ground for it in the individual reality; because the latter, *being more or less similar* to other individual realities, causes the mind to apprehend it by a number of distinct concepts: the individuality whereby it differs really from all other individuals of the same species; the specific, differential and generic grades of being whereby it is conceptually identified with wider and wider classes of things; and the transcendental grades whereby it is conceptually identified with all others. The *similarity* of really distinct individuals, which is the *conceptual identity* of their *qualities*, is the ground on which we conceptually identify their *essences*. Now is there any reason for thinking that these grounds of similarity, as found in the individual, are *really distinct* from one another in the latter? They are certainly conceptually distinct expressions—each less inadequate than the wider ones—of what is really one individual essence. But we must take them to be all really identical in and with this individual essence, unless we are prepared to hold conceptual plurality as such to be real plurality; in which case we should also hold conceptual unity as such to be real unity. But this latter view is precisely the error of extreme realism, of reifying abstract concepts and holding the "*universale a parte rei*": a theory which leads logically to monism.[143]

31. INDIVIDUALITY.—The distinction, therefore, between these grades of being in the individual, is a virtual distinction, *i.e.* a logical distinction with a ground for it in the reality. This is the sort of distinction which exists between the specific nature of the individual, *i.e.* what is contained in the definition of the lowest class to which it belongs, and its *individuality*, *i.e.* what constitutes its *nature or essence as an individual*. No doubt the concrete existing individual contains, besides its individual nature or essence, a variety of accidental characteristics which serve as marks or signs whereby its individuality *is revealed to us*. These are called "individualizing characteristics," "*notae individuantes*," the familiar scholastic list of them being "*forma, figura, locus, tempus, stirps, patria, nomen*," with manifest reference to the individual "man". But though these characteristics enable us to mark off the individual in space and time from other individuals of the same class, thus *revealing* individuality to us in the concrete, it cannot be held that they

constitute the individuality of the nature or substance in each case. If the human substance, essence, or nature, as found in Socrates, were held to differ from the human substance, essence, or nature, as found in Plato, only by the fact that in each it is affected by a different set of accidents, *i.e.* of modes accidental to the substance as found in each, then it would follow that this substance is not merely *conceptually* identical in both, but that it is *really* identical in both; which is the error of extreme realism. As a matter of fact it is the converse that is true: the sets of accidents are distinct because they affect individual substances already really and individually distinct.

It is manifest that the accidents which are *separable* from the individual substance, *e.g.* name, shape, size, appearance, location, etc., cannot constitute its individuality. There are, however, other characteristics which are *inseparable* from the individual substance, or which are *properties* of the latter, *e.g.* the fact that an individual man was born of certain parents. Perhaps it is such characteristics that give its individuality to the individual substance?[144] To think so would be to misunderstand the question under discussion. We are not now inquiring into the *extrinsic* causes whereby actually existing reality is individuated, into the *efficient* principles of its individuation, but into the *formal* and *intrinsic* principle of the latter. There must obviously be something intrinsic to the individual reality itself whereby it is individuated. And it is about this intrinsic something we are inquiring. The individual man is this individual, human nature is thus individuated in him, by something that is essential to human nature as found in him. This something has been called—after the analogy of the *differentia specifica* which differentiates species within a genus—the *differentia individua* of the individual. It has also been called by some the *differentia numerica*, and by Scotists the *haecceitas*. However we are to conceive this something, it is certain at all events that, considered as it is really found in the individual, it cannot be anything *really distinct* from the specific nature of the latter. No doubt, the *differentia specifica*, considered in the abstract, it is not essential and intrinsic to the *natura generica* considered in the abstract: it is extrinsic and accidental to the abstract content of the latter notion; but this is because we are conceiving these grades of being in the abstract. The same is true of the *differentia individua* as compared with the *natura specifica* in the abstract. But we are now considering these grades of reality as they are actually in the concrete individual being: and as they are found here, we have seen that a real distinction between them is inadmissible.

32. THE "PRINCIPLE OF INDIVIDUATION".—How, then, are we to conceive this something which individuates reality? It may be well to point out that for the erroneous doctrine of extreme realism, which issues in monism, the problem of individuation, as here understood, does not arise. For the monist all plurality in being is merely apparent, not real: there can be no question of a real distinction

between individual and individual.[145] Similarly, the nominalist and the conceptualist evade the problem. For these the individual alone is not merely formally real: it alone is fundamentally real: the universal is not even fundamentally real, has no foundation in reality, and thus all scientific knowledge of reality as revealed in sense experience is rendered impossible. But for the moderate realist, while the individual alone is formally real, the universal is fundamentally real, and hence the problem arises. It may be forcibly stated in the form of a paradox: That whereby Socrates and Plato are really distinct from each other as individuals is really identical with the human nature which is really in both. But what individuates human nature in Socrates, or in Plato, is logically distinct from the human nature that is really in Socrates, and really in Plato. We have only to inquire, therefore, whether the intrinsic principle of individuation is to be conceived merely as a negation, as something negative added by the mind to the concept of the specific nature, whereby the latter is apprehended as incapable of multiplication into "others" each of which would be formally that same nature, or, in other words, as incommunicable; or is the intrinsic ground of this incommunicability to be conceived as something positive, not indeed as something really distinct from, and superadded to, the specific nature, but as a positive aspect of the latter, an aspect, moreover, not involved in the concept of the specific nature considered in the abstract.

Of the many views that have been put forward on this question two or three call for some attention. In the opinion of Thomists generally, the principle which individuates *material* things, thus multiplying numerically the same specific nature, is to be conceived as a positive mode affecting the latter and revealing it in a new aspect, whereas the specific nature of the *spiritual* individual is itself formally an individual. The principle of the latter's individuation is already involved in the very concept of its specific nature, and therefore is not to be conceived as a distinct positive aspect of the latter but simply as the absence of plurality and communicability in the latter. In material things, moreover, the positive mode or aspect whereby the specific nature is found numerically multiplied, and incommunicable as it exists in each, consists in the fact that such a specific nature involves in its very constitution a *material* principle which is actually allied with certain *quantitative dimensions*. Hence the principle which individuates material substances is not to be conceived—after the manner in which Scotists conceive it—as an ultimate *differentia* affecting the *formal* factor of the nature, determining the specific nature just as the *differentia specifica* determines the generic nature, but as a *material* differentiating principle. What individuates the material individual, what marks it off as one in itself, distinct or divided from other individuals of the same specific nature, and incommunicable in that condition, is the material factor of that individual's nature—not, indeed, the material factor, *materia prima*, considered in the abstract, but the material factor as proximately capable of actual existence by being allied to certain more or less definite spatial or quantitative dimensions: "matter affected with quantity": "*materia quantitate signata*".[146]

In regard to material substances this doctrine embraces two separate contentions: (*a*) that the principle which individuates such a substance must be conceived as something positive, not really distinct from, but yet not contained in, the specific nature considered in the abstract; (*b*) that this positive aspect is to be found not in the formal but in the material principle of the composite corporeal substance.

To the former contention it might be objected that what individuates the specific nature cannot be conceived as anything *positive*, superadded to this nature: it cannot be anything *accidental* to the latter, for if it were, the individual would be only an accidental unity, a "*unum per accidens*" and would be constituted by an accident, which we have seen to be inadmissible; nor, on the other hand, can it be anything *essential* to the specific nature, for if it were, then individuals should be capable of adequate essential definition, and furthermore the definition of the specific nature would not really give the whole essence or *quidditas* of the individuals—two consequences which are commonly rejected by all scholastics. To this, however, it is replied that the principle of individuation is something essential to the specific nature in the sense that it *is* something intrinsic to, and really identical with, the whole real substance or entity of this nature, though not involved in the abstract concept by the analysis of which we reach the definition or *quidditas* of this nature. What individuates Socrates is certainly essential to Socrates, and is therefore really identical with his human nature; it is intrinsic to the human nature in him, a mode or aspect of his human substance; yet it does not enter into the definition of his nature—"*animal rationale*"—for such definition abstracts from individuality. When, therefore, we say that definition of the specific nature gives the whole *essence* of an individual, we mean that it gives explicitly the abstract (specific) essence, not the individuality which is really identical with this, nor, therefore, the whole substantial reality of the individual. We give different answers to the questions, "What is Socrates?" and "Who is Socrates?" The answer to the former question—a "man," or a "rational animal"—gives the "essence," but not explicitly the whole substantial reality of the individual, this remaining incapable of adequate conceptual analysis. The latter question we answer by giving the notes that *reveal* individuality. These, of course, are "accidental" in the strict sense. But even the principles which constitute the individuality of separate individuals of the same species, and which differentiate these individuals numerically from one another, we do not describe as *essential* differences, whereas we do describe specific and generic differences as *essential*. The reason of this is that the latter are abstract, universal, conceptual, amenable to intellectual analysis, scientifically important, while the former are just the reverse; the universal differences alone are principles about which we can have scientific knowledge, for "all science is of the abstract and universal";[147] and this is what we have in mind when we describe them as "essential" or "formal," and individual differences as "entitative" or "material".

The second point in the Thomistic doctrine is that corporeal substances are individuated by reason of their *materiality*. The formative, specific, determining principle of the corporeal substance is rendered *incommunicable* by its union with the material, determinable principle; and it becomes individually *distinct* or separate by the fact that this latter principle, in order to be capable of union with the given specific form, has in its very essence an exigence for certain more or less determinate dimensions in space. Corporeal things have their natural size within certain limits. The individual of a given corporeal species can exist only because the material principle, receptive of this specific form, has a natural relation to the fundamental property of corporeal things, *viz.* quantity, within certain more or less determinate limits. The form is rendered incommunicable by its reception in the matter. This concrete realization of the form in the matter is individually distinct and separate from other realizations of the same specific form, by the fact that the matter of this realization demands certain dimensions of quantity: this latter property being the root-principle of numerical multiplication of corporeal individuals within the same species.

On the other hand, incorporeal substances such as angels or pure spirits, being "pure" forms, "*formæ subsistentes*," wholly and essentially unallied with any determinable material principle, are *of themselves* not only specific but individual; they are themselves essentially incommunicable, superior to all multiplication or repeated realization of themselves: they are such that each can be actualized only "once and for all": each is a species in itself: it is the full, exhaustive, and adequate expression of a divine type, of an exemplar in the Divine Mind: its realization is not, like that of a material form, the actuation of an indefinitely determinable material principle: it sums up and exhausts the imitable perfection of the specific type in its single individuality, whereas the perfection of the specific type of a corporeal thing cannot be adequately expressed in any single individual realization, but only by repeated realizations; nor indeed can it ever be adequately, exhaustively expressed, by any finite multitude of these.

It follows that in regard to pure spirits the individuating principle and the specific principle are not only really but also logically, conceptually identical; that the distinction between individual and individual is here properly a specific distinction; that it can be described as numerical only in an analogical sense, if by numerical we mean material or quantitative, *i.e.* the distinction between corporeal individuals of the same species.

But the distinction between individual human souls is not a specific or formal distinction. These, though spiritual, are not *pure* spirits. They are spiritual substances which, of their very nature, are essentially ordained for union with matter. They all belong to the same species—the human species. But they do not constitute individuals of this species unless as existing actually united with matter. Each human soul has a transcendental relation to its own body, to the "*materia signata*" for which, and in which, it was created. For each human soul this relation is unique. Just as it is the material principle of each human being, the matter as allied to quantitative dimensions, that individuates the man, so it is the unique relation of his soul to the material principle thus spatially determined, that individuates his soul. Now the soul, even when disembodied and existing after death, necessarily retains in its very constitution this essential relation to its own body; and thus it is that disembodied souls, though not actually allied with matter, remain numerically distinct and individuated in virtue of their essential relation, each to its own body. We see, therefore, that human souls, though spiritual, are an entirely different order of beings, and must be conceived quite differently, from pure spirits.

We must be content with this brief exposition of the Thomistic doctrine on individuation. A discussion of the arguments for and against it would carry us too far.[148] There is no doubt that what *reveals* the individuality of the corporeal substance to us is its material principle, in virtue of which its existence is circumscribed within certain limits of time and space and affected with individual characteristics, "*notae individuantes*". But the Thomistic doctrine, which finds in "*materia signata*" the formal, intrinsic, constitutive principle of individuation, goes much deeper. It is intimately connected with the Aristotelian theory of knowledge and reality. According to this philosophy the formative principle or εἶδος, the *forma subtantialis*, is our sole key to the intelligibility of corporeal things: these are intelligible in so far forth as they are actual, and they are actual in virtue of their "forms". Hence the tendency of the scholastic commentators of Aristotle to use the term "form" as synonymous with the term "nature," though the whole nature of the corporeal substance embraces the material as well as the formal principle: for even though it does, we can understand nothing about this "nature" beyond what is intelligible in it in virtue of its "form." The material principle, on the other hand, is the potential, indeterminate principle, in itself unintelligible. We know that in ancient Greek philosophy it was regarded as the ἄλογον, the surd and contingent principle in things, the element which resisted rational analysis and fell outside the scope of "science," or "knowledge of the necessary and universal". While it revealed the forms or natures of things to sense, it remained itself impervious to intellect, which grasped these natures and rendered them intelligible only by divesting them of matter, by abstracting them from matter. Reality is intelligible only in so far forth as it is immaterial, either in fact or by abstraction. The human intellect, being itself spiritual, is "receptive of forms without matter". But being itself allied with matter, its proper object is none other than the natures or essences of corporeal things, abstracted, however, from the matter in which they are actually "immersed". The only reason, therefore, why any intelligible form or essence which, as abstract and universal, is "one" for intellect, is nevertheless actually or potentially "manifold" in its reality, is because it is allied with a material principle. It is the latter that accounts for the numerical multiplication, in actual reality, of any intelligible form or essence. If the latter is material it can be actualized only by indefinitely repeated, numerically or materially distinct, alliances with matter. It cannot be actualized "*tota simul*," or "once for all," as it were. It is, therefore, the material principle that not merely reveals, but also constitutes, the individuation of such corporeal forms or essences. Hence, too, the individual as such cannot be adequately apprehended by intellect; for all intelligible principles of reality are formal, whereas the individuating principle is material.

On the other hand, if an intelligible essence or form be purely spiritual, wholly unrelated to any indeterminate, material principle, it must be "one" not alone conceptually or logically but also really: it can exist only as "one": it is of itself individual: it can be differentiated from other spiritual essences not materially but only formally, or, in other words, not numerically but by a distinction which is at once individual and specific. Two pure spirits cannot be "two" numerically and "one" specifically, two for sense and one for intellect, as two men are: if they are distinct at all they must be distinct for intellect, *i.e.* they cannot be properly conceived as two members of the same species.

In this solution of the question it is not easy to see how the material principle, which, by its alliance with quantity, individuates the form, is itself individuated so as to be the source and principle of a multiplicity of numerically distinct and incommunicable realizations of this form. Perhaps the most that can be said on this point is that we must conceive quantity, which is the fundamental property of corporeal reality, as being itself essentially divisible, and the material principle as deriving from its essential relation to quantity its function of multiplying the same specific nature numerically.

Of those who reject the Thomistic doctrine some few contend that it is the *actual existence* of any specific nature that should be conceived as individuating the latter. No doubt the universal as such cannot exist; reality in order to exist actually must be individual. Yet it cannot be actual existence that individuates it. We must conceive it as individual before conceiving it as actually existent; and we can conceive it as individual while abstracting from its existence. We can think, for instance, of purely possible individual men, or angels, as numerically or individually distinct from one another. Moreover, what individuates the nature must be essential to the latter, but actual existence is not essential to any finite nature. Hence actual existence cannot be the principle of individuation.[149] Can it be contended that *possible* existence is what individuates reality? No; for possible existence is nothing more than intrinsic capacity to exist actually, and this is essential to all reality: it is the criterion whereby we distinguish real being from logical being; but real being, as such, is indifferent to universality or individuality; as far as the simple concept of real being is concerned the latter may be either universal or individual; the concept abstracts equally from either condition of being.

The vast majority, therefore, of those who reject the Thomistic doctrine on individuation, support the view that what individuates any nature or substance is simply the whole reality, the total entity, of the individual. This total entity of the individual, though really identical with the specific nature, must be conceived as something positive, superadded to the latter, for it involves a something which is logically or mentally distinct from the latter. This something is what we conceive as a *differentia individua*, after the analogy of the *differentia specifica* which contracts the concept of the genus to that of the species; and by Scotists it has been termed "*haecceitas*" or "thisness". Without using the Scotist terminology, most of those scholastics who reject the Thomist doctrine on this point advocate the present view. The individuality or "thisness" of the individual substance is regarded as having no special principle in the individual, other than the whole substantial entity of the latter. If the nature is simple it is of itself individual; if composite, the intrinsic principles from which it results—*i.e.* matter and form essentially united—suffice to individuate it.

In this view, therefore, the material principle of any individual man, for example, is numerically and individually distinct from that of any other individual, *of itself* and independently of its relation either to the formative principle or to quantity. The formative principle, too, is individuated *of itself*, and not by the material principle which is really distinct from it, or by its relation to this material principle. Likewise the union of both principles, which is a substantial mode of the composite substance, is individuated and rendered numerically distinct from all other unions of these two individual principles, not by either or both these, but by itself. And finally, the individual composite substance has its individuation from these two intrinsic principles thus individually united.

It may be doubted, perhaps, whether this attempt at explaining the real, individual "manifoldness" of what is "one" for intellect, *i.e.* the universal, throws any real light upon the problem. No doubt, every element or factor which is grasped by intellect in its analysis of reality—matter, form, substance, accident, quantity, nay, even "individuality" itself—is apprehended as abstract and universal; and if we hold the doctrine of Moderate Realism, that the intellect in apprehending the universal attains to reality, and not merely to a logical figment of its own creation, the problem of relating intelligibly the reality which is "one" for intellect with the same reality as manifestly "manifold" in its concrete realizations for sense, is a genuine philosophical problem. To say that what individuates any real essence or nature, what deprives it of the "oneness" and "universality" which it has for intellect, what makes it "this," "that," or "the other" incommunicable individual, must be conceived to be simply the whole essential reality of that nature itself—leaves us still in ignorance as to why such a nature, which is really "one" for intellect, can be really "manifold" in its actualizations for sense experience. The reason why the nature which is one and universal for abstract thought, and which is undoubtedly not a logical entity but a reality capable of actual existence, can be actualized as a manifold of distinct individuals, must be sought, we are inclined to think, in the relation of this nature to a material principle in alliance with quantity which is the source of all purely numerical, "space and time" distinctions.

33. INDIVIDUATION OF ACCIDENTS.—The rôle of quantity in the Thomistic theory of individuation suggests the question: How are accidents themselves individuated? We have referred already to the view that they are individuated by the individual subjects or substances in which they inhere. If we distinguish again between what *reveals* individuality and what *constitutes it*, there can be no doubt that when accidents of the same kind are found in individually distinct subjects what reveals the numerical distinction between the former is the fact that they are found inhering in the latter. So, also, distinction of individual substances is the *extrinsic*, *genetic*, or *causal* principle of the numerical distinction between similar accidents arising in these substances. But when the same kind of accident recurs successively in the same individual substance—as, for example, when a man performs repeated acts of the same kind—what reveals the numerical or individual distinction between these latter cannot be the individual substance, for it is one and the same, but rather the *time* distinction between the accidents themselves.

The intrinsic constitutive principle which formally individuates the accidents of individually distinct substances is, according to Thomists generally, their essential relation to the individual substances in which they appear. It is not clear how this theory can be applied to the fundamental accident of corporeal substances. If the function of formally individuating the corporeal substance itself is to be ascribed in any measure to *quantity*, it would seem to follow that this latter must be regarded as individuated by itself, by its own total entity or reality. And this is the view held by most other scholastics in regard to the individuation of accidents generally: that these, like substances, are individuated by their own total positive reality.

When there is question of the same kind of accident recurring in the same individual subject, the "time" distinction between such successive individual accidents of the same kind would appear not merely to *reveal* their individuality but also to indicate a different relation of each to its subject as existing at that particular point of space and time: so that the relation of the accident to its individual subject, as here and now existing in the concrete, would be the individuating principle of the accident.

Whether a number of accidents of the same *species infima*, and distinct merely numerically, could exist simultaneously in the same individual subject, is a question on which scholastic philosophers are not agreed: the negative opinion, which has the authority of St. Thomas, being the more probable. Those various questions on the individuation of accidents will be better understood from a subsequent exposition of the scholastic doctrine on accidents.

It may be well to remark that in inquiring about the individuation of substances and accidents we have been considering reality from a static standpoint, seeking how we are to conceive and interpret intellectually, or for abstract thought, the relation of the universal to the individual. If, however, we ascribe to "time" distinctions any function in individuating accidents of the same kind in the same individual substance, we are introducing into our analysis the kinetic aspect of reality, or its subjection to processes of change.

We may call attention here to a few other questions of minor import discussed by scholastics. First, have all individuals of the same species the same *substantial* perfection, or can individuals have different grades of substantial perfection within the same species? All admit the obvious fact that individual differs from individual within the same species in the number, variety, extent and intensity of their accidental properties and qualities. But, having the human soul mainly in view, they disagree as to whether the substantial perfection of the specific nature can be actualized in different grades in different individuals. According to the more common opinion there cannot be different *substantial* grades of the same specific nature, for the simple reason that every such grade of substantial perfection should be regarded as specific, as changing the species: hence, *e.g.* all human souls are substantially equal in perfection. This view is obviously based upon the conception of specific types or essences as being, after the analogy of numbers, immutable when considered in the abstract. And it seems to be confirmed by the consideration that the intrinsic principle of individuation is nothing, or adds nothing, *really distinct* from the specific essence itself.

Another question in connexion with individuation has derived at least an historical interest from the notable controversy to which it gave rise in the seventeenth century between Clarke and Leibniz. The latter, in accordance with the principles of his system of philosophy,—the *Law of Sufficient Reason* and the *Law of Continuity* among the *monads* or ultimate principles of being,—contended that two individual beings so absolutely alike as to be *indiscernible* would be *eo ipso identical*, in other words, that the reality of two such beings is impossible.

Of course if we try to conceive two individuals so absolutely alike both in essence and accidents, both in the abstract and in the concrete, as to be indiscernible either by our senses or by our intellect, or by any intellect—even the Divine Intellect—we are simply conceiving *the same thing* twice over. But is there anything impossible or contradictory in thinking that God could create two perfectly similar beings, distinct from each other only individually, so similar, however, that neither human sense nor human intellect could apprehend them as two, but only as one? The impossibility is not apparent. Were they two material individuals they should, of course, occupy the same space in order to have similar spatial relations, but impenetrability is not essential to corporeal substances. And even in the view that each is individuated by its "*materia signata*" it is not impossible to conceive numerically distinct quantified matters allied at the same time to the same dimensions of space. If, on the other hand, there be question of two pure spirits, absolutely similar specifically, even in the Thomistic view that here the individual distinction is at the same time specific there seems to be no sufficient ground for denying that the Divine Omnipotence could create two or more such individually (and therefore specifically) distinct spirits:[150] such distinction remaining, of course, indiscernible for the finite human intellect.

The argument of Leibniz, that there would be *no sufficient reason* for the creation of two such indiscernible beings, and that it would therefore be repugnant to the Divine Wisdom, is extrinsic to the question of their intrinsic possibility: if they be intrinsically possible they cannot be repugnant to any attribute of the Divinity, either to the Divine Omnipotence or to the Divine Wisdom.

34. IDENTITY.—Considering the order in which we acquire our ideas we are easily convinced that the notion of finite being is antecedent to that of infinite being. Moreover, it is from reflection on finite beings that we arrive at the most abstract notion of being in general. We make the object of this latter notion definite only by dividing it off mentally from nothingness, conceived *per modum entis*, or as an *ens rationis*. Thus the natural way of making our concepts definite is by *limiting* them; it is only when we come to reflect on the necessary implications of our concept of "infinite being" that we realize the possibility of conceiving a being which is *definite* without being really *limited*, which is definite by the very fact of its infinity, by its possession of unlimited perfection; and even then our imperfect human mode of conceiving "infinite being" is helped by distinguishing or dividing it off from all finite being and contrasting it with the latter. All this goes to prove the truth of the teaching of St. Thomas, that the mental function of *dividing* or *distinguishing* precedes our concepts of unity and multitude. Now the concepts of *identity* and *distinction* are closely allied with those of unity and multitude; but they add something to these latter. When we think of a being as one we must analyse it further, look at it under different aspects, and *compare it with itself*, before we can regard it as *the same* or *identical* with itself. Or, at least, we must think of it twice and compare it with itself in the affirmative judgment "This is itself," "A is A," thus formulating the logical *Principle of Identity*, in order to come into possession of the concept of *identity*.[151] Every affirmative categorical judgment asserts *identity* of the predicate with the subject ("*S is P*"): asserts, in other words, that what we apprehend under the notion of the predicate (*P*) is *really identical* with what we have apprehended under the *distinct* notion of the subject (*S*). The synthetic function of the affirmative categorical judgment *identifies* in the real order what the analytic function of mental abstraction had *separated* in the logical order. By saying that the affirmative categorical judgment asserts identity we mean that by asserting that "this is that," "man is rational" we identify "this" with "that," "man" with

"rational," thus *denying* that they are *two*, that they are *distinct*, that they *differ*. Identity is one of those elementary concepts which cannot be defined; but perhaps we may describe it as *the logical relation through which the mind asserts the objects of two or more of its thoughts to be really one.*

If the object formally represented by each of the concepts is one and the same—as, *e.g.* when we compare "*A*" with "*A*," or "man" with "rational animal," or, in general, any object with its definition—the identity is both *real and logical* (or *conceptual, formal*). If the concepts differ in their formal objects while representing *one and the same reality*—as when we compare "St. Peter" with "head of the apostles," or "man" with "rational"—the identity is *real, but not logical* or formal. Finally, if we represent two or more realities, "John, James, Thomas," by the same formal concept, "man," the identity is *merely logical* or formal, *not real.* Of these three kinds of identity the first is sometimes called *adequate*, the second and third *inadequate.*

Logical identity may be *specific* or *generic*, according as we identify really distinct individuals under one specific concept, or really distinct species or classes under one generic concept. Again, it may be *essential* or *accidental*, according as the abstract and universal class-concept under which really distinct members are classified represents a common part of the essence of these members or only a common property or accident. Thus John, James and Thomas are essentially identical in their *human nature*; they are accidentally identical in being all three *fair-haired* and *six feet in height.* Logical identity under the concept of *quality* is based on the real relation of *similarity*; logical identity under the concept of *quantity* is based on the real relation of *equality*. When we say that *essential* (logical) *identity* (*e.g.* the identity of John, James and Thomas under the concept of "man") is based on the fact that the really distinct individuals have really *similar* natures, we merely mean that *our* knowledge of natures or essences is derived from our knowledge of qualities, taking "qualities" in the wide sense of "accidents" generally: that the properties and activities of things are our only key to the nature of these things: *Operari sequitur esse.* It is not implied, nor is it true, that real *similarity* is a partial *real identity*: it is but the ground of a partial *logical* identity,—identity under the common concept of some quality (in the wide sense of this term). For example, the height of John is as really distinct from that of James as the humanity of John is from that of James. If, then, individual things are *really* distinct, how is it that we can represent (even inadequately) *a multitude* of them by *one* concept? To say that we can do so because they reveal themselves to us as *similar* to one another is to say what is undoubtedly true; but this does not solve the problem of the relation between the universal and the individual in human experience: rather it places us face to face with this problem.

Reverting now to *real* identity: whatever we can predicate affirmatively about a being considered as *one*, and as subject of a judgment, we regard as really identical with that being. We cannot predicate a real part of its real whole, or *vice versa*. But our concepts, when compared together in judgment, bear *logical* relations of extension and intension to each other, that is, relations of logical part to logical whole. Thus, the *logical* identity of subject and predicate in the affirmative judgment may be only *inadequate*.[152] But the real identity underlying the affirmative judgment is an adequate real identity. When we say, for example, that "Socrates is wise," we mean that the object of our concept of "wisdom" is in this case really and adequately identical with the object of our concept of "Socrates": in other words that we are conceiving one and the same real being under two distinct concepts, each of which represents, more or less adequately, the whole real being, and one of them in this case less adequately than the other.

We have to bear in mind that while considering being as one or manifold, identical or distinct, we are thinking of it in its *static* mode, as an object of abstract thought, not in its *dynamic and kinetic* mode as actually existing in space and time, and subject to change. It is the identity of being with itself when considered in this static, unchanging condition, that is embodied in the logical *Principle of Identity*. In order, therefore, that this principle may find its application to being or reality *as subject to actual change*—and this is the state in which *de facto* reality is presented to us as an immediate datum of experience—we must seize upon the changing reality and think of it in an indivisible instant apart from the change to which it is actually subject; only thus does the Principle of Identity apply to it—as *being*, not as *becoming*, not *in fieri*, but *in facto esse*. The Principle of Identity, which applies to all real being, whether possible or actual, tells us simply that "a thing is what it is". But for the understanding of actual being as subject to real change we must supplement the Principle of Identity by another principle which tells us that such an actual being not only is actually what it is (Principle of Identity), but also that it *is potentially something other than what it actually is, that it is potentially what it can become actually* (Ch. ii.).

We have seen that, since change is not continuous annihilation and creation, the changing being must in some real and true sense *persist* throughout the process of change. It is from experience of change we derive our notion of time-duration; and the concept of permanence or stability throughout change gives us the notion of a real sameness or abiding self-identity which is compatible with real change. But a being which persists in existence is identical with itself throughout its duration only in so far forth as it has not changed. Only the Necessary Being, whose duration is absolutely exempt from all change, is *absolutely* or *metaphysically* identical with Himself: His duration is eternity—which is one perpetual, unchanging *now*. A being which persists unchanged in its essence or nature, which is exempt from substantial change, but which is subject to accidental change, to a succession of accidental qualities such as vital actions—such a being is said to retain its *physical* identity with itself throughout those changes. Such, for instance, is the identity of the human soul with itself, or of any individual living thing during its life, or even of an inorganic material substance as long as it escapes substantial change. Finally, the persisting identity of a collection of beings, united by some moral bond so as to form a moral unit, is spoken of as *moral* identity as long as the bond remains, even though the constituent members may be constantly disappearing to be replaced by others: as in a nation, a religious society, a legal corporation, etc.

35. DISTINCTION.—Distinction is the correlative of identity; it is the absence or negation of the latter. We express the relation called distinction by the negative judgment, "this is not that"; it is the relation of a being to whatever is not itself, the relation of *one* to *other*.

Distinction may be either *adequate* or *inadequate*, according as we distinguish one total object of thought from another total object, or only from a part of itself. For example, the distinction between John and James is an adequate real distinction, while that between John and his body is an inadequate real distinction; the distinction between John's rationality and his animality is an adequate logical distinction, while the distinction between either of these and his humanity is an inadequate logical distinction.

We have already briefly explained and illustrated the most important classification of distinctions: that into real and logical; the sub-division of the latter into purely logical and virtual; and of the latter again into perfect (complete, adequate) and imperfect (incomplete, inadequate). But the theory there briefly outlined calls for some further analysis and amplification.

36. LOGICAL DISTINCTIONS AND THEIR GROUNDS.—The purely logical distinction must not be confounded with a mere *verbal* distinction, *e.g.* that between an "edifice" and a "building," or between "truthfulness" and "veracity". A logical distinction is a distinction *in the concepts*: these must represent one and the same reality but in different ways: the one may be more explicit, more fully analysed than the other, as a definition is in comparison with the thought-object defined; or the one may represent the object less adequately than the other, as when we compare (in intension) the concepts "man" and "animal"; or the one may be predicated of the other in an affirmative judgment; or the one may represent the object as concrete and individual, the other the same object as abstract and universal.[153]

Comparing, in the next place, the purely logical with the virtual distinction, we see that the grounds for making these distinctions are different. Every distinction made by the mind must have an intelligible ground or reason of some sort—a *fundamentum distinctionis*. Now in the case of the purely logical distinction the ground is understood to consist exclusively in the needs of the mind itself—needs which spring from the mind's own limitations when confronted with the task of understanding or interpreting reality, of making reality intelligible. Purely logical distinctions are therefore seen to be a class of purely logical relations, *i.e.* of those *entia rationis* which the mind must construct for itself in its effort to understand the real. They have no other reality as objects of thought than the reality they derive from the constitutive or constructive activity of the mind. They are modes, or forms, or terms, of the cognitive activity itself, not of the reality which is the object apprehended and contemplated by means of this cognitive activity.

The virtual distinction, on the other hand, although it also, as an object of thought, is only an *ens rationis*—inasmuch as there is no real duality or plurality corresponding to it in the reality into which the mind introduces it, this reality being a real *unity*—the virtual distinction is considered, nevertheless, to have a ground, or reason, or foundation (for making and introducing it) in the nature of this one reality; that is, it is regarded as having a *real* foundation, a *fundamentum in re*. In so far, therefore, as our knowledge is permeated by virtual distinctions, reality cannot be said to be *formally*, but only *fundamentally* what this knowledge represents it to be. Does this fact interfere with the objective validity of our knowledge? Not in the least; for we do not ascribe to the reality the distinctions, and other such modes or forms, which we know by reflection to be formally characteristic *not of things* but *of our thought or cognition of things*. Our knowledge, therefore, so far as it goes, may be a faithful apprehension of reality, even though it be itself affected by modes not found in the reality.

But what is this *real* foundation of the virtual distinction? What *is* the *fundamentum in re*? It is not a real or objective duality in virtue of which we could say that there are, in the object of our thought, two beings or realities one of which is not the other. Such duality would cause a *real* distinction. But just here the difficulties of our analysis begin to arise: for we have to fix our attention on actually existing realities; and, assuming that each and every one of these is an individual, we have to bear in mind the relation of the real to the actual, of reality as abstract and universal to reality as concrete and individual, of the simple to the composite, of the stable to the changing, of essential to accidental unity—in any and every attempt to discriminate in detail between a real and a virtual distinction. Nor is it easy to lay down any general test which will serve even theoretically to discriminate between them. Let us see what grounds have been mainly suggested as real foundations for the virtual distinction.

If a being which is not only one but simple, manifests, in the superior grade of being to which it belongs, a perfection which is equivalent to many lesser perfections found really distinct and separate elsewhere, in separate beings of an inferior order, this is considered a sufficient real ground for considering the former being, though really one and simple, as virtually manifold.[154] The human soul, as being virtually threefold—rational, sentient and vegetative—is a case in point: but only on the assumption that the soul of the individual man can be proved to be one and simple. This, of course, all scholastics regard as capable of proof: even those of them who hold that the powers or faculties whereby it immediately manifests these three grades of perfection are *accidental* realities, *really distinct* from one another and from the *substance* of the soul itself.

Again, the being which is the object of our thought may be so rich in reality or perfection that our finite minds cannot adequately grasp it by any one mental intuition, but must proceed discursively, by analysis and abstraction, taking in partial aspects of it successively through inadequate concepts; while realizing that these aspects, these objects of our distinct concepts, are only partial aspects of one and the same real being. This, in fact, is our common experience. But the theory assumes that we are able to determine when these objects of our concepts are only mental aspects of *one* reality, and when they are several separate realities; nay, even, that we can determine whether or not they are really distinct entities united together to form one *composite* individual being, or only mentally distinct views of one *simple* individual being. For example, it is assumed that while the distinction between the sentient and the rational grades of being in a human individual can be shown to be only a virtual distinction, that between the body and the soul of the same individual can be shown to be a real distinction; or, again, that while the distinction between essence, intellect, and will in God, can be shown to be only a virtual distinction, that between essence, intellect, and will in man, can be shown to be a real distinction.

37. THE VIRTUAL DISTINCTION AND THE REAL DISTINCTION.—Now scholastics differ considerably in classifying this, that, or the other distinction, as logical or as real; but this does not prove that it is impossible ever to determine with certitude whether any particular distinction is logical or real. What we are looking for just now is a general test for discriminating, if such can be found. And this brings us to a consideration of the test suggested in the very definitions themselves. At first sight it would appear to be an impracticable, if not even an unintelligible test: "The distinction is real if it exists in the reality—*i.e.* if the reality is *two* (or more) *beings*, not *one being*—antecedently to, or independently of, the consideration of the mind; otherwise the distinction is logical". But—it might be objected—how can we possibly know whether or not any object of perception or thought is *one* or *more than one* antecedently to, or independently

of, the consideration of the mind? It is certainly impossible for us to know what, or what kind, reality is, or whether it is one or manifold, apart from and prior to, the exercise of our own cognitive activity. This, therefore, cannot be what the test means: to interpret it in such a sense would be absurd. But when we have perceived reality in our actual sense experience, when we have interpreted it, got the meaning of it, made it intelligible, and actually understood it, by the spontaneous exercise of intellect, the judging and reasoning faculty: then, obviously, we are at liberty to reflect critically on those antecedent spontaneous processes, on the knowledge which is the result of them, and the reality which is known through them; and by such critical reflection on those processes, their objects and their products, on the "reality as perceived and known" and on the "perceiving" and "knowing" of it, we may be able to distinguish between two classes of contributions to the total result which is the "known reality": those which we must regard as purely mental, as modes or forms or subjectively constructed terms of the mental function of cognition itself (whether perceptual or conceptual), and those which we must regard as given or presented to the mind as objects, which are not in any sense constructed or contributed by the mind, which, therefore, are what they are independently of our mental activity, and which would be and remain what they are, and what we have apprehended them to be, even if we had never perceived or thought of them. This, according to the scholastics, is the sense—and it is a perfectly intelligible sense—in which we are called on to decide whether the related terms of any given distinction have been merely rendered distinct by the analytic activity of the cognitive process, or are themselves distinct realities irrespective of this process. That it is possible to carry on successfully, at least to some extent, this work of discrimination between the subjective and the objective factors of our cognitive experience, can scarcely be denied. It is what philosophers in every age have been attempting. There are, however, some distinctions about the nature of which philosophers have never been able to agree, some holding them to be real, others to be only virtual: the former view being indicative of the tendency to emphasize the rôle of cognition as a passive representation of objectively given reality; the latter view being an expression of the opposite tendency to emphasize the active or constitutive or constructive factors whereby cognition assimilates to the mind's own mode of being the reality given to it in experience. In all cognition there is an assimilation of reality and mind, of object and subject. When certain distinctions are held to be real this consideration is emphasized: that in the cognitive process, as such, it is the mind that is assimilated to the objective reality.[155] When these same distinctions are held to be logical this other consideration is emphasized: that in the cognitive process reality must also be assimilated to mind, must be mentalized so to speak: *Cognitum est in cognoscente secundum modum cognoscentis*: that in this process the mind must often regard what is *one* reality under *distinct aspects*: and that if we regard these distinct aspects as distinct realities we are violating the principle, *Entia non sunt multiplicanda praeter necessitatem*.

Now those philosophers who hold certain distinctions to be virtual, and not real, thereby ascribe to cognitive experience a larger sphere of constitutive or constructive influence than would be allowed to it by advocates of the reality of such distinctions. But by doing so are they to be regarded as calling into question the objective validity of human knowledge? By no means: the fact that the human mind can understand reality only by processes of abstracting, generalizing, comparing, relating, analysing and synthesizing—processes which involve the production of logical entities—in no way vitiates the value of these modes of understanding: it merely indicates that they are less perfect than intuitive modes of understanding which would dispense with such logical entities,—the modes characteristic of pure, angelic intelligences, or the knowledge of the Deity. The objective validity of human cognition is not interfered with either by enlarging or by restricting the domain of the mind's constitutive activity in forming such logical entities; nor, therefore, by claiming that certain distinctions are real rather than virtual, or *vice versa*. It must be remembered, moreover, that the virtual distinction is not purely logical: it has a foundation in the reality, a "*fundamentum in re*"; and in so far as it has it gives us an insight into the nature of reality.

No doubt, any particular distinction cannot be virtual and at the same time simply real: either view of it must be erroneous: and possibly both, if it happen to be *de facto* a *purely* logical distinction. But the error of confounding a virtual distinction with a real is not so great as that of regarding either as a purely logical distinction. Now the tendency of much modern philosophy, under the influence of Kant, has been to regard all the categories in which the mind apprehends reality as being wholly and exclusively forms of cognition, as being in the reality neither formally nor even fundamentally; and to infer from this an essential, constitutional inability of the mind to attain to a valid knowledge of reality. But if, as a matter of fact, these categories are in the reality formally, nay, even if they are in it only fundamentally, the inference that issues in Kantian subjectivism is unwarranted. And those categories we hold to be in the reality at least fundamentally; we therefore reject the Kantian phenomenism of the speculative reason. Moreover, we can see no valid ground for admitting the Kantian division of the human mind into two totally separate cognitive compartments, the speculative and the practical reason, and ascribing to each compartment cognitive principles and capacities entirely alien to the other. To arrive at a right theory of knowledge human cognitive experience as a whole must be analysed; but provided the analysis is really an analysis of this experience it may be legitimately directed towards discovering what the mental conditions must be—*i.e.* the conditions on the side of the knowing subject, the subject having the experience—which are *necessarily prerequisite* for having such experience. And if it be found by such analysis that cognitive experience presupposes in the knowing subject not merely a sentient and intelligent mind, but a mind which perceives, imagines, remembers reality in certain definite ways; which thinks reality in certain modes and through certain forms which by its own constitutive activity it constructs for itself, and which it recognizes by reflection to be its own constructions (*e.g.* distinctions, relations, affirmations and negations, abstractions, generalizations, etc.: *intentiones logicae*, logical entities),—there is no reason whatever in all this for inferring that because the mind is so constituted, because it has these modes of cognition, it must necessarily fail to reach, by means of them, a true, valid, and genuine knowledge of reality. From the fact that human modes of cognition are human, and not angelic or divine; from the fact that reality can be known *to man* only through these modes, these finite modes of finite human faculties,—we may indeed infer that even our highest knowledge of reality is inadequate, that it does not *comprehend* all that is in the reality, but surely not that it is essentially illusory and of its very nature incapable of giving us any true and valid insight into the nature of reality.

Fixing our attention on the virtual distinction we see that the mind is supposed by means of it to apprehend, through a plurality of distinct concepts, what it knows somehow or other to be *one* being. Now if it knows the reality to be *really one*, it knows that the formal object of every distinct concept of this reality is really identical with the objects of all the other concepts of the latter. This condition of things is certainly verified when the mind can see that each of the distinct concepts, though not *explicitly* presenting the objects of the others, nevertheless *implicitly and necessarily* involves all these other objects:[156] for by seeing that the distinct concepts necessarily involve one another objectively it sees that the reality apprehended through all of them must necessarily be *one reality*. This is what takes place in the *imperfect* virtual distinction: the concepts prescind from one another formally, not objectively. But suppose that the distinct concepts prescind from one another *objectively*, so that they cannot be seen by any analysis to involve one another even implicitly, but present to the mind, so far as they themselves are concerned, adequately distinct modes of being—as happens in the *perfect* virtual distinction, *e.g.* between organic life, sentient life, and intellectual life (in man), or between animality and rationality (in man),—then the all-important question arises: How do we know, in any given case of this kind, whether or not these adequately distinct thought-objects are *identical with one another in the reality*? What is the test for determining whether or not, in a given case, these objects, which are *many* for abstract intellectual thought, are *one being* in the real order? The answer seems to be that *internal and external sense experience* can and does furnish us with embodiments of these intellectual manifolds,—embodiments each of which we apprehend as *a being that is really one*, as an *individual subject* of which they are conceptually distinct predicates.

It would appear, therefore, that we cannot reach a true conception of what we are to regard as *really one*, or *really manifold*, by abstract thought alone. It is external and internal sense experience, not abstract thought, which first brings us into direct and immediate mental contact with *actually existing* reality. What we have therefore to determine is this: Does sense experience, or does it not, reveal reality to us as a *real manifold*, not as *one being* but as *beings* coexisting outside one another in space, succeeding one another in time, interdependent on one another, interacting on one another, and by this interaction causing and undergoing real change, each producing others, or being produced by others, really distinct from itself? In other words, is separateness of existence in time or space, as revealed in sense experience, a sufficient index of the real manifoldness of corporeal being, and of the really distinct individuality of each such being?—or are we to take it that because those space and time distinctions have to be apprehended by thought in order that not merely sense but intellect may apprehend corporeal beings as really manifold, therefore these distinctions are not *in the reality* given to us? Or, again, is each person's own conscious experience of himself as one being, of his own unity, and of his distinctness from other persons, a sufficient index that the distinction between person and person is a real distinction?—or are we to take it that because his *feeling* of his individual unity through sense consciousness must be interpreted by the *thought-concepts* of "one"—"individual"—"person"—"distinct" from "others," these concepts do not truly express what is really given him to interpret? Finally, if we can infer from the actually existing material reality which forms the immediate datum of direct experience, or from the human *Ego* as given in this experience, the actual existence of a real mode of being which is not material but spiritual, by what tests can we determine whether this spiritual mode of being is really one, or whether there is a real plurality of such beings? The solution of these questions bears directly on the validity of the adequate or "greater" real distinction, the "*distinctio realis major seu absoluta*".

The philosophy which defends the validity of this distinction,—which holds that the distinction between individual human beings, and between individual living things generally, is in the fullest and truest sense a real distinction,—is at all events in conformity with universally prevailing modes of thought and language; while the monism which repudiates these spontaneous interpretations of experience as invalid by denying all real manifoldness to reality, can make itself intelligible only by doing violence to thought and language alike. Not that this alone is a disproof of monism; but at all events it creates a presumption against a system to find it running counter to any of those universal spontaneous beliefs which appear to be rooted in man's rational nature. On the other hand, the philosophy which accords with common belief in proclaiming a real plurality in being has to reconcile intellect with sense, and the universal with the individual, by solving the important problem of *individuation*. What is it that makes real being individual, if, notwithstanding the fact that intellect apprehends reality as abstract and universal, reality nevertheless can exist only as concrete and individual?.

38. THE REAL DISTINCTION.—In the next place it must be remembered, comparing the virtual distinction with the real, that philosophers have recognized two kinds of real distinction: the *major* or *absolute* real distinction, and the *minor* real, or *modal* distinction. Before defining these let us see what are the usual signs by which a real distinction in general can be recognized.

The relation of efficient causality, of efficient cause and effect, between two objects of thought, is sometimes set down as a sure sign of a (major) real distinction between them.[157] And the reason alleged is that a thing cannot be the efficient cause of itself: the efficient cause is necessarily extrinsic to the effect and cannot be really identical with the latter. It is to be noted that this test applies to reality as actually existing, as producing or undergoing change, and that it is derived from our sense experience of reality in process of change. But since our concept of efficient causality has its origin in our internal experience of our own *selves* as active agents, as causing some portion of what enters into our experience, the test seems to assume that we have already introduced into this experience a real distinction between the self and what is caused by the self. It is not clear that the relation of efficient cause to effect, as applied to created causes, can precede and reveal, in our experience, the relation of what is *really one* to what is *really other*, in this experience. If the reality revealed to us in our direct experience, the phenomenal universe, has been brought into existence by the creative act of a Supreme Being, this, of course, implies a real distinction between Creator and creature. But it does not seem possible in this case, or indeed in any case, to prove the existence of the causal relation antecedently to that of the real distinction, or to utilize the former as an index to the latter.

Two distinct thought-objects are regarded as *really* distinct (1) when they are found to exist separately and apart from each other in time or space, as is the case with any two individuals such as John and James, or a man and a horse; (2) when, although they are found in the same individual, one of them at least is separable from the other, in the sense that it can actually exist without that other: for example, the soul of any individual man can exist apart from the material principle with which it is actually united to form this living human individual; the individual himself can exist without the particular accidental modes, such as sitting, thinking, speaking, which actually affect his being at any particular instant of his existence.

From this we can gather in the first place that the distinction between two "individuals,"—individual "persons" or individual "things"—is a real distinction in the fullest and plainest sense of this expression, a major or absolute real distinction. It is, moreover, not merely real but actual. Two existing "individuals" are always actually divided and separate from each other, while each is actually one or actually undivided in itself. And they are so "independently of the consideration of the mind".

In the second place, assuming that the mind can apprehend, in the individuals of its experience, a unity resulting from the union or composition of separable factors or principles, whether essential or accidental; and assuming that it can know these factors to be really separable (though actually one and undivided), that is, separable in the sense that each of any two such factors, or at least one of them, could actually exist without the other,—it regards the distinction between such factors as real. They are really distinct because though *actually* one and undivided they are *potentially* manifold. If each has a positive entity of its own, so that absolutely speaking each could exist without the other, the distinction is still regarded as an absolute or major real distinction. For example, the human soul can exist without the body; the body can exist without the soul, being actualized by the new formative principle or principles which replace the soul at death; therefore there is an absolute real distinction between the soul and the body of the living human individual: although both factors form *one actual being*, still, independently of the consideration of the mind *the one factor is not the other*: each is really, though only potentially, other than the factor with which it is united: the relation of "one" to "other" though not *actually* verified of either factor (since there is only *one actual* being: the existing individual man), is potentially and really verified, *i.e. verifiable* of each. Again, the individual corporeal substance can, absolutely speaking, exist without its connatural accident of external or local extension; this latter can, absolutely speaking, exist without its connatural substance;[158] therefore these are absolutely and really distinct.

If only one of the factors is seen to be capable of existing without the other, and the latter to be such that it could not actually exist except as united with the former, so that the separability is not mutual, the distinction is regarded still as real, but only as a *minor* or *modal* distinction. Such, for instance, is the distinction between a body and its location, or its state of rest or motion: and, in general, the distinction between a substance and what are called its accidental modes or modal accidents. The distinction is regarded as real because reflection is held to assure us that it is in the reality itself independently of the mind, and not merely imposed by the mind on the reality because of some ground or reason in the reality. It is called a modal distinction rather than an absolute real distinction because those accidental modes of a substance do not seem to have of themselves sufficient reality to warrant our calling them "things" or "realities," but rather merely "modes" or "determinations" of things or realities. It is significant, as throwing light on the relation of the virtual to the real distinction, that some authors call the modal distinction not a real distinction but a "distinctio *media*," *i.e.* intermediate between a real and a logical distinction; and that the question whether it should be called simply a real distinction, or "intermediate" between a real and a logical distinction is regarded by some as "a purely verbal question."[159] We shall recur to the modal distinction later.

In the third place it must be noted that separability *in the sense explained*, even non-mutual, is not regarded as the *only* index to a real distinction. In other words, certain distinctions are held by some to be real even though this test of separability does not apply. For instance, it is commonly held that not merely in man but in *all* corporeal individuals the formative and the determinable principle of the nature or substance, the *forma substantialis* and the *materia prima*, are really distinct, although it is admitted that, apart from the case of the human soul, *neither* can actually exist except in union with the other. What is held in regard to *accidental* modes is also applied to these essential principles of the corporeal substance: *viz.*

that there is here a special reason why such principles cannot actually exist in isolation. Of their very nature they are held to be such that they cannot be *actualized* or *actually exist* in isolation, but only in union. But this fact, it is contended, does not prove that the principles in question are merely mentally distinct aspects of one reality: the fact that they cannot actually exist as such separately does not prove that they are not really separable; and it is contended that they are really and actually separated whenever an individual corporeal substance undergoes substantial change.

This, then, raises once more the question: What sort of "separation" or "separability" is the test of a real distinction? Is it separateness in and for sense perception, or separateness in and for intellectual thought? The former is certainly the fundamental index of the real distinction; for all our knowledge of reality originates in sense experience, and separateness in time and space, which marks its data, is the key to our knowledge of reality as a manifold of really distinct individual beings; and when we infer from sense-experience the actual existence of a *spiritual* domain of reality we can conceive *its* "individuals" only after the analogy of the corporeal individuals of our immediate sense experience. Scholastic philosophers, following Aristotle, have always taken the manifoldness of reality, *i.e.* its presentation in sense experience in the form of "individuals," of "this" and "that," "τοδὲ τι," "*hoc aliquid*," as an unquestioned and unquestionable *real datum*. Not that they naïvely assumed everything *perceived by the senses* as an individual, in time and space, to be really an individual: they realized that what is perceived by sense as *one* limited continuum, occupying a definite portion of space, may be in reality an aggregate of many individuals; and they recognized the need of scrutinizing and analysing those apparent individuals in order to test their real individuality; but they held, and rightly, that sense experience does present to us some data that are unmistakably real individuals—individual men, for instance. Next, they saw that intellectual thought, by analysing sense experience, amasses an ever-growing multitude of abstract and conceptually distinct thought-objects, which it utilizes as predicates for the interpretation of this sense experience. These thought-objects intellect can unite or separate; can in some cases positively see to be mutually compatible or incompatible; can form into ideal or possible complexes. But whether or not the *conceptually* distinct, though mutually compatible, thought-objects forming any such complex, will be also *really distinct* from one another, is a question which evidently cannot arise until such a complex is considered as an actual or possible *individual being*: for it is the individual only that exists or can exist. They will be *really* distinct when found actualized in *distinct individuals*. Even the *conceptually* one and self-identical abstract thought-object will be *really distinct from itself* when embodied in distinct individuals; the one single abstract thought-object, "humanity," "human nature," is really distinct from itself in John and in James; the humanity of John is *really other* than the humanity of James.

Of course, if conceptually distinct thought-objects are seen to be mutually incompatible they cannot be found realized except in really distinct individuals: the union of them is only an *ens rationis*. Again it may be that the intellect is unable to pronounce positively as to whether they are compatible or not: as to whether the complex forms a possible being or not. But when the intellect positively sees such thought-objects to be mutually compatible—by interpretation of, and inference from, its actual sense experience of them as embodied in individuals—and when, furthermore, it now finds a number of them coexisting in some one actual individual, the question recurs: How can it know whether they are *really distinct* from each other, though actually united to form one (essentially or accidentally composite) individual, or only conceptually distinct aspects of one (simple) individual?

This, as we have seen already, is the case for which it is really difficult to find a satisfactory test: and hence the different views to be found among scholastic philosophers as to the nature of the distinctions which the mind makes or discovers *within the individual*. The difficulty is this. The conceptual distinction between compatible thought-objects is not a proof of real distinction when these thought-objects are found united in *one individual* of sense experience, as *e.g.* animality and rationality in man; and the only distinction given to us by sense experience, at least directly and immediately, as undoubtedly real, is the distinction *between* corporeal *individuals* existing apart in space or time, as *e.g.* between man and man. How then, can we show that any distinctions *within the individual* are real?

Well, we have seen that certain entities, which are objects of sense or of thought, or of both, can disappear from the individual without the residue thereby perishing or ceasing to exist actually as an individual: the human soul survives, as an actual individual reality, after its separation from the material principle with which it formed the individual man; the individual man persists while the accidental modes that affect him disappear. In such cases as these, intellect, interpreting sense experience and reasoning from it, places a real distinction, in the composite individual, between the factors that can continue to exist without others, and these latter. In doing so it is apparently applying the analogy of the typical real distinction—that between one individual and another. The factor, or group of factors, which can continue to exist actually after the separation of the others, is an individual: and what were separated from it were apparently real entities, though they may have perished by the actual separation. But on what ground is the distinction between the material principle and the vital principle of a plant or an animal, for example, regarded as real? Again on the ground furnished by the analogy of the distinction between individuals of sense experience. Note that it is not between the material and the vital principles *as objects of abstract thought, i.e.* between the *materiality* and the *vitality* of the plant or the animal, that a real distinction is claimed: these are regarded only as conceptually distinct aspects of the plant or the animal; nor is it admitted that because one of these thought-objects is found embodied elsewhere in nature without the other—materiality without vitality in the inorganic universe—we can therefore conclude that they are really distinct in the plant or the animal. No; it is between the two principles conceived as coexisting and united in the concrete individual that the real distinction is claimed. And it is held to be a real distinction because substantial change in corporeal things, *i.e.* corruption and generation of individual corporeal substances, is held to be real. If it is real there is a real separation of essential factors when the individual perishes. And the factors continue to be real, as *potential* principles of other individuals, when any individual corporeal substance perishes. Each principle may not continue to exist actually as such in isolation from the other—though some scholastics hold that, absolutely speaking, they could be conserved apart, as actual entities, by the Author of Nature. But they *can* actually exist *as essential principles of other actual individuals*: they are real *potentialities*, which *become actual* in other individuals. Thus we see that they are conceived throughout *after the analogy of the individual*. Those who hold that, absolutely speaking, the material principle as such, *materia prima*, could actually exist in isolation from any formative principle, should apparently admit that in such a case it would be *an individual reality*.

39. SOME QUESTIONABLE DISTINCTIONS. THE SCOTIST DISTINCTION.—The difficulty of discriminating between the virtual and the real distinction in an individual has given rise to the conception of distinctions which some maintain to be real, others to be less than real. The virtual distinction, as we have hitherto understood it, may be described as *extrinsic* inasmuch as it arises in the individual only when we consider the latter under different aspects, or in different relations to things extrinsic to it. By regarding an individual under different aspects—*e.g.* a man under the aspects of animality and rationality—we can predicate contradictory attributes of the individual, *e.g.* of a man that "he is similar to a horse," and that "he is not similar to a horse". Now it is maintained by some that although independently of the consideration of the mind the grounds of these contradictory predications are not *actually* distinct in the individual, nevertheless even before such consideration the individual has a real *intrinsic capacity* to have these contradictory predicates affirmed of him: they can be affirmed of him not merely when he is regarded, and because he is regarded, under conceptually different aspects, but because these principles, "animality" and "rationality," are already really in him not merely as aspects but as distinct capacities, as potentially distinct principles of contradictory predications.

The virtual distinction, understood in this way, is described as *intrinsic*. It is rejected by some on the ground that, at least in its application to finite realities, it involves a violation of the principle of contradiction: it seems to imply that one and the same individual has in itself absolutely (and not merely as considered under different aspects and relations) the capacity to verify of itself contradictory predicates.

Scotus and his followers go even farther than the advocates of this intrinsic virtual distinction by maintaining the existence of a distinction which on the one hand they hold to be less than real because it is not between "thing and thing," and on the other hand to be more than logical or virtual, because it *actually* exists between the various thought-objects or *"formalitates"* (such, *e.g.* as animality and rationality) in the individual, independently of the analytic activity whereby the mind detects these in the latter. This distinction Scotists call a "formal distinction, actual on the part of the thing"—"*distinctio formalis, actualis ex natura rei.*" Hence the name "formalists" applied to Scotists, from their advocacy of this "Scotistic" distinction. It is, they explain, a distinction not between "things" ("*res*") but between "formalities" ("*formalitates*"). By "thing" as opposed to "formality" they mean not merely the individual, but also any positive thought-object which, though it may not be capable of existing apart, can really appear in, or disappear from, a thing which can so exist: for instance, the essential factors of a really composite essence, its accidental modes, and its real relations. By "formality" they mean a positive thought-object which is absolutely inseparable from the thing in which it is apprehended, which cannot exist without the thing, nor the thing without it: for instance, all the metaphysical grades of being in an individual, such as substantiality, corporeity, life, animality, rationality, individuality, in an individual man. The distinction is called "formal" because it is between such "formalities"—each of which is the positive term of a separate concept of the individual. It is called "*actual* on the side of the thing" because it is claimed to be *actually* in the latter apart from our mental apprehension of the individual. What has chiefly influenced Scotists in claiming this distinction to be thus *actually* in the individual, independently of our mental activity, is the consideration that these metaphysical grades are grounds on which we can predicate contradictory attributes of the same individual, *e.g.* of an individual man that "he is similar to a horse" and that "he is not similar to a horse": whence they infer that in order to avoid violation of the principle of contradiction, we must suppose these grounds to be *actually* distinct in the thing.

To this it is replied, firstly, that if such predications were truly contradictory we could avoid violation of the principle of contradiction only by inferring a *real* distinction—which Scotists deny to exist—between these grounds; secondly, that such predications are not truly contradictory inasmuch as "he is similar" really means "he is partially similar," and "he is not similar" means "he is not completely similar"; therefore when we say that a man's rationality "*is not* the principle whereby he resembles a horse," and his animality "*is* the principle whereby he resembles a horse," we mean (*a*) that his rationality is not the principle of complete resemblance, though we know it is the principle of partial resemblance, inasmuch as we see it to be really identical with that which is the principle of partial resemblance, *viz.* his animality; and we mean (*b*) that his animality is the principle of his partial resemblance to a horse, not of total resemblance, for we know that the animality of a man is not perfectly similar to that of a horse, the former being really identical with rationality, the latter with irrationality. When, then, we predicate of one thing that "it is similar to some other thing," and that "it is not similar to this other thing" we are not really predicating contradictories of the same thing; if we take the predicates as contradictories they are true of the same reality undoubtedly, but not under the same aspect. Scotists themselves admit that the *real identity* of these aspects involves no violation of the principle of contradiction; why, then, should these be held to be *actually* distinct formalities independently of the consideration of the mind? How can a distinction that is actual independently of the mind's analysis of the reality be other than real? Is not predication a work of the mind? And must not the conditions on which reality verifies the predication be determined by the mind? If, then, we see that in order to justify this predication—of "similar" and "not similar"—about any reality, it is merely necessary that the mind should apprehend this reality to be in its undivided unity equivalent to manifold grades of being or perfection which the mind itself can grasp as mentally distinct aspects, by distinct concepts, how can we be justified in supposing that these grades of being are not merely *distinguishable*, but *actually distinct* in the reality itself, *independently of the mind*?

The Scotist doctrine here is indicative of the tendency to emphasize, perhaps unduly, the assimilation of reality as a datum with the mind which interprets this datum; to regard the constitution of reality itself as being what abstract thought, irrespective of sense experience, would represent it; and accordingly to place in the reality as being actually there, independently of thought, distinctions which as a matter of fact may be merely the product of thought itself.

Scotists, by advocating an *actual* distinction between these grades of being, as "formalities" in the individual, have exposed themselves to the charge of extreme realism. They teach that each of these "formalities" has, for abstract thought, a *formal* unity which is *sui generis*. And this unity is not regarded as a product of thought, any more than the distinction between such unities. Thus, the materiality apprehended by thought in all material things is one, not because it is made one by the abstracting and universalizing activity of thought, as most if not all other scholastics teach; it is not merely *conceptually one* through our thought-activity, it is *formally one* apart from the latter; and it thus knits into a "formal" unity all material things. And so does "life" all living things; and "animality" all animals; and "rationality" all men. Now, if this "formal unity" of any such essential or metaphysical grade of being were regarded as a real unity, monism would be of course the logically inevitable corollary of the theory.

But the "formal" unity of any such essential grade of being Scotists will not admit to be a real unity, though they hold it to be characteristic of reality independently of our thought. They contend that this unity is quite compatible with the *real plurality* conferred upon being by the principles which individuate the latter; and thus they cannot be fairly accused of monism. Their reasoning here is characteristically subtle. Just as any metaphysical grade of being, considered as an object of thought, is in itself neither manifold individually nor one universally—so that, as Thomists say, designating it in this condition as the *universale directum*, or *metaphysicum*, or *fundamentale*, or *quoad rem conceptam*, we can truly affirm of it in this condition neither that it is one (logically, as a universal) nor that it is manifold (really, as multiplied in actual individuals),[160]—so likewise, Scotists contend, it is in this condition *ontologically*, as an entity in the real order independently of thought, and as such has a unity of its own, a formal unity, which, while uniting in a formal unity all the individuals that embody it, is itself incapable of fitting this grade of being for actual existence, and therefore admits those ultimate individuating principles which make it a real manifold in the actual order.[161]

Thus, the metaphysical grade of being, which, as considered in itself, Thomists hold to be an abstraction, having no other unity than that which thought confers upon it by making it logically universal, Scotists on the contrary hold to be as such something positive in the ontological order, having there a "formal" unity corresponding to the "conceptual" or "logical" unity which thought confers upon it by universalizing it. The metaphysical grade of being, thus conceived as something positive in the real order, Scotists will not admit to be a "reality," nor the unity which characterizes it a "real" unity. But after all, if such a "formality" with its proportionate "unity," is independent of thought; and if on the other hand "universality" is the work of thought, so that the universal as such cannot be real, it is not easy to see how the Scotist doctrine escapes the error of extreme realism. The metaphysical grade of being is a "formality" only because it is *made abstract* by thought; and it has "unity" only because it is *made logically universal* by thought; therefore to contend that as such it is something positive in the real order, independently of thought, is to "reify" the abstract and universal as such: which is extreme realism.

Chapter V.

Reality And The True.

40. ONTOLOGICAL TRUTH CONSIDERED FROM ANALYSIS OF EXPERIENCE.—
We have seen that when the mind thinks of any reality it apprehends it as "one," that ontological unity is a transcendental attribute of being; and this consideration led us to consider the manifoldness and the distinctions which characterize the totality of our experience. Now man himself is a real being surrounded by all the other real beings that constitute the universe. Moreover he finds himself endowed with faculties which bring him into conscious relations both with himself and with those other beings; and only by the proper interpretation of these relations can he understand aright his place in the universe. The first in order of these relations is that of reality to mind. This relation between mind and reality is what we understand by *Truth*.

Now truth is attributed both to knowledge and to things. We say that a person thinks or judges *truly*, that his knowledge is *true* (or correct, or accurate), when things really are as he thinks or judges them to be. The truth which we thus ascribe to knowledge, to the mind interpreting reality, is *logical* truth: a relation of concord or conformity of the mind interpreting reality—or, of the mind's judgment about reality—with the reality itself.[162] Logical truth is dealt with in Logic and Epistemology. We are concerned here only with the truth that is attributed to reality, to things themselves: ontological, metaphysical, transcendental truth, as it is called. There is nothing abstruse or far-fetched about the use of the terms "true" and "truth" as equivalent to "real" and "reality". We speak of "true" gold, a "true" friend, a "veritable" hero, etc. Now what do we mean by thus ascribing truth to a thing? We mean that it corresponds to a mental type or ideal. We call a liquid true wine or real wine, for instance, when it verifies in itself the definition we have formed of the nature of wine. Hence whenever we apply the terms "true" or "truth" to a thing we shall find that we are considering that thing not absolutely and in itself but in reference to an idea in our minds: we do not say of a thing simply that it is true, we say that it is *truly such or such* a thing, *i.e.* that it is really of a certain nature already conceived by our minds. If the appearance of the thing suggests comparison with some such ideal type or nature, and if the thing is seen on examination not really to verify this nature in itself, we say that it is not really or truly such or such a thing: *e.g.* that a certain liquid is not really wine, or is not true wine. When we have no such ideal type to which to refer a thing, when we do not know its nature, cannot classify and name it, we have to suspend our judgment and say that we do not know what the thing *really* is. Hence, for example, the new rays discovered by Röntgen were called provisionally "X rays," their real nature being at first unknown. We see, then, that real or ontological truth is simply reality considered as conformable with an ideal type, with an idea in the mind.

Whence does the human mind derive these ideal types, these concepts or definitions of the nature of things? It derives them from actually experienced reality by abstraction, comparison, generalization, and reflection on the data of its experience.[163] Hence it follows that the ontological truth of things is not known by the mind antecedently to the formation of the mental type. It is, of course, in the things antecedently to any judgment we form about the things; and the logical truth of our judgments is dependent on it, for logical truth is the conformity of our judgments with the real nature of things. But antecedently to all exercise of human thought, antecedently to our conception of the nature of a thing, the thing has not for us *formal* or *actual* ontological truth: it has only fundamental or *potential* ontological truth. If in this condition reality had actual ontological truth for us, there would be no ground for our distinguishing mentally between the reality and the truth of things; whereas the existence of this mental or logical distinction is undeniable. The concept of reality is the concept of something absolute; the concept of ontological truth is the concept of something relative, not of an absolute but of a relative property of being.

But if for the human mind the ontological truth of things is—at least proximately, immediately, and in the first place—their conformity with the abstract concepts of essences or natures, concepts derived by the mind from an analysis of its experience, how can this ontological truth be one for all men, or immutable and necessary? For, since men form different and divergent and conflicting conceptions as to the natures of things, and so have different views and standards of truth for things, ontological truth would seem, according to the exposition just outlined, to be not one but manifold, not immutable but variable: consequences which surely cannot be admitted? The answer to this difficulty will lead us to a deeper and more fundamental conception of what ontological truth really is.

First, then, we must consider that all men are endowed with the same sort of intellect, an intellect capable of some insight at least into the nature of things; that therefore they abstract the same transcendental notions and the same widest concepts from their experience: transcendental concepts of being, unity, truth, goodness; generic concepts of substance, matter, spirit, cause, of accident, quantity, multitude, number, identity, similarity, distinction, diversity, etc. They also form the same *specific* concepts of possible essences. Although, therefore, they may disagree and err in regard to *the application* of those concepts, especially of the lower, richer and more complex specific concepts, to the actual data of their experience, they agree in the fact that they have those common concepts or idea-types of reality; also in the fact that when they apply those concepts *rightly* (*i.e.* by *logically true* judgments) to the things that make up their experience, they have so far grasped the real natures of these things; and finally in recognizing that the ontological truth of these things lies in the conformity of the latter with their true and proper mental types or essences. And just as each of these latter is one, indivisible, immutable, necessary and eternal, so is the ontological truth of things, whether possible or actual, one, indivisible, immutable, necessary and eternal. Of course, just as the human mind does not constitute but only apprehends reality, so the human mind does not constitute the ontological truth of reality, but only apprehends it. Every reality is capable of producing in the human mind a more or less adequate mental representation of itself: in this lies what we may call the potential or fundamental ontological truth of reality. When it does produce such a mental concept of itself its relation of conformity to this concept is its formal ontological truth. Of course the human mind may err in applying to any reality a wrong concept; when it does it has so far failed to grasp the real nature of the thing and therefore the ontological truth which is really identical with this nature. But the thing still has its ontological truth, independently of the erring mind; not only fundamental truth, but also possibly formal truth in so far as it may be rightly apprehended, and thus related to its proper mental type, by other human minds. Reality itself, therefore, is not and cannot be false, as we shall see more fully later; error or falsity is an accident only of the mind interpreting reality.

41. ONTOLOGICAL TRUTH CONSIDERED SYNTHETICALLY, FROM THE STANDPOINT OF ITS ULTIMATE REAL BASIS.—So far we have explained ontological truth as a relation of reality to the human intelligence; but this relation is not one of dependence. The objective term of the relation, the reality itself, is anterior to the human mind, it is not constituted by the latter. The subjective term, the abstract concept, is indeed as a vital product dependent on the mind, but as representative of reality it is determined only by the latter. Is there, however, an Intelligence to which reality is *essentially* conformed, other than the human intelligence? Granted the actual existence of contingent realities, and granted that the human mind can derive from these realities rational principles which it sees to be necessarily and universally applicable to all the data of experience, we can demonstrate the existence of a Necessary Being, a First and Self-Existent Intelligence. Realizing, then, that God has created all things according to Infinite Wisdom, we can see that the essences of things are imitations of exemplar ideas in the Divine Mind. On the Divine Mind they depend essentially for their reality and intelligibility. It is because all created realities, including the human mind itself, are adumbrations of the Divine Essence, that they are intelligible to the human mind. Thus we see that in the ontological order, in the order of real gradation and

dependence among things, as distinct from the order of human experience,[164] the reason why reality has ontological truth for the human mind is because it is antecedently and essentially in accord with the Divine Mind from which it derives its intelligibility. Although, therefore, ontological truth is for us proximately and immediately the conformity of reality with our own conceptions, it is primarily and fundamentally the essential conformity of all reality with the Divine Mind. All reality, actual and possible, including the Divine Essence itself, is actually comprehended by the Divine Mind, is actually in conformity with the exemplar ideas in the Divine Mind, and has therefore ontological truth even independently of its relation to created minds; but "in the (impossible) hypothesis of the absence of all intellect, such a thing as truth would be inconceivable".[165]

The reason, therefore, why things are ontologically true for our minds, why our minds can apprehend their essences, why we can have any true knowledge about them, is in fact because both our minds and all things else, being expressions of the Divine Essence, are in essential conformity with the Divine Intellect. Not that we must know all this in order to have any logical truth, any true knowledge, about things; or in order to ascribe to things the ontological truth which consists in their conformity with our conception of their nature. The atheist can have a true knowledge of things and can recognize in them their conformity with his mental conception of their nature; only he is unaware of the real and fundamental reason why he can do so. Nor can he, of course, while denying the existence of God, rise to the fuller conception of ontological truth which consists in the essential conformity of all reality with the Divine Intellect, and its essential dependence on the latter for its intelligibility to the human intellect.

Naturally, it is this latter and fuller conception of ontological truth that has been at all times expounded by scholastic philosophers.[166] We may therefore, define ontological truth as *the essential conformity of reality, as an object of thought, with intellect, and primarily and especially with the Divine Intellect.*

The conformity of reality with the Divine Intellect is described as *essential* to reality, in the sense that the reality is dependent on the Divine Intellect for its intelligibility; it derives its intelligibility from the latter. The conformity of reality with the human intellect is also essential in the sense that *potential* conformity with the latter is inseparable from reality; it is an aspect really identical with, and only logically distinct from, the latter. But inasmuch as the *actual* conformity of reality with our human conception of it is contingent on the existence of human intelligences, and is not *ultimately* dependent on the latter, inasmuch as reality does not derive its intelligibility *ultimately* from this conception—seeing that rather this conception is derived from the reality and is ultimately dependent on the Divine Exemplar,—this conformity of reality with the human mind is sometimes spoken of as *accidental* to reality in contrast with the relation of dependence which exists between reality and the Divine Mind.

Bearing in mind that reality derives its intelligibility from its essential conformity with the Divine Mind, and that the human mind derives *its* truth from the reality, we can understand how it has been said of truth in general that it is first in the Uncreated Intellect, then in things, then in created intellects; that the primary source and measure of all truth is the Divine Intellect Itself Unmeasured, "mensurans, non mensuratus"; that created reality is measured by, or conformed with, the Divine Intellect, and is in turn the measure of the human intellect, conforming the latter with itself, "mensurans et mensurata"; and that, finally, the human intellect, measured by created reality and the Divine Mind, is itself the measure of no natural things but only of the products of human art, "intellectus noster ... non mensurans quidem res naturales, sed artificiales tantum".[167]

Is truth *one*, then, or is it *manifold*? Logical truth is manifold—multiplied by the number of created intelligences, and by the number of distinct cognitions in each. The primary ontological truth which consists in the conformity of all reality with the Divine Intellect is one: there is no real plurality of archetype ideas in the Divine Mind; they are manifold only to our imperfect human mode of thinking. The secondary ontological truth which consists in the conformity of things with the abstract concepts of created intelligences is conditioned by, and multiplied with, the manifoldness of the latter.[168]

Again to the question: Is truth *eternal* or *temporal?*—we reply in a similar way that the truth of the Divine comprehension of reality, actual and possible, is eternal, but that no other truth is eternal. There is no eternal truth outside of God. Created things are not eternal; and truth is consecutive on reality: where there is no reality there is no ontological truth: the conformity of things with human conceptions and the logical truth of the latter are both alike temporal.[169]

Finally, we may say that the truth of the Divine Intellect is *immutable*; and so is the essential conformity of all reality with the Divine Intellect. The change to which created reality is essentially subject is itself essentially conformed with the Divine Mind; it is, so to speak, part and parcel of the ontological truth of this reality in relation to the Divine Mind, and cannot therefore interfere with this ontological truth. When the acorn grows into the oak the whole process has its ontological truth; that of the acorn changes, not into falsity, but into another truth, that of the oak.[170] We see, then, that as things change, their truth does not change in the sense of being lost or giving place to falsity: the truth of one state changes to the truth of another while the ontological truth of the changing reality perseveres immutably.

The same immutability attaches to the truth of things in relation to the human mind: with the qualification, to which we shall return, that they may occasion false judgments in the human mind, and on that account be designated "false".

Finally, the logical truth which has its seat in created intelligences is *mutable*: it may be increased or diminished, acquired or lost.

42. ONTOLOGICAL TRUTH A TRANSCENDENTAL ATTRIBUTE OF REALITY.—From what has been said it will be apparent that ontological truth is a transcendental attribute of reality. That is to say, whatever is real, whether actual or possible, is ontologically true; or, in scholastic terminology, "*Omne ens est verum; Ens et verum convertuntur.* All being is true; The real and the true are convertible terms". For in the first place there is no mode or category of real being, of which the human mind actually thinks, to which it does not attribute ontological truth in the sense of conformity with the right human conception of it. Moreover, the proper object of the human intellect is reality; all true knowledge is knowledge of reality. Reality of itself is manifestly knowable, intelligible, and thus potentially or fundamentally true; and, on the other hand, intellect is, according to the measure of its capacity, a faculty of insight into all reality, into whatever is real: *intellectus potens fieri omnia; anima ... quodammodo fit omnia.*[171] Deny either of these postulates regarding the terms of the ontological relation, reality and mind, and all rational thought is instantly paralysed. Hence, in so far as a reality becomes an actual object of human knowledge it has formal ontological truth in relation both to the human mind and to the Divine Mind; while antecedently to human thought it is fundamentally true, or intelligible, to the human mind, and of course formally true in relation to the Divine Mind.

Thus we see that whatever is real is ontologically true; that ontological truth is really identical with real being; that, applied to the latter, it is not a mere extrinsic denomination, but signifies an intrinsic, positive aspect of reality, *viz.* the real, essential, or transcendental relation of all real being to Mind or Intellect: a relation which is logically or conceptually distinct from the notion of reality considered in itself.

43. ATTRIBUTION OF FALSITY TO REAL BEING.—If ontological truth is really identical with real being, if it is an essential aspect of the latter, a transcendental relation of reality to mind, it follows immediately that there can be no such thing as transcendental falsity: if whatever is real is ontologically true, then the ontologically false must be the unreal, must be nothingness. And this is really so: ontologically falsity *is* nothingness. We have, therefore, to discover the real meaning of attributing falsity to things, as when we speak of a false friend, false gold, false teeth, a false musical note, a false measure in poetry, etc.

First of all, then, it will be noted that each such object has its own real nature and character, its proper mental correlate, and, therefore, its ontological truth. The false friend is a true or real deceiver, or traitor, or coward, or whatever his real character may be; the false gold is true or real bronze, or alloy, or whatever it may be in reality; the false teeth are true or real ivory, or whatever substance they are made of; a false musical note is a true or real note but not the proper one in its actual setting; and so of a false measure in poetry. Next, when we thus ascribe falsity to a friend, or gold, or such like, we see that the epithet "false" is in reality merely transferred from the false judgment which a person is liable to make about the object. We mean that to judge that person a friend, or that substance gold, or those articles real teeth, would be to form a false judgment. We see that it is only in the judgment there can be falsity; but we transfer the epithet to the object because the object is likely to occasion the erroneous judgment in the fallible human mind, by reason of the resemblance of the object to something else which it really is not. We see, therefore, that falsity is not in the objects, but is transferred to them by a purely extrinsic denomination on account of appearances calculated to mislead. We commonly say, in such cases that "things mislead us," that "appearances deceive us". Things, however, do not deceive or mislead us *necessarily*, but only *accidentally*: they are the *occasions* of our allowing ourselves to be deceived: the fallibility and limitations of our own minds in interpreting reality are the real cause of our erroneous judgments.[172]

Secondly, there is another improper sense in which we attribute falsity to works of art which fail to realize the artist's ideal. In this sense we speak of a "false" note in music, a "false" measure in poetry, a "false" tint in painting, a "false" curve in sculpture or architecture. "False" here means defective, bad, wanting in perfection. The object being out of harmony with the ideal or design in the practical intellect of the artist, we describe it as "false" after the analogy of what takes place when we describe as "false gold" a substance which is out of harmony with the idea of gold in the speculative intellect. It is in relation to the speculative, not the practical, intellect, that things have ontological truth. All created things are, of course, as such, in conformity not only with the Divine Intellect considered as speculative, but also with the Divine Intellect considered as practical. For God, being omnipotent, does all things according to the designs of His Wisdom. For Him nothing is accidental, nothing happens by chance. But the world He has freely willed to create is not the best possible world. Both in the physical and in the moral order there are things and events which are defective, which fall short of their natural perfection. This defectiveness, which is properly physical or moral evil, is sometimes described as falsity, lying, vanity, etc., on account of the discrepancy between those things and the ideal of what they should be. But all such defective realities are known to be what they are by the Divine Mind, and may be known as they really are by the human mind. They have, therefore, their ontological truth. The question of their perfection or imperfection gives rise to the consideration of quite a different aspect of reality, namely its *goodness*. This, then, we must deal with in the next place.

Chapter VI.

Reality And The Good.

44. The Good as "Desirable" and as "Suitable".—The notion of the *good* (L. *bonum*; Gr. ἀγαθόν) is one of the most familiar of all notions. But like all other transcendental or widely generic concepts, the analysis of it opens up some fundamental questions. The princes of ancient Greek philosophy, Socrates, Plato and Aristotle, gave much anxious thought to its elucidation. The tentative gropings of Socrates involved an ambiguity which issued in the conflicting philosophies of Stoicism and Epicureanism. Nor did Plato succeed in bringing down from the clouds the "Idea of the Good" which he so devotedly worshipped as the Sun of the Intellectual World. It needed the more sober and searching analysis of the Stagyrite to bring to light the formula so universally accepted in after ages: The Good of beings is that which all desire: *Bonum est quod omnia appetunt*.[173] Let us try to reach the fundamental idea underlying the terms "good," "goodness," by some simple examples.

The child, deriving sensible pleasure from a sweetmeat, cries out: That is *good!* Whatever gratifies its senses, gives it sensible delight, it *likes* or *loves*. Such things it *desires*, *seeks*, *yearns for*, in their absence; and in their presence *enjoys*. At this stage the good means simply the *pleasure-giving*. But as reason develops the human being apprehends and describes as good not merely what is pleasure-giving, but whatever satisfies any natural need or craving, whether purely organic, or purely intellectual, or more widely human: food is good because it satisfies a physical, organic craving; knowledge is good because it satisfies a natural intellectual thirst; friendship is good because it satisfies a wider need of the heart. Here we notice a transition from "agreeable" in the sense of "pleasure-giving" to "agreeable" in the more proper sense of "suitable" or useful. The good is now conceived not in the narrow sense of what yields sensible pleasure but in the wider sense of that which is useful or suitable for the satisfaction of a natural tendency or need, that which is *the object of a natural tendency*.

Next, let us reflect, with Aristotle, that each of the individual persons and things that make up the world of our direct experience has an end towards which it naturally tends. There is a purpose in the existence of each. Each has a nature, *i.e.* an essence which is for it a principle of development, a source of all the functions and activities whereby it continually adapts itself to its environment and thereby continually fulfils the aim of its existence. By its very nature it tends towards its end along the proper line of its development.[174] In the world of conscious beings this natural tendency is properly called appetite: *sense appetite* of what is apprehended as good by sense cognition, and rational appetite or *will* in regard to what is apprehended as good by intellect or reason. In the world of unconscious things this natural tendency is a real tendency and is analogous to conscious appetite. Hence it is that Aristotle, taking in all grades of real being, describes the good as that which is the object of any natural tendency or "appetite" whatsoever: the good is the "*appetibile*" or "desirable," that which all things seek: *bonum est quod omnia appetunt.*

45. THE GOOD AS AN "END," "PERFECTING" THE "NATURE".—So far, we have analysed the notion of what is "good" *for some being*; and we have gathered that it implies what *suits* this being, what contributes to the latter's realization of its end. But we apply the term "good" to objects, and speak of their goodness, apart from their direct and immediate relation of helpfulness or suitability *for us*. When, for instance, we say of a watch that it is a *good* one, or of a soldier that he is a *good* soldier, what precisely do we mean by such attribution of goodness to things or persons? A little reflection will show that it is intelligible *only in reference to an end or purpose*. And we mean by it that the being we describe as good has the powers, qualities, equipments, which *fit it for its end or purpose*. A being is good whose nature is equipped and adapted for the realization of its natural end or purpose.

Thus we see that the notion of goodness is correlative with the notion of an end, towards which, or for which, a being has a natural tendency or desire. Without the concept of a nature as tending to realize an end or purpose, the notion of "the good" would be inexplicable.[175] And the two formulæ, "The good is that which beings desire, or towards which they naturally tend," and "The good is that which is adapted to the ends which beings have in their existence," really come to the same thing; the former statement resolving itself into the latter as the more fundamental. For the reason why anything is desirable, why it is the object of a natural tendency, is because it is good, and not *vice versa*. The description of the good as that which is desirable, "*Bonum est id quod est appetibile,*" is an *a posteriori* description, a description of cause by reference to effect.[176] A thing is desirable because it is good. Why then is it good, and therefore desirable? Because it *suits* the natural needs, and *is adapted* to the nature, of the being that desires it or tends towards it; because it *helps* this being, *agrees with* it, by contributing towards the realization of its end: *Bonum est id quod convenit naturæ appetentis*: The good is that which suits the nature of the being that desires it. The greatest good for a being is the realization of its end; and the means towards this are also good because they contribute to this realization.

No doubt, in beings endowed with consciousness the gradual realization of this natural tendency, by the normal functioning and development of their activities, is accompanied by pleasurable feeling. The latter is, in fact, not an end of action itself, but rather the natural concomitant, the effect and index, of the healthy and normal activity of the conscious being: *delectatio sequitur operationem debitam*. It is the pleasure felt in tending towards the good that reveals the good to the conscious agent: that is, taking pleasure in its wide sense as the feeling of well-being, of satisfaction with one's whole condition, activities and environment. Hence it is the anticipated pleasure, connected by past association with a certain line of action, that stimulates the conscious being to act in that way again. It is in the first instance because a certain operation or tendency is felt to be *pleasing* that it is desired, and apprehended as *desirable*. Nor does the brute beast recognize or respond to any stimulus of action other than pleasure. But man—endowed with reason, and reflecting on the relation between his own nature and the activities whereby he duly orients his life in his environment—must see that what is pleasure-giving or "agreeable" in the ordinary sense of this term is generally so because it is "agreeable" in the deeper sense of being "suitable to his nature," "adapted to his end," and therefore "good".

The good, then, is whatever suits the nature of a being tending towards its end: *bonum est conveniens naturæ appetentis*. In what precisely does this suitability consist? What suits any nature *perfects* that nature, and suits it precisely in so far as it perfects it. But whatever perfects a nature does so only because and in so far as it is *a realization of the end* towards which this nature tends. Here we reach a new notion, that of "perfecting" or "perfection," and one which is as essentially connected with the notion of "end" or "purpose," as the concept of the "good" itself is. Let us compare these notions of "goodness," "end," and "perfection". We have said that a watch or a soldier are good when they are adapted to their respective ends. But they are so only because the end itself is already good. And we may ask why any such end is itself good and therefore desirable. For example, why is the accurate indication of time good, or the defence of one's country? And obviously in such a series of questions we must come to something which is good and desirable in and for itself, for its own sake and not as leading and helping towards some remoter good. And this something which is good in and for itself is a last or ultimate end—an absolute, not a relative, good. There must be such an absolute good, such an ultimate end, if goodness in things is to be made intelligible at all. And it is only in so far as things tend towards this absolute good, and are adapted to it, that they can be termed good. The realization of this tendency of things towards the absolute good, or ultimate end, is what constitutes the goodness of those things, and it does so because it *perfects their natures*.

The end towards which any nature tends is the cause of this tendency, its *final* cause; and the influence of a final cause consists precisely in its goodness, *i.e.* in its power of actualizing and perfecting a nature. This influence of the good is sometimes described as the "diffusive" character of goodness: *Bonum est diffusivum sui.* Goodness tends to diffuse or communicate itself, to multiply or reproduce itself. This character, which we may recognize in the goodness of finite, created things, is explained in the philosophy of theism as being derived, with this goodness itself, from the uncreated goodness of God who is the Ultimate End and Supreme Good of all reality. Every creature has its own proper ultimate end and highest perfection in its being a manifestation, an expression, a shewing forth, of the Divine Goodness. It has its own actuality and goodness, distinct from, but dependent on, the Divine Goodness; but inasmuch as its goodness is an expression or imitation of the Divine Goodness, we may, by an *extrinsic* denomination, say that the creature is good *by the Divine Goodness*. In a similar way, and without any suspicion of pantheism, we may speak of the goodness of creatures as being a *participation* of the Divine Goodness.

46. THE PERFECT. ANALYSIS OF THE NOTION OF PERFECTION.—It is the realization of the end or object or purpose of a nature that perfects the latter, and so far formally constitutes the goodness of this nature. Now the notion of perfection is not exactly the same as the notion of goodness: although what is perfect is always good, what is good is not always perfect. The term "perfect" comes from the Latin *perficere, perfectum,* meaning fully made, thoroughly achieved, completed, finished. Strictly speaking, it is only finite being, potential being, capable of completion, that can be spoken of as *perfectible*, or, when fully actualized, *perfect.* But by universal usage the term has been extended to the reality of the Infinite Being: we speak of the latter as the Infinitely *Perfect* Being, not meaning that this Being has been "perfected," but that He is the purely Actual and Infinite Reality. Applied to any finite being, the term "perfect" means that this being has attained to the full actuality which we regard as its end, as the ideal of its natural capacity and tendency. The finite being is subject to change; it is not actualized all at once, but gradually; by the play of those active and passive powers which are rooted in its nature it is gradually actualized, and thus perfected, gaining more and more reality or being by the process. But what directs this process and determines the line of its tendency? The *good* which is the *end* of the being, the good towards which the being by its nature tends. This good, which is the term of the being's natural tendency—which is, in other words, its end—is the fundamental principle[177] which perfects the nature of the being, is the source and explanation of the process whereby this nature is perfected: *bonum est*

perfectivum: the good is the perfecting principle of reality. The end itself is "the good which perfects," *bonum quod;* the "perfecting" itself is the formal cause of the goodness of the being that is perfected, *bonum quo;* the being itself which is perfected, and therefore ameliorated or increased in goodness, is the *bonum cui.* In proportion, therefore, to the degree in which a being actually possesses the perfection due to its nature it is "good"; in so far as it lacks this perfection, it is wanting in goodness, or is, as we shall see, ontologically "bad" or "evil".

While, then, the notion of the "good" implies a relation of the appetite or natural tendency of a being towards its end, the notion of "perfection," or "perfecting," conveys to our minds actual reality simply, or the actualizing of reality. The term "perfection" is commonly used as synonymous with actual reality. In so far forth as a reality is actual we say it "has perfection". But we do not call it "perfect" *simply*, unless it has all the actuality we conceive to be due to its nature: so long as it lacks any of this it is only perfect *secundum quid, i.e.* in proportion to the actuality it does possess. Hence we define "the perfect" as *that which is actually lacking in nothing that is due to its nature.* The perfect is therefore not simply the good, but the complete or finished good; and it is even logically distinct from the latter, inasmuch as the actuality connoted by the former has added to it the relation to appetite connoted by the latter. Similarly "goodness" is logically distinct from "perfection" by adding the like relation to the latter. Although a thing has goodness in so far as it has perfection, and *vice versa*, still its perfection is its actuality simply, while its goodness is this actuality considered as the term of its natural appetite or tendency.

47. GRADES OF PERFECTION. REALITY AS STANDARD OF VALUE.—We may distinguish between stages of perfection in the changing reality of the same being, or grades of perfection in comparing with one another different classes or orders of being.

In one and the same being we may distinguish between what is called its *first* or *essential* perfection, which means its essence or nature considered as capable of realizing its purpose in existence by tending effectively towards its end; what is called its *intermediate* or *accidental* perfection, which consists in all the powers, faculties and functions whereby this tendency is gradually actualized; and what is called its *final* or *integral* perfection, which consists in its full actualization by complete attainment of its end.

Again, comparing with one another the individual beings that make up our experience, we classify them, we arrange them in a hierarchical order of relative "perfection," of inferiority or superiority, according to the different grades of reality or perfection which we think we apprehend in them. Thus, we look on living things as a higher, nobler, more perfect order of beings than non-living things, on animal life as a higher form of being than plant life, on intelligence as higher than instinct, on will as superior to sense appetite, on mind or spirit as nobler than matter, and so on. Now all such comparisons involve the apprehension of some standard of value. An estimation of relative values, or relative grades of perfection in things, is unintelligible except in reference to some such standard; it involves of necessity the intuition of such a standard. We feel sure that some at least of our appreciations are unquestionably correct: that man, for instance, is superior to the brute beast, and the latter superior to the plant; that the lowest manifestation of life—in the amœba, or whatever monocellular, microscopic germ may be the lowest—is higher on the scale of being than the highest expression of the mechanical, chemical and physical forces of the inorganic universe. And if we ask ourselves what is our standard of comparison, what is our test or measure, and why are we sure of our application of it in such cases, our only answer is that our standard of comparison is reality itself, actual being, perfection; that we rely implicitly on our intuition of such actual reality as manifested to us in varying grades or degrees within our experience; that without claiming to be infallible in our judgments of comparison, in our classifications of things, in our appreciations of their relative perfection, we may justly assume reality itself to be as such intelligible, and the human mind to be capable of obtaining some true and certain insight into the nature of reality.

48. THE GOOD, THE REAL, AND THE ACTUAL.—Having compared "perfection" with "goodness" and with "being," let us next compare the two latter notions with each other. We shall see presently that every actual being has its ontological goodness, that these are in reality identical. But there is a logical distinction between them. In the first place the term "being" is applied *par excellence* to substances rather than to accidents. But we do not commonly speak of an individual substance, a person or thing, as good in reference to essential or substantial perfection.[178] When we describe a man, or a machine, as "good," we mean that the man possesses those *accidental* perfections, those qualities and endowments, which are suitable to his nature as a man; that the machine possesses those properties which adapt it to its end. In the second place the notion of being is absolute; that of the good is relative, for it implies the notion not of reality simply but of reality as desirable, agreeable, suitable, as perfecting the nature of a subject, as being the end, or conducive to the end, towards which this nature tends. And since what thus *perfects* must be something not potential but actual, it follows that, unlike real truth, real goodness is identical not with potential, but only with actual reality. It is not an attribute of the abstract, possible essence, but only of the concrete, actually existing essence.[179]

From the fact that the notion of the good is relative it follows that the same thing can be simultaneously good and bad in different relations: "What is one man's meat is another man's poison".

49. KINDS OF GOODNESS; DIVISIONS OF THE GOOD.—(*a*) The goodness of a being may be considered in relation to this being itself, or to other beings. What is good for a being itself, what makes it intrinsically and formally good, *bonum sibi*, is whatever perfects it, and in the fullest sense the realization of its end. Hence we speak of a virtuous, upright man, whose conduct is in keeping with his nature and conducive to the realization of his end, as a good man. But a being may also be good to others, *bonum alteri*, by an extrinsic, active, effective goodness, inasmuch as by its action it may help other beings in the realization of their ends. In this sense, a beneficent man, who wishes the well-being of his fellow-men and helps them to realize this well-being, is called a good man. This kind of goodness is what is often nowadays styled *philanthropy*; in Christian ethics it is known as *charity*.

(*b*) We have described the good as the term or object of natural tendency or appetite. In the domain of beings not endowed with the power of conscious apprehension, determinism rules this natural tendency; this latter is always oriented towards the *real* good: it never acts amiss: it is always directed by the Divine Wisdom which has given to things their natures. But in the domain of conscious living agents this natural tendency is consequent on apprehension: it takes the form of instinctive animal appetite or of rational volition. And since this apprehension of the good may be erroneous, since what is not really good but evil may be apprehended as good, the appetite or will, which follows this apprehension—*nil volitum nisi praecognitum*—may be borne towards evil *sub ratione boni*. Hence the obvious distinction between *real good* and *apparent good*—*bonum verum* and *bonum apparens*.

(*c*) In reference to any individual subject—a man, for instance—it is manifest that *other* beings can be good for him in so far as any of them can be his end or a means to the attainment of his end. They are called in reference to him *objective goods*, and their goodness *objective goodness*. But it is equally clear that they are good for him only because he can perfect his own nature by somehow identifying or uniting himself with them, possessing, using, or enjoying them. This possession of the objective good constitutes what has been already referred to as *formal* or *subjective goodness*.[180]

(*d*) We have likewise already referred to the fact that in beings endowed with consciousness and appetite proper, whether sentient or rational, the function of possessing or attaining to what is objectively good, to what suits and perfects the nature of the subject, has for its natural concomitant a feeling of pleasure, satisfaction, well-being, delight, enjoyment. And we have observed that this pleasurable feeling may then become a stimulus to fresh desire, may indeed be desired for its own sake. Now this subjective, pleasure-giving possession of an objective good has been itself called by scholastics *bonum delectabile*—delectable or delight-giving good. The objective good itself considered as an end, and the perfecting of the subject by its attainment, have been called *bonum honestum*— good which is really and *absolutely* such *in itself*. While if the good in question is really such only when considered as a means to the attainment of an end, of something that is good in itself, the former is called *bonum utile*—useful good.[181]

In this important triple division *bonum honestum* is used in the wide sense in which it embraces any *real* good, whether physical or moral. As applied to man it would therefore embrace whatever perfects his physical life as well as whatever perfects his nature considered as a rational, and therefore moral, being. But in common usage it has been restricted to the latter, and is in this sense synonymous with *moral good, virtue*.[182]

Furthermore, a good which is an end, and therefore desirable for its own sake, whether it be physical or moral, can be at the same time a means to some higher good and desired for the sake of this latter. Hence St. Thomas, following Aristotle, reduces all the moral goods which are desirable in themselves to two kinds: that which is desirable only for itself, which is the last end, final felicity; and those which, while good in themselves, are also conducive to the former, and these are the virtues.[183]

When these various kinds of goodness are examined in reference to the nature, conduct and destiny of man, they raise a multitude of problems which belong properly to Ethics and Natural Theology. The fact that man has a composite nature which is the seat of various and conflicting tendencies, of the flesh and of the spirit; that he perceives in himself a "double law," a higher and a lower appetite; that he is subject to error in his apprehension of the good; that he apprehends a distinction between pleasure and duty; that he feels the latter to be the path to ultimate happiness,—all this accentuates the distinction between real and apparent good, between *bonum honestum, bonum utile*, and *bonum delectabile*. The existence of God is established in Natural Theology; and in Ethics, aided by Psychology, it is proved that no finite good can be the last end of man, that God, the Supreme, Infinite Good, is his last end, and that only in the possession of God by knowledge and love can man find his complete and final felicity.

50. GOODNESS A TRANSCENDENTAL ATTRIBUTE OF BEING.—We have shown that there is a logical distinction between the concept of "goodness" and that of "being". We have now to show that the distinction is not real, in other words, that goodness is a transcendental attribute of all actual reality, that all being, in so far

forth as it is actual, has goodness—transcendental or ontological goodness in the sense of *appetibility, desirability, suitability*, as already explained.

When the thesis is formulated in the traditional scholastic statement, "*Omne ens est bonum: All being is good*" it sounds a startling paradox. Surely it cannot be contended that everything is good? A cancer in the stomach is not good; lies are not good; yet these are actual realities; cancers exist and lies are told; therefore not every reality is good. This is unquestionably true. But it does not contradict the thesis rightly understood. The true meaning of the thesis is, not that every being is good in all respects, or possesses such goodness as would justify us in describing it as "good" in the ordinary sense, but that every being possesses some goodness: every being in so far as it has actuality has formal, intrinsic goodness, or is, in other words, the term or object of natural tendency or desire. This goodness, which we predicate of any and every actual being, may be (1) the term of the natural tendency or appetite of that being itself, *bonum sibi*, or (2) it may be conceivably the term of the appetite of some other being, *bonum alteri*. Let us see whether it can be shown that every actual being has goodness in one or both of these senses.

(1) *Bonum sibi.*—Is there any intelligible sense in which it can be said that the actuality of any and every existing being is *good for that being—bonum sibi*? There is. For if we recognize in every such being, as we must, a *nature*, a potentiality of further actualization, a tendency towards a state of fuller actuality which is its *end*; and if, furthermore, we recognize that every such being at any instant not merely *is* or exists, but is *becoming* or *changing*, and thereby tending effectively towards its end; we must admit not merely that the full attainment of its end (its integral or final perfection) is "desired" by, and "perfects," and is "good" for, that being's nature; but also that the partial realization of its end, or, in other words, the actuality it has at any instant in its changing condition of existence (its accidental or intermediate perfection) is similarly "good" for it; and even that its actual existence as compared with its mere possibility (its first or essential perfection) is "desirable" and "good" for its nature. Actually existing beings are intelligible only because they exist for some end or purpose, which, by their very existence, activities, operations, conduct, they tend to realize. If this be admitted we cannot deny that the full attainment of this end or purpose is "good" for them—suitable, desirable, agreeable, perfecting them. In so far as they fail in this purpose they are wanting in goodness, they are bad, evil. For the realization of their end their natures are endowed with appropriate powers, faculties, forces, by the normal functioning of which they gradually develop and grow in actuality. No real being is by nature inert or aimless; no real being is without its connatural faculties, forces and functions. But the natural result of all operation, of all action and interaction among things, is *actualization* of the potential, amelioration,

development, growth in perfection and goodness by gradual realization of ends. If by accident any of these powers is wanting, or acts amiss by failing to contribute its due perfection to the nature, there is in the being a proportionate want of goodness—it is so far bad, evil. But, even so, the nature of the thing preserves its fundamental orientation towards its end, towards the perfection natural to it, and struggles as it were against the evil—tries to make good the deficiency. A cancer in the stomach is never good *for the stomach*, or *for the living subject* of which the stomach is an organ. For the living being the cancer is an evil, a *failure* of one of the organs to discharge its functions normally, *an absence of a good, viz.* the healthy functioning of an organ. But the cancerous growth, considered in itself and for itself, biologically and chemically, has its own nature, purpose, tendencies, laws; nor can we deny that its development according to these laws is "good" for its specific nature,[184] *bonum sibi*.

It may be asked how can the *first* or *essential* perfection of an existing substance, which is nothing else than the actual existence of the nature itself, be conceived as "good" for this nature? It is so inasmuch as the actual existence of the substance is the first stage in the process by which the nature tends towards its end; an existing nature desires and tends towards the conservation of its own being;[185] hence the saying, "Self-preservation is the first law of nature"; and hence, too, the scholastic aphorism, "*Melius est esse quam non esse*".

The argument just outlined tends to show that every nature of which we can have direct experience, or in other words every finite, contingent nature, is *bonum sibi*, formally and intrinsically good for itself.

It is, of course, equally applicable to the Uncreated, Necessary Being Himself. The Infinite Actuality of the Divine Nature is essentially the term and end of the Divine Love. Therefore every actual being has intrinsic, formal goodness, whereby it is *bonum sibi, i.e.* its actuality is, in regard to its nature, really an object of tendency, desire, appetite, a something that really suits and perfects this nature. Thus understood, the thesis formulates no mere tautology. It makes a real assertion about real being; nor can the truth of this assertion be proved otherwise than by an argument based, as ours is, on the recognition of purpose, of final causality, of adaptation of means to ends, in the actual universe of our experience.

Notwithstanding all that has been said, it may still be asked why should those individual beings, whose existence we have claimed to be good for them, exist at all. It will be objected that there exist multitudes of beings whose existence is manifestly *not* good for them. Take, for instance, the case of the reprobate. If they wish their total annihilation, if they desire the total cessation of their being, rather than an existence of eternal punishment, they undoubtedly wish it *as a good*. Is annihilation or absolute non-existence *really* a good *for them*? *De facto* it is *for them*, considered *in their actual condition* which is *accidental to their nature*. Christ said of the scandal-giver what is surely true of the reprobate: "It were better for that man had he never been born". We may admit, therefore, that for the reprobate themselves simple non-existence is more desirable, and better, than their actual concrete state of existence as reprobate: because simple non-existence is for them the simple *negation* of their reality, whereas the absolute and irreparable loss of their last end, the total frustration of the purpose for which they came into being, is for them the greatest conceivable *privation*. But this condition of the reprobate is accidental to their nature, alien to the purpose of their being, a self-incurred failure, a deliberate thwarting of their natural tendency. It remains true, therefore, that their nature is good though incapable of progress, its purpose is good though frustrated. In so far as they have actual reality they have "essential" goodness. Their *natures* still tend towards self-conservation and the realization of their end. They form no *real* exception to the general truth that "it is better to be than not to be: *melius est esse quam non esse*". It is not annihilation as such that is desired by them, but only as a less evil alternative than the eternal privation of their last end.[186] If the evils accidentally and actually attaching to a certain state of existence make the continuance of *this state* undesirable for a being, it by no means follows that the continuance of this being in existence, simply and in itself, is less desirable than non-existence.

(2) BONUM ALTERI.—Even, however, if it were granted that the actual existence of some beings is not good for *themselves*, might it not nevertheless be good for *other beings*, and in relation to the general scheme of things? Is there not an intelligible sense in which *every* actual being is *bonum alteri*, good for other things? Here again the same experience of actual reality, which teaches us that each individual being has a nature whereby it tends to its own good as a particular end, also teaches us that in the general scheme of reality things are helpful to one another, nay, are intended by their interaction and co-operation with one another to subserve the wider end which is the good of the whole system of reality. There is little use in puzzling, as people sometimes do, over the *raison d'être* of individual things or classes of things in human experience, over the good or the evil of the existence of these things, over the question whether or not it would be better that these things should never have existed, until we have consulted not any isolated portion of human experience but *this experience as a whole*. In this we can find sufficient evidence for the prevalence of a beneficent purpose everywhere. Not that we can read this purpose in every detail of reality. Even when we have convinced ourselves that all creation is the work of a Supreme Being who is Infinite Goodness Itself, we cannot gain that full insight into the secret designs of His Providence, which would be needed in order to "justify His ways" in all things. But when we have convinced ourselves that the created universe exists

because God wills it, we can understand that every actual reality in it must be "good," as being an object or term of the Divine Will. Every created reality is thus *bonum alteri* inasmuch as it is good for God, not, of course, in the impossible sense of perfecting Him, but as an imitation and expression of the Goodness of the Divine Nature Itself. The experience which enables us to reach a knowledge of the existence and nature of God, the Creator, Conserver, and Providence of the actual universe, also teaches us that this universe can have no other ultimate end or good than God Himself, *i.e.* God's will to manifest His goodness by the extrinsic glory which consists in the knowledge and love of Him by His rational creatures. The omnipotence of the Creator, His freedom in creating, and our knowledge of the universe He has actually chosen to create from among indefinite possible worlds, all alike convince us that the actual world is neither the best possible nor the worst possible, *absolutely* speaking. But our knowledge of His wisdom and power also convinces us that for the purpose of manifesting His glory in the measure and degree in which He has actually chosen to manifest it by creating the existing universe, and *relatively* to the attainment of this specific purpose, the existing universe is the best possible.

51. OPTIMISM AND PESSIMISM.—Those few outlines of the philosophy of theism—theses established in Natural Theology—will reveal to us the place of theism in relation to "optimist" and "pessimist" systems of philosophy. Pessimism, as an outcome of philosophical speculation, is the proclamation in some form or other of the conviction that human existence, nay, existence in general, is a failure, an evil. It is the analogue, in relation to will, of what scepticism is in relation to intellect; and it is no less self-contradictory than the latter. While the latter points to total paralysis of thought, the former involves a like paralysis of all will, all effort, all purpose in existence—a philosophy of despair, despondency, gloom. Both are equally erroneous, equally indicative of philosophical failure, equally repugnant to the normal, healthy mind. Optimism on the other hand is expressive of the conviction that good predominates in all existence: *melius est esse quam non esse*; that at the root of all reality there is a beneficent purpose which is ever being realized; that there is in things not merely a truth that can be known but a goodness that can be loved. Existence is not an evil, life is not a failure. This is a philosophy of hope, buoyancy, effort and attainment. But is it true, or is it an empty illusion? Well, to maintain that the actual universe is the best absolutely, would, of course, be absurd. If Leibniz's "Principle of Sufficient Reason" obliged him to contend, in face of the painfully palpable facts of physical and moral evil in the universe, that this universe is the best absolutely possible, the best that God could create, we can only say: so much the worse for his "Principle". The true optimism is that of the theist who, admitting the prevalence of evil in the universe, in the sense to be explained presently, at the same time holds that throughout creation the good predominates, that God's

beneficent purpose in regard to individuals does in the main prevail, and that His glory is manifested in giving to rational creatures the perfection and felicity of knowing and loving Himself. For the theist, then, the problem of the existence of evil in the universe assumes the general form of reconciling the fact of evil in God's creation with the fact of God's infinite power and goodness. This is a problem for Natural Theology. Here we have merely to indicate some general principles arising from the consideration of evil as the correlative and antithesis of goodness.

52. EVIL: ITS NATURE AND CAUSES. MANICHEISM.—Admitting the existence of evil in the universe, the scholastic apparently withdraws the admission forthwith by denying the reality of evil. The paradox explains itself by comparing the notions of good and evil, and thus trying to arrive at a proper conception of the latter.

If ontological goodness is really identical with actual being, if being is good in so far as it is actual, then it would appear that ontological evil must be identical with non-being, nothingness. And so it is, in the sense that no evil is a positive, actual reality, that all evil is an absence of reality. But just as the good, though really identical with the actual, is nevertheless logically distinct from the latter, so is evil logically distinct from nothingness, or the absence of reality. As we have seen, the good is that which perfects a nature, that which is due to a nature as the realization of the end of the latter. So, too, is evil the *privation* of any perfection due to a nature, the absence of something positive and something which ought to be present. Evil, therefore, is not a mere negation or absence of being; it is the absence of a good, or in other words the absence of a reality that should be present. All privation is negation, but not *vice versa*; for privation is the negation of something *due*: the absence of virtue is a mere negation in an animal, in man it is a privation. Hence the commonly accepted definition of evil: *Malum est privatio boni debiti. Evil is the privation of the goodness due to a thing.*[187] Evil is always, therefore, a defect, a deficiency. The notion of evil is a relative, not an absolute notion. As goodness is the right relation of a nature to its proper end, so is evil a failure, a defect in this relation: *Malum est privatio ordinis ad finem debitum.*[188]

The very finiteness of a finite being is the absence of further reality in this being; but as this further reality is not due to such a being, its absence, which has sometimes been improperly described as "metaphysical evil," is not rightly regarded as evil at all: except, indeed, we were to conceive it as happening to the Infinite Being Himself, which would be a contradiction in thought.

Evil, then, in its formal concept is nothing positive; it is essentially negative, or rather privative. For this very reason, when we consider evil in the concrete, *i.e.* as affecting actual things, as occurring in the actual universe—we can scarcely speak of it with propriety as "existing,"—we see that it essentially involves some positive, real subject which it affects, some nature which, by affecting, it renders so far evil. Cancer in the stomach is a real evil of the stomach, a defect, a deficiency, a failure, in the adaptation of the stomach to its proper end. It is not itself a positive, absolute, *evil entity*. In so far as it is itself a positive, physical reality, a growth of living cells, it has its own nature, its natural tendency, its development towards an end in accordance with biological laws: in all of which it verifies the definition of ontological goodness. But the existence of such a growth in the stomach is pathological, *i.e.* a disease of the stomach, a prevention of the natural, normal function of the stomach, a *failure of the latter's adaptation to its end*, and hence an *evil for the stomach*. Lying, too, is an evil, a moral evil of man as a moral subject. But this does not mean that the whole physical process of thinking, judging, speaking, whereby a man lies, is itself a positive evil entity. The thinking is itself good as a physical act. So is the speaking in itself good as a physical act. Whatever of positive reality there is in the whole process is good, ontologically good. But there is a *want of conformity* of the language with the thought, entailing a *privation* or *failure of adaptation* of the man as a moral subject with his end, with his real good; and in this failure of adaptation, this privation of goodness, lies the moral evil of lying.

Evil, then, has a *material* or subjective cause, *viz.* some positive, actual reality, which is good in so far forth as it is actual, but which is evil, or wanting in something due to it, in so far as the privation which we have called evil affects it.

But evil has no *formal* cause: formally it is not a reality but a privation: "evil has no formal cause, but is rather the privation of a form".[189]

Nor has evil any *final* cause, for it consists precisely in the failure of a being's natural tendency towards its end, in the want of adaptation of a nature to its end: "nor has evil a final cause, but is rather the privation of a being's due relation to its natural end".[190] Evil cannot be the natural result of a being's tendency towards its end, or a means to the attainment of this end. For that which is really an end must be good, and a means derives its goodness from the end to which it is a means. The good, because it is an end, or a means to an end, is desirable; and so, too, might evil be defined *a posteriori* as that which is the object of no natural tendency or desire, that from which all things are averse: *malum est quod nullum ens appetit, vel a quo omnia aversantur*. Nor can evil be itself an end, or be as such desired or desirable. Real evil is no doubt often sought and desired by conscious beings, sometimes physical evil, sometimes moral evil. But it is always desired and embraced as a good, *sub specie boni*, *i.e.* when apprehended as here and now good in the sense of gratifying, pleasure-giving, *bonum delectabile*. This is possible because *pleasure*, especially organic, sensible pleasure, as distinct from the state of real well-being which characterizes true *happiness*, is not the exclusive concomitant of seeking and possessing a *real* good: it often accompanies the seeking and possessing of a merely apparent good: and in such cases it is itself a merely apparent good, and in reality evil. The unfortunate man who commits suicide does not embrace evil as such. He wrongly judges death to be good, as being in his view a lesser evil than the miseries of his existence, and under this aspect of goodness he embraces death.

Finally we have to inquire whether evil has an *efficient* cause. Seeing that it is not merely a logical figment, seeing that it really affects actual things, that it really occurs in the actual universe, it must have a real source among the efficient causes of these actual things that make up the universe. It is undoubtedly due to the action of efficient causes, *i.e.* to the *failure*, the *defective* action, of efficient causes. But being itself something negative, a privation, it cannot properly be said to have an "efficient" cause; for the influence of an efficient cause is positive action, which in turn must have for its term something positive, something real, and therefore good. Hence St. Augustine very properly says that evil should be described as having a "*deficient*" cause rather than an "efficient" cause.[191] In other words, evil is not the direct, natural or normal result of the activity of efficient causes; for this result is always good. It must therefore be always an indirect, abnormal, accidental consequence of their activity. Let us see how this can be—firstly in regard to physical evil, then in regard to moral evil.

In the action of physical causes we may distinguish between the operative agencies themselves and the subjects in which the effects of these operations are produced. Sometimes the effect is wanting in due perfection, or is in other words imperfect, physically evil, because of some defect in the agencies: the statue may be defective because the sculptor is unskilled, or his instruments bad; offspring may be weak or malformed owing to some congenital or accidental weakness or unfitness in the parents. Sometimes the evil in the effect is traceable not to the agents but to the materials on which they have to work: the sculptor and his instruments may be perfect, but if there be a flaw in the marble the statue will be a failure; the educator may be efficient, but if the pupil be wanting in aptitude or application the results cannot be "good".

All this, however, does not carry us very far, for we must still inquire *why* are the agencies, or the materials, themselves defective. Moreover, physical evil sometimes occurs without any defect either in the agencies or in the materials. The effect produced may be incompatible with some minor perfection already in the subject; it can then be produced only at the sacrifice of this minor perfection: which sacrifice is for the subject *pro tanto* an evil. It is in the natural order of things that the production of a new "form" or perfection excludes the actuality of a pre-existing form or perfection. All nature is subject to change, and we have seen that all change is ruled by the law: *Generatio unius est corruptio alterius*. It might perhaps be said that this privation or supplanting of perfections in things by the actualization in these things of incompatible perfections, is inherent in the nature of things and essential to their finiteness—at least, if we regard the things not individually but as parts of a whole, as members of a system, as subserving a general scheme;—and that therefore such privation should not be regarded as physical evil proper, but rather as "metaphysical" evil, improperly so called. However we regard it, it can have no other first source than the Will of the Creator decreeing the actual order of the existing universe. And the same must be said of the physical evils proper that are incident to the actual order of things. These evils are "accidental" when considered in relation to the individual natures of the created agencies and materials. They are defects or failures of natural tendencies: were these natural tendencies always realized there would be no such evils. But they are not realized; and their "failure" or "evil" is not "accidental" in regard to God; for God has willed and created these agencies with natural tendencies which He has destined to be fulfilled not always and in every detail, but in such measure as will secure the actual order of the universe and show forth His perfections in the finite degree in which He has freely chosen to manifest these perfections. The world He has chosen to create is not the best absolutely possible: there are physical evils in it; but it is the best for the exact purpose for which He created it.

There is also moral evil in the universe. In comparison with moral evil, the physical defects in God's creation—physical pain and suffering, material privations and hardships, decay and death of living things—are not properly evils at all. At least they are not evils in the same profound sense as the deliberate turning away of the moral agent from God, his Last End and Ultimate Good, is an evil. For the physical evils incident to individual beings in the universe can be not only foreseen by God but accepted and approved, so to speak, by His Will, as subserving the realization of the total physical good which He wills in the universe; and as subordinate to, and instrumental in the realization of, the moral good of mankind: for it is obvious that in the all-wise designs of Providence physical evils such as pain, suffering, poverty, hunger, etc., may be the means of realizing moral goodness. But moral evil, on the contrary, or, in the language of Christian ethics, *Sin*—the conscious and deliberate rejection, by the free agent, of God who is his true good—though necessarily foreseen by God in the universe He has actually chosen to create, and therefore necessarily permitted by the Will of God consequently on this foresight, cannot have been and cannot be intended or approved by Him. Having created man an intelligent and free being, God could not will or decree the revolt of the latter from Himself. He loves essentially His own Infinite Goodness: were He to identify His Will with that of the sinning creature He would at the same time be turning away from His Goodness: which is a contradiction in terms. God, therefore, does not will moral evil. Nevertheless He permits it: otherwise it would not occur, for nothing can happen "against His will". He has permitted it by freely choosing to create this actual universe of rational and free creatures, foreseeing that they would sin. He could have created instead a universe of such beings, in which there would be no moral evil: for He is omnipotent. Into the secrets of His election it is not given to finite minds to penetrate. Acknowledging His Infinite Power, Wisdom and Goodness, realizing at the same time the finiteness of our faculties, we see how rational it is to bow down our minds with St. Paul and to exclaim in admiration: "O, the depth of the riches of the wisdom and of the knowledge of God! How incomprehensible are His judgments, and how unsearchable His ways!"[192]

If it be objected that God's permission of moral evil in the universe is really the cause of this evil, and makes God Himself responsible for sin and its consequences, a satisfactory answer is not far to seek. It is absolutely incompatible with God's Infinite Sanctity that He be responsible for sin and its consequences. For these the free will of the creature is *alone* responsible. The creation of intelligent beings, endowed with the power *freely* to love, honour and serve God, is the most marvellous of all God's works. Free will is the noblest endowment of a creature of God, as it is also the most mysterious. Man, who by his intelligence has the power to know God as his Supreme Good, has by his will the power *freely* to tend towards God and attain to the possession of God as his Last End. In so far as man sins, *i.e.* knowingly, deliberately, and freely violates the tendency of his nature towards God by turning away from Him, he and he alone is responsible for the consequences, because he has the power to accomplish what he knows to be God's design in his regard, and to be his true destiny and path to happiness—*viz.* that he tend towards union with God and the possession of God—and he deliberately fails to make use of this power. Such failure and its consequences are, therefore, his own; they leave absolutely untouched and unassailed the Infinite Goodness and Benevolence of God's eternal design in his regard.

In scholastic form, the objection is proposed and answered in this way: "The cause of a cause is the cause of the latter's effects; but God is the cause of man, and sin is the latter's effect; therefore God is the cause of sin". "That the cause of a *non-free* cause is the cause of the latter's effects, we admit. That the cause of a *free* cause is the cause of the latter's effects, at least in the sense of permitting, without intending and being thereby responsible for them, we also admit; always in the sense of intending and being responsible for them, we deny. The *positive effects* of a created free cause, those which the latter by nature is intended to produce, are attributable to the first cause or creator of the free cause, and the first cause is responsible for them. The *failures* of the created free cause to produce its natural and intended effects, are not due to the first cause; they are not intended by, nor attributable to, the first cause; nor is the latter responsible for them: they are failures of the free cause, and of him alone; though they are of course foreseen and permitted by the first cause or creator of the latter. The minor premiss of the objection we may admit—noting, however, that sin is not properly called an effect, but rather, like all evil, a *failure* of some cause to produce its connatural effect: it is a defect, a deficiency, a privation of some effect, of some positive perfection, which the cause ought naturally to have produced. The conclusion of the objection we distinguish, according to our analysis of the major premiss: God is the cause of sin in the proper sense of intending it, willing it, and producing it positively, and being thereby responsible for it, we deny; God is the cause of sin in the improper sense of merely foreseeing and permitting it as incidental to the universe He has actually willed and decreed to create, as occurring in this universe by the deliberate failure of free creatures to conform themselves to His primary benevolent intention in their regard, we may grant. And this Divine permission of moral evil cannot be shown to be incompatible with any attribute of the Divinity."

In the preceding paragraphs we have barely outlined the principles on which the philosophy of theism meets the problem of evil in the universe. We have made assumptions which it is the proper province of Natural Theology to establish, and to that department also we must refer the student for a fuller treatment of the whole problem.

It has been sometimes said that the fact of evil in the universe is one of the greatest difficulties against the philosophy of Theism. If this be taken as an insinuation that the fact of evil can be better explained—or even as well explained—on the assumptions of Pantheism, Monism, Manicheism, or any other philosophy besides Theism, it is false. If it means simply that in accounting for evil—whether on principles of Theism or of any other philosophy—we are forced to raise some ultimate questions in the face of which we must admit that we have come upon depths of mystery which the plummet of our finite intellects cannot hope to fathom, in this sense indeed the assertion may be admitted. As we have already hinted, even with the light of the Christian Revelation to aid the natural light of reason, there are questions about the existence and causes of evil which we may indeed ask, but which we cannot adequately answer. And obviously this is no reflection on Theism; while in the latter system we have a more intelligible and more satisfactory analysis of the problem than in any other philosophy.

Among the ancient Greek philosophers we find "matter" (ὕλη) identified with "vacuum" or "empty space" (τὸ κενόν) and this again with "nothingness" or non-being (τὸ μὴ νὸ). Now the concept of evil is the concept of something negative—a privation of goodness, of being or reality. Thus the notion of evil came to be associated with the notion of matter. But the latter notion is not really negative: it is that of a formless, chaotic, disorderly material. When, therefore, the Manicheans attributed a positive reality to evil—conceiving it as the principle of all disorder, strife, discord—they naturally regarded all matter as the expression of the Evil Principle, in opposition to soul or spirit as the expression of the Good Principle. The Manichean philosophy of Evil, a product of the early Christian centuries, has been perhaps the most notable alternative or rival system encountered by the theistic philosophy of Evil; for, notwithstanding the fantastic character of its conceptions Manicheism has reappeared and reasserted itself repeatedly in after ages, notably in the Middle Ages. Its prevalence has probably been due partly to the concreteness of its conceptions and partly to a certain analogy which they bear towards the conception of Satan and the fallen angels in Christian theology. In both cases there is the idea of conflict, strife, active and irreconcilable opposition, between the powers of good and the powers of evil. But there the analogy ends. While in Christian theology the powers of evil are presented as essentially subject to the Divine Omnipotence, in Manicheism the *Evil Principle*, the *Summum Malum*, is presented as a supreme, self-existent principle, essentially independent of, as well as antagonistic to, the Divine Being, the *Summum Bonum*. Since there is evil in the world, and since good cannot be the cause of evil—so the Manicheans argue—there must be an essentially Evil First Principle which is the primary source of all the evil in the universe, just as there is an essentially Good First Principle which is the source of all its good. Everything in the world—and especially man himself, composed of matter and spirit—is the expression and the theatre of the essential conflict which is being ever waged between the Good and the Evil Principle. Everywhere throughout the universe we find this dualism: between spirit and matter, light and darkness, order and disorder, etc.

From all that has been said in the preceding paragraphs regarding the nature and causes of good and evil the errors of the Manichean system will be apparent. Its fundamental error is the conception of evil as a positive entity. Evil is not a positive entity but a privation. And this being so, its occurrence does not demand a positive efficient cause. It can be explained and accounted for by deficiency or failure in causes that are good in so far forth as they are operative, but which have not all the goodness their nature demands. And we have seen how this failure of created causes is permitted by the First Cause, and is not incompatible with His Infinite Goodness.

Besides, the Manichean conception of an intrinsically evil cause, a cause that could produce only evil, is a contradiction in terms. The operation of an efficient cause must have a positive term: in so far as the term is positive it is good: and therefore its cause cannot have been totally evil, but must have been in some degree good. The crucial point in the whole debate is this, that we cannot conceive evil as a positive entity. By doing so we render reality unintelligible; we destroy the fundamental ground of any possible distinction between good and evil, thus rendering both alike inconceivable. Each is correlative to the other; we cannot understand the one without the other. If, therefore, goodness is an aspect of real being, and identical with reality, evil must be a negation of reality, and cannot be made intelligible otherwise.

Finally, the Manichean conception of two Supreme, Self-Existent, Independent First Principles is obviously self-contradictory. As is shown in Natural Theology, Being that is absolutely Supreme, Self-Existent and Necessary, must by Its very nature be unique: there could not be two such Beings.

Chapter VII.

Reality And The Beautiful.

53. THE CONCEPT OF THE BEAUTIFUL FROM THE STANDPOINT OF EXPERIENCE.—Truth and Goodness characterize reality as related to intellect and to will. Intimately connected with these notions is that of *the beautiful*,[193] which we must now briefly analyse. The fine arts have for their common object the expression of the beautiful; and the department of philosophy which studies these, the philosophy of the beautiful, is generally described as *Esthetics*.[194]

Like the terms "true" and "good," the term "beautiful" (καλόν; *pulchrum, beau, schön*, etc.) is familiar to all. To reach a definition of it let us question experience. What do men commonly mean when, face to face with some object or event, they say "That is *beautiful*"? They give expression to this sentiment in the presence of a natural object such as a landscape revealing mountain and valley, lake and river and plain and woodland, glowing in the golden glow of the setting sun; or in contemplating some work of art—painting, sculpture, architecture, music: the *Sistine Madonna*, the *Moses* of Michael Angelo, the Cathedral of *Notre Dame*, a symphony of Beethoven; or some literary masterpiece: Shakespeare's *Macbeth*, or Dante's *Divina Commedia*, or Newman's *Apologia*, or Kickham's *Knocknagow*. There are other things the sight of which arouses no such sentiment, but leaves us indifferent; and others again, the sight of which arouses a contrary sentiment, to which we give expression by designating them as "commonplace," "vulgar," "ugly". The sentiment in question is one of *pleasure* and *approval*, or of *displeasure* and *disapproval*.

Hence the first fact to note is that *the beautiful pleases us, affects us agreeably,* while the commonplace or the ugly leaves us indifferent or *displeases us, affects us disagreeably.*

But the *good* pleases us and affects us agreeably. Is the beautiful, then, identical with the good? No; the really beautiful is indeed always good; but not everything that is good is beautiful; nor is the pleasure aroused by the good identical with that aroused by the beautiful. Whatever gratifies the lower sense appetites and causes organic pleasure is good—*bonum delectabile*—but is not deemed beautiful. Eating and drinking, resting and sleeping, indulging the senses of touch, taste and smell, are indeed pleasure-giving, but they have no association with the beautiful. Again, the deformed child may be the object of the mother's special love. But the pleasure thus derived from the good, as the object of appetite, desire, delight, is not esthetic pleasure. If we examine the latter, the pleasure caused by the beautiful, we shall find that it is invariably a pleasure peculiar to *knowledge*, to apprehension, perception, imagination, contemplation. Hence in the domain of the senses we designate as "beautiful" only what can be apprehended by the two higher senses, seeing and hearing, which approximate most closely to intellect, and which, through the imagination, furnish data for *contemplation* to the intellect.[195] This brings us to St. Thomas's definition: *Pulchra sunt quæ visa placent*: those things are beautiful whose vision pleases us,—where vision is to be understood in the wide sense of apprehension, contemplation.[196] The owner of a beautiful demesne, or of an art treasure, may derive pleasure from his sense of proprietorship; but this is distinct from the esthetic pleasure that may be derived by others, no less than by himself, from the mere contemplation of those objects. Esthetic pleasure is disinterested: it springs from the mere *contemplation* of an object as beautiful; whereas the pleasure that springs from the object as good is an interested pleasure, a pleasure of *possession*. No doubt the beautiful is really identical with the good, though logically distinct from the latter.[197] The *orderliness* which we shall see to be the chief objective factor of beauty, is itself a perfection of the object, and as such is good and desirable. Hence the beautiful can be an object of interested desire, but only under the aspect of goodness. Under the aspect of beauty the object can excite only the disinterested esthetic pleasure of contemplation.

But if esthetic pleasure is derived from contemplation, is not this identifying the beautiful with the true, and supplanting art by science? Again the consequence is inadmissible; for not every pleasure peculiar to knowledge is esthetic. There is a pleasure in seeking and discovering truth, the pleasure which gratifies the scholar and the scientist: the pleasure of the philologist in tracing roots and paradigms, of the chemist in analysing unsavoury materials, of the anatomist in exploring the structure of organisms *post mortem*. But these things are not "beautiful". The really beautiful is indeed always true, but it cannot well be maintained that all truths are beautiful. That two and two are four is a truth, but in what intelligible sense could it be said to be beautiful?

But besides the scientific pleasure of seeking and discovering truth, there is the pleasure which comes from contemplating the object known. The aim of the scientist or scholar is *to discover truth*; that of the artist is, through knowledge to derive complacency from *contemplating the thing known*. The scientist or scholar may be also an artist, or *vice versa*; but the scientist's pleasure proper lies exclusively in discovering truth, whereas that of the artist lies in contemplating something apprehended, imagined, conceived. The artist is not concerned as to whether what he apprehends is real or imaginary, certain or conjectural, but only as to whether or how far the contemplation of it will arouse emotions of pleasure, admiration, enthusiasm; while the scientist's supreme concern is to know things, to see them as they are. The beautiful, then, is always true, either as actual or as ideal; but the true is beautiful only when it so reveals itself as to arouse in us the desire to see or hear it, to consider it, to dwell and rest in the contemplation of it.

Let us accept, then, the *a posteriori* definition of the beautiful as *that which it is pleasing to contemplate*; and before inquiring what precisely is it, on the side of the object, that makes the latter agreeable to contemplate, let us examine the subjective factors and conditions of esthetic experience.

54. THE ESTHETIC SENTIMENT. APPREHENSION OF THE BEAUTIFUL.—We have seen that both the appetitive and the cognitive faculties are involved in the experience of the beautiful. Contemplation implies cognition; while the feeling of pleasure, complacency, satisfaction, delight, indicates the operation of appetite or will. Now the notion of the beautiful, like all our notions, has its origin in sense experience; but it is itself suprasensible for it is reached by abstraction, and this is above the power of sense faculties. While the senses and imagination apprehend beautiful objects the intellect attains to that which makes these objects beautiful, to the *ratio pulchri* that is in them. No doubt, the perception or imagination of beautiful things, in nature or in art, produces as its natural concomitant, a feeling of sensible pleasure. To hear sweet music, to gaze on the brilliant variety of colours in a gorgeous pageant, to inhale delicious perfumes, to taste savoury dishes—all such experiences gratify the senses. But the feeling of such sensible pleasure is quite distinct from the esthetic enjoyment which accompanies the apprehension of the beautiful; though it is very often confounded with the latter. Such *sentient* states of agreeable feeling are mainly *passive*, organic, physiological; while esthetic enjoyment, the appreciation of the beautiful, is eminently *active*. It implies the operation of a suprasensible faculty, the *intelligence*; it accompanies

the reaction of the latter faculty to some appropriate objective stimulus of the suprasensible, intelligible order, to some "idea" embodied in the object of sense.[198]

The error of confounding esthetic enjoyment with mere organic sense pleasure is characteristic of all sensist and materialist philosophies. A feeling of sensible gratification always, no doubt, accompanies our apprehension and enjoyment of the beautiful; for just as man is not a merely sentient being so neither is he a pure intelligence. Beauty reaches him through the senses; in order that an object be beautiful for him, in order that the contemplation of it may please him, it must be in harmony with his whole *human* nature, which is both sentient and intelligent; it must, therefore, be agreeable to the senses and imagination as well as to the intellect. "There is no painting," writes M. Brunetière,[199] "but should be above all a joy to the eye! no music but should be a delight for the ear!" Otherwise we shall not apprehend in it the order, perfection, harmony, adaptation to human nature, whereby we pronounce an object beautiful and rejoice in the contemplation of it. And it is this intellectual activity that is properly esthetic. "What makes us consider a colour beautiful," writes Bossuet,[200] is the secret judgment we pronounce upon its adaptation to the eye which it pleases. Beautiful sounds, songs, cadences, have a similar adaptation to the ear. To apprehend this adaptation promptly and accurately is what is described as having a good ear, though properly speaking this judgment should be attributed to the intellect.

According to some the esthetic sentiment, the appreciation and enjoyment of the beautiful, is an exclusively subjective experience, an emotional state which has all its sources within the conscious subject, and which has no real, extramental correlative in things. According to others beauty is already in the extramental reality independently of any subjective conditions, and has no mental factors in its constitution as an object of experience. Both of these extreme views are erroneous. Esthetic pleasure, like all pleasure, is the natural concomitant of the full, orderly, normal exercise of the subject's conscious activities. These activities are called forth by, and exercised upon, some *object*. For esthetic pleasure there must be in the object something the contemplation of which will elicit such harmonious exercise of the faculties. Esthetic pleasure, therefore, cannot be purely subjective: there must be an objective factor in its realization. But on the other hand this objective factor cannot provoke esthetic enjoyment independently of the dispositions of the subject. It must be in harmony with those dispositions—cognitive, appetitive, affective, emotional, temperamental—in order to evoke such a mental view of the object that the contemplation of the latter will cause esthetic pleasure. And it is precisely because these dispositions, which are so variable from one individual to another, tinge and colour the mental view, while this in turn determines the quality of the esthetic judgment and feeling, that people disagree and dispute interminably about questions of beauty in art and nature. Herein beauty differs from truth. No doubt people dispute about the latter also; but at all events they recognize its objective character and the propriety of an appeal to the independent, impersonal standard of evidence. Not so, however, in regard to beauty: *De gustibus non est disputandum*: there is no disputing about tastes. The perception of beauty, the judgment that something is or is not beautiful, is the product of an act of *taste, i.e.* of the individual's intelligence affected by numerous concrete personal dispositions both of the sentient and of the spiritual order, not only cognitive and appetitive but temperamental and emotional. Moreover, besides this variety in subjective dispositions, we have to bear in mind the effects of artistic culture, of educating the taste. The eye and the ear, which are the two main channels of data for the intellect, can be made by training more delicate and exacting, so that the same level of esthetic appreciation can be maintained only by a constantly increasing measure of artistic stimulation. Finally, apart from all that a beautiful object *directly conveys* to us for contemplation, there is something more which it may *indirectly suggest*: it arouses a distinct activity of the imagination whereby we fill up, in our own individual degree and according to our own interpretation, what has not been actually supplied in it by nature or art.

All those influences account sufficiently for the subjectivity and variability of the esthetic sentiment, for diversity of artistic tastes among individuals, for the transitions of fashion in art from epoch to epoch and from race to race. But it must not be concluded that the subjective factors in the constitution of the beautiful are wholly changeable. Since human nature is fundamentally the same in all men there ought to be a fund of esthetic judgments and pleasures common to all; there ought to be in nature and in art some things which are recognized and enjoyed as beautiful by all. And there are such. In matters *of detail* the maxim holds: *De gustibus non disputandum*. But there are fundamental esthetic judgments for which it does not hold. Since men have a common nature, and since, as we shall see presently, there are recognizable and stable objective factors to determine esthetic judgments, there is a legitimate foundation on which to discuss and establish some esthetic canons of universal validity.

55. OBJECTIVE FACTORS IN THE CONSTITUTION OF THE BEAUTIFUL.—"Ask the artist," writes St. Augustine,[201] "whether beautiful things are beautiful because they please us, or rather please us because they are beautiful, and he will reply unhesitatingly that they please us because they are beautiful." What, then is it that makes them beautiful, and so causes the esthetic pleasure we experience in contemplating them? In order that an object produce pleasure of any sort in a conscious being it must evoke the exercise of this being's faculties; for the conscious condition which we describe as pleasure is always a reflex of conscious activity. Furthermore, this activity must be *full* and *intense* and *well-ordered*: if it

be excessive or defective, if it be ill-regulated, wrongly distributed among the faculties, it will not have pleasure for its reflex, but either indifference or pain.

Hence the object which evokes the esthetic pleasure of contemplation must in the *first* place be *complete* or *perfect* of its kind. The truncated statue, the stunted oak, the deformed animal, the crippled human being, are not beautiful. They are wanting in the integrity due to their nature.

But this is not enough. To be beautiful, the object must in the *second* place have a certain *largeness* or amplitude, a certain greatness or power, whereby it can act *energetically* on our cognitive faculties and stimulate them to *vigorous* action. The little, the trifling, the commonplace, the insignificant, evokes no feeling of admiration. The sight of a small pasture-field leaves us indifferent; but the vision of vast expanses of meadow and cornfield and woodland exhilarates us. A collection of petty hillocks is uninteresting, while the towering snow-clad Alps are magnificent. The multiplication table elicits no emotion; but the triumphant discovery and proof of some new truth in science, some far-reaching theorem that opens up new vistas of research or sheds a new light on long familiar facts, may fill the mind with ecstasies of pure esthetic enjoyment.[202] There is no moral beauty in helping up a child that has stumbled and fallen in the mud, but there is in risking one's life to save the child from burning or drowning. There must, then, be in the object a certain largeness which will secure energy of appeal to our cognitive faculties; but this energy must not be excessive, it must not dazzle, it must be in proportion to the capacity of our faculties.[203]

A *third* requisite for beauty is that the object be in itself *duly proportioned, orderly, well arranged.* Order generally may be defined as right or proper arrangement. We can see in things a twofold order, *dynamic,* or that of *subordination,* and *static,* or that of *co-ordination*: the right arrangement of means towards ends, and the right arrangement of parts in a whole, or members in a system. The former indicates the influence of *final* causes and expresses primarily the *goodness* of things. The latter is determined by the *formal* causes of things and expresses primarily their *beauty.* The order essential to beauty consists in this, that the manifold and distinct things or acts which contribute to it must form one whole. Hence order has been defined as *unity in variety*: *unitas in varietate*; variety being the material cause, and unity the formal cause, of order. But we can apprehend unity in a variety of things only on condition that they are *arranged, i.e.* that they show forth clearly to the mind a set of mutual relations which can be easily grasped. Why is it that things mutually related to one another in one way make up what we declare to be a chaotic jumble, while if related in another way we declare them to be orderly? Because unless these relations present themselves in a certain way they will fail to unify the manifold for us. We have an intellectual intuition of the numerical series; and of *proportion*, which is equality of numerical relations. In the domains of magnitude and multitude the mind naturally seeks to detect these proportions. So also in the domains of sensible qualities, such as sounds and colours, we have an analogous intuition of a qualitative series, and we naturally try to detect *harmony*, which is the gradation of qualitative relations in this series. The detection of *proportion* and *harmony* in a *variety* of things pleases us, because we are thus enabled to grasp the manifold as exhibiting *unity*; while the absence of these elements leaves us with the dissatisfied feeling of something wanting. Whether this be because order in things is the expression of an intelligent will, of purpose and design, and therefore calls forth our intelligent and volitional activity, with its consequent and connatural feeling of satisfaction, we do not inquire here. But certain it is that order is essential to beauty, that esthetic pleasure springs only from the contemplation of proportion and harmony, which give unity to variety.[204] And the explanation of this is not far to seek. For the full and vigorous exercise of contemplative activity we need objective variety. Whatever lacks variety, and stimulates us in one uniform manner, becomes monotonous and causes *ennui*. While on the other hand mere multiplicity distracts the mind, disperses and weakens attention, and begets fatigue. We must, therefore, have variety, but variety combined with the unity that will concentrate and sustain attention, and thus call forth the highest and keenest energy of intellectual activity. Hence the function of rhythm in music, poetry and oratory; of composition and perspective in painting; of design in architecture.

The more perfect the relations are which constitute order, the more *clearly* will the unity of the object *shine forth*; hence the more fully and easily will it be grasped, and the more intense the esthetic pleasure of contemplating it.

St. Thomas thus sums up the objective conditions of the beautiful: *integrity* or *perfection*, *proportion* or *harmony*, and *clarity* or *splendour*.[205]

56. SOME DEFINITIONS OF THE BEAUTIFUL.—An object is beautiful when its contemplation pleases us; and this takes place when the object, complete and entire in itself, possesses that order, harmony, proportion of parts, which will call forth the full and vigorous exercise of our cognitive activity. All this amounts to saying that the beauty of a thing is the *revelation or manifestation of its natural perfection*.[206] Perfection is thus the *foundation* of beauty; the showing forth of this perfection is what constitutes beauty *formally*. Every real being has a nature which constitutes it, and activities whereby it tends to realize the purpose of its existence. Now the perfection of any nature is manifested by the proportion of its constitutive parts and by the harmony of all its activities. Hence we see that order is essential to beauty because order shows forth the perfection of the beautiful. An

object is beautiful in the degree in which the proportion of its parts and the harmony of its activities show forth the perfection of its nature.

Thus, starting with the subjective, *a posteriori* definition of beauty from its effect: *beauty is that whose contemplation pleases us*—we have passed to the objective and natural definition of beauty by its properties: *beauty is the evident integrity, order, proportion and harmony, of an object*—and thence to what we may call the *a priori* or synthetic definition, which emphasizes the perfection revealed by the static and dynamic order of the thing: *the beauty of an object is the manifestation of its natural perfection by the proportion of its parts and the harmony of its activities.*[207]

A few samples of the many definitions that have been set forth by various authors will not be without interest. Vallet[208] defines beauty as *the splendour of perfection*. Other authors define it as *the splendour of order*. These definitions sacrifice clearness to brevity. Beauty is *the splendour of the true*. This definition, commonly attributed to Plato, but without reason, is inadequate and ambiguous. Cousin[209] defines beauty as *unity in variety*. This leaves out an essential element, the *clarity* or *clear manifestation* of order. Kant defines beauty as *the power an object possesses of giving free play to the imagination without transgressing the laws of the understanding*.[210] This definition emphasizes the necessary harmony of the beautiful with our cognitive faculties, and the fact that the esthetic sentiment is not capricious but subject to the laws of the understanding. It is, however, inadequate, in as much as it omits all reference to the objective factors of beauty.

57. CLASSIFICATIONS. THE BEAUTIFUL IN NATURE.—All real beauty is either *natural* or *artificial*. Natural beauty is that which characterizes what we call the "works of Nature" or the "works of God". Artificial beauty is the beauty of "works of art".

Again, just as we can distinguish the *real* beauty of the latter from the *ideal* beauty which the human artist conceives in his mind as its archetype and exemplar cause, so, too, we can distinguish between the real beauty of natural things and the ideal beauty of their uncreated archetypes in the Mind of the Divine Artist.

We know that the beauty of the human artist's ideal is superior to, and never fully realized in, that of the actually achieved product of his art. Is the same true of the natural beauty of God's works? That the works of God in general are beautiful cannot be denied; His Wisdom "spreads beauty abroad" throughout His works; He arranges all things according to weight and number and measure:*cum pondere, numero et mensura*; His Providence disposes all things strongly and sweetly: *fortiter et suaviter*. But while creatures, by revealing their own beauty, reflect the Uncreated beauty of God in the precise degree which He has willed from all eternity, it cannot be said that they all realize the beauty of their Divine Exemplars according to His primary purpose and decree. Since there is physical and moral evil in the universe, since there are beings which fail to realize their ends, to attain to the perfection of their natures, it follows that these beings are not beautiful. In so far forth as they have real being, and the goodness or perfection which is identical with their reality, it may be admitted that all real beings are *fundamentally* beautiful; for goodness or perfection is the foundation of beauty.[211] But in so far as they fail to realize the perfection due to their natures they lack even the foundation of beauty. Furthermore, in order that a thing which has the full perfection due to its nature be *formally* beautiful, it must actually show forth by the clearness of its proportions and the harmony of its activities the fulness of its natural perfections. But there is no need to prove that this is not universally verified in nature—or in art either. And hence we must infer that formal beauty is not a transcendental attribute of reality.[212]

Real beauty may be further divided into *material* or *sensible* or *physical*, and *intellectual* or *spiritual*. The former reveals itself to hearing, seeing and imagination; the latter can be apprehended only by intellect; but intellect depends for all its objects on the data of the imagination. The beauty of spiritual realities is of course of a higher, nobler and more excellent order than that of the realities of sense. The spiritual beauty which falls directly within human experience is that of the human spirit itself; from the soul and its experiences we can rise to an apprehension—analogical and inadequate—of the Beauty of the Infinite Being. In the soul itself we can distinguish two sources of beauty: what we may call its *natural* endowments such as intellect and will, and its *moral* dispositions, its perfections and excellences as a free, intelligent, moral agent—its *virtues*. Beauty of soul, especially the moral beauty of the virtuous soul, is incomparably more precious than beauty of body. The latter, of course, like all real beauty in God's creation, has its proper dignity as an expression and revelation, however faint and inadequate, of the Uncreated Beauty of the Deity. But inasmuch as it is so inferior to the moral beauty proper to man, in itself so frail and evanescent, in its influence on human passions so dangerous to virtue, we can understand why in the Proverbs of Solomon it is proclaimed to be vain and deceitful in contrast with the moral beauty of fearing the Lord: *Fallax gratia et vana est pulchritudo; mulier timens dominum ipsa laudabitur.*[213]

58. THE BEAUTIFUL IN ART. SCOPE AND FUNCTION OF THE FINE ARTS.—The expression of beauty is the aim of the fine arts. Art in general is "the proper conception of a work to be accomplished": "ars nihil aliud est quam recta ratio aliquorum operum faciendorum".[214] While the *mechanical* arts aim at the production of things useful, the *fine* arts aim at the production of things beautiful, *i.e.* of works which by their order, symmetry, harmony, splendour, etc., will give

such apt expression to human ideals of natural beauty as to elicit esthetic enjoyment in the highest possible degree. The artist, then, must be a faithful student and admirer of all natural beauty; not indeed to aim at exact reproduction or imitation of the latter; but to draw therefrom his inspiration and ideals. Even the most beautiful things of nature express only inadequately the ideal beauty which the human mind may gather from the study of them. This ideal is what the artist is ever struggling to express, with the ever-present and tormenting consciousness that the achievement of his highest effort will fall immeasurably short of giving adequate expression to it.

If each of the things of nature were so wholly simple and intelligible as to present the same ideal type of beauty to all, and leave no room for individual differences of interpretation, there would be no variety in the products of artistic genius, except indeed what would result from perfect or imperfect execution. But the things of nature are complex, and in part at least enigmatical; they present different aspects to different minds and suggest a variety of interpretations; they leave large scope to the play of the imagination both as to conception of the ideal itself and as to the arrangement and manipulation of the sensible materials in which the ideal is to find expression. By means of these two functions, *conception* and *expression*, the genius of the artist seeks to interpret and realize for us ideal types of natural beauty.

The qualities of a work of art, the conditions it must fulfil, are those already enumerated in regard to beauty generally. It must have unity, order, proportion of parts; it must be true to nature, not in the sense of a mere copy, but in the sense of drawing its inspiration from nature, and so helping us to understand and appreciate the beauties of nature; it must display a power and clearness of expression adjusted to the capacity of the normal mind.

We may add—as indicating the connexion of art with morality—that the work of art must not be such as to excite disapproval or cause pain by shocking any normal faculty, or running counter to any fundamental belief, sympathy, sentiment or feeling, of the human mind. The contemplation of the really beautiful, whether in nature or in art, ought *per se* to have an elevating, ennobling, refining influence on the mind. But the beautiful is not the good; nor does the cultivation of the fine arts necessarily enrich the mind *morally*. From the ethical point of view art is one of those indifferent things which the will can make morally good or morally evil. Since man is a moral being, no human interest can fall outside the moral sphere, or claim independence of the moral law; and art is a human interest. Neither the creator, nor the critic, nor the student of a work of art can claim that the latter, simply because it is a work of art, is neither morally good nor morally bad; or that he in his special relation to it is independent of the moral law.

Under the specious plea that science in seeking truth is neither positively moral nor positively immoral, but abstracts altogether from the quality of morality, it is sometimes claimed that, *a pari*, art in its pursuit of the beautiful should be held to abstract from moral distinctions and have no concern for moral good or evil. But in the first place, though science as such seeks simply the true, and in this sense abstracts from the good and the evil, still the man of science both in acquiring and communicating truth is bound by the moral law: he may not, under the plea that he is learning or teaching truth, do anything *morally wrong*, anything that will *forfeit or endanger moral rectitude*, whether in himself or in others. And in the second place, owing to the different relations of truth and beauty to moral goodness, we must deny the parity on which the argument rests. Truth appeals to the reason alone; beauty appeals to the senses, the heart, the will, the passions and emotions: "*Pulchrum trahit ad se desiderium*". The scientist expresses truth in abstract laws, definitions and formulas: a law of chemistry will help the farmer to fertilize the soil, or the anarchist to assassinate sovereigns. But the artist expresses beauty in concrete forms calculated to provoke emotions of esthetic enjoyment from the contemplation of them. Now there are other pleasure-giving emotions, sensual and carnal emotions, the indiscriminate excitement and unbridled indulgence of which the moral law condemns as evil; and if a work of art be of such a kind that it is directly calculated to excite them, the artist stands condemned by the moral law, and that even though his aim may have been to give expression to beauty and call forth esthetic enjoyment merely. If the preponderating influence of the artist's work on the normal human individual be a solicitation of the latter's nature towards what is evil, what is opposed to his real perfection, his moral progress, his last end, then that artist's work is not a work of art or truly beautiful. The net result of its appeal being evil and unhealthy, it cannot be itself a thing of beauty.

"Art for art's sake" is a cry that is now no longer novel. Taken literally it is unmeaning, for art is a means to an end—the expression of the beautiful; and a means as such cannot be "for its own sake". But it may signify that art should subserve no *extrinsic* purpose, professional or utilitarian; that it should be disinterested; that the artist must aim at the conception and expression of the beautiful through a disinterested admiration and enthusiasm for the beautiful. In this sense the formula expresses a principle which is absolutely true, and which asserts the noble mission of the artist to mankind. But the formula is also commonly understood to claim the emancipation of the artist from the bonds of morality, and his freedom to conceive and express beauty in whatever forms he pleases, whether these may aid men to virtue or solicit them to vice. This is the pernicious error to which we have just referred. And we may now add that this erroneous contention is not only ethically but also *artistically* unsound. For surely art ought to be based on truth: the artist should understand human nature, to which his work appeals: he should not regard as truly beautiful a work the contemplation of which will produce a *discord* in the soul, which will *disturb the right order* of the soul's activities, which will solicit the lower faculties to revolt against the higher; and this is what takes place when the artist ignores moral rectitude in the pursuit of his art: by despising the former he is false to the latter. He fails to realize that the work of art must be judged not merely in relation to the total *amount* of pleasure it may cause in those who contemplate it, but also in relation to the *quality* of this pleasure; and not merely in relation to esthetic pleasure, but in relation to the total effect, the whole concrete influence of the work on all the mental faculties. He fails to see that if this total influence is evil, the work that causes it cannot be good nor therefore really beautiful.

Are we to conclude, then, that the artist is bound to aim positively and always at producing a *good moral effect* through his work? By no means. Esthetic pleasure is, as we have said, indifferent. The pursuit of it, through the conception and expression of the beautiful, is the proper and intrinsic end of the fine arts, and is in itself legitimate so long as it does not run counter to the moral law. It has no need to run counter to the moral law, nor can it do so without defeating its own end. Outside its proper limits art ceases to be art; within its proper limits it has a noble and elevating mission; and it can serve indirectly but powerfully the interests of truth and goodness by helping men to substitute for the lower and grosser pleasures of sense the higher and purer esthetic pleasures which issue from the disinterested contemplation of the beautiful.

Chapter VIII.

The Categories Of Being. Substance And Accident.

59. THE CONCEPTION OF ULTIMATE CATEGORIES.—Having examined so far the notion of real being itself, which is the proper subject-matter of ontology, and those widest or transcendental notions which are coextensive with that of reality, we must next inquire into the various modes in which we find real being expressed, determined, actualized, as it falls within our experience. In other words, we must examine the *highest categories of being*, the *suprema genera entis*. Considered from the point of view of the logical arrangement of our concepts, each of these categories reveals itself as a primary and immediate limitation of the extension of the transcendental concept of real being itself. Each is ultimately distinct from the others in the sense that no two of them can be brought under any other as a genus, nor can we discover any intermediate notion between any one of them and the notion of being itself. The latter notion is not properly a genus of which they would be species, nor can it be predicated univocally of any two or more of them. Each is itself an ultimate genus, a *genus supremum*.

By using these notions as predicates of our judgments we are enabled to interpret things, to obtain a genuine if inadequate insight into reality; for we assume as established in the *Theory of Knowledge* that all our universal concepts have real and objective validity, that they give us real knowledge of the nature of those individual things which form the data of our sense experience. Hence the study of the categories, which is for Logic a classification of our widest concepts, become for Metaphysics an inquiry into the modes which characterize real being.[215] By determining what these modes are, by studying their characteristics, by tracing them through the data of experience, we advance in our knowledge of reality.

The most divergent views have prevailed among philosophers both as to what a category is or signifies, and as to what or how many the really ultimate categories are. Is a category, such as substance, or quality, or quantity, a mode of real being revealed to the knowing mind, as most ancient and medieval philosophers thought, with Aristotle and St. Thomas? or is it a mental mode imposed on reality by the knowing mind, as many modern philosophers have thought, with Kant and after him? It is for the Theory of Knowledge to examine this alternative; nor shall we discuss it here except very incidentally: for we shall assume as true the broad affirmative answer to the first alternative. That is to say, we shall hold that the mind is able to see, in the categories generally, modes of reality; rejecting the sceptical conclusions of Kantism in regard to the power of the Speculative Reason, and the principles which lead to such conclusions.

As to the number and classification of the ultimate categories, this is obviously a question which cannot be settled *a priori* by any such purely deductive analysis of the concept of being as Hegel seems to have attempted; but only *a posteriori*, *i.e.* by an analysis of experience in its broadest sense as including Matter and Spirit, Nature and Mind, Object and Subject of Thought, and even the Process of Thought itself. Moreover it is not surprising that with the progress of philosophical reflection, certain categories should have been studied more deeply at certain epochs than ever previously, that they should have been "discovered" so to speak, not of course in the sense that the human mind had not been previously in possession of them, but in the sense that because of closer study they furnished the mind with a richer and fuller power of "explaining" things. It is natural, too, that historians of philosophy, intent on tracing the movement of philosophic thought, should be inclined to over-emphasize the *relativity* of the categories, as regards their "explaining" value—their relativity to the general mentality of a certain epoch or period.[216] But there is danger here of confounding certain large *hypothetical conceptions*, which are found to yield valuable results at a certain stage in the progress of the sciences,[217] with the categories proper of real being. If the mind of man is of the same nature in all men, if it contemplates the same universe, if it is capable of reaching truth about this universe—real truth which is immutable,—then the modes of being which it apprehends in the universe, and by conceiving which it interprets the latter, must be in the universe as known, and must be there immutably. Nowhere do we find this more clearly illustrated than in the futility of the numerous attempts of modern philosophers to deny the reality of the category of *substance*, and to give an intelligible interpretation of experience without the aid of this category. We shall see that as a matter of fact it is impossible to deny *in thought* the reality of substance, or to think at all without it, however philosophers may have denied it *in language*,—or thought that they denied it when they only rejected some erroneous or indefensible meaning of the term.

60. THE ARISTOTELIAN CATEGORIES.—The first palpable distinction we observe in the data of experience is that between *substance* and *accident*. "We might naturally ask," writes Aristotle,[218] "whether what is signified by such terms as *walking, sitting, feeling well*, is a being (or reality).... And we might be inclined to doubt it, for no single one of such acts *exists by itself* (καθ' αὐτὸ πεφυκός), no one of them is separable from *substance* (οὐσία); it is rather to *him who* walks, or sits, or feels well, that we give the name of *being*. That which is a being *in the primary meaning of this term*, a being *simply and absolutely*, and not merely a being *in a certain sense*, or with a qualification, is substance—ὥστε τὸ πρώτως ὂν καὶ οὐ τὶ ὂν ἀλλ' ὂν ἁπλῶς ἡ οὐσία ἂν εἴν."[219] But manifestly, though substances, or what in ordinary language we call "persons" and "things"—men, animals, plants, minerals—are real beings in the fullest sense, nevertheless sitting, walking, thinking, willing, and actions generally, are also undoubtedly realities; so too are states and qualities; and shape, size, posture, etc. And yet we do not find any of these latter actually existing in themselves like substances, but only dependently on substances—on "persons" or "things" that think or walk or act, or are large or small, hot or cold, or have some shape or quality. They are all *accidents*, in contradistinction to substance.

It is far easier to distinguish between accidents and substance than to give an exhaustive list of the ultimate and irreducible classes of the former. Aristotle enumerates *nine*: Quantity (ποσόν), Quality (ποῖον), Relation (πρὸς τι), Action (ποιέιν), Passion (π άσχειν), Where (π οὗ), When (π οτέ), Posture (κεῖσθαι), External Condition or State (ἔχειν). Much has been said for and against the exhaustive character of this classification. Scholastics generally have defended and adopted it. St. Thomas gives the following reasoned analysis of it:[220] Since accidents may be distinguished by their relations to substance, we see that some affect substances intrinsically, others extrinsically; and in the former case, either absolutely or relatively: if relatively we have the category of *relation*; if absolutely we have either *quantity* or *quality* according as the accident affects the substance by reason of the matter, or the form, of the latter. What affects and denominates a substance extrinsically does so either as a cause, or as a measure, or otherwise. If as a cause, the substance is either *suffering* action, or *acting* itself; if as a measure, it denominates the subject as in *time*, or in *place*, or in regard to the relative position of its parts, its *posture*, in the place which it occupies. Finally, if the accident affects the substance extrinsically, though not as cause or as measure, but only as characterizing its external condition and immediate surroundings, as when we describe a man as clothed or armed, we have the category of *condition*.

It might be said that all this is more ingenious than convincing; but it is easier to criticize Aristotle's list than to suggest a better one. In addition to what we have said of it elsewhere,[221] a few remarks will be sufficient in the present context.

Some of the categories, as being of lesser importance, we may treat incidentally when dealing with the more important ones. *Ubi, Quando,* and *Situs,* together with the analysis of our notions of Space and Time, fall naturally into the general doctrine of *Quantity*. The final category, ἔχειν, however interpreted,[222] may be referred to *Quality, Quantity,* or *Relation*.

A more serious point for consideration is the fact, generally admitted by scholastics,[223] that one and the same real accident may belong to different categories if we regard it from different standpoints. *Actio* and *passio* are one and the same *motus* or change, regarded in relation to the agent and to the effect, respectively. *Place*, in regard to the located body belongs to the category *ubi*, whereabouts; in regard to the locating body it is an aspect of the latter's *quantity*. *Relation*, as we shall see, is probably not an entity really distinct from its foundation—quality, quantity, or causality. The reason alleged for this partial absence of real distinction between the Aristotelian categories is that they were thought out primarily from a logical point of view—that of predication.[224] And the reason is a satisfactory one, for real distinction is not necessary for diversity of predication. Then, where they are not really distinct entities these categories are at least aspects so fundamentally distinct and mutually irreducible that each of them is indeed a *summum genus* immediately under the concept of being in general.

It seems a bold claim to make for any scheme of categories, that it exhausts all the known modes of reality. We often experience objects of thought which seem at first sight incapable of reduction to any of Aristotle's *suprema genera*. But more mature reflection will always enable us to find a place for them. In order that any extrinsic denomination of a substance constitute a category distinct from those enumerated, it must affect the substance *in some real* way distinct from any of those nine; and it must moreover *be not a mere complex or aggregate* of two or more of the latter. Hence denominations which objects derive from the fact that they are terms of mental activities which are really immanent, *actiones "intentionales,"*—denominations such as "being known," "being loved,"—neither belong to the category of "*passio*" proper, nor do they constitute any distinct category. They are *entia rationis*, logical relations. Again, while efficient causation resolves itself into the categories of *actio* and *passio*, the causation of final, formal and material causes cannot be referred to these categories, but neither does it constitute any new category. The influence of a final cause consists in nothing more than its being a good which is the term of appetite or desire. The causation of the formal cause consists in its formally constituting the effect: it is always either a substantial or an accidental form, and so must be referred to the categories of substance, or quality, or quantity. Similarly material causality consists in this that the matter is a partial constitutive principle of the composite being; and it therefore refers us to the category of substance. It may be noted, too, that the ontological principles of a composite being—such as primal matter and substantial form—since they are themselves not properly "beings," but only "principles of being," are said to belong each to its proper category, not formally but only referentially, not *formaliter* but only *reductivé*. Finally, the various properties that are assigned to certain accidents themselves are either logical relations (such as "not having a contrary" or "being a measure"), or real relations, or intrinsic modes of the accident itself (as when a quality is said to have a certain "intensity"); but in all cases where they are not mere logical entities they will be found to come under one or other of the Aristotelian categories.

The "real being" which is thus "determined" into the supreme modes or categories of substance and accidents is, of course, "being" considered *substantially* as *essential* (whether possible or actual), and not merely being that is actually existent, *existential* being, in the *participial* sense. Furthermore, it is primarily finite or created being that is so determined. The Infinite Being is above the categories, *super*-substantial. It is because substance is the most perfect of the categories, and because the Infinite Being verifies in Himself in an incomprehensibly perfect manner all the perfections of substance, that we speak of Him as a substance: remembering always that these essentially finite human concepts are to be predicated of Him only *analogically*.

It may be inquired whether "accident" is a genus which should be predicated *univocally* of the nine Aristotelian categories as species? or is the concept of "accident" only *analogical*, so that these nine categories would be each a *summum genus* in the strict sense, *i.e.* an ultimate and immediate determination of the concept of "being" itself? We have seen already that the concept of "being" as applied to "substance" and "accident" is analogical. So, too, it is analogical as applied to the various categories of accidents. For the characteristic note of "accident," that of "affecting, inhering in" a subject, can scarcely be said to be verified "in the same way," "univocally," of the various kinds of accidents; it is therefore more probably correct not to regard "accident" as a genus proper, but to conceive each kind of accident as a *summum genus* coming immediately under the transcendental concept of "being".

61. THE PHENOMENIST ATTACK ON THE TRADITIONAL DOCTRINE OF SUBSTANCE.—Passing now to the question of the existence and nature of substances, and their relation to accidents, we shall find evidences of misunderstandings to which many philosophical errors may be ascribed at least in part. It is a fairly common contention that the distinction between substance and accident is really a groundless distinction; that we have experience merely of transient events or happenings, internal and external, with relations of coexistence or sequence between them; that it is an illusion to suppose, underlying these, an inert, abiding basis called "substance"; that this can be at best but a useless name for each of the collections of external and internal appearances which make up our total experience of the outer world and of our own minds. This is the general position of *phenomenists*. "What do you know of substance," they ask us, "except that it is an indeterminate and unknown something underlying phenomena? And even if you could prove its existence, what would it avail you, since in its nature it is, and must remain, unknown? No doubt the mind naturally supposes this 'something' underlying phenomena; but it is a mere mental fiction the reality of which cannot be proved, and the nature of which is admitted, even by some who believe in its real existence, to be unknowable."

Now there can be no doubt about the supreme importance of this question: all parties are pretty generally agreed that on the real or fictitious character of substance the very existence of genuine metaphysics in the traditional sense depends. And at first sight the possibility of such a controversy as the present one seems very strange. "Is it credible," asks Mercier,[225] "that thinkers of the first order, like Hume, Mill, Spencer, Kant, Wundt, Paulsen, Littré, Taine, should have failed to recognize the substantial character of things, and of the *Ego* or Self? Must they not have seen that they were placing themselves in open revolt against sound common sense? And on the other hand is it likely that the genius of Aristotle could have been duped by the naïve illusion which phenomenists must logically ascribe to him? Or that all those sincere and earnest teachers who adopted and preserved in scholastic philosophy for centuries the peripatetic distinction between substance and accidents should have been all utterly astray in interpreting an elementary fact of common sense?"

There must have been misunderstandings, possibly on both sides, and much waste of argument in refuting chimeras. Let us endeavour to find out what they are and how they gradually arose.

Phenomenism has had its origin in the *Idealism* which confines the human mind to a knowledge of its own states, proclaiming the unknowability of any reality other than these; and in the *Positivism* which admits the reality only of that which falls directly within external and internal sense experience. Descartes did not deny the substantiality of the soul, nor even of bodies; but his idealist theory of knowledge rendered suspect all information derived by his deductive, *a priori* method of reasoning from supposed innate ideas, regarding the nature and properties of bodies. Locke rejected the innatism of Descartes, ascribing to sense experience a positive rôle in the formation of our ideas, and proving conclusively that we have no such intuitive and deductively derived knowledge of real substances as Descartes contended for.[226] Locke himself did not deny the existence of substances,[227] any more than Descartes. But unfortunately he propounded the mistaken assumption of Idealism, that the mind can know only its own states; and also the error of thinking that because we have not an intuitive insight into the specific nature of individual substances we can know nothing at all through any channel about their nature: and he gathered from this latter error a general notion or definition of substance which is a distinct departure from what Aristotle and the medieval scholastics had traditionally understood by substance. For Locke substance is merely a supposed, but unknown, support for accidents.[228] Setting out with these two notions—that all objects of knowledge must be states or phases of mind, and that material substance is a supposed, but unknown and unknowable, substratum of the qualities revealed to our minds in the process of sense perception—it was easy for Berkeley to support by plausible arguments his denial of the reality of any such things as material substances. And it was just as easy, if somewhat more audacious, on the part of Hume to argue quite logically that if the supposed but unknowable substantial substratum of external sense phenomena is illusory, so likewise is the supposed substantial *Ego* which is thought to underlie and support the internal phenomena of consciousness.

Hume's rejection of substance is apparently complete and absolute, and is so interpreted by many of his disciples. But a thorough-going phenomenism is in reality impossible; no philosophers have ever succeeded in thinking out an intelligible theory of things without the concepts of "matter," and "spirit," and "things," and the "Ego" or "Self," however they may have tried to dispense with them; and these are concepts of substances. Hence there are those who doubt that Hume was serious in his elaborate reasoning away of substances. The fact is that Hume "reasoned away" substance only in the sense of an unknowable substratum of phenomena, and not in the sense of a something that exists in itself.[229] So far from denying the existence of entities that exist in themselves, he seems to have multiplied these beyond the wildest dreams of all previous philosophers *by substantializing accidents*.[230] What he does call into doubt is the capacity of the human mind to attain to a knowledge of the specific natures of such entities; and even here the arguments of phenomenism strike the false Cartesian theory of knowledge, rather than the sober and moderate teachings of scholasticism regarding the nature and limitations of our knowledge of substances.

62. The Scholastic View of our Knowledge in regard to the Existence and Nature of Substances.—What, then, are these latter teachings? That we have a direct, intellectual insight into the specific essence or nature of a corporeal substance such as gold, similar to our insight into the abstract essence of a triangle? By no means; Locke was quite right in rejecting the Cartesian claim to intuitions which were supposed to yield up all knowledge of things by "mathematical," *i.e.* deductive, *a priori* reasoning. The scholastic teaching is briefly as follows:—

First, as regards our knowledge of the *existence* of substances, and the manner in which we obtain our concept of substance. We get this concept from corporeal substances, and afterwards apply it to spiritual substances; so that our knowledge of the former is "immediate" only in the relative sense of being prior to the latter, not in the sense that it is a direct intuition of the natures of corporeal substances. We have no such direct insight into their natures. But our concept of them as actually existing is also immediate in the sense that *at first* we *spontaneously* conceive *every* object which comes before our consciousness *as something existing in itself*. The child apprehends each separate stimulant of its sense perception—resistance, colour, sound, etc.—as a "this" or a "that," *i.e.* as a separate something, existing there in itself; in other words it apprehends all realities as substances: not, of course, that the child has yet any reflex knowledge of what a substance is, but unknowingly it applies to all realities at first the concept which it undoubtedly possesses "something existing in itself". It likewise apprehends each such reality as "one" or "undivided in itself," and as "distinct from other things". Such is the child's immediate, direct, and implicit idea of substance. But if we are to believe Hume, what is true of the child remains true of the man: for the latter, too, "every perception is a substance, and every distinct part of a perception a distinct substance".[231] Nothing, however, could be more manifestly at variance with the facts. For as reason is developed and reflective analysis proceeds, the child most undoubtedly realizes that not everything that falls within its experience has the character of "a something existing in itself and distinct from other things". "Walking," "talking," and "actions" generally, it apprehends as realities,—as realities which, however, do *not* "exist in themselves," but in other beings, in the beings that "walk" and "talk" and "act". And these latter beings it still apprehends as "existing in themselves," and as thus differing from the former, which "exist not in themselves but in other things". Thus the child comes into possession of the notion of "accident," and of the further notion of "substance" as something which not only exists in itself (οὐσία, *ens in se subsistens*), but which is also a support or subject of accidents (ὑποκείμενον, *substans, substare*).[232] Nor, indeed, need the child's reason be very highly developed in order to realize that if experience furnishes it with "beings that do not exist in themselves," there must also be beings which do exist in themselves: that if "accidents" exist at all it would be unintelligible and self-contradictory to deny the existence of "substances".

Hence, *in the order of our experience* the first, *implicit* notion of substance is that of "something existing in itself" (οὐσία); the first *explicit* notion of it, however, is that by which it is apprehended as "a subject or support of accidents" (ὑποκείμενον, *sub-stare, substantia*); then by reflection we go back to the *explicit* notion of it as "something existing in itself". In the *real* or *ontological* order the perfection of "existing in itself" is manifestly more fundamental than that of "supporting accidents". It is in accordance with a natural law of language that we name things after the properties whereby they reveal themselves to us, rather than by names implying what is more fundamental and essential in them. "To exist in itself" is an absolute perfection, essential to substance; "to support accidents" is only a relative perfection; nor can we know *a priori* but a substance might perhaps exist without any accidents: we only know that accidents cannot exist without some substance, or subject, or power which will sustain them in existence.

Can substance be apprehended by the senses, or only by intellect? Strictly speaking, only by intellect: it is neither a "proper object" of any one sense, such as taste, or colour, or sound; nor a "common object" of more than one sense, as extension is with regard to sight and touch: it is, in scholastic language, not a "*sensibile per se*," not itself an object of sense knowledge, but only "*sensibile per accidens*," *i.e.* it may be said to be "accidentally" an object of sense because of its conjunction with accidents which are the proper objects of sense: so that when the senses perceive accidents what they are really perceiving is the substance affected by the accidents. But strictly and properly it is by intellect we consciously grasp that which in the reality is the substance: while the external and internal sense faculties make us aware of various qualities, activities, or other accidents external to the "self," or of various states and conditions of the "self," the intellect—which is a faculty of the same soul as the sense faculties—makes us simultaneously aware of corporeal substances actually existing outside us, or of the concrete substance of the "ego" or "self," existing and revealing itself to us in and through its conscious activities, as the substantial, abiding, and unifying subject and principle of these conscious activities.

Thus, then, do we attain to the concept of substance in general, to a conviction of the concrete actual existence of that mode of being the essential characteristic of which is "to exist in itself".

In the next place, how do we reach a knowledge of the *specific natures* of substances?[233] What is the character, and what are the limitations, of such knowledge? Here, especially, the very cautious and moderate doctrine of scholasticism has been largely misconceived and misrepresented by phenomenists and others. About the specific nature of substances we know just precisely what their accidents reveal to us—that and no more. We have no intuitive insight into their natures; all our knowledge here is abstractive and discursive. As are their properties—their activities, energies, qualities, and all their accidents—so is their nature. We know of the latter just what we can infer from the former. *Operari sequitur esse*; we have no other key than this to knowledge of their specific natures. We have experience of them only through their properties, their behaviour, their activities; analysis of this experience, *a posteriori* reasoning from it, inductive generalization based upon it: such are the only channels we possess, the only means at our disposal, for reaching a knowledge of their natures.

63. PHENOMENIST DIFFICULTIES AGAINST THIS VIEW. ITS VINDICATION.—Now the phenomenist will really grant all this. His only objection will be that such knowledge of substance is really no knowledge at all; or that, such as it is, it is useless. But surely the knowledge that this mode of being *really exists*, that there *is* a mode of being which "exists in itself," is already some knowledge, and genuine knowledge, of substance? No doubt, the information contained in this very indeterminate and generic concept is imperfect; but then it is only a starting point, an all-important starting point, however; for not only is it perfectible but every item of knowledge we gather from experience perfects it, whereas without it the intellect is paralysed in its attempt to interpret experience: indeed so indispensable is this concept of substance to the human mind that, as we have seen, no philosopher has ever been really able to dispense with it. When phenomenists say that what *we* call mind is only a bundle of perceptions and ideas; when they speak of the flow of events, which is *ourselves*, of which *we* are conscious,[234] the very language they themselves make use of cries out against their professed phenomenism. For why speak of "we," "ourselves," etc., if there be no "we" or "ourselves" other than the perceptions, ideas, events, etc., referred to?

Of course the explanation of this strange attitude on the part of these philosophers is simple enough; they have a wrong conception of substance and of the relation of accidents thereto; they appear to imagine that according to the traditional teaching nothing of all we can discover about accidents—or, as they prefer to term them, "phenomena"—can possibly throw any light upon the nature of substance: as if the rôle of phenomena were to cover up and conceal from us some sort of inner core (which they call substance), and not rather to reveal to us the nature of that "being, existing in itself," of which these phenomena are the properties and manifestations.

The denial of substance leads inevitably to the substantializing of accidents. It is possible that the manner in which some scholastics have spoken of accidents has facilitated this error.[235] Anyhow the error is one that leads inevitably to contradictions in thought itself. Mill, for instance, following out the arbitrary postulates of subjectivism and phenomenism, finally analysed all reality into present sensations of the individual consciousness, *plus* permanent possibilities of sensations. Now, consistently with the idealistic postulate, these "permanent possibilities" should be nothing more than a certain tone, colouring, quality of the "present" sensation, due to the fact that this has in it, as part and parcel of itself, feelings of memory and expectation; in which case the "present sensation," taken in its concrete fulness, would be the sole reality, and would exist in itself. This "solipsism" is the ultimate logical issue of subjective idealism, and it is a sufficient *reductio ad absurdum* of the whole system. Or else, to evade this issue, the "permanent possibilities" are supposed to be something really other than the "present sensations". In which case we must ask what Mill can mean by a "permanent *possibility*". Whether it be subjective or objective possibility, it is presumably, according to Mill's thought, some property or appurtenance of the individual consciousness, *i.e.* a quality proper to a subject or substance.[236] But to deny that the conscious subject is a substance, and at the same time to contend that it is a "permanent *possibility* of sensation," *i.e.* that it has properties which can appertain only to a substance, is simply to hold what is self-contradictory.

After these explanations it will be sufficient merely to state formally the proof that substances really exist. It is exceedingly simple, and its force will be appreciated from all that has been said so far: Whatever we become aware of as existing at all must exist either in itself, or by being sustained, supported in existence, in something else in which it inheres. If it exists in itself it is a substance; if not it is an accident, and then the "something else" which supports it, must in turn either exist in itself or in something else. But since an infinite regress in things existing not in themselves but in other things is impossible, we are forced to admit the reality of a mode of being which exists in itself—*viz.* substance.

Or, again, we are forced to admit the real existence of accidents—or, if you will, "phenomena" or "appearances"—*i.e.* of realities or modes of being whose nature is manifestly to modify or qualify in some way or other some subject in which they inhere. Can we conceive a *state* which is not a state of something? a phenomenon or appearance which is not an appearance of something? a vital act which is not an act of a living thing? a sensation, thought, desire, emotion, unless of some conscious being that feels, thinks, desires, experiences the emotion? No; and therefore since such accidental modes of being really exist, there exists also the substantial mode of being in which they inhere.

And the experienced realities which verify this notion of "substance" as the "mode of being which exists in itself," are manifestly *not one but manifold*. Individual "persons" and "things"—men, animals, plants—are all so many really and numerically distinct substances. So, too, are the ultimate individual elements in the inorganic universe, whatever these may be. Nor does the universal interaction of these individuals on one another, or their manifold forms of interdependence on one another throughout the course of their ever-changing existence and activities, interfere in any way with the substantiality of the mode of being of each. These mutual relations of all sorts, very real and actual as they undoubtedly are, only constitute the universe a *cosmos*, thus endowing it with *unity of order*, but not with *unity of substance*.

Let us now meet the objection of Hume: that there is no substantial soul distinct from its acts, that it is only the sum-total of the acts, each of these being a substance. The objection has been repeated in the metaphorical language in which Huxley and Taine speak of the soul, the living soul, as nothing more than a *republic* of conscious states, or the movement of a *luminous sheaf* etc. And Locke and Berkeley had already contended that an apple or an orange is nothing more than a collection or sum-total of sensible qualities, so that if we conceive these removed there is nothing left, for beyond these there was nothing there.

Now we admit that the substance of the soul is not *adequately* distinct from its acts, or the substance of the apple or orange from its qualities. As a matter of fact we never experience substance apart from accidents or accidents apart from substance;[237] we do not know whether there exists, or even whether there can exist, a created substance devoid of all accidents; nor can we know, from the light of reason alone, whether any accidents could exist apart from substance.[238] We have, therefore, no ground in natural experience for demonstrating such an *adequate* real distinctionbetween substance and accidents as would involve the separability of the latter from the former. But that the acts of the soul are so many really distinct entities, each "existing in itself," each therefore a substance, so that the term "soul" is merely a title we give to their sum-total; and similarly the terms "apple" and "orange" merely titles of collections of qualities each of which would be an entity existing in itself and really distinct from the others, each in other words a substance,—this we entirely deny. We regard it as utterly unreasonable of phenomenists thus to multiply substances. Our contention is that the individual soul or mind is one substance, and that it is *partially* and *really*, though *not adequately*, distinct from the various conscious acts, states, processes, functions, which are certainly themselves real entities,—entities, however, the reality of which is dependent on that of the soul, entities which this dependent or "inhering" mode of being marks off as distinct in their nature, and incapable of total identification with that other non-inhering or subsisting mode of being which characterizes the substance of the soul.

We cannot help thinking that this phenomenist denial of substance, with its consequent inevitable substantialization of accidents, is largely due to a mistaken manner of regarding the concrete existing object as a mere mechanical bundle of distinct and independent abstractions. Every aspect of it is mentally isolated from the others and held apart as an "impression," an "idea," etc. Then the object is supposed to be constituted by, and to consist of, a sum-total of these separate "elements," integrated together by some sort of mental chemistry. The attempt is next made to account for our total conscious experience of reality by a number of principles or laws of what is known as "association of ideas". And phenomenists discourse learnedly about these laws in apparent oblivion of the fact that by denying the reality of any substantial, abiding, self-identical soul, distinct from the transient conscious states of the passing moment, they have left out of account the only reality capable of "associating" any mental states, or making mental life at all intelligible. Once the soul is regarded merely as "a series of conscious states," or a "stream of consciousness," or a succession of "pulses of cognitive consciousness," such elementary facts as memory, unity of consciousness, the feeling of personal identity and personal responsibility, become absolutely inexplicable.[239]

Experience, therefore, does reveal to us the real existence of substances, of "things that exist in themselves," and likewise the reality of other modes of being which have their actuality only by inhering in the substances which they affect. "A substance," says St. Thomas, "is a thing whose nature it is to exist not in another, whereas an accident is a thing whose nature it is to exist in another."[240] Every concrete being that falls within our experience—a man, an oak, an apple—furnishes us with the data of these two concepts: the being existing in itself, the substance; and secondly, its accidents. The former concept comprises only constitutive principles which we see to be *essential* to that sort of being: the material, the vegetative, the sentient, the rational principle, in a man, or his soul and his body; the material principle and the formal or vital principle in an apple. The latter concept, that of accidents, comprises only those characteristics of the thing which are no doubt real, but which do not constitute the essence of the being, which can change or be absent without involving the destruction of that essence. An intellectual analysis of our experience enables us—and, as we have remarked above, it alone enables us—to distinguish between these two classes of objective concepts, the concept of the principles that are essential to the substance or being that exists in itself, and the concept of the attributes that are accidental to this being; and experience alone enables us, by studying the latter group, the accidents of the being, whether naturally separable or naturally inseparable from the latter, to infer from those accidents whatever we can know about the former group, about the principles that constitute the specific nature of the particular kind of substance that may be under investigation.

It may, perhaps, be urged against all this, that experience does *not* warrant our placing a *real* distinction between the entities we describe as "accidents" and those which we claim to be constitutive of the "substance," or "thing which exists in itself"; that all the entities without exception, which we apprehend by distinct concepts in any concrete existing being such as a man, an oak, or an apple, are only one and the same individual reality looked at under different aspects; that the distinction between them is only a logical or mental distinction; that we separate in thought what is one in reality because we regard each aspect in the abstract and apart from the others; that to suppose in any such concrete being the existence of two distinct modes of reality—*viz.* a reality that exists in itself, and other realities inhering in this latter—is simply to make the mistake of transferring to the real order of concrete things what we find in the logical order of conceptual abstractions.

This objection, which calls for serious consideration, leads to a different conclusion from the previous objection. It suggests the conclusion, not that substances are unreal, but that accidents are unreal. Even if it were valid it would leave untouched the existence of substances. We hope to meet it satisfactorily by establishing presently the existence of accidents really distinct from the substances in which they inhere. While the objection draws attention to the important truth that distinctions recognized in the conceptual order are not always real, it certainly does not prove that all accidents are only mentally distinct aspects of substance. For surely a man's thoughts, volitions, feelings, emotions, his conscious states generally, changing as they do from moment to moment, are not really identical with the man himself who continues to exist throughout this incessant change; yet they are realities, appearing and disappearing and having all their actuality in him, while he persists as an actual being "existing in himself".

64. ERRONEOUS VIEWS ON THE NATURE OF SUBSTANCE.—If we fail to remember that the notion of substance, as "a being existing in itself and supporting the accidents which affect it," is a most abstract and generic notion; if we transfer it in this abstract condition to the real order; if we imagine that the concrete individual substances which actually exist in the real order merely verify this widest notion and are devoid of all further content; that they possess in themselves no further richness of reality; if we forget that actual substances, in all the variety of their natures, as material, or living, or sentient, or rational and spiritual, are indeed full, vibrant, palpitating with manifold and diversified reality; if we rob them of all this perfection or locate it in their accidents as considered apart from themselves,—we are likely to form very erroneous notions both of

substances and of accidents, and of their real relations to one another. It will help us to form accurate concepts of them, concepts really warranted by experience, if we examine briefly some of the more remarkable misconceptions of substance that have at one time or other gained currency.

(*a*) Substance is not a concrete core on which concrete accidents are superimposed, or a sort of kernel of which they form the rind. Such a way of conceiving them is as misleading as it is crude and material. No doubt the language which, for want of better, we have to employ in regard to substance and accidents, suggests fancies of that kind: we speak of substance "supporting," "sustaining" accidents, and of these as "supported by," and "inhering in" the former. But this does not really signify any juxtaposition or superposition of concrete entities. The substance is a subject determinable by its various accidents; these are actualizations of its potentiality; its relation to them is the relation of the potential to the actual, of a "material" or "determinable" subject to "formal" or "determining" principles. But the appearance or disappearance of accidents never takes place in the same concrete subject: by their variations the concrete subject is changed: at any instant the substance affected by its accidents is one individual concrete being, and the inevitable result of any modification in them is that this individual, concrete being is changed, is no longer the same. No doubt, it preserves its substantial identity throughout accidental change, but not its concrete identity,—that is to say, not wholly. This is the characteristic of every finite being, subject to change and existing in time: it has the actuality of its being, not *tota simul*, but only gradually, successively. From this, too, we see that although substance is a more perfect mode of being than accident—because the former exists in itself while the latter has its actuality only in something else,—nevertheless, created, finite substance is a mode of being which is itself imperfect, and perfectible by accidents: another illustration of the truth that all created perfection is only relative, not absolute. To the notion of "inherence" we shall return in connexion with our treatment of accidents.

(*b*) Again, substance is wrongly conceived as an *inert* substratum underlying accidents. This false notion appears to have originated with Descartes: he conceived the two great classes of created substances, matter and spirit, as essentially inert. For him, matter is simply a *res extensa*; extension in three dimensions constitutes its essence, and extension is of course inert: all motion is given to matter and conserved in it by God. Spirit or soul is simply a *res cogitans*, a being whose essence is thought; but in thinking spirit too is passive, for it simply receives ideas as wax does the impress of a seal. Nay, even when soul or spirit wills it is really inert or passive, for God puts all its volitions into it.[241] From these erroneous conceptions the earlier disciples of Descartes took the obvious step forward into Occasionalism; and to them likewise may be traced the conviction of many contemporary philosophers that the human soul—a being that is so eminently vital and active—cannot possibly be a substance: neither indeed could it be, if substance were anything like what Descartes conceived it to be. The German philosophers, Wundt and Paulsen, for example, argue that the soul cannot be a substance. But when we inquire what they mean by substance, what do we find? That with them the concept of substance applies only to the *corporeal* universe, where it properly signifies the atoms which are "the absolutely permanent substratum, qualitatively and quantitatively unchangeable, of all corporeal reality".[242] No wonder they would argue that the soul is not a substance!

No actually existing substance is inert. What is true, however, is this, that when we conceive a being as a substance, when we think of it under the abstract concept of substance, we of course abstract from its concrete existence as an active agent; in other words we consider it not from the *dynamic*, but from the *static* aspect, not as it is in the concrete, but as constituting an object of abstract thought: and so the error of Descartes seems to have been that already referred to,—the mistake of transferring to the real order conditions that obtain only in the logical order.

(*c*) To the Cartesian conception of substances as inert entities endowed only with motions communicated to them *ab extra*, the mechanical or atomist conception of reality, as it is called, Leibniz opposed the other extreme conception of substances as *essentially active entities*. For him substance is an *ens præditum vi agendi*: activity is the fundamental note in the concept of substance. These essentially active entities he conceived as being all *simple* and *unextended*, the corporeal no less than the spiritual ones. And he gave them the title of *monads*. It is unnecessary for our present purpose to go into any details of his ingenious dynamic theory of the universe as a vast system of these monads. We need only remark that while combating the theory of inert substances he himself erred in the opposite extreme. He conceived every monad as endowed essentially with active tendency or effort which is never without its effect,—an exclusively *immanent* effect, however, which is the constant result of constant immanent action: for he denied the possibility of transitive activity, *actio transiens*; and he conceived the immanent activity of the monad as being in its nature *perceptive*,[243] that is to say, *cognitive* or *representative*, in the sense that each monad, though "wrapt up in itself, doorless and windowless," if we may so describe it, nevertheless mirrors more or less inchoatively, vaguely, or clearly, all other monads, and is thus itself a miniature of the whole universe, a microcosm of the macrocosm. Apart from the fancifulness of his whole system, a fancifulness which is, however, perhaps more apparent than real, his conception of substance is much less objectionable than that of Descartes. For as a matter of fact every individual, actually existing substance is endowed with an internal directive tendency towards some term to be realized or attained by its activities. Every substance has a transcendental relation to the operations which are natural to it, and whereby it tends to realize the purpose of its being. But nevertheless substance should not be defined by action, for all action of created substances is an accident, not a substance; nor even by its transcendental relation to action, for when we conceive it under this aspect we conceive it as an *agent* or *cause*, not as a *substance* simply. The latter concept abstracts from action and reveals its object simply as "a reality existing in itself". When we think of a substance as a principle of action we describe it by the term *nature*.

(*d*) A very widespread notion of substance is the conception of it as a "*permanent,*" "*stable,*" "*persisting*" subject of "*transient,*" "*ephemeral*" realities called accidents or phenomena. This view of substance is mainly due to the influence of Kant's philosophy. According to his teaching we can think the succession of phenomena which appear to our sense consciousness only by the aid of a pure intuition in which our sensibility apprehends them, *viz. time*. Now the application of the category of substance to this pure intuition of our sensibility engenders a *schema* of the imagination, *viz.* the *persistence* of the object in time. Persistence, therefore, is for him the essential note of substance.

Herbert Spencer, too, has given apt expression to this widely prevalent notion: "Existence means nothing more than persistence; and hence in Mind that which persists in spite of all changes, and maintains the unity of the aggregate in defiance of all attempts to divide it, is that of which existence in the full sense of the word must be predicated—that which we must postulate as the substance of Mind in contradistinction to the varying forms it assumes. But if so, the impossibility of knowing the substance of Mind is manifest."[244]

Thus, substance is conceived as the unique but hidden and unknowable basis of all the phenomena which constitute the totality of human experience.

What is to be said of such a conception? There is just this much truth in it: that substance is *relatively* stable or permanent, *i.e.* in comparison with accidents; the latter cannot survive the destruction or disappearance of the substance in which they inhere, while a substance can persist through incessant change of its accidents. But accidents are not *absolutely* ephemeral, nor is substance *absolutely* permanent: were an accident to exist for ever it would not cease to be an accident, nor would a substance be any less a substance were it created and then instantaneously annihilated. But in the latter case the human mind could not apprehend the substance; for since all human cognitive experience takes place *in time*, which involves *duration*, the mind can apprehend a substance only on condition that the latter has some permanence, some appreciable duration in existence. This fact, too, explains in some measure the error of conceiving permanence as essential to a substance. But the error has another source also: Under the influence of subjective idealism philosophers have come to regard the individual's consciousness of his own self, the consciousness of the *Ego*, as the sole and unique source of our concept of substance. The passage we have just quoted from Spencer is an illustration. And since the spiritual principle of our conscious acts is a permanent principle which abides throughout all of them, thus explaining the unity of the individual human consciousness, those who conceive substance in general after the model of the *Ego*, naturally conceive it as an essentially stable subject of incessant and evanescent processes.

But it is quite arbitrary thus to conceive the *Ego* as the sole type of substance. Bodies are substances as well as spirits, matter as well as mind. And the permanence of corporeal substances is merely relative. Nevertheless they are really substances. The relative stability of spirit which is immortal, and the relative instability of matter which is corruptible, have nothing to do with the substantiality of either. Both alike are substances, for both alike have that mode of being which consists in their existing in themselves, and not by inhering in other things as accidents do.

(*e*) Spencer's conception of substance as the permanent, unknowable ground of phenomena, implies that substance is one, not manifold, and thus suggests the view of reality known as *Monism*. There is yet another mistaken notion of substance, the notion in which the well known pantheistic philosophy of Spinoza has had its origin. Spinoza appears to have given the ambiguous definition of Descartes—"*Substantia est res quae ita existit, ut nulla alia re indigeat ad existendum*"—an interpretation which narrowed its application down to the Necessary Being; for he defined substance in the following terms: "*Per substantiam intelligo id quod est in se et per se concipitur: hoc est, id cujus conceptus non indiget conceptu alterius rei a quo formari debeat*". By the ambiguous phrase, that substance "requires no other thing for existing," Descartes certainly meant to convey what has always been understood by the scholastic expression that substance "exists *in* itself". He certainly did not mean that substance is a reality which "exists *of* itself," *i.e.* that it is what scholastics mean by *Ens a se*, the Being that has its actuality from its own essence, by virtue of its very nature, and in absolute independence of all other being; for such Being is One alone, the Necessary Being, God Himself, whereas Descartes clearly held and taught the real existence of finite, created substances.[245] Yet Spinoza's definition of substance is applicable only to such a being that our concept of this being shows forth the actual existence of the latter as absolutely explained and accounted for by reference to the essence of this being itself, and independently of any reference to other being. In other words, it applies only to the Necessary Being. This conception of substance is the starting-point of Spinoza's pantheistic philosophy.

Now, the scholastic definition of substance and Spinoza's definition embody two entirely distinct notions. Spinoza's definition conveys what scholastics mean by the Self-Existent Being, *Ens a se*; and this the scholastics distinguish from caused or created being, *ens ab alio*. Both phrases refer formally and primarily, not to the mode of a being's existence when it does exist, but to the origin of this existence in relation to the being's essence; and specifically it marks the distinction between the Essence that is self-explaining, self-existent, essentially actual ("*a se*"), the Necessary Being, and essences that do not themselves explain or account for their own actual existence, essences that have not their actual existence from themselves or of themselves, essences that are in regard to their actual existence contingent or dependent, essences which, therefore, if they actually exist, can do so only dependently on some other being whence they have derived this existence ("*ab alio*") and on which they essentially depend for its continuance.

Not the least evil of Spinoza's definition is the confusion caused by gratuitously wresting an important philosophical term like *substance* from its traditional sense and using it with quite a different meaning; and the same is true in its measure of the other mistaken notions of substance which we have been examining. By defining substance as an *ens in se*, or *per se stans*, scholastic philosophers mean simply that substance does not depend *intrinsically* on any *subjective* or *material* cause in which its actuality would be supported; they do not mean to imply that it does not depend *extrinsically* on an efficient cause from which it has its actuality and by which it is conserved in being. They assert that all *created* substances, no less than all accidents, have their being "*ab alio*" from God; that they exist only by the Divine creation and conservation, and act only by the Divine *concursus* or concurrence; but while substances and accidents are both alike dependent on this extrinsic conserving and concurring influence of a Divine, Transcendent Being, substances are exempt from this other and distinct mode of dependence which characterizes accidents: intrinsic dependence on a subject in which they have their actuality.[246]

When we say that substance exists "*in* itself," obviously we do not attach to the preposition "*in*" any *local* signification, as a part existing "in" the whole. Nor do we mean that they exist "in" themselves in the same sense as they have their being "in" God. In a certain true sense all creatures exist "in" God: *In ipso enim vivimus, et movemur, et sumus* (Acts xxii., 28), in the sense that they are kept in being by His omnipresent conserving power. But He does not sustain them as a subject in which they inhere, as substance sustains the accidents which determine it, thereby giving expression to its concrete actuality.[247] By saying that substance exists "in itself" we mean to exclude the notion of its existing "in another" thing, as an accident does. And this we shall understand better by examining a little more closely this peculiar mode of being which characterizes accidents.

65. THE NATURE OF ACCIDENT. ITS RELATION TO SUBSTANCE. ITS CAUSES.—From all that has preceded we will have gathered the general notion of *accident* as that mode of real being which is found to have its reality, not by existing in itself, but by affecting, determining, some substance in which it inheres as in a subject. What do we mean by saying that accidents *inhere in* substances as their *subjects*? Here we must at once lay aside as erroneous the crude conception of something as located spatially within something else, as contained in container, as *e.g.* water in a vessel; and the equally crude conception of something being in something else as a part is in the whole, as *e.g.* an arm is in the body. Such imaginations are wholly misleading.

The actually existing substance has its being or reality; it is an actual essence. Each real accident of it is likewise a reality, and has an essence, distinct from that of the substance, yet not wholly independent of the latter: it is a determination of the determinable being of the substance, affecting or modifying the latter in some way or other, and having no other *raison d'être* than this rôle of actualizing in some specific way some receptive potentiality of the concrete substance. And since its reality is thus dependent on that of the substance which it affects, we cannot ascribe to it actual essence or being in the same sense as we ascribe this to substance, but only analogically[248]. Hence scholastics commonly teach that we ought to conceive an accident rather as an "entity *of an entity*," "ens *entis*," than as an entity simply; rather as inhering, indwelling, affecting (*in*-esse) some subject, than simply as existing itself (*esse*); as something whose essence is rather the determination, affection, modification of an essence than itself an essence proper, the term "essence" designating properly only a substance: *accidentis esse est inesse*.[249] This conception might, no doubt, if pressed too far, be inapplicable to absolute accidents, like quantity, which are something more than mere modifications of substance; but it rightly emphasizes the dependence of the reality of accident on that of substance, the non-substantial and "diminished" character of the "accident"-mode of being; it also helps to show that the "inherence" of accident in substance is a relation—of determining to determinable being—which is *sui generis*; and finally it puts us on our guard against the errors that may be, and have been, committed by conceiving accidents in the abstract and reasoning about them apart from their substances, as if they themselves were substances.

This "inherence" of accident in substance, this mode of being whereby it affects, determines or modifies the substance, differs from accident to accident; these, in fact, are classified into *suprema genera* by reason of their different ways of affecting substance. To this we shall return later. Here we may inquire, about this general relation of accident to substance, whether it is *essential* to an accident *actually to inhere in* a substance, if not immediately, then at least through the medium of some other accident. We suggest this latter alternative because as we shall see presently there are some accidents, such as colour, taste, shape, which immediately affect the *extension* of a body, and only through this the substance of the body itself. Now the ordinary course of nature never presents us with accidents except as inhering, mediately or immediately, in a substance. Nor is it probable that the natural light of our reason would ever suggest to us the possibility of an exception to this general law. But the Christian philosopher knows, from Divine Revelation, that in the Blessed Eucharist the *quantity* or *extension* of bread and wine, together with the taste, colour, form, etc., which affect this extension, *remain in existence* after their connatural substance of bread and wine has disappeared by transubstantiation. In the supernatural order of His providence God preserves these accidents in existence without a subject; but in this state, though they do not *actually inhere* in any substance, they *retain their natural aptitude and exigence* for such inherence. The Christian philosopher, therefore, will not define accident as "the mode of being which inheres in a subject," but as "the mode of being which *in the ordinary course of nature* inheres in a subject," or as "the mode of being which has *a natural exigence* to inhere in a subject". It is not *actual inherence*, but the *natural exigence to inhere*, that is essential to an accident as such.[250]

Furthermore, an accident needs a substance not formally *qua* substance, or as a mode of being naturally existing in itself; it needs a substance *as a subject* in which to inhere, which it will in some way affect, determine, qualify; but the subject in which it immediately inheres need not always be a substance: it may be some other accident, in which case both of course will naturally require some substance as their ultimate basis.

Comparing now the concept of accident with that of substance, we find that the latter is presupposed by the former; that the latter is prior *in thought* to the former; that we conceive accident as something over and above, something superadded to substance as subject. For instance, we can define matter and form without the prior concept of body, or animality and rationality without the prior concept of man; but we cannot define colour without the prior concept of body, or the faculty of speech without the prior concept of man.[251]

Substance, therefore, is prior *in thought* to accident; but is the substance itself also prior *temporally* (prior *tempore*) to its accidents? It is prior in time to some of them, no doubt; the individual human being is thus prior, for instance, to the knowledge he may acquire during life. But there is no reason for saying that a substance must be prior *in time* to *all* its accidents;[252] so far as we can discover, no created substance comes into existence devoid of all accidents: corporeal substance devoid of internal quantity, or spiritual substance devoid of intellect and will.

If prior in thought, though not necessarily in time, to its accidents, is a substance prior to its accidents *really, ontologically* (prior *natura*)? Yes; it is the real or ontological principle of its accidents; it sustains them, and they depend on it. It is a passive or material cause (using the term "material" in the wide sense, as applicable even to spiritual substances), or a receptive subject, determined in some way by them as formal principles. It is at the same time an efficient and passive cause of some of its own accidents: the soul is an efficient cause of its own immanent processes of thought and volition, and at the same time a passive principle of them, undergoing real change by their occurrence. Of others it is merely a receptive, determinable subject, of those, namely, which have an adequate and necessary foundation in its own essence, and which are called *properties* in the strict sense: without these it cannot exist, though they do not constitute its essence, or enter into the concept of the latter; but it is not prior to them in time, nor is it the *efficient cause* of them; it is, however, a real principle of them, an essence from the reality of which they necessarily result, and on which their own reality depends. Such, for instance, is the faculty of thought, or volition, or speech in regard to man.

The accident-mode of being is, therefore, a mode of being which determines a substance in some real way. Its *formal effect* is to give the substance some real and definite determination: not *esse simpliciter* but *esse tale*. With the substance it constitutes a concrete real being which is *unum per accidens*, not *unum per se*.

The accident has no *formal cause*: it is itself a "form" and its causality is that of a formal cause, which consists in its communicating itself to a subject, and, by its union therewith, constituting some new reality—in this case a concrete being endowed with "accidental" unity.

Accidents have of course, a *material cause*; not, however, in the sense of a *materia ex qua*, a material from which they are constituted, inasmuch as they are simple "forms"; but in the sense of a *subject* in which they are received and in which they inhere; and this "material cause" is, proximately or remotely, *substance*.

Substance also is the *final cause*, the *raison d'être*, of the reality of the accidental mode of being. Accidents exist for the perfecting of substances: *accidentia sunt propter substantiam*. As we have seen already, and as will appear more clearly later on, the fundamental reason for the reality of an accidental mode of being, really distinct from the created or finite substance (for the Infinite Substance has no accidents), is that the created substance is imperfect, limited in its actual perfection, does not exist *tota simul*, but develops, through a process of change in time, from its first or *essential* perfection, through *intermediate* perfections, till it reaches the *final* perfection of its being.

Have all accidents *efficient causes*? Those which are called common accidents as distinct from *proper* accidents or *properties* have undoubtedly efficient causes: the various agencies which produce real but accidental changes in the individual substances of the universe. *Proper* accidents, however, inasmuch as they of necessity exist simultaneously with the substances to which they belong, and flow from these substances by a necessity of the very essence of these latter, cannot be said to have any efficient causes other than those which contribute by their efficiency to the *substantial changes* by which these substances are brought into actual existence; nor can they be said to be *caused efficiently* by these substances themselves, but only to "flow" or "result" necessarily from the latter, inasmuch as they come into existence simultaneously with, but dependently on, these substances. Hence, while substances are universally regarded as *real principles* of their properties—as, for instance, the soul in regard to intellect and will, or corporeal substance in regard to quantity—they are not really efficient causes of their properties, *i.e.* they do not *produce* these properties by *action*. For these properties are antecedent to all *action* of the substance; nor can a created substance *act* by its *essence*, but only through active powers, or faculties, or forces, which meditate between the essence of a created substance and its actions, and which are the proximate principles of these actions, while the substance or nature is their remote principle. Hence the "properties" which necessarily result from a substance or nature, have as their efficient causes the agencies productive of the substance itself.[253]

66. MAIN DIVISIONS OF ACCIDENTS.—These considerations will help us to understand the significance of a few important divisions of accidents: into proper and common, inseparable and separable. We shall then be in a position to examine the nature of the distinction between accidents and substance, and to establish the existence of accidents really distinct from substance.

(*a*) The attributes which we affirm of substance, other than the notes constitutive of its essence, are divided into *proper* accidents, or *properties* in the strict sense (ἴδιον, *proprium*), and *common* accidents, or accidents in the more ordinary sense (συμβεβηκός, *ac-cidens*). A property is an accident which belongs exclusively to a certain class or kind of substance, and is found *always* in *all* members of that class, inasmuch as it has an adequate foundation in the nature of that substance and a necessary connexion therewith. Such, for instance, are the faculties of intellect and will in all spiritual beings; the faculties of speaking, laughing, weeping in man; the temporal and spatial mode of being which characterizes all created substances.[254] When regarded from the logical point of view, as attributes predicable of their substances considered as logical subjects, they are distinguished on the one hand from what constitutes the essence of this subject (as *genus, differentia, species*), but also on the other hand from those attributes which cannot be seen to have any absolutely necessary connexion with this subject. The latter attributes alone are called *logical accidents*, the test being the absence of a necessary connexion in thought with the logical subject.[255] But the former class, which are distinguished from "logical" accidents and called *logical properties* ("*propria*") are none the less *real accidents* when considered from the ontological standpoint; for they do not constitute the essence of the substance; they are outside the concept of the latter, and super-added—though necessarily—to it. Whether, however, all or any of these "properties," which philosophers thus classify as real or ontological accidents, "proper" accidents, of certain substances, are *really* distinct from the concrete, individual substances to which they belong, or are only aspects of the latter, "substantial modes," only *virtually* distinct in each case from the individual substance itself,—is another and more difficult question . Such a property is certainly not really separable from its substance; we cannot conceive either to exist really without the other; though we can by abstraction think, and reason, and speak, about either apart from the other.[256] Real inseparability is, however, regarded by scholastic philosophers as quite compatible with what they understand by a real distinction .

A *common* accident is one which has no such absolutely necessary connexion with its substance as a "property" has; one which, therefore, can be conceived as absent from the substance without thereby entailing the destruction of the latter's essence, or of anything bound up by a necessity of thought with this essence. And such common accidents are of two kinds.

They may be such that in the ordinary course of nature, and so far as its forces and laws are concerned, they are never found to be absent from their connatural substances—*inseparable* accidents. Thus the colour of the Ethiopian is an inseparable accident of his human nature as an Ethiopian; he is naturally black; but if born of Ethiopian parents he would still be an Ethiopian even if he happened to grow up white instead of black. We could not, however, conceive an Ethiopian, or any other human being, existing without the faculties (not the use) of intellect and will, or the faculty (not the organs, or the actual exercise of the faculty) of human speech.

Or common accidents may be such that they are sometimes present in their substances, and sometimes absent—*separable* accidents. These are by far the most numerous class of accidents: thinking, willing, talking, and actions generally; health or illness; virtues, vices, acquired habits; rest or motion, temperature, colour, form, location, etc.

(*b*) The next important division of accidents is that into mere *extrinsic denominations* and intrinsic accidents; the latter being subdivided into *modal* and *absolute* accidents, respectively.

An *absolute* accident is one which not merely affects its substance intrinsically, giving the latter an actual determination or mode of being, of some sort or other, but which has moreover some entity or reality proper to itself whereby it thus affects the substance, an entity really distinct from the essence of the substance thus determined by it. Such, for instance, are all vital activities of living things;[257] knowledge, and other acquired habits; quantity, the fundamental accident whereby corporeal substances are all capable of existing extended in space; and such sensible qualities and energies of matter as heat, colour, mechanical force, electrical energy, etc. Such, too, according to many, are intellect, will, and sense faculties in man.

There are, however, other intrinsic determinations of substance, other modifications of the latter, which do not seem to involve any new or additional reality in the substance, over and above the modification itself. Such, for instance, are motion, rest, external form or figure, in bodies. These are called *modal* accidents. They often affect not the substance itself immediately, but some absolute accident of the latter, and are hence called "accidental modes". Those enumerated are obviously modes of the quantity of bodies. Now the appearance or disappearance of such an accident in a substance undoubtedly involves a real change in the latter, and not merely in our thought; when a body moves, or comes to rest, or alters its form, there is a change in the reality as well as in our thought; and in this sense these accidents are real and intrinsic to their substances. Yet, though we cannot say that motion, rest, shape, etc., are really identical with the body and only mentally distinct aspects of it, at the same time neither can we say that by their appearance or disappearance the body gains or loses any reality other than an accidental determination of itself; whereas it does gain something more than this when it is heated, or electrified, or increased in quantity; just as a man who acquires knowledge, or virtue, is not only really modified, but is modified by real entities which he has acquired, not having actually possessed them before.

Finally, there are accidents which do not affect the substance intrinsically at all, which do not determine any real change in it, but merely give it an extrinsic denomination in relation to something outside it . Thus, while the *quality* of heat is an absolute accident in a body, the *action* whereby the latter heats neighbouring bodies is no new reality in the body itself, and produces no real change in the latter, but only gives it the extrinsic denomination of *heating* in reference to these other bodies in which the effect really takes place. Similarly the *location* of any corporeal substance in *space* or in *time* relatively to others in the space or time series—its *external* place (*ubi*) or time (*quando*), as they are called—or the relative position of its parts (*situs*) in the place occupied by it: these do not intrinsically determine it or confer upon it any intrinsic modification of its substance. Not, indeed, that they are mere *entia rationis*, mere logical fictions of our thought. They are realities, but not realities which affect the substances denominated from them; they are accidental modes of other substances, or of the absolute accidents of other substances. Finally, the accident which we call a "*real relation*" presupposes in its subject some absolute accident such as quantity or quality, or some real and intrinsic change determining these, or affecting the substance itself; but whether relation is itself a reality over and above such foundation, is a disputed question.

From these classifications of accidents it will be at once apparent that the general notion of accident, as a dependent mode of being, superadded to the essence of a substance and in some way determining the latter, is realized in widely different and merely analogical ways in the different ultimate classes of accidents.

67. REAL EXISTENCE OF ACCIDENTS. NATURE OF THE DISTINCTION BETWEEN ACCIDENTS AND SUBSTANCE.—It would be superfluous to prove the general proposition that accidents really exist. In establishing the real existence of substances we have seen that the real existence of some accidents at least has never been seriously denied. These are often called nowadays *phenomena*; and philosophers who have denied or doubted the real existence of substances have been called "phenomenists" simply because they have admitted the real existence only of these phenomena; though, if they were as logical as Hume they might have seen with him that such denial, so far from abolishing substance, could only lead to the substantializing of accidents.

But while undoubtedly there are realities which "exist in themselves," such as individual men, animals and plants, there is no reason for attributing this same mode of existence to entities such as the thoughts, volitions, emotions, virtues or vices, of the individual man; or the instinct, hunger, or illness of the dog; or the colour, perfume, or form of the rose. The concrete individual man, or dog, or rose, reveals itself to our minds as a substantial entity, affected with these various accidental entities which are really distinct from the substantial entity itself and from one another. Nay, in most of the instances just cited, they are physically separable from the substantial entity in which they inhere; not of course in the sense that they could actually exist without it, but in the sense that it can and does continue to exist actually without them ; for it continues to exist while they come and go, appear and disappear.[258] Of course the *concrete individual* man, or dog, or rose, does not continue to *exist actually unchanged*, and *totally* identical with itself throughout the change of accidents , for the accidents are part of the concrete individual reality; nay, even the substance itself of the concrete individual does not remain totally unaffected by the change of the accidents; because if they *really* affect it, as they do, their change cannot leave it totally unaffected; substance is not at all a changeless, concrete core, surrounded by an ever-changing rind or vesture of accidents; or a dark, hidden, immutable and inscrutable background of a panorama of phenomena. But though it is beyond all doubt really affected by the change of its accidents, it is also beyond all doubt independent of them in regard to the essential mode of its being, in as much as it exists and continues to exist in itself throughout all fluctuation of its accidents; while these on the other hand have only that essentially dependent mode of being whereby they are actual only by affecting and determining some subject in which they inhere and which supports their actuality.

The existence, therefore, of some accidents, which are not only really distinct but even physically separable from their substances, cannot reasonably be called into question. To deny the existence of such accidents, or, what comes to the same thing, their real distinction from substance, is to take up some one of these three equally untenable positions: that all the changes which take place within and around us are substantial changes; or, that there is no such thing as real change, all change being a mental illusion; or, that contradictory states can be affirmed of the same reality.[259]

But the nature of the real distinction between accidents and substance is not in all cases so easy to determine. Nor can we discuss the question here in reference to each *summum genus* of accident separately. Deferring to the chapter on *Relation* the question of the distinction of this particular accident from substance and the other categories, we may confine our attention here to the distinction between substance and the three classes of accidents we have called *extrinsic denominations*, *modal* accidents, and *absolute* accidents respectively. "There are accidents," writes Kleutgen,[260] "which place nothing and change nothing in the subject itself, but are ascribed to it by reason of some extrinsic thing; others, again, produce indeed in the subject itself some new mode of being, but without their existing in it as a new reality, distinct from its reality; others, finally, are themselves a new reality, and have thus a being which is proper to themselves, though this being is of course dependent on the substance. These latter alone can be *really* distinct from the substance, in the full sense in which a real distinction is that between thing and thing. Now Cartesian philosophers have denied that there are any such accidents as those of the latter class; rejecting the division of accidents into absolute and modal, they teach that all accidents are mere *modifications* or determinations of substance, that they consist solely of various locations and combinations of the ultimate parts of a substance, or relations of the latter to other substances."

Now all *extrinsic denominations* of a substance do seem on analysis ultimately to resolve themselves partly into relations of the latter to other substances, and partly into modal or absolute accidents of other substances. Hence we may confine our attention here to the distinction between these two classes of accident and their connatural substances.

And, approaching this question, it will be well for us to bear two things in mind. In the first place, our definitions both of substance and of accident are abstract and generic or universal. But the abstract and universal does not exist *as such*. The concrete, individual, actually existing substance is never *merely* "a being that naturally exists in itself," nor is the accident of such a substance *merely* a verification of its definition as "a being that naturally inheres in something else". In every case what really and actually exists is *the individual*, a being concreted of substance and accidents, a being which is ever and always a *real unity*, composite no doubt, but really one; and this no matter what sort of distinction we hold to obtain between the substance and its accidents. This is important; its significance will be better appreciated according as we examine the distinctions in question. Secondly, as scholastics understand a real distinction, this can obtain not merely between different "persons" or "things" which are separate from one another in time or space, but also between different constitutive principles of any one single concrete, composite, individual being . We have seen that they are not agreed as to whether the essence and the existence of any actual creature are really distinct or not . And it may help us to clear up our notion of "accident" if we advert here to their discussion of the question whether or not an accident ought to be regarded as having an existence of its own, an existence proper to itself.

Those who think that the distinction between essence and existence in created things is a real distinction, hold that accidents as such have no existence of their own, that they are actualized by the existence of the substance, or rather of the concrete, composite individual; that since the latter is a real unity—not a mere artificial aggregation of entities, but a being naturally one—it can have only one existence: *Impossibile est quod unius rei non sit unum esse*;[261] that by this one existence the concrete, composite essence of the substance, as affected and determined by its accidents, is actualized. They contend that if each of the principles, whether substantial or accidental, of a concrete individual being had its own existence, their union, no matter how intimate, could not form a natural unitary being, an individual, but only an aggregate of such beings. It is neither the matter, nor the form, nor the corporeal substance apart from its accidents, that exists: it is the substance completely determined by all its accidents and modes that is the proper subject of existence.[262] It alone is actualized, and that by *one* existence, which is the "ultimate actuality" of the concrete, composite, individual essence: *esse est ultimus actus*. Hence it is too, they urge, that an accident should be conceived not properly as "a being," but only as that whereby a being is such or such: *Accidens non est ens, sed ens entis*. But it cannot be so conceived if we attribute to it an existence of its own; for then it would be "a being" in the full and proper sense of the word.

This is the view of St. Thomas, and of Thomists generally. The arguments in support of it are serious, but not convincing. And the same may be said of the reasons adduced for the opposite view: that existence not being really distinct from essence, accidents in so far as they can be said to have an essence of their own have likewise an existence of their own.

Supporters of this view not only admit but maintain that the entity of a real, existing accident is a "diminished" entity, inasmuch as it is dependent in a sense in which a really existing substance is not dependent. They simply deny the Thomist assertion that substantial and accidental principles cannot combine to form a real and natural unit, an individual being, if each be accorded an existence appropriate and proportionate to its partial essence; nor indeed can Thomists *prove* this assertion. Moreover, if existence be not *really* distinct from essence, there is no more inconvenience in the claim that partial existences can combine to form one complete existence, *unum esse*, than in the Thomist claim that partial essences, such as substantial and accidental constitutive principles, can combine to form one complete essence, one individual subject of existence. Then, furthermore, it is urged that the substance exists prior *in time* to some of its accidents; that it is prior *in nature* to its properties, which are understood to *proceed* or *flow* from it; and that therefore its existence cannot be theirs, any more than its essence can be theirs. Finally, it is pointed out that since existence is the actuality of essence, the existence which actualizes a substance cannot be identical with that which actualizes an accident. At all events, whether the one existence of the concrete individual substance as determined by its accidents be as it were a simple and indivisible existential act, which actualizes the composite individual subject, as Thomists hold, or whether it be a composite existential act, really identical with the composite individual subject, as in the other view,[263] this concrete existence of the individual is constantly varying with the variation of the accidents of the individual. This is equally true on either view.

Inquiring into the distinction between substance and its intrinsic accidents, whether modal or absolute, we have first to remark that all accidents cannot possibly be reduced to relations; for if relation itself is something *extrinsic* to the things related, it must at least presuppose a real and *intrinsic* foundation or basis for itself in the things related. Local motion, for instance, is a change in the spatial relations of a body to other bodies. But it cannot be *merely* this. For if spatial relations are not mere subjective or mental fabrications, if they are in any intelligible sense *real*, then a change in them must involve a change of *something intrinsic* to the bodies concerned. Now Descartes, in denying the existence of *absolute* accidents, in reducing all accidents to *modes* of substances, understood by modes not any *intrinsic* determinations of substance, but only extrinsic determinations of the latter. All accidents of *material* substance were for him mere locations, arrangements, dispositions of its extended parts: extension being its essence. Similarly, all accidents of spiritual substance were for him mere modalities and mutual relations of its "thought" or "consciousness": this latter being for him the essence of spirit. We have here not only the error of identifying or confounding accidents such as thought and extension with their connatural substances, spirit and matter, but also the error of supposing that extrinsic relations and modes of a substance, and changes in these, can be real, without there being in the substances themselves any intrinsic, real, changeable accidents, which would account for the extrinsic relations and their changes. If there are no intrinsic accidents, really affecting and determining substances, and yet really distinct from the latter, then we must admit either that all change is an illusion or else that all change is substantial; and this is the dilemma that really confronts the Cartesian philosophy.

68. MODAL ACCIDENTS AND THE MODAL DISTINCTION.—The real distinction which we claim to exist between a substance and its intrinsic accidents is not the same in all cases: in regard to some accidents, which we have called intrinsic modes of the substance, it is a *minor* or *modal* real distinction; in regard to others which we have called absolute accidents, it is a *major* real distinction. Let us first consider the former.

The term *mode* has a variety of meanings, some very wide, some restricted. When one concept determines or limits another in any way we may call it a mode of the latter. If there is no real distinction between the determining and the determined thought-object, the mode is called a *metaphysical* mode: as rationality is of animality in man. Again, created things are all "modes" of being; and the various aspects of a creature may be called "modes" of the latter: as "finiteness" is a mode of every created being. We do not use the term in those wide senses in the present context. Here we understand by a mode some positive reality which so affects another and distinct reality as to determine the latter proximately to some definite way of existing or acting, to which the latter is itself indifferent; without, however, adding to the latter any new and proper entity other than the said determination.[264] Such modes are called *physical* modes. And some philosophers maintain that there are not only *accidental* modes, thus really distinct from the substance, but that there are even some *substantial* modes really distinct from the essence of the substance which they affect: for instance, that the really distinct constitutive principles of any individual corporeal substance, matter and form, are actually united only in virtue of a substantial mode whereby each is ordained for union with the other; or that *subsistence*, whereby the individual substance is made a subsistent and incommunicable "person" or "thing," is a substantial mode of the individual nature.[265] With these latter we are not concerned here, but only with accidental modes, such as external shape or figure, local motion, position, action,[266] etc. Now when a substance is affected by such accidents as these it is impossible on the one hand to maintain that they add any new positive entity of their own to it; they do not seem to have any reality over and above the determination or modification in which their very presence in the substance consists. And on the other hand it cannot be denied that they express some real predicate which can be affirmed of the substance in virtue of their presence in it, and that independently of our thought; in other words it cannot be maintained that they are mere figments or forms of thought, mere *entia rationis*. If a piece of wax has a certain definite shape, this shape is inseparable from the wax: it is nothing except in the wax, for it cannot exist apart from the wax; but in the wax it is something in some real sense distinct from the wax, inasmuch as the wax would persist even if it disappeared. No doubt it is essential to the wax, as extended in space, to have some shape or other; but it is indifferent to any particular shape, and hence something distinct from it is required to remove this indifference. This something is the particular shape it actually possesses. The shape, therefore, is an accidental mode of the extension of the wax, a mode which is really distinct, by a minor real distinction, from this extension which is its immediate subject.[267] Hence we conclude that there are accidental modes, or modal accidents, really distinct from the subjects in which they inhere.

69. DISTINCTION BETWEEN SUBSTANCE AND ITS "PROPER" ACCIDENTS. UNITY OF THE CONCRETE BEING.—Turning next to the distinction between absolute accidents and substance, we have seen already that separable absolute accidents such as acquired habits of mind and certain sensible qualities and energies of bodies are really distinct from their subjects. Absolute accidents which are *naturally inseparable* from their subjects—such as external quantity or spatial extension or volume is in regard to the corporeal substance—are also really distinct from their subjects; though we cannot know by reason alone whether or how far such accidents are *absolutely separable* from these subjects: from Christian Revelation we know that extension at least is separable from the substance of a body, and with extension all the other corporeal accidents which inhere immediately in extension.[268]

But a special difficulty arises in regard to the nature of the distinction between a substance and its *proper* accidents,[269] *i.e.* those which have such an adequate and necessary ground in the essence of the substance that the latter cannot exist without them: accidents which are simultaneous with the substance and proceed necessarily from it, such as the internal quantity of a corporeal substance, or the intellectual and appetitive powers or faculties of a spiritual substance. The medieval scholastic philosophers were by no means unanimous as to the nature of this distinction. Their discussion of the question centres mainly around the distinction between the spiritual human soul and its spiritual faculties, intellect and will, and between these faculties themselves. It is instructive—as throwing additional light on what they understood by a real distinction—to find that while Thomists generally have held that the distinction here in question is a real distinction, many other scholastics have held that it is only a virtual distinction, while Scotists have generally taught that it is a formal distinction.

Kleutgen[270] interprets the formal distinction advocated by Scotus in the present context as really equivalent to the virtual distinction. St. Bonaventure, after referring to the latter distinction, and to the real distinction propounded by St. Thomas, adopts himself an intermediate view: that the faculties of the soul are indeed really distinct from one another, but nevertheless are not really distinct, as accidental entities, from the substance of the soul itself. We see how this can be by considering that the material and formal principles which constitute a corporeal substance, though really distinct from each other, are not really distinct from the substance itself. They are not accidents of the latter but *constitute* its essence, and so are to be referred *reductivé* to the category of substance. So, by analogy, the faculties of the soul, though really distinct from each other, do not belong to any accidental category really distinct from the substance of the soul, but belong *reductivé* to the latter category, not indeed as constituting, but as flowing immediately and necessarily from, the substance of the soul itself.[271] And, like St. Thomas, he finds the ultimate source and explanation of this multiplicity of faculties and forces *in the finiteness* of the created substance as such.[272] But St. Thomas went farther than St. Bonaventure, for he taught—as indeed Thomists generally teach, and many who are not Thomists—that the faculties of the human soul are really distinct from one another, not merely as proximate principles of really distinct vital acts, but as accidental entities or essences; and that as such they are really distinct from the essence or substance itself of the human soul. The arguments in favour of this view will be given in their proper place in connexion with the category of *Quality*. If they are not demonstrative in their force, they are certainly such that the view for which they make is very highly probable; but we are concerned here to show, in this concluding section, that the recognition of a real distinction in general between substance and its accidents does not in any way compromise the real unity of the concrete individual being. It has been widely accused of doing so by philosophers who try to discredit this view without fully understanding it. This characteristically modern attitude is illustrated by the persistent attempts that have been made in recent times to throw ridicule on what they describe as the "faculty psychology".[273]

The source of this groundless charge lies partly in the mistaken conception of accident and substance as concrete entities superadded the one to the other; partly in the mistaken notion that the union of substance and accidents cannot result in a real unity, that there cannot be more or less perfect grades of real unity; and partly in the false assumption that real distinction always implies mutual separability of concrete entities. Of these errors we need only refer to that concerning unity.

Modern philosophers not uncommonly conceive the union of substance and accidents as being necessarily a mere *mechanical* union or aggregation, and oppose it to "organic" unity which they regard as a real unity involving the richness of an energetic, "living" multiplicity. This involves a misrepresentation of the traditional scholastic view. The union of substance and accident is not a mechanical union. Nothing could be farther from the minds of the scholastic interpreters of Aristotle than the conception of the ultimate principles of the universe of our experience as inert entities moved according to purely mechanical laws; or of the individual concrete being as a mere machine, or a mere aggregate of mechanical elements. They recognized even in the individual inorganic substance an internal, unifying, active and directive principle of all the energies and activities of the thing—its substantial form. And if this is all those philosophers mean by the metaphorical transference of the terms "organic unity," "internal living principle of development," etc., to the mineral world, they are so far in accord with the traditional scholastic philosophy;[274] while if they mean that all substances are principles of "vital" energy, or that all reality is one organic unity, in the literal sense of these terms, they are committing themselves either to the palpably false theory of pan-psychism, or to the gratuitous reassertion of a very old and very crude form of monism.

By "organic" unity we understand the unity of any living organism, a unity which is much more perfect than that of the parts of a machine, or than any natural juxtaposition of material parts in an inorganic whole; for the organs, though distinct in number and in nature from one another, are united by an internal principle to form one living individual, so that if any organ were separated from the living organism it would cease to be an organ.[275] But organic unity is not by any means the most perfect kind of unity conceivable.[276] The living organism exists and develops and attains to the perfection of its being only through a multiplicity of integral parts extended in space. The spiritual substance is subject to no such dispersion of its being. From its union with the faculties whereby it attains to its natural development, there results a real unity of a higher order than that of any organism.

And nevertheless, even though the unity of the concrete spiritual substance and its faculties be so far higher than a mechanical or even an organic unity, it is not perfect. Even though the faculties of the soul be determinations of its substance, even though they flow from it as actualities demanded by its essence for the normal and natural development of its being, still it is a complete subsisting essence of its kind without them; it possesses its *essential* perfection without them, so that however intimate be their union with it they can never form one essence with it; it needs them only for the fuller development of its being by acquiring further *intermediate* perfections and thus attaining to its *final* perfection .

And here we touch on the most fundamental ground of the distinction, in all created things, between their substance and their accidental perfections. Unlike the

Necessary, Absolute Being, whose infinite perfection is the eternal actuality of His essence, no creature possesses the actuality of its being *tota simul*, but only by a progressive development whereby it gradually acquires really new intermediate and final perfections, really distinct from, though naturally due to, its essence. Hence, even though some of its accidents—properties such as the powers and faculties we have been discussing—be not really distinct from the essence wherewith they are necessarily connected, this is not true of its acquired habits and dispositions, or of the activities which proceed from these latter as their proximate principles. At the same time the concrete being is, at every moment of its existence and development, a real unity, but a unity which, involving in itself as it does a real multiplicity of distinct principles, must ever fall infinitely short of the perfect type of real unity—that realized only in the Self-Existent, Necessary Being.

Chapter IX.

Nature And Person.

70. SOME DIVISIONS OF SUBSTANCES.—In the preceding chapter we discussed the nature of substance and accident in general, and the relation between a substance and its accidents. We must next examine the category of substance more in detail, terminating as it does in the important concept of personality or person. This latter conception is one which must have its origin for all philosophers in the study of the human individual, but which, for scholastic philosophers, is completed and perfected by the light of Christian Revelation. We shall endeavour to show in the first place what can be gathered from the light of reason about the constitution of personality, and also briefly to note how Christian Revelation has increased our insight into the perfections involved in it. As leading up to the concept of person, we must set forth certain divisions or classifications of substance: into *first* and *second* substances, and into *complete* and *incomplete* substances.[277]

(*a*) The specific and generic natures of substantial entities do not inhere, like accidents, in individual substances; they constitute the essence of the latter, and hence these *universals* are called substances. But the universal as such does not really exist; it is realized only in individuals; in the logical order it pre-supposes the individual as a logical subject of which it is affirmed, a *subjectum attributionis seu praedicationis*. Hence it is called a *second* substance, while the individual substance is called a *first* substance. Of course we can predicate attributes of universal substances, and use these as logical subjects, as when we say "*Man* is mortal". But such propositions have no real meaning, and give us no information about reality, except in so far as we can refer their predicates ("mortal"), through the medium of their universal subjects ("man"), back ultimately to the individual substances (John, James, etc.) which alone are real, and in which alone the universal ("man") has its reality. Hence the individual is, in the logical order, the ultimate and fundamental subject of all our predications. And furthermore, the individual substance cannot be used as a logical predicate of anything underlying itself, while the universal substance can be so used in relation to the individual.

In the ontological order, of course, the universal substance is individualized, and, as individual, it is the subject in which all accidents inhere, their *subjectum inhaesionis*: the *only* subject of many of them, and the *remote* or *ultimate* subject of those of them which inhere *immediately* in other accidents.

Thus while in the ontological order all substances, whether we think of them as universal or as individual, are the ultimate subjects of inhesion for all real accidents, in the logical order it is only the individual substance that is the ultimate subject of attribution for all logical predicates. Hence it was that the individual substance (τόδε τί ὄν), vindicating for itself more fully the rôle of subject, was called by Aristotle οὐσία πρώτη, *substantia prima*, while he called the universal, specific or generic substance, οὐσία δεύτερα, *substantia secunda*.[278] These are, of course, two ways of regarding substance, and not two really distinct species of substance as genus. The distinction between the *membra dividentia* is logical, not real.

The perfectly intelligible sense in which Aristotle and the scholastics designate the universal a substance, the sense of moderate realism, according to which the universal constitutes, and is identical with, the essence of the individual "person" or "thing," is entirely different from the sense in which many exponents of modern monistic idealism conceive the universal as the substance *par excellence*, the *ens realissimum*, determining, expressing, evolving itself in the individual phenomena of mind and of nature, which would be merely its manifestations.[279]

(*b*) The divisions of substance into spiritual and corporeal, of the latter into inorganic and organic, of these again into vegetative and animal, and finally of animal substances into brute animals and human beings,—offer no special difficulties. All purely natural or rational knowledge of the possibility and nature of purely spiritual substances is based on the analogy of our knowledge of the human soul, which, though a spiritual substance, is not a pure spirit, but is naturally allied with matter in its mode of existence. The individual human being offers to human experience the sole example of the sufficiently mysterious conjunction and combination of matter and spirit, of the corporeal mode of being and the spiritual mode of being, to form one composite substance, partly corporeal and partly spiritual.

(*c*) This in turn suggests the division of substances into *simple* and *composite*. The latter are those which we understand to be constituted by the natural and substantial union of two really distinct but incomplete substantial principles, a formative, determining, specifying principle, and a material, determinable, indifferent principle: such are all corporeal substances whether inorganic, vegetative, sentient, or rational. The former, or simple substances, are those which we understand to be constituted by a sole and single substantial principle which determines and specifies their essence, without the conjunction of any material, determinable principle. We have no direct and immediate experience of any *complete* created substance of this kind; but each of us has such direct experience of an *incomplete* simple substance, *viz.* his own soul; while we can infer from our experience the *existence* of other incomplete simple substances, *viz.* the formative principles of corporeal substances, as also the *possibility* of such complete simple substances as pure spirits, and the actual *existence* of the perfectly simple, uncreated substance of the Infinite Being.

(*d*) If there are such things as composite substances, *i.e.* substances constituted by the substantial union of two really distinct principles, then it follows that while the composite substance itself is *complete*, each of its substantial constitutive principles is *incomplete*. Of course there are many philosophers nowadays who reject as mere mental fictions, as products of mere logical distinctions, and as devoid of objective validity, the notions of *composite* substance and *incomplete* substance. Nor is this to be wondered at when we remember what a variety of groundless and gratuitous notions are current in regard to substance itself. But understanding substance in the traditional sense already explained, there is nothing whatever inconsistent in the notion of a composite substance, or of an incomplete substance,—provided these notions are understood in the sense to be explained presently. Nay, more, not only are these notions intrinsically possible: we must even hold them to be objectively valid and real, to be truly expressive of the nature of reality, unless we are prepared to hold that there is no such thing as substantial change in the universe, and that man himself is a mere *aggregate* of material atoms moved according to mechanical laws and inhabited by a conscious soul, or thinking principle, rather than an individual being with one definite substantial nature.

What, then, are we to understand by complete and incomplete substances respectively? A substance is regarded as complete in the fullest sense when it is wanting in no *substantial* principle without which it would be incapable of *existing* and discharging *all* its functions in the actual order as an individual of some definite species. Of course no created substance exists or discharges its functions unless it is endowed with some accidents, *e.g.* with properties, faculties, forces, etc. But there is no question of these here. We are considering only the essential perfections of the substance. Thus, then, any existing individual of any species—a man, a horse, an oak—is a complete substance in this fullest sense. It is complete *in the line of substance*, in *substantial* perfection, "*in ordine substantialitatis*," inasmuch as it can exist (and does actually exist) without being conjoined or united substantially with any other substance to form a composite substance other than itself. And it is complete *in the line of specific perfection*, "*in ordine speciei*," because not only can it exist without such conjunction with any other substantial principle, but it can discharge *all* the functions natural to its species, and thus tend towards its *final* perfection without such conjunction.

But it is conceivable that a substance might be complete in the line of substantial perfections, and thus be capable of *existing* in the actual order and discharging there *some* of the functions of its species without conjunction with any other substantial principle, and yet be incapable of discharging *all* the functions natural to an individual of its species without conjunction with some other substantial principle, in which case it would be *incomplete* in the line of *specific* perfection, though complete in everything pertaining to its *substantiality*. We know of one such substance,—the human soul. Being spiritual and immortal, it can exist apart from the body to which it is united by nature, and in this separated condition retain and exercise its spiritual faculties of intellect and will; it is therefore complete as regards the distinctively substantial perfection whereby it is "capable of existing in itself". But being of its nature destined for union with a material principle, constituting an individual of the human species only by means of such union, and being capable of discharging some of the functions of this species, *viz.* the sentient and vegetative functions, only when so united, it has not *all* the perfections of its species independently of the body; and it is therefore an incomplete substance in the line of specific perfections, though complete in those essential to its substantiality.

Again, if it be true that just as man is composed of two substantial principles, soul and body, so every living thing is composed of a substantial vital principle and a substantial material principle, and that every inorganic individual thing is likewise composed of two really distinct substantial principles, a formative and a passive or material principle; and if, furthermore, it be true that apart from the spiritual principle in man every other vital or formative principle of the composite "things" of our experience is of such a nature that it cannot actually exist except in union with some material principle, and *vice versa*,—then it follows necessarily that all such substantial principles of these complete composite substances are themselves *incomplete* substances: and incomplete not only in regard to perfections which would make them subsisting individuals of a species, but (unlike the human soul) incomplete even in the line of substantiality itself, inasmuch as no one of them is capable of actually existing at all except in union with its connatural and correlative principle.

Thus we arrive at the notion of substances that are *incomplete* in the line of specific perfections, or in that of substantial perfections, or even in both lines. An incomplete substance, therefore, is not one which verifies the definition of substance only in part. The incomplete substance *fully* verifies the definition of a substance.[280] It is conjoined, no doubt, *with another* to form a complete substance; but it does not exist *in the other*, or in the composite substance, as accidents do. It is *a substantial* principle of the composite substance, not an *accidental* determination of the latter, or of the other substantial principle with which it is conjoined. It thus verifies the notion of substance as a mode of being which naturally exists in itself; and united with its correlative substantial principle it discharges the function of supporting all accidental determinations which affect the composite substantial essence. Since, however, it does not exist itself independently as an individual of a species, but only forms the complete individual substance by union with its correlative substantial principle, it may be, and has been, accurately described as not belonging to the category of substance *formally*, but only *referentially*, "*reductive*".

The concepts of composite substance, of complete and incomplete substances, understood as we have just explained them, are therefore perfectly intelligible in themselves. And this is all we are concerned to show in the present context. This is not the place to establish the theses of psychology and cosmology from which they are borrowed. That the human soul is spiritual and immortal; that its union with a really distinct material principle to form the individual human substance or nature is a substantial union; that all living organisms and all inorganic bodies are really composite substances and subject to substantial change: these various theses of scholastic philosophy we here assume to be true. And if they are true the conception of incomplete substances naturally united to form a complete composite substance is not only intelligible as an hypothesis but is objectively true and valid as a thesis; and thus the notion of an incomplete substance is not only a consistent and legitimate notion, but is also a notion which gives mental expression to an objective reality.

We may add this consideration: The concept of an accident really distinct from its substance involves no intrinsic repugnance. Yet an accident is a mode of being which is so weak and wanting in reality, if we may speak in such terms, that it cannot naturally exist except by inhering, mediately or immediately, in the stronger and more real mode of being which is substance. But an incomplete substance is a higher grade of reality than any accident. Therefore if accidents can be real, *a fortiori* incomplete substances can be real.

71. SUBSTANCE AND NATURE.—We have already pointed out that the terms "essence," "substance," and "nature" denote what is really the same thing,

regarded under different aspects. The term "essence" is somewhat wider than "substance," inasmuch as it means "what a thing is," whether the thing be a substance, an accident, or a concrete existing individual including substance and accidents.

The traditional meaning of the term "nature" in Aristotelian and scholastic philosophy is unmistakable. It means the essence or substance of an individual person or thing, regarded as *the fundamental principle of the latter's activities*. Every finite individual comes into existence incomplete, having no doubt its *essential* perfections and properties *actually*, but its *intermediate* and *final* perfections only *potentially*. These it realizes gradually, through the exercise of its connatural activities. Every being is essentially intended for activity of some sort: "Omne ens est propter suam operationem," says St. Thomas. And by the constant interplay of their activities these beings realize and sustain the universal order which makes the world a *cosmos*. There is in all things an immanent purpose or finality which enables us to speak of the whole system which they form as "Universal *Nature*".[281]

Therefore what we call a *substance* or *essence* from the *static* point of view we call a *nature* when we consider it from the *dynamic* standpoint, or as an agent.[282] No doubt the forces, faculties and powers, the active and passive accidental principles, whereby such an agent exerts and undergoes action, are the *proximate* principles of all this action and change, but the *remote* and fundamental principle of the latter is the essence or substance of the agent itself, in other words its *nature*.

Not all modern scholastics, however, are willing thus to identify nature with substance. We have no intuitive insight into what any real essence or substance is; our knowledge of it is discursive, derived by inference from the phenomena, the operations, the conduct of things, in accordance with the principle, *Operari sequitur esse*. Moreover, the actually existing, concrete individual—a man, for instance—has a great variety of activities, spiritual, sentient, vegetative, and inorganic; he has, moreover, in the constitution of his body a variety of distinct organs and members; he assimilates into his body a variety of inorganic substances; the tissues of his body *appear* to be different *in kind*; the vital functions which subserve nutrition, growth and reproduction are at least analogous to mechanical, physical and chemical changes, if indeed they are not really and simply such; it may be, therefore, that the *ultimate material* constituents of his body remain *substantially unaltered* in their passage into, and through, and out of the cycle of his vegetative life; that they retain their elemental *substantial forms* while they assume a *new nature* by becoming parts of the one organic whole, whose higher directive principle dominates and co-ordinates all their various energies.[283] If this be so there is in the same individual a multiplicity of really and actually distinct substances; each of these, moreover, has its own existence proportionate to its essence, since the existence of a created reality is not really distinct from its essence; nor is there any reason for saying that any of these substances is incomplete; what we have a right to say is that no one of them separately is a complete *nature*, that each being an *incomplete nature* unites with all the others to form one *complete nature*: inasmuch as no one of them separately is an adequate intrinsic principle of all the functions which it can discharge, and is naturally destined to discharge, by its natural union with the others, whereas there results from their union a *new fundamental principle* of a co-ordinated and harmonized system of operations—in a word, a *new nature*.

This line of thought implies among other things (*a*) the view that whereas there is no ground for admitting the existence of *incomplete substances*, there is ground for distinguishing between *complete and incomplete natures*; (*b*) the view that from the union or conjunction of an actual multiplicity of substances, each remaining unaltered and persisting in its existence actually distinct from the others, there *can* arise one single complete nature—a nature which will be *one being* simply and really, *unum ens per se et simpliciter*, and not merely an aggregate of beings or an accidental unity, *unum per accidens*,—and there *does* arise such a nature whenever the component substances not merely co-operate to discharge certain functions which none of them could discharge separately (which indeed is true of an accidental union, as of two horses drawing a load which neither could draw by itself), but when they unite in a more permanent and intimate way according to what we call "natural laws" or "laws of nature," so as to form a new fundamental principle of such functions.[284] These views undoubtedly owe their origin to the belief that certain facts brought to light by the physical and biological sciences in modern times afford strong evidence that the elementary material constituents of bodies, whether inorganic or living, remain *substantially unaltered* while combining to form the multitudinous *natural kinds* or *natures* of those living or non-living material things. It was to reconcile this supposed *plurality* of *actually distinct* and *diverse* substances in the individual with the indubitable *real unity* of the latter, that these philosophers distinguished between substance and nature. But it is not clear that the facts alleged afford any such evidence. Of course if the philosopher approaches the consideration of it with what we may call the atomic preconception of material substances as permanent, unchangeable entities, this view will preclude all recognition of *substantial* change in the universe; it will therefore force him to conclude that each individual, composite agent has a unity which must be *less* than substantial, and which, because he feels it to be *more* than a mere accidental or artificial unity, he will describe as *natural*, as a union to form *one nature*. But if he approach the evidence in question with the view that substantial change is possible, this view, involving the recognition of incomplete substances as real, will remove all necessity for distinguishing between substance and nature, and will enable him to conclude that however various and manifold be the activities of the individual, their co-ordination and unification, as proceeding from the individual, point to a *substantial* unity in the latter as their fundamental principle, a unity resulting from the *union of incomplete substances*.

This latter is undoubtedly the view of St. Thomas, of practically all the medieval scholastics, and of most scholastics in modern times. Nor do we see any sufficient reason for receding from it, or admitting the modern distinction between substance and nature.

And if it be objected that the view which admits the reality of incomplete substances and substantial change is as much a preconception as what we have called the atomic view of substance, our answer is, once more, that since we have no intellectual intuition into the real constitution of the substances which constitute the universe, since we can argue to this only by observing and reasoning from their activities on the principle *Operari requitur esse*, the evidence alone must decide which view of these substances is the correct one. Does the evidence afforded us by a scientific analysis of all the functions, inorganic, vegetative, sentient and rational, of an individual man, forbid us to conclude that he is one complete substance, resulting from the union of two incomplete substantial principles, a spiritual soul and a material principle? and at the same time compel us to infer that he is one complete nature resulting from the union of a plurality of principles supposed to be complete as substances and incomplete as natures? We believe that it does not; nor can we see that any really useful purpose is served by thus setting up a real distinction between substance and nature. From the evidence to hand it is neither more nor less difficult to infer unity of substance than unity of nature in the individual. The inference in question is an inference from facts in the phenomenal order, in the domain of the senses, to what must be actually there in the noumenal order, in the domain of nature or substance, a domain which cannot be reached by the senses but only by intellect. Nor will any imagination images which picture for us the physical fusion or coalescence of material things in the domain of the senses help us in the least to conceive in any positive way the mode in which incomplete natures or substances unite to form a complete nature or substance. For these latter facts belong to the domain which the senses cannot reach at all, and which intellect can reach only inferentially and not by direct insight.

Hence we consider the view which regards real unity of nature as compatible with real and actual plurality of complete substances in the individual, as improbable. At the same time we do not believe that this view is a necessary corollary from the real identification of essence with existence in created things. We have seen that even if accidents have their own existence in so far as they have their own essence—as they have if essence and existence be really identical—nevertheless the concrete substance as determined by its accidents can have a really unitary existence, *unum esse* corresponding to and identical with its composite constitution. Similarly, if the existence of each incomplete substance is identical with its incomplete essence, this is no obstacle to the complete substance—which results from the union of two such incomplete substantial principles—having one complete unitary existence identical with its composite essence. Hence it is useless to argue against the view that a plurality of actually distinct and complete substances can unite to form a complete nature which will be really *one being*, on the ground that each complete substance has already its own existence and that things which have and preserve their own existence cannot form *one being*. Such an argument is inconclusive; for although *one being* has of course only one existence, it has not been proved that this one existence cannot result from the union of many incomplete existences: especially if these existences be identical with the incomplete essences which are admittedly capable of uniting to form one complete essence.

It may, however, be reasonably urged against the opinion under criticism that, since the complete substances are supposed to remain complete and unchanged in their state of combination, it is difficult to see how this combination can be a real union and not merely an extrinsic juxtaposition,—one which remains in reality a merely accidental conjunction, even though we may dignify it with the title of a "natural union".

And finally it may be pointed out that in this view the operations of the individual have not really *one ultimate* intrinsic principle at all, since behind the supposed unity of nature there is a more fundamental plurality of actually distinct substances.

72. SUBSISTENCE AND PERSONALITY.—We have already examined the relation between the individual and the universal, between *first* and *second* substances, in connexion with the doctrine of Individuation. And we then saw that whatever it be that individuates the universal nature, it is at all events not to be regarded as anything extrinsic and superadded to this nature in the individual, as anything really distinct from this nature: that, for instance, what makes Plato's human nature to be Plato's is not anything really distinct from the human nature that is in Plato. We have now to fix our attention on the nature as individualized. We have to consider the complete individual nature or substance itself in actually existing individual "things" or "persons".

We must remember that scholastics are not agreed as to whether there is a real distinction or only a virtual distinction between the actual existence and the complete individual essence or substance or nature of created individual beings. Furthermore we have seen that philosophers who study the metaphysics of the inorganic world and of the lower forms of life are unable to say with certainty what is the individual in these domains: whether it is the chemical molecule or the chemical atom or the electron; whether it is the single living cell or the living mass consisting of a plurality of such cells. But we have also seen that as we ascend the scale of living things all difficulty in designating the genuine individual disappears: that a man, a horse, an oak tree, are undoubtedly individual beings.

Bearing these things in mind we have now to inquire into what has been called the *subsistence* or *personality* of the complete individual substance or nature: that perfection which enables us formally to designate the latter a "subsisting thing"[285] or a "person". By personality we mean the subsistence of a complete individual *rational* nature. We shall therefore inquire into the meaning of the generic term *subsistentia* (or *suppositalitas*), *subsistence*, in the abstract. But let us look at it first in the concrete.

A complete individual nature or substance, when it exists in the actual order, really distinct and separate in its own complete entity from every other existing being, exercising its powers and discharging its functions of its own right and according to the laws of its own being, is said to *subsist*, or to have the perfection of *subsistence*. In this state it not only *exists in itself* as every substance does; it is not only *incommunicable* to any other being as every individual is, in contradistinction with *second* or *universal* substances which are, as such, indefinitely communicable to individuals; but it is also a complete whole, incommunicable *as a mere integral or essential part* to some other whole, unlike the incomplete substantial constituents, or integral parts, members or organs of, say, an individual organic body; and finally it is incommunicable in the sense that it is not capable of being assumed into the subsisting unity of some other superior "suppositum" or "person". All those characteristics we find in the individual "subsisting thing" or "person". It "exists in itself" and is not communicable to another substance *as an accident*, because it is itself a substance. It is not communicable *to individuals as a universal*, because it is itself an individual. It is not communicable *as an integral or essential part to a whole*, because it is itself a complete substance and nature.[286] Finally it is not communicable to, and cannot be assumed into, the unity of a higher personality so as to subsist by virtue of the latter's subsistence, because it has a perfection incompatible with such assumption, *viz.* its own proper subsistence, whereby it is already an actually subsisting thing or person in its own right, or *sui juris*, so to speak.

The mention of this last sort of incommunicability would be superfluous, and indeed unintelligible, did we not know from Divine Revelation that the human nature of our Divine Lord and Saviour, Jesus Christ, though it is a complete and most perfect individual nature, is nevertheless *not a person*, because It is assumed into the Personality of the Second Person of the Divine Trinity, and, united hypostatically or personally with this Divine Person, subsists by virtue of the Divine Subsistence of the latter.

We see, therefore, what subsistence does for a complete individual nature in the *static* order. It makes this nature *sui juris*, incommunicable, and entirely independent in the mode of its actual being: leaving untouched, of course, the essential dependence of the created "subsisting thing" or "person" on the Creator. In the *dynamic* order, the order of activity and development, subsistence makes the complete individual nature not only the ultimate principle *by which* all the functions of the individual are discharged, but also the ultimate principle or agent *which* exercises these functions: while the nature *as such* is the ultimate *principium* QUO, the nature *as subsisting* is the ultimate *principium* QUOD, in regard to all actions emanating from this nature. Hence the scholastic aphorism: *Actiones sunt suppositorum*. That is, all actions emanating from a complete individual nature are always ascribed and attributed to the latter *as subsisting*, to the "subsisting thing" or "person". In regard to an individual human person, for instance, whether his intellect thinks, or his will resolves, or his imagination pictures things, or his eyes see, or his hand writes, or his stomach digests, or his lungs breathe, or his head aches, it is the *man*, the *person*, properly, that discharges or suffers all these functions, though by means of different faculties, organs and members; and it is to him properly that we ascribe all of them.[287]

Now the individual human person is neither his soul, nor his body, nor even both conceived as two; he is *one* being, one complete substance or nature composed partly of a spiritual principle or soul and partly of a material principle which the soul "informs" and so constitutes a living human body. Hence the human soul itself, whether we consider it as united to the material principle in the living human person, or as disembodied and separate from its connatural material principle, is not a complete substance, is not capable of *subsisting* and having its human activities referred ultimately to itself as the subsisting, personal principle which elicits these activities. No doubt the disembodied soul has actual *existence*, but it has not the perfection of *subsistence* or *personality*: it is not a complete individual of the human species to which it belongs, and therefore it cannot be properly called a human person, a complete subsisting individual of the human species.[288]

Furthermore, even though an individual nature be complete as a nature, endowed with all the substantial and specific perfections which constitute it a complete individual of the species to which it belongs, nevertheless if it is assumed into the personality of another and higher nature, and subsists in personal union with the latter and by virtue of the latter's subsistence, then that nature, not having its own proper and connatural subsistence, is not itself a person. Nor can the actions which are elicited by means of it be ascribed ultimately to it; they must be ascribed to the person by whose subsistence it subsists and into whose personality it has been assumed. If an individual human nature be thus hypostatically or personally assumed into, and united with, a higher Divine Personality, and subsists only by this Personality, such a human nature will be really and truly an individual nature of the human species; the actions elicited through it and performed by means of it will be really and truly human actions; but it will not be a human person; while its actions will be really and truly the actions of the Divine Person, and will therefore be also really and truly divine: they will be the actions of the God-Man, divine and human, *theandric*. All this we know only from Divine Revelation concerning the hypostatic union of the human nature of Christ with the Person of the Divine Word; nor could we know it otherwise. But all this does not modify, it only supplements and completes, what the light of reason discloses to us regarding the subsistence or personality of any complete individual nature.

We are now in a position to give nominal definitions of subsistence and personality both in the abstract and in the concrete, *i.e.* definitions which will indicate to us what exactly it is that these terms denote,[289] and which will thus enable us to inquire into their connotation, or in other words to ask what is it precisely that constitutes subsistence or personality.

By *"subsistence"* (*"subsistentia,"* *"suppositalitas"*) we mean that perfection whereby a fully complete individual nature is rendered in every way, in its being and in its actions, distinct from and incommunicable to any and every other being, so that it exists and acts *sui juris*, autonomously, independently of every other being save the Creator.[290]

By a *"subsisting being"* in the concrete (ὑπόστασις, *"suppositum,"* *hypostasis*), we mean a being endowed with this perfection of subsistence; in other words, a being that is a complete individual nature existing and acting in every way distinct from and incommunicable to any other being, so that it exists and acts *sui juris*, autonomously.

"Personality" is simply the subsistence of a complete individual nature that is *rational, intelligent.*

A *"person"* is simply a *subsisting* nature that is *rational, intelligent. Persona est suppositum rationale.* The definition given by Boëtius is classic: "*Persona est substantia individua* RATIONALIS *naturae*": "the individual substance of a rational nature,"—where the term *individual* is understood to imply *actually existing and subsisting*.

The special name which has thus been traditionally applied to *rational* or *intelligent* subsisting beings (as distinct from animals, plants, and material "things")—the term "person" ("*persona*," a mask: *per-sonus*; cf. Gr. προσωπέιον, fromπ ροσώπον, the face, countenance)—originally meaning a rôle or character in a drama, came to be applied to the subsisting human individual, and to connote a certain dignity of the latter as compared with the lower or non-rational beings of the universe. And in fact the ascription of its actions to the subsisting being is more deeply grounded in the subsistence of rational, intelligent beings, who, as free agents, can more properly direct and control these actions.[291]

73. DISTINCTION BETWEEN THE INDIVIDUAL NATURE AND ITS SUBSISTENCE. WHAT CONSTITUTES PERSONALITY?—Knowing now what we mean by the terms "subsistence," "suppositum," "person," and "personality," we have next to inquire in what precisely does subsistence consist. What is it that constitutes a complete individual nature a "subsisting being," or if the nature be rational, a "person"? Subsistence connotes, over and above the mode of "existing in itself"

which characterizes all substance, the notion that the substance or nature is individual, that it is complete, that it is in every way incommunicable, that it is *sui juris* or autonomous in its existence and activities. These notions are all positive; they imply positive perfections: even incommunicability is really a positive perfection though the term is negative. But is any one of the positive perfections, thus contained in the notion of subsistence, a positive something *over and above*, and *really distinct from*, the perfection already implied in the concept of *a complete individual nature as such*?

Some of those philosophers who regard the distinction between essence and existence in creatures as a real distinction, identify the *subsistence* of the complete individual nature with its *actual existence*, thus placing a real distinction between nature and subsistence or personality.[292] Apart from these, however, it is not likely that any philosophers, guided by the light of reason alone, would ever have held, or even suspected, that the subsistence of an actually existing individual nature is a positive perfection really distinct from, and superadded to, the latter. For we never, in our natural experience, encounter an existing individual substance, or nature, or agent, that is not distinct, autonomous, independent, *sui juris*, and incommunicable in its mode of being and acting.

Rigorously, however, this would only prove that subsistence is a perfection *naturally inseparable* from the complete individual nature; *conceivably* it *might* still be *really* distinct from the latter. But whether or not such real distinction could be suspected by the unaided light of reason working on natural experience, at all events what we know from Divine Revelation concerning the hypostatic union of the human nature of our Lord Jesus Christ with the Person of the Divine Word, enables us to realize that there *can* be, in the actual order of things, a complete individual nature which is not a "subsisting being" or "person"; for the human nature of our Lord is *de facto* such a nature,—and *ab actu ad posse valet consecutio*. This information, however, is not decisive in determining the character of the distinction between the individual substance or nature and its subsistence.

It may be that the complete individual nature is *eo ipso* and identically a "subsisting being" or "person," that it is always independent, autonomous, *sui juris*, by the very fact that it is a complete individual nature, *unless it is* DE FACTO *assumed into the personality of a higher nature*, so that in this intercommunication with the latter, in the unity of the latter's personality, it is not independent, autonomous, *sui juris*, but dependent, subordinate, and *alterius juris*. In this condition, it loses nothing positive by the fact that it is not now a person and has not its own subsistence; nor does it gain any *natural* perfection, for it was *ex hypothesi* complete and perfect *as a nature*; but it gains something *supernatural* inasmuch as it now subsists in a manner wholly undue to it.[293] According to this view, therefore, subsistence would not be a perfection really distinct from the complete individual nature; it would be a mentally distinct aspect of the latter, a positive aspect, however, consisting in this nature's completeness, its self-sufficing, autonomous character, and consequent incommunicability.[294]

The principal difficulty against this view is a theological difficulty. As formulated by Urraburu,[295] it appears to involve an ambiguity in the expression "substantial union". It is briefly this: If the subsistence proper to a complete individual nature adds no positive perfection to the latter, so that the latter necessarily subsists and is a person unless it is actually assumed into a higher personality, and by the very fact that it is not actually so assumed, then the human nature of Christ "is as complete in every way and in every line of substantial perfection, by virtue of its own proper entity, when actually united with the Divine Person, as it would be were it not so united, or as the person of Peter, or Paul, or any other human person is". But this implies that there are in Christ "two substances complete in every respect". Now between two such substances "there cannot be a substantial union," a union which would constitute "one being," "unum per se ens". Hence the view in question would appear to be inadmissible.

But it is not proved that the union of "two substances complete in every respect" cannot result in the constitution of a being that is really and genuinely one—"unum per se ens"—*in the case in which the union is a personal union*. The hypostatic union of the human nature of Christ with the Divine Person is primarily a *personal* union whereby the former nature subsists by and in the Divine Personality. It has the effect of constituting the united terms "one subsisting being," and therefore has supereminently, if not formally, the effect of a "substantial union". Nay, it is a "substantial" union in the sense that it is a union of two substances, not of a substance and accidents; and also in the sense that it is not a mere accidental aggregation or artificial juxtaposition of substances, resulting merely in the constitution of collective or artificial unity, a *unum per accidens*. But is it a "substantial" union in the sense that it is such a union of substances as results in one "nature"? Most certainly not; for this was the heresy of the Monophysites: that in Christ there is only one nature resulting from the union of the human nature with the Divine. If then, with Urraburu, we mean by "nature" simply "substance regarded as a principle of action", and if, furthermore, the hypostatic union does not result in one "nature," neither does it result in one "substance," nor can it be a "substantial" or "natural" union in this sense.[296] He does not say, of course, that the hypostatic union is a "substantial union" which results in "one nature," or even explicitly that it results in "one substance," but he says that the two substances are "substantially conjoined," "substantialiter conjunguntur"; and he continues, "a substantial union is such a conjunction of two substantial realities that there results from it one substantial something, which is truly and properly one"—"unio enim substantialis, est talis duarum rerum substantialium conjunctio, per quam resultat unum aliquid substantiale quod vere et proprie sit unum,"[297]—and he concludes that "there is something substantial wanting in the human nature of Christ, *viz.* personality, which, of course, is most abundantly supplied in the hypostatic union by the Divine Person"—"reliquum est, ut naturae humanae in Christo aliquid desit substantiale, nempe personalitas, quod per unionem hypostaticam cumulatissime suppleatur a Verbo."[298] Now, this "aliquid substantiale" cannot be "aliquid naturale" in the sense that it is something *constitutive* of the human substance or nature; for the human substance or nature of Christ is certainly complete and perfect as a substance or nature. It must be some complement or mode, that is naturally due to it, but supernaturally supplied by the Person of the Divine Word.[299] This brings us to the view that subsistence is a something positive, distinct in some real way, and not merely in our concepts, from the complete individual substance.

According to the more common view of catholic philosophers (and theologians) subsistence is some positive perfection really distinct from the complete individual nature. But the supporters of this general view explain it in different ways. We have already referred to the view of certain Thomists who, identifying *subsistence* with the *actual existence* of the complete substance or nature, place a real distinction between the existence and the substance or nature. Other Thomists, while defending the latter distinction, point out that actual existence confers no real perfection, but only actualizes the real; they hold, therefore, that subsistence is not existence, but is rather a perfection of the real, essential, or substantial order, as distinct from the existential order—a perfection presupposed by actual existence, and whose proper function is to *unify* all the substantial constituents and accidental determinations of the individual substance or nature, thus making it a really unitary being—"unum ens per se"—proximately capable of being actualized by the simple existential act: which latter is the ultimate actuality of the real being: *esse est ultimus actus*.[300]

The concrete individual nature, containing as it does a plurality of really distinct principles, substantial and accidental, needs some unifying principle to make these one incommunicable reality, proximately capable of receiving a corresponding unitary existential act: without such a principle, they say, each of the substantial and accidental principles in the concrete individual nature would have its own existence: so that the result would be not *really* one being, but a being really *manifold* and only accidentally one—"unum per accidens". This principle is *subsistence*.

The human nature of our Divine Lord has not its own connatural subsistence; this is supplied by the subsistence of the Divine Person. Moreover, since the human nature in question has not its own subsistence, neither has it its own existence; existence is the actuality of the subsisting being; therefore there is in Christ but one existence, that of the Divine Person, whereby also the human nature of Christ exists.[301]

Of those who deny that the distinction between the existence and the essence of any created nature is a real distinction, some hold in the present matter the Scotist view that subsistence is not a positive perfection really distinct from the complete individual nature. Others, however, hold what we have ventured to regard as the more common view: that personality is something positive and really distinct from nature. But they explain what they conceive subsistence to be without any reference to existence, and without distinguishing between the essential and the existential order of reality.

The most common explanation seems to be that subsistence is a unifying principle of the concrete individual nature, as stated above. Thus conceived, it is not an *absolute* reality; nor is the distinction between it and the nature a *major* real distinction. It is a *substantial mode*, naturally superadded to the substance and modally distinct from the latter. It so completes and determines the substance or nature that the latter not only exists in itself but is also, by virtue of this mode, incommunicable in every way and *sui juris*.[302] It gives to the substance that ultimate determinateness which an accidental mode such as a definite shape or location gives to the accident of quantity.[303]

This mode is absent (supernaturally) from the human nature of our Divine Lord; this nature is therefore communicable; and the Personality of the Divine Word supernaturally supplies the function of this absent natural mode.

It must be confessed that it is not easy to understand how this or any other *substantial* mode can be *really* distinct from the substance it modifies. And in truth the distinction is not real in the full sense: it is not between *thing* and *thing*, *inter rem et rem*. All that is claimed for it is that it is not merely mental; that it is not merely an *ens rationis* which the mind projects into the reality; that it is a positive perfection of the nature or substance, a perfection which, though naturally inseparable from the latter, is not absolutely inseparable, and which, therefore, is *de facto* supernaturally absent from the human nature and replaced by the Divine Personality in the case of the hypostatic union.

It belongs, moreover, to the order of substance, not to that of accidents: the substantial mode differs from the accidental mode, or modal accident, in this, that it gives to the substance some ultimate determining perfection which appertains to the substance as such, and whereby the substance is completed in the order of "existing in itself". Subsistence is not an accident, even though it supervenes on the complete nature, for it determines the substance of the latter, not in relation to any line of accidental activity, as a power or faculty, nor as something modifying it accidentally, but as a mode which ultimately determines and perfects it in the order of substantial reality itself, in the order of "existing in itself" in such a full and perfect manner as to be *sui juris* and incommunicable.

The main difficulty against this view is also theological: If subsistence is a positive perfection it either belongs to the complete individual nature or it does not; in the former case the humanity of Christ, assumed by the Divine Word, was not a complete human nature; in the latter case the individual human nature can exist without it: and both consequences are equally inadmissible. But it may be replied that, granting the first member of the disjunctive, the consequence inferred from it does not really follow: subsistence belongs to the complete individual nature as an ultimate natural complement; but when it is absent and supplied supernaturally by the Divine Personality the nature is still complete as a nature: it is wanting in no absolute or entitative perfection, but only in a modality which is supereminently supplied by the Divine Personality. Neither is the consequence from the second member of the disjunctive a valid inference. For though personality as a mode does not belong to the essence of an individual human nature, no such individual nature can exist without *some* personality, either its own or another: just as extension cannot exist without *some* shape, though any particular shape is not essential to it.

To sum up, then, the doctrine of the two preceding sections: What are we to understand by a *person*, and by *personality*? Unquestionably our conception of person and personality (concrete and abstract) is mainly determined, and very rightly so, by an analysis of what constitutes the actually existing individual of the human species. Whatever our concept be, it must certainly be realized and verified in all human individuals: these, before all other beings, must be included in the denotation of our concept of person. In fact, for the philosopher, guided by the natural light of reason alone, the term can have hardly any other connotation. He will, no doubt, ascribe personality, as the highest mode of being he knows of, to the Supreme Being; but he will here ascribe it only in an analogical and supereminent way; and only from Divine Revelation can he know that this Supreme Being has not a single but a threefold Personality. Again, his consideration of the nature of the human soul as an embodied substance which is nevertheless spiritual and immortal will enable him to affirm the possibility of *purely spiritual* created beings; and these he will of course conceive as persons. But, conceiving the human soul itself as a constituent principle of the human individual, he will not conceive the soul itself as a person.

The philosopher who understands the traditional Aristotelian conceptions of substance, of individual substance (*substantia prima*), of incomplete, complete, and composite substances, of substance considered as *nature* or principle of action, of substance considered as *hypostasis*, as the actually existing individual being which is the ultimate logical subject of all predications and the ultimate ontological subject of all real determinations: the philosopher who understands these concepts, and who admits them to be validly grounded in experience, and to offer as far as they go a correct interpretation of reality, will have no difficulty in making up his mind about what is requisite to constitute a person.

Wherever he finds an existing individual being of any species, a being which, even if it is really composite, is nevertheless really one, such a being he will pronounce to be a "subsisting individual being". He may not be able, in the inorganic world or among the lower forms of life, to distinguish for certain what is the real individual from what may be perhaps only an accidental, if natural, colony or group of real individuals. As a test he will always seek for the manifestation of an internal directive principle whereby all the vital functions of the organized mass of matter in question are co-ordinated in such a manner as to make for the preservation, growth and development of the whole throughout a definite life cycle from birth to death. This formative and directive principle is evidence of an individual unity of nature and subsistence; and such evidence is abundantly present in "individuals" of all the higher species in botany and zoology. The "individual subsisting being" will therefore be a "complete individual substance or nature, existing and acting in every way distinct from and incommunicable to any other being, so that it exists and acts *sui juris*, autonomously".

If such an individual nature is not merely corporeal but organic or animate, not merely animate but sentient, and not merely sentient but *rational* or *intelligent, i.e.* constituted at least in part by a *spiritual substantial principle* whereby the individual is *intelligent* and *free*, then that individual is a person. Every individual of the human species is such. And all that is essential to his complete individual human nature enters into and constitutes his person in the concrete. Not merely, therefore, his intellect and will; not merely his soul considered as "mind," *i.e.* as the basis and principle of his whole conscious and subconscious psychic life; or also as the principle of his merely organic life; or also as the actualizing principle of his corporeal nature; but no less also the corporeal principle itself of his composite being, the body itself with all its parts and members and organs: all these without exception belong equally to the human person; all of them without exception go to constitute the *Ego*.[304] This, which is the Aristotelian and scholastic view of the human person, is in perfect accord with the common-sense view of the matter as evidenced by the ordinary usages of language. We speak intelligibly no less than correctly when we say that a man's body is part of his person as well as his soul or mind. And we make a no less accurate, intelligible, and necessary distinction, when we distinguish between all that which *constitutes* the human person and that *whereby we know* ourselves and other human individuals to be persons. Yet this distinction is not kept clearly in mind by many modern philosophers, who, approaching the study of personality exclusively from the side of what the individual consciousness testifies as to the unity and continuity (or otherwise) of mental life in the individual, are scandalized at the assertion that the human body can have anything to do with human personality.

74. CONSCIOUSNESS OF THE PERSONAL SELF.—In order to form the concept of person, and to find that concept verified in the data of our experience, it is absolutely essential that we be endowed with the *faculty of intelligence*, the spiritual power of forming abstract concepts; and secondly, that having formed the concept of person as a "rational or intelligent subsisting being," we be capable, by the exercise of *reflex consciousness*, to find in our own mental life the data from which we can conclude that this concept of person is verified in each and every one of ourselves. It is because we are endowed with intelligence that we can form all the abstract notions—of substance, individual, subsistence, existence, etc.,—which enter into and constitute our concept of person. And it is because we can, by means of this faculty, reflect on our own mental operations, and infer from them that each of us is a complete individual rational nature subsisting independently and incommunicably, that we can know ourselves to be persons.

How the human individual forms these concepts and finds them verified in his own "self," how he gradually comes into conscious possession of the knowledge of his own individual being as an *Ego*, self, or person, are problems for Psychology.[305] It will be sufficient here to point out that there are grounds for distinguishing between the individual's implicit subjective awareness of his subsistence or "selfhood"—an awareness which accompanies all his conscious mental functions, and which becomes more explicit and definite as the power of introspection and reflex consciousness develops—and the "*abstract quasi-objective notion* of his own *personality* habitually possessed by every human being".[306]

The individual human being *immediately* apprehends his own existence, and his abiding unity or sameness throughout incessantly changing states, in the temporal series of his conscious activities; but his knowledge of the *nature* of his own being can be the result only of a long and carefully conducted analysis of his own activities, and of inferences based on the character of these activities. The former or implicit knowledge of the self in the concrete is direct and intuitive. The individual *Ego* apprehends *itself* in *its states*. This knowledge comes mainly from within, and is subject to gradual development. Father Maher thus describes how the child comes gradually into possession of it:—

As thoughts of pleasures and pains repeated in the past and expected in the future grow more distinct, the dissimilarity between these and the permanent abiding self comes to be more fully realized. Passing emotions of fear, anger, vanity, pride, or sympathy, accentuate the difference. But most probably it is the dawning sense of power to resist and overcome rising impulse, and the dim nascent consciousness of responsibility, which lead up to the final revelation, until at last, in some reflective act of memory or choice, or in some vague effort to understand the oft-heard "I," the great truth is manifested to him: the child enters, as it were, into possession of his personality, and knows himself as a *Self-conscious*

Being. The *Ego* does not *create* but *discovers* itself. In Jouffroy's felicitous phrase, it "breaks its shell," and finds that it is *a Personal Agent with an existence and individuality of its own*, standing henceforward alone in opposition to the universe.[307]

After this stage is reached, the human individual easily distinguishes between the "self" as the *cause* or *subject* of the states, and the states as *modifications* of the self. This distinction is implicit in the concomitant awareness of self which accompanies all exercise of direct cognitive consciousness. It is explicit in all deliberate acts of reflex, introspective self-consciousness. The data from which we form the abstract concepts of substance, nature, individual, person, self, etc., and from which we arrive by reasoning at a philosophical knowledge of the nature and personality of the human individual, are furnished mainly by introspection; but also in part by external observation of the universe around us.

Concomitantly, however, with the process by which we become implicitly but immediately aware of the *Ego* or self as an abiding self-identical person in and through our own mental activity, we gradually form a quasi-objective and historical view of our own personality as one of a number of similar personalities around us in the universe. This view, says Father Maher,

gathers into itself the history of my past life—the actions of my childhood, boyhood, youth, and later years. Interwoven with them all is the image of my bodily organism, and clustering around are a fringe of recollections of my dispositions, habits, and character, of my hopes and regrets, of my resolutions and failures, along with a dim consciousness of my position in the minds of other selves.

Under the form of a representation of this composite art, bound together by the thread of memory, each of us ordinarily conceives his complete abiding *personality*. This idea is necessarily undergoing constant modification; and it is in comparing the present form of the representation with the past, whilst adverting to considerable alterations in my character, bodily appearance, and the like, that I sometimes say: "I am completely changed," "I am quite another person," though I am, of course, convinced that it is the same "I" who am changed in accidental qualities. *It is because this complex notion of my personality is an abstraction from my remembered experiences that a perversion of imagination and a rupture of memory can sometimes induce the so-called "illusions or alterations of personality".*[308]

When we remember that this objective conception of the self is so dependent on the function of memory, and that the normal exercise of this faculty is in turn so dependent on the normal functioning of the brain and the nervous system,[309] we can hazard an intelligible explanation of the abnormal facts recorded by most modern psychologists concerning hypnotism, somnambulism and "double" or "multiple" consciousness.[310] Father Maher, ascribing these phenomena partly to dislocations of memory, partly to unusual groupings of mental states according to the laws of mental association—groupings that arise from peculiar physiological connexions between the various neural functionings of the brain centres,—and partly to semi-conscious or reflex nerve processes, emphasizes an important fact that is sometimes lost sight of: the fact that some section at least of the individual's conscious mental life is common to, and present throughout, the two or more "states" or "conditions" between which any such abnormal individual is found to alternate. This consideration is itself sufficient to disprove the theory—to which we shall presently refer—that there is or may be in the individual human being a double, or even a multiple "human personality".

75. FALSE THEORIES OF PERSONALITY.—It is plain that conscious *mental activity* cannot *constitute* human personality, or subconscious mental activity either, for all activity is of the accidental mode of being, is an *accident*, whereas a person must be a *substance*. Of course it is the self-conscious cognitive activity of the human individual that *reveals* to the latter his own self as a person: it is the exercise of reflex consciousness combined with memory that gives us the feeling of personal identity with ourselves throughout the changing events of our mental and bodily life. Furthermore, this self-consciousness has its root in the *rational* nature of the human individual; and rationality of nature is the differentiating principle which makes the subsisting individual a "person" as distinct from a (subsisting) "thing". But then, it is not the feeling of personal identity that *constitutes* the person. Actual consciousness is neither the essence, nor the source, nor even the index of personality; for it is only an activity, and an activity which reveals immediately not the *person* as such, but the *nature* as rational;[311] nor does the rational (substantial) principle of a composite nature constitute the latter a person; but only the subsistence of the complete (composite) individual nature itself.

These considerations are sufficiently obvious; they presuppose, however, the truth of the traditional doctrine already explained in regard to the existence, nature and cognoscibility of *substance*. Philosophers who have misunderstood and rejected and lost this traditional doctrine of substance have propounded many varieties of unsatisfactory and inconsistent theories in regard to what constitutes "person" and "personality". The main feature of all such theories is their identification of personality with the habitual consciousness of self, or habitual feeling of personal identity: a feeling which, however, must be admitted to include *memory* in some form, while the function of memory in any shape or form cannot be satisfactorily explained on any theory of the human *Ego* which denies that there is a human *substance* persisting permanently as a unifying principle of successive mental states.

So far as English philosophy is concerned such theories appear to have had their origin in Locke's teaching on person and personal identity. Discussing the notions of identity and diversity,[312] he distinguishes between the identity of an individual substance with itself in its duration throughout time, and what he terms personal identity; while by identity in general he means not abstract identity but the concrete permanence of a thing throughout time. On this we have to call attention to the fact that just as *duration* is not essential to the *constitution* of a substance, so neither is it essential to the constitution of a complete subsisting individual substance or person; though it is, of course, an essential condition for all human apprehension whether of substance or of person. Locke was wrong, therefore, in confounding what reveals to us the abiding permanence, identity or sameness of a subsisting thing or person (whether the "self" or any other subsisting thing or person) throughout its duration in time, with what constitutes the subsisting thing or person.

Furthermore, his distinction between substantial identity, *i.e.* the sameness of an individual substance with itself throughout time, and personal identity or sameness, was also an error. For as long as there is *substantial* unity, continuity, or identity of the subsisting individual substance, so long is there unity, continuity, or identity of its subsistence, or of its personality if it be a rational substance. The *subsistence* of a complete individual inorganic substance is changed as soon as the individual undergoes *substantial* change: we have them no longer *the same* subsisting individual being. So, too, the subsistence of the organic individual is changed as soon as the latter undergoes *substantial* change by the dissolution of life, by the separation of its formative and vital substantial principle from its material substantial principle: after such dissolution we have no longer *the same* subsisting plant or animal. And, finally, the subsistence of an individual man is changed, or interrupted, or ceases by death, which separates his soul, his vital principle, from his body. We say, moreover, that in the latter case the human *person* ceases to exist when the identity or permanence of his subsisting substance or nature terminates at death; for *personal identity* we hold to be the identity of the complete subsisting substance or nature with itself. But Locke, who practically agrees with what we have said regarding the abiding identity of the subsisting individual being with itself—whether this individual be an inorganic individual, a plant, a brute beast, or a man[313]—distinguishes at this point between identity of the subsisting individual substance and *personal* identity.

Of identity in general he says that "to conceive and judge of it aright, we must consider what idea the word it is applied to stands for; it being one thing to be the same substance, another the same man, and a third the same person, if person, man, and substance, are three names standing for three different ideas".[314] And, struggling to dissociate "person" from "substance," he continues thus:—

To find wherein personal identity consists, we must consider what person stands for; which, I think, is a thinking, intelligent being, that has reason and reflection, and can consider itself as itself, the same thinking thing in different times and places; which it does only by that consciousness which is inseparable from thinking, and, as it seems to me, essential to it. When we see, hear, smell, taste, feel, meditate, or will any thing, we know that we do so. Thus it is always as to our present sensations and perceptions, and by this every one is to himself what he calls self; it not being considered in this case whether the same self be continued in the same or divers substances. For since consciousness always accompanies thinking, and it is that which makes every one to be what he calls self, and thereby distinguishes himself from all other thinking things; in this alone consists personal identity, *i.e.* the sameness of a rational being: and as far as this consciousness can be extended backwards to any past action or thought, so far reaches the identity of that person; it is the same self now it was then; and it is by the same self with this present one that now reflects on it, that that action was done.[315]

The definition of person in this passage as "a thinking, intelligent being," etc., is not far removed from our own definition; but surely conscious thought is not "that which *makes* every one to be what he calls self," seeing that conscious thought is only an *activity* or *function* of the "rational being". It is conscious thought, of course, including memory, that *reveals* the "rational being" to himself as a self, and as the same or identical self throughout time; but unless the "rational being," or the "thinking, intelligent being, that has reason and reflection," etc.—which is Locke's own definition of "person"—were there all the time identical with itself, exercising those distinct and successive acts of consciousness and memory, and unifying them, how could these acts *even reveal* the "person" or his "personal identity" to himself, not to speak of their *constituting* personality or personal identity? It is perfectly plain that these acts *presuppose* the "person," the "thinking, intelligent being," or, as we have expressed it, the "subsisting, rational, individual nature" *already constituted*; and it is equally plain that the "personal identity" which they *reveal* is *constituted by*, and *consists simply in*, the duration or continued existence of this same subsisting individual rational nature; nor could these acts reveal any identity, personal or otherwise, unless they were the acts of one and the same actually subsisting, existing and persisting substance.

Yet Locke thinks he can divorce personal identity from identity of substance, and account for the former independently of the latter. In face of the obvious difficulty that actual consciousness is not continuous but intermittent, he tries to maintain that the consciousness which links together present states with remembered states is sufficient to constitute personal identity even although there may have intervened between the present and the past states a complete change of substance, so that it is really a different substance which experiences the present states from that which experienced the past states. The question

Whether we are the same thinking thing, *i.e.* the same substance or no ... concerns not personal identity at all: the question being, what makes the same person, and not whether it be the same identical substance, which always thinks in the same person: different substances, by the same consciousness (where they do partake in it), being united into one person, as well as different bodies by the same life are united into one animal, whose identity is preserved, in that change of substances, by the unity of one continued life ... [for] animal identity is preserved in identity of life, and not of substance.[316]

Here the contention is that we can have "the same person" and yet not necessarily "the same identical substance," because *consciousness* may give a personal unity to distinct and successive substances in the individual man just as *animal life* gives an analogous unity to distinct and successive substances in the individual animal. This is very superficial; for it only substitutes for the problem of human personality the similar problem of explaining the unity and sameness of subsistence in the individual living thing: a problem which involves the fact of *memory* in animals. For scholastic philosophers unity of life in the living thing, involving the fact of memory in animals, is explained by the perfectly intelligible and will-grounded teaching that there is in each individual living thing a *formative and vital principle* which is *substantial*, a *forma substantialis*, which unites, in the *abiding self-identical unity of a complete individual composite substance*, the material principle of the corporeal substances which thus go, in the incessant process of substantial change known as metabolism, to form partially, and to support the substantial continuity of, the living individual. While the latter is thus in constant process of material, or partial, substantial change, it remains, as long as it lives, the same complete individual substance, and this in virtue of the abiding *substantial* formative and vital principle which actuates and animates it. The abiding permanence or self-identity of the *subsisting individual substance* which feels or thinks, and remembers, is an intelligible, and indeed the only intelligible, ground and explanation of memory, and of our consciousness of personal identity.

But if we leave out of account this abiding continuity and self-identity of the subsisting individual substance or nature, which is the subject, cause and agent of these acts of memory and consciousness, how can these latter, in and by themselves, possibly form, or even indeed reveal to us, our personal identity? Locke felt this difficulty; and he tried in vain to meet it: in vain, for it is insuperable. He merely suggests that "the same consciousness ... can be transferred from one thinking substance to another," in which case "it will be possible that two thinking substances may make one person".[317] This is practically his last word on the question,—and it is worthy of note, for it virtually *substantializes consciousness*. It makes consciousness, which is really only an act or a series of acts, a *something substantial and subsisting*. We have seen already how modern phenomenists, once they reject the notion of substance as invalid or superfluous, must by that very fact equivalently *substantialize accidents*; for substance, being a necessary category of human thought as exercised on reality, cannot really be dispensed with. And we see in the present context an illustration of this fact. The abiding self-identity of the human person cannot be explained otherwise than by the abiding self-identical subsistence of the individual human substance.

If personal identity were constituted and determined by consciousness, by the series of conscious states connected and unified by memory, then it would appear that the human being in infancy, in sleep, in unconsciousness, or in a state of insanity, is not a human person! Philosophers who have not the hardihood to deny human personality to the individual of the human species in these states, and who on the other hand will not recognize the possession of a *rational nature* or substance by the subsisting individual as the ground of the latter's personality and personal identity, have recourse to the hypothesis of a *sub-conscious*, or "*subliminal*" *consciousness* in the individual, as a substitute. If by this they merely meant an abiding *substantial* rational principle of all mental activities, even of those which may be semi-conscious or sub-conscious, they would be merely calling by another name what we call the *rational nature* of man. And the fact that they refer to this principle as the sub-conscious "self" or "Ego" shows how insistent is the rational need for rooting personality and personal identity in something which is a *substance*. But they do not and will not conceive it as a substance; whereas if it is not this, if it is only a "process," or a "function," or a "series" or "stream" of processes or functions, it can no more constitute or explain, or even reveal, personal identity, than a series or stream of *conscious* states can.[318]

Unable as he was to explain how the same consciousness could persist throughout a succession of really and adequately distinct substances (except by virtually substantializing consciousness), Locke nevertheless persisted in holding that consciousness and consciousness alone (including memory, which, however, is inexplicable on any other theory than that of a subsisting and persisting substance or nature which remembers), constitutes personality and personal identity. We have dwelt upon his teaching mainly because all modern phenomenists try to explain personality on the same principles—*i.e.* independently of the doctrine of substance.

As a corollary from his doctrine he inferred that if a man completely and irrevocably loses consciousness [or rather memory] of his past life, though he remains the same "man" he is no longer the same "person": "if it be possible for the same man to have distinct incommunicable consciousness at different times, it is past doubt the same man would at different times make different persons";[319] and he goes on in this sense to give a literal interpretation to the modes of speech we have referred to above.[320] He likewise admitted that two or more "persons," *i.e.* consciousnesses, can be linked with the same individual human being, or the same individual human soul, alternately appearing and disappearing, giving place successively to one another. When any one of these "personalities" or consciousnesses ceases to be actual, it must in Locke's view cease to be in any sense real: so that there could not be two or more personalities at the same time in the same individual human being. Modern psychologists, however, of the phenomenist school, convinced that sub-conscious mental activities are not only possible, but that the fact of such activities is well established by a variety of experiences, have extended Locke's conception of personality (as actual consciousness) to embrace groups of mental activities which may emerge only intermittently "above the threshold of consciousness". Hence they explain the abnormal cases of double or multiple consciousness already referred to, as being manifestations of really distinct "personalities" in one and the same human individual. In normal human beings there is, they say, only one normally "conscious personality". The sub-conscious mental activities of such an individual they bulk together as forming this individual's "sub-liminal" or "sub-conscious" *Ego* or "self": presumably a distinct personality from the conscious one. In the abnormal cases of "double-consciousness" the subliminal self struggles for mastery over the conscious self and is for a time successful: the two personalities thus for a time changing places as it were. In the rarer or more abnormal cases of treble or multiple consciousness, there are presumably three or more "personalities" engaged in the struggle, each coming to the surface in turn and submerging the others.

It is not the fancifulness of this theory that one might object to so much as its utter inadequacy to explain the facts, nay, its utter unintelligibility *on the principles of those who propound it*. For we must not lose sight of the fact that it is propounded by philosophers who purport to explain mental life and human personality without recourse to a *substantial soul*, to any *substantial* basis of mental life, or indeed to the concept of *substance* at all: by philosophers who will talk of a mental process without admitting mind or soul as a *substance* or *subject* of that process, of a "series" or "stream" of mental functions or activities without allowing any *agent* that would exercise those functions, or any *substantial abiding principle* that would unify the series or stream and know it as such; philosophers who regard the *Ego*, "self," or "person," as *nothing other than* the group or series or stream of mental states, and not as anything of which these are the states; and, finally, who speak of these groups of functions or activities as "personalities"—which they describe as "struggling" with one another—apparently oblivious of the fact that by using such language they are *in their thought at least* transforming these *activities* into *agents*, these *states* into *subjects of states*, in a word, these *accidents* into *substances*; or else they are making their language and their thought alike unintelligible.[321]

Of course those numerous modern philosophers who, like James, try to "find a place for all the experiential facts unencumbered by any hypothesis [like that of an individual substantial soul, presumably] save that of passing states of mind" [*ibid.*, p. 480], do not really leave these "states" suspended in mid-air as it were. The imperative need for admitting the reality of substance always ultimately asserts itself: as when James recognizes the necessity of admitting something "more than the bare fact of co-existence of a passing thought with a passing brain-state" [*Principles of Psychology*, i., p. 346—*apud* MAHER, *ibid.*, p. 483]. Only his speculation as to what constitutes this "something 'more' which lies behind our mental states" [*ibid.*, p. 485] is not particularly convincing: "For my own part," he says, "I confess that the moment I become metaphysical and try to define the *more*, I find the notion of some sort of an *anima mundi* thinking in all of us to be a more promising hypothesis, in spite of all its difficulties, than that of a lot of absolutely individual souls" [*ibid.*, p. 346—apud MAHER, *ibid.*]. This restatement of the medieval pantheistic theory known as Averroïsm, Monopsychism, or the theory of the *intellectus separatus* [*cf.* DE WULF, *History of Medieval Philosophy*, pp. 381 *sqq.*], is a somewhat disappointing contribution to Metaphysics from the most brilliant of our modern psychologists. The "difficulties" of this "more promising hypothesis" had discredited it a rather long time before Professor James resurrected it [*cf.* criticisms—*apud* MAHER, *ibid.*].

Chapter X.

Some Accident-Modes Of Being: Quality.

76. ONTOLOGY AND THE ACCIDENT-MODES OF BEING.—Under the ultimate category or *genus supremum* of Substance experience reveals to us two broadly distinct sub-classes: corporeal substances, "bodies" or "material" things, and spiritual substances or "spirits". Of these latter we have direct experience only of one class, *viz. embodied* spirits or human souls. The investigation of the nature of these belongs to *Psychology*, and from the data of that science we may infer, by the light of reason, the *possibility* of another class of spirits, *viz. pure* spirits, beings of whose actual existence we know from Divine Revelation. The existence of a Supreme Being, Whom we must conceive analogically as substance and spirit, is demonstrated by the light of reason in *Natural Theology*. The investigation of the nature of corporeal substances belongs properly to *Cosmology*. Hence in the present treatise we have no further direct concern with the substance-mode of reality;[122] but only with its accident-modes, and not with all of these.

Not with all of them; for those which belong properly to spiritual substances, or properly to corporeal substances, call for special treatment in Psychology and Cosmology respectively. In the main, only such species of accidents as are common to matter and spirit alike, will form the subject of the remaining portion of the present volume. Only the broader aspects of such categories as Quality, Quantity and Causality—aspects which have a more direct bearing on the Theory of Being and the Theory of Knowledge in general,—call for treatment in General Metaphysics. A more detailed treatment must be sought in other departments of Philosophy.

77. NATURE OF THE ACCIDENT CALLED QUALITY.—In the widest sense of the term, *Quality* is synonymous with *logical attribute*. In this sense whatever can be predicated of a subject, whatever *logically* determines a subject in any way for our thought is a quality or "attribute" of that subject. In a sense almost equally wide the term is used to designate any *real* determination, whether substantial or accidental, of a subject. In this sense the differential element, or *differentia specifica*, determines the generic element, or genus, of a substance: it tells us what *kind* or *species* the substance is: *e.g.* what kind of animal a man is, *viz.* rational; what kind of living thing an animal is, *viz.* sentient; what kind of body or corporeal thing a plant is, *viz.* living. And hence scholastics have said of the predicable "*differentia specifica*" that it is predicated adjectivally, or as a *quality*, to tell us in *what the thing consists*, or what is its nature: differentia specifica praedicatur *in quale quid*: it gives us the determining principle of the specific nature. Or, again, quality is used synonymously with any *accidental* determination of a substance. In this sense magnitude, location, action, etc., though they determine a subject in different accidental ways, nevertheless are all indiscriminately said to "qualify" it in the sense of determining it somehow or other, and are therefore called "qualities" in the wide sense of "accidents". Hence, again, the scholastics have said that inasmuch as all accidents determine or qualify their subjects, they are predicated of these *qualitatively*, and may be called in a wide sense "qualifications" or "qualities": omnia genera accidentium qualificant substantiam et praedicantur *in quale*.

It is in this wide sense that we use the term when we say that the (specific) nature (or "kind") of a thing is revealed by its "qualities"; for the nature of a thing is revealed by all its accidents. And when we infer the nature of a thing from its activities, in accordance with the maxim *Qualis est operatio talis est natura*, we must take the term "*operatio*" or "activity" to include the operation of the thing on our cognitive faculties, the states of cognitive consciousness thus aroused in us, and all the other accidents thus revealed to us in the thing by its "knowledge-eliciting" action on our minds.

But the term *Quality* has been traditionally restricted, after Aristotle, to designate properly one particular category of accidents distinct from the others and from substance.

A definition proper of any *genus supremum* is of course out of the question. But it is not easy to give even a description which will convey an accurate notion of the special category of Quality, and mark it off from the other accident-categories. If we say with Aristotle that quality is "that whereby we are enabled to describe *what sort* (ποιόν, *quale*) anything is"[323]—*e.g.* that it is white by whiteness, strong by strength, etc.—we are only illustrating the abstract by the concrete. But even this serves the purpose of helping us to realize what quality in general means. For we are more familiar with the concrete than with the abstract: and we can see a broad distinction between the question: "*What sort* is that thing? *Qualis* est ista res?" (Quality), and the question: "*How large* is that thing? *Quanta* est ista res?" (Quantity), or "*Where* is that thing?" (Place), or "What is it *doing*? What is *happening* to it?" (*Actio et Passio*), or "What does it *resemble*?" (*Relation*), etc. This will help us to realize that there are accidental modes of being which affect substances in a different way from all the extrinsic denominations of the latter, and also in a different way from Quantity, Relation, and Causality; and these modes of being, whereby the substance is *of such a sort*, or *in such a condition*, we call *qualities*. And if we inquire what special kind of *determination* of the substance is common to qualities, and marks these off from the other accidents, we shall find it to consist in this, that quality is an accidental mode of being which so affects the substance that it disposes the latter well or ill in regard to the perfections natural to this particular kind of substance: it *alters* the latter accidentally by increasing or diminishing its natural perfection. We have seen that no created substance has all the perfection natural to its kind, *tota simul* or *ab initio*; that it fulfils its rôle in existence by development, by tending towards its full or final perfection. The accidental realities which supervene on its essence, and thus *alter* its perfection *within the limits of its kind or species*, are what we call qualities. They diversify the substance accidentally in its perfection, in its concrete mode of existing and behaving: by their appearance and disappearance they do not change the *essential perfection* of the substance, they do not effect a substantial change; but they change its intermediate, accidental perfection; and this qualitative change is technically known and described as *alteration*[24].

Hence we find *Quality* described by St. Thomas as the sort of accident which modifies or disposes the substance in itself: "*accidens modificativum sen dispositivum substantiaein seipsa*," and by Albertus Magnus somewhat more explicitly as "the sort of accident which completes and perfects substance in its existence and activity: *accidens complens ac perficiens substantiam tarn in existendo quam in operando*".[325] This notion will be conveyed with sufficient clearness if we describe *Quality* as *that absolute accident which determines a substance after the manner of an accidental "differentia," affecting the essential perfection of the substance in regard to its existence or to its activity.*

Hence (I) the Pure Actuality of the Infinitely Perfect Being cannot admit qualities, inasmuch as quality implies only a relative and limited perfection; (2) the qualities of a corporeal substance are grounded in the *formative* principle which gives that substance its specific nature and is the principle of its tendency and development towards its final perfection, whereas its *quantity* is grounded in its determinable or *material* principle; (3) the *essential* differentiating principles of substances—being known to us not intuitively, but only abstractively and discursively, *i.e.* by inference from the behaviour of these substances, from the effects of their activities—are often designated not by what constitutes them intrinsically, but by the *accidental perfections* or *qualities* which are our only key to a knowledge of them. For instance, we differentiate the nature of man from that of the brute beast by describing the former as *rational*: a term which really designates not the essence or nature itself, but one of its fundamental qualities, *viz.* the faculty of reason.

78. IMMEDIATE SUB-CLASSES OF QUALITY AS *Genus Supremum*.—On account of the enormous variety of qualities which characterize the data of our experience, the problem of classifying qualities is not a simple one. Its details belong to the special sciences and to the other departments of philosophy. Here we must confine ourselves to an attempt at indicating the immediate sub-classes of the *genus supremum*. And in this context it will not be out of place to call attention to a remarkable, and in our view quite erroneous, trend of modern thought. It accompanied the advent of what is known as *atomism* or *the mechanical conception of the universe*, a conception much in vogue about half a century ago, but against which there are already abundant evidences of a strong reaction. We refer to the inclination of scientists and philosophers to eliminate Quality altogether as an ultimately distinct category of human experience, by reducing all qualities to *quantity*, *local relations*, and *mechanical* or *spatial motions* of matter. In this theory all the sensible qualities of the material universe would be really and objectively nothing more than locations and motions of the ultimate constituents of perceptible matter. All the chemical, physical and mechanical energies or forces of external nature would be purely quantitative dispositions or configurations of matter in motion: realities that could be *exhaustively* known by mathematical analysis and measurement. And when it was found that *qualitative* concepts stubbornly resisted all attempts at elimination, or reduction to *quantitative* concepts, even in the investigation of the material universe or external nature, scientists and philosophers of external nature thought to get rid of them by locating them exclusively in the human mind, and thus pushing them over on psychologists and philosophers of the mind for further and final exorcism. For a time extreme materialists, less wise than daring, endeavoured to reduce even mind and all its conscious states and processes to a mere subjective aspect of what, looked at objectively, would be merely matter in motion.[326] It can be shown in Cosmology, Psychology, and Epistemology that all such attempts to analyse qualities into something other than qualities, are utterly unsatisfactory and unsuccessful. And we may see even from an enumeration of some of the main classes of qualities that such attempts were foredoomed to failure.

Scholastic Philosophy has generally adopted Aristotle's division of qualities into four great groups:[327] (1) ἕξις ἢ διάθεσις, *habitus vel dispositio*; (2) δύναμις φυσικὴ ἢ ἀδυναμία, potentia *naturalis vel impotentia*; (3) ποιότητες παθητικαί καὶ πάθη, *potentiae passivae et passiones*; (4) μορφὴ ἢ σχῆμα, *forma vel figura*. St. Thomas offers the following ground for this classification. Since quality, he says,[328] is an accidental determination of the substance itself, *i.e.* of the perfection of its concrete existence and activity, and since we may distinguish four aspects of the substance: its nature itself as perfectible; its intrinsic principles of acting and receiving action, principles springing from the *formative*, specific constituent of its nature; its receptivity of change effected by such action, a receptivity grounded in the determinable or *material* principle of its nature; and finally its quantity, if it be a corporeal substance,—we can likewise distinguish between (1) *acquired habits or dispositions*, such as health, knowledge, virtue, vice, etc., which immediately determine the perfection of the substance, disposing it well or ill in relation to its last end; (2) intrinsic *natural forces, faculties, powers of action, aptitudes, capacities*, such as intellect, will, imagination, instinct, organic vital forces, physical, chemical, mechanical energies; (3) states resulting in a corporeal being from the action of its *milieu* upon it: the *passions* and emotions of sentient living things, such as sensations of pleasure, pain, anger, etc.; the *sensible qualities* of matter, such as colour, taste, smell, temperature, feel or texture, etc.; and, finally (4) the quality of *form or shape* which is a mere determination of the quantity of a corporeal substance.

This classification is not indeed perfect, for the same individual quality can be placed in different classes when looked at from different standpoints: heat, for instance, may be regarded as a *natural operative power* of a substance in a state of combustion, or as a *sensible quality* produced in that substance by the operation of other agencies. But it has the merit of being an exhaustive classification; and philosophers have not succeeded in improving on it.

Qualities of the third and fourth class do not call for special treatment. In the third class, Aristotle's distinction between οιότητες παθητικαί (*qualitates passibiles*) and πάθη (*passiones*) is based upon the relatively permanent or transient character of the quality in question. The transient quality, such as the blush produced by shame or the pallor produced by fear, would be a *passio*;[329] whereas the more permanent quality, such as the natural colour of the countenance, would be a *passibilis qualitas*. The "passions" or sensible changes which result from certain conscious states, and affect the organism of the sentient living being, are included in this class as *passiones*; while the visible manifestations of more permanent mental derangement or insanity would be included in it as *passibiles qualitates*. We may, perhaps, get a fairly clear and comprehensive notion of all that is contained in this class as "sensible qualities" by realizing that these embrace whatever is the immediate *cause* or the immediate *result* of the *sense modification involved in any act or process of sense consciousness*. Such "sensible qualities," therefore, belong in part to the objects which provoke sense perception, and in part to the sentient subject which elicits the conscious act. One of the most important problems in the Theory of Knowledge, and one which ramifies into Cosmology and Psychology, is that of determining the precise significance of these "sensible qualities,"—and especially in determining whether they are qualities of an extramental reality, or merely states of the individual mind or consciousness itself.

Form or *figure*, which constitutes the fourth class of quality, is a mode of the quantity of a body, being merely the particular surface termination of its extension or volume. Considered as a mode of abstract or mathematical quantity, it belongs to the domain of mathematics. Considered in the concrete body, it is the physical, sensible form, shape, or figure, of the latter; and here it may be either natural or artificial, according as it results from the unimpeded action of natural forces or from these forces as manipulated and directed by intelligent agents. It is worthy of special note that while extension or volume is indicative of the *material* principle of corporeal substances, the figure or shape naturally assumed by this volume is determined by their *formative* principle, and is thus indicative of their specific nature. This is already noticeable in the inorganic world, where many of the chemically different substances assume each its own distinctive crystalline form. But it is particularly in the domains of botany and zoology that the natural external form of the living individual organism is recognized as one of the most important grounds of its classification and one of the surest tests of its specific nature.[330]

79. HABITS AND DISPOSITIONS.—Every created being is subject to change, capable of development or retrogression, endowed with a natural tendency towards some end which it can reach by a natural process of activity, and which constitutes for it, when attained, its full and final perfection. Through this process of change it acquires accidental modes of being which help it or hinder it, dispose it or indispose it, in the exercise of its natural activities, and therefore also in the concrete perfection of its nature as tending towards its natural end. Such an accidental mode of being is acquired by a series of transient actions and experiences, *actiones et passiones*: after these have passed away it remains, and not merely as a state or condition resulting from the changes wrought in the subject by these experiences, but as a *disposition* towards easier repetition of such experiences. Moreover, it may be not a mere transient disposition, but something stable and permanent, not easily removed or annulled, a *dispositio difficile mobilis*. And just as it is essentially indicative of past actions whereby it was

acquired, so, too, the very *raison d'être* of its actuality is to dispose its subject for further and future changes, for operations and effects which are not yet actual but only potential in this subject. Such an accidental mode of being is what Aristotle called ἕξις, and the scholastics *habitus*. With Aristotle, they define *habit* as a *more or less stable disposition whereby a subject is well or ill disposed in itself or in relation to other things*. *Habitus dicitur dispositio difficile mobilis secundum quam bene vel male disponitur subjectum aut secundum se aut in ordine ad aliud.*[331]

The difference between a *habit* (ἕξις) and a simple *disposition* (διάθεσις) is that the former is by nature a more or less *stable* quality while the latter is unstable and transient. Moreover, the facilities acquired by repeated action of the organs or members of men or animals, and the particular "set" acquired by certain tools or instruments from continued use, are more properly called *dispositions* than *habits*: they are not habits in the strict sense, though they are often called habits in the ordinary and looser usage of common speech. A little reflection will show that *the only proper subjects of natural habits in the strict sense are the spiritual faculties of an intelligent and free agent.*

Since all natural habits are acquired by the past activities, and dispose for the future activities, of a being not absolutely perfect, but partly potential and partly actual, and subject to change, it follows that only finite beings can have habits. But, furthermore, beings that are not free, that have not control or dominion of their own actions, that have not freedom of choice, are determined by their nature, by a necessary law of their activity, to elicit the actions which they do actually elicit: such beings are by their nature *determinata ad unumn*; they are confined necessarily to the particular lines of action whereby they fulfil their rôle in the actual order of things. As Aristotle remarks, you may throw the same stone repeatedly in the same direction and with the same velocity: it will never acquire a *habit* of moving in that direction with that velocity.[332] The same is true of plants and animals; for a habit in the strict sense implies not merely a certain mutability in its subject; it implies, and consists in, a stable modification of some power or faculty *which can have its activities directed indifferently in one or other of a variety of channels or lines*: the power or faculty which is the proper subject of a habit must be a *potentia dirigibilis vel determinabilis ad diversa*. Hence merely material powers of action—such as the mechanical, physical and chemical forces of inorganic nature, or the organic powers of living bodies, whether vegetative or merely sentient,—since they are all *of themselves*, of *their nature*, determined to certain lines of action, and to these only,—such powers cannot become the subjects of habits, of stable dispositions towards one line of action rather than another. "The powers of material nature," says St. Thomas, "do not elicit their operations by means of habits, for they are of themselves [already adequately] determined to their particular lines of action."[333]

Only the spiritual faculties of free agents are, then, the proper seat of real habits. Only of free agents can we say strictly that "habit is second nature". Only these can direct the operations of their intellect and will, and through these latter the operations of their sense faculties, both cognitive and appetitive, in a way conducive to their last end or in a way that deviates therefrom, by attaching their intellects to truth or to error, their wills to virtue or to vice, and thus forming in these faculties stable dispositions or *habits*.[334]

Is there any sense, then, in which we can speak of the sentient (cognitive and appetitive) and executive powers of man as the seat of habits? The activities of those faculties are under the control of intellect and will; the acts *elicited* by the former are *commanded* by the latter; they are acts that issue primarily from the latter faculties; and hence the dispositions that result from repetition of these acts and give a facility for further repetition of them—acts of talking, walking, singing, playing musical instruments, exercising any handicraft—are partly, though only secondarily, *dispositions* formed in these sentient faculties (the "trained" eye, the "trained" ear, the "discriminating" sense of taste, the "alert" sense of touch in the deaf, dumb, or blind), or in these executive powers, whereby the latter more promptly and easily obey the "command" of the higher faculties; but they are primarily and principally *habits* of these higher faculties themselves rendering the latter permanently "apt" to "command" and utilize the subordinate powers in the repetition of such acts.[335]

Unquestionably the bodily organs acquire by exercise a definite "set" which facilitates their further exercise. But this "set" is not something that they can use themselves; nor is it something that removes or lessens a natural indeterminateness or indifference of these powers; for they are not indifferent: they *must* act, at any instant, in the *one* way which their concrete nature in all its surroundings actually demands. They themselves are only instruments of the higher faculties; these alone have freedom of choice between lines of action; it is only the stable modifications which these acquire, which they themselves can use, and which *dispose* them by lessening their indeterminateness, that are properly called habits. There are, therefore, in the organic faculties of man *dispositions* which give facility of action. There are, moreover, organic dispositions which dispose the organism not for *action* but for its union with the *formative principle* or soul: *habituales dispositiones materiae ad formam*.[336] Aristotle gives as instances bodily health or beauty.[337] But these *dispositiones materiales ad formam* he does not call *habits*, any more than the organic *dispositiones ad operationem* just referred to: and for this reason, that although all these dispositions have a certain degree of stability in the organism—a stability which they derive, moreover, from the soul which is the formative principle that secures the continuity and individual identity of the organism,—yet they are not of themselves, of their own nature, stable; whereas the acquired dispositions of the spiritual faculties, intellect and will, rooted as they are in a subject that is spiritual and substantially immutable, are of their own nature stable and permanent. Nor are all dispositions of these latter faculties to be deemed habits, but only those which arise from acts which give them the special character of stability. Hence mere *opinion* in the intellectual order, as distinct from *science*, or a mere *inclination* resulting from a few isolated acts, as distinct from a *virtue* or a *vice* in the moral order, are not habits.[338] Habits, therefore, belong properly to the faculties of a spiritual substance; indirectly, however, they extend their influence to the lower or organic powers dependent on, and controlled by, the spiritual faculties.

To the various dispositions and facilities of action acquired by animals through "training," "adaptation," "acclimatization," etc., we may apply what has been said in regard to the sense faculties and executive powers of the human body. Just as we may regard the internal sense faculties (memory, imagination, sense appetite) in man as in a secondary and subordinate way subjects of habits, in so far as these faculties act under the direction and control of human reason and will,[339] so also the organic dispositions induced in irrational animals by the direction and guidance of human reason may indeed be regarded as extensions or effects of the habits that dispose the rational human faculties, but not as themselves in the strict sense habits.[340]

If, then, habits belong properly to intellect and will, and if their function is to dispose or indispose the human agent for the attainment of the perfection in which his last end consists, we must naturally look to *Psychology* and *Ethics* for a detailed analysis of them. Here we must be content with a word on their origin, their effects, and their importance.

Habits are produced by acts. The act modifies the faculty. If, for instance, nothing remained in our cognitive faculties after each transient cognitive act had passed, memory would be inexplicable and knowledge impossible; nor could the repetition of any act ever become easier than its first performance. This something that remains is a habit, or the beginning of a habit A habit may be produced by a single act: the mind's first intuition of an axiom or principle produces a *habit or habitual knowledge* of that principle. But as a rule it requires a repetition of any act, and that for a long time at comparatively short intervals, to produce a *habit* of that act, a stable disposition whereby it can be readily repeated; and to strengthen and perfect the habit the acts must be formed with a growing degree of intensity and energy. Progress in virtue demands sustained and increasingly earnest efforts.

The natural effect of habit is to perfect the faculty,[341] to increase its energy, to make it more prompt to act, and thus to *facilitate* the performance of the act for which the habit disposes it. It also engenders and develops a natural *need* or *tendency* or *desire* to repeat the act, and a natural aversion from the acts opposed to the habit. Finally, according as the habit grows, the performance of the act demands less effort, calls for less actual attention; thus the habit diminishes the feeling of effort and tends to bring about a quasi-automatic and semi-conscious form of activity.

Good habits are those which *perfect* the nature of the agent, which advance it towards the realization of its end; bad habits are those which retard and prevent the realization of this end. Hence the *ethical* importance, to the human person, of forming, fostering and confirming good habits, as also of avoiding, resisting and eradicating bad habits, can scarcely be exaggerated.

The profound and all-pervading influence of habit in the mental and moral life of man is unfortunately far from being adequately appreciated even by those responsible for the secular, moral and religious education of the young. This is perhaps mainly due to the fact that the influence of habit on the conduct of life, enormous as it is in fact, is so secret, so largely unconscious, that it easily escapes notice. Careful reflection on our actions, diligent study of the springs of action in our everyday life, are needed to reveal this influence. But the more we analyse human conduct in ourselves and others, the more firmly convinced we become that human character and conduct are *mainly* dependent on *the formation of habits*. Habits are the grand conserving and perfecting—or the terrible undermining and destroying—force of life. They are the fruit of our past and the seed of our future. In them the words of Leibniz find their fullest verification: "the present is laden with the past and pregnant with the future". By forming good habits we escape the disheartening difficulties of perpetual beginnings; and thus the labour we devote to the acquisition of wisdom and virtue has its first rich recompense in the facility it gives us to advance on the path of progress.

It has been truly and rightly said that all genuine education consists in the formation of good habits.

80. POWERS, FACULTIES AND FORCES.—A natural operative power, faculty, or force (δύναμις, *potentia, facultas, virtus agendi*) is a quality which renders the nature of the individual agent apt to elicit certain actions. By *impotence* or *incapacity* (ἀδυναμία, *impotentia, incapacitas*) Aristotle meant not an opposite kind of quality, in contradistinction to power or faculty, but only a *power of a weaker order*, differing *in degree*, not *in kind*, from the real power which renders

an agent proximately capable of acting; such weaker capacities, for instance, as the infant's power to walk, or the defective eyesight of the aged.

It is to the individual subsisting person or thing that all the actions proceeding from the latter are ascribed: *actiones sunt suppositorum*: the "*suppositum*" or person is the *principium* QUOD *agit*. And it acts in accordance with its nature; this latter is the *principium* QUO *agens agit*: the nature is the substance or essence as a principle of the actions whereby the individual tends to realize its end. But is a created, finite nature the *immediate* or *proximate* principle of its activities, so that it is operative *per se*? Or is it only their *remote principle*, eliciting them not by itself but *only* by means of *powers, faculties, forces*, which are themselves accidental perfections of the substance and *really distinct* from it, qualities intermediate between the latter and its actions, being the *proximate* principles of the latter?

No doubt when any individual nature is acted upon by other agencies, when it undergoes real change under the influence of its environment, its *passive potentiality* is being so far forth actualized. Moreover when the nature itself acts *immanently*, the term of such action remaining within the agent itself to actualize or perfect it, some *passive potentiality* of the agent is being actualized. In these cases the nature before being thus actualized was really capable of such actualization. This *passive potentiality*, however, is itself nothing actual, it implies no actual perfection in the nature. But we must distinguish carefully from this *passive or receptive potentiality* of a nature its *active or operative powers— potentiae operativae*. These may be themselves *actual perfections* in the nature, *accidental* perfections actually in the nature, and perhaps really distinct from it.

That they are indeed *actual* perfections of the nature is fairly obvious: it is an actual perfection of a nature to be *proximately* and *immediately*, and without any further complement or addition to its reality, *capable of acting*, and this is true whether the action in question be immanent or transitive: if it be immanent, the perfection resulting from the action, the term of the latter, will be a perfection of the agent itself, and in this case the agent by virtue of its operative power will have had *the capacity of perfecting itself*, while if the action be transitive the agent will have had, in virtue of its operative power, *the capacity of producing perfections in other things*. In either case such capacity is undoubtedly an actual perfection of the agent that possesses it. Hence the truth of the scholastic formula: *Omne agens agit in quantum est in* ACTU, *patiatur vero inquantum est in* POTENTIA.

Furthermore, all such operative powers are *really distinct from the actions* which immediately proceed from them: this, too, is obvious, for while the operative power is a stable, abiding characteristic of the agent, the actions elicited by means of it are transient.

But what is the nature of this operative power in relation to the nature itself of the agent? It is an actual perfection of this nature. It is, moreover, unlike acquired habits, native to this nature, born with it so to speak, naturally inseparable from it. Further still, operative powers would seem to be all *properties* of their respective natures: inasmuch as it is only in virtue of the operative power that the nature can act, and there can be no nature without connatural operations whereby it tends to realize the full and *final* perfection of its being, the perfection which is the very *raison d'être* of its presence in the actual order of things. The question therefore narrows itself down to this: Are operative powers, which perfect the nature of which they are properties, really distinct from this nature, or are they only virtually distinct aspects under which we view the nature itself? For example, when we speak of intellect and will as being faculties of the human soul, do we merely mean that intellect is the soul itself regarded as capable of reasoning, and will the soul itself regarded as capable of willing? Or do we mean that the soul is not *by itself* and *in virtue of its own essence* capable of reasoning and willing; that it can reason and will only through the instrumentality of two realities of the accidental order, really distinct from, though at the same time *necessarily* rooted in and springing from, the substance of the soul itself: realities which we call *powers* or *faculties*? Or again, when we speak of a man or an animal as having various *sense faculties*—internal and external, cognitive, appetitive, executive—do we merely mean that the living, sentient organism is itself directly capable of eliciting acts of various kinds: of imagining, desiring, seeing, hearing, etc.? Or do we mean that the organism can elicit these various acts only by means of several accidental realities, really distinct from, and inhering in, itself?

If such operative powers or faculties are naturally inseparable from the substance in which they inhere, if they are so necessarily consequent on the nature of the latter that it cannot exist without them, are they anything more than virtually distinct aspects of the substance itself? On this question, as we have already seen, scholastics are not agreed. St. Thomas, and Thomists generally, maintain that intellect and will are really distinct from the substance of the soul, and likewise that the sense faculties are really distinct from the substance of the animated organism in which they inhere.[342] In this view the distinction is not merely a virtual distinction between different aspects of the soul (or the organism) itself, grounded in the variety and complexity of the acts which emanate from the latter: the faculties are real entities of the accidental order, mediating between the substance and its actions, and involving in the concrete being a plurality which, however, is not incompatible with the real unity of the latter.

The following are some of the arguments urged in proof of a real distinction:—

(*a*) Existence and action are two really distinct actualities; therefore the potentialities which they actualize must be really distinct: for such is the transcendental relation between the potential and the actual that any potential subject and the corresponding perfection which actualizes it must belong to the same *genus supremum*: the one cannot be a substance and the other an accident.[343] Now existence is the actuality of *essence* and action is the actuality of *operative power* or *faculty*. But action is certainly an accident; therefore the operative power which it actualizes must also be an accident, and must therefore be really distinct from the substance of which it is a power, and of which existence is the actuality. This line of argument applies with equal force to all created natures.[344]

In the Infinite Being alone are operation and substance identical. No creature is operative in virtue of its substance. The actions of a creature cannot be actualizations *of its substance*: existence is the actualization of its substance; therefore its actions must be actualizations of potentialities which are *accidents* distinct from its substance; in other words, of operative powers which belong indeed necessarily to its substance but are really distinct from the latter.

This argument rests on very ultimate metaphysical conceptions. But not all scholastics will admit the assumptions it involves. How, for instance, does it appear that the created or finite substance as such cannot be *immediately* operative? Even were it immediately operative its actions would still be accidents, and the distinction between Creator and creature would stand untouched. The operative power must be an accident because the action which actualizes it, the "*actus secundus*," is an accident. But the *consequentia* has not been proved, and it is not self-evident. On the theory of the real distinction, is not the operative power itself an *actual perfection* of the substance, and therefore in some sort an actualization of the latter? And yet they are not in the same ultimate category, *in eodem genere supremo*. The nature which is the potential subject, perfected by the operative power, is a substance, while the operative power which perfects the substance by actualizing this potentiality is an accident. Of course there is not exactly the same correlation between substance and operative power as between the latter and action. But anyhow the action is in some true sense an actualization of the substance, at least through the medium of the power, unless we are prepared to break up the concrete unity of the agent by referring the action solely to the power of the agent, and isolating the substance of the latter as a sort of immutable core which merely "exists": a mode of conceiving the matter, which looks very like the mistake of reifying abstract concepts. And if the action is in any true sense an actualization of the substance, we have, after all, a *potentia* and *actus* which are not in the same ultimate category.

These considerations carry us, of course, right into what is perhaps the most fundamental of all metaphysical problems: that of the mode in which finite reality is actual. In its concrete actuality every finite real being is essentially subject to change: its actuality is not *tota simul*: at every instant it not only *is* but is *becoming*: it is a mixture of potentiality and actuality: it is ever really changing, and yet the "it" which changes can in some real degree and for some real space of time persist or endure identical with itself as a "subsisting thing" or "person". How, then, are we to conceive aright the mode of its actuality? Take the concrete existing being at any instant of its actuality: suppose that it is not merely undergoing change through the influence of other beings in its environment, or through its own immanent action, but that it is itself "acting," whether immanently or transitively. If we consider that at this instant its *existence* is "really distinct" from its *action* we cannot mean by this that there is in it an unchanging substantial core, which is actually merely "existing," and a vesture of active and passive accidental principles, which is just now actual (though always in a state of flux or change) by "acting" or "being acted on".[345] Such a conception would conflict with the truth that the existing substance is ever being really and actually, though accidentally, determined, changed, modified, improved or disimproved, in its total concrete existing reality. Even when these changes are not so profound as to destroy its substantial identity and thus terminate its actuality as an individual being, even when, in other words, they are not substantial, they are none the less real and really affect the substance. Since they are real they necessarily involve the recognition of really distinct principles in the concrete being and preclude the view that the distinctions which we recognize in the ever-changing modes of its actuality, as revealed to us in time and space, are all *merely* conceptual or logical distinctions projected by the mind into what would therefore be in fact a simple and immutable reality. The denial of any real distinction between successive actual states, or between co-existing principles of those states, in any finite being, would lead logically to the Eleatic doctrine, *i.e.* to denial of the reality of change. On the other hand, while recognizing that change is a reality and not a subjective mental illusion, and that real change can be grounded only in a plurality of really distinct principles in the finite individual being, we must at the same time hold that this plurality of really distinct principles in the individual does not destroy a real unity, stability, and self-identical continuity of the individual being in the mode of its actuality throughout time. Not, of course, that this stability or sameness of the individual throughout time is complete and adequate to the exclusion of all real change, but it is certainly a *real* continuity of one and the same individual being: to deny this would be to remove all permanence from reality and to reduce all real being to flux or change, *i.e.* to the πάντα ρέι of the Ionian philosopher, Heraclitus.

We cannot get a true conception of any finite reality by considering it merely from the *static* point of view, which is the natural standpoint of abstract thought; we must view it also from the *dynamic-kinetic* standpoint, *i.e.* not merely as an essence or principle of existence, but as a power or principle of action, and of consequent change, evolution, or decay. And the philosophy which is the latest fashion among contemporary systems, that of the brilliant French thinker and writer, Bergson, has at all events the merit of emphasizing this important truth, that if our philosophical analysis of experience is to be fruitful we must try to grasp reality not merely as it presents itself to abstract thought at any section drawn by the latter through the incessant process of its *fieri* or continuous actualization in time, but also to grasp and analyse as far as possible the *fieri* or process itself, and bring to light whatever we find that this process implies.

These considerations may help the student to estimate for himself the value and the limitations of the argument which has suggested them.

(*b*) A thing cannot be really identical with a variety of things that are really distinct from one another; but the faculties of the soul are really distinct from one another; therefore they must be really distinct from the substance of the soul. The minor premiss is supported by these considerations: The vegetative and sentient operations of the human individual are operations of the living *organism*, while the higher operations of rational thought and volition are operations of the *soul alone*, the spiritual or immaterial principle in the individual. But the immaterial principle cannot be really and adequately identical with the animated organism. Therefore the *powers* or *immediate principles* of these two classes of functions, belonging as they do to two really (though not adequately) distinct substantial principles, cannot be really identical with one of them, *viz.* with the soul itself, the spiritual principle. Again: The exercise of certain functions by the human individual is subordinate to, and dependent on the previous exercise of other functions. For example, actual volition is necessarily dependent and consequent on actual thought: we cannot will or desire any good without first knowing it as a good. But the immediate principle of any function or activity cannot be dependent on or subordinate to itself. Therefore the immediate principles of such controlling and controlled activities—intellect and will, for example—must be really distinct faculties.[346]

(*c*) Suppose the substance or nature of an agent—the human individual, for instance—were really identical with all its powers or faculties, that these were merely the nature itself viewed under different aspects, so that there would be in reality only one operative power in the individual, then there would be no reason why the individual could not or should not at any instant elicit one single action or operation which would be simultaneously an act of thinking, willing, seeing, hearing, etc., *i.e.* which would have at once in itself the modalities of all human activities. But universal experience testifies, on the contrary, that the operations of the individual are each of some particular mode only, that he cannot elicit every mode of human activity simultaneously, that he never elicits one single act having a variety of modes. But why could he not, if his substance or nature itself were the one and only *proximate principle* of all his modes of activity? Because the conditions for the *full and adequate* exercise of this one single or proximate principle (at once substance and power) are never realized! But it is arbitrary to assume the existence of a power which could never pass fully into the act connatural to it. And moreover, even if these conditions are partially realized we should see as a consequence of this some human activity which would manifest *in some degree at least* all the modalities of the various human actions of which we have experience. But we have no experience of a single human activity manifesting *in any degree* the modalities of the numerous and really distinct human activities which experience reveals to us. Hence the variety of these really distinct modes of activity can be explained only by the fact that the human individual elicits them through proximate operative principles or powers which are really distinct from one another and from the nature itself of the individual.[347]

The problem of analysing and classifying the forces, faculties, or powers of the subsisting things and persons in the universe of our experience, belongs partly to Cosmology and partly to Psychology. In the latter it becomes mainly a problem of classifying our mental acts, functions, or processes—our states of consciousness. Apart from the question whether or not our mental faculties are really distinct from one another and from the human nature or substance itself of the individual, the problem of their proper classification is important from the point of view of *method* and of *accurate psychological analysis*. We have seen already that the greatest scholastic philosophers are not unanimous in declaring the distinction to be real. But it is at least a virtual distinction; and even as such it gives rise to the problem of classification. It will be sufficient here to indicate the general principle on which the classification proceeds: Wherever the *acts* are *adequately distinct* they proceed from distinct powers; and the acts are adequately distinct when they have adequately distinct *formal objects*.[348] *Potentiae specificantur per actus et objecta*. The operation or act is the correlative of the power or faculty; and the *formal object* or *term* of the operation is the *final cause* of the latter, the end for which it is elicited. On this basis Aristotle and the scholastics distinguish two mental faculties of the higher or spiritual order, intellect and will; and in the lower or sense order of mental life they distinguish one appetitive faculty, sense appetite, and several cognitive sense faculties. These latter comprise the internal sense faculties, *viz.* the *sensus communis* or unifying and associating sense, the imagination, sense memory, and instinct; and the external sense faculties comprise sight, sound, taste, smell and touch.

81. SOME CHARACTERISTICS OF QUALITIES.—(*a*) *Qualities have contraries.* Health and illness, virtue and vice, science and error, etc., are opposed as contraries. This, however, is not a *property* of qualities; it is not verified in powers, or in forms and figures; and it is verified in accidents which are not qualities, *e.g.* in *actio* and *passio*.

(*b*) *Quality is the basis or "fundamentum" of all relations of similarity and dissimilarity.* This attribute seems to be in the strict sense a *property* of all qualities. Substances are *similar* in so far as they have the same kind of qualities, *dissimilar* in so far as they have different kinds. *Similarity* of substances is the main index to *identity of nature or kind*; but it must not be confounded with the latter. The latter cannot always be inferred even from a high degree of similarity: some specifically distinct classes of things are very similar to one another. Nor, on the other hand, is full and complete similarity a necessary consequence of identity of nature: individuals of the same species are often very dissimilar, very unlike one another.

(c) *Qualities admit of varying degrees of intensity.* They can increase or diminish in the same substance, while numerically (and specifically) distinct substances can have the same kind of quality in different degrees. This is manifest in regard to "habits," "passions" and "sensible qualities". On the other hand, it is clearly not true of "form" or "figure". Different individuals can have the same kind of "natural power" in different degrees. One man may be naturally of keener intellect and stronger will than another: the *weak* power was what Aristotle called ἀδυναμία (*impotentia*). But whether the natural powers of the same individual can *themselves* increase or decrease in strength or intensity—and not merely the *habits* that affect these powers—is not so clear. Operative powers are certainly perfected (or injured) by the acquisition of good (or bad) habits. In the view of those who deny a real distinction between natural operative power or faculty and substance, it is, of course, the substance itself that is so perfected (or injured).

This attribute, therefore, is *not* found in *all* qualities; but it is found in qualities *alone*, and not in any other category or mode of being.

How are we to conceive this variation in intensity, this growth or diminution of any quality, in a substance in which such change takes places? On this point philosophers are not agreed. By "degree of intensity"—"*intensio vel remissio qualitatis*"—we understand the degree (or change of degree) in which the same numerical quality affects *the same part* or *the same power* of its subject, thus rendering this part or power formally more or less "qualified" in some particular way. This is clearly something quite different from the *extension* of the same quality to different parts (or its withdrawal from different parts) of the same extended subject. In a corporeal, extended substance, there can accordingly be question of both kinds of change, *intensive* and *extensive*; while in a simple, spiritual substance there can obviously be question only of *intensive* change of qualities. And the fact of intensive change of qualities is an undeniable fact of experience. In what manner does it take place? Some authors conceive it as an addition or subtraction of *grades* or *degrees* of the same quality. Others, conceiving qualities as simple, indivisible entities or "forms," and thence denying the possibility of distinct grades of any quality, conceive such change to take place by this simple entity affecting its subject *more or less intimately*, becoming *more or less firmly rooted*, as it were, in its subject.[349] And they explain this more or less perfect mode of inherence in a variety of ways, all of which are grounded on certain texts of St. Thomas:[350] the quality receives a new accidental mode whereby it "communicates itself to" the subject, and "informs" the latter, more or less perfectly; or, it is educed more or less fully from the potentiality of its subject, thus qualifying the latter in the degree in which it is educed from, and rooted in, the latter.

These explanations are instructive, as illustrating the view that the actual reality of the accidental mode of being consists in its affecting, determining, the subject in which it inheres. St. Thomas, professing that he can attach no intelligible meaning to addition or substraction of grades,[351] teaches that the habit of charity, for example, can be increased "secundum essentiam" by "inhering more perfectly," "being more firmly rooted" in its subject; for, he says, since it is an accident, "ejus esse est inesse. Unde nihil est aliud ipsam secundum essentiam augeri, quam eam magis inesse subjecto, quod est magis eam radicari in subjecto. Augetur ergo essentialiter... ita quod magis ac magis in subjecto esse incipiat."[352] And elsewhere he concludes with the words: "Ponere igitur quod aliqua qualitas non augeatur secundum essentiam, sed augeatur secundum radicationem in subjecto vel secundum intensionem actus, est ponere contradictoria esse simul".[353]

Chapter XI.

Quantity, Space And Time.

82. ANALYSIS OF THE CONCEPT OF QUANTITY.—A detailed study of Quantity, including Space and Time, and the Aristotelian categories *Ubi*, *Quando* and *Situs*, belongs to Cosmology. Here we shall confine ourselves mainly to the exposition of certain elementary notions preparatory to such detailed study; and we shall assume the validity of the Scholastic Theory of Knowledge: that a real, material world exists independently of our minds; that it consists of material substances or bodies, animate and inanimate, endowed with the fundamental accident of quantity or extension; that these bodies possess, moreover, many other real accidents such as qualities and energies, chemical, physical and mechanical; that they are subject to real change, local, quantitative, qualitative and substantial; that our concepts of space and time, derived from those of extension and change, are not purely subjective or mental forms of cognition, but are objectively valid notions grounded in the reality of the corporeal universe and giving us a genuine, if inadequate, insight into the nature of this reality.

Among the characteristics recognized by physicists in all perceptible matter— divisibility, commensurability, impenetrability, passivity or inertia, subjection to external forces or energies, external extension or volume, internal quantity or mass—there are none more fundamental than those of volume and mass, or extension and quantity.[354] Nowhere, however, do we find a better illustration of the fact that it is impossible to give a definition proper of any supreme category, or even a description of it by the aid of any more elementary notions, than in the attempts of philosophers to describe *Quantity*. When, for instance, we describe *external, actual, local,* or *spatial extension* as *that accident of a corporeal substance or body in virtue of which the latter so exists that it has parts outside parts in space*, we have to admit at once that the notions expressed by the terms "parts," "outside" and "space" are no simpler than the notion of extension itself: in fact our notions of "place" (*locus*) and "space" (*spatium*) are derived from, and presuppose, that of extension. This, however, is no serious disadvantage; for the description, such as it is, indicates what we mean by the terms "local, spatial, external, actual extension," and declares this latter to be an accident of corporeal substances.

Extension, as it is actually in the concrete body, affected by a variety of sensible qualities, is called *physical* extension; regarded in the abstract, apart from these qualities, it is called *geometrical* or *mathematical* extension: *trina dimensio*, or extension in three dimensions, length, breadth and depth. If we abstract from one of these we have extension in *two* dimensions, *superficial* extension; if we abstract from *two*, we have extension in *one* dimension, *linear* extension; and if we abstract from all three we have the extreme *limiting concept* of the *mathematical point*. Of these four abstract mathematical concepts, "point," "line," "surface," and "volume," each expresses the *mathematical limitation* of the succeeding one.

We cannot conceive a body existing by having parts outside parts in space, each part occupying exclusively a place appropriated to itself, unless we conceive the body, the corporeal *substance*, as having already a plurality of *really distinct* or *distinguishable* parts *in itself*, and abstracting from all relation to space. The *substance* must be conceived as having a plurality of really distinct or distinguishable *integral* parts of itself, before these parts can be conceived as existing *outside* one another, each in its own place. And the property in virtue of which the corporeal substance has in itself this plurality of distinct integral parts, whereby it is *capable* of occupying space, and of being impenetrable, divisible, measurable, etc., is called *internal, radical, potential quantity* or *extension*.[355]

The corporeal substance itself is, of course, *essentially* composite, essentially divisible into two *essential* constitutive principles, the passive, determinable, or material principle (*materia prima*), and the specifying, determining, formative principle (*forma substantialis*). Then we conceive this essentially composite substance as necessarily endowed with the *property* of *internal quantity* whereby it is composite in another order: composed of, and divisible into, really distinct *integral* parts, each of which is, of course, essentially composite like the whole itself.[356] Finally we conceive that the corporeal substance, endowed with this property, has also, as a connatural but really distinct and absolutely separable effect of the latter, the accidental mode of being, called external or local extension, in virtue of which it actually occupies space, and thus becomes the subject of all those qualities whereby it is perceptible to our senses.

We have next to inquire into the relations between these three distinct objective concepts, corporeal substance, internal quantity, and local or external extension.

83. CORPOREAL SUBSTANCE, QUANTITY AND EXTENSION.—The corporeal substance is an essentially composite substance, resulting from the union of two distinct essential constitutive principles. It exists in itself and is the ultimate subject of all the determinations whereby it reveals itself to our senses. Its actual extension in space is a fundamental mode or determination of its reality, but it is a mode which is distinct from the reality itself of the corporeal substance. Aristotle regarded the distinction as real. In his *Metaphysics* he declares that the three dimensions of bodies are quantities, not substances, that quantity is not a substance, whereas that in which it ultimately inheres is a substance;[357] in his *Physics* he says that substance is of itself indivisible and is made divisible by its quantity or extension;[358] in his *De Anima*[359] he observes that [external] quantity is directly perceptible by the senses (*sensibile* per se) while substance is only indirectly perceptible (*sensibile* per accidens):[360] from which it is inferred that substance and extension cannot be really identical. Again, St. Thomas argues that a corporeal substance as such, and so far as its essence is concerned, is indifferent to greater or less extension in space, that the whole nature or substance of a man, for instance, is indifferent to, and independent of, his particular size at any point of time, that while he grows from childhood to manhood it is his external quantity that changes, but not his humanity, his human essence, nature, or substance.[361]

Considerations such as these, though they do not indeed amount to cogent proofs of a real distinction between spatial extension and corporeal substance, should make any serious philosopher hesitate to identify these absolutely, as Descartes and his followers did when they declared the essence of corporeal substance to consist in three dimensions of spatial extension. Even looking at the matter from the point of view of natural reason alone, and apart altogether from any light that may be thrown upon it for the Christian philosopher by Divine Revelation, it is only the superficial thinker who will conclude that because extension—which reveals to his intellect through the medium of external sense perception the presence of a corporeal substance—is naturally inseparable from the latter, therefore it is really and absolutely identical with this latter. The philosopher who remembers how little is known for certain about the ultimate, essential constitution of bodies or corporeal substances, will be slow to conclude that the spatially extended mode of their being enters into the constitution of their essence, and is not rather an accidental determination whereby these substances have their integral parts dispersed or extended in space and thus revealed to the human intellect through sense perception.

And if he be a Christian philosopher he will naturally inquire whether any truth of the Christian Revelation will help indirectly to determine the question. Descartes and his followers were Christian philosophers; and hence it was all the more rash and imprudent of them, in spite of what they knew concerning the Blessed Eucharist, to identify the corporeal substance with its spatial extension. They knew that by transubstantiation the bread and wine are changed *substantially* into the Body and Blood of Christ. But all the *appearances* or *phenomena* of bread and wine remain after transubstantiation, the Eucharistic *species* as they are called, the taste, colour, form, etc., in a word, all the sensible qualities of these substances, including the *extension* in which they immediately inhere. From the revealed truth that the *substances* disappear, and from the manifest fact that all their *accidents* remain, Christian philosophers and theologians have rightly drawn the sufficiently obvious inference that the spatially extended quantity, which immediately supports all the other sensible qualities, must be itself an *absolute* accident not only *really distinct*, but by the absolute power of God *really separable*, from its *connatural substance*, the bread and the wine respectively; and that this extended quantity remains in this state of actual separation miraculously supported by the direct influence of the Divine Omnipotence. And while Christian philosophers who hold this view can defend it from all charges of inconsistency, unreasonableness and impossibility, Descartes and his followers can defend their particular view only by the admission that in the case of the consecrated Eucharist our senses are deceived. In this view, while no accidents of the bread and wine remain objectively, God Himself produces directly in our minds the subjective, mental states which the bread and wine produced before consecration.[362] This gratuitous aspersion is cast on the trustworthiness of sense perception, simply on account of the preconceived theory identifying the corporeal substance with its extension. According to the common view, on the other hand, the senses are not really deceived. That to which they testify is really there, *viz.* the whole collection of natural accidents of bread and wine. It is not the function of the senses, but of the intellect, to testify to the presence of the substance. Of course the unbeliever looking at the consecrated species, or the believer who looks at them not knowing that they have been consecrated, thinks that the substance of bread and the substance of wine are there. Each is deceived intellectually, the one by his unbelief of a truth, the other by his ignorance of a fact. If both knew of the fact of consecration, and if the former believed in the effect of it, neither would be deceived.[363]

While the Cartesian view is thus open to such serious objections, the only plausible difficulty against the traditional view is that of conceiving how the reality of a merely accidental mode of being, such as extension, can be sustained in the actual order of things apart from its connatural substance, and yet not become itself *eo ipso* a substance. Needless to say we have no *positive* conception of the manner in which the Divine Omnipotence thus sustains extension; but since this latter, being an absolute accident, and not a mere modal determination of the substance, has a reality of its own, the miraculous persistence of this reality cannot be shown to be impossible. Nor is it, in this separated condition, itself a substance, for it still retains its natural aptitude for inherence in its connatural substance; and this *aptitude* alone, not *actual* inherence, is of its essence as an accident: retaining this natural aptitude it cannot possibly become a substance, it cannot be identified with the *substantial* mode of being which has essentially the very opposite aptitude, that of *existing in itself*.

External extension, then, is an absolute accident, really distinct from the corporeal substance, and naturally though not absolutely inseparable from the latter. It is the natural concomitant or consequence of the *internal quantity* whereby the corporeal substance has in itself a plurality of distinct integral parts. This *internal quantity* itself is either an aspect of the corporeal substance itself, only virtually distinct from the latter, or else in the strict sense a *property*, absolutely inseparable, if really distinct, from the substance. Natural experience furnishes no example of a corporeal substance actually existing devoid of internal quantity or internal distinction of integral parts.[364] But scholastic philosophers are not agreed as to whether the corporeal substance is itself and by its own essence a manifold of really distinct integral parts (in which case internal quantity would be merely the aspect under which the essence is thus regarded as an integral whole constituted by a plurality of distinct integral parts; while, looked at as an essence, it would be an essential whole constituted by the union of two essential parts or principles)—or whether it is formally constituted an integral whole, not by its essence (which makes it only an essential whole, an essentially composite substance), but by a property really distinct, though necessarily flowing, from this essence, *viz.* internal quantity. According to the former view the material principle (*materia prima*) of the composite corporeal substance is such that the essence resulting from its union with the formative principle (*forma substantialis*) is necessarily an integral whole with distinguishable integral parts, each of which naturally demands the spatially extended mode of being which external extension *de facto* confers upon it. According to the latter view, which is that of St. Thomas and his followers generally, the corporeal substance as such has no mode of composition other than *essential* composition: it is not of itself an *integral* whole, compounded of distinct or distinguishable integral parts (each of which would be, like the whole, essentially composite): of itself it is *indivisible* into integral parts: it is, therefore, in this order of being, simple and not composite. It has, no doubt, by reason of its material principle, an absolutely necessary exigence for divisibility into distinct integral parts, for integral composition in other words. But this actual integral composition, this actual divisibility, is the formal effect of a property really distinct from the substantial essence itself; and this property is internal quantity: the connatural, but absolutely separable, complement of this internal quantity being, as in the other view, local or spatial extension.

In both views external extension is an absolute accident of the corporeal substance; and in the Thomist view internal quantity would also appear to be an absolute accident, and not a mere mode.

It is instructive to reflect how far this scholastic doctrine removes us from the Cartesian view which sets up an absolute antithesis between mind or spirit, and matter or body, placing the essence of the former in *thought* and that of the latter in *extension*. According to the scholastic view the spiritual substance is an immaterial "actuality" or "form"; it is *essentially simple*, and not like a corporeal substance an *essentially composite* substance resulting from the union of a formative principle or "form" with a passive, determinable, material principle. And since it is the material principle that demands the property of internal quantity and the accident of external extension, whereby the corporeal substance becomes an integral whole with its parts extended in space, it follows that the spiritual substance, having no material principle in its constitution, is not only *essentially* simple—to the exclusion of distinct principles of its essence,—but is also and as a consequence *integrally* simple, to the exclusion of distinct integral parts, and of the extended or characteristically corporeal mode of occupying space. So far there is contrast between the two great substantial modes of finite being, matter and spirit; but the contrast is by no means an absolute antithesis. For if we look at the essence alone of the corporeal substance it is not *of itself* actually extended in space: in the Thomist view it is not even of itself divisible into distinct integral parts. It differs from spirit in this that while the latter is essentially simple the former is essentially composite and has by reason of this compositeness a natural aptitude for divisibility into parts and for the extension of these parts in space, an aptitude which spirit does not possess. But the corporeal substance *may* exist without actual extension, and consequently without any of those other attributes such as impenetrability, solidity, colour, etc., through which it is perceptible to our senses. In this condition, how does it differ from spirit? In being essentially composite, and in being perhaps endowed with distinguishable integral parts.[365] But in this condition the essential mode of its being has a relation to space which closely resembles the mode in which spirit exists in space: it is related to space somewhat in the manner in which the soul is in the space occupied by the body—whole in the whole of this space and whole in every assignable portion of this space. So that after all, different as matter and spirit undoubtedly are, the difference between them is by no means that sort of Cartesian chasm which human thought must for ever fail to bridge.

By virtue of its external extension the corporeal substance exists by having distinguishable parts outside parts in space. We can conceive any perceptible volume of matter as being *perfectly continuous*, if it has no *actual* limits or *actual* distinction of parts within itself, but is *one* individual being *completely filling* the whole space within its outer surface; or *imperfectly continuous*, if while being one and undivided it has within its volume pores or interstices, whether these be empty or filled with some other sort of matter; or as made up of *contiguous* integral parts if each or these is really distinct and actually divided from every other, while each actually touches with its outer limits the adjacent limits of the parts lying next to it, so that all the internal parts or limits are co-terminous; or as made up of separate, *discrete* or distant parts no one of which actually touches any other.

It is clear that there must be, in any actually extended volume of matter, *ultimate parts* which are really *continuous*—unless we are to hold, with dynamists, that our perception of extension is produced in our minds by the action of extramental points or centres of force which are themselves *simple* or *unextended*. But the physical phenomena of contraction, expansion, absorption, undulatory and vibratory motions accompanying our sensations of light, heat and sound, as well as many other physical phenomena, all point to the fact that volumes of matter which are *apparently* continuous are really porous: the molecular structure of perceptible matter is an accepted physical theory; and scientists also universally accept as a working hypothesis the existence of an imperceptible material medium pervading and filling all real space, though there is no agreement as to the properties with which they suppose this hypothetical medium, the "ether," to be endowed.

Again, as regards the *divisibility* of extended matter, it is obvious that if we conceive extension in three dimensions *geometrically*, *mathematically* or *in the abstract*, any such volume or extension is *indefinitely divisible* in thought. But if we inquire how far any concrete, actually existing volume of matter is divisible, we know in the first place that we cannot divide the body of any actual organic living thing indefinitely without destroying its life, and so its specific character. Nor can we carry on the division of inorganic matter indefinitely for want of sufficiently delicate dividing instruments. But apart from this the science of chemistry points to the fact that every inorganic chemical compound has an ultimate individual unit, the chemical molecule, which we cannot sub-divide without destroying the specific nature of the compound by resolving it into its elements or into less complex compounds. Furthermore, each "elementary" or "chemically simple" body—such as gold, oxygen, carbon, etc.—seems resolvable into units called "atoms," which appear to be ultimate *individual* units in the sense that if their mass *can* be subdivided (as appears possible from researches that have originated in the discovery of radium) the subdivisions are specifically different kinds of matter from that of the atom so divided.

In the inorganic world the perceptible mass of matter is certainly not an *individual* being, a *unum per se*, but only a collection of individual atoms or molecules, a *unum per accidens*. Whether the molecule or the atom of the chemically elementary body is the "individual," cannot be determined with any degree of certitude. It would appear, however, that every specifically distinct type of inorganic matter, whether compound or elementary, requires for its existence a certain minimal volume, by the sub-division of which the type is substantially changed; and this is manifestly true of organic or living matter: so that matter *as it naturally exists* would appear not to be indefinitely divisible.

If in a chemically homogeneous mass of *inorganic* matter (such as carbon or water) the chemical molecule be regarded as the "individual," this cannot be the case in any *organic, living thing*, for whatever matter is assimilated into the living substance of such a being *eo ipso* undergoes substantial change whereby it loses the nature it had and becomes a constituent of the living individual. The *substantial*, "*individual*" unity of the organic living being seems to be compatible not merely with qualitative (structural and functional) heterogeneity of parts, but also with (perhaps even *complete*) spatial separateness of these parts. If the structure of the living body is really "molecular," *i.e.* if it has *distances* between its ultimate integral units, so that these are not in spatial contact, then the fact that the formative, vital principle (*forma substantialis, anima*) unifies this material manifold, and constitutes it an "individual" by actualizing and vitalizing each and all of the material units, spatially separate as they are,—this fact will help us to realize that the *formative principle* of the composite corporeal substance has not *of itself* the *spatial, extended* mode of being, but that the substance derives the latter from its material principle (*materia prima*).

84. PLACE AND SPACE.—From the concept of the volume or actual extension of a body we pass immediately to that of the "place" (*locus*) which it occupies. We may distinguish between the *internal* and the *external* place of a body. By the former we understand *the outer (convex) surface of the body itself, regarded as a receptacle containing the volume of the body*. If, therefore, there were only one body in existence it would have its own internal place: this is independent of other bodies. Not so, however, the external place; for by the external place of a body we mean *the immediately surrounding (concave) surface*, formed by the bodies which circumscribe the body in question, and *considered formally as an immovable container of this body*. This is a free rendering of Aristotle's definition: *Place is the first (or immediate) immovable surface (or limit) of that which contains a body: prima immobilis superficies ejus quod continet*.[366] If a hollow sphere were filled with water, the inner or concave surface of the sphere would be the "external place" of the water. Not, however, this surface considered materially, but *formally as a surface*, so that if the sphere could be removed, and another instantaneously substituted for it, the water would still be contained within the same *formal* surface; its *locus externus* would remain the same. And, again, it is the containing surface considered as *immovable* or as circumscribing that definite portion of space, that constitutes the *locus externus* or "external place" of the located body: so that if the sphere with the water were moved the latter would thereby obtain a new external location, for though the containing surface be still materially and formally the same, it is no longer the same *as a locating* surface, seeing that it now marks off a portion of space different from that marked off by it before it was moved.

Aristotle's definition defines what is known as the *proper* external place of a body. From this we distinguish the *common* external place or location of a body:

understanding by the latter, or "locus *communis*," the whole collection of spatial relations of the body in question to all the bodies in its immediate neighbourhood. It is by indicating these relations, or some of them, that we assign the Aristotelian category, or extrinsic denomination, *Ubi*.[367]

Regarded ontologically, the internal place of a body is an absolute accident: it is the accident which gives the latter concrete volume or external extension, and it is not really distinct from the latter. The external place of a body includes in addition the spatial relations of the latter to other bodies, relations grounded in the volumes of those bodies.

It is by reason of these spatial relations with certain bodies, that a being is said to be "present" in a certain place. A corporeal extended substance is said to occupy space *circumscriptivé*, or by having parts outside parts in the place it occupies. A finite or created spiritual substance is said to occupy space *definitivé* inasmuch as it can naturally exercise its influence only within certain more or less extended spatial limits: as the human soul does within the confines of the body.[368] The Infinite Being is said to occupy space *repletivé*. The actual presence of God in all real space, conserving in its existence all created, contingent reality, is called the Divine *Ubiquity*. The perfection whereby God can be present in other worlds and other spaces which He may actualize is called the Divine *Immensity*.

The local presence of a finite being to other finite beings is itself a positive perfection—based on its actual extension if it be an extended corporeal substance, or on its power of operating within a certain space if it be a spiritual substance. The fact that in the case of a finite being this local presence is itself limited, is at once a corollary and an index of the finiteness of the being in question. Only the Infinite Being is omnipresent or ubiquitous. But every finite being, whether corporeal or spiritual, from the very fact that it exists at all, must exist somewhere or have some *locus internus*, and it must have some local presence if there are other corporeal, extended beings in existence. Thus the *local presence* of a being is a (finite) perfection which seems to be grounded in the very nature itself of the creature.[369]

From the concept of *place* we pass naturally to the more complex and abstract notion of *space*. It is, of course, by cognitive processes, both sentient and intellectual, that we come into possession of the abstract concept of space. These processes are subjective in the sense that they are processes of the individual's mental faculties. Distinguishing between the processes and the object or content which is brought into consciousness, or put in presence of the mind, by means of them; and assuming that this object or content is not a *mere* form or groove of our cognitive activity, not a *mere* antecedent condition requisite on the mental side for the conscious exercise of this activity on its data, but that on the contrary it is, or involves, an objective, extramental reality apprehended by the mind,—we go on to inquire in what this objective reality consists. In approaching the question we must first note that what is true of every abstract and universal concept is true of the concept of space, *viz.* that the *abstractness* and *universality* ("*intentio universalitatis*") of real being, as apprehended by the intellect, are modes or forms of thought, *entia rationis*, logical conditions and relations which are created by thought, and which exist only in and for thought; while the reality itself is the object apprehended in these modes and under these conditions: *Universale est formaliter in mente et fundamentaliter in re.* Now through the concept of space we apprehend a reality. Our concept of real space has for its object an actual reality. What is this reality? If space is real, in what does its reality consist? We answer that the reality which we apprehend through this concept is *the total amount of the actual extension or magnitude of all created and coexisting bodies*; not, however, this total magnitude considered absolutely and in itself, but *as endowed with real and mutual relations of all its parts to one another*;[370] relations which are apprehended by us as distances, linear, superficial, and voluminal.

Such, then, is the reality corresponding to our concept of real and actual space. But no sooner have we reached this concept than we may look at its object in the abstract, remove mentally all limits from it, and conceive all extended bodies as actually non-existent. What is the result? The result is that we have now present to our minds the *possibility* of the existence of extended bodies, and a concomitant imagination image (which memory will not allow us to banish from consciousness) of a vast and boundless emptiness, an indefinite and unmeasurable vacuum in which bodies were or may be. The intellectual concept is now not a concept of any *actual* object, but of a mere *possibility*: the possibility of a corporeal, extended universe. This is the concept of what we call *ideal* or *possible space*; and like the concept of any other possible reality it is derived by us from our experience of actual reality,—in this case from our experience of extended bodies as actually existing. The corporeal universe has not existed from all eternity, but it was possible from all eternity. When we think of that possibility as antecedent to all creation, we are thinking of bodies, and of their extension, as possible; and the concept of their total extension as possible is the concept of ideal or possible space. This concept is, through a psychological necessity, accompanied by an imagination image of what we call *imaginary space*: the unlimited vacuity which preceded corporeal creation, which would still persist were the latter totally annihilated, which reaches out indefinitely beyond its actual limits, which imagination pictures for us as a receptacle in which bodies may exist but which all the time our reason assures us is actually nothing, being really only the known possibility of corporeal creatures. This familiar notion of an empty receptacle for bodies is what we have in mind when we think of bodies as existing "*in* space". Hence we say that space, as conceived by the human mind, is not a mere subjective form of cognition, a mere *ens rationis*, inasmuch as our concept has a foundation in reality, *viz.* the actual extension of all existing bodies; nor is it on the other hand simply a real entity, because this actual extension of bodies does not really exist in the manner in which we apprehend it under the abstract concept of space, as a mere possibility, or empty receptacle, of bodies. Space is therefore an *ens rationis cum fundamento in re*.

A great variety of interesting but abstruse questions arise from the consideration of space; but they belong properly to Cosmology and Natural Theology. For example: Is real space actually infinite in magnitude, or finite? In other words, besides the whole solar system—which is in reality merely one star *plus* its planets and their satellites,—is there in existence an actually infinite multitude of such stellar worlds? It is not likely that this can ever be determined empirically. Many philosophers maintain that the question must be answered in the negative, inasmuch as an actually infinite multitude is *impossible*. Others, however, deny that the impossibility of an actually infinite multitude can be proved.[371] Again, within the limits of the actual corporeal universe, are there really *vacant* spaces, or is all space within these limits actually (or even necessarily) filled with an all-pervading ether or corporeal medium of some sort? How would local motion be possible if all space were full of impenetrable matter? How would the real interaction of distant bodies on one another be possible if there were only vacant space between them? Is the *real* volume or extension of a corporeal substance (as distinct from its *apparent* volume, which is supposed to include interstices, or spaces not filled with that body) actually or necessarily unchangeable? Or is the internal quantity of a body actually or necessarily unchangeable? Can more than one individual corporeal substance simultaneously occupy exactly the same space? (This is not possible naturally, for impenetrability is a natural consequence of local extension; but it is possible miraculously—if all the bodies, or all except one, be miraculously deprived of local or spatial extension.) Can the same individual body be present at the same time in totally different and distant places? (Not naturally, of course; but how it can happen even miraculously is a more difficult question than the preceding one. It is in virtue of its actual or local extension that a body is present sensibly in a definite place. Deprived miraculously of this extension it can be simultaneously in several places, as our Blessed Lord's Body is in the Eucharist. But if a body has its natural local extension at one definite place, does this extension so confine its presence to this place that it cannot be simultaneously present—miraculously, and without its local extension—at other places? The most we can say is that the absolute impossibility of this is neither self-evident nor capable of cogent proof. The Body of our Lord has its natural local extension in heaven—for heaven, which will be the abode of the glorified bodies of the blessed after the general resurrection, must be not merely a state or condition, but a place—and at the same time it is sacramentally present in many places on earth.)

85. Time: its Apprehension and Measurement.—If the concept of space is difficult to analyse, and gives rise to some practically insoluble problems, this is still more true of the concept of time. "What, then, is time?" exclaims St. Augustine in his *Confessions*.[372] "If no one asks me, I know; but if I am asked to explain it, then I do not know!" We reach the notion of space through our

external perception of *extension* by the senses of sight and touch. So also we derive the notion of time from our perception of *motion* or *change*, and mainly from our consciousness of change and succession in our own conscious states. The concept of time involves immediately two other concepts, that of *duration*, and that of *succession*. Duration, or continuance in existence, is of two kinds, *permanent* and *successive*. Permanent duration is the duration of an *immutable* being, formally and in so far as it is immutable. Successive duration is the continued existence or duration of a being that is *subject* to change, formally and in so far as it is mutable. Now real change involves a continuous *succession* of real states, it is a continuous *process* or *fieri*; and it is the duration of a being subject to such change that we call *time* or *temporal duration*. Had we no consciousness of change, or succession of states, we could have no notion of time; though we might have a notion of unchanging duration if *per impossibile* our cognitive activity were itself devoid of any succession of conscious states and had for its object only unchanging reality. But since our cognitive activity is *de facto* successive we can apprehend permanent or unchanging duration, not as it is in itself, but only after the analogy of successive or temporal duration. The continuous series of *successive states involved in change* is, therefore, the real and objective content of our notion of time; just as the *co-existing* total of *extension* forms the content of our notion of space. The concept of space is the concept of something static; that of time is the concept of something kinetic. Time is the continuity of change: where there is change there is time; without change time would be inconceivable. Change involves succession, and succession involves the temporal elements of "before" and "after," separated by the indivisible limiting factor called the "now" or "present instant". The "past" and the "future" are the two *parts* of time, while the "present instant" is not a part of time, but a *point of demarcation* at which the future flows into the past. Change is a reality; it is a real mode of the existence of mutable things; but neither the immediately past state, nor the immediately future state of a changing reality, are actual at the present instant: it is only to the permanent, abiding mind, apprehending real change, and endowed with memory and expectation, that the past and the future are actually (and, of course, only *ideally*, not *really*) present. And it is only by holding past and future in present consciousness, by distinguishing mentally between them, by counting or measuring the continuous flow of successive states from future to past, through the present instant, that the mind comes into possession of the concept of time.[373] The mind thus apprehends time as the measure of the continuous flow of successive states in things subject to change. As thus apprehended, time is not merely the reality of change: it is the successive continuity or duration of change considered as a measure of change. It is that within which all changes are conceived to happen: just as space is conceived as that within which all extended things are conceived to exist. We have said that without real change or motion there could be no time. We can now add that without a mind to apprehend and measure this motion there could be no time. As St. Thomas declares, following Aristotle: *Si non esset anima non esset tempus*.[374] For time, as apprehended by means of our abstract and universal concept, is not simply a reality, but a reality endowed with logical relations, or, in other words, a logical entity grounded in reality, an *ens rationis cum fundamento in re*.

This brings us to Aristotle's classic definition,[375] which is at once pithy and pregnant: Τοῦτο γάρ ἐστιν ὁ χρόνος, ἀριθμὸς κινήσεως κατὰ τὸ πρότερον καὶ ὕστερον: *Tempus est numerus motus secundum prius et posterius*: Time is the measure of motion or change by what we conceive as *before* and *after*, or *future* and *past*, in its process. Every change involves its own intrinsic flow of states from future to past. It is by mentally distinguishing these states, and by thus computing, counting, numbering, the continuous flow or change, that we derive from the latter the notion of time.[376] If, then, we consider all created things, all things subject to change, we shall realize that real time commenced with the creation of the first of them and will continue as long as they (or any of them) continue to exist. We thus arrive at a conception of time in general, analogous to that of space: *the whole continuous series of successions, in changing things, from future to past, regarded as that in which these changes occur, and which is the measure of them*.

Here, too, as in the case of space, we can distinguish *real time*, which is the total duration of actual changes, from *ideal or imaginary time* which is the conceived and imagined duration of merely possible changes.

But a more important distinction is that between *intrinsic* or *internal time*, or the duration of any concrete mutable reality considered in itself, and *extrinsic* or *external time*, which is some other extrinsic temporal duration with which we compare, and by which we may measure, the former duration. Every change or motion has its own internal time; and this is what we have been so far endeavouring to analyse. If two men start at the same instant to walk in the same direction, and if one walk three miles and the other four, while the hands of a watch mark the lapse of an hour, the *external time* of each walk will be the same, will coincide with one and the same motion of the hands of the watch used as a measure. But the internal time of the four-mile walk will be greater than that of the three-mile walk. The former will be a greater amount of change than the latter; and therefore its internal time, estimated by this amount absolutely, will be greater than that of the latter estimated by its amount absolutely.[377] The greater the amount of a change the greater the internal time-duration or series of successive states which measures this change absolutely.[378]

Just as the category *Where* is indicated by the spatial relations of a body to other bodies, so the category *When* is indicated, in regard to any event or process, by its commensuration or comparison with other events or processes.

This brings us to the notion of measurement. To measure anything quantitatively is to apply to it successively some quantitative unit taken as a standard and to count the number of times it contains this unit. This is a process of mentally breaking up continuous quantity or *magnitude*—whether permanent or successive, *i.e.* whether extension or motion—into discontinuous quantity or *multitude*. If the measurement of permanent quantity by spatial units, and the choosing of such units, are difficult processes,[379] those of measuring successive quantity and fixing on temporal units are more difficult still. Is there any natural motion or change of a general character, whereby we can measure (externally) the time-duration of all other changes? The motions of the earth itself—on its axis and around the sun— at once suggest themselves. And these motions form in fact the *natural* general standard for measuring the time of all other events in the universe. All *artificial* or mechanical devices, such as hour-glasses, watches, clocks, chronometers, etc., are simply contrivances for the more convenient application of that general and natural standard to all particular events.

It requires a little reflection to realize that all our means of measuring time-duration can only attain to *approximate* accuracy, inasmuch as our faculties of sense perception, no matter by what devices they are aided, are so limited in range and penetration that fluctuations which fall below the *minima sensibilia* cannot be detected. It is a necessary condition of any motion used as a standard for time-measurement that it be *regular.* That the standard motions we actually employ are *absolutely* regular we have no guarantee. We can test their regularity only up to the point at which our power of detecting irregularity fails.

Reflection will also show that our appreciation of time-duration is also *relative*, not absolute. It is always a comparison of one flow or current of conscious experiences with another. It is the greater regularity of astronomical motions, as compared with changes or processes experienced as taking place within ourselves, that causes us to fix on the former as the more suitable standard for the measurement of time. "There is indeed," writes Father Maher,[380] "a certain rhythm in many of the processes of our organic life, such as respiration, circulation, and the recurrent needs of food and sleep, which probably contribute much to our power of estimating duration.... The irregular character and varying duration of conscious states, however, soon bring home to us the unfitness of these subjective phenomena to serve as a standard measure of time." Moreover, our estimate of duration is largely dependent on the nature of the estimated experiences and of our mental attitude towards them: "A period with plenty of varied incident, such as a fortnight's travel, passes rapidly *at the time*. Whilst we are interested in each successive experience we have little spare attention to notice the duration of the experience. There is almost complete lapse of the 'enumerating' activity. But *in retrospect* such a period expands, because it is estimated by the number and variety of the impressions which it presents to recollection. On the other hand a dull, monotonous, or unattractive occupation, which leaves much of our mental energy free to advert to its duration, is over-estimated whilst taking place. A couple of hours spent impatiently waiting for a train, a few days in idleness on board ship, a week confined to one's room, are often declared to constitute an 'age'. But when they are past such periods, being empty of incident, shrink up into very small dimensions.... Similarly, recent intervals are exaggerated compared with equal periods more remote. Whilst as we grow older and new experiences become fewer and less impressive, each year at its close seems shorter than its predecessor."[381]

From those facts it would seem perfectly legitimate to draw this rather surprising inference: that if the rate of *all* the changes taking place in the universe were to be suddenly and simultaneously altered in the same direction—all increased or all diminished in the same degree—and *if our powers of perception were simultaneously* so altered as to be *readjusted to this new rate* of change, *we could not become aware of the alteration*.[382] Supposing, for instance, that the rate of motion were doubled, the same amount of change would take place in the new day as actually took place in the old. The *external or comparative* time of all movements—that is to say, the time of which alone we can have any appreciation—would be the same as of old. The new day would, of course, appear only half as long as the old to a mind not readjusted to the new conditions; but this would still be external time. But would the *internal, intrinsic* time of each movement be unaltered? It would be the same for the readjusted mind as it was previously for the mind adjusted to these previous conditions. By an unaltered mind, however, by the Divine Mind, for instance, the same amount of motion would be seen to constitute the same movement under both conditions, but to take place twice as quickly under the new conditions as it did under the old. This again, however, involves a comparison, and thus informs us merely of external or relative time. If we identify intrinsic time with *amount of change*, making the latter the measure of the former, we must conclude that alteration in the *rate* of a motion does not alter its absolute time: and this is evident when we reflect that the very notion of a *rate* of motion involves the comparison of the latter with some other motion.[383] Finally, we have no positive conception of the manner in which time duration is related to, or known by, the Divine Eternal Mind, which is present to all time—past, present and future.

Besides the question of the relativity of time, there are many other curious and difficult questions which arise from a consideration of time-duration, but a detailed consideration of them belongs to Cosmology. We will merely indicate a few of them. How far is time *reversible*, at least in the case of purely mechanical movements?[384] Had time a beginning? We know from Revelation that *de facto* it had. But can we determine by the light of reason alone whether or not it *must* have had a beginning? The greatest philosophers are divided as to possibility or impossibility of *created* reality existing *from all eternity*. St. Thomas has stated, as his considered opinion, that the impossibility of *creatio ab aeterno* cannot be proved. If a series of creatures could have existed successively from all eternity, and therefore without any *first* term of the series, this would involve the possibility of an *actually infinite multitude* of creatures; but an actually infinite multitude of creatures, whether existing simultaneously or successively, is regarded by most philosophers as being self-contradictory and intrinsically impossible. And this although the Divine Essence, being infinitely imitable *ad extra*, and being clearly comprehended as such by the Divine Mind, contains virtually the Divine exemplars of an infinite multitude of possible creatures. Those who defend the possibility of an actually infinite multitude of creatures consider this fact of the infinite imitability of the Divine Essence as the ground of this possibility. On the other hand, those who hold that an actually infinite multitude is self-contradictory deny the validity of this argument from possibility to actuality; and they bring forward such serious considerations and arguments in favour of their own view that this latter has been at all times much more commonly advocated than the former one.[385] Will time have an end? All the evidence of the physical sciences confirms the truth of the Christian faith that external time, as measured by the motions of the heavens, will have an end. But the internal or intrinsic time which will be the measure of the activities of immortal creatures will have no end.[386]

86. DURATION OF IMMUTABLE BEING: ETERNITY.—We have seen that *duration* is the perseverance or continuance of a being in its existence. The duration of the Absolutely Immutable Being is a positive perfection identical with the essence itself of this Being. It is a duration without beginning, without end, without change or succession, a *permanent* as distinct from a *successive* duration, for it is the duration of the Necessary Being, whose essence is Pure Actuality. This duration is eternity: *an interminable duration existing all together. Aeternitas est interminabilis duratio tota simul existens.* This is the common definition of eternity in the proper sense of the term—absolute or necessary eternity. The word "*interminabilis*" connotes a *positive* perfection: the exclusion of beginning and end. The word "*tota*" does not imply that the eternity has parts. The expression "*tota simul*" excludes the imperfection which is characteristic of time duration, *viz.* the *succession* of "before" and "after". The definition given by Boëtius[387] emphasizes these points, as also the indefectible character of immutable life in the Eternal Being: *Aeternitas est interminabilis vitae tota simul et prefecta possessio.*

There is, in the next place, a kind of duration which has been called *hypothetical, relative,* or *borrowed* eternity: *aeternitas hypothetica, relativa, participata,* also called by scholastics "*aeviternitas*". It is the duration in existence of a being that is contingent, but *of its nature incorruptible, immortal,* such as the human soul or a pure spirit. Even if such a being existed from all eternity its existence would be contingent, dependent on a real principle distinct from itself: its duration, therefore, would not be eternity in the strict sense. On the other hand, once created by God, its nature would demand conservation without end; nor could it naturally cease to exist, though absolutely speaking it could cease to exist were God to withdraw from it His conserving power. Its duration, therefore, differs from the duration of corporeal creatures which are by nature subject to change, decay, and cessation of their being. A contingent spiritual substance has by nature a beginning to its duration, or at least a duration which is not essential to it but dependent on the Necessary Being, a duration, however, which is naturally without end; whereas the duration of the corporeal being has by nature both a beginning and an end.

But philosophers are not agreed as to the nature and ground of the distinction between these two kinds of duration in contingent beings. No contingent being is self-existent, neither has any contingent being the principle of its own duration in its own essence. Just as it cannot begin to exist of itself, so neither can it continue to exist of itself. At the same time, granted that it has obtained from God actual existence, some kind or degree of duration, of continuance in that existence, seems to be naturally due to its essence. Otherwise conservation would be not only really but formally a continued creation. It is such indeed on the part of God: in God there is no variety of activity. But on the part of the creature, the preservation of the latter in existence, and therefore some degree of duration, seems to be due to it on the hypothesis that it has been brought into existence at all. The *conserving* influence of God is to its duration in existence what the *concurring* influence of God is to the exercise of its activities.[388] In this sense the duration of a finite being in existence is a positive perfection which we may regard as a property of its nature. But is this perfection or property of the creature which we call *duration*, (*a*) essentially *successive* in all creatures, spiritual as well as corporeal? And (*b*) is it really identical with their actual existence (or with the reality of whatever change or actualization occurs to their existence), or it is a *mode* of this existence or change, really distinct from the latter and conferring upon the latter the perfection of continuity or persistence?

This, at all events, is universally admitted: that *we* cannot become aware of any duration otherwise than through our apprehension of *change*; that we have direct knowledge only of *successive* duration; that we can conceive the *permanent* duration of immutable reality only after the analogy of successive duration, or as the co-existence of immutable reality with the successive duration of mutable things.

Now some philosophers identify successive duration with change, and hold that successive duration is formally the duration of things subject to change; that in so far as a being is subject to change its duration is successive, and in so far as it is free from change its duration approaches the essentially permanent duration of the Eternal, Immutable Being; that therefore the duration of corporeal, corruptible, mortal beings is *par excellence* successive or temporal duration (*tempus*); that spiritual beings, which are substantially immutable, but nevertheless have a successive series of spiritual activities, have a sort of duration more perfect, because more permanent, than mere temporal duration, but less perfect, because less permanent, than eternal duration (*aevum, aeviternitas*); while the

Absolutely Immutable Being alone has perfect permanent duration (*aeternitas*).[389] It is not clear whether according to this view we should distinguish between the duration of spiritual *substances* as permanent, and that of their *acts* as successive; or why we should not attribute *permanent* duration to corporeal *substances* and their *permanent accidents*, confining successive duration formally to motion or change itself. It is, moreover, implied in this view that duration is not any really distinct perfection or mode superadded to the actuality of the being that endures.

Other philosophers hold that *all* duration of *creatures* is *successive*; that no individual creature has a mixture of permanent and successive duration; that this successive duration is really distinct from that which endures by means of it; that it is really distinct even from the reality of change or motion itself; that it is a *real mode* the formal function of which is to confer on the enduring reality a series of *actualities in the order of* "*succession of posterior to prior*," a series of intrinsic *quandocationes* (analagous to the intrinsic locations which their extension confers upon bodies in space). These philosophers distinguish between *continuous* or (indefinitely) *divisible* successive duration, the (indefinitely divisible) parts of which are "past" and "future," and the present not a "part" but only an "indivisible limit" between the two parts; and *discontinuous* or *indivisible* successive duration, whose parts are separate and indivisible units of duration succeeding one another discontinuously: each part being a real but indivisible duration, so that besides the parts that are *past* and *future*, the *present* is also a *part*, which is—like an instant of time—indivisible, but which is also—unlike an instant of time—a real duration. The former kind of successive duration they ascribe to corporeal, corruptible creatures; the latter to spiritual, incorruptible creatures. This view is defended with much force and ingenuity by De San in his *Cosmologia*,[390] where also a full discussion of most of the other questions we have touched upon will be found.

Chapter XII.

Relation; The Relative And The Absolute.

87. IMPORTANCE OF THE PRESENT CATEGORY.—An analysis of the concept of *Relation* will be found to have a very direct bearing both on the Theory of Being and on the Theory of Knowledge. For the human mind knowledge is embodied in the mental act of judgment, and this is an act of *comparison*, an act whereby we *relate* or *refer* one concept to another. The act of cognition itself involves a relation between the knowing subject and the known object, between the mind and reality. Reality itself is understood only by our mentally recognizing or establishing relations between the objects which make up for us the whole knowable universe. This universe we apprehend not as a multitude of isolated, unconnected individuals, but as an *ordered whole* whose parts are *inter-related* by their mutual *co-ordinations* and *subordinations*. The *order* we apprehend in the universe results from these various inter-relations whereby we apprehend it as a *system*. What we call a *law of nature*, for instance, is nothing more or less than the expression of some constant relation which we believe to exist between certain parts of this system. The study of *Relation*, therefore, belongs not merely to Logic or the Theory of Knowledge, but also to the Theory of Being, to Metaphysics. What, then, is a relation? What is the object of this mental concept which we express by the term *relation*? Are there in the known and knowable universe of our experience *real* relations? Or are all relations *merely logical*, pure creations of our cognitive activity? Can we classify relations, whether real or logical? What constitutes a relation formally? What are the properties or characteristics of relations? These are some of the questions we must attempt to answer.

Again, there is much ambiguity, and not a little error, in the use of the terms "absolute" and "relative" in modern philosophy. To some of these sources of confusion we have referred already. It is a commonplace of modern philosophy, a thing accepted as unquestioned and unquestionable, that we know, and can know, only the relative. There is a true sense in this, but the true sense is not the generally accepted one.

Considering the order in which our knowledge of reality progresses it is unquestionable that we first simply perceive "things" successively, things more or less *similar* or *dissimilar*, without realizing *in what* they agree or differ. To realize the latter involves *reflection* and *comparison*. Similarly we perceive "events" in succession, events some of which *depend on* others, but without at first noting or realizing this dependence. In other words we apprehend at first *apart from their relations*, or *as absolute*, things and events which are really relative; and we do so spontaneously, without realizing even that we perceive them as absolute.

The seed needs soil and rain and sunshine for its growth; but these do not need the seed. The turbine needs the water, but the water does not need the turbine. When we realize such facts as these, *by reflection*, contrasting what is dependent with what is independent, what is like or unlike, before or after, greater or less than, other things, with what each of these is in itself, we come into conscious possession of the notion of "the relative" and oppose this to the notion of "the absolute".

What we conceive as dependent we conceive as relative; what we conceive, by negation, as independent, we conceive as absolute. Then by further observation and reflection we gradually realize that what we apprehended as independent of certain things is dependent on certain other things; that the same thing may be independent in some respects and dependent in other respects. The rain does not depend on the seed which it causes to germinate, but it does depend on the clouds. The water which turns the turbine does not depend on the turbine, but it does depend on the rain; and the rain depends on the evaporation of the waters of the ocean; and the evaporation on the solar heat; and this again on chemical and physical processes in the sun; and so on, as far as sense experience will carry us: until we realize that everything which falls directly within this sense experience is dependent and therefore relative. Similarly, the accident of quantity, in virtue of which we pronounce one of two bodies to be *larger* than the other, is something *absolute* as compared with this *relation* itself; but as compared with the substance in which it inheres, it is dependent on the latter, or *relative* to the latter, while the substance is *absolute*, or free from dependence on it. But if substance is absolute as compared with accident, in the sense that substance is not dependent on a subject in which to inhere, but exists *in itself*, it is not absolute in the sense understood by Spinoza, in the sense of existing *of itself*, independently of any efficient cause to account for its origin . All the substances in the universe of our direct sense experience are contingent, dependent *ab alio*, and therefore in this sense relative, not absolute.

This is the true sense in which relativity is an essential note of the reality of all the data of the world of our sense experience. They are all contingent, or relative, or conditioned existences. And, as Kant rightly taught, this experience forces us inevitably to think of a Necessary, Absolute, Unconditioned Being, on whom these all depend. But, as can be proved in *Natural Theology* against Kant, this concept is not a mere regulative idea of the reason, a form of thought whereby we systematize our experience: it is a concept the object of which is not merely a necessity of thought but also an objectively existing reality.[391]

But in the thought of most modern philosophers relativism, or the doctrine that "we can know only the relative," is something very different from all this. For positivists, disciples of Auguste Comte (1798-1857), it means that we can know only the phenomena which fall under the notice of our senses, and the laws of resemblance, succession, etc., according to which they occur. All "theological" quests for supra-mundane causes and reasons of these events, and all "metaphysical" quests for suprasensible forces, powers, influences, in the events themselves, as explaining or accounting for these latter, are according to this theory necessarily futile: the mind must rest content with a knowledge of the *positive facts* of sense, and their relations. Relativism is thus another name for Positivism.

For the psychological sensism of English philosophers from Hobbes [1588-1679] and Locke [1632-1704] down to Mill [1806-73] and Bain [1818-1903] relativism means that all conscious cognition—which they tend to reduce to modes and complexes of *sensation*—must be, and can only be, a cognition of the changing, the transitional, the relative.[392] According to an extreme form of this theory the mind can apprehend only relations, but not the terms of any of these relations: it can apprehend nothing as absolute. Moreover the relations which it apprehends it creates itself. Thus all reality is reduced to a system of relations. For Mill the supreme category of real being was *Sensation*: but sensation can be only a feeling of a relation: thus the supreme category of real being would be *Relation*.[393]

But the main current of relativism is that which has issued from Kant's philosophy and worked itself out in various currents such as Spencer's Agnosticism, Hegel's Monism, and Renouvier's Neo-criticism.[394] The mind can know only what is related to it, what is present to it, what is in it; not what is apart from it, distinct from it. The mind cannot know the real nature of the extramental, nor even if there be an extramental real. Subject and object in knowledge are really one: individual minds are only self-conscious phases in the ever-evolving reality of the One Sole Actual Being.

These are but a few of the erroneous currents of modern relativism. A detailed analysis of them belongs to the *Theory of Knowledge*. But it may be pointed out here that they are erroneous because they have distorted and exaggerated certain profound truths concerning the scope and limits of human knowledge.

It is true that we have no positive, proper, intuitive knowledge of the Absolute Being who is the First Cause and Last End of the universe; that all our knowledge of the nature and attributes of the Infinite Being is negative, analogical, abstractive. In a certain sense, therefore, He is above the scope of our faculties; He is Incomprehensible. But it is false to say that He is Unknowable; that our knowledge of Him, inadequate and imperfect as it is, is not genuine, real, and instructive, as far as it goes.

Again, a *distinct* knowledge of any object implies *defining, limiting, distinguishing, comparing, relating, judging, analysing and synthesizing*. It implies therefore that we apprehend things *in relations* with other things. But this supposes an antecedent, if indistinct, apprehension of the "things" themselves. Indeed we cannot help pronouncing as simply unintelligible the contention that all knowledge is of relations, and that we can have no knowledge of things as absolute. How could we become aware of relations without being aware of the terms related? Spencer himself admits that the very reasoning whereby we establish the "relativity of knowledge" leads us inevitably to assert as necessary the existence of the non-relative, the Absolute:[395] a necessity which Kant also recognizes.

Finally, the fact that reality, in order to be known, must be present to the knowing mind—or, in other words, that knowledge itself is a relation between object and subject—in no way justifies the conclusion that we cannot know the real nature of things as they are in themselves, absolutely, but only our own subjective, mental impressions or representations of the absolute reality, in itself unknowable.[396] The obvious fact that any reality in order to be known must be related to the knowing mind, seems to be regarded by some philosophers as if it were a momentous discovery. Then, conceiving the "thing-in-itself," the absolute, as a something standing out of all relation to mind, they declare solemnly that we cannot know the absolute: a declaration which may be interpreted either as a mere truism—that we cannot know a thing without knowing it!—or as a purely gratuitous assertion, that besides the world of realities which reveal themselves to our minds there is another world of unattained and unattainable "things-in-themselves" which are as it were the *real* realities! These philosophers have yet to show that there is anything absurd or impossible in the view that there is simply one world of realities—realities which exist absolutely in themselves apart from our apprehension of them and which in the process of cognition come into relation with our minds.[397] Moreover, if besides this world of known and knowable realities there were such a world of "transcendental" things-in-themselves as these philosophers discourse of, such a world would have very little concern for us,[398] since by definition and *ex hypothesi* it would be *for us* necessarily as if it were not: indeed the hypothesis of such a transcendental world is self-contradictory, for even did it exist we could not think of it.

The process of cognition has indeed its difficulties and mysteries. To examine these, to account for the possibility of truth and error, to analyse the grounds and define the scope and limits of human certitude, are problems for the *Theory of Knowledge*, on the domain of which we are trenching perhaps too far already in the present context. But at all events to conceive reality as absolute in the sense of being totally unrelated to mind, and then to ask: Is reality so transformed in the very process of cognition that the mind cannot possibly apprehend it or represent it as it really is?—this certainly is to misconceive and mis-state in a hopeless fashion the main problem of Epistemology.

88. ANALYSIS OF THE CONCEPT OF RELATION.—Relation is one of those ultimate concepts which does not admit of definition proper. And like other ultimate concepts it is familiar to all. Two lines, each measuring a yard, are *equal* to each other *in length*: *equality* is a *quantitative* relation. The number 2 is *half* of 4, and 4 is *twice* 2: *half* and *double* express each a *quantitative* relation of *inequality*. If two twin brothers are *like* each other we have the *qualitative* relation of *resemblance* or *similarity*; if a negro and a European are *unlike* each other we have the *qualitative* relation of *dissimilarity*. The steam of the locomotive moves the train: a relation of *efficient causality*, of efficient cause to effect. The human eye is adapted to the function of seeing: a relation of *purpose* or *finality*, of means to end. And so on.

The objective concept of relation thus establishes a *conceptual unity* between a pair of things in the domain of some other category. Like quantity, quality, *actio* and *passio*, etc., it is an ultimate mode of reality as apprehended through human experience. But while the reality of the other accident-categories appertains to substances considered absolutely or in isolation from one another, the reality of this category which we call *relation* appertains indivisibly to two (or more) together, so that when one of these is taken or considered apart from the other (or others) the relation formally disappears. Each of the other (absolute) accidents is formally "something" ("*aliquid*"; "τι"), whereas the formal function of *relation* is to refer something "to something" else ("*ad aliquid*"; "πρός τι"). The other accidents formally inhere in a subject, "habent *esse in* subjecto"; relation, considered formally as such, does not inhere in a subject, but gives the latter a respect, or bearing, or reference, or ordination, *to* or *towards* something else: "relatio dat subjecto respectum vel *esse ad* aliquid aliud". The length of each of two lines is an *absolute* accident of that line, but the *relation* of equality or inequality is intelligible only of both together. Destroy one line and the relation is destroyed, though the other line retains its length absolutely and unaltered. And so of the other examples just given. Relation, then, considered formally as such, is not an absolute accident inhering in a subject, but is a reference of this subject to some other thing, this latter being called the *term* of the relation. Hence relation is described by the scholastics as the *ordination or respect or reference of one thing to another: ordo vel respectus vel habitudo unius ad aliud*. The relation of a subject to something else as term is formally not anything absolute, "*aliquid*" in that subject, but merely refers this subject to something else as term, "*ad aliquid*". Hence Aristotle's designation of relation as " ρός τι," "*ad aliquid*," "to or towards something". "We conceive as relations [π ρός τι]," he says, "those things whose very entity itself we regard as being somehow *of* other things or *to* another thing."[399]

To constitute a relation of whatsoever kind, three elements or factors are essential: the *two extremes* of the relation, viz. the *subject* of the relation and the *term* to which the subject is referred, and what is called the *foundation*, or basis, or ground, or reason, of the relation (*fundamentum* relationis). This latter is the cause or reason on account of which the subject bears the relation to its term. It is always something absolute, in the extremes of the relation. Hence it follows that we may regard any relation in two ways, either *formally* as the actual bond or link of connexion between the extremes, or *fundamentally, i.e.* as in its cause or foundation in these extremes. This is expressed technically by distinguishing between the relation *secundum esse in* and *secundum esse ad, i.e.* between the absolute entity of its foundation in the subject and the purely relative entity in which the relation itself formally consists. Needless to say, the latter, whatever it is, does not add any *absolute entity* to that of either extreme. But in what does this relative entity itself consist? Before attempting an answer to this question we must endeavour to distinguish, in the next section, between *purely logical* relations and relations which are in some true sense *real.* Here we may note certain corollaries from the concept of relation as just analysed.

Realities of which the objective concept of relation is verified derive from this latter certain *properties* or special characteristics. The *first* of these is *reciprocity*: two related extremes are as such intelligible only in reference to each other: father to son, half to double, like to like, etc., and *vice versa*: *Correlativa se invicem connotant.* The *second* is that things related to one another are collateral or concomitant in *nature*: *Correlativa sunt simul natura*: neither related extreme is as such naturally prior to the other. This is to be understood of the relation only in its *formal* aspect, not fundamentally. Fundamentally or *materialiter,* the cause for instance is *naturally prior* to its effect. The *third* is that related things are concomitant *logically*, or in the order of knowledge: *Correlativa sunt simul cognitione*: a reality can be known and defined as relative to another reality only by the simultaneous cognition of both extremes of the relation.

89. LOGICAL RELATIONS.—Logical relations are *those which are created by our own thought, and which can have no being other than the being which they have in and for our thought.* That there are such relations, which are the exclusive product of our thought-activity, is universally admitted. The mind can reflect on

its own direct concepts; it can compare and co-ordinate and subordinate them among themselves; it thus forms ideas of relations between those concepts, ideas which the scholastics call *reflex* or *logical* ideas, or "*secundæ intentiones mentis*". These relations are *entia rationis*, purely logical relations. Such, for instance, are the relations of *genus* to *species*, of predicate to subject, the relations described in Logic as the *prædicabilia*. Moreover we can compare our direct universal concepts with the individual realities they represent, and see that this feature or mode of *universality* in the concept, its "*intentio universalitatis*" is a *logical relation* of the concept to the reality which it represents: a logical relation, inasmuch as its *subject* (the concept) and its *foundation* (the *abstractness* of the concept) are in themselves pure products of our thought-activity. Furthermore, we are forced by the imperfection of the thought-processes whereby we apprehend reality— conception of *abstract* ideas, *limitation* of concepts in extension and intension, *affirmation* and *negation*, etc.—to apprehend *conceptual* limitations, negations, comparisons, etc., in a word, all *logical entities*, as if they were *realities*, or after the manner of realities, *i.e.* to conceive what is really "nothing" as if it were really "something," to conceive the *non-ens* as if it were an *ens*, to conceive it *per modum entis*. And when we compare these logical entities with one another, or with real entities, the relations thus established by our thought are all *logical relations*. Finally, it follows from this same imperfection in our human modes of thought that we sometimes understand things only by attributing to these certain logical relations, *i.e.* relations which affect not the reality of these things, their *esse reale*, but only the mode of their presence in our minds, their *esse ideale*.

In view of the distinction between logical relations and those we shall presently describe as real relations, and especially in view of the prevalent tendency in modern philosophy to regard all relations as merely logical, it would be desirable to classify logical relations and to indicate the ways in which they are created by, or result from, our thought-processes. We know of no more satisfactory analysis than that accomplished by St. Thomas Aquinas in various parts of his many monumental and enduring works. In his *Commentaries on the Sentences*[400] he enumerates four ways in which logical relations arise from our thought-processes. In his *Quaestiones Disputatae*[401] he reduces these to two: some logical relations, he says, are invented by the intellect reflecting on its own concepts and are attributed to these concepts; others arise from the fact that the intellect can understand things only by relating, grouping, classifying them, only by introducing among them an *arrangement* or *system of relations* through which alone it can understand them, relations which it could only erroneously ascribe to these things as they really exist, since they are only projected, as it were, into these things by the mind. Thus, though it consciously thinks of these things as so related, it deliberately abstains from asserting that these relations really affect the things themselves. Now the mistake of all those philosophers, whether ancient, medieval or modern, who deny that any relations are real, seems to be that they carry this abstention too far. They contend that all relations are simply read into the reality by our thought; that none are in the reality in any true sense independently of our thought. They thus exaggerate the rôle of thought as a *constitutive* factor of known or experienced reality; and they often do so to such a degree that according to their philosophy human thought not merely *discovers* or *knows* reality but practically *constitutes* or *creates* it: or at all events to such a degree that cognition would be mainly a process whereby reality is assimilated to mind and not rather a process whereby mind is assimilated to reality. Against all such idealist tendencies in philosophy we assert that not all relations are logical, that there are some relations which are not mere products of thought, but which are themselves real.

90. REAL RELATIONS; THEIR EXISTENCE VINDICATED.—A real relation is *one which is not a mere product of thought, but which obtains between real things independently of our thought.* For a real relation there must be (*a*) a *real*, individual *subject*; (*b*) a *real foundation*; and (*c*) a *real*, individual *term*, really distinct from the subject. If the subject of the relation, or its foundation, be not real, but a mere *ens rationis*, obviously the relation cannot be more than logical. If, moreover, the term be not a really distinct entity from the subject, then the relation can be nothing more than a mental comparison of some thing with itself, either under the same aspect or under mentally distinct aspects. A relation is real in the fullest sense when the extremes are *mutually* related in virtue of a foundation really existing in both. Hence St Thomas' definition of a real relation as a *connexion between some two things in virtue of something really found in both*: *habitudo inter aliqua duo secundum aliquid realiter conveniens utrique.*[402]

Now the question: Are there in the real world, among the things which make up the universe of our experience, relations which are not merely logical, which are not a mere product of our thought?—can admit of only one reasonable answer. That there are relations which are in some true sense real and independent of our thought-activity must be apparent to everyone whose mental outlook on things has not been warped by the specious sophistries of some form or other of Subjective Idealism. For *ex professo* refutations of Idealist theories the student must consult treatises on the *Theory of Knowledge*. A few considerations on the present point will be sufficiently convincing here.

First, then, let us appeal to the familiar examples mentioned above. Are not two lines, each a yard long, *really equal* in length, whether we know it or not? Is not a line a yard long *really greater than* another line a foot in length, whether we know it or not? Surely our thought does not *create* but *discovers* the equality or inequality. The twin brothers *really resemble* each other, even when no one is thinking of this resemblance; the resemblance is there whether anyone adverts to it or not. The motion of the train *really depends* on the force of the steam; it is not our thought that produces this relation of dependence. The eye is *really* so constructed as to perceive light, and the light is really such by nature as to arouse the sensation of vision; surely it is not our thought that produces this relation of mutual adaptation in these realities. Such relations are, therefore, in some true sense real and independent of our thought: unless indeed we are prepared to say with idealists that the lines, the brothers, the train, the steam, the eye, and the light—in a word, that not merely relations, but all accidents and substances, all realities—are mere products of thought, ideas, states of consciousness.

Again, *order* is but a system of relations of co-ordination and subordination between really distinct things. But there is real order in the universe. And therefore there are real relations in the universe. There is real order in the universe: In the physical universe do we not experience a real subordination of effects to causes, a real adaptation of means to ends? And in the moral universe is not this still more apparent? The domestic society, the family, is not merely an aggregate of individuals any one of whom we may designate indiscriminately husband or wife, father or mother, brother or sister. These relations of order are real; they are obviously not the product of our thought, not produced by it, but only discovered, apprehended by it.

It is a profound truth that not all the reality of the universe which presents itself to the human mind for analysis and interpretation, *not all* the reality of this universe, is to be found in the mere sum-total of the individual entities that constitute it, considering these entities each absolutely and in isolation from the others. Nor does *all* its real perfection consist in the mere sum-total of the absolute perfections intrinsic to, and inherent in, those various individual entities. Over and above these individual entities and their absolute perfections, there is a domain of reality, and of real perfections, consisting in the real *adaptation, interaction, interdependence, arrangement, co-ordination* and *subordination*, of those absolute entities and perfections among themselves. And if we realize this profound truth[403] we shall have no difficulty in recognizing that, while the thought-processes whereby we interpret this universe produce logical relations which we utilize in this interpretation, there is also in this universe itself a system of relations which are real, which are not invented, but are merely detected, by our minds.

According to idealists, relation is a subjective category of the mind. It belongs to phenomena only on the introduction of the latter into the understanding. "Laws no more exist in phenomena," writes Kant,[404] "than phenomena exist in themselves; the former are relative to the subject in which the phenomena inhere, in so far as this subject is endowed with understanding; just as the latter are relative to this same subject in so far as it is endowed with sensibility." This is ambiguous and misleading. Of course, laws or any other relations do not exist *for us*, are *not known* by us, are not *brought into relation to our understanding*, as long as we do not consciously grasp the two terms and the foundation on which the law, or any other relation, rests. But there are relations whose terms and foundations are anterior to, and independent of, our thought, and which consequently are not a product of thought.

"Sensations, or other feelings being given," writes J. S. Mill,[405] "succession and simultaneousness are the two conditions to the alternative of which they are subjected by the nature of our faculties." But, as M. Boirac pertinently asks,[406] "why do we apply in any particular case the one alternative of the two-faced category rather than the other? Is it not because in every case the concrete application made by our faculties is determined by the objects themselves, by an objective and real foundation of the relation?"

91. MUTUAL AND MIXED RELATIONS; TRANSCENDENTAL RELATIONS.—There are, then, relations which are in some true sense real. But in what does the reality of a real relation consist? Before answering this question we must examine the main classes of real relations.

We have already referred to the *mutual* relation as one which has *a real foundation in both* of the extremes, such as the relation between father and son, or between a greater and a lesser quantity, or between two equal quantities, or between two similar people.[407] Such a relation is called a *relatio aequiperantiae*, a relation of *the same denomination*, if it has the same name on both sides, as "*equal—equal*," "*similar—similar*," "*friend—friend*," etc. It is called a *relatio disquiperantiae*, of *different denomination*, if it has a different name, indicating a different kind of relation, on either side, as "*father—son*," "*cause—effect*," "*master—servant*," etc.

Distinct from this is the *non-mutual* or *mixed* relation, which has a real foundation only in one extreme, so that the relation of this to the other extreme is real, while the relation of the latter to the former is only logical.[408] For instance, the relation of every creature to the Creator is a real relation, for the essential dependence of the creature on the Creator is a relation grounded in the very nature of the creature as a contingent being. But the relation of the Creator to the creature is only logical, for the creative act on which it is grounded implies in the Creator no reality distinct from His substance, which substance has no necessary relation to any creature. Similarly, the relation of the (finite) knowing mind to the known object is a real relation, for it is grounded in a new quality, *viz.* knowledge, whereby the mind is perfected. But the relation of the object to the mind is not a real relation, for by becoming actually known the object itself does not undergo any real change or acquire any new reality or perfection. We have seen already that all reality has a *transcendental* or *essential* relation to intellect and to will, ontological truth and ontological goodness. These relations of reality to the

Divine Intellect and Will are *formally* or *actually* verified in all things; whereas the transcendental truth and goodness of any thing in regard to any created intellect and will are formal or actual only when that thing is *actually* known and willed by such created faculties: the relations of a thing to a mind that does not actually know and desire that thing are only *fundamental* or *potential* truth and goodness. This brings us to a second great division of relations, into *essential* or *transcendental* and *accidental* or *predicamental*.

An essential or transcendental relation is *one which is involved in the very essence itself of the related thing*. It enters into and is inseparable from the concept of the latter. Thus in the concept of the *creature* as such there is involved an *essential* relation of the latter's dependence on the *Creator*. So, too, every individual reality involves essential relations of *identity* with itself and *distinction* from other things, and essential relations of *truth* and *goodness* to the Divine Mind and created minds. Knowledge involves an essential relation to a known object. *Accidents* involve the essential relation of an aptitude to inhere in *substances*. *Actio* involves an essential relation to an *agens*, and *passio* to a *patiens*; matter to form and form to matter. And so on. In general, wherever any subject has an intrinsic and essential exigence or aptitude or inclination, whereby there is established a connexion of this subject with, or a reference to, something else, an ordination or "*ordo*" to something else, there we have an "essential" relation.[409] Such a relation is termed "transcendental" because it can be verified of a subject in any category; and, since it adds nothing real to its subject it does not of itself constitute any new category of real being. Like the logical relation it is referred to here in order to bring out, by way of contrast, the accidental or predicamental relation which is the proper subject-matter of the present chapter.

92. PREDICAMENTAL RELATIONS; THEIR FOUNDATIONS AND DIVISIONS.—An accidental or predicamental relation is one which is *not essential to the related subject, but superadded to, and separable from, the latter*. Such, for instance, are relations of equality or inequality, similarity or dissimilarity. It is not involved in the nature of the subject itself, but is superinduced on the latter by reason of some real foundation really distinct from the nature of this subject. Its sole function is to refer the subject to the term, while the essential or transcendental relation is rather an intrinsic attribute or aptitude of the nature itself as a principle of action, or an effect of action. The real, accidental relation is the one which Aristotle placed in a category apart as one of the ultimate accidental modes of real being. Hence it is called a "predicamental" relation. What are its principal sub-classes?

Real relations are divided according to the nature of their foundations. But some relations are real *ex utraque parte*—mutual relations, while others are real only on the side—mixed relations. Moreover, some real relations are transcendental, others predicamental. Aristotle in assigning three distinct grounds of predicamental relations seems to have included some relations that are transcendental.[410] He distinguishes[411] (*a*) relations grounded in unity and multitude; (*b*) relations grounded in efficient causality; and (*c*) relations grounded in "commensuration".

(*a*) By "unity and multitude" he is commonly interpreted to mean identity or diversity not merely in *quantity*, but in any "formal" factor, and therefore also in *quality*, and in *nature* or *substance*. Things that are one in quantity we term *equal*; one in quality, *similar*; one in substance, *identical*. And if they are not one in these respects we call them *unequal*, *dissimilar*, *distinct* or *diverse*, respectively. About quantity as a foundation for real, predicamental relations there can be no difficulty. Indeed it is in a certain sense implied in all relations—at least as apprehended by the human mind. For we apprehend relations, of whatsoever kind, by mental comparison, and this involves the consciousness of *number* or *plurality*, of *two* things compared.[412] And when we compare things on the basis of any *quality* we do so only by distinguishing and measuring *intensive grades* in this quality, after the analogy of *extensive* or *quantitative* measurement. Nevertheless just as quality is a distinct accident irreducible to quantity, so are relations based on quality different from those based on quantity. But what about substance or nature as a foundation of *predicamental* relations? For these, as distinct from transcendental relations, some accident really distinct from the substance seems to be required. The substantial, individual *identity* of any real being with itself is only a logical relation, for there are not two really distinct extremes. The specific identity of John with James in virtue of their common human nature is a real relation but it would appear to be transcendental.[413] The relation of the real John and the real James to our knowledge of them is the transcendental relation of any reality to knowledge, the relation of ontological truth. This relation is *essentially* actual in regard to the Divine mind, but only potential, and *accidentally* actual, in regard to any created mind. The relation of real distinction between two individual substances is a real but *transcendental* relation, grounded in the transcendental attribute of *oneness* which characterizes every real being.

(*b*) Efficient causality, *actio et passio*, can undoubtedly be the ground of real predicamental relations. If the action is transitive[414] the *patiens* or recipient of the real change acquires by this latter the basis of a relation of real dependence on the cause or *agens*. Again, if the action provokes reaction, so that there is real interaction, each *agens* being also *patiens*, there arises a mutual predicamental relation of interdependence between the two agencies. Furthermore, if the agent itself is in any way really perfected by the action there arises a real predicamental relation which is mutual: not merely a real relation of effect to agent but also of agent to effect. This is true in all cases of what scholastics call "univocal" as distinct from "equivocal" causation. Of the former, in which the agent produces an effect *like in nature to itself*, the propagation of their species by living things is the great example. Here not only is the relation of offspring to parents a real relation, but that of parents to offspring is also a real relation. And this real relation is permanent because it is grounded not merely in the transient generative processes but in some real and abiding result of these processes—either some physical disposition in the parents themselves,[415] or some *specific* perfection attributed by extrinsic denomination to the *individual* parents: the parents are in a sense continued in their offspring: "generation really perpetuates the species, the specific nature, and in this sense may be said to perfect the individual parents".[416] In cases of "equivocal" causation—*i.e.* where the effect is different in nature from the cause, as when a man builds a house—the agent does not so clearly benefit by the action, so that in such cases, while the relation of the effect to the cause is real, some authors would regard that of the cause to the effect as logical.[417] When, however, we remember that the efficient activity of all *created* causes is necessarily dependent on the Divine *Concursus*, and necessarily involves *change in the created cause itself*, we can regard this change as in all cases the ground of a real relation of the created cause to its effect. But the creating and conserving activity of the Divine Being cannot ground a real relation of the latter to creatures because the Divine Being is Pure and Unchangeable Actuality, acquiring no new perfection, and undergoing no real change, by such activity.[418]

(*c*) By commensuration as a basis of real relations Aristotle does not mean quantitative measurement, but the determination of the perfection of one reality by its being essentially conformed to, and regulated by, another: as the perfection of knowledge or science, for instance, is determined by the perfection of its object. This sort of commensuration, or essential ordination of one reality to another, is obviously the basis of *transcendental* relations. Some authors would consider that besides the transcendental relation of science to its object, a relation which is independent of the actual existence of the latter, there also exists an accidental relation in science to its object as long as this latter is in actual existence. But rather it should be said that just as the transcendental truth-relation of any real object to intellect is fundamental (potential) or formal (actual) according as this intellect merely *can* know this object or actually *does* know it, so also the transcendental relation of knowledge to its object is fundamental or formal according as this object is merely possible or actually existing.

We gather from the foregoing analysis that the three main classes of predicamental relations are those based on *quantity*, *quality*, and *causality*, respectively.

93. IN WHAT DOES THE REALITY OF PREDICAMENTAL RELATIONS CONSIST?— We have seen that not all relations are purely logical. There are real relations; and of these some are not merely aspects of the other categories of real being, not

merely transcendental attributes virtually distinct from, but really identical with, these other absolute modes of real being which we designate as "substance," "quantity," "quality," "cause," "effect," etc. There are real relations which form a distinct accidental mode of real being and so constitute a category apart. The fact, however, that these predicamental relations have been placed by Aristotle and his followers in a category apart does not of itself prove that the predicamental relation is a special reality *sui generis*, really and adequately distinct from the realities which constitute the other categories. If the predicamental relation be not a *purely logical entity*, if it be an *ens rationis cum fundamento in re*, or, in other words, if the object of our concept of "predicamental relation," has a foundation in reality (*e.g.* like the concepts of "space" and "time"), then it may reasonably be placed in a category apart, even although it may not be itself formally a reality. We have therefore to see whether or not the predicamental relation is, or embodies, any mode of real being adequately distinct from these modes which constitute the other categories.

The predicamental relation is real in the sense that it implies, in addition to two really distinct extremes, a real foundation in one or both of these extremes, a real accident such as quantity, quality, or causality. That is to say, considered in its foundation or cause, considered fundamentally or *secundum suum esse in subjecto*, the predicamental relation is real, inasmuch as its foundation is a reality independently of the consideration of the mind. No doubt, if the predicamental relation, adequately considered, implies no other reality than that of its foundation and terms, then the predicamental relation does not contain any special reality *sui generis*, distinct from substances, quality, quantity, and other such absolute modes of real being. This, however, does not prevent its ranking as a distinct category provided it adds a virtually distinct and altogether peculiar aspect to those absolute realities. Now, considered adequately, the predicamental relation adds to the reality it has in its foundation the *actual reference* of subject to term. In fact, it is in this reference of subject to term, this "*esse ad*," that the relation *formally* consists. The question therefore may be stated thus: Is this formal relation of subject to term, this "*esse ad*" a real entity *sui generis*, really distinct from the absolute entities of subject, term and foundation, and in contradistinction to these and all absolute entities a "relative entity," actually existing in the real universe independently of our thought? Or is it, on the contrary, itself formally a mere product of our thought, a product of the mental act of comparison, an *ens rationis* an aspect superadded by our minds to the extremes compared, and to the foundation in virtue of which we compare them?

A good many scholastics, and some of them men of great name,[419] have espoused the former alternative, considering that the reality of the predicamental relation cannot be vindicated—against idealists, who would reduce all relations to mere logical entities—otherwise than by according to the relation considered *formally*, i.e. *secundum suum "esse ad,"* an entity in the actual order of things independent of our thought: adding as an argument that if relation formally as such is anything at all, if all relation be not a mere mental fabrication, it is essentially a "relative" entity, and that manifestly a "relative" entity cannot be really identical with any "absolute" entity. And they claim for this view the authority of St Thomas.[420]

The great majority of scholastics, however, espouse the second alternative: that the relation, considered *formally*, "secundum *esse ad*," is a product of our mental comparison of subject with term. It is not itself a real entity or a real mode, superadded to the reality of extremes and foundation.

In the first place there is no need to suppose the reality of such a relative entity. *Entia non sunt multiplicanda præter necessitatem.* It is an abuse of realism to suppose that the *formal* element of a relation, its *"esse ad,"* is a distinct and separate reality. The reality of the praedicamental relation is safeguarded without any such postulate. Since the predicamental relation, considered *adequately*, i.e. not merely formally but fundamentally, not merely *secundum esse ad* but *secundum esse in*, involves as its foundation an absolute accident which is real independently of our thought, the predicamental relation is not a *mere ens rationis*. It has a foundation in reality. It is an *ens rationis cum fundamento in re*. This is a sufficient counter-assertion to Idealism, and a sufficient reason for treating relation as a distinct category of real being.

That there is no need for such a relative entity will be manifest if we consider the simple case of two bars of iron each a yard long. The length of each is an absolute accident of each. The length of either, considered absolutely and in itself, is not formally the *equality* of this with the other. Nor are both lengths considered separately the formal relation of equality. But both considered together are the adequate foundation of this formal relation; both considered together are this relation *potentially, fundamentally*, so that all that is needed for the *actual, formal* relation of *equality* is the mental apprehension of the two lengths together. The mental process of comparison is the only thing required to make the potential relation actual; and the product of this mental process is the *formality* or *"esse ad"* of the relation, the actual reference of the extremes to each other. Besides the absolute accidents which constitute the foundation of the relation something more is required for the constitution of the adequate predicamental relation. This "something more," however, is a mind capable of comparing the extremes, and not any real entity distinct from extremes and foundation. Antecedently to the act of comparison the formally relative element of the relation, its *"esse ad,"* was not anything actual; it was the mere *comparability* of the extremes in virtue of the foundation. If the *"esse ad"* were a separate real entity, a relative entity, really distinct from extremes and foundation, what sort of entity could it be? Being an accident, it should inhere in, or be a mode of its subject. But if it did it would lose its formally relative character by becoming an inherent mode of an absolute reality. While to conceive it as an entity astride on both extremes, and bridging or connecting these together, would be to substitute the crude imagery of the imagination for intellectual thought.

In the second place, if a subject can acquire a relation, or lose a relation, *without undergoing any real change*, then the relation considered formally as such, or *secundum "esse ad,"* cannot be a reality. But a subject can acquire or lose a relation without undergoing any real change. Therefore the relation considered formally, as distinct from its foundation and extremes, is not a reality.

The minor of this argument may be proved by the consideration of a few simple examples. A child already born is neither larger nor smaller than its brother that will be born two years hence.[421] But after the birth of the latter child the former can acquire those relations successively *without any real change in itself*, and merely by the growth of the younger child. Again, one white ball *A* is similar in colour to another white ball *B*. Paint the latter black, and *eo ipso* the former loses its relation of resemblance *without any real change in itself*.

And this appears to be the view of St. Thomas. If, he writes, another man becomes equal in size to me by growing while I remain unchanged in size, then although *eo ipso* I become equal in size to him, thus acquiring a new relation, *nevertheless I gain or acquire nothing new*: "nihil advenit mihi de novo, per hoc quod incipio esse alteri aequalis per ejus mutationem". Relation, he says, is an extramental reality *by reason of its foundation or cause*, whereby one reality is referred to another.[422] Relation itself, considered formally as distinct from its foundation, is not a reality; it is real only inasmuch as its foundation is real.[423] Again, relation is something inherent, but not formally as a relation, and hence it can disappear without any real change in its subject.[424] A real relation may be destroyed in one or other of two ways: either by the destruction or change of the foundation in the subject, or by the destruction of the term, entailing the cessation of the reference, *without any change in the subject*.[425] Hence, too, the reason alleged by St. Thomas why relation, unlike the other categories of real being, can be itself divided into logical entity and real entity, *ens rationis* and *ens reale*: because formally it is an *ens rationis*, and only fundamentally, or in virtue of its foundation, is it an *ens reale*.[426] And hence, finally, the reason why St. Thomas, following Aristotle, describes relation as having a "lesser reality," an "esse debilius,"[427] than the other or absolute categories of real being: not as if it were a sort of diminutive entity, intermediate between nothingness and the absolute modes of reality, but because being dependent for its formal actuality not merely on a foundation in its subject, but also on a term to which the latter is referred, it can perish not merely by the destruction of its subject like other accidents, but also by the destruction of its term while subject and foundation remain unchanged.

If, then, the real relation, considered formally or "*secundum esse ad*" is not a reality, the relation under this aspect is a *logical*, not a *real*, accident.

To constitute a mutual real relation there is needed a foundation in *both* of the extremes. As long as the term of the relation does not actually exist, not only does the relation not exist formally and actually, but it is not even *adequately potential*: the foundation in the subject alone is not an adequate foundation.

To this view, which denies any distinct reality to the predicamental relation considered formally, it has been objected that the predicamental relation is thus confounded with the transcendental relation. But this is not so; for the transcendental relation is always essential to its subject, whatever this subject may be, while the predicamental relation, considered formally, is a logical accident separable from its subject, and considered fundamentally it is some absolute accident really distinct from the substance of the related extremes. For instance, the *action* which mediates between cause and effect is itself transcendentally related to both; while it is at the same time the adequate foundation whereby cause and effect are predicamentally related to each other.[428]

If what we have called the formal element of a relation be nothing really distinct from the extremes and foundation, it follows that some real relations between creatures are really identical with their substances;[429] and to this it has been objected that no relation *in creatures* can be, *quoad rem*, substantial: "Nulla relatio," says St. Thomas,[430] "est substantia secundum rem in creaturis". To this it may be replied that even in these cases the relation itself, considered adequately, is not wholly identical with the substance of either extreme. It superadds a separable logical accident to these.[431]

Finally it is objected that the view which denies a distinct reality to the formal element of a real relation, to its "*esse ad*," equivalently denies all reality to relations, and is therefore in substance identical with the idealist doctrine already rejected. But this is a misconception. According to idealists, relations grounded on quality, quantity, causality, etc., are exclusively in the intellect, in our mental activity and its mental products, in our concepts alone, and are in no true sense characteristic of reality. This is very different from saying that our concepts of such relations are grounded in the realities compared, and that these realities are really endowed with everything that constitutes such relations, the comparative act of the intellect being required merely to apprehend these characteristics and so to give the relation its formal completeness.[432] There is all the difference that exists between a theory which so exaggerates the constitutive function of thought as to reduce all intellectual knowledge to a knowledge of mere subjective mental appearances, and a theory which, while recognizing this function and its products, will not allow that these cast any cloud or veil between the intellect and a genuine insight into objective reality. These mental processes are guided by reality; the *entia rationis* which are their products are grounded in reality; moreover we can quite well distinguish between these *mental* modes and products of our intellectual activity and the *real* contents revealed to the mind in these modes and processes. So long, therefore, as we avoid the mistake of ascribing to the objective reality itself any of these mental modes (as, for instance, extreme realists do when they assert the extramental reality of the *formal* universal), our recognition of them can in no way jeopardize the objective validity of intellectual knowledge. Perhaps an excessive timidity in this direction is in some degree accountable for the "abuse of realism" which ascribes to the formal element of a relation a distinct extramental,[433] objective reality.

Chapter XIII.

Causality; Classification Of Causes.

94. TRADITIONAL CONCEPT OF CAUSE.—The modes of real being which we have been so far examining—substance, quality, quantity, relation—are modes of reality considered as *static*. But it was pointed out in an early chapter that the universe of our experience is subject to change, that it is ever *becoming*, that it is the scene of a continuous world-process which is apparently regulated by more or less stable principles or laws, these laws and processes constituting the *universal order* which it is the duty of the philosopher to study and explain. We must now return to this *kinetic* and *dynamic* aspect of reality, and investigate the principles of change in things by a study of *Causes*.

As with the names of the other ultimate categories, so too here, the general sense of the term "cause" (*causa*, αἴτιον) is familiar to all, while analysis reveals a great variety of modalities of this common signification. We understand by a cause *anything which has a positive influence of any sort on the being or happening of something else*. In philosophy this is the meaning which has been attached traditionally to the term since the days of Aristotle; though in its present-day scientific use the term has almost lost this meaning, mainly through the influence of modern phenomenism.[434] The traditional notion of cause is usually expounded by comparing it with certain kindred notions: *principle, condition, occasion, reason*.

A *principle* is *that from which anything proceeds in any way whatsoever*.[435] Any sort of intrinsic connexion between two objects of thought is sufficient to constitute the one a "principle" of the other; but a mere extrinsic or time sequence is not sufficient. A *logical* principle is some *truth* from which further truths are or may be derived. A *real* principle is some *reality* from which the *being* or *happening* of something originates and proceeds.[436] If this procession involves a real and positive influence of the principle on that which proceeds from it, such a real principle is a cause. But there may be a real and intrinsic connexion without any such influence. For instance, in the substantial changes which occur in physical nature the generation of the new substantial formative principle necessarily presupposes the *privation* of the one which antecedently "informed" the material principle; but this "*privatio formae*" has no positive influence on the generation of the new "form"; it is, however, the necessary and natural antecedent to the generation of the latter; hence although this "*privatio formae*" is a real principle of substantial change (the process or *fieri*) it is not a *cause* of the latter. The notion of principle, even of real principle, is therefore wider than the notion of cause.[437]

A *condition*, in the proper sense of a necessary condition or *conditio sine qua non*, is something which must be realized or fulfilled before the event or effect in question can happen or be produced. On the side of the latter there is real dependence, but from the side of the former there is no real and positive influence on the happening of the event. The influence of the condition is negative; or, if positive, it is only indirect, consisting in the removal of some obstacle—"*removens probibens*"—to the positive influence of the cause. In this precisely a condition differs from a cause: windows, for instance, are a condition for the lighting of a room in the daylight, but the sun is the cause. The distinction is clear and intelligible, nor may it be ignored in a philosophical analysis of causality. At the same time it is easy to understand that where, as in the inductive sciences, there is question of discovering *all* the antecedents, positive and negative, of any given kind of phenomenon, in order to bring to light and formulate the law or laws according to which such phenomenon occurs, the distinction between cause and condition is of minor importance.[438]

An *occasion* is *any circumstance or combination of circumstances favourable to the action of a free cause*. For instance, a forced sale is an occasion for buying cheaply; night is an occasion of theft; bad companionship is an occasion of sin. An occasion has no intrinsic connexion with the effect as in the case of a principle, nor is it necessary for the production of the effect as in the case of a condition. It is spoken of only in connexion with the action of a free cause; and it differs from a cause in having no positive and direct influence on the production of the effect. It has, however, a real though indirect influence on the production of the effect by soliciting and aiding the determination of the free efficient cause to act. In so far as it does exert such an influence it may be regarded as a partial efficient cause, not a physical but a moral cause, of the effect.

To ask for the *reason* of any event or phenomenon, or of the nature or existence of any reality, is to demand an *explanation* of the latter; it is to seek what *accounts* for the latter, what makes this *intelligible* to our minds. Whatever is a cause is therefore also a reason, but the latter notion is wider than the former. Whatever explains a *truth* is a *logical* reason of the latter. But since all truths are concerned with realities they must have ultimately *real* reasons, *i.e.* explanatory principles inherent in the realities themselves. The knowledge of these real or ontological principles of things is the logical reason of our understanding of the things themselves. But the ontological principles, which are the real reasons of the things, are wider in extent than the causes of these things, for they include principles that are not causes.

Furthermore, the grades of reality which we discover in things by the activity of abstract thought, and whereby we compare, classify and define those things, we apprehend as explanatory principles of the latter; and these principles, though really in the things, and therefore real "reasons," are not "causes".

Thus, life is a real reason, though not a cause, of sensibility in the animal organism; the soul's independence of matter in its mode of existence is a real reason, though not a cause, of its spiritual activities. Hence, between a reason and that which it accounts for there may be only a logical distinction, while between a cause and that which it causes there must be a real distinction.

To understand all the intrinsic principles which constitute the *essence* of anything is to know the *sufficient reason* of its *reality*. To understand all the extrinsic principles which account for its actual *existence* is to know the sufficient reason of its *existence*; and to understand this latter adequately is to realize that the thing depends ultimately for its actual existence on a Reality or Being which necessarily exists by virtue of its own essence.

What has been called the *Principle of Sufficient Reason* asserts, when applied to reality, that every existing reality must have a sufficient reason for existing and for being what it is.[439] Unlike the *Principle of Causality* which is an axiomatic or self-evident truth, this principle is rather a necessary postulate of all knowledge, an assumption that *reality is intelligible*. It does not mean that all reality, or even any single finite reality, is adequately intelligible to our finite minds. In the words of Bossuet, we do not know everything about anything: "nous ne savons le tout de rien".

In regard to contingent *essences*, if these be composite we can find a sufficient reason why they are such in their constitutive principles; but in regard to simple essences, or to the simple constitutive principles of composite essences, we can find no sufficient reason why they are such in anything even logically distinct from themselves: they are what they are because they are what they are, and to demand why they are what they are, is, as Aristotle remarked, to ask an idle question. At the same time, when we have convinced ourselves that their actual existence involves the existence of a Supreme, Self-Existent, Intelligent Being, we can see that the essence of this Being is the ultimate ground of the intrinsic possibility of all finite essences.

In regard to contingent *existences* the Principle of Sufficient Reason is coincident with the Principle of Causality, inasmuch as the sufficient reason of the actual existence of any contingent thing consists in the extrinsic real principles which are its causes. The existence of contingent things involves the existence of a Necessary Being. We may say that the sufficient reason for the existence of the Necessary Being is the Divine Essence Itself; but this is merely denying that there is outside this Being any sufficient reason, *i.e.* any cause of the latter's existence; it is the recognition that the Principle of Causality is inapplicable to the Necessary Being. The Principle of Sufficient Reason, in this application of it, is logically posterior to the Principle of Causality.[440]

95. CLASSIFICATION OF CAUSES: ARISTOTLE'S FOURFOLD DIVISION.—In modern times many scientists and philosophers have thought it possible to explain the order and course of nature, the whole cosmic process and the entire universe of our experience, by an appeal to the operation of *efficient causes*. Espousing a mechanical, as opposed to a teleological, conception of the universe, they have denied or ignored all influence of *purpose*, and eschewed all study of *final causes*. Furthermore, misconceiving or neglecting the category of substance, and the doctrine of substantial change, they find no place in their speculations for any consideration of *formal* and *material* causes. Yet without final, formal and material causes, so fully analysed by Aristotle[441] and the scholastics, no satisfactory explanation of the world of our experience can possibly be found. Let us therefore commence by outlining the traditional fourfold division of causes.

We have seen already that change involves composition or compositeness in the thing that is subject to change. Hence two *intrinsic* principles contribute to the constitution of such a thing, the one a passive, determinable principle, its *material cause*, the other an active, determining principle, its *formal cause*. Some changes in material things are superficial, not reaching to the substance itself of the thing; these are *accidental*, involving the union of some *accidental* "form" with the concrete pre-existing substance as material (*materia "secunda"*). Others are more profound, changes of the substance itself; these are *substantial*, involving the union of a new *substantial* "form" with the primal material principal (*materia "prima"*) of the substance undergoing the change. But whether the change be substantial or accidental we can always distinguish in the resulting composite thing two intrinsic constitutive principles, its *formal cause* and its *material cause*. The agencies in nature which, by their activity, bring about change, are *efficient causes*. Finally, since it is an undeniable fact that there is *order* in the universe, that its processes give evidence of *regularity*, of operation according to *law*, that the cosmos reveals a *harmonious co-ordination of manifold* agencies and a *subordination of means to ends*, it follows that there must be working in and through all nature a directive principle, a principle of plan or design, a principle according to which those manifold agencies work together in fulfilment of a purpose, *for the attainment of ends*. Hence the reality of a fourth class of causes, *final causes*.

The separate influence of each of those four kinds of cause can be clearly illustrated by reference to the production of any work of art. When, for instance, a sculptor chisels a statue from a block of marble, the latter is the material cause (*materia secunda*) of the statue, the form which he induces on it by his labour is the formal cause (*forma accidentalis*), the sculptor himself as agent is the efficient cause, and the motive from which he works—money fame, esthetic pleasure, etc.—is the final cause.

The formal and material causes are *intrinsic* to the effect; they constitute the effect *in facto esse*, the distinction of each from the latter being an inadequate real distinction. It is not so usual nowadays to call these intrinsic constitutive principles of things *causes* of the latter; but they verify the general definition of cause. The other two causes, the efficient and the final, are *extrinsic* to the effect, and really and adequately distinct from it,[442] extrinsic principles of its production, its *fieri*.

This classification of causes is adequate;[443] it answers all the questions that can be asked in explanation of the production of any effect: *a quo? ex quo? per quid? propter quid?* Nor is there any sort of cause which cannot be brought under some one or other of those four heads. What is called an "exemplar cause," *causa exemplaris, i.e.* the ideal or model or plan in the mind of an intelligent agent, according to which he aims and strives to execute his work, may be regarded as an extrinsic formal cause; or again, in so far as it aids and equips the agent for his task, an efficient cause; or, again, in so far as it represents a good to be realized, a final cause.[444]

The objects of our knowledge are in a true sense causes of our knowledge: any such object may be regarded as an efficient cause, both physical and moral, of this knowledge, in so far as by its action on our minds it determines the activity of our cognitive faculties; or, again, as a final cause, inasmuch as it is the end and aim of the knowledge.

The essence of the soul is, as we have seen, not exactly an efficient cause of the faculties which are its properties; but it is their final cause, inasmuch as their *raison d'être* is to perfect it; and their subjective or material cause, inasmuch as it is the seat and support of these faculties.

The fourfold division is analogical, not univocal: though the matter, the form, the agent, and the end or purpose, all contribute positively to the production of the effect, it is clear that the character of the causal influence is widely different in each case.

Again, its members do not demand distinct subjects: all four classes of cause may be verified in the same subject. For instance, the human soul is a formal cause in regard to the composite human individual, a material cause in regard to its habits, an efficient cause in regard to its acts, and a final cause in regard to its faculties.

Furthermore, the fourfold division is not an immediate division, for it follows the division of cause in general into *intrinsic* and *extrinsic* causes. Finally, it is a division of the causes which we find to be operative *in* the universe. But the philosophical study of the universe will lead us gradually to the conviction that itself and all the causes in it are themselves *contingent*, themselves caused by and dependent on, a Cause *outside* or extrinsic to the universe, a *First, Uncaused, Uncreated, Self-Existent, Necessary Cause* (*Causa Prima, Increata*), at once the *efficient* and *final* cause of all things. In contrast with this *Uncreated, First Cause*, all the other causes we have now to investigate are called *created* or *second* causes (*causae secundae, creatae*).

A cause may be either *total, adequate*, or *partial, inadequate*, according as the effect is due to its influence solely, or to its influence in conjunction with, or dependence on, the influence of some other cause or causes *of the same order*. A created cause, therefore, is a total cause if the effect is due to its influence independently of other created causes; though of course all created causes are dependent, both as to their existence and as to their causality, on the influence of the First Cause. Without the activity of created efficient and final causes the First Cause can accomplish directly whatever these can accomplish—except their very causality itself, which cannot be actualized without them, but for which He can supply *eminenter*. Similarly, while it is incompatible with His Infinite Perfection that He discharge the function of material or formal cause of finite composite things, He can immediately create these latter by the simultaneous production (*ex nihilo*) and union of their material and formal principles.

A cause is said to be *in actu secundo* when it is actually exercising its causal influence. Antecedently to such exercise, at least *prioritate naturae*, it is said to be *in actu primo*: when it has the expedite power to discharge its function as cause it is *in actu primo proximo*, while if its power is in any way incomplete, hampered or unready, it is *in actu primo remoto*.

Many other divisions of cause, subordinate to the Aristotelian division, will be explained in connexion with the members of this latter.

96. MATERIAL AND FORMAL CAUSES.—These are properly subject-matter for *Cosmology*. We will therefore very briefly supplement what has been said already concerning them in connexion with the doctrine of *Change*. By a material cause we mean *that out of which anything is made*: *id ex quo aliquid fit*. Matter is correlative with form: from the union of these there results a composite reality endowed with either essential or accidental unity—with the former if the material principle be absolutely indeterminate and the correlative form substantial, with the latter if the material principle be some actually existing individual reality and the form some supervening accident. Properly speaking only corporeal substances have material causes,[445] but the term "material cause" is used in an extended sense to signify any potential, passive, receptive subject of formative or actuating principles: thus the soul is the subjective or material cause of its faculties and habits; essence of existence; *genus of differentia*, etc.

In what does the positive causal influence of a material cause consist? How does it contribute positively to the actualization of the composite reality of which it is the material cause? It *receives* and *unites with* the form which is educed from its potentiality by the action of efficient causes, and thus contributes to the generation of the concrete, composite individual reality.[446]

It is by reason of the causality of the *formal cause* that we speak of a thing being *formally* such or such. As correlative of material cause it finds its proper application in reference to the constitution of corporeal things. The formative principle, called *forma substantialis*, which actuates, determines, specifies the material principle, and by union with the latter constitutes an individual corporeal substance of a definite kind, is the (substantial) formal cause of this composite substance.[447] The material principle of corporeal things is of itself indifferent to any species of body; it is the form that removes this indefiniteness and determines the matter, by its union with the latter, to constitute a definite type of corporeal substance.[448] The existence of different species of living organisms and different types of inorganic matter in the universe implies in the constitution of these things a common material principle, *materia prima*, and a multiplicity of differentiating, specifying, formative principles, *formae substantiales*. That the distinction between these two principles in the constitution of any individual corporeal substance, whether living or inorganic, is not merely a virtual distinction between metaphysical (generic and specific) grades of being in the individual, but a real distinction between separable entities, is a scholastic thesis established in the Special Metaphysics of the organic and inorganic domains of the universe.[449]

Since the *form* is a perfecting, actuating principle, the term is often used synonymously with *actus, actuality*. And since besides the essential perfection which a being has by virtue of its substantial form it may have accidental perfections by reason of supervening accidental forms, these, too, are formal causes.

In what does the causal influence of the formal cause consist? In communicating itself intrinsically to the material principle or passive subject from whose potentiality it is evoked by the action of efficient causes; in actuating that potentiality by intrinsic union therewith, and thus determining the individual subject to be actually or formally an individual of such or such a kind.

The material and formal causes are *intrinsic* principles of the constitution of things. We next pass to an analysis of the two *extrinsic* causes, and firstly of the efficient cause and its causality.

97. EFFICIENT CAUSE; TRADITIONAL CONCEPT EXPLAINED.—By efficient cause we understand that *by which* anything takes place, happens, occurs: *id a quo aliquid fit*. The world of our external and internal experience is the scene of incessant *changes*: men and things not only are, but are constantly *becoming*. Now every such change is originated by some active principle, and this we call the efficient cause of the change. Aristotle called it τὸ κινητικόν or ἡ ἀρχὴ κινητική, the *kinetic* or *moving* principle; or again, ἀρχὴ κινησέως ἢ μεταβολῆς ἐν ἑτέρῳ, *principium motus vel mutationis in alio*, "the principle of motion or change in some other thing". The result achieved by this change, the actualized potentiality, is called the *effect*; the causality itself of the efficient cause is called *action* (ποίησις), *motion, change*—and, from the point of view of the effect, *passio* (παθήσις). The perfection or endowment whereby an efficient cause acts, *i.e.* its efficiency (ἐνέργεια), is called *active power* (*potentia seu virtus activa*); it is also called *force* or *potential energy* in reference to inanimate agents, *faculty* in reference to animate agents, especially men and animals. This active power of an efficient cause or agent is to be carefully distinguished from the *passive potentiality* acted upon and undergoing change. The former connotes a perfection, the latter an imperfection: *unumquodque agit inquantum est in actu, patitur vero inquantum, est in potentia*. The scope of the active power of a cause is the measure of its actuality, of its perfection in the scale of reality; while the extent of the passive potentiality of *patiens* is a measure of its relative imperfection. The actuation of the former is *actio*, that of the latter *passio*. The point of ontological

connexion of the two *potentiae* is the *change* (*motus*, κίνησις), this being at once the formal perfecting of the passive potentiality in the *patiens* or effect, and the immediate term of the efficiency or active power of the *agens* or cause. *Actio* and *passio*, therefore, are not expressions of one and the same concept; they express two distinct concepts of one and the same reality, *viz.* the change: *actio et passio sunt idem numero motus*. This change takes place *formally* in the subject upon which the efficient cause acts, for it is an actuation of the potentiality of the former under the influence of the latter: ἡ κίνησις ἐν τῷ κινητῷ; ἐντελέχεια γὰρ ἐστι τούτου. Considered in the potentiality of this subject—"τὸ τοῦδέ ἐν τῷδε: *hujus in hococ*"—it is called *passio*. Considered as a term of the active power of the cause—"τοῦδε ὑπο τοῦδε: *hujus per hoc*"—it is called *actio*.

The fact that *actio* and *passio* are really and objectively one and the same *motus* does not militate against their being regarded as two separate supreme categories, for they are objects of distinct concepts,[450] and this is sufficient to constitute them distinct categories.

Doubts are sometimes raised, as St. Thomas remarks,[451] about the assertion that the action of an agent is not formally in the latter but in the *patiens*: *actio fit in passo*. It is clear, however, he continues, that the action is formally in the *patiens* for it is the actuation not of any potentiality of the agent, but of the passive potentiality of the *patiens*: it is in the latter that the *motus* or change, which is both *actio* and *passio*, takes place, dependently of course on the influence of the agent, or efficient cause of the change. The active power of an efficient cause is an index of the latter's actuality; the exercise of this power (*i.e. action*) does not formally perfect the agent, for it is not an actuation of any passive potentiality of the latter; it formally perfects the *patiens*. Only *immanent* action perfects the agent, and then not as agent but as *patiens* or receiver of the actuality effected by the action.

We may, then, define efficient cause as *the extrinsic principle of the change or production of anything by means of action*: *principium extrinsicum a quo fluit motus vel productio rei mediante actione*.

It is a "first" principle as compared with material and formal causes for its influence is obviously prior in nature to theirs; also as compared with the other extrinsic cause, the final cause, *in ordine executionis*, not, however, *in ordine intentionis*. The "end," not as realized but as realizable, not in execution but in intention, discharges its function and exerts its influence as "final *cause*" and in this order the final cause, as will appear later, is *the first of all causes*: *finis est ultimus in executione sed primus in intentione*.

"Change or production," in the definition, is to be understood not in the strict sense in which it presupposes an existing subject or material, but in the wide sense in which it includes any production of new reality, even creation or production *ex nihilo*.

"Action," too, is to be understood in the wide sense in which it includes the action of the First Cause, which action is really identical with the essence of the latter. We conceive creation after the analogy of the efficient action of created or "second" causes: we have no *proper* concept of the infinite perfection of the Divine activity. In all created efficient causes not only is the action itself, but also the efficiency, force, power, faculty, which is its *proximate* principle, really distinct from the nature or essence of the agent; the former is a substance, the latter an accident.

Finally, the action of a created efficient cause is either transitive (*transiens*) or immanent (*immanens*) according as the change wrought by the action takes place in something else (as when *the sun* heats or lights *the earth*) or in the cause itself (as when a man reasons or wills). In the former case the action perfects not the agent but the other thing, the *patiens*; in the latter case it perfects the agent itself, *agens* and *patiens* being here the same identical concrete individual.[452]

98. SOME SCHOLIA ON CAUSATION. THE PRINCIPLE OF CAUSALITY.—Before enumerating the principal kinds of efficient cause, and analysing the nature of efficient causality, we may set down here certain self-evident axioms and aphorisms concerning causation in general. (*a*) The most important of these is the *Principle of Causality*, which has been enunciated in a variety of ways: *Whatever happens has a cause*; *Whatever begins to be has a cause*; *Whatever is contingent has a cause*; *Nothing occurs without a cause*. Not everything that begins to be has necessarily a *material* cause, or a *formal* cause, really distinct from itself. For instance, simple spiritual beings, like the human soul, have no material cause, nor any formal cause or constitutive principle distinct from their essence. Similarly, the whole universe, having been created *ex nihilo*, had no pre-existing material cause. All the material beings, however, which are produced, generated, brought into actual existence in the course of the incessant changes which characterize the physical universe, have both material and formal causes. But the Principle of Causality refers mainly to extrinsic causes. It is commonly understood only of efficient causes; and only in regard to these is it self-evident. We shall see that as a matter of fact nothing happens without a *final* cause: that intelligent purpose pervades reality through and through. This, however, is a conclusion, not a principle. What is really a self-evident, axiomatic, necessary principle is that *whatever happens has an* EFFICIENT *cause*. Only the Necessary, Self-Existing, Eternal Being, has the sufficient reason of His actual existence in Himself, in His

own essence. That any being which is contingent could exist *independently of some other actual being* as the cause of this existence; that it could have come into existence or begun to exist *from absolute nothingness, or be produced or brought into actual existence without any actual being to produce it*; or that, once existing and subject to change, it could undergo change and have its potentialities actualized *without any actual being to cause such change*—all this is positively unthinkable and absolutely repugnant to our intelligence; all this our reason peremptorily declares to be intrinsically impossible. Nor is there question of a mere psychological inconceivability, such as might be due to a long-continued custom of associating the idea of a "beginning" with the idea of a "cause" of this beginning—as phenomenists generally contend.[453] There is question of an impossibility which our reason categorically dictates to be a real, ontological impossibility. The Principle of Causality is therefore a necessary, *a priori*, self-evident principle.

(*b*) *Every effect must have an adequate efficient cause*, i.e. a cause sufficiently perfect, sufficiently high on the scale of being, to have the active power to produce the effect in question; otherwise the effect would be partially uncaused, which is impossible.

(*c*) *An effect cannot as such be actually more perfect than its adequate (created) cause.* The reason is that the effect as such is really dependent for its actuality on its adequate created cause. It derives its actuality from the latter. Now it is inconceivable that an agent could be the active, productive principle of a greater perfection, a higher grade of actuality, than itself possesses. Whatever be the nature of efficient causality, *actio* and *passio*, or of the dependence of the produced actuality upon the active power of its adequate efficient cause, the reality of this dependence forbids us to think that in the natural order of efficient causation a higher grade of reality can be actualized than the agent is capable of actualizing, or that the agent can naturally actualize a higher or more perfect grade of reality than is actually its own. We must, however, bear in mind that there is question of the *adequate* created cause of an effect; and that to account *fully* for the actualization of any potential reality whatsoever we are forced to recognize in all causation of created efficient causes the *concursus* of the *First Cause*.

(*d*) The actuality of the effect is in its adequate created cause or causes, *not actually and formally, but potentially* or *virtually*. If the cause produce an effect of the same kind as itself (*causa univoca*), as when living organisms propagate their species, the perfection of the effect is said to be in the cause *equivalently* (*aequivalenter*); if it produce an effect of a different kind from itself (*causa analoga*), as when a sculptor makes a statue, the perfection of the effect is said to be in the cause *eminently* (*eminenter*).

(*e*) *Omne agens agit inquantum est in actu.* The operative power of a being is in proportion to its own actual perfection: the higher an agent is on the scale of reality, or in other words the more perfect its grade of being, the higher and more perfect will be the effects achieved by the exercise of its operative powers. In fact our chief test of the perfection of any nature is analysis of its operations. Hence the maxim so often referred to already:—

(*f*) *Operari sequitur esse; qualis est operatio talis est natura; modus operandi sequitur modum essendi.* Operation is the key to nature; we know what any thing is by what it does.

(*g*) *Nihil agit ultra suam speciem*; or, again, *Omne agens agit simile sibi.* These are inductive generalizations gathered from experience, and have reference to the natural operation of agents, especially in the organic world. Living organisms reproduce only their own kind. Moreover, every agency in the universe has operative powers of a definite kind; acting according to its nature it produces certain effects and these only; others it cannot produce: this is, in the natural order of things, and with the natural *concursus* of the First Cause. But created causes have a passive *obediential capacity* (*potentia obedientialis*) whereby their nature can be so elevated by the First Cause that they can produce, with His special, supernatural *concursus*, effects of an entirely higher order than those within the ambit of their natural powers.[454]

(*h*) From a known effect, of whatsoever kind, we can argue with certainty, *a posteriori*, to the *existence* of an adequate efficient cause, and to *some knowledge* of the *nature* of such a cause.[455] By virtue of the principle of causality we can infer the existence of an adequate cause containing either equivalently or eminently all the perfections of the effect in question.

99. CLASSIFICATION OF EFFICIENT CAUSES.—(*a*) We have already referred to the distinction between the *First* Cause and *Second* or *Created* Causes. The former is absolutely independent of all other beings both as to His power and as to the exercise of this power. The latter are dependent, for both, upon the former.

The distinction between a first, or primary, or independent cause, and second, or subordinate, or dependent causes can be understood not only of causes universally, but also as obtaining among created causes themselves. In general the *subordination* of a cause to a superior or anterior cause may be either *essential* or *accidental*: essential, when the second cause depends—either for its existence or for an indispensable complement of its efficiency—on the *present* actual influence of the other cause; accidental when the second cause has indeed received its existence or efficiency from this other cause, but is now no longer dependent, for its existence or action, on the latter. Thus, living organisms are, as causes, accidentally subordinate to their parent organisms: they derived their existence from the latter, but are independent of these when in their maturity they continue to exist, and live, and act of themselves and for themselves. But all creatures, on the other hand, are, as causes, *essentially* subordinate to the Creator, inasmuch as they can exist and act only in constant dependence on the ever present and ever actual conserving and concurring influence of the Creator.

It is obvious that all the members of any series of causes *essentially* subordinate the one to the other *must exist simultaneously*. Whether such a series could be infinite depends, therefore, on the question whether an *actually infinite multitude* is intrinsically possible. This difficulty cannot be urged with such force against an infinite regress in causes *accidentally* subordinate to one another; for here such a regress would not involve an actually infinite multitude of things existing simultaneously. In the case of essentially subordinate causes, moreover, the series, whatever about its infinity, must contain, or rather imply *above* it, *one* cause which is *first* in the sense of being *independent*, or exempt from the subordination characteristic of all the others. And the reason is obvious: Since no one of them can exist or act except dependently on another, and this on another, and so on, it is manifest that the series cannot exist at all unless there is some one cause which, unlike all the others, exists and acts without such subordination or dependence. Hence, *in essentially subordinate causes an infinite regress is impossible.*[456] In Natural Theology these considerations are of supreme importance.

(*b*) An efficient cause may be described as *immanent* or *transitive* according as the term of its action remains within the cause itself, or is produced in something else. The action of the First Cause is formally immanent, being identical with the Divine Nature itself; it is virtually transitive when it is creative, or operative among creatures.

(*c*) An efficient cause is either a *principal* or an *instrumental* cause. When two causes so combine to produce an effect that one of them uses the other the former is called the principal and the latter the instrumental cause. Thus I am the principal cause of the words I am writing; my pen is the instrumental cause of them. Such an effect is always attributed to the principal cause, not to the instrumental. The notion of an instrument is quite a familiar notion. An instrument helps the principal agent to do what the latter could not otherwise do, or at least not so easily. An instrument therefore is really a cause. It contributes positively to the production of the effect. How does it do so? By reason of its nature or structure it influences, modifies, and directs in a particular way, the efficiency of the principal cause. But this property of the instrumental cause comes into play only when the latter is being actually used by a principal cause. A pen, a saw, a hammer, a spade, have each its own instrumentality. The pen will not cut, nor the saw mould iron, nor the hammer dig, nor the spade write, for the agent that uses them. Each will produce its own kind of effect when used; but none of them will produce any effect except when used: though each has in itself permanently and inherently the power to produce its own proper effect in use.[457] We have instanced the use of *artificial* instruments. But nature itself provides some agencies with what may be called *natural* instruments. The *semen* whereby living organisms propagate their kind is an instance. In a less proper sense the various members of the body are called instruments of the human person as principal cause, "instrumenta *conjuncta*".

The notion of an instrumental cause involves then (*a*) subordination of the latter, in its instrumental activity, to a principal cause, (*b*) incapacity to produce the effect otherwise than by modifying and directing the influence of the principal cause. This property whereby the instrumental cause modifies or determines in a particular way the influence of the principal cause, is called by St. Thomas an *actio* or *operatio* of the former; the distinction between the principal and the instrumental cause being that whereas the former acts by virtue of a power permanently inherent in it as a natural perfection, the latter acts as an instrument only by virtue of the transient motion which it derives from the principal cause which utilizes it.[458]

We may, therefore, define an *instrumental* cause as *one which, when acting as an instrument, produces the effect not by virtue of its inherent power alone, but by virtue of a power communicated to it by some principal cause which acts through it.* A *principal* cause, on the other hand, is *one which produces its effect by virtue of an active power permanently inherent in itself.*

The designations *principal* and *instrumental* are obviously correlative. Moreover, *all created* causes may be called *instrumental* in relation to the *First Cause*. For, not only are they dependent on the latter for the *conservation* of their nature and active powers; they are also dependent, in their action, in their actual exercise of these powers, on the First Cause (for the *concursus* of the latter).[459] Yet some created causes have these powers permanently, and can exercise them without subordination to other creatures; while others need, for the exercise of their proper functions, not only the Divine *concursus*, but also the motion of other creatures. Hence the former are rightly called *principal* created causes, and the latter *instrumental* created causes.

(*d*) Efficient causes are divided into *free* causes and *necessary* causes. A free or self-determining cause is *one which is not determined by its nature to one line of action*, but *has the power of choosing, or determining itself*, to act or abstain, when all the conditions requisite for acting are present. Man is a free agent, or free cause, of his deliberate actions. A necessary cause, or natural cause as it is sometimes called, is *one which is determined by its nature to one invariable line of action*, so that, granted the conditions requisite for action, it cannot naturally abstain from acting in that invariable manner. All the physical agencies of the inorganic world, all plant and animal organisms beneath man himself, are necessary causes.

The freedom of the human will is established against determinism in Psychology.[460] The difficulties of determinists against this doctrine are for the most part based on misconceptions, or on erroneous and gratuitous assumptions. We may mention two of them here.[461] Free activity, they say, would be *causeless* activity: it would violate the "law of universal causation". We reply that free activity is by no means causeless activity. The free agent himself is in the fullest and truest sense the efficient cause of his free acts. It is by his causal, efficient influence that the act of free choice is determined and elicited. Free causality evidently does not violate the necessary, *a priori* principle set forth above under the title of the Principle of Causality. But—they urge in the second place—it violates the "law of universal causation," *i.e.* the law that every event in nature must be the result of some set of phenomenal antecedents which *necessitate* it, and which, therefore, whenever verified, *must* produce this result and no other; and by violating this law it removes all supposed "free" activities from the domain of that regularity and uniformity without which no scientific knowledge of such phenomena would be possible. To this we reply, firstly, that the law of uniform causation in nature, the law which is known as the "Law of the Uniformity of Nature," and which, under the title of the "Law of Universal Causation" is confounded by determinists and phenomenists with the entirely distinct "Principle of Causality"—is not by any means a law of *necessary* causation.[462] The statement that Nature is uniform in its activities is not the expression of an *a priori*, necessary truth, like the Principle of Causality. It is a generalization from experience. And experience testifies to the existence of grades in this all-prevailing uniformity. In the domain of physical nature it is the expression of the Free Will of the Author of Nature, who may miraculously derogate from this physical uniformity for higher, moral ends. In the domain of deliberate human activities it is the expression of that less rigorous but no less real uniformity which is dependent on the free will of man. And just as the possibility of miracles in the former domain does not destroy the regularity on which the generalizations of the physical sciences are based, so neither does the fact of human free will render worthless or unreliable the generalizations of the human sciences (ethical, social, political, economic, etc.) about human conduct. Were the appearance of miracles in the physical domain, or the ordinary play of free will in the human domain, entirely *capricious, motiveless, purposeless*, the results would, of course, be chaotic, precarious, unaccountable, unintelligible, and scientific knowledge of them would be impossible: for the assumption that reality is the work of intelligent purpose, and is therefore a regular, orderly expression of law, in other words, the assumption that the universe is intelligible, is a prerequisite condition for scientific knowledge about the universe. But determinists seem to assume that Divine Providence and human free will must necessarily imply that the whole universe of physical phenomena and human activities would be an unintelligible chaos; and having erected this philosophical scarecrow on a gratuitous assumption they think it will gradually exorcise all belief in Divine Providence and human freedom from the "scientific" mind!

(*e*) Efficient causes are either *physical* or *moral*. A physical efficient cause is *one which produces its effect by its own proper power and action*—whether immediately or by means of an instrument. For instance, the billiard player is the physical cause of the motion he imparts to the balls by means of the cue. A moral cause is one which produces its effect by the representation of something as good or evil to the mind of a free agent; by inducing the latter through example, advice, persuasion, promises, threats, commands, entreaties, etc., to produce the effect in question. For instance, a master is the moral cause of what his servant does in obedience to his commands. The motives set forth by way of inducement to the latter are of course *final* causes of the latter's action. But the former, by setting them forth, is the moral cause of the action: he is undoubtedly more than a mere condition; he contributes positively and efficiently to the effect. His physical causation, however, does not reach to the effect itself, but only to the effect wrought in the mind of the servant by his command. It is causally connected with the physical action of the servant by means of an intermediate link which we may call *mental* or *psychical causation*—actio "*intentionalis*,"—the action of cognition on the mind of a cognitive agent.

The agent employed by a moral cause to produce an effect physically may be called an instrumental cause in a wide and less proper sense of this term, the instrumentality being moral, not physical. Only free agents can be moral causes; and as a rule they are termed moral causes only when they produce the effect through the physical operation of another free agent. What if they employ not free agents, nor yet inanimate instruments, but agents endowed with sense cognition and sense appetite, to produce effects? If a man set his dog at another, is he the *moral* or the *physical* cause of the injuries inflicted by the dog? That he is the principal *efficient* cause is unquestionable. But is he the principal *physical* cause and the dog the *instrument*? We think it is more proper to call the principal efficient cause a *moral* cause in all cases where there intervenes between his physical action and the effect an intermediate link of "psychical" or "intentional" action, even though, as in the present example, this psychical link is of the sentient, not the intellectual, order.

(*f*) The efficient cause, like other causes, may be either *partial* or *total*, according as it produces the effect by co-operation with other causes, or by itself alone. The aim of the inductive sciences is to discover for each kind of natural event or phenomenon the "total cause" in the comprehensive sense of the whole group of *positive* agencies or causes proper, and *negative* antecedent and concomitant *conditions* which are *indispensable* and *necessitating* principles of the happening of such kind of event.[463]

(*g*) We can distinguish between the *immediate or determining*, the more or less *proximate*, and the more or less *remote*, efficient causes of an event. Thus, the application of the fuse to the charge of dynamite in a rock is the immediate or determining cause of the explosion which bursts the rock; the lighting of the fuse, the placing of the charge, etc., the more proximate causes; the making of the fuse, dynamite, instruments, etc., the more remote causes. Again the aim of the inductive sciences is to discover the "total *proximate* cause" of events,[464] leaving the investigation of ultimate causes, as well as the analysis of causality itself, to philosophy.

(*h*) Finally, we must distinguish between the *individual* agent itself as cause (the *suppositum* or person that acts); the agent's *nature* and *active power* as causes; and the *action*, or exercise of this power as cause. The former, the individual, concrete agent, is the "principium *quod* agit," and is called the "causa *ut quae*". The nature and the active power of the agent are each a "principium *quo* agens agit," the remote and the proximate principle of action respectively; and each is called a "causa *ut qua*". The action of the agent is the cause of the effect in the sense that the actual production or *fieri* of anything is the immediate cause of this thing *in facto esse*. Corresponding to these distinctions we distinguish between the cause *in actu primo remoto*, *in actu primo proximo*, and *in actu secundo*. These distinctions are of no little importance. By ignoring them, and by losing sight of the intrinsic (formal and material) causes of natural phenomena, many modern scientists and philosophers have confounded cause and effect with the process itself of causation, and declared that cause and effect are not distinct realities, but only two mental aspects of one and the same reality.[465]

The same may be said of all the distinctions so far enumerated. They are absolutely essential to the formation of clear ideas on the question of causality. No term in familiar use is of more profound philosophical significance, and at the same time more elastic and ambiguous in its popular meanings, than the term *cause*. This is keenly felt in the Logic of the Inductive Sciences, where not only the discovery, but the exact measurement, of physical causes, is the goal of research.

"When we call one thing," writes Mr. Joseph,[466] "the cause of another, the real relation between them is not always the same.... We say that molecular action is the cause of heat, that the heat of the sun is the cause of growth, that starvation is sometimes the cause of death, that jealousy is a frequent cause of crime. We should in the first case maintain that cause and effect are reciprocally necessary; no heat without molecular motion and no molecular motion without heat. In the second the effect cannot exist without the cause, but the cause may exist without the effect, for the sun shines on the moon but nothing grows there. In the third the cause cannot exist without the effect, for starvation must produce death, but the effect may exist without the cause, since death need not have been produced by starvation. In the fourth case we can have the cause without the effect, and also the effect without the cause; for jealousy may exist without producing crime, and crime may occur without the motive of jealousy. It is plain then that we do not always mean the same thing by our words when we say that two things are related as cause and effect; and anyone who would classify and name the various modes in which two things may be causally related would do a great service to clear thinking."

In the popular acceptation of the term *cause*, the same kind of event can have a *plurality of (efficient) causes*. Death, for example, may be brought about in different cases by different diseases or accidents. But if we understand by the total efficient cause of any given kind of effect the sum-total of agencies and conditions which when present *necessitate* this kind of an effect, and which are collectively and severally *indispensable* for its production, then it is obvious that a given *kind* of effect can have *only one kind* of such total group of antecedents as total cause, just as any one individual effect can have only one individual total cause, *viz.* the one which actually produced it; a *similar* total cause would produce a *similar* effect, but could not produce the numerically identical individual effect of the other similar cause.[467]

The medieval scholastics discussed the question in connexion with the problem of individuation: "Would Alexander the Great have been the same individual had he been born of other parents than Philip and Olympia?" The question is hardly intelligible. The person born of these other parents might indeed have been as similar as you will to the actual Alexander of history, but would not and could not have been the actual Alexander of history. Nowadays the question discussed in this connexion is not so much whether the same kind of natural phenomenon can be produced by different kinds of total cause—for the answer to this question depends wholly on the wider or the narrower meaning attached to the term "total cause,"[468]—but rather whether or how far the inductive scientist's ideal of searching always for the *necessitating and indispensable* cause (or, as it is also called, the "reciprocating" or "commensurate" cause) is a practical ideal.

Chapter XIV.

Efficient Causality; Phenomenism And Occasionalism.

100. OBJECTIVE VALIDITY OF THE TRADITIONAL CONCEPT OF EFFICIENT CAUSALITY.—We have seen how modern sensists, phenomenists, and positivists have doubted or denied the power of the human mind to attain to a knowledge of any objective reality corresponding to the category of substance. They treat in a similar way the traditional concept of efficient causality. And in delivering their open or veiled attacks on the real validity of this notion they have made a misleading use of the proper and legitimate function of the inductive sciences. The chief aim of the natural scientist is to seek out and bring to light the *whole group of necessitating and indispensable* (phenomenal) *antecedents* of any given kind of event, and to formulate the natural law of their connexion with this kind of event. There is no particular objection to his calling these antecedents the *invariable*, or even the *necessary* or *necessitating*, antecedents of the event; provided he does not claim what he cannot prove—and what, as we shall see later, is not true, *viz.*—that the invariability or necessity of this connexion between phenomenal antecedents and consequents is wholly inviolable, fatal, absolute in character. He may rightly claim for any such established connexion the hypothetical, conditional necessity which characterizes all inductively established laws of physical nature. There are such antecedents and consequents in the universe; there are connexions between them which are more than mere *casual* connexions of *time sequence*, which are connexions of physical law, inasmuch as they are connexions based on the *natures* of agencies in an *orderly* universe, connexions of these agencies with their natural effects. All this is undeniable. Moreover, so long as *the scientist* confines himself

to inferences concerning such connexions between phenomena, to inferences and generalizations based on the assumed uniformity of nature, he is working in his proper sphere. Nay, even if he chooses to designate these groups of invariable phenomenal antecedents by the title of "physical causes" we know what he means; though we perceive some danger of confusion, inasmuch as we see him arrogating to the notion of regularity or uniformity of connexion *i.e.* to the notion of *physical law*, a term, *causality*, which traditionally expressed something quite distinct from this, *viz.* the notion of *positive influence* of one thing on the being or happening of another. But when *phenomenist philosophers* adopt this usage we cannot feel reassured against the danger of confusion by such protestations as those of Mill in the following passage:—[469]

I premise, then, that when in the course of this inquiry I speak of the cause of any phenomenon, I do not mean a cause which is not itself a phenomenon; I make no research into the ultimate or ontological cause of anything. To adopt a distinction familiar in the writings of the Scotch metaphysicians, and especially of Reid, the causes with which I concern myself are not *efficient*, but *physical* causes. They are causes in that sense alone, in which one physical fact is said to be the cause of another. Of the efficient causes of phenomena, or whether any such causes exist at all I am not called upon to give an opinion. The notion of causation is deemed, by the schools of metaphysics most in vogue at the present moment, to imply a mysterious and most powerful tie, such as cannot, or at least does not, exist between any physical fact and that other physical fact on which it is invariably consequent, and which is popularly termed its cause; and thence is deduced the supposed necessity of ascending higher, into the essences and inherent constitution of things, to find the true cause, the cause which is not only followed by, but actually produces, the effect. No such necessity exists for the purposes of the present inquiry, nor will any such doctrine be found in the following pages. The only notion of a cause, which the theory of induction requires, is such a notion as can be gained by experience. The Law of Causation, which is the main pillar of inductive science, is but the familiar truth, that invariability of succession is found by observation to obtain between every fact in nature and some other fact which has preceded it; independently of all considerations respecting the ultimate mode of production of phenomena, and of every other question regarding the nature of "Things in themselves".

This passage—which expresses fairly well the phenomenist and positivist attitude in regard to the reality, or at least the cognoscibility, of *efficient* causes—fairly bristles with inaccuracies, misconceptions, and false insinuations.[470] But we are concerned here only with the denial that any notion of an *efficient* cause "can be gained from experience," and the doubt consequently cast on the objective validity of this notion. The Sensism which regards our highest intellectual activities as mere organic associations of sentient states of consciousness, has for its logical issue the Positivism which contends that all valid knowledge is confined to the existence and time and space relations of sense phenomena. In thus denying to the mind all power of attaining to a valid knowledge of anything suprasensible—such as substance, power, force, efficient cause, etc.—Positivism passes over into Agnosticism.

In refutation of this philosophy, in so far as it denies that we have any grounds in experience for believing in the real existence of efficient causes, we may set down in the first place this universal belief itself of the human race that there are in the universe efficient causes of the events that happen in it. Men universally believe that they themselves as agents contribute by a real and positive influence to the actual occurrence of their own thoughts, reasonings, wishes, desires, sensations; that their mental resolves to speak, walk, write, eat, or perform any other external, bodily works do really, positively, and efficiently produce or cause those works; that external phenomena have a real influence on happenings in their own bodies, that fire burns them and food nourishes them; that external phenomena also have a real and positive influence on their sense organs, and through these on their minds by the production there of conscious states such as sensations; finally that external phenomena have a real and positive influence on one another; that by action and interaction they really produce the changes that are constantly taking place in the universe: that the sun does really heat and light the earth, that the sowing of the seed in springtime has really a positive influence on the existence of crops in the harvest, that the taking of poison has undoubtedly a real influence on the death which results from it. And if any man of ordinary intelligence and plain common sense is told that such belief is an illusion, that in all such cases the connexion between the things, facts or events which he designates as "cause" and "effect," is a mere connexion of invariable time sequence between antecedents and consequents, that in no case is there evidence of any *positive, productive influence* of the one fact upon the other, he will either smile incredulously and decline to take his objector seriously, or he will simply ask the latter to *prove* the universal belief to be an illusion. His conviction of the real and objective validity of his notion of efficient cause, as something which positively influences the happening of things, is so profound and ineradicable that it must necessarily be grounded in, and confirmed by, his constant experience of the real world in which he lives and moves. Not that he professes to be able to explain the *nature* of this efficient influence in which he believes. Even if he were a philosopher he might not be able to satisfy himself or others on this point But being a plain man of ordinary intelligence he has sense enough to distinguish between the *existence* of a fact and its *nature*, its explanation, its *quomodo*; and to believe in the real existence of a *positive efficient, productive* influence of cause on effect, however this influence is to be conceived or explained.

A second argument for the objective validity of the concept of efficient cause may be drawn from a consideration of the *Principle of Causality*. The experience on which the plain man grounds his belief in the validity of his notion of cause is not mere uninterpreted sense experience in its raw and brute condition, so to speak; it is this sense experience rationalized, assimilated into his intelligence—spontaneously and half unconsciously, perhaps—by the light of the self-evident Principle of Causality, that whatever happens has a cause. When the plain man believes that all the various agencies in nature, like those enumerated above, are not merely *temporal* antecedents or concomitants of their effects, but are *really productive* of those effects, he is really applying the universal and necessary truth—that an "event," a "happening," a "change," a "commencement" of any new actual mode of being demands the existence of another actual being as cause—the truth embodied in the Principle of Causality, to this, that, and the other event of his experience: he is *locating* the "causes" of these events in the various persons and things which he regards as the agents or producers of these events. In making such applications he may very possibly err in detail. But no actual application of the principle at all is really required for establishing the objective validity of the concept of cause. There are philosophers who—erroneously, as we shall see—deny that the Principle of Causality finds its application in the domain of *created* things, who hold, in other words, that no created beings can be efficient causes, and who nevertheless recognize, and quite rightly, that the concept of efficient cause is an objectively valid concept. And they do so because they see that since events, beginnings, happenings, changes, are real, there must be really and objectively existent an efficient cause of them—whatever and wherever such efficient cause may be: whether it be one or manifold, finite or infinite, etc.

We have already examined Hume's attempt to deny the ontological necessity of the Principle of Causality and to substitute therefor a subjectively or psychologically necessary "feeling of expectation" grounded on habitual association of ideas. Kant, on the other hand, admits the self-evident, necessary character of the Principle; but holds that, since this necessity is engendered by the mind's imposing a subjective form of thought on the data of sense consciousness, the principle is validly applicable only to connexions within the world of mental appearances, and not at all to the world of real being. He thus transfers the discussion to the domain of Epistemology, where in opposition to his theory of knowledge the Principle of Causality can be shown to be applicable to all contingent reality, and to be therefore legitimately employed in Natural Theology for the purpose of establishing the real existence of an Uncaused First Cause.

101. ORIGIN OF THE CONCEPT OF EFFICIENT CAUSE.—We have seen that universal belief in the real existence of efficient causes is grounded in experience. The formation of the concept, and its application or extension to the world within and around us, are gradual.[471] Active power, force, energy, efficiency, faculty, or by whatever other name we may call it, is of course experienced only in its actual exercise, in action, motion, production of change. Our first experience of its

exercise is found in our consciousness of our own personal activities, mental and bodily: in our thinking, willing or choosing, in our deliberate control of our mental processes, and in the deliberate exercise of our sense faculties and bodily organs. In all this we are conscious of exerting power, force, energy: we apprehend *ourselves* as agents or efficient causes of our mental processes and bodily movements. We apprehend these happenings as due to the exercise of *our own power to produce them*. Seeing other human beings behave like ourselves, we infer by analogy that they also possess and exercise active powers like our own, that they, too, are efficient causes. Finally, observing that effects like to those produced by ourselves, whether in ourselves or in the material world around us, are also consequent on certain other changes in external nature, whether organic or inorganic, we infer by analogy that these corporeal things have also powers, forces, energies, whereby they produce these effects. While our senses testify only to time and space connexions between physical happenings in external nature, our intellect apprehends action and interaction, *i.e.* causal dependence of events on the active influence or efficiency of physical things as agents or causes.[472] Thus, our knowledge of the existence and nature of the forces, powers and energies which constitute *material* things efficient causes is posterior to, and derived by analogy from, our knowledge of the *mental* and bodily powers which reveal themselves to us in our conscious vital processes as constituting our own personal efficient causality.

This conception of efficient causality even in the inanimate things of external nature, *after the analogy of our own vital powers* as revealed in our conscious activities, is sometimes disparaged as naïve anthropomorphism. It just depends on the manner and degree in which we press the analogy. Observing that our earlier notion of cause is "the notion of power combined with a purpose and an end" (thus including *efficient* and *final* causality), Newman remarks[473] that "Accordingly, wherever the world is young, the movements and changes of physical nature have been and are spontaneously ascribed by its people to the presence and will of hidden agents, who haunt every part of it, the woods, the mountains and the streams, the air and the stars, for good or for evil—just as children again, by beating the ground after falling, imply that what has bruised them has intelligence". This is anthropomorphism. So, too, would be the conception of the forces or powers of inanimate nature as powers of sub-conscious "*perception*" and "*appetition*" (Leibniz), or, again, as rudimentary or diminished "will-power" (Cousin).[474] "Physical phenomena, as such, are without sense," as Newman rightly observes; and consequently we may not attribute to them any sort of conscious efficiency, whether perceptive or appetitive. But Newman appears to err in the opposite direction when he adds that "experience teaches us nothing about physical phenomena as causes".[475] The truth lies between these extremes. Taking experience in the wide sense in which it includes rational interpretation of, and inference from, the data of internal and external sense perception, experience certainly reveals to us the *existence* of physical phenomena as efficient causes, or in other words that there is real and efficient causality not only in our own persons but also in the external physical universe; and as to the *nature* of this causality it also gives us at least some little reliable information.

By pursuing this latter question a little we shall be led to examine certain difficulties which lie at the root of *Occasionalism*: the error of denying that creatures, or at least merely corporeal creatures, can be in any true sense efficient causes. A detailed inquiry into the nature of the active powers, forces or energies of the inorganic universe, *i.e.* into the nature of *corporeal* efficient causality, belongs to Cosmology; just as a similar inquiry into *vital, sentient* and *spiritual* efficient causality belongs to Psychology. Here we have only to ascertain what is common and essential to all efficient causality as such, what in general is involved in the exercise of efficient causality, in *actio* and *passio*, and what are the main implications revealed in a study of it.

102. ANALYSIS OF EFFICIENT CAUSALITY, OR *Actio* AND *Passio*: (*a*) THE FIRST CAUSE AND CREATED CAUSES.—We have already referred to the universal dependence of all created causes on the First Cause; and we shall have occasion to return to it in connexion with Occasionalism. God has created all second causes; He has given them their powers of action; He conserves their being and their powers in existence; He applies these powers or puts them in act; He concurs with all their actions; He is therefore the *principal* cause of all their effects; and in relation to Him they are as instrumental causes: "Deus est causa actionis cujuslibet inquantum *dat* virtutem agendi, et inquantum *conservat* eam, et inquantum *applicat* actioni, et inquantum *ejus virtute* omnis alia virtus agit."[476]

In our analysis of change we saw why no finite, created agent can be the *adequate* cause of the *new actualities* or perfections involved in change, and how we are therefore obliged, by a necessity of thought, to infer the existence of a First Cause, an Unchanging, Infinite Source of these new actualities.[477]

The principle upon which the argument was based is this: that the actuality of the effect is something over and above the reality which it had in the passive potentiality of its created material cause and in the active powers of its created efficient cause antecedently to its production: that therefore the production of this actuality, this *novum esse*, implies the influence—by way of co-operation or *concursus* with the created efficient cause—of an Actual Being in whom the actuality of all effects is contained in an eminently perfect way. Even with the Divine *concursus* a created cause cannot itself *create*, because even with this *concursus* its efficiency attains only to the modifying or changing of pre-existing being: and in creation there is no pre-existing being, no material cause, no real passive potentiality to be actuated. But *without* this *concursus* not only can it not create; it cannot even, as an efficient cause, actuate a real pre-existing potentiality. And why? Because its efficiency cannot attain to the *production of new actuality*. It determines the mode of this actuality, and therein precisely lies the efficiency of the created cause. But *the positive entity or perfection* of this new actuality can be produced only by the Infinite, Changeless, Inexhaustible Source of all actuality, co-operating with the created cause[478].

But, it might be objected, perhaps created efficient causes are themselves the adequate and absolutely independent principles of the whole actuality of their effects? They cannot be such; and that for the simple reason that they are not always *in act*. Were they such they should be always and necessarily in act: they should always and necessarily contain in themselves, and that actually and in an eminently perfect manner, all the perfections of all the effects which they gradually produce in the universe. But experience shows us that created causes are not always acting, that their active power, their causality *in actu primo* is not to be identified with their action, their causality *in actu secundo*; and reason tells us that since this is so, since action is something more than *active power*, since a cause acting has more actuality than the same cause not acting, it must have been determined or reduced to action by some actuality other than itself. This surplus of actuality or perfection in an acting cause, as compared with the same cause prior to its acting, is the Divine *concursus*. In other words, an active power which is really distinct from its action requires to be moved or reduced to *its* act (which is *actio*) no less than a passive potentiality required to be moved to *its* act (which is *passio*), by some really distinct actual being. A created efficient cause, therefore, by passing from the state of rest, or mere power to act, into the state of action, is perfected by having its active power actualized, *i.e.* by the Divine *concursus*: in this sense action is a perfection of the agent. But it is not an entitative perfection of the latter's essence; it is not a permanent or stable elevation or perfection of the latter's powers; it is not the completion of any passive potentiality of the latter; nor therefore is it properly speaking a *change* of the agent as such; it is, as we have said already, rather an index of the latter's perfection in the scale of real being.[479] Action really perfects the *patiens*; and only when this is identical in its concrete individuality with the *agens* is the latter permanently perfected by the action.

The action of created causes, therefore, depends on the action of the First Cause. We derive our notion of action from the former and apply it analogically to the latter. If we compare them we shall find that, notwithstanding many differences, the notion of action in general involves a "simple" or "unmixed" perfection which can, without anthropomorphism, be applied analogically to the Divine Action. The Divine Action is identical with the Divine Power and the Divine Essence. In creatures essence, power and action are really distinct. The Divine Action, when creative, has not for its term a *change* in the strict sense, for it produces being *ex nihilo*, whereas the action of creatures cannot have for term the production of new being *ex nihilo*, but only the change of pre-existing being. The Divine Action, whether in creating or conserving or concurring with creatures, implies in God no real transition from power to act; whereas the action of creatures does imply such transition in them. Such are the differences; but with them there is this point of agreement: the Divine Action implies in God an efficiency which has for its term *the origin of new being dependently on this efficiency*.[480] So, too, does the *action of creatures*. *Positive efficient influence on the one side, and the origin, production, or "fieri" of new actual being on the other, with a relation of real dependence on this efficiency*: such is the essential note of all efficient causality, whether of God or of creatures.[481]

103. (*b*) ACTIO IMMANENS AND ACTIO TRANSIENS.—Let us compare in the next place the perfectly immanent spiritual causality of thought, the less perfectly immanent organic causality of living things, and the transitive physical causality of the agencies of inorganic nature. The term of an immanent action remains either within the very faculty which elicits it, affecting this faculty as a habit: thus acts of thought terminate in the intellectual habits called *sciences*, acts of free choice in the habits of will called *virtues* or *vices*.[482] Or it remains at least within the agent: as when in the vital process of nutrition the various parts and members of the living organism so interact as procure the growth and development of the living individual which is the cause of these functions.[483] In those cases the agent itself is the *patiens*, whereas every agency in the inorganic universe acts not upon itself, but only on some other thing, *transitively*. But immanent action, no less than transitive action, is productive of real change—not, of course, in the physical sense in which this term is identified with "motion" and understood of corporeal change, but in the metaphysical sense of an *actuation of some passive potentiality*.[484]

What, then, do we find common to the immanent and the transitive causality of created causes? *An active power or influence on the side of the agent, an actuation of this active power*, either by the action of other causes on this agent, or by the fulfilment of all conditions requisite for the action of the agent, and in all cases by the concursus of the First Cause; and, *on the side of the effect, the production of some new actuality, the actuation of some passive potentiality, dependently on the cause* now in action.

Thus we see that in all cases *action*, or the exercise of efficient causality, implies that *something which was not actual becomes actual*, that *something which was not, now is*; and that this *becoming*, this *actuation*, this *production*, is really and essentially dependent on the influence, the efficiency, of some actual being or beings, which we therefore call *efficient causes*.

104. ERRONEOUS THEORIES OF EFFICIENT CAUSALITY. IMAGINATION AND THOUGHT.—Are we certain of anything more about the nature of this connecting link between efficient cause and effect, which we call *action*? Speculations and theories there are indeed in abundance. Some of these can be shown to be false; and thus our knowledge of the real nature of action may be at least negatively if not positively perfected. Our concept of action is derived, like all our concepts, from experience; and although we are conscious of *spiritual* action in the exercise of intellect and will, yet it is inseparably allied with sentient action and this again with organic and corporeal action. Nor can we conceive or describe spiritual action without the aid of imagination images, or in language other than that borrowed from the domain of corporeal things, which are the proper object of the human intellect.[485] Now in all this there is a danger: the danger of mistaking imagination images for thoughts, and of giving a literal sense to language in contexts where this language must be rightly understood to apply only analogically.

In analysing the nature of efficient causality we might be tempted to think that we understood it by imagining some sort of a *flow* or *transference* of some sort of actual reality from *agens* to *patiens*. It is quite true that in describing *action*, the actual connecting link between *agens* and *patiens*, we have to use language suggestive of some such imagination image. We have no option in the matter, for all human language is based upon sense consciousness of physical phenomena. When we describe efficiency as an "influence" of cause on effect, or the effect as "dependent" on the cause, the former term suggests a "flowing," just as the latter suggests a "hanging". So, too, when we speak of the effect as "arising," "originating," "springing," or "emanating," from the cause.[486] But we have got to ask ourselves what such language *means*, *i.e.*, what concepts it expresses, and not what imagination images accompany the use of it.

Now when we reflect that the senses testify only to time and space sequences and collocations of the phenomena which we regard as causally connected, and when we feel convinced that there is something more than this in the causal connexion,—which something more we describe in the terms illustrated above,—we must inquire whether we have any rational ground for thinking that this something more is really anything in the nature of a spatial transference of some actual reality from *agens* to *patiens*. There are indeed many philosophers and scientists who seem to believe that there is such a local transference of some actuality from cause to effect, that efficient causality is explained by it, and cannot be intelligibly explained otherwise. As a matter of fact there is no rational ground for believing in any such transference, and even were there such transference, so far from its being the only intelligible explanation of efficient causality, it would leave the whole problem entirely unexplained—and not merely the problem of spiritual, immanent causality, to which it is manifestly inapplicable, but even the problem of corporeal, transitive causality.[487]

We have already referred at some length to the philosophy which has endeavoured to reduce all change, or at least all corporeal change, to mechanical change; all qualities, powers, forces, energies of the universe, to ultimate particles or atoms of matter in motion; and all efficient causality to a flow or transference of spatial motion from particle to particle or from body to body. A full analysis of all such theories belongs to Cosmology. But we may recall a few of the more obvious considerations already urged against them.

In the first place, the attempt to explain all *qualities* in the material universe—all the powers, forces, energies, of matter—by maintaining that objectively and extramentally they are all purely *quantitative* realities, all spatial motions of matter—does not explain the qualitative factors and distinctions in the world of our sense experience at all, but simply transfers the problem of explaining them from the philosophy of matter to the philosophy of mind, by making them all subjective after the manner of Kant's analysis of experience.

In the second place, when we endeavour to conceive, to apprehend intellectually, how *motion*, or indeed any other physical or real entity, could actually pass or be transferred from *agens* to *patiens*, whether these be spatially in contact or not, we find such a supposition positively unintelligible. Motion is not a substance; and if it is an accident it cannot migrate from subject to subject. The idea that corporeal efficient causality—even mechanical causality—can be explained by such a transference of actual accidental modes of being from *agens* to *patiens* is based on a very crude and erroneous conception of what an accidental mode of being really is.

The more we reflect on the nature of real change in the universe, and of the efficient causality whereby it is realized, the more convinced we must become that there can be no satisfactory explanation of these facts which does not recognize and take account of this great fundamental fact: that contingent real being is *not all actual*, that it is partly potential and partly actual; that therefore our concepts of "passive potentiality" and "active power" are not mere subjective mental motions, with at best a mere regulative or systematizing function (after the manner of Kant's philosophy), but that they are really and objectively valid concepts—concepts which from the time of Aristotle have given philosophers the only insight into the nature of efficient causality which is at any rate satisfactory and intelligible as far as it goes.

Of this great fact the advocates of the mechanical theory of efficient causality have, in the third place, failed to take account. And it is partly because with the revival of atomism at the dawn of modern philosophy this traditional Aristotelian conception of contingent being as potential and actual was lost sight of, that such a crude and really unintelligible account of efficient causality, as a "flow of motion," has been able to find such continued and widespread acceptance.

Another reason of the prevalence of this tendency to "explain" all physical efficient causality as a propagation of spatial motions of matter is to be found in the sensist view of the human mind which confounds intellectual thought with mental imagery, which countenances only *picturable* factors in its "explanations," and denounces as "metaphysical," "occult," and "unverifiable" all explanatory principles such as forces, powers, potentialities, etc., which are not directly picturable in the imagination.[488] And it is a curious fact that it is such philosophers themselves who are really guilty of the charge which they lay at the door of the traditional metaphysics: the charge of offering explanations—of efficient causality, for instance—which are really no explanations. For while they put forward their theory of the "flow of motion" as a real explanation of the *quomodo* of efficient causality—and the ultimate and only explanation of it within reach of the human mind, if we are to accept their view of the matter—the exponent of the traditional metaphysics more modestly confines himself to setting forth the inevitable implications of the fact of efficient causality, and, without purporting to offer any positive explanation of the real nature of action or efficient influence, he is content to supplement his analysis negatively by pointing out the unintelligible and illusory character of their proffered "explanations".

In the exact methods of the physical sciences, their quantitative evaluation of all corporeal forces whether mechanical, physical, or chemical, in terms of mechanical work, which is measured by the motion of matter through space, and in the great physical generalization known as the law of the equivalence of energies, or of the equality of action and reaction,—we can detect yet further apparent reasons for the conception of efficient causality as a mere transference or interchange of actual physical and measurable entities among bodies. It is an established fact not only that all corporeal agents gradually lose their energy or power of action by actually exercising this power, but that this loss of energy is in direct proportion to the amount of energy gained by the recipients of their action; and this fact would naturally suggest the mental picture of a transference of some actual measurable entity from cause to effect. But it does not necessarily imply such transference—even if the latter were intelligible, which, as we have seen, it is not. The fact is quite intelligibly explained by the natural supposition that in proportion as the *agens* exhausts its active power by exercise the *patiens* gains in some form of actuality. Similarly, the fact that all forms of corporeal energy can be measured in terms of mechanical energy does not at all imply that they all *really are* mechanical energy, but only that natural agents can by the use of one form of energy produce another form in equivalent quantity. And finally, the law of the conservation of corporeal energy in the universe is explained by the law of the equality of action and reaction, and without recourse to the unintelligible supposition that this sum-total of energy is one unchanging and unchangeable *actuality*.

There is just one other consideration which at first sight appears to favour the "transference" theory of causality, but which on analysis shows how illusory the proffered explanation is, and how unintelligible the simplest phenomenon of change must be to those who fail to grasp the profound significance of the principle that all real being which is subject to change must of necessity be *partly potential and partly actual*. We allude to the general assumption of physical scientists that corporeal action of whatsoever kind takes place *only on contact*, whether mediate or immediate, between the bodies in question.[489] Now it is well to bear in mind that this is not a self-evident truth or principle, but only an hypothesis, a very legitimate hypothesis and one which works admirably, but still only an hypothesis. It implies the assumption that some sort of substance—called the universal ether—actually exists and fills all space, serving as a medium for the action of gravitation, light, radiant heat, electricity and magnetism, between the earth and the other planets, the sun and the stars. This whole supposition is the only thinkable alternative to *actio in distans*. If those bodies really act on one another—and the fact that they do is undeniable,—and if there were no such medium between them, then the causal influence of one body should be able to produce an effect in another body spatially distant from, and not physically connected by any material medium with, the former. Hence two questions: Is this alternative, *actio in distans*, imaginable? *i.e.* can we form any *positive imagination image* of *how* this would take place? And secondly: Is it *thinkable, conceivable, intrinsically possible?* We need not hesitate to answer the former question in the negative. But as to the latter question all we can say is that we have never met any cogent proof of the intrinsic impossibility of *actio in distans*. The efficient action of a finite cause implies that it has active power and is conserved in existence with this power by the Creator or First Cause, that this power is reduced to act by the Divine *concursus*, and that *dependently on this cause so acting* some change takes place, some potentiality is actualized in some other finite being. Nothing more than this is involved in the general concept of efficient causality. Of course real influence on the one side, and real dependence on the other, imply some *real* connexion of cause with effect. But is *spatial* connexion a necessary condition of real connexion? Is a *physical, phenomenal, imaginable, efflux* of some entity out of the cause into the effect, either immediately or through some medium as a channel, a necessary condition for real influence? There is nothing of the kind in spiritual causality; and to demand anything of the kind for causality in general would be to make imagination, not thought, the test and measure of the real. But perhaps *spatial* connexion is essential to the real connexion involved in *this particular kind* of causality, *corporeal* causality? Perhaps. But it has never been proved. Too little is known about the reality of space, about the ultimate nature of material phenomena and their relation to our minds, to justify anything like dogmatism on such an ultimate question. It may well be that if we had a deeper insight into these things we could pronounce *actio in distans* to be absolutely incompatible with the essences of the things which do as a matter of fact constitute the actual corporeal universe. But in the absence of such insight we cannot pronounce *actio in distans* to be intrinsically impossible. Physical scientists assume that as a matter of fact bodies do not act *in distans*. Granted the assumption to be correct, it still remains an open question whether by a miracle they could act *in distans*, *i.e.* whether or not such action would be incompatible with their nature as finite corporeal causes.

Owing to a very natural tendency to rest in imagination images we are inclined not only to pronounce as impossible any process the mode of which is not positively imaginable, but also to think that we rightly understand a process once we have provided ourselves with an imagination image of it—when as a matter of fact this image may cover an entirely groundless conception or theory of the process. Hence the fairly prevalent idea that while *actio in distans* is impossible, *the interaction of bodies on contact* is perfectly intelligible and presents no difficulties. When a billiard ball in motion strikes another at rest it communicates some or all of its motion to the other, and that is all: nothing simpler! And then all the physical, chemical, and substantial changes in the material universe are reducible to this common denominator! The atomic philosophy, with its two modest postulates of matter and motion, is a delightfully simple philosophy; but unfortunately for its philosophical prestige *it does not explain causality or change*. Nor can these facts be explained by any philosophy which ignores the most elementary implication of all real change: the implication that changing reality involves real passive potentialities and real active powers or forces in the phenomena which constitute the changing reality of the universe.

105. THE SUBJECT OF EFFICIENT CAUSALITY. OCCASIONALISM.—We have established the objective validity of the concept of efficient causality and analysed its implications. There have been philosophers who, while admitting the objective validity of the concept, have maintained that no creature, or at least no corporeal creature, can be an efficient cause. Efficient influence is, in their view, incompatible with the nature of a corporeal substance: only spiritual substances can be efficient causes: corporeal things, conditions, and happenings, are all only the *occasions* on which spiritual substances act efficiently in and through all created nature. Hence the name of the theory: *Occasionalism*. There are two forms of it: the milder, which admits that created spirits or minds are efficient causes; and the more extreme view, according to which no creature can be an efficient cause, inasmuch as efficient causality is essentially a Divine attribute, a prerogative of the Divinity.

This error was not unknown in the Middle Ages,[490] but it was in the seventeenth century that certain disciples of Descartes,—Geulincx (1625-1669) and Malebranche (1638-1715),—expressly inferred it from the Cartesian antithesis of matter and spirit and the Cartesian doctrine that matter is essentially inert, or inactive. According to the gratuitous and unproven assertion laid down by Geulincx as a principle: *Quod nescis quomodo fiat, id non facis*,—we do not cause our own sensations or reasoning processes, nor our own bodily movements, inasmuch as we do not know *how* these take place; nor can bodies cause them, any more than our own created spirits, inasmuch as bodies are essentially inactive. According to Malebranche the mind can perceive no necessary *nexus* between effects and any cause other than the Divine Will;[491] moreover reflection convinces us that efficient causality is something essentially Divine and incommunicable to creatures;[492] and finally neither bodies can be causes, for they are essentially inert, nor our minds and wills, for we do not know how a volition could move any organ or member of our bodies.[493] Yet Malebranche, at the cost of inconsistency with his own principles, safeguards free will in man by allowing an exclusively *immanent* efficiency to spiritual causes.[494]

Such is the teaching of Occasionalism. Our criticism of it will be brief.[495]

(1) Against the doctrine that creatures generally are not, and cannot be, efficient causes, we direct the first argument already outlined against Phenomenism and Positivism,—the argument from the universal belief of mankind, based on the testimony of consciousness as rationally interpreted by human intelligence. Consciousness testifies not merely that processes of thought, imagination, sensation, volition, etc., *take place* within our minds; not merely that our bodily movements, such as speaking, walking, writing, *occur*; but that *we are the causes of them*.[496] It is idle to say that we do not efficiently move our limbs because we may not be able to understand or explain fully "*how* an unextended volition can move a material limb".[497] Consciousness testifies to the fact that the volition does move the limb; and that is enough.[498] The fact is one thing, the *quomodo* of the fact is quite another thing. Nor is there any ground whatever for the assertion that a cause, in order to produce an effect, must *understand how* the exercise of its own efficiency brings that effect about. Moreover, Malebranche's concession of at least immanent activity to the will is at all events an admission that there is in the nature of the creature as such nothing incompatible with its being an efficient cause.

(2) Although Malebranche bases his philosophy mainly on deductive, *a priori* reasonings from a consideration of the Divine attributes, his system is really derogatory to the perfection of the First Cause, and especially to the Divine Wisdom. To say, for instance, that God created an organ so well adapted to discharge the function of seeing as the human eye, and then to deny that the latter discharges this or any function, is tantamount to accusing God of folly. There is no reason in this system why any created thing or condition of things would be even the appropriate *occasion* of the First Cause producing any definite effect. Everything would be an equally appropriate occasion, or rather nothing would be in any intelligible sense an appropriate occasion, for any exercise of the Divine causality. The admirable order of the universe—with its unity in variety, its adaptation of means to ends, its gradation of created perfections—is an intelligible manifestation of the Divine perfections on the assumption that creatures efficiently co-operate with the First Cause in realizing and maintaining this order. But if they were all inert, inoperative, useless for this purpose, what could be the *raison d'être* of their diversified endowments and perfections? So far from manifesting the wisdom, power and goodness of God they would evidence an aimless and senseless prodigality.

(3) Occasionalism imperils the distinction between creatures and a personal God. Although Malebranche, fervent catholic that he was, protested against the pantheism of "le misérable Spinoza," his own system contains the undeveloped

germ of this pernicious error. For, if creatures are not efficient causes not only are their variety and multiplicity meaningless, as contributing nothing towards the order of the universe, but their very existence *as distinct realities* seems to have no *raison d'être*. Malebranche emphasizes the truth that *God does nothing useless: Dieu ne fait rien d'inutile*. Very well. If, then, a being *does nothing*, what purpose is served by its existence? Of what use is it? What is the measure of a creature's reality, if not its action and its power of action? So intimately in fact is this notion of causality bound up with the notion of the very reality of things that the concept of an absolutely inert, inactive reality is scarcely intelligible. It is almost an axiom in scholastic philosophy that every nature has its correlative activity, every being its operation: *Omne ens est propter suam operationem; Omnis natura ordinatur ad propriam operationem*. Hence if what we call creatures had really no proper activity distinct from that of the First Cause, on what grounds could we suppose them to have a real and proper existence of their own distinct from the reality of the Infinite Being? Or who could question the lawfulness of the inference that they are not really creatures, but only so many phases, aspects, manifestations of the one and sole existing reality? Which is Pantheism.

(4) Occasionalism leads to Subjective Idealism by destroying all ground for the objective validity of human science. How do we know the real natures of things? By reasoning from their activities in virtue of the principle, *Operari sequitur esse*.[499] But if things have no activities, no operations, such reasoning is illusory. How, for instance, do we justify by rational demonstration, in opposition to subjectivism, the common-sense interpretation of the data of sense consciousness as revealing to us the real and extramental existence of a material universe? By arguing, in virtue of the principle of causality, from our consciousness of our own passivity in external sense perception, to the real existence of bodies outside our minds, as *excitants* of our cognitive activity and *partial causes* of these conscious, perceptive processes. But if occasionalism were true such inference would be illusory, and we should infer, with Berkeley, that only God and minds exist, but not any material universe. Malebranche admits the possible validity of this inference to immaterialism from his principles, and grounds his own belief in the existence of an external material universe solely on faith in Divine Revelation.[500]

It only remains to answer certain difficulties urged by occasionalists against the possibility of attributing real efficiency to creatures.

(1) They argue that efficient causality is something essentially Divine, and therefore cannot be communicated to creatures.

We reply that while the absolutely independent causality of the First Cause is essentially Divine, another kind or order of causality, dependent on the former, but none the less real, can be and is communicated to creatures. And just as the fact that creatures have real being, real existence, distinct from, but dependent on, the existence of the Infinite Being, does not derogate from the supremacy of the latter, so the fact that creatures have real efficient causality, distinct from, but dependent on, the causality of the First Cause, does not derogate from the latter's supremacy.

(2) They urge that efficient causality is creative, and therefore infinite and incommunicable.

We reply that there is a plain distinction between creative activity and the efficient activity we claim for creatures. Creation is the production of new being from nothingness. God alone, the Infinite Being, can create; and, furthermore, according to the common view of Theistic philosophers a creature cannot even be an instrument of the First Cause in this production of new being from nothingness. And the main reason for this appears to be that the efficiency of the creature, acting, of course, with the Divine *concursus*, necessarily presupposes some pre-existing being as material on which to operate, and is confined to the *change or determination of new forms or modes* of this pre-existing reality. Such efficiency, subordinate to the Divine *concursus* and limited to such an order of effects, is plainly distinct from creative activity.

(3) But the creature, acting with the Divine *concursus*, either contributes something real and positive to the effect or contributes nothing. The former alternative is inadmissible, for God is the cause of everything real and positive: *omne novum ens est a Deo*. And in the latter alternative, which is the true one, the *concursus* is superfluous; God does all; and creatures are not really efficient causes.

We reply that the former alternative, not the latter, is the true one. But the former alternative does not imply that the creature produces any new reality *independently of the First Cause*; nor is it incompatible with the truth that God is the author and cause of all positive reality: *omne novum ens est a Deo*. No doubt, were we to conceive the co-operation of God and the creature after the manner of the co-operation of two partial causes of the same order, producing by their joint efficiency some one total effect—like the co-operation of two horses drawing a cart,—it would follow that the creature's share of the joint effect would be independent of the Divine *concursus* and attributable to the creature alone, that the creature would produce some reality independently of the First Cause. But that is *not* the way in which the First Cause concurs with created causes. They are not partial causes of the same order. Each is a total cause in its own order. They so co-operate that God, besides having created and now conserving the second cause, and moving the latter's power to act, produces Himself the whole effect directly and immediately by the efficiency of His *concursus*; while at the same time the second cause, thus reduced to act, and acting with the *concursus*, also directly and immediately produces the whole effect. There is one effect, one change *in facto esse*, one change *in fieri*, and therefore one action as considered in the subject changed, since the action takes place in this latter: *actio fit in passo*. This change, this action considered thus passively, or "*in passo*," is the total term of each efficiency, the Divine and the created, not partly of the one and partly of the other. It is one and indivisible; it is wholly due to, and wholly attained by, each efficiency; not, however, under the same formal aspect. We may distinguish in it two formalities: it is a *novum ens*, a new actuality, something positive and actual superadded to the existing order of real, contingent being; but it is not "being in general" or "actuality in general," it is some specifically, nay individually, determinate mode of actuality or actual being. We have seen that it is precisely because every real effect has the former aspect that it demands for its adequate explanation, and as its only intelligible source, the presence and influence of a purely actual, unchanging, infinite, inexhaustible productive principle of all actual contingent reality: hence the necessity and efficacy of the Divine *concursus*. And similarly it is because the new actuality involved in every change is an individually definite mode of actuality that we can detect in it the need for, and the efficacy of, the created cause: the nature of this latter, the character and scope and intensity of its active power is what determines the individuality of the total result, to the total production of which it has by the aid of the Divine *concursus* attained.

(4) But God can Himself produce the total result *under both formalities* without any efficiency of the creature. Therefore the difficulty remains that the latter efficiency is superfluous and useless: and *entia non sunt multiplicanda praeter necessitatem*.

We reply that as a matter of fact the effects produced in the ordinary course of nature are produced by God under both formalities; but also by the created cause under both formalities: inasmuch as the formalities are but mentally distinct aspects of one real result which is, as regards its extrinsic causes, individual and indivisible. The distinction of these formal aspects only helps us to realize how *de facto* such an effect is due to the cooperation of the First Cause and created causes. That God *could* produce all such effects without any created causes—we must distinguish. Some such effects He could not produce without created causes, for such production would be self-contradictory. He could not produce, for instance, a volition except as the act of a created will, or a thought except as the act of a created intellect, or a vital change except as the act of a living creature. But apart from such cases which would involve an intrinsic impossibility, God could of course produce, without created agents, the effects which He does produce through their created efficiency. It is, however, not a question of what *could be*, but of what *actually is*. And we think that the arguments already set forth prove conclusively that creatures are not *de facto* the inert, inactive, aimless and unmeaning things they would be if Occasionalism were the true interpretation of the universe of our actual experience; but that these creatures are in a true sense efficient causes, and that just as by their very co-existence with God, as contingent beings, they do not derogate from His Infinite Actuality but rather show forth His Infinity, so by their cooperation with Him as subordinate and dependent efficient causes they do not derogate from His supremacy as First Cause, but rather show forth the infinite and inexhaustible riches of His Wisdom and Omnipotence.

Chapter XV.

Final Causes; Universal Order.

106. TWO CONCEPTIONS OF EXPERIENCE, THE MECHANICAL AND THE TELEOLOGICAL.—We have seen that all change in the universe demands for its explanation certain real principles, *viz.* passive potentiality, actualization, and active power or efficiency; in other words that it points to material, formal and efficient causes. Do these principles suffice to explain the course of nature to the inquiring mind? Mechanists say, Yes; these principles explain it so far as it is capable of explanation. Teleologists say, No; these principles do not of themselves account for the universe of our experience: this universe reveals itself as a *cosmos*: hence it demands for its explanation real principles or causes of another sort, *final causes*, the existence of which implies purpose, plan or design, and therefore also intelligence.

The problem whether or not the universe manifests the existence and influence of final causes has been sometimes formulated in this striking fashion: Is it that birds have wings in order to fly, or is it merely that they fly because they have wings? Such a graphic statement of the problem is misleading, for it suggests that the alternatives are mutually exclusive, that we must vote either for final causes or for efficient causes. As a matter of fact we accept both. Efficient causes account for the course of nature; but they need to be determined by the influence of final causes. Moreover, the question how far this influence of final causes extends— *finality* (*finalitas*), as it is technically termed—is a secondary question; nor does the advocate of final causality in the universe undertake to decide its nature and scope in every instance and detail, any more than the physical scientist does to point out all the physical laws embodied in an individual natural event, or the biologist to say whether a doubtful specimen of matter is organic or inorganic, or whether a certain sort of living cell is animal or vegetable. The teleologist's thesis, as against that of mechanism, is simply that *there are final causes in the universe, that the universe does really manifest the presence and influence of final causes.*[501]

There are two ways, however, of conceiving this influence as permeating the universe. The conception of final causality in general is, as we shall see, the conception of acting *for an end*, from a *motive*, with a *purpose, plan* or *design* for the attainment of something. It implies arrangement, ordination, adaptation of means to ends. Now at least there *appears* to be, pervading the universe everywhere and directing its activities, such an adaptation. The admirable equilibrium of forces which secures the regular motions of the heavenly bodies; the exact mixture of gases which makes our atmosphere suitable for organic life; the distance and relative positions of the sun and the earth, which secure conditions favourable to organic life; the chemical transformations whereby inorganic elements and compounds go to form the living substance of plants and are thus prepared for assimilation as food by animal organisms; the wonderfully graded hierarchy of living species in the animate world, and the mutual interdependence of plants and animals; the endless variety of instincts which secure the preservation and well-being of living individuals and species; most notably the adaptability and adaptation of other mundane creatures to human uses by man himself,—innumerable facts such as these convince us that the things of the universe are *useful to one another*, that they are constituted and disposed in relation to one another *as if they had been deliberately chosen* to suit one another, to fit in harmoniously together in mutual co-ordination and subordination so that by their interaction and interdependence they work out a plan or design and *subserve as means to definite ends*. This suitability of things *relatively to one another*, this harmony of the nature and activity of each with the nature and activity of every other, we may designate as *extrinsic* finality. The Creator has willed so to arrange and dispose all creatures in conditions of space and time that such harmonious but purely extrinsic relations of mutual adaptation do *de facto* obtain and continue to prevail between them under His guidance.

But are these creatures themselves, in their own individual natures, equally indifferent to any definite mode of action, so that the orderly concurrence of their activities is due to an initial collocation and impulse divinely impressed upon them from without, and not to any purposive principle intrinsic to themselves individually? Descartes, Leibniz and certain supporters of the theory of atomic dynamism regarding the constitution of matter, while recognizing a relative and extrinsic finality in the universe in the sense explained, seem to regard the individual agencies of the universe as mere efficient causes, not of themselves endowed with any immanent, intrinsic directive principle of their activities, and so contributing by mere extrinsic arrangement to the order of the universe. Scholastic philosophers, on the contrary, following the thought of Aristotle,[502] consider that every agency in the universe is endowed with an *intrinsic principle of finality* which constantly directs its activities towards the realization of a perfection which is proper to it and which constitutes its intrinsic end. And while each thus tends to its own proper perfection by the natural play of its activities, each is so related to all others that they simultaneously realize the extrinsic purpose which consists in the order and harmony of the whole universe. Thus the extrinsic and relative finality whereby all conspire to constitute the universe a *cosmos* is secondary and posterior and subordinate to the deeper, intrinsic, immanent and absolute finality whereby each individual created nature moves by a tendency or law of its being towards the realization of a *good* which *perfects* it as its natural end.

In order to understand the nature of this intrinsic and extrinsic finality in the universe, and to vindicate its existence against the philosophy of Mechanism, we must next analyse the concept, and investigate the influence, of what are called *final causes*.

107. THE CONCEPT OF FINAL CAUSE; ITS OBJECTIVE VALIDITY IN ALL NATURE. CLASSIFICATION OF FINAL CAUSES.—When we speak of the *end* of the year, or the *end* of a wall, we mean the extreme limit or ultimate point; and the term conveys no notion of a cause. Similarly, were a person to say "I have got to the *end* of my work," we should understand him to mean simply that he had finished it. But when people act deliberately and as intelligent beings, they usually act for some *conscious purpose*, with some *object in view*, for the achievement or attainment of something; they continue to act until they have attained this object; when they have attained it they cease to act; its attainment synchronizes with the *end* of their action, taking this term in the sense just illustrated. Probably this is the reason why the term *end* has been extended from its original sense to signify the *object* for the attainment of which an intelligent agent acts. This object of conscious desire *induces* the agent to seek it; and because it thus influences the agent to act it verifies the notion of a *cause*: it is a *final cause*, an *end* in the causal sense. For instance, a young man wishes to become a medical doctor: the *art of healing* is the *end* he wishes to secure. For this purpose he pursues a course of studies and passes certain examinations; these acts whereby he qualifies himself by obtaining a certain fund of knowledge and skill are *means* to the end intended by him. He need not desire these preparatory labours *for their own sake*; but he does desire them as *useful for his purpose*, as *means* to his end: in so far as he wills them as means he wills them not for their own sake but because of the end, *propter finem*. He *apprehends* the end as a *good*; he *intends* its attainment; he *elects* or *selects* certain acts or lines of action as means suitable for this purpose. An end or final cause, therefore, may be defined as *something apprehended as a good, and which, because desired as such, influences the will to choose some*

action or line of action judged necessary or useful for the attainment of this good. Hence Aristotle's definition of end as τὸ οὗ ἕνεκα: id cujus gratia aliquid fit: *that for the sake of which an agent acts.*

The end understood in this sense is a *motive* of action; not only would the action not take place without the agent's intending the end, showing the latter to be a *conditio sine qua non*; but, more than this, the end as a good, apprehended and willed, *has a positive influence* on the ultimate effect or issue, so that it is really a *cause*.

Man is conscious of this "finality," or influence of final causes on his own deliberate actions. As an intelligent being he acts "for ends," and orders or regulates his actions as means to those ends; so much so that when we see a man's acts, his whole conduct, utterly unrelated to rational ends, wholly at variance and out of joint with the usual ends of intelligent human activity, we take it as an indication of loss of reason, insanity. Furthermore, man is free; he *chooses* the ends for which he acts; he acts *electivé propter fines*.

But in the domain of animal life and activity is there any evidence of the influence of final causes? Most undoubtedly. Watch the movements of animals seeking their prey; observe the wide domain of animal instincts; study the elaborate and intricate lines of action whereby they protect and foster and preserve their lives, and rear their young and propagate their species: could there be clearer or more abundant evidence that in all this conduct they are *influenced* by objects which they *apprehend* and seek as *sensible goods*? Not that they can conceive in the abstract the *ratio bonitatis* in these things, or freely choose them as good, for they are incapable of abstract thought and consequent free choice; but that these sensible objects, apprehended by them in the concrete, do really influence or move their sense appetites to desire and seek them; and the influence of an object on sense appetite springs from the goodness of this object. They tend towards *apprehended* goods; they act *apprehensivé propter fines*.[503]

Finally, even in the domains of unconscious agencies, of plant life and inorganic nature, we have evidence of the influence of final causes. For here too we witness innumerable varied, complex, ever-renewed activities, constantly issuing in results useful to, and good for, the agents which elicit them: operations which contribute to the *development* and *perfection* of the natures of these agents. Now if similar effects demand similar causes how can we refuse to recognize even in these activities of physical nature the influence of final causes? Whenever and wherever we find a great and complex variety of active powers, forces, energies, issuing invariably in effects which suit and develop and perfect the agents in question,—in a word, which are *good* for these agents,—whether the latter be conscious or unconscious, does not reason itself dictate to us that all such domains of action must be subject to the influence of final causes? Of course it would be mere unreflecting anthropomorphism to attribute to *unconscious* agencies a *conscious* subjection to the attracting and directing influence of such causes. But the recognition of such influence in this domain implies no naïve supposition of that sort. It does, however, imply this very reasonable view: that there must be some reason or ground in the nature or constitution of even an inanimate agent for its acting always in a uniform manner, conducive to its own development and perfection; that there must be in the nature of each and every one of the vast multitude of such agents which make up the whole physical universe a reason or ground for each co-operating constantly and harmoniously with all the others to secure and preserve that general order and regularity which enables us to pronounce the universe not a *chaos* but a *cosmos*. Now that ground or reason in things, whereby they act in such a manner—not indifferently, chaotically, capriciously, aimlessly, *unintelligibly*, but definitely, regularly, reliably, purposively, *intelligibly*—is a real principle of their natures, impressing on their natures a definite tendency, directive of their activities towards results which, as being suited to these natures, bear to these latter the relation of final causes. A directive principle need not itself be conscious; the inner directive principle of inanimate agents towards what is *good* for them, what *perfects* them, what is therefore in a true and real sense their end, is not conscious. But in virtue of it they act as if they were conscious, nay intelligent, *i.e.* they act *executive propter fines*.

Of course the existence of this principle in inanimate agencies necessarily *implies* intelligence: this indeed is our very contention against the whole philosophy of mechanism, positivism and agnosticism. But is this intelligence really identical with the agencies of nature, so that all the phenomena of experience, which constitute the *cosmos* or universe, are but phases in the evolution of One Sole Reality which is continually manifesting itself under the distinct aspects of nature and mind? Or is this intelligence, though *virtually immanent* in the universe, really distinct from it—*really transcendent*,—a Supreme Intelligence which has created and continues to conserve this universe and govern all its activities? This is a distinct question: it is the question of Monism or Theism as an ultimate interpretation of human experience.

We conclude then that what we call *finality*, or the influence of final causes, pervades the whole universe; that in the domain of conscious agents it is *conscious*, *instinctive* when it solicits *sense appetite*, *voluntary* when it solicits *intelligent will*; that in the domain of unconscious agencies it is not conscious but "*natural*" or "*physical*" soliciting the "*nature*" or "*appetitus naturalis*" of these agencies.

Before inquiring into the nature of final causality we may indicate briefly the main divisions of final causes: some of these concern the domain of human activity and are of importance to Ethics rather than to Ontology.

(*a*) We have already distinguished between *intrinsic* and *extrinsic* finality. An intrinsic final cause is an end or object which perfects the nature itself of the agent which tends towards it: nourishment, for instance, is an intrinsic end in relation to the living organism. An extrinsic final cause is not one towards which the nature of the agent immediately tends, but one which, intended by some other agent, is *de facto* realized by the tendency of the former towards its own intrinsic end. Thus, the general order of the universe is an extrinsic end in relation to each individual agency in the universe: it is an end intended by the Creator and *de facto* realized by each individual agency acting in accordance with its own particular nature.

(*b*) Very similar to this is the familiar distinction between the *finis operis* and the *finis operantis*. The former is the end necessarily and *de facto* realized by the act itself, by its very nature, independently of any other end the agent may have expressly intended to attain by means of it. The latter is the end expressly intended by the agent, and which may vary for one and the same kind of act. For instance, the *finis operis* of an act of almsgiving is the actual aiding of the mendicant; the *finis operantis* may be charity, or self-denial, or vanity, or whatever other motive influences the giver.

(*c*) Akin to those also is the distinction between an unconscious, or physical, or "natural" end, and a conscious, or mental, or "intentional" end. The former is that towards which the nature or "*appetitus naturalis*" of unconscious agencies tends; the latter is an end apprehended by a conscious agent.

(*d*) An end may be either *ultimate* or *proximate* or *intermediate*. An ultimate end is one which is sought for its own sake, as contrasted with an intermediate end which is willed rather as a means to the former, and with a proximate end which is intended last and sought first as a means to realizing the others. It should be noted that proximate and intermediate ends, in so far as they are sought for the sake of some ulterior end, are not ends at all but rather means; only in so far as they present some good desirable for its own sake, are they properly ends, or final causes. Furthermore, an ultimate end may be such absolutely or relatively: absolutely if it cannot possibly be subordinated or referred to any ulterior or higher good; relatively if, though ultimate in a particular order as compared with means leading up to it, it is nevertheless capable of being subordinated to a higher good, though not actually referred to this latter by any explicit volition of the agent that seeks it.

(*e*) We can regard the end for which an agent acts either *objectively*,—finis "*objectivus*,"—or *formally*,—finis "*formalis*". The former is the objective good itself which the agent wishes to realize, possess or enjoy; the latter is the act whereby the agent formally secures, appropriates, unites himself with, this objective good. Thus, God Himself is the objective happiness (*beatitudo objectiva*) of man, while man's actual possession of, or union with, God, by knowledge and love, is man's formal happiness (*beatitudo formalis*).

(*f*) We may distinguish also between the *real* end (finis "*qui*" or "*cujus*", and the *personal* end (finis "*cui*"). The former is the good *which* the agent desires, the good for the sake of *which* "*cujus*" *gratia*) he acts. The latter is the subject or person *to whom* he wishes this good, or *for whom* he wishes to procure it. Thus, a labourer may work to earn *a sustenance* for *himself* or also for *his family*. The real and the personal end are never willed separately, but always as one concrete good.

(*g*) The distinction between a *principal* end and an *accessory* end (motivum "*impulsivum*") is obvious. The former can move to act of itself without the latter, but the latter strengthens the influence of the former. A really charitable person, while efficaciously moved to give alms by sympathy with the poor, may not be uninfluenced by vanity to let others know of his charity.

(*h*) Finally we may note the theological distinction between the *natural* end, and the *supernatural* end, of man as a rational and moral agent. The former is the end *due* to man's nature, the latter is an end which is gratuitous and undue to his nature. God might not have created the world or man, and in this sense even the natural end of man is a gratuitous gift of God; but granted that God did decree to create the world and man, an end corresponding to man's nature and powers was due to him: the knowledge, service and love of God as known to man by the light of natural reason. But as a matter of fact God, in His actual providence, has decreed for man an incomparably higher and purely gratuitous end, an end revealed to man by God Himself, an end entirely undue not only to man but to any and every possible creature: the Beatific Vision of the Divine Essence for ever in heaven.

108. CAUSALITY OF THE FINAL CAUSE; RELATION OF THE LATTER TO EFFICIENT, FORMAL, AND MATERIAL CAUSES.—We can best analyse the influence of the final cause by studying this influence as exerted on conscious and intelligent agents. The final cause has a positive influence of some sort on the production, happening, actualization of effects. What is the nature of this influence? The final cause exerts its influence by being *a good*, an apprehended good; it exerts this influence on the appetite of the agent, soliciting the latter to perform certain acts for the realization, attainment, possession, or enjoyment of this good. But it must not be conceived as the *efficient cause* of this movement of the appetite, nor may its influence be conceived as *action*. An efficient cause must

actually exist in order to act; but when the final cause, as an apprehended good, exerts its influence on the appetite *it is not yet actual*: not until the agent, by his action, has realized the end and actually attained it, does the end, as a good, actually exist. We must distinguish between the end *as attained* and the end *as intended*, between the *finis in executione* and the *finis in intentione*. It is not the end as attained that is a final cause; as attained it is an effect pure and simple. It is the end as intended that is a final cause; and as intended it does not yet actually exist: hence its influence cannot be by way of *action*. Perhaps it is the *idea* or *cognition* of the intended end that exerts the peculiar influence of final cause? No; the *idea* or *cognition* of the end actually exists, no doubt, in the conscious agent, but this is only a condition, a *conditio sine qua non*, for the apprehended good, the final cause, to exert its influence: *nil volitum nisi praecognitum*. It is not the cognition of the good, however, that moves the agent to act, it is not the idea of the good that the agent desires or strives for, but the good itself. It is the good itself, the known good, that exerts the influence, and this influence consists in the *passive inclination* or *attraction* or *tendency* of the appetite towards the good: a tendency which necessarily results from the very presence of the good (not really or physically of course, but representatively, mentally, "*intentionally*," by "*esse intentionale*") in the agent's consciousness, and which is formally the actualization of the causal power or influence of the final cause. "Just as the efficient cause influences by acting," says St. Thomas,[504] "so the final cause influences by being yearned for and desired".

Looked at from the side of the agent that undergoes it, this influence is a *passive yielding*: this next becomes an *active* motion of appetite; and in the case of free will a deliberate act of intending the end, followed by acts of choosing means, and finally by acts commanding the executive faculties to employ these means.

Looked at from the side of the final cause, the influence consists in an *attraction* of appetite towards union with itself as a good. The matter cannot be analysed much further; nor will imagination images help us here any more than in the case of efficient causality. It must be noted, however, that the influence of the final cause is the influence not of a reality as actual, or in its *esse actuale*, but of a reality as present to a perceiving mind, or in its *esse intentionale*. At the same time it would be a mistake to infer from this that the influence of the final cause is not *real*. It is sometimes described as "intentional" causality, "*causalitas intentionalis*"; but this must not be taken to mean that it is not real: for it is not the "*esse intentionale*" of the good, *i.e.* the cognition of the good, its presence in the mind or consciousness of the agent, that moves the latter's appetite: it is the apprehended good, apprehended *as real*, as possible of actual attainment, that moves the agent to act. The influence may not be *physical* in the sense of being productive of, or interchangeable with, or measurable by, corporeal energy, or in terms of mechanical work; nor is it; but it is none the less real.

But if the influence of a final cause really reaches to the effect of the agent's actions only through the medium of the latter's appetite, and therefore through a link of "intentional" causality, does it not at once follow that the attribution of final causality to the domain of unconscious and inorganic activities, can be at best merely metaphorical? The attribution to such agencies of an "*appetitus naturalis*" is intelligible indeed as a striking and perhaps not unpoetic metaphor. But to contend that it is anything more than a metaphor, to claim seriously that inanimate agencies are swayed and influenced by "ends,"—is not this really to substitute mysticism and mystery for rational speculation and analysis?

Mechanists are wont to dismiss the doctrine of final causes in the physical universe with offhand charges of this kind. They are but too ready to attribute it to a mystical attitude of mind. Final causes, they say, are not discovered in inanimate nature by the cold, calculating, unemotional analysis to which reason submits its activities, but are read into it by minds which allow themselves to be prompted by the imagination and emotions to personify and anthropomorphize inanimate agencies. The accusation is as plausible as it is unjust. It is plausible because the attribution of final causes to inanimate nature, and of an "*appetitus naturalis*" to its agencies, *seems* to imply the recognition of conscious, mental, "intentional" influence in this domain. But it really implies nothing of the sort; and hence the injustice of the charge. What it does imply is the existence of a genuine *analogy* between the nature and natural activities of physical agencies on the one hand and the appetite and appetitive activities of conscious agencies on the other. The existence of this analogy is absolutely undeniable. The orderly, invariable and uniformly suitable character of physical activities, simply forces our reason to recognize in physical agencies *natures* which tend towards their development, and which by their activities attain to what is *good* for them, to what *perfects* them. In other words we have to recognize that each by its natural line of activity attains to results that are good and useful to it *just as if* it apprehended them as such and consciously tended towards them. The analogy is there; and the recognition of it, so far from being a "mystic" interpretation of facts, is an elementary logical exercise of our reasoning faculty. The scholastics emphasized their recognition of the analogy by calling the *nature* of an unconscious agent,—the principle of its active tendencies towards the realization of its own perfection—an "*appetitus naturalis*": an expression into which no one familiar with scholastic terminology would venture to read any element of mysticism.[505]

Every separate agency in nature has a uniform mode of activity; by following out this line of action each co-operates with all the others in maintaining the orderly course of nature. These are facts which call for explanation. They are not explained by the supposition of mechanists that these agencies are mere efficient causes: efficient causality does not account for order, it has got simply nothing to do with order or regularity. Consequently the last word of the mechanical philosophy on the fact of order in the universe is—Agnosticism. In opposition to this attitude we are far from contending that there is no mystery, or that all is clear either in regard to the fact of *change* or the fact of *regularity*. Just as we cannot explain everything in *efficient* causality, so neither can we explain everything in *final* causality. But we do contend that the element of order, development, evolution, even in the physical universe, can be partially explained by recognizing in its several agencies a *nature*, a principle of development, a passive inclination implanted in the very being of these agencies by the Intelligent Author of their being.

In conscious agencies this inclination or tendency to actions conformable or *connatural* to their being is not always in act; it is aroused by conscious cognition, perception, or imagination of a *good*, and operates intermittently. In unconscious agencies it is congenital and constantly in act, *i.e.* as a tendency, not as actually operative: for its actual development due conditions of environment are required: the seed will not grow without a suitable soil, temperature, moisture, etc. In conscious agencies the tendency, considered entitatively or as a reality in them, is an *accidental form*; in unconscious agencies it is their *forma substantialis*, the formative substantial principle, which determines the specific type to which their nature belongs.[506]

In all agencies the inclination or appetite or tendency to action arises from a form; an elicited appetite from an "intentional" form, a natural appetite from a "natural" form: *Omnis inclinatio seu appetitus consequitur formam; appetitus elicitus formam intentionalem, appetitus naturalis formam naturalem*. The scholastic view that final causality pervades all things is expressed in the aphorism, *Omne agens agit propter finem*: Every agency acts for an end.

From our analysis of final causality it will be seen that the "end" becomes a cause by exercising its influence on the agent or efficient cause, and thus initiating the action of the latter. We have seen already that material and formal causes exercise their causality dependently on the efficient cause of the change or effect produced by the latter. We now see that the final cause, the end as *intended*, determines the action of the efficient cause; hence its causality holds the primacy as compared with that of the other causes: it is in this sense the cause of causes, *causa causarum*.[507] But while the end *as intended* is the starting point of the whole process, the end *as attained* is the ultimate term of the latter. Hence the scholastic aphorism: *Finis est primus in intentione et ultimus in executione*. And this is true where the process involves a series of acts attaining to means subordinate to an end: this latter is the first thing intended and the last attained.

The final cause, the end as intended, is extrinsic to the effect. It is intrinsic to the efficient cause. It is a *"forma"* or determinative principle of the latter: a *forma intentionalis* in conscious agents, a *forma naturalis* in unconscious agents.

109. NATURE AND THE LAWS OF NATURE. CHARACTER AND GROUNDS OF THEIR NECESSITY AND UNIVERSALITY. SCIENTIFIC DETERMINISM AND PHILOSOPHIC FATALISM.—By the term *nature* we have seen that Aristotle and the scholastics meant the essence or substance of an agent regarded as inner principle of the latter's normal activities, as determining the bent or inclination of these, and therefore as in a real sense their final cause. Hence Aristotle's definition of *nature* as *a certain principle or cause of the motion and rest of the thing in which that principle is rooted fundamentally and essentially and not merely accidentally*.[508] The scholastics, recognizing that this *intentio naturae*, this subjection to finality, in *unconscious* agencies must be the work and the index of intelligence, in other words that this *analogical* finality in inanimate things must connote a *proper* finality, a properly purposive mode of action, in the author of these things, conceived this *nature* or *intentio naturae* as the impression of a divine art or plan upon the very being of all creatures by the Creator Himself. Hence St. Thomas's profound and well-known description of *nature* as *"the principle of a divine art impressed upon things, in virtue of which they move towards determinate ends"*. Defining *art* as *the just conception of external works to be accomplished*,[509] he observes that nature is a sort of art: "as if a ship-builder were to endow his materials with the power of moving and adapting themselves so as to form or construct a ship".[510] And elsewhere he remarks that nature differs from art only in this that the former is an intrinsic, the latter an extrinsic, principle of the work which is accomplished through its influence: so that if the art whereby a ship is constructed were intrinsic to the materials, the ship would be constructed by nature as it actually is by art.[511]

Such, then, is the teleological conception of the nature of each individual agency in the universe. When we speak of "universal *nature*," "external *nature*," "physical *nature*," "the course of *nature*," "the laws of *nature*," etc. we are using the term in a collective sense to signify the sum-total of all the agencies which constitute the whole physical universe; and furthermore in all such contexts we usually understand by *nature* the world of *corporeal* things as distinct from the domain of *mind* or *spirit*.

The proof of this view,—that the agencies of the physical universe are not merely efficient causes, but that they act under the influence of ends; that they have definite lines of action which are natural to them, and whereby they realize their own individual development and the maintenance of the universe as a *cosmos*; that by doing so they reveal the influence of *intelligent purpose*,—the proof of this view lies, as we have seen, in the fact that their activities are regular, uniform, and mutually useful, or, in other words, that they are productive of *order*. Bearing this in mind let us inquire into the various meanings discernible in the very familiar expressions, "laws of nature," "physical laws," "natural laws".[512]

We may understand firstly by a law of nature this innate tendency we have been describing as impressed upon the very being of all created things by the Creator. It is in this sense we speak of a thing acting "naturally," or "according to the *law* of its nature," or "according to its nature," when we see it acting according to what we conceive to be the end intended for it, acting in a manner conducive to the development of its own individuality, the preservation of its specific type or kind, and the fulfilment of its rôle in the general scheme of things. What this "natural" mode of action is for this particular kind of thing, we gather from our experience of the regular or normal activity of things of its kind. Thus, we say it is a *law* of oxygen and hydrogen to combine in definite proportions, under suitable conditions, to form water; a *law* of all particles of matter in the universe to tend to move towards one another with a definite acceleration; a *law* of living organisms to reproduce their kind. This usage comes nearest to the original meaning of the term *law*: a precept or command imposed on intelligent agents by a superior. For we conceive this natural tendency impressed on physical agencies by the Creator after the analogy of a precept or command. And we have good reason to do so: because *uniformity of conduct* in intelligent agents is the normal result of their obedience to a law imposed upon them; and we see in the activities of the physical universe an *all-pervading feature of regularity*.

Secondly, we transfer the term *law* to *this result itself* of the natural tendency of the being, of the convergence of its activities towards its end. That is to say, we call *the uniform mode of action* of an agent a *law of nature*, a *natural* or *physical law*. This usage, which is common in the positive sciences, implies a less profound, a more superficial, but a perfectly legitimate mode of apprehending and studying the changes and phenomena of the physical universe.

Thirdly, since the several agencies of the universe co-exist in time and space, since they constantly interact on one another, since for the exercise of the natural activities of each *certain extrinsic conditions of relationship with its environment* must be fulfilled, an accurate knowledge and exact formulation of these relations are obviously requisite for a scientific and practical insight into the mode of activity of any natural agency. In fact the physical scientist may and does take for granted the natural tendency and the uniformity of action resulting therefrom, and confines himself to *discovering and formulating the relations between any given kind of action and the extrinsic conditions requisite for its exercise*. Such, for instance, would be any chemical "law" setting forth the measure, and the conditions of temperature, pressure, etc., in which certain chemical elements combine to form a certain chemical compound. To all such formulae scientists give the title of *physical laws*, or *laws of physical nature*. These formulae, descriptive of the manner in which a phenomenon takes place, setting forth with the greatest possible quantitative exactness the phenomenal factors[513] that enter into and precede and accompany it, are laws in a still more superficial and still less philosophical sense, but a sense which is most commonly—and justly—accepted in the positive or physical sciences.

Before examining the feature and characteristic of *necessity and universality* which enters into all these various conceptions of a "physical law" we have here to observe that it would make for clearness, and for a better understanding between physics and metaphysics, between science and philosophy, between the investigator who seeks by observation and experiment for the proximate phenomenal conditions and "physical" causes of phenomena, and the investigator who seeks for the ultimate real ground and explanation of these latter by speculative analysis of them, and by reasoning from the scientist's discoveries about them,—if it were understood and agreed that investigation into the scope and significance and ultimate ground of this feature of stability in the laws of physical nature belongs to the philosopher rather than to the scientist. We have already called attention to the fact that the propriety of such an obviously reasonable and intelligible division of labour is almost universally admitted in theory both by scientists and by philosophers; though, unfortunately, it is not always remembered in practice.

In theory the scientist assumes, and very properly assumes, that the agencies with which he deals are not capricious, unreliable, irregular, but stable, reliable, regular in their mode of action, that in similar sets of conditions and circumstances they will act uniformly. Without inquiring into the ultimate grounds of this assumption he premises that all his conclusions, all his inductive generalizations about the activity of these agencies, will hold good of these latter just in so far as they do act according to his general postulate as to their regularity. He then proceeds, by the inductive processes of hypothesis and experimental verification, to determine what agencies produce such or such an event, under what conditions they bring this about, what are all the phenomenal conditions, positive and negative, antecedent and concomitant, in the absence of any one of which this event will not happen, and in the presence of all of which it will happen. These are, in accordance with his assumption, *determining* causes of the event; the knowledge of them is from the speculative point of view extremely important, and from the practical standpoint of invention and applied science extremely useful. As a scientist he has no other knowledge in view: he aims at discovering the "how," the *quomodo*, of natural phenomena,—how, for instance, under what conditions and in what measure, water is produced from oxygen and hydrogen. When he has discovered all these positive and negative conditions his *scientific* knowledge of the formation of water is complete.

But there are other questions in regard to natural phenomena to which the experimental methods of the positive sciences can offer no reply. They can tell us nothing about the *wider* "how" which resolves itself into a "why." They can give no information about the ultimate causes, origins, reasons, or essences, of those phenomena. As Pasteur and other equally illustrious scientists have proclaimed, experimental science is essentially positive, *i.e.* confined to the proximate phenomenal conditions and causes of things; it has nothing to say, nor has it any need or any right to say anything, about the ultimate nature, or first origin, or final destiny, of the things and events of the universe.

Yet such questions arise, and clamour insistently for solution. *How* is it, or *why* is it, that natural phenomena are uniformly linked to certain other phenomenal antecedents or "physical" causes? Is it absolutely impossible, inconceivable, that this sequence should be found not to obtain in even a single individual instance? Why should there be such uniform "sequences" or "laws" at all? Are there exceptions, or can there be exceptions to these "laws of physical nature"? What is the character and what are the grounds of the *necessity* of these laws? Every living organism comes from a living cell—not from *any* living cell, but from *some particular kind* of living cell. But *why* are there such kinds of cells? Why are there living cells at all? Whence their first origin? Again, granted that there are different kinds or types of living cells, *why* should a particular kind of cell give rise, by division and evolution, to an organism of the same kind or type as the parent organisms? Why does it not *always* do so? Why are what biologists describe as "monsters" in the organic kingdom possible? And why, since they are possible, are they not as numerous as what are recognized as the normal types or kinds of living organisms?

Now these are questions in regard to which not only every professing physical scientist and every professing metaphysician, but every thinking man, *must* take up some attitude or other. A refusal to consider them, on the plea that they are insoluble, is just as definite an attitude as any other; nor by assuming this attitude does any man, even though he be a specialist in some department of the positive or physical sciences, escape being a "metaphysician" or a "philosopher," however much he may deprecate such titles; for he is taking up a reasoned attitude—we presume it is such, and not the outcome of mere prejudice—on ultimate questions. And this is philosophy; this is metaphysics. When, therefore, a physical scientist either avows or insinuates that *because* the methods of physical science, which are suitable for the discovery of the *proximate* causes of phenomena, can tell him nothing about *ultimate* questions concerning these phenomena, *therefore* there is nothing to be known about these questions, he is not only committing himself, *nolens volens*, to definite philosophical views, but he is doing a serious disservice to physical science itself by misconceiving and mis-stating its rightful scope and limits. He has just an equal right with any other man to utilize the established truths of physical science to help him in answering ultimate questions. Nay, he may even use the unverified hypotheses and systematic conceptions[514] of physical science for what they are worth in helping him to determine his general world-view. But his competence as a specialist in physical science does not confer upon him any *special* qualification for estimating the value of these truths and hypotheses as evidence in the domain of ultimate problems. Nor can he, because he is a scientist, or even because he may go so far as to assert the right of speaking in the name of "science," claim for his particular interpretation the privilege of exemption from criticism; and this is true no matter what his interpretation may be— whether it be agnosticism, mechanism, teleologism, monism, or theism. These observations may appear elementary and obvious; but the insinuation of positivism and phenomenism, that whatever is not itself phenomenal and verifiable by the experimental methods of the physical sciences is in no wise knowable, and the insinuation of mechanists that their world-view is the only one compatible with the truths of science and therefore the only "scientific" philosophy, justify us in reiterating and emphasizing even such obvious methodological considerations. Bearing them in mind, let us now examine the uniformity and necessity of the laws of physical nature.

Understanding by natural law the natural inclination or tendency of the creature to a definite line of activity, this law is of itself determining or necessitating. Moreover, it is absolutely inseparable from the essence of the creature. Granted that the creature exists, it has this tendency to exert and direct all its forces and energies in a definite, normal way, for the realization of its end. This *nisus naturae* is never absent; it is observable even where, as in the generation of "monsters" by living organisms, it partially fails to attain its end. A law of nature, taken in this sense, is absolutely necessary to, and inseparable from, the created agent; it admits of no exceptions; no agent can exist without it; for it is identical with the very being of the agent

But the uniformity of action resulting from this natural tendency, the uniform series of normal operations whereby it realizes its end, is not absolutely necessary, inviolable, unexceptional. In the first place the Author of Nature can, for a higher or moral purpose, prevent any created agency supernaturally, miraculously, from actually exercising its active powers in accordance with its nature for the prosecution of its natural end. But apart altogether from this, abstracting from all special interference of the First Cause, and confining our attention to the natural order itself, we have to consider that for any physical agency to act in its natural or normal manner certain extrinsic conditions are always requisite: oxygen and hydrogen, for instance, will combine to produce water, but only under certain conditions of contact, pressure, temperature, etc. This general requirement arises from the fact already mentioned, that physical agencies co-exist in time and space and are constantly interacting. These extrinsic conditions are, of course, not expressly stated in the formulation of those uniformities and quantitative descriptions called "laws of nature" in the second and third interpretations of this expression as explained above. It is taken as understood that the law applies only if and when and where all such conditions are verified. The law, therefore, as stated categorically, does not express an absolutely necessary, universal, and unexceptional truth. It may admit of exceptions.

In the next place, when we come to examine these exceptions to uniformity, these failures or frustrations of the normal or natural activities of physical agencies, we find it possible to distinguish roughly, with Aristotle, between two groups of such "uniformities" or "laws". There are firstly those which, so far as our experience goes, seem to prevail *always* (ἀεὶ), unexceptionally; and secondly, those which seem to prevail *generally, for the most part* (ἐπὶ τὸ πολὺ), though not unexceptionally. The former would be the outcome of active powers, energies, forces, *de facto* present and prevalent always and everywhere in all physical agencies, and of such a character that the conditions requisite for their actual operation would be always verified. Such, for instance, would be the force of gravity in all ponderable matter; and hence the law of gravitation is regarded as all-pervading, universal, unexceptional. But there are other natural or normal effects which are the outcome of powers, forces, energies, not all-pervading, but restricted to special groups of agencies, dependent for their actual production on the presence of a great and complex variety of extrinsic conditions, and liable therefore to be impeded by the interfering action of numerous other natural agencies. Such, for instance, would be the natural powers and processes whereby living organisms propagate their kind. The law, therefore, which states it to be a uniformity of nature that living organisms reproduce offspring similar to themselves in kind, is a general law, admitting exceptions.

Operations and effects which follow from the nature of their causes are called natural (καθ' αὑτό, καὶ μὴ κατὰ συμβεβηκός).[515] Some causes produce their natural effects *always* (τὰ ἐξ ἀνάνκης καὶ ἀεὶ γιγνομένα), others produce their natural effects *usually, as a general rule* (τὰ ὡς ἐπι πολὺ γιγνόμενα).[516] Operations and effects which are produced by the interfering influence of extrinsic agencies (τὸ βίαιον "violent," as opposed to natural), and not in accordance with the nature of their principal cause, are called by Aristotle *accidental* (τὰ κατὰ συμβεβηκός, τὰ ἐνδεχόμενα γυγνέσθαι); and these, he remarks, people commonly describe as due to chance (καὶ ταῦτα πάντες φασὶν εἶναι ἀπο τύχης).[517]

All are familiar with events or happenings described as "fortuitous," "accidental," "exceptional," "unexpected," with things happening by "chance," by (good or bad) "luck" or "fortune".[518] There are terms in all languages expressive of this experience—*casus, sors, fortuna,* τύχη, etc. The notion underlying all of them is that of something occurring unintentionally, *praeter intentionem agentis*. Whether chance effects result from the action of intelligent agents or from the operation of physical causes they are not "intended,"—by the deliberate purpose of the intelligent agent in the one case, or by the natural tendency, the *intentio naturae*, of the mere physical agency in the other. Such an effect, therefore, has not a *natural* cause; hence it is considered *exceptional*, and is always more or less unexpected. *Nature*, as Aristotle rightly observes,[519] never produces a chance effect. His meaning is, that whenever such an effect occurs it is not brought about in accordance with the natural tendency of any physical agency. It results from a collision or coincidence of two or more such agencies, each acting according to its nature. The hunter's act of firing at a wild fowl is an intentional act. The boy's act of coming into the thicket to gather wild flowers is an intentional act. The accidental shooting of the boy is the result of a coincidence of the two intentional acts. Similarly, each of all the various agencies which bring about the development of an embryo in the maternal womb has its own immediate and particular natural effect, and only mediately contributes to the general effect of bringing the embryo to maturity. As a rule these particular effects are favourable to the general effect. But sometimes the immediate ends do not subserve this ulterior purpose. The result is accidental, exceptional, a deviation from the normal type, an anomaly, a "monster" in the domain of living organisms.

Aristotle's analysis, correct so far, is incomplete. It assigns no ultimate explanation of the fact that there are such encounters of individual natural tendencies in the universe, such failures in the subordination of particular ends to wider ulterior ends. As a matter of fact these chance effects, although not "intended" by the natures of individual created agencies, are not wholly and entirely unintended. They are not wholly aimless. They enter into the general plan and scheme of things as known and willed by the Author of Nature. They are known to His Intelligence, and willed and ruled by His Providence. For Him there can be no such thing as chance. Effects that are accidental in relation to created causes, effects that run counter to the nature or *intentio naturae* of these, are foreseen and willed by Him and made to subserve that wider and more general end which is the universal order of the world that He has actually willed to create. It is only in relation to the natures of individual agencies, and to the limited horizon of our finite intelligences, that such phenomena can present the aspect of fortuitous or chance occurrences.

Before passing on to deal, in our concluding section, with the great fact of order, let us briefly compare with the foregoing explanation of nature and its laws the attempt of mechanists to explain these without recognizing in the physical universe any influence of final causes, or any indication of a purposive intelligence. We have ventured to describe their attitude as philosophic fatalism.[520] According to their view there is no ground for the distinction between phenomena that happen "naturally" and phenomena that happen "accidentally" or "by chance". All alike happen by the same kind of general necessity: the generation of a "monster" is as "natural" as the generation of normal offspring; the former, when it occurs, is just as inevitably the outcome of the physical forces at work in the particular case as the latter is the outcome of the particular set of efficient causes which do actually produce the normal result: the only difference is that the former, occurring less frequently and as the result of a rarer and less known conjunction of "physical" causes than the latter, is not expected by us to occur, and is consequently regarded, when it does occur, as exceptional. Now it is quite true that what we call "chance" effects, or "exceptional" effects, result just as inevitably from the set of forces operative in their case, as normal effects result from the forces operative in theirs. But this leaves for explanation something which the mechanist cannot explain. He regards a physical law merely as a generalization, beyond experience, of some experienced uniformity; and he holds that all our physical laws are provisional in the sense that a wider and deeper knowledge of the actual conditions of interaction among the physical forces of the universe would enable us to eliminate exceptions—which are all apparent, not real—by restating our laws in such a comprehensive way as to include all such cases. We may, indeed, admit that our physical laws are open to revision and restatement in this sense, and are *de facto* often modified in this sense by the progress of science. But the important point is this, that the mechanist does not admit the existence, in physical agencies, of any law in the sense of a *natural inclination towards an end*, or in any sense in which it would imply intelligence, design, or purpose. On the contrary, claiming as he does that all physical phenomena are *reducible to mechanical motions of inert masses, atoms, or particles of matter in space*, he is obliged to regard all physical agencies as being, so far as their nature is concerned, wholly *indifferent* to any particular form of activity.[521] Committed to the indefensible view that all qualitative change is reducible to quantitative, and all material differences to differences in the location of material particles and in the velocity and direction of the spatial motion impressed upon each by others extrinsic to itself, he has left himself no factors wherewith to explain the actual order and course of the universe, other than the purely *indifferent* factors of essentially or naturally homogeneous particles of inert matter endowed with local motion. We emphasize this feature of indifference; for the conception of an inert particle of matter subject to mechanical motion impressed upon it from without, is the very type of an indifferent agency. What such an entity will do, whether or not it will move, with what velocity and in what direction it will move—in a word, its entire conduct, its rôle in the universe, the sum-total of its functions—nothing of all this is dependent on itself; everything depends on agencies extrinsic to it, and on its extrinsic time-and-space relations to these agencies; and these latter in turn are in the same condition as itself. Now is it conceivable that agencies of this kind, of themselves absolutely indifferent to any particular kind of effect, suitable or unsuitable, regular or irregular, orderly or disorderly, could actually produce and maintain the existing order of the universe?

If they were themselves *produced by an All-Wise and All-Powerful Being*, and *definitely arranged* in spatial relations to one another, and *initial mechanical motion in definite directions and velocities* impressed on the different parts of the system, there is no denying that Infinite Wisdom and Power could, by Divine concurrence even with such indifferent agencies, realize and maintain a *cosmos*, or *orderly* universe. Such *purely extrinsic finality* could, absolutely speaking, account for the existence of order, uniformity, regularity, system; though all the evidence furnished by the universe of our actual experience points to the existence of *intrinsic finality* also as understood by Aristotle and the scholastics. But the mechanist will not allow even extrinsic finality; he will not recognize in the actual universe of our experience any evidence of a Ruling Intelligence realizing a plan or design for an intelligent purpose; he denies the necessity of the inference from the data of human experience to the existence of a Guiding Intelligence. And what are his alternatives? He may choose one or other of two.

He may restate in the more scientific and imposing terminology of modern mechanics the crude conception of the ancient Greek atomists: that the actual order of the universe is the absolutely inevitable and fatal outcome of a certain collocation of the moving masses of the physical universe, a collocation favourable to order, a collocation which *just happened to occur* by some happy chance from the essentially aimless, purposeless, indifferent and *chaotic* motions of those material masses and particles. We say "chaotic," for *chaos* is the absence of *cosmos*; and *order* is the fact that has got to be explained. In the concept of *indifferent, inert* atoms of matter moving through space there is emphatically no principle of order;[522] and hence the mechanist who will not admit the necessity of inferring an Intelligence to give these moving masses or atoms the collocation *favourable to order* is forced to "explain" this supposed collocation by attributing it to pure chance—the *concursus fortuitus atomorum* of the ancient Greeks. When, however, we reflect that the more numerous these atoms and the more varied and complex their motions, the smaller is the chance of a collocation favourable to order; that the atoms and motions are supposed actually to surpass any assignable number; that therefore the chance of any such favourable collocation occurring is indefinitely smaller than any measurable proportion,—we can draw our own conclusions about the value of such a speculation as a rational "explanation" of the existing *cosmos*. And this apart altogether from the consideration that the fact to be explained is not merely the *momentary* occurrence of an orderly collocation, but the *maintenance* of an orderly system of cosmic phenomena *throughout the lapse of all time*. No orderly finite system of mechanical motions arranged by human skill can preserve its orderly motions indefinitely without intelligent human supervision: the neglected machine will get out of order, run down, wear out, if left to itself; and we are asked to believe that the whole universe is one vast machine which not only goes on without intelligent supervision, but which actually made itself by chance![523]

Naturally such an "explanation" of the universe does not commend itself to any man of serious thought, whatever his difficulties may be against the argument from the fact of order in the universe to the existence of an Intelligent Designer. Add to this the consideration that the mechanist theory does not even claim to account for the first origin of the universe: it postulates the existence of matter in motion. In regard to this supreme problem of the *first origin* of the universe the attitude of the mechanist is avowedly *agnostic*; and in view of what we have just remarked about the "chance" theory as an "explanation" of the *existing order* of the universe, it is no matter for surprise that most mechanists reject this theory and embrace the agnostic attitude in regard to this latter problem also. Whether the agnostic attitude they assume be negative or positive, *i.e.* whether they are content to say that they themselves at least fail to find any satisfactory rational explanation of the *origin* and *nature* of the *cosmos*, or contend further that no rational solution of these problems is within the reach of the human mind, their teaching is refuted in Natural Theology, where the theistic solution of these problems is set forth and vindicated.

110. THE ORDER OF THE UNIVERSE; A FACT AND ITS IMPLICATIONS.—The considerations so far submitted in this chapter, as pointing to the existence and influence of final causes in the universe, will be strengthened and completed by a brief analysis of *order* and its implications.

We have seen already that the apprehension of order in things implies the recognition of *some unifying principle in what is manifold*. What, in general, is the nature of this principle? It is the *point of view*, the *standpoint* from which the unifying arrangement or disposition of the manifold is carried out; in other words it is the *end, object,* or *purpose*, of the orderly arrangement. The arrangement, and the order resulting from it, will vary according to the end in view—whether, for instance, it be an arrangement of books in a library, of pictures in a gallery, of materials in an edifice, of parts in a machine. Hence St. Thomas's definition of order as the due adaptation of means to ends: *recta ratio rerum ad finem*. When this adaptation is the work of human intelligence the order realized is *artificial*, when it is the work of nature the order realized is *natural*. Art is an extrinsic principle of order, nature implies indeed also an intelligent extrinsic principle of order, but is itself an intrinsic principle of order: the works of nature and those of art have this feature in common, that they manifest adaptation of means to ends.[524]

The *subordination* of means to ends realizes an order which has for its unifying principle the influence of an *end*, a *final cause*. The group of *dynamic* relations thus revealed constitutes what is called *teleological* order, the order of *purpose* or *finality*. The realization or execution of such an order implies the simultaneous existence of *co-ordinated* parts or members in a system, a realized whole with complex, co-ordinated, orderly parts, the principle of unity in this system being the *form* of the whole. This realized, disposed, or constituted order, is called the *esthetic* order, the order of co-ordination, composition, constitution. In ultimate analysis, however, these two orders, the *teleological* and the *esthetic*, having as respective unifying principles the *final* cause and the *formal* cause, are not two really distinct orders, but rather two aspects of one and the same order: we have seen that in the things of nature the intrinsic end or final cause of each is identical with its *forma substantialis* or formal cause. But the final cause is naturally prior to the formal cause, and consequently the teleological order is more fundamental than the esthetic.

St. Augustine's definition of order as "the arrangement of a multiplicity of things, similar and dissimilar, according its proper place to each,"[525] reveals the *material* cause of order in the multiplicity of varied elements, the *formal* cause of order in the group of relations resulting from the arrangement or *dispositio*, and the *efficient* cause of order in the agent that disposes or arranges them. The *final* cause, though not directly mentioned, is implied in the fact that the place of each factor in the system is necessarily determined by the function it has to fulfil, the part it is suited by its nature to play, in contributing to the realization of the end or purpose of the arrangement.

If, then, order is *the right arrangement or disposition of things according to their destination, or in the mutual relations demanded by their ends*, it necessarily follows that the very existence of *natural* order in the universe implies that this universe is not a work of *chance* but a *purposive* work, just as the existence of *artificial* order in products of human art implies that these products are not the result of chance but of activity influenced by final causes.[526]

It is in fact impossible to conceive order except as resulting from the influence of final causes. Right reason rejects as an utterly inadequate explanation of the natural order of the universe the fantastic and far-fetched supposition of a chance collocation of indifferent, undetermined and aimless physical agencies.[527] If we find in the actual physical universe difficulties against the view that this universe reveals the influence of final causes, such difficulties do not arise from the fact that there is order in the universe, but rather from the fact that with this order there seems to coexist some degree of disorder also. In so far forth as there is natural order there is *cogent* evidence of the influence of final causes. And so necessary is this inference that even one single authentic instance of natural order in an otherwise chaotic universe would oblige us to infer the existence and influence of a final cause to account for that solitary instance. We mean by an authentic instance one which evidences a real and sustained uniformity, regularity, mutual co-ordination and subordination of factors in the behaviour of any group of natural agencies; for we allow that transient momentary collocations and concurrences of *indifferent* agencies, acting aimlessly and without purpose as a matter of fact, might present to our minds, accustomed to seek for orderly and purposive phenomena, the deceptive appearance of order.

Order, then, we take it, necessarily implies the existence and influence of final causes. This in turn, as we have already observed, implies with equal necessity the existence of *Intelligent Purpose*. If, then, there is natural order in the universe, there must exist an *Intelligent Will* to account for this natural order.

Leaving the development of this line of argument to its proper place in Natural Theology, there remains the simple question of fact: Is the physical universe a *cosmos*? Does it reveal order—a natural order distinct from the artificial order realized by the human mind in the mechanical and fine arts, an order, therefore, realized not by the human mind but by some other mind, by the Divine Mind? The evidences of such order superabound. We have already referred to some of them, nor is there any need to labour the matter. Two points, however, in connexion with this universally recognized fact of order in the universe, call for a brief mention before we conclude. They are in the nature of difficulties against the ordinary, reasonable view of the matter, the view on which the theistic argument from order is based.

In accordance with the Kantian theory of knowledge it is objected that the order which we apprehend, or think we apprehend, in the universe, is not *really in* the universe of our experience, but is as it were *projected into* this universe by our own minds in the very process of cognition itself. It is therefore not real but only apparent, not noumenal but only phenomenal. It is simply a product of the categorizing, unifying, systematizing activity of our minds. It is a feature of the phenomenon or mental product, *i.e.* of the noumenal *datum as invested with a category of thought.* But whether or not it is a characteristic of the real universe itself man's speculative reason is by its very constitution essentially incapable of ever discovering. The theory of knowledge on which this difficulty is based can be shown to be unsound and erroneous. For a criticism of the theory we must refer the reader to scholastic works on Epistemology. It may be observed, however, apart from the merits or demerits of the theory, that the experienced fact of order is by no means demolished or explained away by any questions that may be raised about the exact *location* of the fact, if we may so express it. Order is a fact, an undeniable, experienced fact; and it looms just as large, and cries out just as insistently for explanation, with whichever of the imposing adjectives "noumenal" or "phenomenal" a philosopher may choose to qualify it; nor do we diminish its reality by calling it phenomenal one whit more than we increase that reality by calling it noumenal.

The other difficulty arises from the existence of *disorder* in the universe. Pessimists of the type of Schopenhauer or Nietzsche concentrate their attention so exclusively on the evidences of disorder, the failures of adaptation of means to ends, the defects and excesses, the prodigality and penury, the pain and suffering, which abound in physical nature—not to speak of moral evil,—that they become blind to all evidences of order, and proclaim all belief in order an illusion.

The picture of

Nature, red in tooth and claw
With ravine[528]

is, however, the product of a morbid and distraught imagination rather than a sane view of the facts. The undeniable existence of disorder, of physical evils, defects, failures, frustrations of natural tendency in the universe, does not obscure or conceal from the normal, unbiassed mind the equally undeniable evidences of a great and wide and generally prevailing order. Nor does it conceal from such a mind the fact that the existence of order in any measure or degree implies of necessity the existence of plan or design, and therefore of intelligent purpose also. Inferring from this fact of order the existence of a Supreme Intelligence, and inferring by other lines of reasoning from the data of experience the dependence of the universe on this Intelligence as Creator, Conserver and Ruler, the theist is confronted with the reality of moral and physical evil, *i.e.* of *disorder* in the universe. But he does not see in this disorder anything essentially incompatible with his established conclusion that the universe is a finite creation of Infinite Wisdom, and a free manifestation of the latter to man. If the actual universe is imperfect, he knows that God created it freely and might have created a more perfect or a less perfect one. Knowing that God is All-Powerful as He is All-Wise, he knows that the actual universe, though imperfect *absolutely*, is perfect *relatively*, in that it infallibly reveals the Divine Wisdom and Goodness exactly in the measure in which God has willed to reveal Himself in His works. Conscious on the one hand that his finite mind cannot trace in detail all the purposes of God in nature, or assign to all individual events their divinely appointed ends, he is confident on the other hand that the whole universe is intelligible only as the working out of a Divine plan, and not otherwise. To his mind as a theist these lines are a clearer expression of rationally grounded optimism than they were perhaps even to the poet who penned them:—

I trust in nature for the stable laws
Of beauty and utility. Spring shall plant
And Autumn garner to the end of time.
I trust in God—the right shall be the right
And other than the wrong, while He endures;
I trust in my own soul, that can perceive
The outward and the inward, Nature's good
And God's.[529]

We have seen that the agencies which constitute the universal order have each its own inner principle of finality; that these agencies are not isolated but mutually related in such ways that the ends of each subserve an extrinsic and remoter end which is none other than this universal order whereby we recognize the world as a *cosmos*. The maintenance of this order is the *intrinsic* end of the universe as a whole: an end which is *immanent* in the universe, an end which is of course *a good*. But this universal order itself is *for an end*, an *extrinsic, transcendent* end, distinct from itself; and this end, too, must be *a good*. "The universe," says St. Thomas,[530] "has the good of order and another distinct good." The universal order, says Aristotle, has itself an end, a *good*, which is *one*, and to which all else is ordained: "πρὸς ἕν ἅπαντα συντέτακται".[531] What can this Supreme Good be, this absolutely Ultimate End, this Transcendent Principle of all nature, and of all nature's tendencies and activities? Whence comes this universal tendency of all nature, if not from the Being who is the One, Eternal, Immutable Prime Mover,[532] and whose moving influence is Love?[533] Such is the profound thought of Aristotle, a thought re-echoed so sublimely by the immortal poet of Christian philosophy in the closing line of the *Paradiso*:—

L'amor che muove il Sole e l'altre stelle.

The immediate factors of the universal order of nature, themselves devoid of intelligence, must therefore be the work of Intelligent Will. To arrange these factors as parts of one harmonious whole, as members of one orderly system, Supreme Wisdom must have conceived the plan and chosen the means to realize it. The manifestation of God's glory by the realization of this plan, such is the ultimate transcendent end of the whole created universe. "The whole order of the universe," writes St. Thomas, developing the thought of Aristotle,[534] "is for the Prime Mover thereof; this order has for its purpose the working out in an orderly universe of the plan conceived and willed by the Prime Mover. And hence the Prime Mover is the principle of this universal order."

The truths so briefly outlined in this closing chapter on the order and purpose of the universe have nowhere found more apt and lucid philosophical formulation than in the monumental writings of the Angel of the Christian Schools; nor perhaps have they ever elsewhere appeared in a more felicitous setting of poetic imagery than in these stanzas from the immortal epic of the Poet of the Christian Schools:—

... Le cose tutte quante
Hann' ordine tra lora; e questa è forma
Che l'universo a Dio fa simigliante.
Qui veggion l'alte creature l'orma
Dell'eterno Valore, il quale è fine
Al quale è fatta la toccata norma.
Nell' ordine ch'io dico sono accline
Tutte nature per diverse sorti
Più al Principio loro e men vicine;
Onde si muovono a diversi porti
Per lo gran mar dell'essere, e ciascuna
Con instinto a lei dato che la porti.
Questi ne porta il fuoco inver la Luna:
Questi ne' cuor mortali è permotore;
Questi la terra in se stringe ed aduna.
Nè pur le creature, che son fuore
D'intelligenza, quest' arco saetta
Ma quelle ch' hanno intelletto ed amore.
La Providenza, che cotanto assetta,
Del suo lume fa il ciel sempre quieto,
Nel qual si volge quel ch'ha maggior fretta:
Ed ora li, com' a sito decreto,
Cen porta la virtù di quella corda,
Che ciò che scocca drizzo in segno lieto.[535]

Footnotes

1. 2 vols. Longmans, 1912.

2. *Institutions Metaphysica, quas Roma, in Pontificia Universitate Gregoriana tradiderat* P. JOANNES JOSEPHUS URRABURU, S.J. Volumen Secundum: *Ontologia* (Rome, 1891).

3. French version by SIERP, 4 vols. Paris, Gaume, 1868.

4. *Ontologie, ou Métaphysique Générale*, par D. MERCIER. Louvain, 3me édit., 1902.

5. Τὴν ὀνομαζομένην σοφίαν περὶ τὰ πρῶτα αἴτια καὶ τὰς ὑπολαμβάνουσι πάντες.—ARISTOTLE, *Metaph.*, I., I. "Sapientia [philosophia] est scientia quae considerat primas et universales causas."—ST. THOMAS, *In Metaph.*, I., I. 2.

6. *Cf.* DE WULF, *Scholasticism Old and New*, pp. 59-61, 191-4; *History of Medieval Philosophy*, pp. 311-13; also two articles in the *Irish Ecclesiastical Record* (March and May, 1906) on *Thoughts on Philosophy and Religion*, and an article in the *Irish Theological Quarterly* (October, 1910) on *Philosophy and Sectarianism in Belfast University*, by the present writer.

7. *Cf.* Encyclical *Aeterni Patris*, on Philosophical Studies, by Pope Leo XIII., August 4,1880.

8. Introduction, § I.

9. As a brief general statement of the matter this is sufficiently accurate and will not be misunderstood. Of course the general standpoint of ultimate causes and reasons admits within itself some variety of aspects. Thus Epistemology and Psychology deal with human thought, but under different aspects; Psychology and Ethics deal with human volition, but under different aspects, etc.

10.

"Theoreticus sive speculativis intellectus, in hoc proprie ab operativo sive practico distinguitur, quod speculativus habet pro fine veritatem quam considerat, practicus autem veritatem consideratam ordinat in operationem tamquam in finem; et ideo differunt ab invicem fine; finis speculativae est veritas, finis operativae sive practicae actio."—ST. THOMAS, *In lib. Boetii de Trinitate.*

11.

Here is St. Thomas' exposition and justification of the doctrine in the text: "Sapientis est ordinare. Cujus ratio est, quia sapientia est potissima perfectio rationis, cujus proprium est cognoscere ordinem.... Ordo autem quadrupliciter ad rationem comparatatur. Est enim quidam ordo quem ratio non facit, sed solum considerat, sicut est ordo rerum naturalium. Alius autem est ordo, quem ratio considerando facit in proprio actu, puta cum ordinat conceptus suos ad invicem, et signa conceptuum, quae sunt voces significativae. Tertius autem est quem ratio considerando facit in operationibus voluntatis. Quartus autem est ordo quem ratio considerando facit in exterioribus rebus, quarum ipsa est causa, sicut in arca et domo. Et quia consideratio rationis per habitum perficitur, secundum hos diversos ordines quos proprie ratio considerat, sunt diversae scientiae. Nam ad *philosophiam naturalem* pertinet considerare ordinem rerum quem ratio humana considerat sed non facit; ita quod sub naturali philosophia comprehendamus *et metaphysicam*. Ordo autem quem ratio considerando facit in proprio actu, pertinet ad *rationalem philosophiam*, cujus est considerare ordinem partium orationis ad invicem et ordinem principiorum ad invicem et ad conclusiones. Ordo autem actionum voluntariarum pertinet ad considerationem *moralis philosophiae*. Ordo autem quem ratio considerando facit in rebus exterioribus constitutis per rationem humanam, pertinet ad *artes mechanicas*."—*In X. Ethic. ad Nichom.*, i., lect. I.

12.

Cf. Science of Logic, i., Introduction, ch. ii. and iii.

13.

ARISTOTLE and the scholastics distinguished between the domain of the practical (πρᾶσσω, πρᾶξις, *agere, agibilia*) and the operative or productive (ποιεῖν, ποίησις, *facere, factibilia*).

14.

Cf. Science of Logic, i., § 8.

15.

"Quaedam igitur sunt *speculabilium* quae dependent a materia secundum esse, quia non nisi in materia esse possunt, et haec distinguuntur quia dependent quædam a materia secundum esse et intellectum, sicut illa in quorum definitione ponitur materia sensibilis: unde sine materia sensibili intelligi non possunt; ut in definitione hominis oportet accipere carnem et ossa: et de his est *physica* sive scientia naturalis. Quædam vero sunt quæ, quamvis dependeant a materia sensibili secundum esse, non tamen secundum intellectum, quia in eorum definitionibus non ponitur materia sensibilis, ut linea et numerus: et de his est *mathematica*. Quædam vero sunt speculabilia quæ non dependent a materia secundum esse, quia sine materia esse possunt: sive nunquam sint in materia, sicut Deus et angelus, sive in quibusdam sint in materia et in quibusdam non, ut substantia, qualitas, potentia et actus, unum et multa, etc., de quibus omnibus est *theologia*, id est scientia divina, quia præcipuum cognitorum in ea est Deus. Alio nomine dicitur *metaphysica*, id est, transphysica, quia post physicam dicenda occurrit nobis, quibus ex sensibilibus competit in insensibilia devenire. Dicitur etiam *philosophia prima*, in quantum scientiae aliæ ab ea principia sua accipientes eam sequuntur."—ST. THOMAS, *In lib. Boetii de Trinitate*, q. 5, a. I.

16.
Ἔττιν ἐπιστήμη τις ἥ θεωοεῖ τὸ ὄν και τούτῳ ὑπάρχοντα καθ' αὐτό.—*Metaph.* III., I (ed. Didot).

17.
Metaph. X., ch. vii., 5 and 6.

18.
Cf. *Science of Logic*, ii., §§ 251-5.

19.
When the term "science" is used nowadays in contradistinction to "philosophy," it usually signifies the knowledge embodied in what are called the special, or positive, or inductive sciences—a knowledge which Aristotle would not regard as strictly or fully scientific.

20.
Aristotle's conception of the close relation between *Physics* (or the *Philosophy* of Nature) and those analytic studies which we nowadays describe as the physical sciences, bears witness to the close alliance which he conceived to exist between sense observation on the one hand and rational speculation on the other. This sane view of the continuity of human knowledge, a view to which the Schoolmen of the Middle Ages were ever faithful, was supplanted at the dawn of modern philosophy in the sixteenth and seventeenth centuries by the opposite view, which led to a divorce between physics and metaphysics, and to a series of misunderstandings which still prevail with equal detriment to science and philosophy alike.

21.
Cf. DE WULF, *History of Medieval Philosophy*, pp. 28-9, 66; MERCIER, *Ontologie*, Introd., p. v., n.

22.
"Dicitur metaphysica [scientia] id est, transphysica, quia post physicam dicenda occurrit nobis, quibus ex sensibilibus competit in insensibilia devenire."—ST. THOMAS, *In Lib. Boetii de Trinitate*, q. 5, a. 1.

23.
This is also the title of the social and ethnological study of the various races of men, their primitive habits, customs, institutions, etc.

24.
Not entirely; for instance, what is perhaps the most comprehensive course of philosophy published in recent times, the *Philosophia Lacensis* (11 vols., Herder, 1888-1900) apparently follows the arrangement of metaphysics outlined above. The fundamental questions on *knowing* and *being*, which usually constitute distinct departments under the respective titles of *Epistemology* and *Ontology*, are here treated under the comprehensive title of *Institutiones Logicales* (3 vols.). However, they are really metaphysical problems, problems of speculative philosophy, wherever they be treated; and the fact that the questions usually treated in Ontology are here treated in a volume apart (vol. iii. of the *Institutiones Logicales*: under the peculiar title of *Logica Realis*), and not in the volumes assigned to general metaphysics, shows the necessity and convenience of the more modern arrangement. General metaphysics are dealt with in 2 vols. of *Institutiones Philosophiae Naturalis* and 3 vols. of *Institutiones Psychologicae*; special metaphysics in the *Institutiones Theodicœae* (1 vol.); ethics in 2 vols. of *Institutiones Juris Naturae*.

25.
Cf. TURNER, *History of Philosophy*, p. 525.

26.
MERCIER, *Logique*, Introd., § 9.

27.
pp. 45, 51.

28.
Cf. *Science of Logic*, i., § 17.

29.
Cf. *ibid.* i., Introd., ch. i.

30.
CAJETAN, *In 2 Post Anal.*, ch. xiii.

31.
Cf. MERCIER, *Ontologie*, §§ 6-13; LADD, *A Theory of Reality*, ch. i.

32.

33. *infra*, ch. viii.; *Cf. Science of Logic*, ii., Part IV., ch. iii.-vi.; Part V., ch. i.

34. p. 18—in which context will be found a masterly analysis and criticism of current prejudices and objections against systematic metaphysics.

35. *ibid.* pp. 19-20.

36. ROYCE, *The Conception of God*, p. 207.

37. MERCIER, *Logique*, Introd., § 14.

38. Encyclical, *Aeterni Patris*, on philosophical studies.

39. *Summa Theologica*, I, q. 1, a. 8, ad. 2.

40. *Cf.* MERCIER, *Origines de la psychologie contemporaine*, ch. viii.; DE WULF, *Scholasticism Old and New* (*passim*).

41. *Cf.* LADD, *op. cit.*, pp. 9, 10.

42. EUCKEN, *Gesammelte Aufsaetze zur Philosophie und Lebensanschauung*, § 157 (Leipzig, 1903).

43. *Cf.* art. *Philosophy and the Sciences at Louvain*, in the *Irish Ecclesiastical Record*, May, 1905, reprinted as Appendix in DE WULF'S *Scholasticism Old and New.*

Hence the necessity of equipping the student of philosophy with a knowledge of the main conclusions and theories of the sciences that have an immediate bearing on philosophy: chemistry, physics, geology, astronomy, mechanics, the axioms and postulates of pure and applied mathematics, cellular biology, embryology, the physiology of the nervous system, botany and zoology, political economy, sociology and ethnology. Nowhere is the system of combining the scientific with the philosophical formation of mind more thoroughly carried out at the present time than in the curriculum of the Philosophical Institute at the University of Louvain. In the College of Maynooth not only is the study of philosophy completed by a fuller course of Christian Theology,—both disciplines thus combining to give the student all the essential elements of a complete *Philosophy of Life* (ii.),—but it is preceded by an elementary training in the physical sciences and accompanied by courses on the history of scientific theories in chemistry, physics, physiology, and general biology.

44.
"We may mention it in passing," writes Mercier in his general introduction to philosophy (*Logique*, § I, p. 6)—"it was this feeling of individual impotence in face of the task confronting the philosopher at the present day, that inspired the foundation of the Philosophical Institute at the University of Louvain". He had previously outlined the project in his *Rapport sur les études philosophiques* at the Congress of Mechlin in 1891. Here are a few brief extracts from that memorable document: "Since individual effort feels itself well nigh powerless in the presence of the field of observation which goes on widening day by day, association must make up for the insufficiency of the isolated worker; men of analysis and men of synthesis must come together and form, by their daily intercourse and united action, an atmosphere suited to the harmonious development of science and philosophy alike...." "Man has multiplied his power of vision; he enters the world of the infinitely small; he fixes his scrutinizing gaze upon regions where our most powerful telescopes discern no limits. Physics and Chemistry progress with giant strides in the study of the properties of matter and of the combinations of its elements. Geology and Astronomy reconstruct the history of the origin and formation of our planet. Biology and the natural sciences study the minute structure of living organisms, their distribution in space and succession in time; and Embryology explores their origin. The archæological, philological and social sciences reconstruct the past ages of our history and civilizations. What an inexhaustible mine is here to exploit, what regions to explore and materials to analyse and interpret; finally what pioneers we must engage in the work if we are to have a share in garnering those treasures!"

45.
Grammar of Assent, p. 229.

46.
Lucerna pedibus meis verbum tuum, et lumen semitis meis.—Ps. cxviii., 105.

47.
TENNYSON, *In Memoriam*.

48.
Cf. *Logic*, i., § 123.

49.
Cf. *Logic*, i., pp. 204-6.

50.
Cf. SCOTUS, *Summa Theologica*, edit. by Montefortino (Rome, 1900), i., p. 106, *Ad tertium*.

51.

52. *Cf. Logic*, i., pp. 119-20.

53. *Cf.* SCOTUS, *op. cit.*, i., pp. 104, 129; also URRABURU, *Ontologia*, Disp. III., Cap. II., Art. III., p. 155.

54. Hence St. Thomas calls the things about which a generic or specific concept is predicated "*analoga secundum esse et non secundum intentionem*" (*In I Sent.*, Dist. xix., q. 5, a. 2, ad a am): we bring them under the same notion or "*intentio*" (*e.g.* "living being"), but the content of this notion is realized in the various things (*e.g.* in Socrates, this horse, that rose-tree, etc.) in varying and unequal degrees of perfection. Hence, too, this univocal relation of the genus to its subordinate subjects is sometimes (improperly) called "analogy of inequality".

55. *Cf. infra*, ch. viii.

56. *Cf.* KLEUTGEN, *Philosophie der Vorzeit*, §§ 599, 600.

57. This, of course, is the proper sort of analogical predication: the predication based upon similarity of proportions or relations. Etymologically, analogy means equality of proportions (*Cf. Logic*, ii., p. 160). On the whole subject the student may consult with profit Cajetan's *Opusculum de Nominum Analogia*, published as an appendix to vol. iv. of St. Thomas' *Quæstiones Disputatæ* in De Maria's edition (1883).

58. *Cf.* KLEUTGEN, *op. cit.*, §§ 40-42.

59. *Cf.* SCOTUS, *op. cit.*, i., pp. 318-22, 125-131, 102-7 (especially p. 128, *Ad tertium*); p. 131, *Ad sextum*; p. 321, *Ad tertium*.

60. KLEUTGEN, *op. cit.*, § 599.

61. *ibid.*, § 600.

62. SUAREZ, *Metaph.*, Dist. xxviii., § 3; Dist. xxxii., § 2.

63. SCOTUS, *op. cit.*, i., pp. 106-7, 128-9.

64. *ibid.*, p. 107.

Cf. KLEUTGEN, *La philosophie scolastique* ("*Die Philosophie der Vorzeit*"). Fr. trans. by Sierp (Paris, 1868), vol. i., p. 66, § 35.

65.
The logical copula, which expresses this relation and asserts the truth of the judgment, expresses, of course, a logical entity, an *ens rationis*. True judgments may be stated about logical entities as well as about realities. But since the former can be conceived only after the manner of the latter, the appropriateness of using the verb which expresses existence or reality, as the logical copula, will be at once apparent. *Cf. Logic*, i., p. 249, n. 1.

66.
SUAREZ, *Metaph.*, Dist. 54, § i., 6.

67.
Cf. Logic, i., pp. 28-9.

68.
Cf. KLEUTGEN, *op. cit.*, §§ 551-2.

69.
Cf. Logic, i., pp. 70-1.

70.
"Esse actum quondam nominat: non enim dicitur esse aliquid ex hoc, quod est in potentia, sed ex hoc, quod est in actu."—ST. THOMAS, *Contra Gent.* i., c. xxii., 4.

71.
Certain medieval philosophers had made the same mistake. St. Thomas points out their error frequently. *Cf. Contra Gentes*, i., c. xxvi: "Quia id, quod commune est, per additionem specificatur vel individuatur, æstimaverunt, divinum esse, cui nulla fit additio, non esse aliquid proprium, sed esse commune omnium: non considerantes, quod id, quod commune est, vel universale, sine additione esse non potest, sed sine additione consideratur. Non enim animal potest esse absque rationali vel irrationali differentia, quamvis sine his differentiis consideretur; licet enim cogitetur universale absque additione, non tamen absque receptibilitate additionis est. Nam si animali nulla differentia addi posset, genus non esset; et similiter est de omnibus aliis nominibus. Divinum autem esse est absque additione, non solum cogitatione, sed etiam in rerum natura; et non solum absque additione, sed absque receptibilitate additionis. Unde ex hoc ipso quod additionem non recipit, nec recipere potest, magis concludi potest quod Deus non sit esse commune, sed esse proprium. Etenim ex hoc ipso suum esse ab omnibus aliis distinguitur, quia nihil ei addi potest."

72.
Cf. ST. THOMAS, QQ. DD. *De Potentia*, q. i. art. 1, ad. 18.

73.
ARISTOTLE, *Metaph.*, c. iv., v., *apud* KLEUTGEN, *op. cit.*, iii., p. 60.

74.

75. *Contra Gentes*, II., c. vii.

76. Cf. LAMINNE, *Cause et Effet—Revue neo-scolastique*, February, 1914, p. 38.

77. St. Thomas uses what is for him strong language when he describes such a view as ridiculous: "Ridiculum est dicere quod ideo corpus non agat, quia accidens non transit de subjecto in subjectum; non enim hoc modo dicitur corpus calidum calefacere, quod idem numero calor, qui est in calefaciente corpore, transeat ad corpus calefactum; sed quia virtute caloris, qui est in calefaciente corpore, alius calor numero fit actu in corpore calefacto, qui prior erat in eo in potentia. Agens enim naturale non est traducens propriam formam in alterum subjectum, sed reducens subjectum quod patitur de potentia in actum."—*Contra Gentes*, L. III., c. lxix.

78. Cf. ZIGLIARA, *Ontologia* (8), ix., *Quintum*. Cf. also ARISTOTLE, *Metaph.* v., ST. THOMAS, *In Metaph.*, v., § 14, and *Contra Gentes*, i., c. xvi., where he emphasizes the truth that potential being presupposes actual being: "Quamvis id quod quandoque est in potentia, quandoque in actu, prius sit tempore in potentia quam in actu, tamen simpliciter actus est prior potentia; quia potentia non educit se in actum, sed opportet quod educatur in actum per aliquid quod sit in actu. Omne igitur quod est aliquo modo in potentia, habet aliquid prius se".

79. KLIMKE, *Der Monismus und seine philosophischen Grundlagen*, p. 185. Cf. *Irish Theological Quarterly*, vol. vii. (April, 1912), p. 157 *sqq.*, art. *Reflections on Some Forms of Monism*.

80. For relations of *potentia* and *actus*, cf. MERCIER, *Ontologie*, § 214.

81. Cf. *Physics*, v., 1; *De Anima*, i., 3.

82. Λεγώ δ' ὕλην, ἢ καθ' αὑτὴν μήτε τὶ, μήτε ποσὸν, μήτε ποίον, μήτε ἄλλο μεδὲν λέγεται οἷς ὥρισται τὸ ὄν.—*Metaph.* vi., c. iii.

"Decepit antiquos philosophos hanc rationem inducentes, ignorantia formae substantialis. Non enim adhuc tantum profecerant ut intellectus eorum se elevaret ad aliquid quod est supra sensibilia: et ideo illas formas tantum consideraverunt, quæ sunt sensibilia propria vel communia. Hujusmodi autem manifestum est esse accidentia, ut album et nigrum, magnum et parvum, et hujusmodi. Forma autem substantialis non est

83. sensibilis nisi per accidens, et ideo ad ejus cognitionem non bervenerunt, ut scirent ipsam materiam distinguere."—*In Metaph.* vii., 2.

84. "Esse actum quemdam nominat: non enim dicitur esse aliquid, ex hoc quod est in potentia, sed ex hoc quod est in actu."—ST. THOMAS, *Contra Gentes*, i., ch. xxii., 4.

85. The etymology of Aristotle's description of the essence as τὸ τί ἦν εἶναι is not easy to explain. The expression τὸ εἶναι supposes a dative understood, *e.g.* τὸ ἀνθρώπῳ εἶναι, the being proper to man. To the question τί ἐστι τὸ ἀνθρώπῳ εἶναι; what is the being or essence proper to man? the answer is: that which gives the definition of man, that which explains what he is—τί ἦν. Is the imperfect, τὶ ἦν, an archaic form for the present, τὶ ἐστι; or is it a deliberate suggestion of the profound doctrine that the essence as ideal, or possible, is anterior to its actual, physical realization? Commentators are not agreed. *Cf.* MATTHIAS KAPPES, Aristoteles-Lexicon, p. 25 (Paderborn, 1894); MERCIER, *Ontologie*, p. 30 n.

86. Essentia est illud per quod res constituitur in proprio genere vel specie, et quod significamus per definitionem indicantem quid est res.—*De Ente et Essentia*, ch. i.

87. ARISTOTLE, *Metaph.*, v., 4; ST. THOMAS, *De Potentia Dei*, q. ix., art. I.

88. Sometimes, however, the expression "metaphysical essence" is used to signify those objective concepts, and those only, *without which the thing cannot be conceived,* (or sometimes, even the one which is considered most fundamental among these), and therefore as not explicitly involving the concepts of properties which follow necessarily from the former; while the "physical essence" is understood to signify all those real elements *without which the thing cannot actually exist,* including, therefore, all such necessary properties. Taken in this sense the physical essence of man would include not merely soul and body, but also such properties as the capacity of speech, of laughter, of using tools, of cooking food, etc.

Et ex hoc patet ratio, writes St. Thomas, quare genus et species et differentia se habeant proportionaliter ad materiam, formam et compositum in natura, quamvis non sint idem cum illis; quia neque genus est materia, sed sumitur a materia ut significans totum; nec differentia est forma, sed sumitur a forma ut significans totum. Unde dicimus hominem esse *animal rationale*, et non *ex animali et rationali*; sicut dicimus eum esse ex corpore et anima. Ex corpore enim et anima dicitur esse homo, sicut ex duabus rebus quædam tertia res constituta, quæ neutra illarum est: homo enim nec est anima neque corpus; sed si homo aliquo modo ex animali et rationali dicatur esse, non erit sicut res tertia ex duabus rebus sed sicut intellectus [conceptus] tertius ex duobus intellectibus. Intellectus enim *animalis* est sine determinatione formae specialis naturam exprimens rei, ex eo quod est materiale respectu ultimae perfectionis. Intellectus autem hujus differentiae, *rationalis*, consistit in determinatione formae specialis: ex quibus duobus intellectibus constituitur intellectus speciei vel definitionis. Et ideo sicut res constituta ex aliquibus non recipit prædicationem earum rerum ex quibus constituitur; ita nec intellectus recipit prædicationem eorum intellectuum ex quibus constituitur; non enim dicimus, quod definitio sit genus vel differentia.—*De Ente et Essentia*, cap. iii.

89.

Cf. MERCIER, *Psychologie*, vol. ii., § 169 (6th edit., 1903, pp. 24-5).

90.

Cf. ARISTOTLE, *Metaph.*, L. viii., 10; ST. THOMAS, *In* viii., *Metaph.*, Lect. iii., par. i.

91.

Cf. MERCIER, *Ontologie*, pp. 42-3. How do we know that not only water (H^2O) is a possible essence but also hydrogen di-oxide (H^2O^2)? Because the latter substance has been *actually formed* by chemists (*Cf.* ROSCOE, *Elementary Chemistry*, Lesson VI.). Is hydrogen tri-oxyde (H^2O^3) a possible substance? We may ask chemists,—and they may not be able to tell us with any certainty whether it is or not.

92.

The actual existence of a thinking mind is of course a necessary condition, in the actual order, for the apprehension of objects in this abstract way. But such existence is no part of the apprehended object. That the human mind, which is itself finite, contingent, allied with matter, and dependent on the activity of corporeal sense organs for the objects of its knowledge, should nevertheless have the power to apprehend contingent realities apart from their contingent actual existence in time and space,—is a fact of the greatest significance as regards the nature of the mind itself. But if we try to prove the existence of God from a consideration of the nature and powers of the human mind, our argument proceeds from the actual, and is distinct from any argument based exclusively on the nature and properties of possible essences as such. St. Augustine's argument assumes as a fact that the human mind represents to itself possible essences as having reality independently both of its own thought and of any actual existence of such

93.
> essences (*Cf.* DE MUNNYNCK, *Praelectiones de Dei Existentia*, p. 23). But *is* this a fact? This is the really debatable point.

94.
> Among others Henry of GHENT († 1293; *Cf.* DE WULF, *History of Medieval Philosophy*, pp. 364-6; KLEUTGEN, *Philosophie der Vorzeit*, Dissert. vi., cap. ii., 2 §§ 581-5), Capreolus (1380-1444), certain Scotists, and certain theosophists of the thirteenth and fourteenth centuries, are credited with this peculiar view. For numerous references, *Cf.* URRABURU, *Ontologia*, Disp. iii., cap. ii., art. v. pp. 650-63.

95.
> *Cf.* URRABURU, *op. cit.*, pp. 652-3, for references; among others, to ST. THOMAS, *De Potentia*, q. 3, art. 1, ad 2um; art. 7, ad 10um; art. 5, argum. 2°; *ibid.*, ad 2um. *Summa Theol.*, i., q. 14, art. 9; q. 45, art. 1; *ibid.*, art. 2, ad 2um; q. 61, art. 2, corp.

96.
> Among others, BALMES (*Fundamental Philosophy*, bk. iv., ch. xxvi.), LEPIDI (*Ontologia*, quoted by DE MUNYNCK, *Praelectiones de Dei Existentia*, Louvain, 1904, p. 19); DE MUNYNCK (*ibid.*, pp. 19-23, 46-7, 75); HICKEY (*Theologia Naturalis*, pp. 31-4); DRISCOLL (*God*, pp. 72 sqq.); LACORDAIRE (*God*, p. 21); KLEUTGEN, *Philosophie der Vorzeit*, Dissert. iv., § 476.

97.
> Truth is not the work of any human intelligence, says St. Augustine, nor can any one arrogate to himself the right to say "*my* truth," or "*thy* truth," but all must say simply "*the* truth": "Quapropter, nullo modo negaveris esse incommutabilem veritatem, haec omnia, quae incommutabiliter vera sunt, continentem, quam non possis dicere vel tuam vel meam, vel cujuscumque hominis, sed omnibus incommutabilia vera cernentibus, tamquam miris modis secretum et publicum lumen, praesto esse ac se praebere communiter: omne autem quod communiter omnibus ratiocinantibus atque intelligentibus praesto est, ad ullius eorum proprie naturam pertinere quis dixerit?"—*De Libero Arbitrio*, lib. ii., ch. xii. *Cf.* his striking expression of the same thought in his Commentary, *Super Genesim ad Litteram*, lib. ii., cap. vii.: "We may conceive the heavens and the earth, that were created in six days, ceasing to exist; but can we conceive the number 'six' ceasing to be the sum of six units?": "Facilius coelum et terra transire possunt, quae secundum numerum senarium fabricata sunt, quam effici possit ut senarius numerus suis partibus non compleatur" (*apud* MERCIER, *Ontologie*, pp. 35-6).

Cf. BALMES (*Fundamental Philosophy*, bk. iv., ch. xxvi.), who, analysing the truth of the proposition "Two circles of equal diameters are equal," as an example of the necessary, eternal, immutable characteristics of possible essences, goes so far as to write (italics ours): "What would happen, if, withdrawing all bodies, all sensible representations, *and even all intelligences*, we should imagine absolute and universal nothing? We see the truth of the proposition even on this supposition: for it is impossible for us to hold it to be false. On every supposition, our understanding sees a connection which it cannot destroy: the condition once established, the result will infallibly follow.

"An absolutely necessary connection, founded neither on us, nor on the external world, which exists before anything we can imagine, and subsists after we have annihilated all by an effort of our understanding, must be based upon something, it cannot have nothing for its origin: to say this would be to assert a necessary fact without a sufficient reason.

"It is true that in the proposition now before us nothing real is affirmed, but if we reflect carefully we find even here the greatest difficulty for those who deny a real foundation to pure possibility. What is remarkable in this phenomenon, is precisely this, that our understanding feels itself forced to give its assent to a proposition which affirms an absolutely necessary connection *without any relation to an existing object*. It is conceivable that an intelligence affected by other beings may know their nature and relations; but it is not so easy of comprehension how it can discover their nature and relations in an absolutely necessary manner, when it abstracts all existence, when the ground upon which the eyes of the understanding are fixed, is the abyss of nothing.

"We deceive ourselves when we imagine it possible to abstract all existence. Even when we suppose our mind to have lost sight of every thing, a very easy supposition, granting that we find in our consciousness the contingency of our being, the understanding still perceives a possible order, and imagines it to be all occupied with pure possibility, *independent of a being upon which it is based.* We repeat, that this is an illusion, which disappears so soon as we reflect upon it. In pure nothing, nothing is possible; there are no relations, no connections of any kind; in nothing there are no combinations, it is a ground upon which nothing can be pictured.

"The objectivity of our ideas and the perception of necessary relations in a possible order, reveal *a communication of our understanding with a being on which is founded all possibility.* This possibility can be explained on no supposition except that which makes the communication consist in *the action of God giving to our mind faculties* perceptive of the necessary relation of certain ideas, based upon necessary being, and representative of His infinite essence."

Balmes, therefore, does not mean that we could continue to see essences as possible were we to imagine withdrawn not merely finite minds but even the Divine Mind. In such an absurd hypothesis, nothing would appear true or false, possible or impossible. But he contends that even when we *try* to think away *all* minds, even the Divine Mind, we still see possible essences to be possible. And from this he argues that, since we have successfully thought away finite minds and the actuality of essences, while the possibility of these latter still persists, these must be grounded in the Mind of God, the Actual, Eternal, Necessary Being, where they have eternal ideal being.

Cf. DE MUNNYNCK (*op. cit.*, pp. 22-3): "Ponamus mundum non esse, nec supponamus Dei existentiam. In nihilo illo, omne ens actuale excludens, remanet intacta—hoc certissime scimus ex objectivo valore intellectus nostri—realitas aeterna, immutabilis, ordinis idealis. [Illa realitas essentiarum, he adds (*ibid.*, n. 2), independens ab omni actuali existentia, atque ab omni actu intellectus, est fundamentum metaphysicum realismi platonici.—Habet praeterea mirum hoc systema, ut omnes sciunt, fundamentum criteriologicum.] Essentiae *sunt*, nec tamen existunt. Illa realitas, praeter mundum totum, praeter entia rationis, indestructibilis perseverat, nec tamen actualis est. Haec quomodo intelligi possit nescimus, nisi ponatur illam fundari in plenitudine aeterna, infinita, absoluta τοῦ Esse absoluti. Hoc ente supremo posito, omnia lucidissima se praebent intellectui; illo Deo optimo—quem non possumus, perspectis illis altissimis, non adorare—sublato, admittendae sunt essentiae rerum ab aeterno reales sine actuali existentia; atque proinde quid non-individuale est reale in se, quod tamen concipi non potest nisi objective in mente."

98.   *Cf.* ST. AUGUSTINE, *De Libero Arbitrio*, lib. ii., ch. viii.

99.   *Cf.* especially MERCIER, *Ontologie*, pp. 40-49.

100.   It is, for example, just as necessarily and immutably true of any actually existing man that he cannot be at the same time existing and not existing as it is that a man cannot be an irrational animal.

101.

"Unde, etiamsi intellectus humanus non esset, adhuc res dicerentur verae in ordine ad intellectum divinum. Sed si uterque intellectus, quod est impossibile, intelligeretur auferri, nullo modo ratio veritatis remaneret."—ST. THOMAS, *De Veritate*, q. i., art. ii.

102.

Phædo, 100, C. ff.

103.

MERCIER, *Ontologie*, pp. 45-7.

104.

Cf. DE MUNNYNCK, *op. cit.*, pp. 24-5.

105.

Cf. DE MUNNYNCK, *op. cit.*, pp. 24-5.

106.

ibid., pp. 22, 24.

107.

"Quæ objecta non divina esse, luce clarius apparet. Attamen ilia ponderando, *modumque inspiciendo quo representantur a mente humana*, atque praesupponendo valorem objectivum intellectus, concludimus ex ideis ad realitates illas quæ in Esse divino fundantur ... ratione horum [objectorum *scil.* idearum nostrarum] percipimus, ope ratiocinii, illa positive aeterna et immutabilia, quæ reapse in Deitate fundantur, atque sunt ipse Deus quatenus imitabilis."—*ibid.*, pp. 24-5. *Cf.* extract quoted above, p. 91 n.

108.

"Non ideo voluit Deus mundum creare in tempore, quia vidit melius sic fore, quam si creasset ab æterno; *nec voluit tres angulos trianguli æquales esse duobus rectis, quia cognovit aliter fieri non posse.* Sed contra, quia voluit creare mundum in tempore, ideo sic melius est, quam si creatus fuisset ab æterno, *et quia voluit tres angulos trianguli necessario æquales esse duobus rectis, idcirco jam verum est, et aliter fieri non potest*, atque ita de reliquis."—DESCARTES, in *Resp. ad Sext. Objectiones*, ad 6um scrupulum.

109.

MERCIER, *op. cit.*, pp. 58-60.

110.

URRABURU (*op. cit.* Disp. iii., cap. ii., § iii., p. 671) mentions Wolff, Leibniz, Genuensis and Storchenau as holding this view.

111.

Among others, Liberatore, Lahousse, Pesch, Harper. *Cf.* URRABURU, *op. cit., ibid.*

112.

113. Dupasquier, Mastrius and Rada, *apud* URRABURU, *op. cit., ibid.,* pp. 679-81.

114. Urraburu, Schiffini, Mendive. *Cf.* URRABURU, *op. cit., ibid.,* p. 671.

115. I Cor. xiii. 12.

116. "Ex hoc ipso quod quidditati esse attribuitur, non solum esse, sed ipsa quidditas creari dicitur: quia antequam esse habeat, nihil est, nisi forte in intellectu creantis, ubi non est creatura, sed creatrix essentia."—ST. THOMAS, *De Potentia,* q. iii., art. v., ad 2 um.

"Ipsum esse competit primo agenti secundum propriam naturam: esse enim Dei est ejus substantia, ut ostensum est (*C. G.,* Lib. i., c. 22). Quod autem competit alicui secundum naturam suam, non convenit aliis nisi per modum participationis, sicut calor aliis corporibus ab igne [*i.e.* as caused or produced in them. *Cf.* Kleutgen, *op. cit.,* Dissert., i., c. iii., § 61]. Ipsum igitur esse competit aliis omnibus a primo agente per participationem quamdam. Quod autem alicui competit per participationem, non est substantia ejus. Impossibile est igitur quod substantia alterius entis praeter agens primum sit ipsum esse. Hinc est quod Exod. iii., proprium nomen Dei ponitur esse *qui est,* quia ejus solius proprium est, quod sua substantia non sit aliud quam suum esse."—ST. THOMAS, *Contra Gentes,* L. ii., cap. 52, n. 7.

"Quod inest alicui ab agente, oportet esse actum ejus; agentis enim est facere aliquid actu. Ostensum est autem supra, quod omnes aliae substantiæ habent esse a primo agente, et per hoc ipsæ substantiæ creatæ sunt, quod esse ab alio habent. Ipsum igitur esse inest substantiis creatis ut quidam actus earum. Id autem, cui actus inest, potentia est: nam actus in quantum hujusmodi ad potentiam refertur. In qualibet igitur substantia creata est potentia et actus."—*ibid.,* cap. 53, n. 2.

"Omne quod recipit aliquid ab alio, est in potentia respectu illius: et hoc quod receptum est in eo, est actus ejus; ergo oportet, quod ipsa forma vel quidditas, quæ est intelligentia [*i.e.* a pure spirit], sit in potentia respectu esse, quod a Deo recipit, et illud esse receptum est per modum actus, et ita invenitur actus et potentia in intelligentiis [*i.e.* pure spirits], non tamen forma et materia nisi aequivoce."—*De Ente et Essentia,* cap. v. *Cf.* also *Summa Theol.,* P. i., q. iii., art. 4; q. xiii., art. 11; q. lxxv., art. 5, ad 4 um. *Quodlibeta,* ii., art. 3; ix., art. 6. *De Potentia,* q. vii., art. 2. *In Metaph.,* iii.,

Dist. vi., q. 2, art. 2. *Contra Gentes*, L. ii., cap. 54, 68. St. Thomas is usually interpreted as teaching that the distinction between essence and existence in created things is a real distinction. But there are some who have been unable to convince themselves that the Angelic Doctor has made his mind entirely clear on the subject. Kleutgen, for instance, writes (*op. cit.*, Dissert. vi., c. ii., § 574, n. 2): "In the extracts quoted above St. Thomas clearly states that the distinction made by our thought is based on the nature of created things, but not that this distinction is that which exists between different parts, dependent on one another, each having its own proper being or reality."

117.
Cf. URRABURU, *op. cit.*, § 249, 5°.

118.
Cf. REINSTADLER, *Ontologia*, lib. ii., cap. i., art. ii., § 2.

119.
Zigliara (*Ontologia* (14), iii. iv.) gives the virtual distinction as a sub-class of the real distinction; adding, however (according to Goudin, *Metaph.*, Disp. i., q. iii. art. ii., § i) that "this virtual distinction is not so much a [real] distinction as the basis of a [mental] distinction".

120.
op. cit., p. 110.

121.
These may be seen in abundance in the works of any of the scholastic writers, medieval or modern, who discuss the question. *Cf., e.g.* URRABURU, *op. cit.*, §§ 251-4.

122.
Besides St. Thomas (*cf. supra*, p. 102, n. 2), Albertus Magnus (1193-1280), Aegidius Romanus († *circa* 1300), Capreolus (1380-1444), Soncinas († 1494), Cajetan (1468-1534), Sylvester Ferrariensis (1474-1528), Dominicus Bañez (1528-1604), John of St. Thomas (1589-1644), Goudin (1639-95), are among the most noted scholastics to hold this view. It is supported by the members of the Dominican Order generally; and by not a few Jesuits among recent scholastic writers; also by MERCIER, *op. cit.*, §§ 48-51.

123.
Cf. KLEUTGEN, *op. cit.*, § 575.

124.
ibid., § 577.

125.
Cf. URRABURU, *op. cit.*, Disp. iv., cap. i., art. 2, pp. 730-31.

126.

"Esse rei quamvis sit aliud ab ejus essentia, non tamen est intelligendum, quod sit aliquod superadditum, ad modum accidentis, sed quasi constituitur per principia essentiae. Et ideo hoc nomen, quod imponitur ab esse (ens) significat idem cum nomine quod imponitur ab ipsa essentia."—ST. THOMAS, *In Metaph.*, L. iv., l. 2.

127.

Among the advocates of this view are Alexander of Hales († 1245), Aureolus († 1322), Durandus († 1332), Gabriel Biel († 1495), Suarez (1548-1617), Toletus (1532-1596), Vasquez (1551-1604), Gregory of Valentia († *circa* 1600), and the Jesuits generally: some few regarding the distinction as *purely* logical, *e.g.* Franzelin (*apud* MERCIER, *op. cit.*, § 47, p. 110, n. 2). For details and arguments on both sides, *cf.* URRABURU, *op. cit.*, Disp. iv., cap. i., art. 2.

128.

"Compositum ex esse et essentia dicitur de ratione entis creati secundum fundamentum, quod in ipso ente creato habet; hoc autem fundamentum non est aliud nisi quia creatura non habet ex se actu existere, sed tantum est ens potentiale, quod ab alio potest esse participare: nam hinc fit, ut essentia creaturae concipiatur a nobis ut potentiale quid, esse vero ut modus seu actus, quo talis essentia ens in actu constituitur."—SUAREZ, *Metaph.*, Disp. xxxi., § 13.

129.

When we speak of an essence as *receiving* existence, we do not necessarily imply a real distinction between receiver and received: "Non est imaginandum quod una res sit, quae participat sicut essentia, et alia quae participatur sicut esse, sed quia una et eadem res est realitas modo participato et per vim alterius sicut per vim agentis: haec enim realitas de se non est nisi sub modo possibili; quod autem sit et vocari possit actus, hoc habet per vim agentis."—ALEXANDER OF HALES, *In Metaph.*, L. vii., text 22. "Non omne acceptum," writes St. Thomas, "est receptum in aliquo subjecto; alioquin non posset dici quod tota substantia rei creatae sit accepta a Deo, cum totius substantiae non sit aliquod subjectum receptivum"—*Summa Theol.*, I., q. xxvii., art. ii., ad. 3um.

130.

Cf. MERCIER, *op. cit.*, § 49. Some of these doctrines we shall examine later, by way of illustration, in connexion with the *Unity* of being.

131.

Cf. URRABURU, *ibid.*, art. iii., Obj. 9, Resp.

132.

This view is advocated by, among others, Duns Scotus (1266-1308), Henry of Ghent († 1293), Francis de Vittoria (1480-1566), Dominicus de Soto (1496-1560), Molina (1535-1600), Fonseca (1548-97), and Scotists generally.

133. ARISTOTLE, *Metaph.*, lib. 5, text ii., cap. 6; ST. THOMAS, *in loc.* et alibi.

134. "Si ... modus entis accipiatur ... secundum divisionem unius ab altero, ... hoc exprimit hoc nomen *aliquid*, dicitur enim aliquid quasi *aliud quid.* Unde sicut ens dicitur *unum* inquantum est *indivisum in se*, ita dicitur *aliquid* inquantum est *ab aliis diversum.*"—ST. THOMAS, *De Veritate*, q. I, a. I.

135. "Nam omne ens est aut simplex, aut compositum. Quod autem est simplex, est indivisum et actu et potentia. Quod autem est compositum, non habet esse, quamdiu partes ejus sint divisae, sed postquam constituunt et componunt ipsum compositum. Unde manifestum est quod esse cujuslibet rei consistit in indivisione; et inde est, quod unumquodque sicut custodit suum esse, ita custodit suam unitatem."—ST. THOMAS, *Summa Theol.*, i., q. xi., a. I.

136. "Unum vero quod est principium numeri, addit supra substantiam *rationem mensurae*, quae est propria passio quantitatis, et primo invenitur in unitate. Et dicitur per privationem vel negationem divisionis, quae est secundum quantitatem continuam. *Nam numerus ex divisione continui causatur.*"—ST. THOMAS, *In Metaph.*, lib. 4, lect. 2, par. *b*.

137. Those who regard the distinction between the essence and the existence of an actually existing substance as real consider the latter as an *ens unum per se*. The existence of a real distinction between the essential constitutive factors of a composite substance is universally regarded by scholastics as compatible with essential unity—unitas *per se*—in the latter. Such factors are really distinct, and separable or divisible, but actually undivided. So also, the union of an individual nature and its subsistence forms a *unum per se* (unum *compositionis*) in the view of those who place a real distinction between these factors.

138. Of course essential unity of composition is also "natural". *Cf.* KLEUTGEN, *op. cit.*, §§ 631-8.

139. "Unum quod convertitur cum ente ponit quidem ipsum ens, sed nihil superaddit, nisi negationem divisionis. Multitudo autem ei correspondens addit supra res, quæ dicuntur multæ, quod unaquæque earum sit una, et quod una earum non sit altera.... Et sic, cum unum addat supra ens unam

negationem, secundum quod aliquid est indivisum in se, multitudo addit duas negationes, prout scilicet aliquid est in se indivisum, et prout est ab alio divisum, et unum eorum non esse alterum."—ST. THOMAS, *De Potent.*, q. 9, a. 7.

140.

"Sic ergo primo in intellectu nostro cadit *ens*, et deinde *divisio*, et post hoc *unum* quod divisionem privat, et ultimo *multitudo* quæ ex unitatibus constituitur."—ST. THOMAS, *In Metaph.*, lib. 10, lect. 4, par. *c.*

141.

Omnis pluralitas consequitur aliquam divisionem. Est autem duplex divisio: una materialis quæ fit secundum divisionem continui, et hanc sequitur numerus, qui est species quantitatis. Unde talis numerus, non est nisi in rebus materialibus habentibus quantitatem. Alia est divisio formalis, quæ fit per oppositas vel diversas formas: et hanc divisionem sequitur multitudo quæ non est in aliquo genere, sed est de transcendentibus, secundum quod ens dividitur per unum et multa. Et talem multitudinem solam contingit esse in rebus immaterialibus.—ST. THOMAS, *Summa Theol.*, i., q. xxx., art. 3.

142.

We may confine our attention here to substances, assuming for the present that accidents are individuated by the individual substances in which they inhere. We may note further that it is only corporeal individuals that fall directly within our experience. We can, of course, infer from the latter the actual existence of individual spiritual realities subsisting apart from matter, *viz.* human souls after death, and also the possibility of purely spiritual individual beings such as angels. But when we conceive these as individuals we must conceive them after the analogy of individuals in the domain of corporeal reality: it is only through concepts derived from this domain, and finding their *proper* application within it, that we can have any knowledge of suprasensible or spiritual realities, *viz.* by applying those concepts *analogically* to the latter.

143.

The "*formal-actual*" distinction, which Scotists advocate between these grades of being, we shall examine later.

144.

Cf. URRABURU, *op. cit.*, p. 280: "Principium ... intrinsicum vel formale est aliquid insitum rei, pertinensque ad intrinsecam et ultimam individui constitutionem, et fundans formalitatem illam, quae *individitatio* dicitur. Sicut enim materia est in homine, v.g. principium et fundamentum propter quod est, ac praedicatur *materialis*, et forma fundat in eodem praedicatum *rationalis*, totaque natura composita, *humanitas*, praedicatum *hominis*; ita quaerimus quid sit illud primum principium, unde existit in quovis individuo sua peculiaris ac propria individuatio."

145.

In ancient Greece the Eleatics argued against the possibility of real plurality somewhat in this wise: If there were really different beings any two of them would differ from each other only by some third reality, and this again from each of the former by a fourth and a fifth reality, and so on *ad infinitum*: which would involve the absurdities of infinite number and infinite regress. A similar argument was used by the medieval pantheist, David of Dinant, to identify God with the material principle of corporeal reality: God and primary matter exist and do not differ; therefore they are identical: for if they differed they should differ by something distinct from either, and this again should differ from both by something distinct from all three, and so on *ad infinitum*: which is absurd. Such sophisms arise from accepting the purely abstract view of reality as adequate. We have seen already, in dealing with the abstract notion of being, that from this point of view it must be recognized and admitted that the reality whereby things differ (*viz.* being) is also the reality wherein they agree (*viz.* being, also). The paradox is restated below in regard to individuation.

146.

Materia ... dupliciter accipitur, scilicet, ut signata et non signata. Et dicitur signata, secundum quod consideratur cum determinatione dimensionum harum scilicet vel illarum; non signata autem, quæ sine determinatione dimensionum consideratur. Secundum hoc igitur est sciendum, quod materia signata est individuationis principium.—ST. THOMAS, *De Veritate*, q. ii., art. 6, ad. 7[am].

147.

Cf. URRABURU, *op. cit.*, Disp. ii., cap. 2, § iii., pp. 271-3.

148.

These will easily be found in any of the fuller scholastic treatises. *Cf.* URRABURU, *op. cit.*, Disp. ii., cap. 2, art. 4. *Philosophia Lacencis, Logica*, §§ 1282 *sqq.*; MERCIER, *Ontologie*, §§ 36-42; KLEUTGEN, *Philosophie Scolastique*, §§ 610 *sqq.*; BULLIAT, *Thæsaurus Philosophiæ Thomisticae* (Nantes, 1899), pp. 171 *sqq.*—a useful book of reference for the teaching of St. Thomas.

149.

A kindred view to this is the view that subsistence ("*subsistentia*," "*suppositalitas*") or personality ("*personalitas*") is the principle of individuation. We shall see later in what subsistence or personality is supposed to consist. Here it is sufficient to observe that the individual nature as such has not necessarily subsistence or personality; hence it cannot be individuated by this latter.

150.

The consistent attitude for the Thomist here would, however, appear to be a denial that such a thing would be intrinsically possible.

151.

Hujusmodi relatio non potest consistere nisi in quodam ordine, quem ratio adinvenit alicujus ad seipsum secundum aliquas ejus duas considerationes.—ST. THOMAS, *Summa Theol.*, i., q. xxviii., art. 3, ad. 2^{am}.

152.

Cf. Science of Logic, vol. i., § 59.

153.

It is only the concrete and individual that as such can exist actually; the abstract and universal as such cannot exist actually: abstractness and universality are mental modes—*entia rationis*—annexed by the mind to the real content of its concepts: considered as thought-objects they are themselves not real entities: they do not affect reality as given to us in our experience. But perhaps concreteness and individuality are also mere mental modes, affecting reality not as given to us in our experience but only as subjected to the process of intellectual conception, or at least as subjected to the process of sense perception? This would appear to be part of the general Kantian theory of knowledge: that we can apprehend reality as concrete and individual only because space and time, which characterize the concrete and individual mode of being, are mental modes which must be applied to reality as a prerequisite condition for rendering the latter capable of apprehension in our experience. This contention is examined in another context..

154.

Thus the recognition of a virtual distinction in a being is a sign of the *relative perfection* of the latter: the being involves in its higher sort of unity perfections elsewhere dispersed and separate. The being is of a higher order than if the principles of these perfections in it were really distinct from one another. But the virtual distinction also seems to imply a *relative imperfection* when it is found in creatures, inasmuch as here the thought-objects so distinguished are always principles of a plurality of really distinct accidental perfections: and real plurality in a being is less perfect than unity.—*Cf.* KLEUTGEN, *op. cit.*, § 633.

155.

"Omnis cognitio est a potentia et objecto, sive a cognoscente et cognito. Ratio a priori est, quia omnis cognitio saltem creata est expressio et imitatio atque imago vitalis objecti. Inquantum igitur est vitalis, procedit a cognoscente; implicat enim cognoscentem vivere per aliquid, quod ab ipso non est, sed pure illud recipit ab alio mere passive se habendo; inquantum vero cognitio est expressio, imitatio et imago objecti, procedit ab objecto"—SILVESTER MAURUS, *Quaest. Philos.*, q. 2. This is the common scholastic distinction: cognition as a product representative or expressive of reality is a product determined by the influence of reality (as active) on the mind (as passive); cognition as a vital process is active, a reaction of mind to the influence of reality. It may be remarked, however, that the cognitive process, as vital, has always a positive term. Our cognitive processes are partly at least processes of abstracting, comparing, relating, universalizing: processes which produce "*intentiones logicas*" or "*entia rationis*," such as the "*intentio universalitatis*" the relation of subject to predicate, and other logical relations and logical distinctions: and hence arises the difficulty, when we come to reflect on our cognitive experience, of discriminating between these "logical entities" and the reality which we interpret by means of them: of discriminating, in other words, between logical and real distinctions.

156.

It is not necessary of course that this implicit embodiment of all the others, by any one of them, be seen to be *mutual*. It is sufficient, for instance, that of the concepts *a, b, c* and *d, a* be seen implicitly to involve *b, b* to involve *c*, etc., though not *vice versa*. However, it must be remarked that in the exercise of *thought* upon its *abstract* objects we feel something wanting to our intellectual insight as long as the relations we apprehend are not *reciprocal*. In the sciences of abstract quantity we approximate to the ideal of establishing reciprocal relations throughout the whole system of the concepts analysed. But abstract thought does not give us an adequate apprehension of the real: it represents reality only under the *static* aspect, and as *abstract, i.e.* apart from the individualizing conditions of time and space which affect its *concrete, actual existence* as revealed in sense experience. Were we to neglect the latter, and consider merely what abstract thought gives us, we should regard as *really one* what is *one for thought*. But what is one for thought is *the universal*; and the logical issue of holding the universal as such to be real is monism. Or again, to put the matter in another way, in so far as intellect sees the objects of its various abstract concepts to involve one another necessarily, it has no reason—as long as it ignores the verdict of sense experience on the real manifoldness of actually existing being—to abstain from attributing a *real unity* to the whole system of abstract thought-objects which it contemplates as reciprocally and necessarily interrelated. On the contrary, it should pronounce that whatever plurality can be unified by the dialectically necessary relations discovered by thought, is *really one*, and must be regarded as *one reality*: which, again, is monism. But a philosophy which thus ignores sense experience must be one-sided and misleading.

157.

Cf. URRABURU, *op. cit.*, Disp. ii., cap. ii., art. 5 (p. 319).

158.

Cf. infra, § 83.

159.

Cf. URRABURU, *op. cit., ibid.* p. 322.

160.

ST. THOMAS, *De Ente et Essentia*, cap. iv.: "Ideo, si quaeratur utrum ista natura possit dici una vel plures, neutrum concedendum est: quia utrumque est extra intellectum [conceptum] humanitatis, et utrumque potest sibi accidere. Si enim pluralitas esset de ratione ejus, nunquam posset esse una: cum tamen una sit secundum quod est in Sorte. Similiter si unitas esset de intellectu et ratione ejus, tunc esset una et eadem natura Sortis et Platonis, nec posset in pluribus plurificari." *Cf.* ZIGLIARA, *Summa Philos., Ontologia* (I), iv., v.; (3) iv.

161.

"Licet enim (natura) nunquam sit sine aliquo istorum, non tamen est de se aliquod istorum, ita etiam in rerum natura secundum illam entitatem habet verum 'esse' extra animam reale: et secundum illam entitatem habet unitatem sibi proportionabilem, quae est indifferens ad singularitatem, ita quod non, repugnat illi unitati de se, quod cum quacumque unitate singularitatis ponatur."—SCOTUS, *In L. Sent.*, 2, dist. iii., q. 7.—*Cf.* DE WULF, *History of Medieval Philosophy*, p. 372.

162.

Cf. Science of Logic, ii., § 248. *Moral* truth or veracity—the conformity of language with thought—is treated in Ethics.

163.

Cf. MERCIER, *Ontologie*, P. ii., § 4, i.

164.

Cf. Science of Logic, ii., §§ 252-4.

165.

"Si omnis intellectus (quod est impossibile) intelligeretur auferri, nullo modo ratio veritatis remaneret."—ST. THOMAS, *De Veritate*, q. i., art I, 2 in fine.

166.

Cf. ST. THOMAS, *De Veritate*, q. i., and *passim*.

167.

ST. THOMAS, *De Veritate*, q. i., art. 2.

168.

169. ST. THOMAS, *De Veritate*, q. i., art. 4; *Summa Theol.*, i., q. 16, art. 6.

170. "Si intellectus humanus non esset, adhuc res dicerentur veræ in ordine ad intellectum divinum. Sed si uterque intellectus, quod est impossibile, intelligeretur auferri, nullo modo ratio veritatis remaneret."—ST. THOMAS, *De Veritate*, q. i., art. 2.

171. "Si ergo accipiatur veritas *rei* secundum ordinem ad intellectum divinum, tunc quidem mutatur veritas rei mutablis in aliam veritatem, non in falsitatem."—ST. THOMAS, *ibid.* q. i., art. 6.

172. *Cf.* ARISTOTLE, *De Anima*, iii.; ST. THOMAS, *De Veritate*, q. i., art. 1.

173. "Res per se non fallunt, sed per accidens. Dant enim occasionem falsitatis; eo quod similitudinem eorum gerunt quorum non habent existentiam.... Res notitiam sui facit in anima per ea quae de ipsa exterius apparent ... et ideo quando in aliqua re apparent sensibiles qualitates demonstrantes naturam quae eis non subest, dicitur res illa esse falsa.... Nec tamen res est hoc modo causa falsitatis in anima, quod necessario falsitatem causat."—ST. THOMAS, *Summa Theol.*, i., q. 17, art. 1, ad. 2; *De Veritate*, q. i., art. 10, c.

174. Καλῶς ἀπεφήναντο τἀγαθὸν, οὗ πάντα ἐφίεται.—ARISTOTLE, *Eth.*, i.

175. *Cf. Science of Logic*, ii., § 217.

176. "Bonum autem, cum habeat notionem appetibilis, importat habitudinem causæ finalis."—ST. THOMAS, *Summa Theol.*, i., q. 5, art. 2, ad. 1.

177. "Prima autem non possunt notificari per aliqua priora, sed notificantur per posteriora, sicut causæ per proprios effectus. Cum autem bonum proprie sit motivum appetitus, describitur bonum per motum appetitus, sicut solet manifestari vis motiva per motum. Et ideo dicit (Aristoteles) quod philosophi bene enunciaverunt bonum esse id quod omnia appetunt."—ST. THOMAS, *Comment. in Eth. Nich.*, i., lect. 1ª.

The "end," which is last in the order of actual attainment, is first as the ideal term of the aim or tendency of the nature: *finis est ultimus in executione, sed primus in intentione*: it is that for the sake of which, and with a view to which, the whole process of actualization or "perfecting" goes on. *Cf. infra*, § 108.

178.

"Licet bonum et ens sint idem secundum rem; quia tamen differunt secundum rationem, non eodem modo dicitur aliquid ens simpliciter et bonum simpliciter. Nam, cum ens dicat aliquid esse in actu, actus autem proprie ordinem habeat ad potentiam, secundum hoc simpliciter aliquid dicitur esse ens secundum quod primo secernitur ab eo quod est in potentia tantum; hoc autem est esse substantiale rei uniuscujusque. Unde per suum esse substantiale dicitur unumquodque ens simpliciter; per actus autem superadditos dicitur aliquid esse secundum quid.... Sic ergo secundum primum esse, quod est substantiale, dicitur aliquid ens simpliciter et bonum secundum quid, id est, inquantum est ens; secundum vero ultimum actum dicitur aliquid ens secundum quid, et bonum simpliciter."—ST. THOMAS, *Summa Theol.*, i., q. 5, art. I, ad. I.

179.

"Respectus ... qui importatur nomine boni est *habitudo perfectivi* secundum quodaliquid natum est perficere non solum secundum rationem speciei [*i.e.* the abstract essence], sed secundum esse quod habet in rebus; hoc enim modo finis perficit ea quae sunt ad finem."—ST. THOMAS, *De Veritate*, q. 26, art. 6.

180.

Cf. the familiar ethical distinction between objective, and formal or subjective happiness, *beatitudo objectiva* and *beatitudo formalis seu subjectiva*.

181.

"In motu appetitus, id quod est appetibile terminans motum appetitus secundum quid, ut medium per quod tenditur in aliud, vocatur *utile*. Id autem quod appetitur ut ultimum terminans totaliter motum appetitus sicut quaedam res in quam per se appetitus tendit, vocatur *honestum*; quia honestum dicitur quod per se desideratur. Id autem quod terminat motum appetitus, ut quies in se desiderata, est *delectabile*."—ST. THOMAS, *Summa Theol.*, i., q. 5, art. 3.

182.

Excellentia hominis maxime consideratur secundum virtutem, quae est dis positio perfecti ad optimum, ut dicitur in 6 Physic. Et ideo, honestum, *proprie loquendo*, in idem refertur cum virtute.—*ibid.*, 2^a 2^{ae}, q. 145, art. I, c.

183.

"Eorum quae propter se apprehenduntur, quaedam apprehenduntur solum propter se, et nunquam propter aliud, sicut felicitas, quae est ultimus finis; quaedam vero apprehenduntur et propter se, in quantum habent in seipsis aliquam rationem bonitatis, etiamsi nihil aliud boni per ea nobis accideret, et tamen sunt appetibilia propter aliud, in quantum scilicet perducunt nos

184.
    in aliquod bonum perfectius: et hoc modo virtutes sunt propter se apprehendendae."—*ibid.*, ad I.

185.
    Cf. MERCIER, *op. cit.*, p. 236.

186.
    "Omnia ... quae jam habent esse, illud esse suum naturaliter amant, et ipsam tota virtute conservant.... Ipsum igitur esse habet rationem boni. Unde sicut impossibile est quod sit aliquod ens quod non habeat esse, ita necesse est quod omne ens sit bonum ex hoc ipso quod habet esse."—ST. THOMAS, *De Veritate*, q. 21, art. 2, c.

187.
    "Non-esse secundum se non est appetibile, sed per accidens, inquantum scilicet ablatio alicujus mali est appetibilis; quod malum quidem aufertur per non-esse; ablatio vero mali non est appetibilis, nisi inquantum per malum privatur quoddam esse. Illud igitur, quod per se est appetibile, est esse; non-esse vero, per accidens tantum, inquantum scilicet quoddam esse appetitur, quo homo non sustinet privari; et sic etiam per accidens non-esse dicitur bonum."—ST. THOMAS, *Summa Theol.*, i., q. 5, art. 2, ad. 3.

188.
    "Malum est defectus boni quod natum est et debet haberi."—ST. THOMAS, *Summa Theol.*, i., q. 49, art. I, c.

189.
    ibid.

190.
    "Causam formalem malum non habet, sed est magis privatio formae."—St. THOMAS, *Summa Theol.*, i., q. 49, art. I, c.

191.
    "Nec causam finalem habet malum, sed magis est privatio ordinis ad debitum finem."—*ibid.*

192.
    "Non est causa efficiens sed *deficiens* mali, quia malum non est effectio sed *defectio*."—*De Civ. Dei*, xii., 7.

193.
    "O, altitudo divitiarum sapientiae, et scientiae Dei! Quam incomprehensibilia sunt judicia ejus, et investigabiles viae ejus!"—Rom. xi., 33.

194.
    Connected with the transcendental notion of unity is another concept, that of *order*, which will be more fully examined when we come to treat of causes.

BAUMGARTEN, a German philosopher of the eighteenth century, was the first to use the term *Aesthetica* in this sense.

195.

"Dicendum est quod pulchrum est idem bono sola ratione differens. Cum enim bonum sit quod omnia appetunt, de ratione boni est, quod in eo quietetur appetitus; sed ad rationem pulchri attinet quod *in ejus aspectu seu cognitione* quietetur appetitus; unde et illi sensus præcipue respiciunt pulchrum, qui maxime cognoscitivi sunt, scilicet visus et auditus rationi deservientes; dicimus enim pulchra visibilia et pulchros sonos; in sensibilibus autem aliorum sensuum non utimur nomine pulchritudinis; non enim dicimus pulchros sapores, aut odores."—ST. THOMAS, *Summa Theol.*, iª. iiæ., q. 27, art. I, ad. 3.

196.

"Ad rationem pulchri pertinet, quod in ejus aspectu seu *cognitione* quietetur appetitus ... ita quod pulchrum dicatur id, cujus ipsa *apprehensio* placet."—ST. THOMAS, *Summa Theol.*, iª. iiæ., q. 27, art. I, ad. 3. And the Angelic Doctor justifies the extended use of the term *vision*: "De aliquo nomine dupliciter convenit loqui, uno modo secundum ejus primam impositionem, alio modo secundum usum nominis, sicut patet in nomine *visionis*, quod primo impositum est ad significandum actum sensus visus; sed propter dignitatem et certitudinem hujus sensus extensum est hoc nomen, secundum usum loquentium, ad omnem *cognitionem aliorum* sensuum; dicimus enim: Vide quomodo sapit, vel quomodo redolet, vel quomodo est calidum; et ulterius etiam ad *cognitionem intellectus*, secundum illud Matt. v. 8: Beati mundi corde quoniam ipsi Deum videbunt."—i., q. 67, art. I, c.

197.

"Pulchrum et bonum in subjecto quidem sunt idem, quia super eandem rem fundantur, scilicet super formam, et propter hoc bonum laudatur ut pulchrum: sed ratione differunt: nam bonum proprie respicit appetitum: ... et ideo habet rationem finis.... Pulchrum autem respicit vim cognoscitivam: pulchra enim dicuntur quæ visa placent."—ST. THOMAS, *Summa Theol.*, i., q. 5, art. 4, ad. I.

198.

Cf. DE WULF, *La Valeur esthétique de la moralité dans l'art*, pp. 28-9.

199.

L'Art et la Morale, p. 29.

200.

De la connaissance de Dieu et de soi-même, ch. i., § 8.

201.

De Vera Religione, c. 32.

202.

202. *Cf.* POINCARÉ, *Conférence sur les rapports de l'analyse et de la physique mathematique.—apud* MERCIER, *Ontologie*, § 274, pp. 546-7 n.

203. When the object so excels in greatness or grandeur as to exceed more or less our capacity to realize it we speak of it as *sublime*. The sublime calls forth emotions of self-abasement, reverence, and even fear. If an object possessing the other requisites of beauty is wanting in due magnitude, we describe it as *pretty* or *elegant*. The terms *grace*, *graceful*, apply especially to gait, gesture, movement.

204. On this point all the great philosophers are unanimous. For Plato, beauty whether of soul or of body, whether of animate or of inanimate things, results not from chance, but from order, rectitude, art: οὐχ οὕτως εἰκῇ κάλλιστα παραγίγνεται ἀλλὰ τάξει καὶ ὀρθότητι καὶ τέχνῃ, ἥτις ἑκάστῳ ἀποδέδοται αὐτῶν (Plato, *Gorg.* 506D). Aristotle places beauty in grandeur and order: Τὸ γὰρ καλὸν ἐν μεγέθει καὶ τάξει ἐστί (*Poetics*, ch. viii., n. 8). Τοῦ δὲ καλοῦ μέγιστα εἴδη τάξις καὶ συμμετρία καὶ τὸ ὡρισμένον (*Metaph.*, xii., ch. iii., n. 11). "Nihil," writes St. Augustine, "est ordinatum quod non sit pulchrum." "Pulchra," says St. Thomas, "dicuntur quae visa placent; unde pulchrum in debita proportione consistit" (*Summa Theol.*, i., q. 5, art. 4, ad. 1).

205. "Ad pulchritudinem tria requiruntur; primo quidem integritas sive perfectio; quae enim diminuta sunt, hoc ipso turpia sunt; et debita proportio sive consonantia; et iterum claritas."—*Summa Theol.*, i., q. 39, art. 8, c. Elsewhere he omits integrity, supposing it implied in order: "ad rationem pulchri sive decori concurrit et claritas et debita proportio". And elsewhere again he omits clarity, this being a necessary effect of order: "pulchrum in debita proportione consistit".

206. By "natural perfection" is meant the perfection which a nature acquires by the realization of its end : Τέλειον δὲ τὸ ἔχον τέλος (Aristotle).

207. This definition coincides with that found in a medieval scholastic treatise *De Pulchro et Bono*, attributed to St. Thomas or Albertus Magnas: "Ratio pulchri in universali consistit in resplendentia formae super partes materiae proportionatas, vel super diversas vires vel actiones." *Cf.* MERCIER, *Ontologie*, p. 554.

208.

209. *L'Idée du beau dans la philosophie de S. Thomas d'Aquin*, p. 2.

210. *Du Vrai, du Beau et du Bien*, viie leçon.

211. *Kritik der Urtheilskraft*, Th. i., Abschn. I, B. I, passim.

212. "Omnis corporea creatura ... bonum est infimum, *et in genere suo pulchrum* quoniam forma et specie continetur."—ST. AUGUSTINE, *De Vera Relig.*, c. 20.

213. At the same time it must be borne in mind that many of the judgments by which things are pronounced "ugly" or "commonplace" are erroneous. This is partly because they are based on first and superficial sense impressions: beauty must be apprehended and judged by the *intellect*, and by the intellect "informed" with genuine knowledge; to the eye of enlightened intelligence there are beauties of structure and organization in the beetle or the tadpole as well as in the peacock or the spaniel. It is partly, too, because we unconsciously or semi-consciously apply standards of human beauty to beings that are merely animal: "To know really whether there are ugly monkeys we should have to consult a monkey; for the beauty we unconsciously look for, and certainly do not find, in the monkey, is the beauty of the human form; and when we declare the monkey ugly what we really mean is that it would be ugly if it were a human being; which is undeniable."—SULLY-PRUDHOMME, *L'Expression dans les beaux arts*, p. 104.

214. Proverbs, xxxi. 30.

215. ST. THOMAS, *Summa Theol.*, i[a], ii[ae], q. 57, art. 3, c.

216. *Cf. Science of Logic*, i., §§ 70 *sqq.*

217. *Cf.* WINDELBAND, *History of Philosophy* (tr. Tufts), *Introduction*.

218. *Cf. Science of Logic*, ii. P. iv., ch. v.

219. *Metaph.*, vi., 1.

220. *Cf.* ST. THOMAS, *Summa Theol.*, i., q. 90, art. 2: "Illud proprie dicitur esse quod ipsum habet esse quasi in suo esse subsistens. Unde *solæ substantiæ proprie et vere dicuntur entia*; accidens vero non habet esse sed eo aliquid est, et hac ratione ens dicitur ... accidens dicitur *magis entis quam ens.*"

221. *In Metaph.*, L. v., lect. 9; cf. *In Physic.*, L. iii., lect. 5.

222. *Science of Logic*, i., §§ 71, 73-76.

223. *ibid.*, §§ 74, 76.

224. Cf. URRABURU, *op. cit.*, § 268 (p. 668); MERCIER, *Logique*, § 33 (4th edit., p. 99).

225. Cf. ST. THOMAS, *In Metaph.*, L. xi., lect. 9: "Sed sciendum est quod prædicamenta diversificantur secundum diversos modos prædicandi. Unde idem, secundum quod diversimode de diversis prædicatur, ad diversa prædicamenta pertinet.... Similiter motus secundum quod prædicatur de subjecto in quo est, constituit prædicamentum passionis. Secundum autem quod prædicatur de eo a quo est, constituit prædicamentum actionis."

226. *Ontologie*, § 138 (3rd edit., p. 263).

227. Cf. *Essay concerning Human Understanding*, book iv., ch. vi., § 11: "Had we such ideas of substances, as to know what real constitutions produce those sensible qualities we find in them, and how these qualities flowed from thence, we could, by the specific ideas of their real essences in our own minds, more certainly find out their properties, and discover what properties they had or had not, than we can now by our senses: and to know the properties of gold, it would be no more necessary that gold should exist, than it is necessary for the knowing the properties of a triangle, that the triangle should exist in any matter; the idea in our minds would serve for the one as well as the other."

228. "Sensation convinces us that there are solid, extended substances; and reflection, that there are thinking ones: experience assures us of the existence of such beings."—*ibid.*, book ii., ch. xxiii., § 29. Locke protested repeatedly against the charge that he denied the existence of substances.

The notion one has of pure substance is "only a supposition of he knows not what support of such qualities, which are capable of producing simple ideas in us; which qualities are commonly called accidents.... The idea then we have, to which we give the general name substance, being nothing but the supposed, but unknown support of those qualities we find existing, which we imagine cannot subsist, 'sine re substante,' without something to support them, we call that support *substantia*."—book ii., ch. xxiii., § 2. In the following passage we may detect the idealistic insinuation that knowledge reaches only to "ideas" or mental states, not to the extramental reality, the "secret, abstract nature of substance": "Whatever therefore be the secret abstract nature of substance in general, all the ideas we have of particular distinct sorts of substances, are nothing but several combinations of simple ideas, co-existing in such, though unknown, cause of their union, as makes the whole subsist of itself". It belongs, of course, to the Theory of Knowledge, not to the Theory of Being, to show how groundless the idealistic assumption is.

229.

Inquiring into the causes of our "impressions" and "ideas," he admits the existence of "bodies" which cause them and "minds" which experience them: "We may well ask, *What causes induce us to believe in the existence of body*? but 'tis vain to ask, *Whether there be body or not*? That is a point, which we must take for granted in all our reasonings."— *A Treatise on Human Nature*, Part iv., § ii.

230.

Of the definition of a substance as *something which may exist by itself*, he says: "this definition agrees to everything that can possibly be conceiv'd; and will never serve to distinguish substance from accident, or the soul from its perceptions.... Since all our perceptions are different from each other, and from everything else in the universe, they are also distinct and separable, and may be consider'd as separately existent, and may exist separately, and have no need of anything else to support their existence. They are, therefore, substances, as far as this definition explains a substance."—*ibid.*, § v. "We have no perfect idea of substance, but ... taking it for *something that can exist by itself*, 'tis evident every perception is a substance, and every distinct part of a perception a distinct substance."—*ibid.*

231.

Cf. MERCIER, *op. cit.*, § 142 (p. 272).

232.

Cf. KLEUTGEN, *op. cit.*, Dissert. vi., ch. iii., li, § 592.

233.

Assuming for the moment that we can know substance to be not *one* but *manifold*: that experience reveals to us a plurality of numerically or *really*, and even specifically and generically, distinct substances..

234.

Cf. HUXLEY, *Hume*, bk. ii., ch. ii. TAINE, *De L'Intelligence*, t. i., Preface, and *passim*.

235.

Cf. § 65, *infra*.

236.

Such terms as "corruptible," "destructible," etc., imply certain attributes *of a thing* which can be corrupted, destroyed. Conceiving this attribute in the abstract we form the terms "corruptibility," "destructibility," etc. So, too, the term "possibility" formed from the adjective "possible," simply implies in the abstract what the latter implies in the concrete—an active or passive power *of a thing* to cause or to become something; or else the mind's conception of the non-repugnance of this something. To substantialize a possibility, therefore, is sufficiently absurd; but to speak of a possibility as real and at the same time to deny the reality of any subject in which it would have its reality, is no less so.

237.

except in the Blessed Eucharist: here we know from Divine Revelation that the accidents of bread and wine exist apart from their connatural substance. We cannot, by the light of reason, prove *positively* the possibility of such separate existence of accidents; at the most, men of the supreme genius of an Aristotle may have strongly suspected such possibility, and may have convinced themselves of the futility of all attempts to prove in any way the impossibility of such a condition of things. Nor can we, even with the light of Revelation, do any more than show the futility of such attempts, thus *negatively* defending the possibility of what we know from Revelation to be a fact.

238.

Cf. n. 1.

239.

Cf. MAHER, *Psychology*, ch. xxii., for a full analysis and refutation of phenomenist theories that would deny the substantiality of the human person.

240.

"Substantia est res, cujus naturae debetur esse non in alio; accidens vero est res, cujus naturae debetur esse in alio."—*Quodlib.*, ix., a. 5, ad. 2.

241.

Cf. DESCARTES, *Oeuvres*, edit. Cousin, tome ix., p. 166—*apud* MERCIER, *Ontologie*, p. 280.

242.

PAULSEN, *Einleitung in die Philosophie*, Berlin, 1896, S. 135—*apud* MERCIER, *loc. cit.*

243.

and also *appetitive*; as in mental life appetition is a natural consequent of perception. It is in accordance with this latter idea that Wundt conceives all reality as being in its ultimate nature appetitive activity: the *Ego* is a "volitional unit" and the universe a "collection of volitional units".—*Cf.* WUNDT, *System der Philosophie*, Leipzig, 1889, S. 415-421.

244.

Principles of Psychology, Pt. ii., ch. i., § 59.

245.

But from Descartes' doctrine of two passive substances so antithetically opposed to each other the transition to Spinozism was easy and obvious. If mind and matter are so absolutely opposed as thought and extension, how can they unite to form one human individual in man? If both are purely passive, and if God alone puts into them their conscious states and their mechanical movements respectively, what remains proper to each but a pure passivity that would really be common to both? Would it not be more consistent then to refer this thought-essence or receptivity of conscious activities, and this extension-essence or receptivity of mechanical movements, to God as their proper source, to regard them as two attributes of His unique and self-existent substance, and thus to regard God as substantially immanent in all phenomena, and these as only different expressions of His all-pervading essence? This is what Spinoza did; and his monism in one form or other is the last word of many contemporary philosophers on the nature of the universe which constitutes the totality of human experience.—*Cf.* HÖFFDING, *Outlines of Psychology*, ch. ii., and criticism of same *apud* MAHER, *Psychology*, ch. xxiii.

246.

"Esse substantiæ non dependet ab esse alterius sicut ei inhærens, licet omnia dependeant a Deo sicut a causa prima."—ST. THOMAS, *De Causa Materiæ*, cap. viii.

247.

Cf. KLEUTGEN, *op. cit.* § 594.

248.

Ibid., §§ 597-600.

249.

"Illud proprie dicitur esse, quod ipsum habet esse, quasi in suo esse subsistens. Unde solæ substantiæ proprie et vere dicuntur entia; accidens vero non habet esse, sed eo aliquid est, et hac ratione ens dicitur: sicut albedo dicitur ens quia ea aliquid est album. Et propter hoc dicitur in *Metaph.*, l. 7 [al. 6], c. i. [Arist.], quod accidens dicitur magis entis quam ens."—ST. THOMAS, *Summa Theol.*, i. q. 90, art. 2. "Illud cui advenit accidens, est ens in se completum consistens in suo esse, quod quidem esse naturaliter præcedit accidens, quod supervenit: et ideo accidens superveniens, ex conjunctione sui cum eo, cui supervenit, non causat illud esse in quo res subsistit per quod res est ens per se: sed causat quoddam esse secundum, sine quo res subsistens intelligi potest esse, sicut primum potest intelligi sine secundo, vel prædicatum sine subjecto. Unde ex accidente et subjecto non fit unum per se, sed unum per accidens, et ideo ex eorum conjunctione non resultat essentia quædam, sicut ex conjunctione formæ cum materia: propter quod accidens neque rationem completæ essentiæ habet, neque pars completæ essentiæ est, sed sicut est ens secundum quid, ita et essentiam secundum quid habet."—*De Ente et Essentia*, ch. vii.

250.

"Non est definitio substantiæ, ens per se sine subjecto, nec definitio accidentis, ens in subjecto; sed quidditati seu essentiæ substantiæ *competit* habere *esse* non in subjecto; quidditati autem sive essentiæ accidentis *competit* habere *esse* in subjecto."—ST. THOMAS, *Summa Theol.*, iii., q. 77, art. I, ad. 2.

251.

Cf. KLEUTGEN, *op. cit.*, §§ 595-596.

252.

ibid., § 619.

253.

Cf. URRABURU, *op. cit.*, §§ 320-325.

254.

KLEUTGEN, *op. cit.*, §§ 618, 624.

255.

This logical usage is applied equally to attributes of a logical subject which is not itself a substance but an accident; it turns solely on the point whether the concept of the logical predicate of a judgment is or is not connected by an absolute logical connexion, a connexion of thought, with the concept of the logical subject.

256.

Cf. ST. THOMAS, *Quaest. Disp., De Spir. Creat.*, art. II, ad. 7.

257.

Cf., however, § 68, p. 246, n. 2, *infra.*

258.

St. Thomas, whose language is usually so moderate, thus expresses his view of the doctrine afterwards propounded by Descartes when the latter declared the essence of the soul to be thought: "Quidquid dicatur de potentiis animae, tamen nullus unquam opinatur, nisi insanus, quod habitus et actus animae sint ipsa ejus essentia."—*Quaest. Disp., De Spir. Creat.*, art. II, ad I. For a very convincing treatment of this question, *cf.* KLEUTGEN, *op. cit.*, §§ 625-626.

259.

DE SAN, *Cosmologia*, § 323, *apud* MERCIER, *op. cit.*, § 158.

260.

op. cit., § 625.

261.
St. Thomas, *Summa Theol.*, iii., q. 17, art. 2, c.

262.
Hence St. Thomas says, in regard to the Blessed Eucharist, that the accidents of bread and wine had not an existence of their own as long as the substance of bread and wine was there; that this is true of accidents generally; that it is not they that exist, but rather their subjects; that their function is to determine these subjects to exist as characterized in a certain way, as whiteness gives snow a white existence: "Dicendum quod accidentia panis et vini, manente substantia panis et vini non habebant ipsa *esse* sicut nec alia accidentia, sed subjecta eorum habebant hujusmodi *esse* per ea, sicut nix est alba per albedinem."—*Summa Theol.*, iii., q. 77, art. I, ad. 4.

263.
For the arguments on both sides *cf.* Mercier, *Ontologie*, § 156 (pp. 308 *sqq.*). The indirect argument which the author derives from the fact that the Divine *Concursus* is necessary for the activity of creatures, while offering an intelligible explanation of this necessity on Thomistic principles, does not touch the probability of other explanations.

264.
Cf. Urraburu's definition: "entitas vel realitas a subjecto realiter distincta, cujus totum esse consistit in ultima determinatione rei ad aliquod munus obeundum, vel ad aliquam realem denominationem actu habendam, sine qua, saltem in individuo sumpta, res eadem potest existere absolute".—*op. cit.*, § 120 (p. 380).

265.
Cf. Urraburu, *op. cit.*, § 291 (p. 854, *quarta opinio*), p. 854.

266.
Whether immanent vital acts—especially of the spiritual faculties in man: thoughts, volitions, etc.—are mere modes, or whether they are absolute accidents, having their own proper and positive reality which perfects their subject by affecting it, is a disputed question. Habits, acquired by repetition of such acts, *e.g.* knowledge and virtue, belonging as they do to the category of quality, are more than mere modalities of the human subject: they have an absolute, positive entity, whereby they add to the total perfection of the latter.

267.
Cf. Urraburu, *op. cit.*, § 121 (pp. 386 *sqq.*).

268.
The fact that Aristotle [*Metaph.*, lib. vii. (al. vi.), ch. iii.] seems to have placed a *real distinction* between extension and corporeal substance, while he could not have suspected the absolute *separability* of the former from

269. Obviously we are not concerned herewith *all* the attributes which by a necessity of thought we ascribe to an essence, *e.g.* the *corruptibility* of a corporeal substance, or the *immortality* of a spiritual substance. These are not entities really distinct from the substance, but only aspects which we recognize to be necessary corollaries of its nature. We are concerned only with properties which are real powers, faculties, forces, aptitudes of things.—*Cf.* KLEUTGEN, *op. cit.*, § 627.

270. *op. cit.*, § 628.

271. "Tertii sunt, qui dicunt, quod potentiae animae nec adeo sunt idem ipsi animae, sicut sunt ejus principia intrinsica et essentialia, nec adeo diversae, ut cedant in aliud genus, sicut accidentia; sed in genere substantiae sunt per reductionem ... et ideo quasi medium tenentes inter utramque opinionem dicunt, quasdam animae potentias sic differre ad invicem, ut nullo modo dici possint una potentia: non tamen concedunt, eas simpliciter diversificari secundum essentiam, ita ut dicantur diversae essentiae, sed differre essentialiter in genere potentiae, ita ut dicantur diversa instrumenta ejusdem substantiae."—*In lib.* ii., dist. xxiv., p. I, art. 2, q. I.

In the same context he explains what we are to understand by referring anything to a certain category *per reductionem*: "Sunt enim quaedam, quae sunt in genere *per se*, aliqua *per reductionem* ad idem genus. Illa per se sunt in genere, quae participant essentiam completam generis, ut species et individua; illa vero per reductionem, quae nan dicunt completam essentiam.... Quaedam reducuntur sicut principia ... aut essentialia, sicut sunt materia et forma in genere substantiae; aut integrantia, sicut partes substantiae.... Quaedam reducuntur sicut *viae* ... aut sicut *viae ad res*, et sic motus et mutationes, ut generatio, reducuntur ad substantiam; aut sicut *viae a rebus*, et sic habent reduci potentiae ad genus substantiae. Prima enim agendi potentia, quae egressum dicitur habere ab ipsa substantia, ad idem genus reducitur, quae non adeo elongatur ab ipsa substantia, ut dicat aliam essentiam completam."—*ibid.*, ad. 8.

272. "Quoniam potentia creaturae arctata est, non potuit creatura habere posse perfectum, nisi esset in ea potentiarum multitudo, ex quarum collectione

273.
    sive adunatione, una supplente defectum alterius, resultaret unum posse completum, sicut manifeste animadverti potest in organis humani corporis, quorum unumquodque indiget a virtute alterius adjuvari."—*In lib.* ii., dist. xxiv., p. I, art. 2, q. 8.

274.
    The student will find in MAHER'S *Psychology* (ch. iii.) a clear and well-reasoned exposition of the inconsistency and groundlessness of such attacks on the doctrine of faculties.

275.
    Cf. KLEUTGEN, *op. cit.*, § 636-637.

276.
    "Cum corpus hominis aut cujuslibet alterius animalis sit quoddam totum naturale, dicit unum ex eo quod unam formam habeat qua perficitur non solum secundum aggregationem aut compositionem, ut accidit in domo et in aliis hujusmodi. Unde opportet quod quaelibet pars hominis et animalis recipiat esse [*i.e.* sibi proprium] et speciem ab anima sicut a propria forma. Unde Philosophus dicit (l. ii. de anima, text. 9), quod recedente anima neque oculus neque caro neque aliqua pars manet nisi aequivoce."—ST. THOMAS, *Quaest. Disp. de anima*, art. 10—*apud* KLEUTGEN, *op. cit.*, § 632.

277.
    The most perfect real unity is of course that which includes all perfection in the simplicity of its actual essence, without any dispersion or plurality of its being, without any admixture of accident or potentiality. Such is the unity of the Infinite Being alone. No finite being possesses its actuality *tota simul*. And the creature falls short of perfect unity in proportion as it attains to this actuality only by a multiplicity of real changes, by a variety of really distinct principles and powers, essential and accidental, in its concrete mode of being. In proportion as created things are higher or lower in the scale of being, they realize a higher or a lower grade of unity in their mode of individual existence.

278.
    We are concerned here only with finite, created substances, as distinct from the Divine Uncreated Substance on whom these depend.

279.
    ARISTOTLE, *Categ.* ch. iii., *passim*; *Metaph.*, l. v. (al. vi.), ch. viii.; ST. THOMAS, *In Metaph.*, l. v. lect. 10; KLEUTGEN, *op. cit.*, § 589-591.

280.
    Cf. KLEUTGEN, *op. cit.*, §§ 587, 602-603.

281.
    Cf. URRABURU, *op. cit.*, §§ 277, 279.

282.
    Cf. Science of Logic, ii., § 217 (pp. 66 *sqq.*).

283.
    Sciendum est quod nomen naturae significat quodlibet principium intrinsicum motus; secundum quod Philosophus dicit quod *natura est principium motus in eo in quo est per se, et non secundum accidens.*—ST. THOMAS, *Summa Theol.*, iii., q. 2, art. 1 in c.

284.
    And here we are reminded of the view of many medieval scholastics of high authority, that the same material entity can have at the same time a plurality of formative principles or *substantial forms* of different grades of perfection.

285.
    Cf. URRABURU, *op. cit.*, § 282 (p. 825).

286.
    For want of a more appropriate rendering we translate the Latin term *suppositum* (Gr. ὑπόστασις) by the phrase "subsisting thing"; though the classical terms are really generic: *suppositum* being a genus of which there are two species, *suppositum irrationale* ("*thing*" or "subsisting *thing*") and *suppositum rationale* ("*person*").—*Cf. infra*, pp. 265-6.

287.
    Complete in every way: in *substantial* and in *specific* perfections. The separated soul, though it is an existing individual substance, retains its essential communicability to its connatural material principle, the body. Hence it has not "subsistence," it is not a "person".—*Cf. infra*.

    "Per se agere *convenit per se existenti*. Sed per se existens quandoque potest dici aliquid, si non sit inhærens ut accidens, vel ut forma materialis, etiamsi sit pars. Sed proprie et per se subsistens dicitur quod neque est praedicto modo inhærens neque est pars. Secundum quem modum oculus aut manus non potest dici per se subsistens, et per consequens nec per se operans. Unde et operationes partium attribuuntur toti per partes. Dicimus enim quod homo videt per oculum et palpat per manum."—ST. THOMAS, *Summa Theol.*, i., q. 75, art. 2, ad. 2.

288.
    Cf. preceding note. St. Thomas continues: "Potest igitur dici quod anima intelligit, sicut oculus videt, sed magis proprie dicitur quod homo intelligat per animam" (ibid.); and elsewhere he writes: "Dicendum quod anima est pars humanae speciei [*i.e.* naturae]. Et ideo, licet sit separata, quia tamen retinet naturam unibilitatis, non potest dici substantia individua quae est hypostasis vel substantia prima, sicut nec manus, nec quaecumque alia partium hominis; et sic non competit ei neque definitio personae, neque nomen."—*Summa Theol.*, i., q. 29, art. 1, ad. 5.

289.
    Cf. Science of Logic, i., §§ 54-5.

290.
    All *created* subsisting things and persons depend, of course, essentially on the Necessary Being for their existence and for their activity. This Necessary Being we know from Revelation to be *Triune*, Three in Persons, One in Nature. The subsistence of each Divine Person of the Blessed Trinity excludes *all* modes of dependence.

291.
    "Hoc ... quod est per se agere, excellentiori modo convenit substantiis rationalis naturae quam aliis. Nam solae substantiae rationales habent dominium sui actus, ita quod in eis est agere et non agere; aliae vero substantiae magis aguntur quam agunt. Et ideo conveniens fuit ut substantia individua *rationalis* naturae speciale nomen haberet."—ST. THOMAS, *Quaest. Disp. de Potentia*, q. ix., art. 1, ad. 3.

292.
    Cf. BILLOT, *De Verbo Incarnato*, q. ii.—*apud* MERCIER, *op. cit.*, § 151 (pp. 299-300).

293.
    Cf. URRABURU, *op. cit.*, § 291, for an exhaustive list of the authorities in favour of each of the various views propounded in this present context.

294.
    "Natura singularis et integra per se consituitur in sua independentia, non aliquo positivo addito ultra illam entitatem positivam, qua est haec natura."—SCOTUS, iii., Dist. i. q. 1, n. 9 and n. 11, ad. 3. *Cf.* SUAREZ, *Metaph.*, Disp. xxxiv. § 2; KLEUTGEN, *op. cit.*, § 616; FRANZELIN, *De verbo Incarnato*, Th. xxix.

295.
    op. cit., § 293 (p. 861).

296.
    Neither is it a *natural* union in the sense of being *due* to the human nature; it is wholly *undue* to the latter, and is in this sense *supernatural*.

297.
    op. cit., § 293 (p. 861).

298.
    ibid. Farther on (p. 863) he says it is certain that the Divine Nature of the Word is *substantially* united with humanity in a unity of person or subsistence: "certum est eamdem [naturam divinam] substantialiter uniri cum humanitate in unitate suppositi;" and for this he considers that the human nature must be incomplete "in ratione personae". But this proves nothing; for of course the human nature must be wanting in personality. But it is complete *as a nature*. Nor does the aphorism he quotes—

299.
"Quidquid substantiae in sua specie completae accedit, accidens est,"—apply to subsistence or personality supervening on a complete substance.

300.
"Humanitas illa [*scil.* Christi], quamvis completa in *esse* naturae, non tamen habet ultimum complementum in genere substantiae cum in se non subsistat."—*ibid.*, § 296 (p. 866).

301.
This view, which has many supporters, is clearly explained and ably defended by MERCIER in his *Ontologie*, § 151 (pp. 298-302), § 52 (pp. 134-5), § 49 (p. 127, n. 1).

302.
Cf. MERCIER, *op. cit.*, § 49 (p. 127, n. 1).

303.
Hence Urraburu gives this *real* definition of subsistence: *ultimus naturae terminus in ordine substantiali* sive in ratione existentis per se: the ultimate term (or determination) of a nature in the order of substantiality or of "existing by itself"—*op. cit.*, § 296 (p. 866).

304.
"Sicut enim modus accidentalis figurae terminat quantitatem, et modus ubicationis constituit rem hic et non alibi, ita modus substantialis personalitatis terminans naturam reddit illam incommunicabilem alieno supposito."—URRABURU, *op. cit.*, § 291 (p. 854).

305.
The terms "Self," "*Ego*," and "Person" we take to be identical in reference to the human individual. The *mind* is not the *Ego*, self, or person, but only a part of it.—*Cf.* MAHER, *Psychology*, ch. vi., p. 104.

306.
Cf. MAHER, *Psychology*, ch. xvii.

307.
ibid., p. 365.

308.
Cf. MAHER, *Psychology*, p. 363.

309.
Cf. MAHER, *Psychology*, p. 365 (italics in last sentence ours).

310.
Cf. RICKABY, *First Principles*, p. 370.

311.
Cf. MAHER, *ibid.*, pp. 487-92; MERCIER, *Psychologie*, ii., pp. 197-224 (6th edit.); *Ontologie*, § 153 (p. 304).

There are cogent theological reasons also against the view that consciousness constitutes personality. For instance, the human nature of

312. our Divine Lord has its own proper consciousness, which, nevertheless, does not constitute this nature a person.

313. *Essay Concerning Human Understanding*, bk. ii., ch. xxvii.

"That being then one plant which has such an organization of parts in one coherent body partaking of one common life, it continues to be the same plant as long as it continues to partake of the same life, though that life be communicated to different particles of matter vitally united to the living plant, in a like continued organization conformable to that sort of plants....

"The case is not so much different in brutes, but that anyone may hence see what makes an animal and continues it the same....

"This also shows wherein the identity of the same man consists: *viz.* in nothing but a participation of the same continued life, by constantly fleeting particles of matter, in succession vitally united to the same organized body.... For if the identity of soul alone makes the same man, and there be nothing in the nature of matter why the same individual spirit may be united [*i.e.* successively] to different bodies, it will be possible that ... men living in distant ages, and of different tempers, may have been the same man...."—*Essay Concerning Human Understanding*, bk. ii. ch. xxvii. § 4-6. Yet though "identity of soul" does not make "the same man," Locke goes on immediately to assert that identity of *consciousness*, which is but a function of the soul, makes *the same person*.

314. *Essay Concerning Human Understanding*, bk. ii., ch. xxvii., § 7. Names do not stand for ideas or concepts but for *conceived* realities; and the question here is: What is the conceived reality (in the existing human individual) for which the term "person" stands?

315. *ibid.*, § 9.

316. *Essay Concerning Human Understanding*, bk. ii., ch. xxvii., §§ 13, 14.

317. *Essay Concerning Human Understanding*, bk. ii., ch. xxvii., § 13.

318. For a searching criticism of such theories of the Ego or human person, *cf.* MAHER, *Psychology*, ch. xxii.

319.
: *ibid.*, § 19.

320.
: p. 276.

321.
: *Cf.* MAHER'S criticism of Professor James' theory on double personality (*op. cit.*, ch. xxii., pp. 491-2): "Professor James devotes much space to these 'mutations' of the Ego, yet overlooks the fact that they are peculiarly fatal, not to his adversaries, but to his own theory that 'the present thought is the only thinker,' and that seeming identity is sufficiently preserved by each thought 'appropriating' and 'inheriting' the contents of its predecessor. The difficulties presented to this process of inheritance by such facts as sleep and swooning have been already dwelt upon [*cf. ibid.*, p. 480 (c)]; but here they are if possible increased. The last conscious thought of, say, Felida 2 has to transmit its gathered experience not to its *proximate* conscious successor, which is Felida 1, but across seven months of vacuum until on the extinction of Felida 1 the next conscious thought which constitutes Felida 2 is born into existence. If the single personality is hard for Mr. James to explain, 'double-personality' at least doubles his difficulties."

322.
: *Cf. infra*, § 82.

323.
: Ποιότητα δὲ λέγω, καθ᾽ ἥν ποιοί τινες εἶναι λέγονται.—*Categ.*, ch. iv. *Cf.* ST. THOMAS: "Haec est ratio formalis qualitatis, per quam respondemus interroganti qualis res sit."

324.
: The other accidents, *e.g. actio* and *passio*, in so far as they change the perfection of the substance, do so only by producing qualities in it. Quantity, which is the connatural accident of all corporeal substance, adds of itself no special complement or degree of accidental perfection to the latter, in the sense of disposing (or indisposing) the latter for the attainment of the full and final perfection due to its specific nature; but only in the sense that it supposes more or less of that kind of substance to exist, or in the sense in which it is understood to include the *qualities* of which it may be the *immediate* subject.—*Cf.* URRABURU, *op. cit.*, § 326.

325.
: *In Praedicamenta*, ch. i.

326.
: *Cf.* MAHER, *Psychology*, ch. xii, xiii, xxiii, xxv. BERGSON rightly recognizes the irreducibility of quality to quantity (*Essai sur les données immediates de la conscience, passim*). But he wrongly infers from this

"fundamental antinomy," as he calls it, the existence, in each human individual, of a two-fold *Ego*, a deeper self where all is quality, and a superficial self which projects conscious states, in static and numerical isolation from one another, into a homogeneous space where all is quantitative, mathematical. The reasonable inference is merely that the human mind recognizes in the data of its experience a certain richness and variety of modes of real being.

327. *Metaph.* V., ch. xiv., where the four groups are finally reduced to two.

328. *Summa Theol.*, ia, ii^{ae}, q. 49, art. 2.

329. To be distinguished from the *passio* which is correlative of *actio* and which consists in the actual undergoing of the latter, the actual reception of the accidental form which is the term of the latter.

330. "Inter omnes qualitates, figurae maxime sequuntur et demonstrant speciem rerum. Quod maxime in plantis et animalibus patet, in quibus nullo certiori indicio diversitas specierum dijudicari potest, quam diversitate figurae."—ST. THOMAS, *In* VII. *Physic*, lect. 5.

331. Every natural habit, as we have just seen, has an essential relation to *activity*. Every such habit inheres immediately in some operative faculty, as science in the intellect, or justice in the will. All natural habits are *operative*. There is, however, as we know from Divine Revelation, an "entitative" habit, a *habitus entitativus*, which affects the substance itself of the human soul, ennobling its natural mode of being and so perfecting it as to raise it to a higher or supernatural plane of being, to an order of existence altogether undue to its nature: the *supernaturally infused* habit of *sanctifying grace*.

332. *Eth. Eud.*, ii., 2.

333. "Vires naturales non agunt operationes suas mediantibus aliquibus habitibus, quia secundum seipsas sunt determinatae ad unum."—*Summa Theol.*, i^a ii^{ae}, q. 49, art. 4, ad 2.

334. "Intellectus ... est subjectum habitus. Illi enim competit esse subjectum habitus quod est in potentia ad multa; et hoc maxime competit intellectui...."—ST. THOMAS, *Summa Theol.*, i^a, ii^e, q. 50, art. 4, ad. I. "Omnis potentia quae diversimode potest ordinari ad agendum, indiget habitu, quo bene disponatur ad suum actum. Voluntas autem cum sit

potentia rationalis, diversimode potest ad agendum ordinari: et ideo oportet in voluntate aliquem habitum ponere, quo bene disponatur ad suum actum ...,"—*ibid.* art. 5, in c.

335.

"Habitualis dispositio requiritur ubi subjectum est in potentia ad multa. Operationes vero quae sunt ab anima per corpus, principaliter quidem sunt ipsius animae, secundario vero ipsius corporis. Habitus autem proportionantur operationibus; unde ex similibus actibus similes habitus causantur, ut dicitur in 2 Ethic., cap. I et 2; in corpore vero possunt esse secundario, inquantum scilicet corpus disponitur et habilitatur ad prompte deserviendum operationibus animae."—*Summa Theol.*, iª iiᵃᵉ, q. 49, art. I, in c.

336.

Cf. ST. THOMAS, *ibid.*, q. 50, art. I.—MERCIER, *Ontologie*, § 164.

337.

According to the scholastic theory of matter and form the matter must be predisposed by certain qualities for the reception of a given substantial form. The chemical elements which form a compound will not do so in any and every condition, but only when definitely disposed and brought together under favourable conditions. These elementary qualities, considered in themselves, are not habits or dispositions: "Unde qualitates simplices elementorum, quae secundum unum modum determinatum naturis elementorum conveniunt, non dicimus *dispositiones* vel *habitus*, sed *simplices qualitates.*"—ST. THOMAS, *ibid.*, q. 49, art. 4, in C. They are natural qualities and not dispositions produced by disposing causes.

338.

St. Thomas regards the distinction between *habits* and mere dispositions as a distinction not of *degree* but of *kind*. "Dispositio et habitus possunt distingui sicut diversae species unius generis subalterni, ut dicantur *dispositiones* illae qualitates primae speciei quibus convenit secundum propriam rationem ut de facili amittantur, quia habent causas mutabiles, ut aegritudo et sanitas; *habitus* vero dicantur illae qualitates quae secundum suam rationem habent quod non de facili transmutentur quia habent causas immobiles; sicut scientia et virtutes; et secundum hoc disposito non fit habitus."—ST. THOMAS, *Summa Theol.*, iª, iiᵃᵉ, q. 49, art. 2, ad. 3.

339.

"Vires sensitivae *dupliciter* possunt considerari: *uno modo*, secundum quod operanter ex instinctu naturae; *alio modo*, secundum quod operantur ex imperio rationis. Secundum igitur quod operantur ex instinctu naturae, sic ordinantur ad unum, sicut et natura; et ideo sicut in potentiis naturalibus non sunt aliqui habitus, ta etiam nec in potentiis sensitivis, secundum quod ex instinctu naturae operantur. Secundum vero quod operantur ex imperio rationis, sic ad diversa ordinari possunt: et sic possunt esse in eis aliqui habitus, quibus bene aut male ad aliquid disponuntur."—ST. THOMAS, *ibid.*, q. 50, art. 3, in c. In this context the angelic doctor, following Aristotle, places the virtues of temperance and fortitude in the sense *appetite* as controlled by the rational will. For the same reason he admits the possibility of habits in the faculties of *internal* sense perception, though not in the *external* senses (*ibid.*, ad. 3).

340.

"Quia bruta animalia a ratione hominis per quandam consuetudinem disponuntur ad aliquid operandum sic, vel aliter, hoc modo in brutis animalibus habitus quodammodo poni possunt.... Deficit tamen ratio habitus quantum ad usum voluntatis quia non habent dominium utendi vel non utendi, quod videtur ad rationem habitus pertinere; et ideo, proprie loquendo, in eis habitus esse non possunt."—*ibid.*, ad. 2.

341.

It must not be forgotten that habit is an *accident*, an accidental perfection of the substance or nature of an individual agent; it immediately affects the operative power of the agent, which operative power is itself an accident of this agent's nature (constituting the second sub-class of the accident, *Quality*). Habit is thus at once an *actuality* or actualization of the operative power and a *potentiality* of further and more perfect acts. It is intermediate between the operative power and the complete actualization which the power receives by the acts that spring from the latter as perfected by the habit. Faculty and habit form one complete proximate principle of those acts: a principle which is at once a partial actualization of the individual agent's nature and a potentiality of further actualization of this nature.

342.

"Si potentiae animae non sunt ipsa essentia animae, sequitur quod sint accidentia in aliquo novem generum contenta. Sunt enim in secunda specie qualitatis, quæ dicitur potentia vel impotentia naturalis."—*Q. Disp. de Spir. Creat.*, art. II, in c.

343.

Cf. ST. THOMAS, *Summa Theol.*, i., q. 76, art. I, in c.—"Cum potentia et actus dividant ens, et quodlibet genus entis, opportet quod ad idem genus referatur potentia et actus; et ideo si actus non est in genere substantiae, potentia, quæ dicitur ad illum actum, non potest esse in genere substantiae. Operatio autem animae non est in genere substantiae, sed in solo Deo, cujus operatio est ejus substantia."—*Cf.* ZIGLIARA, *Ontologia* (9), xi.: "Actus et potentia essentialiter ad illum actum ordinata sunt in eodem genere supremo."

344.

> "Nec in angelo, nec in aliqua creatura, virtus vel potentia operativa est idem quod sua essentia.... Actus ad quem comparatur potentia operativa est operatio. In angelo autem non est idem intelligere et esse; nec aliqua alia operatio, aut in ipso aut in quocunque alio creato, est idem quod ejus esse. Unde essentia angeli non est ejus potentia intellectiva, nec alicujus creati essentia est ejus operativa potentia."—*ibid.*, q. 54, art 3.

345.

As we shall see later, action as such does not perfect or change the *agens*, unless when, as in immanent action, the *agens* is identical with the *patiens*. Action formally actualizes or perfects the *patiens*: *actio fit in passo*. But the exercise of any activity by an agent undoubtedly connotes or implies a perfection of this agent. It is not, however, that the actual operation as such (unless it is immanent) adds a new perfection to the agent. Rather the agent's *power* of acting, revealed to us in its exercise, is for us a measure of the actual perfection of the agent. But the question remains: Is this power or perfection, so far as we know it, a *substantial* perfection? Is it *the very perfection itself of the agent's substance or nature* as known to us? Or is it an *accidental* perfection which is for us an index of a corresponding degree of substantial perfection? In getting our knowledge of the nature of a substance from a consideration of its *sensible* accidents, its *phenomena*, its *operations*—according to the rule, *Operari sequitur esse: qualis est operatio talis est natura*—can we use a *single* inference, from *action* to *nature*, or must we use a *double* inference, from action to power, and from power to nature? But even if we have to make the double inference, this *of itself* does not prove any more than a conceptual distinction between *power* and *nature*.

346.

Cf. ST. THOMAS, *Q. Disp. de spir. creat.*, art. 11, in c.—MAHER, *Psychology* ch. iii.

347.

Cf. MERCIER, *Ontologie*, § 168.

348.

Cf. ibid., op. cit., § 169; MAHER, *Psychology*, ch. iii. (p. 29, n. 3.)

349.

Of course all accidents are "forms" in the sense of being *determining principles* of their subjects, these being considered as *determinable* or *receptive* principles. Even quantity is a form in this sense. But quantity itself does not appear to be a "simple" principle in the sense of being "indivisible": its very function is to make the corporeal substance divisible into integral parts. What then of all those qualities which inhere *immediately* in the quantity of corporeal substances? They are determinations or affections of a composite, extended, divisible subject. Conceived in the abstract they have, of course, the attributes of indivisibility, immutability, etc., characteristic of all *abstract* essences (14). But in their physical actuality in what intelligible sense can they be said to be simple, indivisible entities?

350.

Summa Theol., i^a, ii^{ae}, q. 52, art. 2; ii^a, ii^{ae}, q. 24, art. 4, 5.—*Q. Disp. de Virtutibus in communi*, q. i, art. II, in c.—I. *In Sentent., Dist.*, 17, q. 2, art. 2.—*Cf.* URRABURU, *op. cit.*, §§ 329-332, for arguments and authorities. The author himself defends the former view, according to which alteration takes place by a real addition or substraction of grades of the same quality.

351.

I. *In Sentent., Dist.*, 17, q. 2, art. 2.

352.

ii^a, ii^{ae}, q. 24, art. 4, ad. 3.

353.

Q. Disp. de Virtut., q. I, art. II, in c.

354.

The scientific concept of "volume" is identical with the common and philosophical concept of "external, actual, local, or spatial extension". The functions ascribed by physics and mechanics to the "mass" of a body have no other source, in the body, than what philosophers understand by the "internal extension" or "quantity" of the body.—*Cf.* Nys, *Cosmologie* (Louvain, 1903), §§ 192-203.

355.

The terms *quantity* and *extension* are commonly taken as synonymous; but *quantity* is more properly applied to the internal plurality of integral parts of the substance itself, *extension* to the dispersion of these parts outside one another in space.

356.

Hence Aristotle's definition in *Metaph.*, iv.: "Quantum dicitur, quod [est] in insita divisibile, quorum utrumque aut singula unum quid et hoc quid apta sunt esse": a quantified substance is one which is divisible into parts that are really in it [*i.e. partes integrantes*], parts each of which is capable of becoming a distinct subsisting individual thing.—*Cf.* NYS, *Cosmologie*, § 154.

357.

"Longitudo, latitudo et profunditas quantitates quaedam, sed non substantiae sunt. Quantitas enim non est substantia, sed magis cui haec ipsa primo insunt illud est substantia."—*Metaph.*, L. vii., ch. iii.

358.

359. *Physic*, L. i., ch. ii.

360. L. ii., ch. iv.

361. Cf. § 62 *supra*.

362. "Propria ... totalitas substantiae continetur indifferenter in parva vel magna quantitate; sicut ... tota natura hominis in magno, vel parvo homine."—*Summa Theol.*, iii., q. 76, art. I, ad. 3.

363. No argument in favour of this view can be based on the use of the term *species* ("*manentibus dumtaxat speciebus panis et vini*") by the Fathers of the Council of Trent. For them, as for all Catholic philosophers and theologians of the time, the scholastic term *species*, used in such a context, meant simply the objective, perceptible accidents of the substance. Cf. NYS, *op. cit.*, § 175.

Hence the significance of the lines in ST. THOMAS' hymn, *Adoro Te devote*:—

Visus, tactus, gustus in te fallitur,
Sed *auditu* solo tuto creditur.

364. and neither does Revelation. The Body of our Blessed Lord exists in the Eucharist without its connatural external extension and consequent impenetrability. But according to the common teaching of Catholic theologians it has its *internal quantity*, its distinct integral parts, organs and members—really distinct from one another, though interpenetrating and not spatially external to one another. Its mode of existence in the space occupied by the sacramental species is thus analogous to the mode in which the soul is in the body, or a pure spirit in space.

365. We know from Revelation that the Body of our Lord exists in this way in the Eucharist. We know, too, from Revelation that after the general resurrection the glorified bodies of the just will be *real* bodies, real *corporeal substances*, and nevertheless that they will be endowed with properties very different from those which they possess in the present state: that they will be immortal, incorruptible, impassible, "spiritual" (*cf.* I Cor. xv.). The Catholic philosopher who adds those scattered rays of revealed light to what his own rational analysis of experience tells him

about matter and spirit, will understand the possibility of such a kinship between the latter as will make the fact of their union in his own nature and person not perhaps any less wonderful, but at any rate a little less surprising and inscrutable: and this without committing himself to the objective idealism whereby Berkeley, while endeavouring to show the utter unreality of matter, only succeeded in persuading himself that its reality was not independent of all mind.

366.

"Ὥστε τὸ τοῦ περιέχοντος πέρας ἀκίνητον πρῶτον, τουτ' ἔστιν ὁ τόπος."—*Physic*, L. iv., ch. iv. (6).

367.

The category *Situs* is commonly interpreted to signify the *mutual* spatial relations or dispositions of the various parts of a body in the place actually occupied by the latter.

368.

A body deprived of its connatural extension exists in space in a manner analogous to that in which the soul is in the body. The Body of our Divine Lord is in the Eucharist in this manner—"*sacramentaliter*".

369.

Cf. KLEUTGEN, *op. cit.*, § 624.

370.

Cf. ZIGLIARA, *Ontologia* (35), iv.

371.

Cf. NYS, *La Notion d'Espace* (Louvain, 1901), pp. 95 *sqq.*—*La Notion de Temps* (Louvain, 1898), pp. 123 *sqq.*

372.

"Quid est ergo tempus? Si nemo ex me quaerat, scio; si quaerenti explicare velim, nescio."—*Confess.* L. xi., ch. xiv.

373.

"Cum enim intelligimus extrema diversa alicujus medii, et anima dicat, illa esse duo *nunc,* hoc *prius,* illud *posterius* quasi numerando *prius* et *posterius* in motu, tunc hoc dicimus esse tempus."—ST. THOMAS, in *Phys.*, L. iv. lect. 17[a].

374.

Sentent., Dist. xix., q. ii., art. 1.—*Cf.* Lect. xxiii. in iv. *Physic.*

375.

Physic., iv., ch. xi.—*Cf.* ST. THOMAS *in loc.*

376.

"The conception of variation united with sameness is not, however, the whole cognition of time. For this the mind must be able to combine in thought two different movements or pulsations of consciousness, so as to represent an interval between them. It must hold together two *nows*, conceiving them, in succession, yet uniting them through that intellectual synthetic activity by which we *enumerate* a collection of objects—a process or act which carries concomitantly the consciousness of its own continuous unity."—MAHER, *Psychology*, ch. xvii.

377.

That is, provided we abstract from all comparison of this internal time duration with that of any other current of conscious experiences in the estimating mind. As a matter of fact we always and necessarily compare the time duration of any particular experienced change with that of the remaining portion of the whole current of successive conscious states which make up our mental life. And thus we feel, not that the four-mile walk had a longer time duration than the three-mile walk, but rather that it took place at a quicker *rate*, more rapidly, than the latter. But if a mind which had no other consciousness of change whatsoever than, *e.g.* that of the two walks experienced successively, no other standard change with which to compare each of them as it occurred—if such a mind experienced each in this way, would it pronounce the four-mile walk to have occupied a longer time than the three-mile walk?—*Cf. infra*, p. 327.

378.

This is true on the assumption that the intrinsic *time-duration* of a successive, continuous change, its divisibility into distinct "nows" related as "before" and "after," is *really identical with* the continuous, successive *states constituting the change* itself, and is not *a really distinct mode* superadded to this change, a continuous series of "*quandocationes*," distinct from the change, and giving the latter its temporal duration. But many philosophers hold that in all creatures *duration* is a mode of their existence really distinct from the creatures themselves that have this duration or continued existence.—*Cf. infra*, § 86.

379.

Cf. Science of Logic, ii., § 246, pp. 201 *sqq.*

380.

op. cit., c. xvii.

381.

op. cit., c. xvii.

382.

Cf. NYS, *La Notion de Temps* (Lovain, 1898), p. 104.

383.

The fact that we can perceive and estimate temporal duration only *extrinsically*, and in ultimate analysis by comparison with the flow of our own conscious states, and that therefore we can have no perception or conception of the intrinsic time duration of any change, seems to have been overlooked by DE SAN *(Cosmologia,* pp. 528-9) when he argues from our perception of different *rates* of motion, in favour of the view that time *duration* is not really identical with motion or change, but a superadded mode, really distinct from the latter.

384.

Cf. NYS, *La Notion de Temps,* pp. 85 *sqq.*

385.

Cf. NYS, *op. cit.,* pp. 120 *sqq.,* for a defence of the view that an actually infinite multitude involves no contradiction.

386.

ibid., pp. 162-9.

387.

De Consolatione, L. v., *pr. ult.*

388.

Cf. KLEUTGEN, *op. cit.,* § 624.

389.

"Est ergo dicendum, quod, cum aeternitas sit mensura esse permanentis secundum quod aliquid recedit a permanentia essendi, secundum hoc recedit ab aeternitate. Quaedam autem sic recedunt a permanentia essendi, quod esse eorum est subjectum transmutationis, vel in transmutatiose consistit; et hujusmodi mensurantur *tempore,* sicut omnis motus, et etiam esse omnium corruptibilium. Quaedam vero recedunt minus a permanentia essendi, quia esse eorum nec in transmutatione consistit nec est subjectum transmutationis; tamen habent transmutationem adjunctam vel in actu vel in potentia ... patet de angelis, quod scilicet habent esse intransmutabile cum transmutabilitate secundum electionem, quantum ad eorum naturam pertinet, et cum transmutabilitate intelligentiarum, et affectionum, et locorum suo modo. Et ideo hujusmodi mensurantur *aevo,* quod est medium inter aeternitatem et tempus. Esse autem quod mensurat *aeternitas,* nec est mutabile nec mutabilitati adjunctum. Sic ergo tempus habet prius et posterius, aevum non habet in se prius et posterius, sed ei conjungi possunt; aeternitas autem non habet prius neque posterius, neque ea compatitur."—ST. THOMAS, *Summa Theol.,* i., q. x., art. 5, in c.

390.

pp. 517-57.

391.

Invisibilia enim ipsius a creatura mundi, per ea quae facta sunt intellecta, conspiciuntur, sempiterna quoque ejus virtus et divinitas, ita ut [qui veritatem Dei in injustitia detinent] sint inexcusabiles.—Rom. ii. 20 [18].

392.

Cf. MAHER, *Psychology* (4th edit.), pp. 90-2.

393.

394. For a clear and trenchant criticism of modern relativist theories, *cf.* VEITCH, *Knowing and Being*, especially ch. iv., "Relation," pp. 129 *sqq.*

395. *Cf.* MERCIER, *op. cit.*, §§ 179-80.

396. *Principles of Psychology*, P. ii., ch. iii., § 88.

397. *Cf.* MAHER, *Psychology*, pp. 157-9.

398. "We cannot of course *perceive* an *unperceived* world, nor can we conceive a world the conception of which is not in the mind; but there is no contradiction or absurdity in the proposition: 'A material world of three dimensions has existed for a time unperceived and unthought of by any created being, and then revealed itself to human minds'."—MAHER, *Psychology*, p. iii, n.

399. "I do not pretend to demonstrate anything, nor do I feel much concern, about any unknowable *noumenon* which never reveals itself in my consciousness. If there be in existence an inscrutable 'transcendental Ego,' eternally screened from my ken by this self-asserting 'empirical Ego,' I confess I feel very little interest in the nature or the welfare of the former. *The only soul about which I care is that which immediately presents itself in its acts, which thinks, wills, remembers, believes, loves, repents, and hopes.*"—MAHER, *op. cit.*, p. 475. *Cf.* MERCIER, *op. cit.*, § 180, pp. 363.

400. Πρός τι δὲ τὰ τοιαῦτα λέγεται, ὅσα αὐτά, ἅπερ ἐστὶν, ἑτέρων εἶναι λέγεται, ἢ ὁπωσοῦν ἄλλως πρὸς ἕτερον.—*Categ.* v. 1.

401. I *Sentent.*, Dist. xxvi., q. 2, art. 1.

"Sicut realis relatio consistit in ordine rei ad rem, ita relatio rationis consistit in ordine intellectuum [ordination of concepts]; quod quidem dupliciter potest contingere. Uno modo secundum quod iste ordo est adinventus per intellectum, et attributus ei, quod relative dicitur; et hujusmodi sunt relationes quae attribuuntur ab intellectu rebus intellectis, prout sunt intellectae, sicut relatio generis et speciei; has enim relationes ratio adinvenit considerando ordinem ejus, quod est in intellectu ad res, quae sunt extra, vel etiam ordinem intellectuum ad invicem. Alio modo secundum quod hujusmodi relationes consequuntur modum intelligendi, videlicet quod intellectus intelligit aliquid in ordine ad aliud; licet illum ordinem intellectus non adinveniat, sed magis ex quadam necessitate consequatur modum intelligendi. Et hujusmodi relationes intellectus non attribuit ei, quod est in intellectu, sed ei, quod est in re. Et hoc quidem contingit secundum quod aliqua non habentia secundum se ordinem, ordinate intelliguntur; licet intellectus non intelligit ea habere ordinem, quia sic esset falsus. Ad hoc autem quod aliqua habeant ordinem, oportet quod utrumque sit ens, et utrumque ordinabile ad aliud. Quandoque autem intellectus accipit aliqua duo ut entia, quorum alterum tantum vel neutrum est ens; sicut cum accipit duo futura, vel unum praesens et aliud futurum, et intelligit unum cum ordine ad aliud, dicit alterum esse prius altero; unde istae relationes sunt rationis tantum, utpote modum intelligendi consequentes. Quandoque vero accipit unum ut duo, et intelligit ea cum quodam ordine; sicut cum dicitur aliquid esse idem sibi: et sic talis relatio est rationis tantum. Quandoque vero accipit aliqua duo ut ordinabilia ad invicem, inter quae non est ordo medius, immo alterum ipsorum essentialiter est ordo; sicut cum dicit relationem accidere subjecto; unde talis relatio relationis ad quodcumque aliud est rationis tantum. Quandoque vero accipit aliquid cum ordine ad aliud, inquantum est terminus ordinis alterius ad ipsum, licet ipsum non ordinetur ad aliud: sicut accipiendo scibile ut terminum ordinis scientiae ad ipsum."—*De Potentia*, q. vii., art. II; cf. *ibid.* art. 10.

"Cum relatio requirit duo extrema, tripliciter se habet ad hoc quod sit res naturae aut rationis. Quandoque enim ex utraque parte est res rationis tantum, quando scilicet ordo vel habitudo non potest esse inter aliqua nisi secundum apprehensionem intellectus tantum, utpote cum dicimus idem eidem idem. Nam secundum quod ratio apprehendit bis aliquod unum statuit illud ut duo; et sic apprehendit quandam habitudinem ipsius ad seipsum. Et similiter est de omnibus relationibus quae sunt inter ens et non ens, quas format ratio, inquantum apprehendit non ens ut quoddam extremum. Et idem est de omnibus relationibus quae consequuntur actum rationis, ut genus, species, et hujusmodi...."—*Summa Theol.*, i., q. xiii., art. 7.

402.

Summa Theol., I. q. xiii. art. 7. Elsewhere he points the distinction in these terms: "Respectus ad aliud aliquando est in ipsa natura rerum, utpote quando aliquae res secundum suam naturam ad invicem ordinatae sunt, et ad invicem inclinationem habent; et hujusmodi relationes oportet esse reales.... Aliquando vero respectus significatus per ea, quae dicuntur *Ad aliquid*, est tantum in ipsa apprehensione rationis conferentis unum alteri; et tunc est relatio rationis tantum, sicut cum comparat ratio hominem animali, ut speciem ad genus."—*ibid.*, q. xxviii., art. 1.

403. St. Thomas gives expression to it in these sentences: "Perfectio et bonum quae sunt in rebus extra animam, non solum attenduntur secundum aliquid absolute inhaerens rebus, sed etiam secundum ordinem unius rei ad aliam; sicut etiam in ordine partium exercitus, bonum exercitus consistit: huic enim ordini comparat Philosophus [Aristot., xii. (x.) *Metaph.*, Comment. 52 *sqq.*] ordinem universi. Oportet, ergo in ipsis rebus ordinem quemdam esse; hic autem ordo relatio quaedam est.... Sic ergo oportet quod res habentes ordinem ad aliquid, realiter referantur ad ipsum, et quod in eis aliqua res sit relatio."—*QQ. Disp. De Potentia*, q. vii., art. 9.

404. *Kritik der reinen Vernunft*, bk. i., Hauptst. ii., Abschn. ii., § 26.

405. *Logic*, bk. i., ch. iii., § 10.

406. *L'Idée du phénomène*, p. 181—*apud* MERCIER, *op. cit.*, § 173.

407. "Quaedam vero relationes sunt quantum ad utrumque extremum res naturae, quando scilicet est habitudo inter aliqua duo secundum aliquid realiter conveniens utrique; sicut patet de omnibus relationibus quae consequuntur quantitatem, ut magnum et parvum, duplum et dimidium, et hujusmodi; nam quantitas est in utroque extremorum: et simile est de relationibus quae consequuntur actionem et passionem, ut motivum et mobile, pater et filius, et similia."—ST. THOMAS, *Summa Theol.*, i., q. xiii., art. 7.

408. "Quandoque vero relatio in uno extremorum est res naturae, et in altero est res rationis tantum: et hoc contingit quandocunque duo extrema non sunt unius ordinis; sicut sensus et scientia referuntur ad sensibile et scibile; quae quidem, inquantum sunt res quaedam in esse naturale existentes, sunt extra ordinem esse sensibilis et intelligibilis. Et ideo in scientia quidem et sensu est relatio realis, inquantum ordinantur ad sciendum vel sentiendum res; sed res ipsae in se consideratae sunt extra ordinem hujusmodi; unde in eis non est aliqua relatio realiter ad scientiam et sensum, sed secundum rationem tantum, inquantum intellectus apprehendit ea ut terminos relationum scientiae et sensus. Unde Philosophus dicit in 5 Metaph., text. 20, quod non dicuntur relative, eo quod ipsa referantur ad alia, sed quia alia referantur ad ipsa."—*ibid.*

409.

Being really and adequately identical with its foundation, which is the essence of its subject, this relation does not necessarily need the *actual* existence of its term. Thus actual knowledge or science, which is a habit of the mind, has a transcendental relation to its object even though this latter be not actual but only a pure possibility. Similarly the accident of quantity sustained without its connatural substance in the Eucharist, retains its transcendental relation to the latter.—*Cf.* URRABURU, *op. cit.*, § 335 (p. 997).

410.

Cf. URRABURU, *op. cit.*, § 336 (p. 990).

411.

Metaph., L. v., ch. xv. *Cf.* ST. THOMAS, *in loc.*, lect. 17, where, approving of this triple division, he writes: "Cum enim relatio quae est in rebus, consistat in ordine unius rei ad aliam, oportet tot modis hujusmodi relationes esse, quot modis contingit unam rem ad aliam ordinari. Ordinatur autem una res ad aliam, vel secundum esse, prout esse unius rei dependet ab alia, et sic est tertius modus. Vel secundum virtutem activam et passivam, secundum quod una res ab alia recipit, vel alteri confert aliquid; et sic est secundus modus. Vel secundum quod quantitas unius rei potest mensurari per aliam; et sic est primus modus."

412.

Cf. MERCIER, *op. cit.*, § 175. For transcendental and predicamental unity, *cf. supra*, §§ 26, 28.

413.

Cf. infra. Some authors hold that the relation in question is predicamental. *Cf.* URRABURU, *op. cit.*, p. 987. The nature or essence of any individual would seem to imply in its very concept a transcendental relation of specific identity with all other actual and possible individual embodiments of this essence. The point is one of secondary importance.

414.

Even virtually, though not formally. The creative act is not formally transitive; it is virtually so: and in the creature it grounds the latter's relation of real dependence on the Creator.

415.

Cf. URRABURU, *op. cit.*, § 336 (p. 989), § 341 (p. 1011); ST. THOMAS, iii. *Sentent.*, Dist., viii., q. i., art. 5.

416.

MERCIER, *op. cit.*, § 175.

417.

MERCIER, *ibid.*

418.

"Cum igitur Deus sit extra totum ordinem creaturae, et omnes creaturae ordinentur ad ipsum et non e converso; manifestum est quod creaturae realiter, referuntur ad ipsum Deum; sed in Deo non est aliqua realis relatio ejus ad creaturas, sed secundum rationem tantum, inquantum creaturae referantur ad ipsum."—ST. THOMAS, *Summa Theol.*, i., q. xiii., art. 7.

419. Among others Cajetan, Ferriariensis, Capreolus, Bañez, Joannes a St. Thoma. *Cf.* URRABURU, *op. cit.*, § 338 (p. 994); MERCIER, *op. cit.*, § 174. It would be interesting to know how precisely those authors conceived this "relative" entity, this "*esse ad*" as a reality independent of their own thought-activity. *Cf.* art. by the present writer in the *Irish Theological Quarterly* (vol. vii., April, 1912: "Reflections on some Forms of Monism," pp. 167-8): "The whole universe of direct experience displays a unity of order or design which pervades it through and through; it is a revelation of intelligent purpose. Now a *Cosmos*, an orderly universe—which is intelligible only as the expression of intelligent purpose, and not otherwise—is a system of *interrelated* factors. But *relating* is unintelligible except as an expression of the activity of mind or spirit, that is, of something at least analogous to our mental activity of comparing and judging. Scholastic philosophers, as we know, discuss the question whether or how far the exact object of our 'relation' concept is real; that is, whether this object is, in itself and apart from the terms related [and the foundation], a mere *ens rationis*, a product of our thought, or whether it is in itself something more than this; and some of them hold that there are relations which, in themselves and formally as relations, *are* something more than mere products of our thought. Now if there be such relations, since they are not products of *our* thought, we may fairly ask: Must they be the product of *some* thought? And from our analysis of our very notion of what a relation is, it would seem that they must be in some sort or other a product or expression of some thought-activity: even relations between *material* things. It is in determining how precisely this is, or can be, that the theist and the monist differ. The theist regards all material things, with their real relations—and all our finite human minds, which apprehend the material world and its relations and themselves and one another—as being indeed in a true sense terms or objects of the Thought of God; not, however, as therefore identical or consubstantial with the Divine Spirit, but as distinct from It though dependent on It: inasmuch as he holds the Divine Thought to be creative, and regards all these things as its *created* terms. The kinship he detects between matter and spirit lies precisely in this, that matter is for him a created term of the Divine Thought. For him too, therefore, matter can have no existence except as a term of thought—the creative Thought of

God." Not that "the intelligible relations apprehended by us in matter are ... identical in reality with the thought-activity of the Divine Mind," as Ontologists have taught; nor that we can directly infer the existence of a Supreme Spirit from the existence of matter, as Berkeley tried to do by erroneously regarding the latter merely as an essentially mind-dependent phenomenon; because "for the orthodox theist matter is in its own proper nature not spiritual, mental, psychical; not anything after the manner of a thought-process, or endowed with the spirit-mode of being". If predicamental relations, such as *quality* or *similarity* of material things, are, as those medieval scholastics contended, real entities, "relative" in their nature, and really distinct from their extremes and foundations, did those scholastics conceive such "relative entities" as essentially mind-dependent entities? If they did they would probably have conceived them in the sense of Berkeley, as created terms of the Divine Thought, rather than in the Ontologist sense which would identify them with the Divine Thought itself. But it is not likely that they conceived such relative entities as essentially thought-dependent, any more than the absolute material realities related to one another by means of these relative entities. On the other hand it is not easy to see how such relative entities can be anything more than mere products of some thought-activity or other.

420.

They rely especially on this text from the *De Potentia* (q. vii., art. 9): "Relatio est debilioris esse inter omnia praedicamenta; ideo putaverunt quidam eam esse ex secundis intellectibus. Secundum ergo hanc positionem sequeretur quod relatio non sit in rebus extra animam sed in solo intellectu, sicut intentio generis et speciei, et secundarum substantiarum. Hoc autem esse non potest. In nullo enim praedicamento ponitur aliquid nisi res praeter animam existens. Nam ens rationis dividitur contra ens divisum per decem praedicamenta.... Si autem relatio non est in rebus extra animam non poneretur *ad aliquid* unum genus praedicamenti."

421.

Cf. ST. ANSELM, *Monolog.*, ch. xxvi.

422.

"Relatio habet quod sit res naturae ex sua causa per quam una res naturalem ordinem habet ad alteram."—*Quodl.* I, art. 2.

423.

"In hoc differt *Ad Aliquid* [*i.e.* Relation] ab aliis generibus; quod alia genera ex propria sui ratione habent, quod aliquid sint, sicut quantitas ex hoc ipso quod est quantitas, aliquid ponit: et similiter est de aliis. Sed *Ad Aliquid* ex propria sui generis ratione non habet, quod ponat aliquid, sed

424.
ad aliquid.... Habet autem relatio quod sit aliquid reale ex eo, quod relationem causat."—*Quodl.* 9, art. 4. *Cf. De Potentia*, q. ii., art. 5.

425.
"Relatio est aliquid inhaerens *licet non ex hoc ipso quod est relatio*.... Et ideo nihil prohibet, *quod esse desinat hujusmodi accidens sine mutatione ejus in quo est.*"—*De Potentia*, q. vii., art. 9, ad. 7.

426.
"Et utroque modo contingit in realibus relationibus destrui relationem: vel per destructionem quantitatis [or other foundation], unde ad hanc mutationem quantitatis sequitur per accidens mutatio relationis: vel etiam secundum quod cessat respectus ad alterum, *remoto illo ad quod referebatur*; et tunc *relatio cessat, nulla mutatione facta in ipsa*. Unde in illis in quibus non est relatio nisi secundum hunc respectum, *veniunt et recedunt relationes sine aliqua mutatione ejus, quod refertur.*"—In i. *Sent.*, Dist. xxvi., q. ii., art. I, ad. 3.

427.
"Relationes differunt in hoc ab omnibus aliis rerum generibus, quia ea quae sunt aliorum generum, ex ipsa ratione sui generis habent, quod sint res naturae, sicut quantitates ex ratione quantitatis, et qualitates ex ratione qualitatis. Sed relationes non habent quod sint res naturae ex ratione respectus ad alterum.... Sed relatio habet quod sit res naturae ex sua causa, per quam una res naturalem ordinem habet ad alteram, qui quidem ordo naturalis et realis est ipsis ipsa relatio."—*Quodl.*, I, art. 2.

428.
Cf. supra, , n. I; in which context we may reasonably suppose him to be arguing that relation *considered adequately* is not a *mere logical entity*, "ex secundis intellectibus," inasmuch as, having *a real foundation* in things outside the mind, it is in this respect real, independently of our thought.

429.
Cf. URRABURU, *op. cit.*, § 341 (p. 1008).

430.
ibid., p. 1007; *cf. supra.*

431.
In i. *Sentent.*, Dist. iv., q. I, art. I, ad. 3.

Cf. URRABURU, *ibid.*, pp. 1006-7: "Deinde *nullam relationem esse substantiam* scripsit [S. Thomas] vel quia plerumque ratio fundandi non est substantia ... vel potius quia semper relatio, etiam cum in substantia fundatur, aliquid addit supra substantiam cujuslibet extremi relati singillatim sumpti, quia non identificatur cum fundamento prout se tenet ex parte solius subjecti, vel solius termini, sed prout se tenet ea parte utriusque. Quare relatio ... semper exprimit denominationem contingentem et accidentaliter supervenientem subjecto, utpote quae adesse vel abesse potest, prout adsit vel deficiat terminus."

432.

"Illi enim [the reference is to certain medieval idealists] quamvis agnoscerent duo alba existentia negabant dari actu in rebus formalem similaritatem [*i.e.* even after the comparative activity of thought], sed formalem similitudinem, et aliam quamvis relationem, reponebant in actu intellectus unum cum alio comparantis; nos vero ante actum intellectus agnoscimus in rebus, quidquid sufficit ad constituendam relationem similitudinis, diversitatis, paternitatis, etc., ita ut hujusmodi denominationes non verificentur de actu intellectus unum cum alio comparantis, sed plenam habeant in rebus ipsis verificationem."— URRABURU, *op. cit.*, p. 1010.

433.

In what sense "extramental"?—*Cf. supra*, p. 350, n. I (end).

434.

Cf. Science of Logic, ii., § 218. For the concepts of "cause" and "causality" in the inductive sciences, as well as for much that cannot be repeated here, the student may consult with advantage vol. ii., p. iv., ch. iii., iv. and vi. of the work referred to.

435.

"Id a quo aliquid procedit quocunque modo."—ST. THOMAS, *Summa Theol.*, i., q. xxxiii., art. I.

436.

Hence Aristotle's definition of principle, including both logical and real principles: Πασῶν μὲν οὖν κοινὸν τῶν ἀρχῶν τὸ πρῶτον εἶναι ὅθεν ἢ ἐστιν ἢ γίγνεται ἢ γιγνώσκεται.—*Metaph.* IV., ch. i.

437.

A *cause* must be prior *in nature* to its effect, but not necessarily prior *in time*. In fact the *action* of the cause and the *production* of the effect must be simultaneous. *Cf. Science of Logic*, ii., § 220. Considered formally as correlatives they are *simul natura*. A *principle* must likewise be in some sense *prior* to what proceeds from it, not necessarily, however, by priority of time, nor by priority of nature involving real dependence. The Christian Revelation regarding the Blessed Trinity involves that the First Divine Person is the "principle" from which the Second proceeds, and the First and the Second the "principle" from which the Third proceeds; yet here there is no dependence or inequality, or any priority except the "relation of origin" be called priority.

438.

Cf. Science of Logic, ii., § 216.

439.
: Cf. *Science of Logic*, i., § 16; ii., §§ 214, 224 (p. 113).

440.
: Cf. MERCIER, *op. cit.*, § 252.

441.
: Cf. *Physic.*, Lib. ii., cap. 3; *Metaph.*, Lib. i., cap. 3; v., cap. 2.

442.
: *i.e.* from the effect considered *formally* as a term of the activity; in the case of *immanent* activity, as, *e.g.* thought or volition, where the effect remains within the agent (as a *verbum mentale* or other mental term), uniting with the concrete reality of the latter, the effect is not adequately distinct from the agent as affected by this term or product.

443.
: Cf. ST. THOMAS, *In Physic.*, ii., lect. 10: "Necesse est quatuor esse causas: quia cum causa sit, ad quam sequitur esse alterius, esse ejus quod habet causam potest considerari dupliciter: uno modo absolute, et sic causa essendi est forma per quam aliquid est ens in actu; alio modo secundum quod de potentia ente fit actu ens: et quia omne quod est in potentia, reducitur ad actum per id quod est actu ens, ex hoc necesse est esse duas alias causas, scilicet materiam, et agentem quod reducit materiam de potentia in actum. Actio autem agentis ad aliquod determinatum tendit, sicut ab aliquo determinato principio procedit; nam omne agens agit quod est sibi conveniens. Id autem ad quod intendit actio agentis dicitur causa finalis. Sic igitur necesse est esse causas quatuor."

444.
: Cf. MERCIER, *op. cit.*, §§ 247-8.

445.
: Certain medieval scholastics, especially of the Franciscan School, regarded spiritual substances as having in their constitution a certain potential, determinable principle, which they called "*materia*". St. Thomas, without objecting to the designation, insisted that such potential principle cannot be the same as the *materia prima* of corporeal substances (cf. *De Substantis Separatis*, ch. vii.).

446.
: Cf. ST. THOMAS: "Actio est actus activi *et passio est actus passivi*" (iii. *Physic.*, l. 5); "*Materia* non fit *causa in actu* nisi *secundum quod alteratur et mutatur*" (i. *Contra Gentes*, xvii.); "Materia est causa formae, inquantum forma non est nisi in materia" (*De Princip. Naturae*).

447.
: Cf. ST. THOMAS, *De Princip. Naturae, ibid.*: "... et similiter forma est causa materiae, inquantum materia non habet esse in actu nisi per formam;

448.

materia enim et forma dicuntur relative ad invicem; dicuntur etiam relative ad compositum, sicut pars ad totum".

"Materia cum sit infinitarum formarum determinatur per formam, et per eam consequitur aliquam speciem."—ST. THOMAS, *Summa Theol.*, i., q. vii., art. I.

449.

To Special Metaphysics also belongs the controverted question whether or not a plurality of really distinct substantial forms can enter into the constitution of an individual corporeal substance. When we classify corporeal things into *genera* and *species* according to their *natural kinds* (*cf. Science of Logic*, i., § 67), these latter are determined by the *formae substantiales* of the things classified, and are called *infimæ species*. Numerically distinct individuals which have (conceptually) the same *forma substantialis*, fall into the same *infima species*; while if such individuals have (conceptually and numerically) distinct *formae substanialis* they fall into distinct *infimae species* of some higher common genus. The wider the generic concept the larger the group of individuals which it unifies: it is a principle of conceptual unity, *i.e.* of universality. The objects of our *generic, differential,* and *specific* concepts, throughout this process of classification, are only virtually distinct metaphysical grades of being in the individuals. Now if the *forma substantialis* which yields the unifying concept of the *species infima* for the individuals, and the material principle which is the ground of the numerical distinction between these latter, were likewise regarded by the scholastics as being merely virtually distinct metaphysical grades of being, in each individual, then the question of a plurality of really distinct forms in one and the same individual would have no meaning: all "forms" in the latter would be only virtually distinct from one another and from the material principle. But the scholastics did not conceive that the real ground for grouping individuals into *species infimae* was the same as that for grouping these latter into wider genera. They regarded the relation between the *forma substantialis* and the *materia prima* in the individual as quite different from that between the generic and specific grades of being in the individual (*cf. supra*, § 38; *Science of Logic*, i., § 44; JOSEPH, *Introduction to Logic*, pp. 93-6). While they considered the latter a relation of virtual distinction they held the former to be one of real distinction. And while they recognized the concept of the *species infima* to be a principle of conceptual unity in grouping the individuals together mentally, St. Thomas emphasized especially the rôle of the *forma substantialis* (on which that concept was founded) as a principle of *real unity* in the individual: "Ab eodam habet res *esse* et *unitatem*. Manifestum est autem quod res habet esse per formam. Unde et per formam res habet unitatem" (*Quodlib.* i., art. 6). If we accept this doctrine of St. Thomas the arguments which he bases on it against the possibility of a plurality of distinct substantial forms in the same corporeal individual are unanswerable (*Cf.* MERCIER, *Ontologie*, § 215).

450.

"Idem actus secundum rem est duorum secundum diversam rationem: agentis quidem, secundum quod est ab eo, patientis autem, secundum quod est in ipso.... Ex eo quod actio et passio sunt unus motus non sequitur quod actio et passio, vel doctio et doctrina, sint idem; sed quod motus cui inest utrumque eorum, sit idem. Qui quidem motus secundum unam rationem est actio, et secundum aliam rationem est passio; alterum enim est secundum rationem esse actus hujus, ut *in hoc*, et esse actus hujus, ut *ab hoc*; motus autem dicitur actio secundum quod est actus agentis ut ab hoc; dicitur autem passio secundum quod est actus patientis ut in hoc. Et sic patet quod licet motus sit idem moventis et moti, propter hoc quod abstrahit ab utraque ratione: tamen actio et passio differunt propter hoc quod diversas rationes in sua significatione habent."—ST. THOMAS, *In Phys.*, iii. 1. 5.

451.

"Solet dubium esse apud quosdam, utrum motus sit in movente, aut in mobili.... Sed manifestum est quod actus cujuslibet est in eo cujus est actus; actus autem motus est in mobili, cum sit actus mobilis, causatus tamen in eo a movente ... cum motus sit actus existentis in potentia, sequitur quod motus non sit actus alicujus inquantum est movens, sed inquantum est mobile."—*ibid.*, 1. 4.

452.

Some languages mark the distinction between these two kinds of action: "Differt autem *facere* et *agere*: quia *factio* est actio transiens in exteriorem materiam, sicut aedificare, secare et hujusmodi; *agere* autem est actio permanenslin ipso agente sicut videre, velle et hujusmodi."—ST. THOMAS, *Summa Theol.* i[ae] ii[a], q. lxvii., art. 4, c.

453.

Hume went even farther, at least in language; for he alleged (whether he really believed is another question) that he could overcome the supposed merely psychological difficulty, that he could easily—and, presumably, without doing violence to his rational nature—conceive a non-existent thing as coming into existence without a cause! He proclaimed that he could achieve the feat of thinking what the universal voice of mankind has declared to be unthinkable: *an absolute beginning of being from nothingness.* "The knowledge of this relation (causality) is not," he writes, "in any instance attained by reasonings *a priori*; but arises entirely from experience, when we find that any particular objects are *constantly conjoined* with each other "(*Works*, ed. Green and Grose, iv., 24). "All distinct ideas are separable from each other, and, as the ideas of cause and effect are evidently distinct, 'twill be easy for us (!) to conceive any object as nonexistent this moment, and existent the next, without conjoining to it the distinct idea of a cause or producing principle" (*Treatise on Human Nature*, p. 381). On this argument (?) even such an ardent admirer of the pan-phenomenist as Huxley was, is forced to remark that "it is of the circular sort, for the major premise, that all distinct ideas are separable in thought, assumes the question at issue" (HUXLEY'S *Hume*, p. 122).

454.
Thus, for instance, man, elevated by sanctifying grace, can perform acts which merit the supernatural reward of the Beatific Vision.

455.
Cf. *Science of Logic*, ii., § 231.

456.
Cf. ARISTOTLE, *Metaph.*, ii., cap. 2.

457.
Cf. URRABURU, *op. cit.*, § 392 (p. 1123): "Unde adaequata virtus instrumentalis videtur conflari ex naturali instrumenti virtute vel efficacitate et ex virtute causae principalis sibi transeunter addita, docente S. Thoma: *Instrumentum virtutem instrumentalem acquirit dupliciter scilicet quando accipit formam instrumenti et quando movetur a principali agente ad effectum* (*Summa Theol.*, iii., q. xix., art. 3, ad. 2)."

458.
"Ad aliquem effectum aliquid operatur dupliciter. Uno modo sicut per se agens; et dicitur per se agere quod agit per aliquam formam sibi inhaerentem per modum naturae completae, sive habeat illam formam a se, sive ab alio.... Alio modo aliquid operatur ad effectum aliquem instrumentaliter, quod quidem non operatur ad effectum per formam sibi inhaerentem, sed solum inquantum est motum a per se agente. Haec est ratio instrumenti, inquantum est instrumentum, ut moveat motum; unde sicut se habet forma completa ad per se agentem, ita se habet motus, quo movetur a principale agente, ad instrumentum, sicut serra operatur ad scamnum. Quamvis enim serra habeat aliquam actionem quae sibi competit secundum propriam formam, ut dividere; tamen aliquem effectum habet qui sibi non competit, nisi inquantum est mota ab artifice, scilicet facere rectam incisionem, et convenientem formae artis: et sic instrumentum habet duas operationes; unam quae competit ei secundam rationem propriam; aliam quae competit ei secundam quod est motum a per se agente, quae transcendit virtutem propriae formae."—*De Veritate*, q. xxvii., art. 4. It is not clear, however, that St. Thomas regarded these

two "*operationes*" of the instrumental cause as really distinct, for he says that it acts as an instrument (*i.e.* modifies the efficiency of the principal cause) only by exercising its own proper function: "Omne agens instrumentale exsequitur actionem principalis agentis per aliquam operationem propriam, et connaturalem sibi, sicut calor naturalis generat carnem dissolvendo et digerendo, et serra operatur ad factionem scamni secando" (*Contra Gentes*, ii., ch. xxi.): from which he goes on to argue that no creature can act even as an instrumental cause *in creating.*—*Cf.* iv. *Sent.*, Dist. i., q. i., art. 4, sol. 2.—*De Potentia*, q. iii., art. 7.—*Summa Theol.*, iii., q. lxii., art. I, ad. 2.

459.

St. Thomas, proving the necessity of the Divine *concursus* for all created causes, illustrates the general distinction between a *principal* and an *instrumental* cause: "Virtus naturalis quae est rebus naturalibus in sua institutione collata, inest eis *ut quaedem forma habens esse ratum et firmum in natura.* Sed id quod a Deo fit in re naturali, quo actualiter agat, est ut intentio sola, habens esse quoddam incompletum, per modum quo ... virtus artis [est] in instrumento artificis. Sicut ergo securi per artem dari potuit acumen, ut esset forma in ea permanens, non autem dari ei potuit quod *vis artis* esset in ea quasi quaedam forma permanens, *nisi haberet intellectum*; ita rei naturali potuit conferri virtus propria, ut forma in ipsa permanens, non autem *vis qua agit ad esse* ut instrumentum primae causae, *nisi daretur ei quod esset universale essendi principium*; nec iterum virtuti naturali conferri potuit ut moveret seipsam, nec ut conservaret se in esse: unde sicut patet quod instrumento artificis conferri non oportuit quod operaretur absque motu artis; ita rei naturali conferri non potuit quod operaretur absque operatione divina."—*QQ. DD. De. Pot.*, q. iii., art. 7.

460.

Cf. MAHER, *Psychology*, ch. xix.—MERCIER, *Psychologie*, ii., ch. i. § 2.

461.

For a fuller treatment of this whole subject, *cf. Science of Logic*, ii., Part iv., chs. iii., iv.; Part v., ch. i.—MAHER, *Psychology*, ch. xix., pp. 423-4.

462.

Cf. NEWMAN, *Grammar of Assent*, Part i., ch. iv., § I (5), (6); § 2, remark I.

463.

Cf. Science of Logic, ii., §§ 216, 218, 219.

464.

ibid., § 216.

465.

ibid., § 220.

466.

467.
    Introduction to Logic, pp. 64-5.

468.
    "Whenever science tries to find the cause not of a particular event, such as the French Revolution (whose cause must be as unique as that event itself is), but of an event of a kind, such as consumption, or commercial crises, it looks in the last resort for a *commensurate* cause. What is that exact state or condition of the body, given which it must and without which it cannot be in consumption? What are those conditions in a commercial community, given which there must and without which there cannot be a commercial crisis?"—JOSEPH, *op. cit.*, p. 65. *Cf. Science of Logic*, ii., § 221.

    Cf. what was said above about the causal or extrinsic, as distinct from the intrinsic, principle of individuation.

469.
    System of Logic, iii., v., § 2.

470.
    For instance: (*a*) The "ontological" or "true" cause, which "actually produces" the effect, need not necessarily be the "ultimate" cause of the latter. (*b*) A "physical fact" can be the cause of another in the sense of being the invariable antecedent (or *physical* cause) of the latter, but not "in that sense alone"; it may also be an *efficient* cause of the latter by exerting an active influence on the happening of this latter. (*c*) Whether or not efficiency is "a mysterious and most powerful tie," at any rate it does exist between "physical facts" in the universe. (*d*) Its analysis reveals not a "supposed necessity of ascending ... to ... the true cause, ... which ... produces the effect," as if the proximate causes did not also truly produce the latter; but a real necessity of ascending to a First Cause as the source and support and complement of the real efficiency of these proximate causes. (*e*) A merely *logical* theory of Induction does not indeed demand any inquiry either into the efficiency of natural agencies, or into the nature and grounds of the "invariability" or "necessity" or "law" whereby these are connected with their effects. But a *philosophical* theory of Induction does imply such inquiries. And here phenomenist writers like Mill have laid themselves open to two accusations. For while professing merely to abstract from the problem of *efficiency* they have tried equivalently to deny its existence by proclaiming it superfluous and insoluble, besides consciously or unconsciously misrepresenting it. And similarly, in dealing with the *invariability* of causal sequences in the universe, with the *necessary* character of its physical laws, they have misconceived this necessity as being mechanical, fatal, absolutely inviolable; and have wrongly proclaimed its ultimate grounds to be unknowable

(Agnosticism). Cf. *infra*, § 104; *Science of Logic*, ii., Part IV., chs. iii., iv., and v.; Part V., ch. i. Thus, while eschewing the genuine Metaphysics, which seeks the real nature and causes of the world of our experience, as superfluous and futile, they have substituted for it a masked and spurious metaphysics which they have wrongly fathered on Physical Science: a mass of more or less superficial speculations which have not even the merit of consistency. No philosopher, starting with their views on the nature of the human mind, can consistently claim for the latter any really valid or reliable knowledge of *laws*, any more than of causes. For the knowledge of a *law*, even as a *generalized* fact, is a knowledge that claims to pass beyond the limits of the individual's present and remembered experiences. But there can be no rational justification, whether psychological or ontological, for the certain reliability of such a step, in the philosophy which logically reduces all certain knowledge to the mere awareness of a flow of successive sensations supposed to constitute the total content of the individual consciousness and the total reality of human experience.

471.

Cf. MAHER, *Psychology*, ch. xvii., pp. 368-70.—MERCIER, *op. cit.*, § 229.

472.

"When an *effort* of attention combines two ideas, when one billiard ball moves another, when a steam hammer flattens out a lump of solid iron, when a blow on the head knocks a man down, in all these cases there is something more than, and essentially different from, the mere *sequence* of two phenomena: there is *effective force—causal action* of an agent endowed with *real energy*."—MAHER, *op. cit., ibid.*, p. 370.

473.

Grammar of Assent, p. 66.

474.

Cf. DOMET DE VORGES, *Cause efficiente et cause finale*, p. 39. Volitional activity is no doubt the most prominent type of efficient causality in our mental life. But it is not the only type; we have direct conscious experience of intellectual effort, of the work of the imagination, of the exercise of organic and muscular energy. There is no warrant therefore for conceiving all efficient power or energy, after the model of will-power, as Newman among others appears to have done when he wrote in these terms: "Starting, then, from experience, I consider a cause to be an effective will: and by the doctrine of causation, I mean the notion, or first principle, that all things come of effective will" (*ibid.*, p. 68). No doubt, all things do come ultimately from the effective will of God. This, however, is not a first principle, but a remote philosophical conclusion.

475.

476.
    ibid., p. 66.

477.
    St. Thomas, *QQ. Disp. De Potentia*, q. iii., art. 7, in c.

478.
    "Nulla res per seipsam movet vel agit, nisi sit movens non motum.... Et quia natura inferior agens non agit nisi mota ... et hoc non cessat quousque perveniatur ad Deum, sequitur de necessitate quod Deus sit causa actionis cujuslibet rei naturalis, ut movens et applicans virtutem ad agendum."—St. Thomas, *De Potentia Dei*, q. iii., art. 7.

    This is the principle repeatedly expressed by St. Thomas: "Unde quarto modo unum est causa alterius, sicut principale agens est causa actionis instrumenti: et hoc modo etiam oportet dicere, quod Deus est causa omnis actionis rei naturalis. Quanto enim aliqua causa est altior, tanto est communior et efficacior, tanto profundius ingreditur in effectum, et de remotiori potentia ipsum reducit in actum. In qualibet autem re naturali invenimus *quod est ens* et quod est res naturalis, et quod est talis vel talis naturae. Quorum primum est commune omnibus entibus; secundum omnibus rebus naturalibus; tertium in una specie; et quartum, si addamus accidentia, est proprium huic individuo. Hoc ergo individuum agendo non potest constituere aliud in simili specie, nisi prout est instrumentum illius causae *quae respicit totam speciem* et ulterius *totum esse* naturae inferioris. Et propter hoc nihil agit in speciem in istis inferioribus ... nec aliquid agit *ad esse* nisi per virtutem Dei. *Ipsum enim esse est communissimus effectus, primus et intimior omnibus aliis effectibus; et ideo soli Deo competit secundum virtutem propriam talis effectus*: unde etiam, ut dicitur in *Lib. de Causis* (prop. 9), intelligentia non dat esse, nisi prout est in ea virtus divina. Sic ergo Deus est causa omnis actionis prout quodlibet agens est instrumentum divinae virtutis operantis."—St. Thomas, *De Potentia Dei*, q. iii. art 7.—*Cf. supra*, 99 (*c*), n. 2.

479.
    Why, then, is a finite cause not capable of acting uninterruptedly? why are its powers, forces, energies, fatigued, lessened, exhausted by exercise? Simply because its action is proportionate to its powers, and these to its *finite* nature.

480.
    "Creatio non est mutatio nisi secundum modum intelligendi tantum. Nam de ratione mutationis est quod aliquid idem se habeat aliter nunc et prius.... Sed in creatione, per quam producitur tota substantia rei, non potest accipi aliquid idem aliter se habens nunc et prius, nisi secundum intellectum tantum; sicut si intelligatur aliqua res prius non fuisse totaliter, et postea esse. Sed cum actio et passio conveniant in una substantia motus,

et differant solum secundum habitudines diveras ... oportet quod subtracto motu, non remaneant nisi diversae habitudines in creante et creato. Sed quia modus significandi sequitur modum intelligendi ... creatio significatur per modum mutationis; et propter hoc dicitur quod creare est ex nihilo aliquid facere; quamvis facere et fieri magis in hoc conveniant quam mutare et mutari; quia facere et fieri important habitudinem causae ad effectum et effectus ad causam, sed mutationem ex consequenti."—ST. THOMAS, *Summa Theol.*, i., q. xlv., art. 2, ad. 2.

481.

"Remoto motu, actio nihil aliud importat quam ordinem originis [effectus] secundum quod [effectus] a causa aliqua procedit."—*op. cit.*, i. q. xli., art. I, ad 2.

482.

The act of the will is, of course, virtually transitive when it wills or determines bodily movements.—*Cf.* MAHER, *Psychology*, chs. x., xxiii. (pp. 517-24).

483.

At the same time it must be noted that organic vital activity is transitive in the sense that no part or member of the organism acts upon itself, but only on other parts, in the production of the local, quantitative and qualitative changes involved in nutrition. It is subject to the inductively established law which seems to regulate all *corporeal* action: that all such action involves *reaction* of the *patiens* on the *agens*. Mental activity is outside this law. Cognitive and appetitive faculties do not react on the objects which reduce these faculties to act, thus arousing their immanent activity.—*Cf.* MERCIER, *op. cit.*, § 227.

484.

Cf. MERCIER, *op. cit.*

485.

Cf. MAHER, *Psychology*, chs. xiii. and xiv.

486.

Cf. URRABURU: "Vel, si mavis, dic causam efficientem esse causam, a qua fit aliquid, vel a quo proprie oritur actio, intelligendo per actionem emanationem et fluxum ac dependentiam effectus a causa."—*op. cit.*, § 389 (p. 1112).

487.

Cf. MERCIER, *op. cit.*, § 229: "L'action, l'efficience, qu'est elle, en quoi consiste-t-elle? Est-ce une sorte d'écoulement de la cause dans l'effet? Évidemment non. Lorsque nous voulons nous élever à une conception métaphysique, nous nous raccrochons à une image sensible, et nous nous persuadons volontiers, que la netteté de la première répond à la facilité avec laquelle nous nous figurons la seconde. Il faut se défier de cette illusion. Puisque l'action, même corporelle, ne modifie point l'agent, la causalité efficiente ne peut consister dans un influx physique, qui passerait de la cause dans l'effet."

488.

Cf. Science of Logic, ii., §§ 228-9.

489.

We might add this other fact: that *all* kinds of corporeal activity and change seem to involve *motion* or local change. This does not prove that they all *are* motion or local change. The significance of the fact lies probably in this, that local motion is necessary for procuring and continuing physical contact between the interacting physical agencies.—*Cf.* NYS, *Cosmologie*, §§ 227-9.

490.

Cf. ST. THOMAS, *Contra Gentes*, iii., 69.

491.

"Une cause véritable est une cause, entre laquelle et son effet l'esprit aperçoit une liaison nécessaire: c'est ainsi que je l'entendes. [This is ambiguous.] Or il n'y a que l'être infiniment parfait entre la volonté duquel et les effets l'esprit aperçoive une liaison nécessaire. Il n'y a donc que Dieu qui soit véritable cause, et il semble même qu'il y ait contradiction à dire que les hommes puissent l'être"—*De la récherche de la vérité*, Liv. 6me, 2e partie, ch. iii.

492.

"Si l'on vient à considérer attentivement l'idée que l'on a de cause ou de puissance d'agir, on ne peut en douter que cette idée ne présente quelque chose de divin."—*ibid.*

493.

"Il n'y a point d'homme qui sache seulement ce qu'il faut faire pour remuer un de ses doigts par le moyen des esprits animaux."—*ibid.*

494.

"J'ai toujours soutenue que l'âme était l'unique cause de ses actes, c'est à dire de ses déterminations libres ou de ses actes bons ou mauvais.... J'ai toujours soutenu que l'âme était active, mais que ses actes ne produisaient rien de physique."—*Réflexions sur la prémotion physique.* "Je crois que la volonté est une *puissance active*, qu'elle a un véritable pouvoir de se déterminer; mais son action est *immanente*; c'est une action qui ne produit rien par son efficace propre, pas même le mouvement de son bras."—*Réponse à la 3me lettre d'Arnauld.*

495.

Cf. MERCIER, *op. cit.*, §§ 230-2; ZIGLIARA, *Ontologia* (45); URRABURU, *op. cit.*, §§ 393 *sqq.*

496.

497.

> We may reasonably ask the occasionalist to suppose for the moment that we are efficient causes of our mental processes and to tell us what better proof of it could he demand, or what better proof could be forthcoming, than this proof from consciousness.

MAHER, *Psychology*, ch. x., p. 220.

498.

> Should anyone doubt that consciousness does testify to this fact, we may prove it inductively from the constant correlation between the mental state and the bodily movement: "I will to move my arm, it moves; I will that it remain at rest, it does not move; I will that its movement be more or less strong and rapid, the strength and rapidity vary with the determination of my will. What more complete inductive proof can we have of the efficiency of our will-action on the external world?"—

MERCIER, *op. cit.*, § 231.

499.

> "Si effectus non producuntur ex actione rerum creatarum, sed solum ex actione Dei, impossibile est quod per effectus manifestetur virtus alicujus causae creatae: non enim effectus ostendit virtutem causae nisi ratione actionis, quae a virtute procedens ad effectum terminatur. Natura autem causae non cognoscitur per effectum, nisi inquantum per ipsum cognoscitur virtus, quae naturam consequitur. Si igitur res creatae non habent actiones ad producendum effectum, sequitur, quod nunquam naturam alicujus rei creatae poterit cognosci per effectum; et sic subtrahitur nobis omnis cognitio scientiae naturalis, in qua praecipuae demonstrationes per effectum sequuntur."—ST. THOMAS, *Contra Gentes*, L. iii., cap. 69.

500.

> "Je demeure d'accord que la foi oblige à croire qu'il y a des corps; mais, pour l'évidence, il me semble qu'elle n'est point entière, et que nous ne sommes point invinciblement portés à croire qu'il y ait quelqu'autre chose que Dieu et notre esprit."—*Récherche de la vérite*, 6me éclaircissement.

501.

Cf. Science of Logic, ii., § 217.

502.

Metaph., v., 17.

503.

> "Quaedam vero ad bonum inclinantur cum aliqua cognitione; non quidem sic quod cognoscant ipsam rationem boni, sed cognoscunt aliquod bonum particulare.... Inclinatio autem hanc cognitionem sequens dicitur appetitus *sensitivus*. Quaedam vero inclinantur ad bonum cum cognitione qua

cognoscant ipsam boni rationem; et haec inclinatio dicitur *voluntas*."—St. Thomas, *Summa Theol.*, i., q. xlix., art. 1.

504.

"Sicut influere causae efficientis est agere, ita influere causae finalis est appeti et desiderari."—*De Veritate*, q. xxii., art. 2.

505.

In its modern usage the term "intention" is inseparable from the notion of *conscious* direction. The scholastics used the term "*intentio*" in a *wider* and *deeper* sense to connote the natural tendency of all created agencies towards their natural activities and lines of development. And in unconscious agencies they did not hesitate to refer to it as "*intentio naturae*" or "*appetitus naturalis*".

506.

"Res naturalis per *formam* qua perficitur in sua specie, habet inclinationem in proprias operationes et proprium finem, quem per operationes consequitur; quale enim unumquodque est, talia operatur, et in sibi convenientia tendit."—St. Thomas, *Contra Gentes*, iv., 19.

"Omnia suo modo per appetitum inclinantur in bonum, sed diversimode. Quaedam enim inclinantur in bonum per solam naturalem habitudinem absque cognitione, sicut plantae et corpora inanimata; et talis inclinatio ad bonum vocatur appetitus naturalis."—*Summa Theol.*, i., q. xlix., art. 1.

507.

"Causa efficiens et finis sibi correspondent invicem, quia efficiens est principium motus, finis autem terminus. Et similiter materia et forma: nam forma dat esse, materia autem recipit. Est igitur efficiens causa finis, finis autem causa efficientis. Efficiens est causa finis quantum ad esse, quidem, quia movendo perducit efficiens ad hoc, quod *sit* finis. Finis autem est causa efficientis non quantum ad esse sed quantum ad *rationem causalitatis*. Nam efficiens est causa in quantum agit; non autem agit nisi causa [gratia] finis. Unde ex fine habet suam causalitatem efficiens."—St. Thomas, *In Metaph.*, v., 2.

"Sciendum quod licet finis sit ultimus in esse in quibusdam, in causalitate tamen est prior semper, unde dicitur *causa causarum*, quia est causa causalitatis in omnibus causis. Est enim causa causalitatis efficientis, ut jam dictum est. Efficiens autem est causa causalitatis et materiae et formae."—*ibid.*, lect. 3.

508.

Φύσις ἐστιν ἀρχή τὶς καὶ αἰτία του κινεῖσθαι καὶ ἠρεμεῖν ἐν ᾧ ὑπάχει πρώτως καθ᾽ αὐτο, καὶ μὴ κατὰ συμβεβηκός. Natura est principium quoddam et causa cur id moveatur et quiescat, in quo inest primum, per se et non secundum accidens.—*Physic.*, L. ii., cap. I.

509.

"Ars nihil aliud est quam recta ratio aliquorum operum faciendorum."—*Summa Theol.* i^a ii^{ae}, q. lvii., art. 3.—*Cf. In Post. Anal.*, l. I.

510.

"Natura nihil aliud est quam ratio cujusdam artis, scilicet divinae, indita rebus qua ipsae res moventur ad finem determinatum; sicut si artifex factor navis posset lignis tribuere quod ex seipsis moverentur ad navis formam inducendam."—*In II Phys.*, lect. 14.

"Omnia naturalia, in ea quae eis conveniunt, sunt inclinata, habentia in seipsis aliquod inclinationis principium, ratione cujus eorum inclinatio naturalis est, *ita ut quodammodo ipsa vadant, et non solum ducantur in fines debitos.*"—*De Veritate*, q. xxii., art. 7.

511.

"In nullo enim alio natura ab arte videtur differre, nisi quia natura est principium intrinsecum, et ars est principium extrinsicum. Si enim ars factiva navis esset intrinseca ligno, facta fuisset navis a natura, sicut modo fit ab arte."—*In II. Phys.*, lect. 13.

512.

Cf. Science of Logic, ii., § 217.

513.

Cf. Science of Logic, ii., § 227.

514.

Cf. Science of Logic, ii., §§ 226-31.

515.

ARISTOTLE, *Metaph.*, iv., ch. v.

516.

Physic., ii., ch. v.

517.

ibid.

518.

Cf. Science of Logic, ii., §§ 264, 268-9.

519.

Οὐδὲν γὰρ ὡς ἔτυχε ποιεῖ ἡ φυσις.—*De Coelo*, ii., 8.

520.

521.
Fatalism is the view that all things happen by a blind, inevitable, eternally foredoomed and unintelligible necessity. Thus SENECA (*Nat. Quaest.*, L. III., cap. 36) describes *fatum* as *necessitas omnium rerum actionumque, quam nulla vis rumpat*. This *necessitas ineluctabilis* is totally different from the conditional physical necessity of the course of Nature dependently on the *Fiat* of a Supreme Free Will guided by Supreme Intelligence (*Cf. Science of Logic*, §§ 224, 249, 253, 257). If the necessity of actual occurrences is not ultimately traceable to the *Fiat* of an Intelligent Will—and mechanists deny that it can be so traced—it is rightly described as fatalistic, blind, purposeless, unintelligible.

522.
Cf. MERCIER, *op. cit.*, §§ 259, 260.

523.
"Expliquer par une rencontre fortuite, la convergence d'éléments, dont chacun a sa poussée propre, c'est rendre raison de la *convergence* par des principes de *divergence*.... Il est donc contradictoire d'attribuer au hasard la raison explicative de l'ordre."—MERCIER, *op. cit.*, § 260.

524.
Cf. Science of Logic, ii., §§ 224, 250, and *passim*.

525.
"Similiter ex prioribus pervenitur ad posteriora in arte et in natura: unde si artificialia, ut domus, fierent a natura, hoc ordine fierent, quo nunc fiunt per artem: scilicet prius institueretur fundamentum, et postea erigerentur parietes, et ultimo supponeretur tectum.... Et similiter si ea quae fiunt a natura fierent ab arte, hoc modo fierent sicut apta nata sunt fieri a natura; ut patet in sanitate, quam contigit fieri, et ab arte et a natura.... Unde manifestum est quod in natura est alterum propter alterum, scilicet priora propter posteriora, sicut et in arte."—ST. THOMAS, *In II. Phys.*, lect. 13.—*Cf. supra*, n. 3.

526.
"Ordo est parium dispariumque rerum sua cuique loca tribuens dispositio."—*De Civ. Dei*, xix., 13.

527.
Cf. MERCIER, *op. cit.*, §§ 257-61.

528.
"*La convergence de causes indifférentes qui réalisent d'une manière harmonieuse et persistante un même objet ordonné, ne s'explique point par des coincidences fortuites; elle réclame un principe interne de convergence.*"—*Ibid.*, § 260.

529.
TENNYSON, *In Memoriam*, lvi.

BROWNING, *A Soul's Tragedy*, Act. I.

530.

"Universum habet bonum ordinis et bonum separatum."—*In Metaph.*, xii., l. 12.

531.

ARISTOTLE, *Metaph.*, xi., 10. Does Aristotle teach that God moves the universe only as its Final Cause, as the Supreme Good towards which it tends, or also as Efficient Cause? His thought is here obscure, and has given rise to much controversy among his interpreters.

532.

Ἡ ἀρχὴ καὶ τὸ πρῶτον τῶν ὄντων ἀκίνητον καὶ καθ᾿ αὑτὸ καὶ κατὰ συμβεβηκός, κινοῦν δὲ τὴν πρώτην ἀΐδιον καὶ μίαν κίνησιν.—*Ibid.*, xi., 8.

533.

Κινεῖ δὲ (οὗ ἕνεκα) ὡς ἐρώμενον, κινούμενον δὲ τἆλλα κινει.—*ibid.*, 7.

534.

"Totus ordo universi est propter primum moventem, ut scilicet explicetur in universo ordinato id quod est in intellectu et voluntate primi moventis. Et sic oportet quod a primo movente sit tota ordinatio universi."—*Ibid.*, xii., l. 12.

535.

... Among themselves all things
Have order; and from hence the form, which makes
The universe resemble God. In this
The higher creatures see the printed steps
Of that eternal worth, which is the end
Whither the line is drawn. All natures lean
In this their order, diversely, some more,
Some less approaching to their primal source.
Thus they to different havens are moved on
Through the vast sea of being, and each one
With instinct giv'n, that bears it in its course;
This to the lunar sphere directs the fire,
This prompts the hearts of mortal animals,
This the brute earth together knits and binds.
Nor only creatures, void of intellect,
Are aim'd at by this bow; but even those
That have intelligence and love, are pierced.
That Providence, who so well orders all,

With her own light makes ever calm the heaven,
In which the substance that hath greatest speed
Is turned: and thither now, as to our seat
Predestin'd, we are carried by the force
Of that strong cord, that never looses dart,
But at fair aim and glad ...

—DANTE, *Paradiso*, Cant. i. (tr. by CARY).

www.ingramcontent.com/pod-product-compliance
Lightning Source LLC
Chambersburg PA
CBHW081208230426
43666CB00015B/2676